D1496421

THE FUTURE OF AFRICAN CUSTOMARY LAW

Customary laws and traditional institutions in Africa constitute comprehensive legal systems that regulate the entire spectrum of activities from birth to death. Once the sole source of law, customary rules now exist in the context of pluralist legal systems with competing bodies of domestic constitutional law, statutory law, common law, and international human rights treaties.

The Future of African Customary Law is intended to promote discussion and understanding of customary law and to explore its continued relevance in sub-Saharan Africa. This volume considers the characteristics of customary law and efforts to ascertain and codify customary law, and how this body of law differs in content, form, and status from legislation and common law. It also addresses a number of substantive areas of customary law, including the role and power of traditional authorities; customary criminal law; customary land tenure, property rights, and intestate succession; and the relationship between customary law, human rights, and gender equality.

Jeanmarie Fenrich is the Director of Special Projects in Africa for the Leitner Center for International Law and Justice at Fordham Law School in New York. She graduated magna cum laude from Fordham Law School, where she served as editor-in-chief of the *Fordham Law Review*. She has conducted field research and authored publications on issues related to domestic violence, discrimination faced by women with HIV/AIDS, women's property rights, and women in customary-law marriage under domestic and international human rights law.

Paolo Galizzi is Clinical Associate Professor of Law and Director of the Sustainable Development Legal Initiative (SDLI) at the Leitner Center for International Law and Justice at Fordham Law School. He previously held academic positions at Imperial College London and the Universities of Nottingham, Verona, and Milan. Professor Galizzi's research interests lie in international law, environmental law, and law of sustainable development, and he has conducted fieldwork in several African countries.

Tracy E. Higgins co-founded the Leitner Center for International Law and Justice at Fordham Law School where she is a co-director and a law professor. She is a former editor of the *Harvard Law Review*, a Women's Law and Public Policy Fellow, and an Adjunct Professor at Georgetown University Law Center. Higgins has published numerous academic articles focusing on feminist jurisprudence, international human rights, and constitutional law in many of the nation's leading law journals.

The Future of African Customary Law

Edited by

JEANMARIE FENRICH

School of Law, Fordham University

PAOLO GALIZZI

School of Law, Fordham University

TRACY E. HIGGINS

School of Law, Fordham University

CAMBRIDGE
UNIVERSITY PRESS

CAMBRIDGE UNIVERSITY PRESS
Cambridge, New York, Melbourne, Madrid, Cape Town,
Singapore, São Paulo, Delhi, Mexico City

Cambridge University Press
The Edinburgh Building, Cambridge CB2 8RU, UK

Published in the United States of America by Cambridge University Press, New York

www.cambridge.org
Information on this title: www.cambridge.org/9781107625044

© Cambridge University Press 2011

First published 2011
First paperback edition 2013

A catalogue record for this publication is available from the British Library

Library of Congress Cataloging in Publication data
The future of African customary law / [edited by] Jeanmarie Fenrich,
Paolo Galizzi, Tracy E.Higgins.
p. cm.
Includes index.
ISBN 978-0-521-11853-8 (hardback)
1. Customary law – Africa. I. Fenrich, Jeanmarie. II. Galizzi, Paolo.
III. Higgins, Tracy. IV. Title.
KQC99.F88 2011
340.5′26–dc22   2011001813

ISBN 978-0-521-11853-8 Hardback
ISBN 978-1-107-62504-4 Paperback

Contents

Notes on Contributors

Ernest Kofi Abotsi is a lecturer at the Faculty of Law at Kwame Nkrumah University of Science & Technology (KNUST) in Ghana and specializes in constitutional and international law. He holds an LLB degree from the University of Ghana, Legon, and an LLM from Harvard Law School, together with a Barrister-at-Law Certificate from the Ghana School of Law. He holds significant publications to his credit in leading peer-review journals, and his research interests span the fields of law and development, legal aid, comparative constitutional law, and customary law reform. Abotsi also consults for justice sector institutions in Ghana and is counsel to the Constitutional Review Commission.

Justice **Joseph B. Akamba** is a Justice of the Court of Appeal of Ghana and Acting Director, Judicial Training Institute (JTI) Ghana. He started his legal career at the Attorney General's office in Ghana and later joined the bench as a Magistrate. Appointed as a High Court Judge in Ghana in 1989, he was seconded to the Gambia as a Director of Public Prosecutions (DPP) in 1994. He joined the Gambia Court of Appeal in 1999 and returned to the judiciary of Ghana in January 2002. Justice Akamba's competencies and interests are in credibility assessment, judicial ethics, and criminal and customary law. He is a proud associate of the National Judicial Institute (NJI) and a Fellow of Commonwealth Judicial Education Institute (CJEI), both of Canada; he also has contributed significantly to and spearheaded the adoption of modern adult education learning principles at the JTI. He is a Board member of the International Organisation of Judicial Trainers (IOJT).

Kristina Scurry Baehr served as the Yale Law School Bernstein Fellow (2008–2009) with the Carter Center in Liberia, where she assisted the Ministry of Justice in launching a Sexual and Gender-Based Violence (SGBV) Crimes Unit. She also co-supervised the Fordham Leitner Clinic's project for the Carter Center and the Justice and Peace Commission. She graduated from Yale Law School, where she founded and directed the Domestic Violence Clinic. She previously lived and worked in

Namibia, South Africa, and Uganda, focusing primarily on women and HIV/AIDS. She received her A.B. from the Woodrow Wilson School at Princeton University and has published in the areas of HIV/AIDS, violence against women, and sentencing. Baehr now represents survivors of domestic violence in Massachusetts and has been clerking for Judge Nancy Gertner since the fall of 2010.

Janet L. Banda is Chief Law Reform Officer in the Malawi Law Commission. She is currently pursuing doctoral studies in Law at Birkbeck College, University of London, researching African land tenure issues in relation to international development policies. She holds an LLM from the University of Georgia, where she specialized in international legal studies. She was also a Stanford Summer Fellow on Democracy and Development (2005). She has worked on land reforms in Malawi, providing technical legal support to the Ministry responsible for land matters. She has written on the relevance and centrality of law reform in promoting good governance, democracy, and sustainable development.

Thomas W. Bennett is a professor in the Department of Public Law and a Fellow of the University of Cape Town. Although his teaching involves mainly international law, his research interests have led him to African customary law, a subject on which he has published several monographs. Formerly a member of the South African Law Reform Commission's special project committee on customary law, he was extensively engaged in preparing reports and bills on marriage, succession, and traditional courts. His work for the Commission also entailed South Africa's contribution to International Judicial Co-operation. He is currently working on traditional African religions and ubuntu jurisprudence.

Johanna E. Bond joined Washington and Lee University in Virginia as an Associate Professor of Law in 2008. Professor Bond's teaching and scholarship focus on international human rights law and gender and the law. In 2001, Professor Bond was selected as a Senior Fulbright Scholar and traveled to Uganda and Tanzania to conduct research that later resulted in a book that she edited, *Voices of African Women: Women's Rights in Ghana, Uganda, and Tanzania*. Before joining the faculty of Washington and Lee University School of Law, Professor Bond was an Associate Professor of Law at the University of Wyoming and before that a Visiting Associate Professor of Law at Georgetown University Law Center for several years. She has published extensively in the area of women's human rights, with a particular focus on Africa.

Dr. Fatou K. Camara is an Associate Professor of Law at Cheikh Anta Diop University in Dakar, Senegal, specializing in Alternative Dispute Resolution, Family Law, Conflict of Laws, and African Customary Law. She received her Bachelor's degree in Law, a Master's degree in International and European Law, and two pre-doctoral degrees in Law at Paris II Assas – Panthéon University (France). She received her PhD in Law at Cheikh Anta Diop University in 1998. Dr. Camara has written and lectured extensively, in English and in French, on pre-colonial African culture and customary law. Her publications in English include "Women and the Law – A Critique of the Senegalese Family Law," an article in the November issue of the *Social Identities Journal for the Study of Race, Nation and Culture*, and "State and Religion in West Africa: Problems and Perspectives" in *ICLARS – International Consortium for Law and Religion Studies*.

Willemien du Plessis is a Professor at the North-West University (Potchefstroom Campus) in South Africa. She teaches land law, environmental law, and legal history as well as indigenous law to students at the Practical Legal School. She has published several articles on indigenous law in various journals and participated in national and international conferences in this regard. She participated in the drafting of the South African White Paper on Land Reform and was also a member of an inter-university Traditional Authorities Research Group.

Jeanmarie Fenrich is the Director of Special Projects in Africa for the Leitner Center for International Law and Justice at Fordham Law School in New York. She graduated magna cum laude with her J.D. from Fordham Law School, where she served as editor-in-chief of the *Fordham Law Review*. Following graduation, she served as law clerk to the Honorable John F. Keenan, U.S. District Court for the Southern District of New York. She has also held positions as the Human Rights Fellow for the Crowley Program in International Human Rights and Secretary for the International Human Rights Committee of the New York City Bar Association. She has conducted field research and authored publications focusing on issues related to domestic violence, stigma and discrimination faced by women with HIV/AIDS, women's property and inheritance rights, and the situation of women in customary-law marriage under domestic and international human rights law. She has also taught classes on specialized human rights topics, civil procedure, and the United Nations Security Council.

Paolo Galizzi is a Clinical Associate Professor of Law and Director of the Sustainable Development Legal Initiative (SDLI) at the Leitner Center for International Law and Justice at Fordham Law School. He previously held academic positions at Imperial College London, and the Universities of Nottingham, Verona, and Milan. Professor Galizzi graduated summa cum laude from the Faculty of Law of the University of Milan and continued his legal education at the School of Oriental and African Studies, University of London, where he obtained an LLM, and then went on to receive his PhD in International Environmental Law from the University of Milan. Professor Galizzi's research interests lie in international law, environmental law, and law of sustainable development, and he has conducted fieldwork in several African countries.

Roelof H. Haveman (LLM 1983; PhD 1998) works as a Field Programme Manager for the International Development Law Organization supporting the justice institutions of Southern Sudan, based in Juba. From 2005 to 2010, he worked in Rwanda, initially supporting two law faculties, and since 2008 as the Vice Rector of Academic Affairs of the ILPD/Institute of Legal Practice and Development. From its establishment in 2002 until 2005, he was the program director of the Grotius Centre for International Legal Studies at Leiden University, the Netherlands, where he also served as an associate professor of (international) criminal law. In 1998, he defended his PhD dissertation on trafficking in women. Over the past twenty-five years, he has published many articles and a number of books on gender-related crimes, trafficking in persons, the principle of legality, Indonesian adat law, Rwandan *gacaca*, and supranational criminology and victimology. He is the editor-in-chief of the series *Supranational Criminal Law*.

Tracy E. Higgins co-founded the Leitner Center for International Law and Justice at Fordham Law School, an institution that seeks to promote respect for human rights around the world. She co-directs the Leitner Center and is a law professor at Fordham University. Professor Higgins received her Bachelor of Arts degree from Princeton University and attended Harvard Law School, where she served as an editor of the *Harvard Law Review*. After graduating magna cum laude with her Juris Doctor, Professor Higgins became the Women's Law and Public Policy Fellow and an Adjunct Professor at Georgetown University Law Center. Professor Higgins has published numerous academic articles focusing on feminist jurisprudence, international human rights, and constitutional law in many of the nation's leading law journals, and she has conducted human rights research in eighteen countries, including Ghana, Kenya, Malawi, South Africa, and Rwanda.

Chuma Himonga is a Professor of Law at the University of Cape Town, South Africa, and holds a PhD and LLM from London University and an LLB from the University of Zambia. She also collaborated in researching the Sonderforschungsbericht 214: Identitat in Afrika – Prozesse ihre Entstehung und Veranderung inter-disciplinary research project at the University of Bayreuth, Germany. Her research interests and publications cover the law of persons and marriage, African customary law, women's rights in Southern Africa, and children's rights.

Manfred O. Hinz studied law and philosophy at the University of Mainz, Germany, from which he graduated in 1960. He obtained his doctorate degree in law from the University of Mainz in 1964. After studying anthropology, sociology, and African and Oriental languages at the same university, he became assistant lecturer, teaching anthropology and public law. In 1971, he was appointed full professor at the University of Bremen, Germany. He went to Namibia at the country's independence and helped build the first institution for legal education on Namibian soil: the Faculty of Law of the University of Namibia, which he joined in 1993. Professor Hinz holds the UNESCO Chair: Human Rights and Democracy in the Law Faculty's Human Rights and Documentation Centre.

Sandra F. Joireman is a Professor of Politics and International Relations at Wheaton College in Illinois. She specializes in comparative political economy with an emphasis on Africa. A political scientist and the author of three books and numerous articles on property rights and legal development, her research currently focuses on the enforcement of property rights in common-law Africa. Joireman received her MA and PhD in political science from the University of California, Los Angeles. She was a Fulbright scholar at the University of Addis Ababa and a visiting research scholar at Oxford University in the United Kingdom and Makerere University in Uganda. She has also taught at Meserete Kristos College in Ethiopia.

Laurence Juma is Associate Professor of Law at the Faculty of Law at Rhodes University in Grahamstown, South Africa. Before joining Rhodes, he held faculty positions at the University of Nairobi, the National University of Lesotho, and University of Fort Hare. From 2001 to 2002, he was a research Fellow at the Danish Centre for Human Rights in Copenhagen and was involved in various research projects focusing on the congruence between human rights and African customary law. His interests are in the fields of African customary law, international human rights law, and conflict studies, and he has written extensively on these subjects. Currently, his research focuses on the relationship between customary institutions and democratic practice in the Kingdom of Lesotho and South Africa.

Digby Sqhelo Koyana is a law professor at Fort Hare University, South Africa. He holds LLB and LLM degrees. He also earned the LLD degree from the University of South Africa in 1988 and the LLD degree from the University of Pretoria in 1992. He practiced as an Attorney and later as an Advocate of the High Court of South Africa. He is the author of two textbooks, one on customary law entitled *Customary Law in a Changing Society* and one on criminal law entitled *The Influence of the Transkei Penal Code on South African Criminal Law*. He has published numerous articles in journals in the fields of customary law and criminal law.

Chi Mgbako is a Clinical Associate Professor of Law and Director of the Leitner International Human Rights Clinic at Fordham Law School in New York City, which partners with NGOs and foreign law schools on human rights projects in Africa, Asia, Latin America, the Middle East, and the United States. Previously, she was Fordham's Crowley Fellow in International Human Rights. Before joining Fordham's faculty, she was based in Dakar, Senegal, as Harvard Henigson Human Rights Fellow with the International Crisis Group. She has conducted human rights fieldwork and reporting in Ethiopia, Liberia, Nigeria, Malawi, Sierra Leone, Rwanda, and Uganda, and she has taught African women's history and human rights in Accra, Ghana. She is a graduate of Harvard Law School and Columbia University and has published in the areas of sex workers rights, reproductive rights, the feminization of HIV/AIDS, justice sector reform, and transitional justice.

Wazha G. Morapedi is a senior lecturer in the history department of the University of Botswana. He teaches Latin American, Central African, and Botswana history. Dr. Morapedi obtained his BA from the University of Botswana in 1989 and joined the university as a Staff Development Fellow in the department of history in 1990. He obtained his MA and PhD in comparative history at Essex University in the United Kingdom in 1992 and 1998, respectively. Dr. Morapedi has written on traditional leadership in Africa, migrant labor, and agrarian and peasant issues in Botswana. His research areas are in comparative agrarian and peasant studies in Africa and Latin America, traditional leadership (chieftaincy) in Africa, and migration studies. Dr. Morapedi is currently working on land restitution in the Tati District of North Eastern Botswana.

Abdulmumini A. Oba is a senior lecturer at the faculty of law, University of Ilorin, in Ilorin, Nigeria, where he served as Head of the Department of Jurisprudence and International Law from 1998 to 2002. His research interests are African customary law, administration of Islamic and customary laws in Nigeria, and human rights from the perspectives of legal, religious, and cultural pluralism. He has published extensively in these areas.

George Otieno Ochich is an advocate of the High Court of Kenya and a Senior Lecturer at the School of Law, Moi University, Eldoret, Kenya. He specializes in customary law, which he has taught at the law school since 1999. Ochich also teaches and researches on the law relating to disabilities, international trade, and the environment. He holds a Bachelor of Laws degree from the University of Nairobi and Master of Laws in international and commercial law from the University of Buckingham. He is currently pursuing doctoral studies at the University of South Africa.

Christa Rautenbach Christa Rautenbach is a Professor of Law at the faculty of law, North-West University (Potchefstroom Campus), South Africa, where she obtained the degrees B Iuris (cum laude), LLB (cum laude), and LLD. She is actively involved in researching issues pertaining to African customary law and has published extensively on the subject in national and international journals. She is co-editor of *Potchefstroom Electronic Law*. Since 2006, she is an Alexander von Humboldt scholar and she has co-edited and authored a number of textbooks including *Customary Law of Succession and Inheritance* in *Law of South Africa: Vol 32*; *Introduction to Legal Pluralism in South Africa*; and *Law of Succession in South Africa*. She is an Advocate of the High Court of South Africa and a Commissioner of the Small Claims Court of Potchefstroom.

Isidore Kwadwo Tufuor is Leitner Center Lecturer in Law at the Law School of the Ghana Institute for Management and Public Administration (GIMPA), Accra, Ghana. A 2010 graduate of the International Law and Justice LLM program of Fordham Law School in New York, he holds a BA in French and Law and an LLB, both from the Kwame Nkrumah University of Science and Technology (KNUST), Kumasi, Ghana. He also holds a Barrister-at-Law Certificate from the Ghana School of Law in Accra. Mr. Tufuor is supervising the implementation of the "Access to Justice" and "Right to Health" clinical projects in Ghana, under the auspices of the Leitner Center for International Law and Justice at Fordham Law School in New York.

Dr. Ben Kiromba Twinomugisha is an Associate Professor and Dean, at the Faculty of Law, Makerere University, Uganda. He is also an advocate of the Courts of Judicature in Uganda and has undertaken research and published in the areas of human rights and environmental law. He has taught law for more than twenty years at both college and university levels. He is a member of the IUCN Academy of Environmental Law and a visiting professor at the Centre for Human Rights, University of Pretoria, South Africa.

Janine Ubink is Senior Lecturer in law at the Van Vollenhoven Institute, Faculty of Law, Leiden University in The Netherlands. She holds a Bachelor of Law together with a Master of International Law from Leiden University. She wrote her PhD about customary land management in Ghana. Her areas of specialization include customary law, traditional authorities, land tenure, legal anthropology, and legal empowerment. Her regional focus is on Africa, but she has also been involved in comparative research in Africa, Asia, and Latin America. She is the executive secretary of the Commission on Legal Pluralism. Since 2010, she has also held the position of Hauser Global Faculty Professor at the New York University School of Law.

Gordon R. Woodman is Emeritus Professor of Comparative Law at the University of Birmingham in the United Kingdom. He took his first degrees at the University of Cambridge. Since 1961, he has studied and written about customary law in many countries. He worked in university law faculties in Ghana and Nigeria for fifteen years before moving to the Faculty of Law of the University of Birmingham. He has been President of the Commission on Legal Pluralism and is editor of the *Journal of Legal Pluralism*. His publications include *Customary Land Law in the Ghanaian Courts* (1996); *African Law and Legal Theory* (co-edited with Akintunde O. Obilade 1995); *Local Land Law and Globalization: A Comparative Study of Peri-urban Areas in Benin, Ghana and Tanzania* (co-edited with Ulrike Wanitzek and Harald Sippel, 2004); and *Law and Religion in Multicultural Societies* (co-edited with Rubya Mehdi, Hanna Petersen, and Erik Reenberg Sand, 2008).

Acknowledgments

The editors wish to acknowledge the incredible efforts of Elizabeth Mooers, Program Assistant at the Leitner Center for International Law and Justice, who coordinated all the logistics necessary for this book as well as the arrangements for the two-day conference in October 2008 at the University of Botswana, where earlier versions of many of the chapters in this book were first presented. The editors are also grateful to the Faculty of Law at the University of Botswana, and especially to Dr. Onkemetse BashiTshosa and Dr. Kholisani Solo, for their valuable contributions in organizing the conference and for the wonderful hospitality they showed to all conference participants in Botswana. We would also like to thank the post-graduate Dean's Fellows at Fordham Law School who provided research and editorial assistance on the chapters included in this book, including John Christopher Moellering, Shabbir Chaudhury, and Abisola Fatade. We would like to thank Fordham Law students Joseph Nussbaum, Chauncee Smith, Marni von Wilpert, Ashley Pope, Jesse Melman, and Amy Rossnagel, who provided excellent research assistance on this book. Finally, we would like to express our gratitude to Alena Herklotz, the Leitner Center's Fellow in International Law of Sustainable Development, and to Liz Shura, the Leitner Center's Dean's Fellow, for their assistance in the final stages of the editorial process for this volume.

Introduction

Jeanmarie Fenrich, Paolo Galizzi, and Tracy E. Higgins

Pluralism is part of the fabric of legal systems in most, if not all, African countries. The traditional institutions and customary law that regulated ancient civilizations and societies on the African continent have changed over the years to keep pace with historical events and the evolution that the continent has witnessed. Once the sole source of law, customary rules have had to adapt to significant change brought by colonial rule and then decolonization. In addition to customary law, most sub-Saharan African countries are now bound by domestic constitutional law, statutory law, and common law, as well as international and regional human rights treaties.

In many countries, constitutional law, statutory law, and common law have superseded most or all customary law. In others, domestic constitutions now enshrine the right to culture and oblige courts to apply customary law where applicable, although subject to constitutional and statutory law.[1] Yet this picture of customary legal systems subordinated to constitutional and formal legal rules does not accurately portray the much more complex reality on the ground. In villages, towns, and cities across the African continent, peoples' lives continue to be regulated by customary laws. Traditional legal systems are often the only ones functioning in remote corners of the continent, where the reach of the State is at best limited and at times non-existent. Even where available, the formal legal system, with its linguistic obstacles, intricate rules, formalities, and expense, is often out of reach of the poor or uneducated. In addition, the persistence of long-standing expectations and social practices informed by customary law has given rise to many problems in enforcing contradictory constitutional or statutory law.

---

[1] See, e.g., S. AFR. CONST. 1996, §31(1) ("Persons belonging to a cultural, religious or linguistic community may not be denied the right, with other members of that community-(a) to enjoy their culture, practise their religion and use their language;"); §211(3) ("The courts must apply customary law when that law is applicable, subject to the Constitution and any legislation that specifically deals with customary law.").

Customary laws and institutions constitute comprehensive legal systems that regulate the entire spectrum of activities from birth to death. In many places, customary law continues to govern civil and criminal affairs, including family relations, traditional authority, property rights, and succession. In some instances, the application of customary law is problematic as there is potential conflict between the protection and application of customary law and other domestic and international human rights norms, such as gender equality. The editors of this book, who are all affiliated with the Leitner Center for International Law and Justice at Fordham Law School in New York, have conducted fieldwork in a number of different countries in Africa and authored publications that illustrate the ongoing importance of customary law and the difficulties that arise in navigating competing bodies of law.[2]

Notwithstanding the significant role customary law continues to play in people's lives, there has been a notable lack of contemporary scholarship on the status and role of customary law across the African continent. In response to this lack of scholarship, the Leitner Center convened a two-day conference in October 2008 in partnership with the Faculty of Law at the University of Botswana. The conference brought together leading academics, judges, stakeholders, policy makers, and experts to discuss the future of African customary law. A total of twenty-eight papers were presented at the conference along with remarks from the Attorney General of Botswana and traditional leaders from Sierra Leone and a roundtable discussion with members of the judiciary from South Africa, Botswana, and Ghana.

This volume, *The Future of African Customary Law*, includes revised versions of a number of the papers that were presented at the conference, in addition to new contributions from scholars and experts in the field, and is aimed at policy makers, scholars, members of the judiciary and legal profession, students, and at a broader audience including all those with an interest, either personal or professional, in African customary law. This volume is intended to promote research to understand customary law, explore its continued relevance, its rules, and its evolution to ensure that this legal system contributes to addressing the needs of the continent. The arguments and insights offered by the authors are the authors' own. The editors have attempted to include authors who present many of the divergent views that exist on the subject of the appropriate role and future

---

[2] *See, e.g.*, Jeanmarie Fenrich & Tracy Higgins, *Promise Unfulfilled: Law, Culture, and Women's Inheritance Rights in Ghana*, 25 FORDHAM INT'L L.J. 259 (2001); Tracy E. Higgins, Jeanmarie Fenrich & Ziona Tanzer, *Gender Equality and Customary Marriage: Bargaining in the Shadow of Post-Apartheid Legal Pluralism*, 30 FORDHAM INT'L L.J. 1653 (2007); Chi Mgbako, Jeanmarie Fenrich & Tracy Higgins, *We Will Still Live: Confronting Stigma and Discrimination Against Women Living with HIV/AIDS in Malawi*, 31 FORDHAM INT'L L.J. 528, 576–578 (2008); Mehlika Hoodboy, Martin Flaherty, & Tracy E. Higgins, *Exporting Despair: The Human Rights Implications of Restriction on U.S. Health Care Funding in Kenya*, 29 FORDHAM INT'L L.J. 1 (2005).

significance of customary law in Africa. Accordingly, the editors do not necessarily endorse all arguments included in this volume. The book primarily focuses on Anglophone African countries, with the exception of chapters focusing on Rwanda and Senegal.

The book is divided into six parts. Part One, titled "The Nature and Future of Customary Law," considers broadly what constitutes customary law and how this body of law differs from legislation and common law. In Chapters 1 and 3, Gordon R. Woodman and Abdulmumini A. Oba offer views on the significant characteristics of customary law. Chapter 3 also discusses the historical development of customary law and the impact of colonialism on the normative content of customary law. The chapters included in Part One also discuss the legal context in which customary law currently operates in various states in West and Southern Africa, and consider state recognition of customary law today and the existence of, and difference between, "official" customary law and "living" customary law. These chapters also discuss the future relevance and influence of customary law with respect to both official and unofficial law and, in Chapter 2, Chuma Himonga considers the potential of living customary law to protect human rights.

Part Two, titled "Ascertainment, Application, and Codification of Customary Law," considers the process to determine the content of customary law; the form and status of customary law; and how the scope of its application has been limited in some countries. In Chapter 4, Janine Ubink considers various methods utilized to ascertain rules of customary law by scholars and judges in African state courts. The chapter focuses in particular on the difficulties presented by situations of change and conflict when customary norms are contested, and utilizes a case study regarding customary land management in Ghana to illustrate many of the issues that arise in such cases. In Chapter 5, George Otieno Ochich considers the historical and current place of customary law in Kenya's legal system, and the manner in which the application of customary law has been severely limited in Kenya.

Part Two also discusses efforts to codify customary law and evaluates the effect of codification projects on the development of customary law and coherency in its application. In Chapter 6, Laurence Juma examines the experiences of the Kingdom of Lesotho with the codification of its customary law in the Code of Lerotholi. Juma attempts to determine what, if any, influence the Code has had on the administration of justice, the institution of chieftaincy, the structure of the legal system, and the practice of democracy.

In contrast to the codification project in Lesotho, Manfred O. Hinz in Chapter 7 discusses a project in Namibia undertaken by traditional communities to "self-state" or make and ascertain the customary law themselves. Hinz discusses how the self-stating project differs in process and effect from codification, although both result in written texts. Interestingly, and in contrast to the efforts elsewhere to alter the customary law of intestate succession through national legislation or case law, Hinz discusses efforts to develop and harmonize the customary law of intestate succession in Namibia through the process of self-stating to improve the plight of widows. In Chapter 8, Chi Mgbako and Kristina Scurry Baehr consider the work of paralegal organizations to resolve justice disputes in Sierra Leone and Liberia. Mgbako and Baehr examine some of the challenges paralegals encounter in working in legal dualist systems and document how paralegals advocate for the positive development of customary law, utilize the formal system to check injustice in customary forums, and provide mediation as an alternative to both the formal and customary systems, among other approaches.

In the final chapter of Part Two, Justice Joseph B. Akamba and Isidore Kwadwo Tufuor consider the sources and scope of customary law in Ghana. Akamba and Tufuor focus in part on the development of customary law through court decisions and maintain that courts today apply emerging principles of social development and public policy to shape and modify customary law rules. This chapter also considers the future of customary law in Ghana and a new customary law ascertainment and codification project being undertaken by the National House of Chiefs and the Law Reform Commission in Ghana.

Part Three considers the role and power of traditional authorities. Digby S. Koyana analyzes the evolution and the primary features and functions of traditional courts in South Africa in Chapter 10. Koyana considers some of the unique aspects of traditional courts that are often criticized, including the prohibition of legal representation, basic record keeping and lack of codification of the customary law, the informal distinction between civil and criminal cases in these courts, and the conciliatory rather than retributive nature of traditional courts. Koyana also discusses advantages traditional courts offer over magistrate or other state courts, and argues for the continued utility of the traditional courts based on their strengths, such as accessibility, affordability, simple procedures, and use of the local language of the parties, among others.

In Chapter 11, Wazha G. Morapedi discusses a surprising resurgence of the institution of chieftaincy in the 1990s in many African countries and offers reasons for this resurgence. Morapedi then discusses in detail the institution of chieftaincy in Botswana, both historically and post-independence, and the roles and duties chiefs have been accorded by the state and how customary law has enabled the institution to remain relevant with respect to judicial and administrative functions in Botswana. Finally, in Chapter 12, Ernest Kofi Abotsi and Paolo Galizzi consider traditional leadership and governance in Ghana. Abotsi and Galizzi examine the history, challenges, and opportunities for the institution of traditional leadership within a modern democracy and evaluate the effect of the current constitutional guarantee for chieftaincy and its practical workability and structural efficiency under the current governance system.

Part Four considers customary land tenure, property rights and intestate succession, and efforts to reform these areas of customary law. In Chapter 13, Sandra F. Joireman examines the relationship between customary land tenure and the role and authority of customary leaders throughout Sub-Saharan Africa. Joireman first discusses the different systems of land holding introduced in the colonial period (private and customary) with the different attendant rights and control and enforcement systems. Joireman then considers the various groups who benefit from customary systems of land tenure, such as the customary leaders who control customary land, and those who are left in a more vulnerable position with respect to property rights due to customary tenure systems, such as migrants and women. Joireman then proposes a set of criteria that can be used to evaluate the impact of customary land tenure and customary authority structures on social welfare and offers recommendations for the future based on the outcome of her analysis.

In Chapter 14, Janet L. Banda considers the variety and efficacy of contemporary land reforms targeting customary tenure. Banda critiques the approach of the World Bank and others that emphasize transformation of existing indigenous tenure systems, and in particular formalization of customary interests in land through title and registration as a means of achieving tenure security and economic growth. Banda offers other approaches for reform that affirm customary tenure systems while working to correct inequitable access to land and enhancing tenure security.

In Chapter 15, Christa Rautenbach and Willemien du Plessis consider the status of the customary law of succession in South Africa and whether this body of law has been improved or abolished by the many judicial and legislative changes that attempt to bring it in line with the constitutional guarantees of gender equality and other rights.

Part Five addresses customary criminal law. Thomas W. Bennett, in Chapter 16, discusses the place of customary criminal law in the South African legal system. Bennett focuses on the jurisdiction recently given to traditional courts to hear cases involving certain customary criminal offenses and considers whether such recognition of customary crimes presents issues with respect to South Africa's constitutional law, political structure and human rights guarantees. In Chapter 17, Roelof H. Haveman considers the *Gacaca* or the traditional justice system in Rwanda and its transformation for use to try suspects involved in the 1994 genocide in that country. Haveman examines important characteristics of the transformed *Gacaca*, which are intended to help rebuild the country by ending impunity for perpetrators of the 1994 genocide and fostering reconciliation among Rwandans.

Finally, Part Six includes chapters that consider the relationship between customary law, human rights, and gender equality. In Chapter 18, Tracy E. Higgins and

Jeanmarie Fenrich explore the tension between traditional legal systems and the commitment to gender equality embodied in international treaties and the domestic constitutions of many African states. Higgins and Fenrich consider whether a pluralist legal structure provides a means of reconciling this tension and examine case studies from Ghana, Tanzania, and South Africa in order to illustrate the strengths and limitations of such a model.

Also in Part Six, Ben Kiromba Twinomugisha considers the relationship between customary law and women's rights in Uganda. Although he recognizes that many customary norms and practices are discriminatory, Twinomugisha rejects the view that customary law is universally contrary to gender equality. Rather, he argues that there are aspects of customary law that are empowering for women and that, given that customary law is a flexible, living system of law, areas of customary law that are discriminatory can be adapted to comply with international and domestic obligations regarding women's rights. Johanna E. Bond in Chapter 20 considers the extent to which international and regional human rights treaties, and in particular the new Protocol to the African Charter on Human and People's Rights on the Rights of Women in Africa, can be used to reform customary law so that it better complies with international human rights norms regarding gender equality.

Finally, in Chapter 21, Fatou K. Camara investigates pre-colonial African customary laws and practices in an effort to identify human-rights-friendly rules and values that different African communities have in common and that can be relied on to promote socio-legal reforms and thereby achieve a long-awaited "African Renaissance."

PART ONE

The Nature and Future of Customary Law

1

A Survey of Customary Laws in Africa in Search of Lessons for the Future

Gordon R. Woodman

1.1. INTRODUCTION

The role of customary laws in the twenty-first century, whether in Africa or elsewhere, is of great theoretical interest. It is important, however, that the present discussion makes a contribution to legal development in Africa. I seek here to discern the lessons that can be learned from past experience of customary laws in Africa and that may assist in determining future policies toward customary law.

I do not argue for the adoption of particular policies. As an outside, although fascinated, observer of customary laws in Africa, it is not for me to say what ought to be done about them in the future. An observer may only help by suggesting the various future courses of action that are open, pointing out what, in the light of experience, may be feasible and what is not. This is an attempt to draw useful generalizations from the considerable volume of information in the literature.

Two further qualifications are needed. First, I concern myself here with Sub-Saharan Africa only. Second, the abundant evidence of the vast variety in the content and form of customary laws in Sub-Saharan Africa entails that there is almost certainly an exception to any generalization somewhere. Attempts have been made to generalize about the substance of specific branches of customary laws in Africa.[1] These are instructive, but still it may be suggested that every particular customary law needs to be studied before it can be concluded that any such generalization of it is true. In this chapter I consider generalizations about the nature of customary laws in Africa in less specific terms, but nevertheless skepticism is needed. Although the propositions I suggest may be true of many instances of customary laws, all that follows in this chapter should be understood with this qualification.

---

[1] *See, e.g.,* TASLIM OLAWALE ELIAS, THE NATURE OF AFRICAN CUSTOMARY LAW (Manchester University Press 1956).

The only completely accurate generalization is that there are no completely accurate generalizations.[2]

1.2. IDENTIFICATION OF THE SUBJECT MATTER

Our subject matter is customary laws that exist in Africa. We do not intend to engage in much theoretical debate. Nevertheless, if we are not clear about our topic of discussion, we shall not produce realistic conclusions, and to define our topic, some theoretical discussion is necessary.

In referring to customary laws that exist in Africa, I use the plural term to avoid any possible implication of a denial of the variety of customary laws on the continent. Furthermore, I refer to those existing in Africa, not to African customary laws, to avoid implying that there is necessarily a distinctive difference between African customary laws and non-African customary laws.

A customary law may be defined as a normative order observed by a population, having been formed by regular social behavior and the development of an accompanying sense of obligation. A normative order is a body of interrelated norms, or of rules and principles. It has been argued that customary laws in Africa, at least those which existed in the past, should not be seen as bodies of norms, because "rules per se had no particular value for African societies" in the period before colonization.[3] Because of concern over this possibility, scholarship on customary law concentrated for a time on the study of disputing processes.[4]

It is not possible to debate this issue fully here. However, it may be noted that studies of disputing processes show that, although the outcomes of disputes may not be determined by the mechanical application of previously published norms, the disputes have originated in and been structured by norms. Disputes are conflicting claims over normatively defined entitlements and obligations, not warfare between total strangers. Moreover, disputing processes follow procedures set by norms.[5]

---

[2] For a similar cautionary preliminary statement, *see* Thomas W. Bennett, *Comparative Law and African Comparative Law*, in THE OXFORD HANDBOOK OF COMPARATIVE LAW 641, 643 (Mathias Reimann & Reinhard Zimmermann eds., Oxford University Press 2006).

[3] THOMAS W. BENNETT, HUMAN RIGHTS AND AFRICAN CUSTOMARY LAW UNDER THE SOUTH AFRICAN CONSTITUTION 2 (Juta 1995); *cf.* THOMAS W. BENNETT, CUSTOMARY LAW IN SOUTH AFRICA 1–33 (Juta 2004).

[4] *See, e.g.,* Richard L. Abel, *Case Method Research in the Customary Law of Wrongs in Kenya I*, 5 E. AFR. L.J. 247 (1969); Richard L. Abel, *Customary Law of Wrongs in Kenya: An Essay in Research Method*, 17 AM. J. COMP. L 573 (1969); Richard L. Abel, *A Comparative Theory of Dispute Institutions in Society*, 8 LAW & SOC'Y REV. 217 (1973); SIMON ROBERTS, ORDER AND DISPUTE: AN INTRODUCTION TO LEGAL ANTHROPOLOGY (Penguin Books 1979).

[5] *See* PHILIP H. GULLIVER, SOCIAL CONTROL IN AN AFRICAN SOCIETY: A STUDY OF THE ARUSHA: AGRICULTURAL MASAI OF NORTHERN TANGANYIKA (Routledge & Kegan Paul 1963); Philip H.

Consequently a study of a customary law may include a study of disputes in the community, but legal studies cannot be limited to this. In many societies, extensive areas of their normative orderings rarely or never give rise to disputes. In many customary laws in Africa, for example, there is never a dispute over the content of the principal norms determining membership of the lineage or "family" that is party to many legal relations.

Customary law is sometimes contrasted with legislation, or the statute law of the modern state. Legislation is ideally formed at a specific moment in time by a formal decision of an individual or a group consisting (except in the case where a popular referendum is held) of a minute portion of the community. The contrast between customary law and legislation may appear especially persuasive in Africa, because here the state, as we know it today, was originally an alien imposition. The customary laws were here before the colonizers arrived, bringing their legislative processes that produced definitive written texts. Even in the field of received law, however, some of the colonies – the Anglophones – also placed emphasis on case law, or precedent. It is questionable how that source of law should be classified, falling as it does somewhere between statute and custom.

The dividing line between customary law and legislation is thus not entirely clear. It becomes still hazier when it is noted that customary laws in Africa have often authorized legislative activity and have enabled the enforcement of the regulations so made.[6] Furthermore, it may be argued that even the statutes of the modern state are effective only because of a social acceptance of the authority of the legislators. Thus the legal nature or legitimacy of legislation is founded on customary law. Indeed, if customary law is said not to be law because of its mode of creation, then neither are many portions of state laws. This applies not only to precedent in the narrow common-law sense but also to the modes of interpreting and applying legislative rules in administrative and judicial processes that are often multifarious and elaborate but not reduced into writing (or not until they have been settled in reported cases). Furthermore, the boundaries of the category of state laws are vague and ultimately indefinable. Even if a state law does not explicitly recognize customary laws as forming part of the legal system – and in all common law systems it does

Gulliver, *Negotiations as a Mode of Dispute Settlement: Towards a General Model* 7 LAW & SOC'Y REV 667 (1973); DISPUTES AND NEGOTIATIONS: A CROSS-CULTURAL PERSPECTIVE, at 190–194 (Philip H. Gulliver ed., Academic Press 1979); JOHN L. COMAROFF & SIMON ROBERTS, RULES AND PROCESSES: THE CULTURAL LOGIC OF DISPUTE IN AN AFRICAN CONTEXT (University of Chicago Press 1981).

6 *See* Elias, *supra*, note 1, at 187–211; Chukwuemeka Ebo, *Indigenous Law and Justice: Some Major Concepts and Practices*, 76 VIERTELJAHRESBERICHTE 139 (1979) (F.R.G.), *reprinted in* AFRICAN LAW AND LEGAL THEORY 33, 35 (Gordon R. Woodman & Akintunde O. Obilade, eds., Aldershot 1995); Mikano Emmanuel Kiye, The Importance of Customary Law in Africa: A Cameroonian Case Study, at 89–91 (2007) (unpublished PhD dissertation, Vrije Universiteit Brussel) (Belgium).

recognize at least some[7] – the processes of interpreting and applying state law, legislative and otherwise, in every legal system involve reference to numbers of socially accepted norms. These are not merely used but are determinative of specific legal issues. They are authoritative, if to some degree manipulable, and thus are legal principles,[8] while being customary norms. It would seem untenable to assert that only formal legislation is true law.

Attempts are made also to contrast customary law with state law. The debates on this are mentioned later, because the issues are especially acute in Africa as a consequence of the colonial origins of the modern African state.

This chapter considers customary laws as just defined. First I consider some of the principal features of customary laws in Africa and their development in recent centuries. Then, in the following section, I consider them as parts of a wider legal picture that includes modern state laws.

1.3. CHARACTERISTICS OF CUSTOMARY LAWS

Certain general characteristics of customary laws in Africa tend to be overlooked, or their existence denied, but are especially significant for current policies.

1.3.1. *Customary Laws Reflect and Tend to Sustain Inequalities in the Social Order of Their Communities*

The notion of a customary law as emerging from the whole body of a community and being generally accepted within the community could be thought to entail that it emerges from processes of popular, democratic debate in which each person's interest carries the same weight as everybody else's. In practice, inequality is universal. In virtually all communities, disproportionate advantages are held, and disproportionate influence is exercised, by males. For example, even though the social meaning of the marriage payment made by the groom or his lineage to the parents or lineage of the bride in many customary laws is subject to debate, the different laws that define the need for and consequences of this payment can hardly be claimed to treat male and female parties equally. Again, succession laws generally give preference to male claimants to property and status, either explicitly or in their effects. A further form of inequality lies in the principle of most customary laws according to which members of the oldest living generation by law exercise more power in social and political arenas than younger members. Especially parents (or at least

---

[7] *See* Gordon R. Woodman, *The Involvement of English Common Law with Other Laws, in* LA QUÊTE ANTHROPOLOGIQUE DU DROIT: AUTOUR DE LA DÉMARCHE D'ÉTIENNE LE ROY (Christoph Eberhard & Genevié ve Vernicos, eds. éditions Karthala 2006).

[8] *See* RONALD DWORKIN, TAKING RIGHTS SERIOUSLY (Harvard University Press 1977).

fathers), while alive, have more authority than their sons and daughters, no matter the age and achievements of the latter. This is made explicit not only in customary laws governing the functions of age sets, but also in those determining the processes of accession to positions of responsibility and power, from caretakers of property to chieftaincy, and in the processes by which marriages are concluded. Further, in nearly all communities, there are some sections – typically lineages or clans – with greater access to benefits and power than the others. For example, in many communities, eligibility for certain public offices rests only in members of a "royal family." Conversely, in some communities, categories of persons of especially low status are excluded from some of the liberties and powers available to others. Examples are the Osus among the Igbo of Nigeria,[9] as well as persons of slave descent in many other societies. The customary laws generally both reflect and tend to perpetuate these inequalities of gender, age, and lineage status.[10]

This characteristic of customary laws might appear to conflict with the notion that such laws exist through acceptance within their communities. How, it may be asked, can an individual who resents discrimination be said to "accept" the normative order that incorporates it? Acceptance may arise from a variety of reasons. Members of communities may have been enculturated to acceptance by their upbringing within the communities. Those who are dissatisfied may nevertheless be unable to envisage any alternative social environment. The active and articulate dissatisfied member may think it preferable to work for change in those portions of the customary law that cause dissatisfaction, and in the meantime to accept the system as a whole, rather than attempting to replace the entire system. There may be a perception that the portions of a customary law that one disapproves of are structurally inseparable from the entire edifice, and maintenance of the existing law may reasonably be seen as preferable to its total destruction. Today the customary laws are often appreciated as inextricable parts of the local, indigenous cultures that are the basis of members' identities.

1.3.2. *Customary Laws Are Complex Bodies of Norms That Have Different Degrees of Mandatory Force*

A certain stereotypical analysis of law says that each legal system consists of a self-consistent body of imperative rules stipulating what must or must not be done. It is

---

[9] Chinua Achebe, No Longer at Ease (Heineman 1960); S. N. C. Obi, The Customary Law Manual: A Manual of Customary Laws Obtaining in the Anambra and Imo States in Nigeria, para. 285 (Ministry of Justice, Anambra State 1977) (Nigeria).

[10] *See* Martin Chanock, *Making Customary Law: Men, Women and Courts in Colonial Northern Rhodesia, in* African Women and the Law: Historical Perspectives (M. J. Hay & M. Wright eds., Boston University African Studies Center 1982); Kiye, *supra* note 6, at 98–101.

often added that sanctions must be prescribed for every case of non-compliance.[11] In practice, however, the norms of customary laws in Africa vary in the degree to which they are compulsory. Thus, for example, a customary law may permit a head of family to allocate the enjoyment of family resources, such as accommodation in a family house, but disapprove a refusal to allocate to a family member thought to be deserving, and more strongly disapprove an allocation to a non-member. The sanctions for failure to observe the norms may vary from a severe publicly imposed penalty, through a requirement to explain and justify an act and apologize if the explanation is thought unsatisfactory, or a liability to lose formal or de facto authority, to critical gossip and a loss of respect. Moreover, the appropriate penalty for breach of a particular norm may vary according to the circumstances, including the attitude of the parties. This variation is well exhibited in the very common practice of dispute processing by mediation, conducted by senior members of the community. In this process, an established infringement of a norm may be penalized to a minor degree, or not at all, if in the process of mediated negotiation this seems most likely to restore peace in the community.[12] Instances of the complexity that this produces in customary law bodies of norms are demonstrated in a number of sources.[13]

One implication of this feature is that customary law is present in hierarchical relations that the observer might at first think place some above the law. Unanimous displays of deep respect are sometimes given to rulers. There is evidence, however, that established customary norms govern the accession to office of the powerful, including traditional rulers, and then also prescribe the ruler's conduct and constrain his or her decision making. This is the case even if infringements are tolerated or seen as justifiable in particular instances. The idea of a *Rechtsstaat* is not foreign to African communities, and the rule of law prevails.[14] This conclusion

[11] *See, e.g.,* JOHN AUSTIN, THE PROVINCE OF JURISPRUDENCE DETERMINED (Weidenfeld & Nicolson 1955) (1832).
[12] *See* Gulliver, SOCIAL CONTROL, *supra* note 5; Gulliver, *Negotiations, supra* note 5; DISPUTES AND NEGOTIATIONS, *supra* note 5; Comaroff & Roberts, *supra* note 5.
[13] *See* Johan F. Holleman, *Trouble-cases and Trouble-less Cases in the Study of Customary Law and Legal Reform,* 7 LAW & SOC'Y REV. 585 (1973), *reprinted in* FOLK LAWS: ESSAYS IN THE THEORY AND PRACTICE OF LEX NON SCRIPTA, VOL. II (Alison D. Renteln & Alan Dundes eds., Garland 1994), *also reprinted in* AFRICAN LAW, *supra* note 6; JACQUES VANDERLINDEN, ANTHROPOLOGIE JURIDIQUE 26 (Dalloz 1996). Vanderlinden's report of the response he received to certain questions seems representative of many customary laws:
    When, in the Zande country, I on the first occasion asked a question designed to establish the order of succession to a deceased, the response was at the same time simple for my informants and devastating for me: "It all depends." The essential was not in effect to have rules in the matter of succession, but to ensure the most efficient transmission possible, in terms of a multitude of diverse parameters, of the powers of the deceased over both a patrimony and a lineage, to the person indicated to be the best for this end.
    Id., at 26 (translated).
[14] *See, e.g.,* ROBERT S. RATTRAY, ASHANTI LAW AND CONSTITUTION 406–407 (Oxford University Press 1929); George P. Hagan, *The Rule of Law in Asante, a Traditional Akan State,* 113 PRÉSENCE AFRICAINE 193 (1980) (Fr.); Vanderlinden, *supra* note 13, at 107–116.

would seem to follow from a number of useful works on chieftaincy published in the past twenty years.[15]

1.3.3. Customary Laws Constantly Change

It is sometimes asserted that it is of the essence of norms of customary law that they have existed "since time immemorial," or that in Africa, the authentic, "true" customary law is that which existed before the colonial period. It is implied that any recent change in the body of norms previously observed by a population is a deviation from the genuine customary law. These assertions may be countered by considering both the definition of customary law and empirical evidence.

The definition I have proposed is in terms of norms that are existing, meaning they are observed. If a community today no longer observes certain customary norms, these cannot be said to be existing customary laws. As lawyers we are usually interested in discovering or stating the law of the present day, unless we explicitly opt to examine the law of an earlier date. In an oft-quoted dictum of a Nigerian court, "the native law and custom which the Court is empowered and directed to observe ... must be existing native law or custom and not the law or custom of a bygone age."[16] It follows that a norm of a customary law need not have a longer history than the length of time it takes for the community to adopt it as part of its scheme of social obligations.

There is abundant empirical evidence that the content of the customary laws of Africa has changed significantly in the past century and continues to change today. A few general examples will accord with many particular laws. The considerable growth in the past century of the incidence of individually owned property rights has resulted in the emergence of norms to respond to issues such as the mode of disposal of property following the death of the owner. Indeed, an entire law of inheritance, intestate and testate, has been developed in many customary laws.[17] The widespread

---

[15] See LEGITIMATION VON HERRSCHAFT UND RECHT (Wilhelm J.G. Möhlig & Trutz von Trotha eds., Rüdiger Köppe 1992); AFRICAN CHIEFTAINCY IN A NEW SOCIO-POLITICAL LANDSCAPE (E. Adriaan B. van Rouveroy van Nieuwaal & Rijk van Dijk eds., Lit Verlag 1999); THE DYNAMICS OF POWER AND THE RULE OF LAW: ESSAYS ON AFRICA AND BEYOND (Wim van Binsbergen ed., Lit Verlag 2003); BARBARA OOMEN, CHIEFS IN SOUTH AFRICA: LAW, POWER AND CULTURE IN THE POST-APARTHEID ERA (James Currey 2005). But cf., e.g., Bennett, HUMAN RIGHTS, supra note 3, at 75; Bennett, SOUTH AFRICA, supra note 3, at 101–106.

[16] Lewis v. Bankole [1908] 1 N.L.R. 81, 83 (Nigeria).

[17] E.g., NII A. OLLENNU, THE LAW OF TESTATE AND INTESTATE SUCCESSION IN GHANA (Sweet & Maxwell and Waterville Publishing House 1966); Nwakamma Okoro, THE CUSTOMARY LAWS OF SUCCESSION IN EASTERN NIGERIA (Sweet & Maxwell and Waterville Publishing House 1966); Patricia G. Kameri-Mbote, Gender Dimensions of Law, Colonialism and Inheritance in East Africa: Kenyan Women's Experiences, 35 VERFASSUNG UND RECHT IN ÜBERSEE 373 (2002) (F.R.G); A.K.P. KLUDZE, MODERN LAW OF SUCCESSION IN GHANA (Foris 1988).

development of cash crops has produced new types of interests in land, especially various new forms of tenancies.[18] In these, as in other transactions such as marriage presentations, there has developed a use of modern currency, with principles emerging as to the appropriate sums to be paid on various occasions. Equally striking has been the use of written documents to evidence or even to effectuate customary-law transactions. In recent times, the phenomena of international migration and of diasporas of Africans who continue to be involved in the activities of their home communities while residing for long periods abroad have resulted in the emergence of norms concerning the participation of absent members and the duties owed by and to them.[19]

Some of these changes may have resulted from internally generated changes of social attitudes within communities. However, the most significant changes in customary laws, as in any laws in any society, seem to ensue from external forces. The increasing degree of incorporation of African communities into national and international economies, political communities, and societies are the cause of most changes in customary laws. Often changes occur because different communities come into close contact, and activities in one impinge on the other. Persons observing different customary laws may find themselves living in close proximity. Some persons may, as a result of economic or other activities, come to observe different customary laws in different spheres of their lives. In broader terms, the monetarization and commoditization brought about by global commerce have produced changes in customary laws in Africa. It seems likely that the pace and extent of change has been increasing in recent times. None of this is to deny that communities themselves exercise degrees of independence in determining their reactions to these forces.[20]

However, the recent increase in the rate of change does not justify its depiction as a rising curve on a track that was horizontal until the colonists arrived. For many centuries before the inception of government by European colonial powers, social change had been induced by shifting patterns of long-distance trade, including intercontinental trade, and population migrations. Thus, to take examples from the West African region, intercontinental trade by sea from Europe supplemented and to a great extent replaced overland trade from North Africa from the fifteenth century. In the seventeenth and eighteenth centuries, the slave trade caused considerable changes in the relations between different communities, and within the

---

[18] *See* GORDON R. WOODMAN, CUSTOMARY LAND LAW IN THE GHANAIAN COURTS 115–141 (Ghana Universities Press 1996).

[19] *See id.* at 324; AT HOME IN THE WORLD: CONTEMPORARY MIGRATION AND DEVELOPMENT IN GHANA AND WEST AFRICA (Takwiyaa Manuh ed., Sub-Saharan Publishers 2005).

[20] *See* LOCAL LAND LAW AND GLOBALIZATION: A COMPARATIVE STUDY OF PERI-URBAN AREAS IN BENIN, GHANA AND TANZANIA (Gordon R. Woodman et al. eds., Lit Verlag 2004).

communities of both those conducting and those suffering from the trade. Then, when the slave trade was suppressed in the first half of the nineteenth century, a huge expansion of the production and export of palm oil occurred to replace it.[21] We do not have detailed records from these earlier periods, but it would seem very likely that these developments brought about considerable changes in the economies of African communities, and so in their social structures and customary laws.[22] It is likely that change and adaptation have occurred continuously in each customary law since the first emergence of the community – itself a transformative process or event.

We may sometimes need to take the advent of colonialism as a marker – for example, when seeking to assess the effects of this transfer of power. In seeking through history an understanding of current law, we may compare it with the law that existed at such a moment. We should recognize, however, that every customary law was in flux at that date and had been long before.

1.3.4. *Parts of a Customary Law Are Often Uncertain and Objects of Controversy*

An increasing number of students of customary law have found that fundamental norms of a customary law may be matters of contestation within a community.[23] The resultant uncertainty may exist not only with regard to the content of the norms of parts of a law, but also with regard to the extent of the field of observance of a law. The very boundaries of a customary law – that is, of the population that observes a law – may be contested. There have long been possibilities of persons switching membership from one community to another, or belonging to more than one community sequentially or simultaneously. Global population movements today increase these possibilities.[24] This uncertainty is often compounded by variations within a community. There may be differences between the customary laws observed in different villages, clans, lineages, or households that, for many purposes, belong to one community.[25]

---

[21] *See* A.G. HOPKINS, AN ECONOMIC HISTORY OF WEST AFRICA 124–135 (Longman 1973).

[22] *See* Gordon R. Woodman, *Common Rights for the Private Good: The Allocation of Proprietary Rights in Ghanaian Agricultural Land* 13 RECHT DER WERKELIJKHEID 27 (1992) (Neth.).

[23] *See* Comaroff & Roberts, *supra* note 5; SARA BERRY, NO CONDITION IS PERMANENT: THE SOCIAL DYNAMICS OF AGRARIAN CHANGE IN SUB-SAHARAN AFRICA (University of Wisconsin Press 1993); ANNE M. O. GRIFFITHS, IN THE SHADOW OF MARRIAGE: GENDER AND JUSTICE IN AN AFRICAN COMMUNITY (University of Chicago Press 1997); Kiye, *supra* note 6.

[24] *See* Ralph Grillo & Valentina Mazzucato, *Africa<>Europe: A Double Engagement*, 34 J. ETHNIC & MIGRATION STUD. 175 (2008).

[25] *See*, *e.g.*, Obi, *supra* note 9 (throughout which sub-clauses set out local variations from the general norms stated).

This is not to claim that customary laws are totally indeterminate. I have suggested already that customary laws exist as bodies of norms, and also that they are elements in social orders that govern even powerful rulers, both of which claims make sense only if at least parts of a customary law are well settled. It is suggested only that total determinacy is not to be expected, especially in fields that are controversial within a community.

This feature arises in part from the nature of human communities: People persistently disagree about their customary laws. It arises also from other features of customary laws that we have already noted. Customary laws reflect and support inequalities in the social order. Norms that effectuate inequalities are likely to be contested by the disadvantaged. Customary laws frequently undergo change, and changes in power and influence are, again, likely to be contested and to give rise to uncertainty about the content of customary laws.

Of the four characteristics of customary laws noted, the first – a tendency to reflect and sustain inequalities – is a common feature of state laws. The other three – complexity with varying mandatory authority of norms, constant change, and contestability – have all been used in the literature to support claims that customary laws, when compared to state laws, are not truly laws. It may be suggested in response that many state laws display these same characteristics to similar degrees. In state laws, rules and principles carry different weight,[26] norms are very frequently changed (as every practitioner struggling to keep abreast of legal developments is aware), and there is a good deal of indeterminacy (as even those who reject the more extreme claims of legal realism and critical legal studies would admit).

1.4. THE LEGAL CONTEXT OF THE ROLE OF CUSTOMARY LAWS TODAY

In modern times, customary laws have generally been conceptualized as portions of wider legal scenarios. They are elements of a ubiquitous legal pluralism – that is, the situation in which a population observes more than one body of law. A consideration of this context casts further light on the nature of customary laws and the possibilities for their future development.

The colonizing powers established states in Africa, asserting jurisdiction in terms of territory and seeking to exercise authority over all the inhabitants of areas enclosed by the boundaries that they had drawn on maps. These were incompatible with customary law principles of jurisdiction, which are not primarily territorial. The populations that observe different customary laws have normally been communities of persons related to each other by common descent and long association.

---

[26] This is demonstrated in Dworkin, *supra* note 8.

Many communities had settled and were associated with particular territories, but the boundaries of these were frequently disregarded by colonial state boundaries, which grouped together communities that had been separate and divided single communities between different states. They established in each state that they created legal institutions such as legislatures and courts. These they designed in forms familiar to themselves. They then enacted the "reception" of their own laws (often themselves "traditional" and customary[27]), which were to be observed and applied in their institutions.

Initially the colonial state was administered by natives of the colonizing state, imbued with its general culture, including its legal culture. Subsequently during the colonial period, portions of the African populations acquired skills necessary to operate within the colonialists' cultures, and some joined the communities of state administrators. It was mainly this class that eventually came to exercise governmental functions in the independent nation-states.

This state law was an additional influence on customary laws, contributing to the extent and character of the changes that occurred. Thus, for example, the great increase in the incidence of individually owned property has been fostered by the individualism of state laws. Again, the development of the use of writing for customary-law transactions was encouraged by people's experience in the use of writing in state law processes. Moreover, the particular forms of documents used for customary-law transactions were often closely copied from the documents of received law, even when their words were inappropriate.[28]

Students of customary law have to contend with a further feature of the received state laws – their claim to legal monopoly. The laws of modern nation-states have frequently been accompanied by ideologies that asserted that only the state had the legitimate authority to create law. In the common-law world, this was put in its most extreme form by the British jurist John Austin. He claimed that law "properly and strictly so called" consisted of commands issued by the established sovereign individual or body of a politically independent state.[29] Customary law was "merely a rule of positive morality" until it was adopted by the courts of a state "and clothed with the legal sanction."[30] It is arguable that this is only one strand in the historical doctrines of common law, which also have a long history of recognizing and seeking

---

[27] See Vanderlinden, *supra* note 13, at 56–58.

[28] See Omoniyi Adewoye, *Legal Practice in Ibadan, 1904–1960*, 24 J. LEGAL PLURALISM 57, 67–68 (1986); Woodman, *supra* note 18, at 366–368; Ahonagnon N. Gbaguidi & Ulrich Spellenberg, *Benin: Globalization and Land Tenure Changes in Per-Urban Areas, in* LOCAL LAND LAW, *supra* note 20; Kasim Kasanga & Gordon R. Woodman, *Ghana: Local Law Making and Land Conversion in Kumasi, Asante, in* LOCAL LAND LAW, *supra* note 20.

[29] Austin, *supra* note 11.

[30] *Id.* at 31.

to give effect to customary laws.[31] Nevertheless, the strand that denies customary law has prevailed on important occasions. In the civil-law world, the same ideology was manifested most clearly in the enactment by the nation-state of codes intended to replace all other forms of law, which gave rise to the notion that law must be written.[32] The result was that many state officials held the conviction that law did not exist in Africa until the colonial powers brought and imposed their own state laws. Consequently customary laws could not be law unless the state had conferred that status on them, and then were law only insofar as it had done so.

The theoretical question whether customary law is properly classified as law has been debated elsewhere.[33] The definition adopted at the start of this paper suggests that customary law does indeed exist. I have suggested in the previous section that the characteristics of customary laws are present in state laws also. For the present purpose, the pressing question is whether customary law or state law should be seen as the primary law.

The order of discussion in this chapter is based on the premise that in Africa, customary law is the first and more fundamental law. An Asante verse, told in the language of the *ntumpane* drums ("talking drums"), reflects the question of which came first, as well as the necessary answer:

> The stream crosses the path,
> The path crosses the stream
> Which of them is the elder?
> Did we not cut a path to go and meet this stream?
> The stream had its origin long, long ago
> The stream had its origin in the Creator...[34]

Trained lawyers, like those who cut a path through the forest with their cutlasses, are prone to assume that the product of their skill, the elaborated state law, is the more fundamental one. The social reality is that the customary laws existed first, and have continued to be generally observed, whether or not they are in accord with state laws.[35]

---

[31] *See* Woodman, *supra* note 7, at 477.

[32] *See* P-F. GONIDEC, LES DROITS AFRICAINS: EVOLUTION ET SOURCES (Libraire Générale de Droit et de Jurisprudence 1976).

[33] *See* Gordon R. Woodman, *Ideological Combat and Social Observation: Recent Debate About Legal Pluralism*, 42 J. LEGAL PLURALISM 21 (1998).

[34] ROBERT S. RATTRAY, ASHANTI 89 (Oxford University Press 1923).

[35] *Cf.* MARTIN CHANOCK, LAW, CUSTOM AND SOCIAL ORDER: THE COLONIAL EXPERIENCE IN MALAWI AND ZAMBIA (Cambridge University Press 1985); Martin Chanock, *Neither Customary nor Legal: African Customary Law in an Era of Family Law Reform*, 3 INT'L J.L. & FAM. 72 (1989), *reprinted in* AFRICAN LAW, *supra* note 6, at 171.

The claim that state laws have exclusive legal authority is usually accompanied by a value judgment that received state law is preferable as a social regulator.[36] This judgment, which is not restricted to state officials, although it seems to be more strongly believed by people more exposed to the influence of the state,[37] has been behind many policy decisions in the development and extension of state laws. However, the legal ideologies and preference for state law of the colonial rulers and some of their African successors have not prevailed in social reality. In every part of Africa, customary laws coexist with state laws. Nevertheless, just as state law has not eliminated customary law, so the observance of customary law has not prevented state law from becoming firmly established. The modern state has power and influence. And the law that academics and officials teach, conduct research into, and apply is primarily state law.

In the modern world, the authority of state law is being challenged by increasingly effective international law and by regional laws such as that of the African Union.[38] These laws also, like state law, generally claim authority to override customary laws. Occasionally they endorse the observance of customary laws when they declare a right to practice a culture or recognize claims of indigenous peoples based on their customary laws, although it is difficult to determine the status of these rights in relation to other human rights.[39] An investigation is needed into the relations between these supra-national state laws and customary laws in Africa, but it is not possible to embark on that in the present chapter.

The relationship between customary law and state law is competitive, but to depict the two as in direct opposition would be to oversimplify the African legal landscape. State laws follow to some extent the practice of "recognizing" customary laws. This means that state laws expressly or impliedly declare that customary laws, or elements of them, already exist as valid laws, and seek to incorporate them into the state laws.[40]

Recognition of a customary law by a state law takes one or both of two forms. First, *normative recognition* occurs when state institutions treat substantive norms (rules, principles or both) of customary law as valid norms of state law. Second, *institutional recognition* occurs when state law treats acts of customary law institutions, such as dispute processing decisions of traditional authorities, as having valid effect in state law. In this case, state law may classify the traditional authorities as state courts, or it

---

[36] Vanderlinden recalls a phrase in a writing by a prominent African intellectual: "When the Europeans disembarked in Africa, bringing us civilisation…" Vanderlinden, *supra* note 13, at 17.

[37] See Kiye, *supra* note 6, at 71–82.

[38] See GLOBAL LAW WITHOUT A STATE (Gunther Teubner ed., Dartmouth 1997).

[39] SEE PATRICK THORNBERRY, INDIGENOUS PEOPLES AND HUMAN RIGHTS (Manchester University Press 2002); Manuela Zips-Mairitsch, Verlorenes Land? Indigene (Land)Rechte am Beispiel der San in Botswana (2008)(unpublished J.D. thesis, Vienna University).

[40] See generally Bennett, SOUTH AFRICA, *supra* note 3, at 34–75.

may go no further than restraining state institutions from exercising jurisdiction or otherwise intervening when customary law institutions operate.

State laws in Africa in which the received law is common law (or English law) have from the earliest colonial times adopted normative recognition through statutory provisions such as those that required state courts to "observe and enforce" customary laws[41] or to "be guided by" them,[42] or gave a discretion to decide issues according to them.[43] They adopted institutional recognition as a policy in the colonial period of indirect rule,[44] and many have done so to a certain degree since then. State laws in Africa in which the received law is civil law have engaged less explicitly in either form of recognition, but they have in practice observed a certain degree of institutional recognition by limiting the authority of their state institutions, preventing them from attempting to nullify or diverge from decisions by customary institutions when they affected persons who had not been "assimilated" into the colonialist culture and law.[45]

Because state law initially claims unlimited legal authority, when it concedes authority to other laws, it does so only on conditions and in circumstances that it defines. Consequently state institutions sometimes determine issues as to the existence of a customary law institution, the form of a customary law process, or the content of a customary law norm. This has implications for both the prevalent concept of customary law and the realities of the processes of state law. What the state institutions determine to be customary law is not always an accurate representation of the customary law observed by the population concerned, for two reasons.

The first reason is that the administrators of state law do not always have accurate or complete information about the customary laws. Recognition requires state court judges to decide cases by reference to particular norms of particular customary laws. Colonial judges were unlikely to have any significant experience of the customary law in practice. They had to rely on evidence, and they were sometimes misled.[46] Today judges are usually nationals by birth of the countries in which they sit, and so have some experience of at least one community's customary law. But a judge's upbringing will not necessarily have given him or her a comprehensive,

---

[41] *See, e.g.,* Supreme Court Ordinance, Lagos and Gold Coast.

[42] *See, e.g.,* Judicature Act, *Laws of Kenya*, chap. 8; Tanganyika Order in Council, 1920.

[43] *See, e.g.,* South Africa, albeit at a relatively late stage of colonization: Native Administration Act, 1927.

[44] *See* HENRY F. MORRIS & JAMES S. READ, INDIRECT RULE AND THE SEARCH FOR JUSTICE: ESSAYS IN EAST AFRICAN LEGAL HISTORY (Clarendon Press 1972).

[45] *See* AFRIKA-INSTITUUT LEIDEN, THE FUTURE OF CUSTOMARY LAW IN AFRICA. L'AVENIR DU DROIT COUTUMIERE EN AFRIQUE (Universitaire Pers Leiden 1956); ETIENNE LE ROY, LES AFRICAINS ET L'INSTITUTION DE LA JUSTICE: ENTRE MIMÉTISMES ET MÉTISSAGES (Dalloz 2004).

[46] *See* Gordon R. Woodman, *Some Realism About Customary Law – The West African Experience,* 1969 WIS. L. REV. 128 (1969), *reprinted in* FOLK LAW, *supra* note 13, *also reprinted in* AFRICAN LAW, *supra* note 6.

reliable knowledge and understanding of the totality of their customary law of birth. Moreover, in the multi-ethnic states of Africa, the judge is likely to be a stranger to the relevant community in most cases. Thus even today the judge needs to rely on evidence of customary law, either given in person to the court by an "expert" who is familiar with it or recorded in writing that can be consulted by the court.

Recognition of the problems in this procedure has been one of the grounds for demands across the continent for authoritative, written statements of customary law, in the form of codes, restatements or other commentaries. It is not clear that any such statement can be sufficiently detailed and extensive to answer many of the questions that could arise in even one of the varied and numerous customary laws in each country.

The problem is exacerbated by the constant changes in the content of customary laws. Even if the evidence available to a court provides accurate information about the content of a customary law as it was at a particular date, it is always possible that it has since changed. This renders unsafe reliance on a system of judicial precedent for determining a customary law, and also reduces still further the usefulness of codification and restatement of customary laws.

The second reason why state institutions do not always recognize accurately the customary law that is in reality observed by the population is that the structures of state institutions render it impossible for them to replicate the popular observance of customary law. This problem arises from two other features of customary law mentioned in the previous section.

First, the norms of each customary law vary in their degrees of mandatory force. State institutions, on the other hand, can only call on the coercive powers of the state to enforce norms. It would be neither appropriate nor possible for state institutions to enforce all the norms relevant in the cases that come before them. They must of necessity select some norms for enforcement. These will then be said officially to be truly law, and will be enforced by sanctions different from, and so either more or less effective than, those of the observed customary law. Other norms of the customary law they will not enforce through their powers, because it would be impractical to attempt to do so.

The same distinction occurs in institutional recognition. If the state law recognizes a customary law institution such as a traditional authority, that institution comes to be supported by the coercive power of the state. The office holder may find that he or she is no longer dependent on local approval to exercise authority, but rather on the approval of state officials. This is likely to produce changes in the ways in which authority can be exercised.[47] If, on the other hand, a customary law institution is not

---

[47] See, e.g., KOFI A. BUSIA, THE POSITION OF THE CHIEF IN THE MODERN POLITICAL SYSTEM OF ASHANTI (Oxford University Press 1951); LEGITIMATION, supra note 15; AFRICAN CHIEFTAINCY, supra note 15; THE DYNAMICS OF POWER, supra note 15.

recognized by the state, the continued exercise of authority by that institution may bring it into conflict with the state.

Second, as I have also suggested, it is common for some portions of a customary law to be uncertain and controversial at any particular time. But if state institutions are required to recognize such a customary law, they have to determine what that law is, for their purposes. They must either decide that an alleged norm is customary law, and direct the coercive powers of the state toward its enforcement, or decide that it is not law and decline to enforce it.

Both of these factors may be illustrated by an example. Suppose that, in a community in which a market in land has developed, the male head of a family takes control of the individually owned plot of his recently deceased brother. Then, with the agreement of some senior members of the family, he sells it to an outsider. The validity of this sale is contested in a state court by the widow of the deceased, and by another brother who, working abroad, was not asked about the sale. They claim that in his lifetime, the deceased had used the rental income from the land to pay the school fees of some of the children of the family. It is established that the popularly observed customary law in this community:

(a) provides that on a man's death, his individually owned land becomes the property of his family;

(b) permits family land to be sold to a stranger by the head of family acting with the consent of the senior members;

(c) states that the widow of a family member should be provided with property for her upkeep; and

(d) states that family land should not be sold unless this will be beneficial to the family members as a whole.

We may take it that the court will recognize (a) and (b) (and we may ignore for the present purpose the difficulty that may arise in determining the norms that define membership of a "family" of a deceased, and so in determining precisely which individuals constitute that family). However, it will need to decide whether to recognize (c), and so commit itself to deciding whether the land in issue was necessary for the appropriate upkeep of the widow; and whether to recognize (d), and so commit itself to deciding in this case (and presumably innumerable other cases) just what is beneficial to the family members as a whole. Finally, in endeavoring to recognize (b), the court is likely to find that there is uncertainty as to who exactly are to be considered senior members of a family, and as to whether action with their consent requires that every one of them should agree, or should even be consulted in circumstances involving different degrees of difficulty of communication.

The effect in summary is that the norms enforced by the state as customary law inevitably differ from the norms observed by the population. There arises a "lawyers' customary law," "judicial customary law," or "official customary law" that differs from "sociologist's customary law," as well as "practiced customary law" or "living customary law."[48] Lawyers' customary law may be seen as a portion of that "invented tradition" that colonial rule created but which has continued in existence.[49] Thus there is in Africa a more complex legal pluralism than that consisting of the coexistence of state law with customary laws. State law itself is plural, including both received law and lawyers' customary law.[50]

This sketch of the recognition of customary laws by state laws must note also the state law principles that on special policy grounds deny recognition to customary law norms that would otherwise be recognized. In the past, these were the repugnancy clauses of common-law countries and the public-order (*ordre publique*) principles of civil law countries. In many countries, these remain parts of state law. In some they have been added to or replaced by provisions giving overriding force to human rights principles, usually through constitutional laws. These have not often been expressly employed, although they may have tacitly influenced the attitudes of state judges to evidence of customary laws.[51] The recent growth of international human rights law may be strengthening this tendency.

The legal context of customary laws cannot be adequately described as simply the processes of state and other external laws operating on customary laws. We need also to consider the policies and principles of customary laws toward state laws. Generally customary laws give institutional recognition to state laws in that customary law administrators and rulers accept that state institutions control certain processes. There is little normative recognition of state law, because customary institutions decline to deal with matters where claims are made or opposed under state law. In some fields, customary laws may operate as means of resistance to state power. Thus customary-law principles such as those that require mediation and conciliation of conflicts, and which require disputes within the household or family not to be taken outside those social circles, have developed in some communities to enjoin people not to have recourse to state courts and other institutions.

---

[48] *See* Woodman, *supra* note 46; Antony N. Allott, *What Is to Be Done with African Customary Law?*, 28 INT'L & COMP. L.Q. 56, 60 (1984); Kludze, *supra* note 17, at 132; Evadené Grant, *Human Rights, Cultural Diversity and Customary Law in South Africa*, 50 J. AFR. L. 2, 12–13 (2006) (citing *Bhe v. Magistrate Khayelitsha* 2005 (1) BCLR 1 (CC) at Para. 222 (S. Afr.)).

[49] TERENCE O. RANGER, THE INVENTION OF TRADITION IN COLONIAL AFRICA, IN THE INVENTION OF TRADITION (Eric J. Hobsawm & Terence O. Ranger eds., Cambridge University Press 1983).

[50] *See* Gordon R. Woodman, *Unification or Continuing Pluralism in Family Law in Anglophone Africa: Past Experience, Present Realities, and Future Possibilities*, 4 LESOTHO L.J. 33 (1988). This would seem to be the main reason for the apparent weakness of the official attempts to define customary law. *See* Henrietta J.A.N. Mensa-Bonsu, *Of 'Nuts in the Ground Not Being Groundnuts' – The Current State of Customary Law in Ghana*, 22 UNIV. GHANA L.J. 1 (2004).

[51] *See* GORDON R. WOODMAN, HOW STATE COURTS CREATE CUSTOMARY LAW IN GHANA AND NIGERIA, IN INDIGENOUS LAW AND THE STATE 181 (Gordon R. Woodman & B.W. Morse eds., Foris 1988).

The effect of these legal developments more generally is that lawyers' customary law to some extent, and living customary law to a greater extent, continue to be of considerable significance in guiding people's lives in the fields of family law (including marriage law) and property law. Principles of state law that purport to nullify portions of customary laws do not eliminate the observance of those laws. Consequently the difference between lawyers', official customary law and practiced, living customary law, is increased, at least for the period required for the standards in these rules of exclusion to become incorporated into the living customary laws.[52] In addition, customary law governmental institutions, in the form of traditional authorities, generally remain significant, although they often perform subordinate functions under the control of state law.

On the other hand, many fields of activity that have developed in recent times are governed only by state laws, and by those parts of state laws that are derived from or modeled on received laws. Thus modern economic activities, from banking to the exploitation of intellectual property, are generally governed by versions of received laws, sometimes adapted to meet local circumstances. State criminal law retains few customary law elements in most states, with the exception of South Africa where the legal history produces a different situation,[53] while in many states living customary law is still strong in the criminal law field. In the fields of contract and tort, it is common to say that received law prevails. Certainly the law reports suggest that state institutions apply only the received laws, not customary laws of tort (with a few exceptions such as defamation and matters related to family relations such as seduction) and contract. However, one suspects that in popular observance, in the vast numbers of acts and transactions with subject matter too small in value to be taken to state institutions, living customary law, however great its difference from received law, may still govern.

1.5. CONCLUSIONS FOR THE TWENTY-FIRST CENTURY

We may seek to look to the future on the basis of analysis of the present for two purposes: to predict the future, or to prepare action in the future. To take or plan action is more useful. In considering action that can be taken, the past provides assistance

[52] So, for example, the Eastern Nigerian legislature enacted in 1956 the Abolition of the Osu System Law (Laws of Anambra State of Nigeria, Rev. Ed. 1979 Cap. 1). But a quasi-official restatement of customary law in 1977, based on extensive interview evidence, stated: "Being an *osu* or an *oru* carries with it a legal disability with regard to marriage. An *osu* or an *oru* has no capacity to inter-marry with a free-born and vice versa" (Obi, *supra* note 9, at para. 285.), and anecdotal evidence suggests that the "system" is still effective to a certain extent today. *e.g.* http://www.nigeriancuriosity.com/2007/01/osu-or-not-to-osu-that-is-question.html (last visited October 5, 2008); International Humanist and Ethical Union http://www.iheu.org/node/3223 (last visited October 5, 2008).
[53] *See* T. W. Bennett, *State Systems of Criminal Justice and Customary Law Crimes*, Chapter 16 in this volume.

in defining the extent of choice. It may enable us to see that the aims of some policies cannot be achieved, however desirable they might seem, and that of other policies some are more feasible than others.

1.5.1. *Policies of State Agents*

Most discussion about planned legal change in African countries is carried on by
professional lawyers and others who adopt the perspective of the state. It debates
those actions that may be taken by state agents. These need to be considered here,
although there is a lack of empirical information on the effects of state laws on
African societies, and so the discussion is largely impressionistic and speculative.

Policies adopted by state agents toward customary laws are inevitably concerned
with the regulation of the relationship between state law and customary laws. In this
respect, two trends seem likely to continue. The first, already noted, is the constant
and now increasingly rapid rate of change in the customary laws. The second is the
tendency for the makers of state law to attempt to govern people's conduct to an
increasing extent and in increasing detail: The immediate inclination, when something is adjudged objectionable or defective in society, to try to remedy it by state
legal regulation is universal. Certainly the state is unlikely to opt to reduce its power
and authority by enabling the operation of customary laws to expand.

The regulation of the relationship between state law and customary laws, taken
in its widest possible sense, includes measures by the state to suppress all customary
laws. This logical possibility is not, it is suggested, a practical possibility. All experience of state laws in Africa shows that, for the foreseeable future, virtually all people
will continue to observe customary laws, at least in some parts of their lives. The abolition of customary laws is no more feasible than the deliberate abolition of state laws
(although a state law may collapse in some circumstances, either totally or within a
certain part of the state's population).

The object of legal development may be the unification of the laws in a state.[54]
This in practice normally means not the unification of all the laws observed by the
population of the state, but the unification of the various types of state law, including particularly received law and lawyers' customary laws. Insofar as this entails any
changes to or abolition of elements of lawyers' customary law, it is likely to increase
the divergence between living customary law and state law, except insofar as communities can be induced to change their observance of law. The main advantage
of unification would be a less complex state law. It is sometimes suggested that the

---

[54] *See* Antony N. Allott, *Towards the Unification of Laws in Africa*, 14 INT'L & COMP. L.Q. 366, 375–379
(1965); K. Chanda, *Continuing Legal Pluralism with Gradual Juridical Integration: The Way Forward
for Post-Colonial Africa, in* THE SHADE OF NEW LEAVES: GOVERNANCE IN TRADITIONAL AUTHORITY
47 (Manfred O. Hinz ed., Lit Verlag 2006).

process could contribute toward nation-building by fostering a sense of national unity. It is possible, however, that it could have the opposite effect by giving members of some ethnic groups the impression that their identities were at risk of being eroded by the intrusion of the state.

An alternative objective may be the harmonization – or, expressed more strongly, the integration – of the various laws in a state. It has been said that "unification imposes a uniform law; integration creates a law which brings together, without totally obliterating, laws of different origins ..."[55] It may be limited to the integration of the various types of state law, in which case its objective is to remove anomalies, contradictions, and complexity in state law.[56] However, integration may also be attempted of state law and living customary law. It is likely that the latter is intended in most discussions because this would have the more fundamental and presumably more deeply desired objective of removing from the total set of laws that all people observe anomalies, contradictions, and complexity. Because it retains the various types of law, integration requires a body of choice of law principles to determine which law applies in any particular circumstances. It is likely that for many cases, especially those concerning marriage and land transactions, the principle will be that the intention of some or all of the parties will prevail. Thus people will be able to opt for the law that they wish to govern them in these activities. If that is done, it seems reasonable to envisage that for many years to come, the majority of people will opt for their customary laws. This is currently noticeable in countries where people have, on marrying, a choice between received law and their customary laws; the great majority of marriages are concluded under customary laws.

It is likely that the normative recognition of customary laws will continue to be a feature of state laws, because it is now quite widely recognized by policy makers that the observance of customary laws cannot be suppressed, even if this were desired. Institutional recognition has ceased in some countries, and its scope has declined in others. It is less likely to be accepted because it entails the abstention by state law from the exercise of authority and power in certain fields, as when powers in the decision of disputes or the discretionary approval of land sales are given to traditional authorities and withheld from state institutions. Where this happens, the traditional authorities may seek to extend their powers, and sometimes may succeed.[57] On the other hand, if choice of law norms enable people to choose between the institutions they use, some will opt for state institutions because they hope thereby to escape

---

[55] Allott, *What Is to Be Done, supra* note 48, at 65. *See also* Allott, *Unification, supra* note 54.

[56] *See* Allott, *Unification, supra* note 54, at 376–377 (citing University of Ife Institute of African Studies, INTEGRATION OF CUSTOMARY AND MODERN LEGAL SYSTEMS IN AFRICA (University of Ife Press 1971)).

[57] Janine Ubink, *Traditional Authority Revisited: Popular Perceptions of Chiefs and Chieftaincy in Peri-Urban Kumasi, Ghana*, 55 J. LEGAL PLURALISM 123 (2007).

from traditional restraints, as where women find that state courts are more favorable to them than traditional rulers' courts.[58]

Normative recognition is apt to give rise to concern over aspects of the customary law such as its uncertainty and liability to change independently of state control. These concerns have already led to widespread attempts to restate or codify customary laws, and these appear to be continuing.[59] I have expressed doubt as to whether these projects can achieve their objectives. In the process of codification, the record made of the law is inevitably distorted by the imposition of certainty where there was uncertainty, and the selection of norms to receive endorsement while others do not. Furthermore, codification, or any manner of "fixing" official customary law such as the establishment of judicial precedents laying down norms of customary law, renders that state-approved customary law inaccessible to subsequent change, except through the cumbersome processes of state legislation, while changes in living customary law will continue. Thus a codified law will inevitably start life at variance with living customary law, and the divergence between them is likely to grow.[60] Attempts at codification are made mainly by state officials, perhaps because they want certainty of information through writing, or even more because they want power. If they had to go back to the people to ascertain the customary law each time they applied it, they would lose authority. Perhaps also there is an element in some communities of a desire on the part of some members to use codification to prevent change.

Finally, there will continue to be concerns that some aspects of living customary law, whether attempts are made to recognize it or not, are objectionable and ought to be suppressed. Many of these arise from the inequalities that are seen to be sustained by customary laws, and perhaps especially from gender inequalities. As we consider the feasibility of effecting changes through state law, we should note that generally state law has made only a limited impact on many people's lives, and that many of the changes that have occurred in living customary laws are not attributable to the rise of state laws.

Another consideration relevant to decisions to make or attempt to make extensive changes in customary laws concerns the interrelation and interdependence between different parts of a customary law. The modification or suppression of the

---

[58] See Griffiths, *supra* note 23.

[59] See William Twining, *The Restatement of African Customary Law: A Comment*, 1 J. Mod. Afr. Stud. 221 (1963); Eugene Cotran, Restatement of African Law. Kenya. Vol 1. The Law of Marriage and Divorce (Sweet & Maxwell 1968); Obi, *supra* note 9, at para. 285; Thomas W. Bennett & T. Vermeulen, *Codification of Customary Law*, 24 J. Afr. L. 206 (1980); Allott, *What Is to Be Done*, *supra* note 48, at 67–68; Towards a Restatement of Nigerian Customary Law 270 (Yemi Osinbajo & Awa U. Kalu eds., Federal Ministry of Justice 1991); Chanda, *supra* note 54; *Customary Law Project Gets a Permanent Secretariat*, Ghana News Agency, July 25, 2008, *available at* http://www.ghanaweb.com/ghanahomepage/newsarchive/artikel/php?ID=147418.

[60] See Bennett & Vermeulen, *supra* note 59; Nigerian Customary Law, *supra* note 59, at 270.

observance of one objectionable norm may have the effect of weakening or destroying other norms, and so may affect the entire system. For example, it may well be
thought desirable to repeal the norms in many customary laws in Africa, which
discriminate against wives and widows, leaving them with limited access to rights
to land and other property and so little freedom of action in their lives. There is a
widespread desire to change these norms by whatever means are effective. However,
they are embedded in a wider social context. This is a system of norms defining and
regulating family relations, such that the principal landholding unit is usually the
unilineal descent group, not the conjugal family based on exogamous marriage.
Developments that improve the property rights of wives in relation to their husbands, or of widows in relation to members of their husbands' lineages, can undermine the cohesion of the lineage generally. It may be that means can be found to
avoid this further effect. If it cannot be avoided, it may nevertheless be judged that
the avoidance of gender discrimination should be rated as more important. All that
is suggested here is that these factors need to be taken into account.

1.5.2. *A Final Note: Policies of Civil Society*

There is a paradox in any debate about the use of state law, with its professional
officials, to remove, reform, or even maintain a customary law. In a democratic,
participatory state, state law is reformed through the regular democratic processes
involving the general population of the state. A customary law of a community exists
because members of the community observe it. It might be expected that it should
be reformed by the decisions and activities of the membership of that community,
not by a state apparatus run primarily by outsiders to the community.

A qualification on this argument arises from the observation made earlier that
there are often inequalities in the authority wielded by different sections of customary-law communities in Africa. Some external pressure may be thought necessary
and desirable. However, in this case, there also may be a greater probability of effecting change in a customary law if, rather than attempts to use state law to replace
portions of customary law with norms newly formulated by state agencies, the policy
is to use external influences to bring about social change, which then will lead to the
development of the customary law away from the inequalities.[61]

Customary laws lie primarily within the knowledge and control of the communities that observe them. For those communities, customary law is their social life.
Indeed, for them, the notion of "revisiting" customary law is quite foreign. They have
never visited customary law, and so could not revisit it: Now as always, they live it.

---

[61] *See also* Manfred O. Hinz, *Jurisprudence and Anthropology, in* THE SHADE OF NEW LEAVES, *supra*
note 54, at 468.

2

The Future of Living Customary Law in African Legal Systems in the Twenty-First Century and Beyond, with Special Reference to South Africa

Chuma Himonga

2.1. INTRODUCTION

Alleged imminent demise of customary law, or some aspects of it, has been and still remains a subject of intense debate among scholars, individuals, and in conferences. The following statements often characterize this debate: "the end of the road for customary law,"[1] "the final nail in the customary law coffin,"[2] "withering province of customary law,"[3] "obituary of customary succession law,"[4] "death shadows,"[5] "killing it softly."[6]

Specific contexts in which these statements have arisen vary. They include the challenge to customary law posed by individual human rights with which much of customary law is said to conflict; encroachments on the authority of customary law made by legislative or judicial actions in contexts of customary law reform in post-colonial states; the shrinking sphere of the operation of customary law due to its

---

[1] Elmarie Knoetze, *End of the Road for the Customary Law of Succession? Bhe v Magistrate, Khayelitsha; Shibi v Sithole*, 67(3) THRHR 515 (2004) (S. Afr.).

[2] Christa Rautenbach & Willemien du Plessis, *Reform of Customary Law of Succession and Regulation of Related Matters Bill: The Final Nail in the Customary Law of Succession Coffin?*, (abstract) for the Leitner Center Conference on African Customary Law Revisited: The Role of Customary Law in the 21st Century, Botswana, October 23–24, 2008, at http://www.customarylawrevisited.com/abstracts.lc; M. Pieterse, *The Promotion of Equality and Prevention of Unfair Discrimination Act 4 of 2000: Final Nail in the Customary Law Coffin*, 117 SALJ 627 (2000).

[3] George O. Otieno Ochich, *The Withering Province of Customary Law in Kenya: A Case of Design or Indifference?*, (abstract) for the Leitner Center Conference (*see supra* note 2).

[4] Manfred O. Hinz, *Bhe v Magistrate Khayelitsha, or: African Customary Law before the Constitution*, in THE SHADE OF NEW LEAVES: GOVERNANCE IN TRADITIONAL AUTHORITY: A SOUTHERN AFRICAN PERSPECTIVE 267 (Manfred O. Hinz ed., Lit Verlag & Transaction Publishers 2006) (referring to a paper presented at a conference).

[5] Chuma Himonga, Achievements, Death Shadows, and Future Directions of Jurisprudence on Customary Law (unpublished paper presented at the Law, Dignity and Transformative Constitutionalism Conference, University of Cape Town, July 26–27, 2007).

[6] M. Pieterse, *Killing it Softly: Customary Law in the New Constitutional Order*, 33 DE JURE 35 (2000).

restriction to private law matters of family law, succession, and land tenure; and the reduced role of customary law in modern African societies due to rapidly changing social and economic conditions, or in contexts of conferences on the future role of African customary law.

As already intimated, the common denominator of all the previously mentioned and similar metaphors as they relate to African customary law is the anticipation of an uncertain future for this system of law. However, this chapter argues that while challenges about its application persist, living customary law is likely to assume, if not maintain, a prominent position in African legal systems and to continue to regulate the lives of the majority of Africans on the African continent in the twenty-first century and beyond.

The basis of this argument is not "deep" or "strong" legal pluralism as a theoretical perspective[7] per se, but rather observable contemporary indicators, the main ones of which are: the toning down of the legal theoretical debates about the idea of customary law; the explicit and implicit constitutional and judicial recognition of the concept of living customary law; the perception that living customary law is suited to protect human rights; and, finally, the judicial engagement with the issue of the ascertainment of customary law.

Viewed against the backdrop of these indicators, it is submitted that statements anticipating the end or looming demise of customary law or about the uncertain future of this system of law must be restricted to official customary law[8] as opposed to living customary law. By its nature, official customary law is unresponsive to change; it becomes obsolete with the passage of time. Additionally, official customary law is often viewed as inimical to the rights of women and children generally. In contrast, living customary law's adaptability to change underscores its potential to live on and to become the customary law of the twenty-first century and beyond. Although not all living customary law is held out to be good in relation, for example, to human rights, it has the ability to change. In contemporary times, this feature seems to commend this form of law in comparison to its official counterpart. It is, therefore, necessary to distinguish between the concepts of official customary law and living customary law when assessing the future of customary law in African legal systems.

---

[7] For a discussion of aspects of legal pluralism as a theoretical perspective see, e.g., John Griffiths, (4) *What Is Legal Pluralism?*, 24 JOURNAL OF LEGAL PLURALISM AND UNOFFICIAL LAW 1 (1986); Gordon R. Woodman, *The Decline of Folk-Law Social Security in Common-Law Africa, in* BETWEEN KINSHIP AND THE STATE: SOCIAL SECURITY AND LAW IN DEVELOPING COUNTRIES 69–88 (Franz von Benda-Beckmann et al. eds., Foris Publications 1988); Manfred O. Hinz, *Legal Pluralism in Jurisprudential Perspective, in* THE SHADE OF NEW LEAVES, *supra* note 4, at 29–45 ; Gardiol J. van Niekerk, *Legal Pluralism, in* INTRODUCTION TO LEGAL PLURALISM IN SOUTH AFRICA 1–18 (J. C. Bekker et al. eds., LexisNexis & Butterworths 2002).

[8] In fact, we would argue that official customary law should be put in its coffin and buried in the shortest time possible.

The argument about the prominence of living customary law does not seek to establish a case for the continued separate existence of this system of law. To the contrary, features such as the increasing constitutional recognition of living customary law, an increasing body of case law implicating this system of law, and the traditional authorities referring more and more to formal courts for the resolution of their own disputes suggest a shrinking rather than an expanding horizon for the existence of living customary law as a separate system. However, we submit that, to the extent that the shrinkage of living customary law's horizon arises as a result of these factors, it represents an interesting indicator of a convergence of two systems of law – living customary law and constitutional law. This convergence in turn shows the dynamism of living customary law – its ability to harmonize with constitutional law rather than signifying its death, as suggested by the metaphors listed earlier in the chapter. In advancing its argument, this chapter will also show that this convergence process is already underway, especially through the courts.

The "indicators" on which the argument of this chapter is built relate to South Africa, but they are relevant to other African countries as well. This is so because of, firstly, these countries' shared history of colonialism and, secondly, the influence the emerging South African jurisprudence is likely to have on the laws of other African countries.[9]

This chapter is divided into four sections. The second part, following this introduction, is devoted to the elucidation of the concepts of official customary law and living customary law. However, the meaning of these concepts is not discussed in great detail here, because this subject is sufficiently covered by existing literature. The third part discusses the various indicators to living customary law's current and future status in African legal systems. The fourth section concludes the chapter with observations on some of the outstanding challenges arising from the emerging significance of living customary law in African legal systems.

2.2. THE CONCEPTS OF OFFICIAL CUSTOMARY LAW AND LIVING CUSTOMARY LAW

The distinction between living and official customary law is controversial. Scholars have debated, and continue to question, whether a rigid line can be drawn between these systems of law and, if so, what factors inform the demarcation of the two spheres of law. This debate is the subject of comment elsewhere;[10] it is not the intention of

---

[9] On the influence South African jurisprudence has already had on customary law in other countries, such as Namibia, see Hinz, *supra* note 4, at 267–268.

[10] See, e.g., CHUMA HIMONGA, FAMILY AND SUCCESSION LAWS IN ZAMBIA: DEVELOPMENTS SINCE INDEPENDENCE 13–27 (Lit Verlag 1995); Gordon R. Woodman, *Customary Law State Courts, and the Notion of Institutionalisation of Norms in Ghana and Nigeria, in* PEOPLE'S LAW AND STATE LAW: THE BELLAGIO PAPERS 143, 148 (A. Allott & Gordon R. Woodman eds., Mouton de Gruyter 1985).

this chapter to go into it. Suffice it to say that both sides of the debate seem to agree that there is a point when official customary law ceases to represent the living customary law; it is transformed to the point where it is alien to the people whose customary law it allegedly represents. For instance, rules and norms of living customary law of a given community that were codified in a piece of legislation several decades ago may no longer correspond to the living customary law of that community.

Thus, the dichotomy between living official and customary law should be thought of in relative terms and not in terms of rigid categorization. The focus in this chapter is on the features that distinguish between the two systems of law. In addition, we show the extent to which the concept of living customary law has been recognized by the courts and the legislature in South Africa, through the references made to it, and by scholars.

From the outset, we need to mention that the South African Constitutional Court and other courts recognize the dichotomy between living customary law and official customary law.[11] This is evident from *Bhe v Magistrate Khayelitsha*.[12] In that case, the majority Court acknowledged the difference between living and official customary law in the following terms:

> The official rules of customary law are sometimes contrasted with what is referred to as "living customary law", which is an acknowledgment of the rules that are adapted to fit in with changed circumstances. The problem with the adaptations is that they are ad hoc and not uniform. However, magistrates and the courts responsible for the administration of intestate estates continue to adhere to the rules of official customary law, with the consequent anomalies and hardships as a result of changes which have occurred in society.[13]

The uncompromising distinctive characteristics of official customary law implied by this statement are ossification and stagnation. This system of law, also referred to as lawyers' customary law or state customary law,[14] is the law applied by the courts and other state institutions. It has its sources in codes of customary law,[15] legislation,[16]

---

[11] See *Alexkor Ltd. and Another v Richtersveld Community and Others* 2004 (5) SA 460 (CC), 2003 (12) BCLR 1301 ¶ 52 (S. Afr.); *Bhe v Magistrate Khayelitsha* 2005 (1) SA 580 (CC), 2005 (1) BCLR 10 ¶ 152 (S. Afr.) (for comments on this case see, Chuma Himonga, *The Advancement of African Women's Rights in the First Decade of Democracy in South Africa: The Reform of the Customary Law of Marriage and Succession*, 2005 CILSA 82 (2005); Chuma Himonga, *African Customary Law in South Africa: Many Faces of Bhe v Magistrate Khayelitsha*, 2 RECHT IN AFRIKA 163 (2005); Hinz, *supra* note 4; *Mabena v Letsoalo* 1998 (2) SA 1068 (T) at 1074.

[12] (1) SA ¶ 152 (S. Afr.).

[13] See *id.* ¶ 87.

[14] See Gordon R. Woodman, *How State Courts Create Customary Law in Ghana and Nigeria*, in INDIGENOUS LAW AND THE STATE 181–220 (Gordon R. Woodman ed., Foris Pubns USA 1988).

[15] See, e.g., Natal Code of Zulu Law Proclamation of 1987 and the KwaZulu Act on the Code of Zulu Law 16 of 1985.

[16] See, e.g., Black Administration Act 38 of 1927 (S. Afr.) (repealed).

court precedents, academic texts, and other written materials sanctioned by the state as its sources. Because of its ossification, official customary law may not represent the customary law of the people whose customary law it purports to be.[17]

Living customary law represents the unwritten practices observed, and invested with binding authority, by the people whose customary law is under consideration. The test of validity of its rules and norms is its acceptance by these people, rather than the command of a sovereign or pronouncement of a legislator. Acceptance in this context means that the customs and practices that compose living customary law are observed by the customary community concerned as a matter of obligation. The rule or norm must be in existence at the time it is sought to be enforced. The opposite in respect of a specific rule or norm would indicate its disuse or obsoleteness. Such a rule or norm, though once observed, would have lost its validity.[18]

A prominent and, apparently, enduring attribute of living customary law worthy of note is that it adapts and develops according to changing socio-economic, political, and other conditions in society. As far back as 1908, Chief Justice Osborne observed in *Lewis v Bankole*[19] that "one of the most striking features of West African native law and custom is its flexibility; it appears to have been always subject to motives of expediency, and it shows unquestionable adaptability to alternated circumstances without entirely losing its character."[20]

This element of adaptability continues to be acknowledged in modern times, and it has been the basis of important court decisions in South Africa. A case in point is that of *Shilubana and Others v Nwamitwa and Other*.[21] The Constitutional Court distinguished customary law from custom as a source of law under the common law.[22] It observed that the latter was envisaged as "an immemorial practice that could be regarded as filling in normative gaps in the common law."[23] In this sense, custom no longer served as an original source of law capable of independent development, but survived merely as a useful accessory whose continued validity was rooted in and dependent on its unbroken antiquity. In contrast, customary law was seen to be an independent and original source of law, which "is adaptive by its very nature."[24]

---

[17] For further discussion of the meaning of official customary law, see Woodman, *supra* note 14; Chuma Himonga & C. Bosch, *The Application of African Customary Law under the Constitution of South Africa: Problems Solved or Just Beginning?*, 117 SALJ 306 (2000).

[18] Zingisile Ntozintle Jobodwana, *Customary Courts and Human Rights: Comparative African Perspective*, 2000 SAPL 26, 32 (2000) (S. Afr.).

[19] [1908] 1 N.L.R. 81, 9, cited by Jobodwana, *supra* note 18, at 32.

[20] *Id.*

[21] 2009 (2) SA 66 (CC). For a complete history of the case as it presented itself in the various courts, see also *Nwamitwa v Phillia and Others* 2005 (3) SA 536 (T), *Shilubana and Others v Nwamitwa (Commission for Gender Equality as Amicus Curiae)* 2007 (2) SA 432 (SCA).

[22] As espoused by *Van Breda v Jacobs* 1921 A.D. 330.

[23] *Id.* ¶ 54.

[24] *Id.*

The Court went on to say, "by definition, then, while change annihilates custom as a source of law, *change is intrinsic to and can be invigorating of customary law*."[25] It accordingly rejected the concept of a customary law that is likened to custom as a source of law under common law in preference for a notion of customary law that adapts to changing conditions. And, in essence, it applied the latter to the case before it.

The changeability of living customary law is closely related to its evolving nature. This was, again, recognized by the Constitutional Court in *Exparte Chairperson of the Constitutional Assembly: In re Certification of the Constitution of the Republic of South Africa*.[26] The role of the Constitutional Court in this case was to certify the compliance of the text of the final Constitution of 1996 to the Principles set out by the interim Constitution of 1993.[27] The relevant Principle to customary law was Constitutional Principle (CP) XIII, which stated, among other things, that "[t]he institution, and role of traditional leadership, according to customary law, shall be recognized and protected in the Constitution. Indigenous law, like common law, shall be recognized and applied by the courts...." In certifying the provisions of the final Constitution in respect of this Principle, the Court held that this principle acknowledged the existence of three culturally relevant traditional African elements, namely institutions of traditional leadership, customary law, and, at the provincial level, the traditional monarchy.[28] The Court went on to hold that the Constitution complied with CP XIII by giving express guarantees of the continued existence of traditional leadership and the survival of "*an evolving customary law*."[29] It observed, however, that how such leadership should function in the wider democratic society, and how customary law should develop, was left to, among other things, "*future social evolution*."[30]

Thus, the Court not only underscored the adaptability and evolving nature of living customary law, but it also implicitly declared it to be the legitimate authoritative system of customary law under the new constitutional legal order. This statement is, in our view, a significant judicial pronouncement on the recognition of living customary law as part of the South African legal system.

The adaptability of living customary law also seems to be the feature that has most attracted the courts to this system of law in relation to the protection of human rights in customary law. This aspect of living customary law is discussed further in Section 2.3.

---

[25] *Id.* (emphasis added).
[26] 1996 (4) SA 744, 1996 (10) BCLR 1253.
[27] Act 200 of 1993 (S. Afr.).
[28] *Id.* ¶ 195.
[29] *Id.* ¶ 197.
[30] *Id.*

The features of living customary law espoused earlier are also manifest in definitions of customary law given by legislation designed to bring customary law in line with constitutional and international human rights. This may be illustrated by the Recognition of Customary Marriages Act[31] and the Reform of Customary Law of Succession and Regulation of Related Matters Act.[32] This legislation constitutes the most comprehensive and prominent attempts in South Africa to reform the customary laws of marriage and succession under the influence of the Constitution and international human rights. Both Acts define customary law as "the customs and usages traditionally observed among the indigenous African peoples of South Africa which form part of the culture of those people."[33] It is submitted that the reference in these provisions to "tradition" emphasizes the fact that customary law is rooted in the practices of the people, whereas the reference to "culture" signifies the inherent evolving nature of living customary law (as culture changes, so does the normative system regulating the lives of people under the culture concerned).

With regard to recognition by scholars, the concept of living customary law is now so common in contemporary legal literature on African legal systems that it needs no further elaboration. A reading of any major work on customary law, especially in southern Africa, confirms this.[34]

Thus, it needs to be emphasized, firstly, that the concept of living customary law is now readily accepted by courts, scholars, and legislation dealing with customary law, and, secondly, that the recognition of this concept in this manner signifies the status of living customary law and its future as a part of African legal systems. This conclusion receives further support from "indicators" discussed in the next section.

2.3. "INDICATORS" OF LIVING CUSTOMARY LAW'S STATUS AND FUTURE

Indicators do not guarantee the fulfillment of that which is indicated. Nevertheless, they provide an informed basis for anticipating the expected fulfillment. Two everyday life examples will suffice. A flashing indicator on a motor vehicle causes other drivers to anticipate the turning of the car in the indicated direction, but the actual

---

[31] Act 120 of 1998 (S. Afr.).

[32] Act 11 of 2009 (S. Afr.).

[33] *See* § 1 of the Act and of the Bill, respectively.

[34] *See, e.g.*, T. W. BENNETT, CUSTOMARY LAW IN SOUTH AFRICA 29 (Juta & Co. 2004) ; Himonga & Bosch, *supra* note 17, at 319–328; C. S. van der Waal, *Formal and Informal Dispute Resolution in Limpopo Province, South Africa*, in THE SHADE OF NEW LEAVES, *supra* note 4, at 154; WILLE'S PRINCIPLES OF SOUTH AFRICAN LAW 104 (Francois du Bois ed., Juta & Co. 2007); T. W. Bennett, *"Official" vs "Living" Customary Law: Dilemmas of Description and Recognition*, in LAND, POWER AND CUSTOM 138, 144–145 (Aninka Claassens & Ben Cousins eds., UCT Press 2008).

fulfillment only happens when the indicating driver turns the car in the direction indicated. Equally, a terminal illness does not guarantee death, though it provides a basis for anticipating it. In this section, we discuss some of the main "indicators" that form the basis of the argument regarding the contemporary and future prominence of living customary law in Africa.

2.3.1. *The Toning Down of the Legal Theoretical Debates about the Idea of Living Customary Law*

It is striking that the concept of living customary law is admitted into major legal textbooks,[35] scholarly writings, legislation, and judicial proceedings.[36] And this is without any apology to dominant legal theory in the form of legal positivism or centralism. It is as though most academics and judges no longer see the need to rationalize or justify their entertainment of the idea of living customary law as law. Thus, while the wrangle about the concept of law in relation to customary law and other non-state legal systems continues in some academic circles,[37] there is a significant body of legal literature and court decisions that simply ignore this debate. In other words, it seems there is a sense in which contemporary scholars and judges increasingly view engagement with dogmatic legal theories rooted in state centralism or in "the hegemonic domination of Euro-modern conceptions of sovereignty"[38] to be irrelevant or not critical to legal discourses concerning Africa.

It could be argued that the apparent recession of centralist legal theories in relation to living customary law increasingly reflects an acceptance of the African social and legal realities and contexts, in which living customary law continues to be observed even where it has not been overtly recognized by the state. In South Africa, in addition, this seems to be influenced by the Courts' interpretation of the Constitution regarding the status of different systems of law under the new constitutional dispensation.[39] In these contexts, it makes little sense to devote time and energy to legal theoretical debates about whether or not living customary law is law. It would be interesting to find out what the exact reasons for this development are.[40] But whatever the reasons, the apparent contemporary toning down of legal theoretical debates in African legal literature says something about the acceptance and status of living customary law in the legal system.

---

[35] *See supra* note 34.
[36] *See* the cases cited in this paper.
[37] *See, e.g.*, Hinz, *supra* note 7, at 31; Bennett (2004), *supra* note 34, at 1–33.
[38] Drucilla Cornell, Professor, *Ubuntu, Pluralism and the Responsibility of Legal Academics to the New South Africa*, Inaugural Lecture at the University of Cape Town (Sept. 10, 2008), at 1.
[39] *See, e.g., Ryland v Edros* 1997 (2) SA 690 (C); *Amod v Multilateral Motor Vehicle Accidents Fund (Commissioner for Gender Equality Intervening)* 1999 (4) SA 1319 (SCA).
[40] Bennett, *supra* note 34, at 1–33, offers a useful summary of relevant developments in concepts and theory.

2.3.2. *The Recognition of Living Customary Law*

As some scholars have observed, "the concept of living law has a long history in legal anthropology and sociology, [starting with the time] when lawyers and anthropologists accepted that customary law, recorded in textbooks, codes or court cases was not necessarily the customary law practiced by the people."[41] However, the appearance of this concept as it relates to customary law in African legal systems seems to be quite recent. It apparently traces its origins to studies by Women and Law in Southern Africa (WLSA), which was inaugurated in 1988.[42] By the early 1990s, courts were making reference to this concept of law in some parts of Africa. For example, it was reported that some judges in Tanzania were beginning to take a critical look at the nature of customary law, leading to the recognition of the dichotomy between official and living customary law.[43] In one such case, a judge is reported to have stated: "[Tanzanian] customary law (particularly the uncodified customary law) is a living law, capable of adaptation and development. It is not immutable."[44]

In South Africa, the recognition of customary law by the Constitution since 1994 and the cases decided on customary law under the new dispensation have sparked an unprecedented interest in living customary law and customary law generally among judges, academics, and the legal profession alike.[45]

In this section, we discuss the manifestation of living customary law in African constitutional provisions and South African courts, as a significant indicator of the future and status of this system of law in African legal systems. As already noted, the importance of South African jurisprudence on this subject is underlined by the influence it is likely to have on the development of customary law on the continent.

2.3.2.1. The Manifestation of Living Customary Law in Constitutional Law

The enactment of new constitutions on the African continent since the early 1990s has ushered in a special dispensation for customary law. Constitutions of several

---

[41] *See* Hinz, *supra* note 4, at 274; van Niekerk, *supra* note 7.

[42] *See* Legal Situation of Women in Southern Africa (Alice Armstrong & Julie Stewart eds., University of Zimbabwe Publications 1990). Concepts with similar meaning, such as the "people's law," were, however, already known and used by legal and other scholars. *See, e.g.,* Allott & Woodman, *supra* note 10.

[43] *See* Bart A. Rwezaura, *Gender Justice and Children's Rights: A Banner for Family Law Reform in Tanzania*, in The International Survey of Family Law 413, 443 (Andrew Bainham ed., 1997).

[44] *Maagwi Kimito v Gibeno Werema*, cited in Rwezaura, *supra* note 43.

[45] It would be interesting for future research to study on how the notion of living customary law found its way into the courts where it is increasingly becoming prominent. What were the factors that got living customary law into the minds of judges? This kind of study would, firstly, reveal the origins and development of concepts of law in African customary law generally and, secondly, show how changes in factors associated with the origins of living customary law might affect its future. Regrettably, this inquiry is beyond the scope of this work, due both to the dearth of relevant information on the subject and the limited scope of this work.

countries enacted in this period carry provisions entrenching cultural rights that courts have used, and may continue to use, to enlarge the sphere of living customary law in African legal systems. The forms of entrenchment of cultural rights vary from one country to another, as also their limitations. For example, under both the South African and Malawian Constitutions, everyone has the right to participate in the cultural life of their choice.[46] But the South African Constitution, unlike its Malawian counterpart, in addition confers a group right to persons belonging to a cultural community "to enjoy their culture, practice their religion and use their language; and ... to form, join and maintain cultural, religious and linguistic associations and other organs of civil society."[47] In the case of Uganda, the right to "enjoy, practise, profess, maintain and promote any culture, cultural institution, language, tradition ..."[48] is coupled with the provision on cultural objectives under the rubric of National Objectives and Directive Principles of State Policy. The cultural objectives state, *inter alia*, that "cultural and customary values which are consistent with the fundamental rights and freedom, human dignity, democracy, and with the Constitution may be developed and incorporated in aspects of Ugandan life."[49] In addition, the state is under an obligation to promote and preserve, among other things, "those cultural values and practices which enhance the dignity and well-being of Ugandans."[50]

Tradition and custom are also specially protected by some constitutions. The South African Bill of Rights, for example, states that the right to freedom of religion, belief, and opinion "does not prevent legislation recognizing marriages concluded under any *tradition* ... or systems of personal and family law under any *tradition*...."[51]

With regard to limitations, some constitutions limit the cultural rights by subjecting them to the Constitution or Bill of Rights, in addition to their limitation by general limitation clauses;[52] others limit the cultural rights only in terms of the latter.[53]

Some of the older constitutions also protect the people's cultures, though not as fundamental rights.[54] But some of these countries, like those with newer constitutions,

---

[46] *See* S. AFR. CONST. 1996 § 30; Const. of the Republic of Malawi of 1999 § 26.
[47] CONST. OF THE REPUBLIC OF UGANDA OF 1995 § 31.
[48] *Id.* § 37.
[49] *Id.* at Cultural objectives XXIV.
[50] *Id.* at Cultural objectives XXIV (a).
[51] *See* S. AFR. CONST. 1996 § 15(3)(a).
[52] *See, e.g.*, the South African limitation clauses state that the cultural rights "may not be exercised in a manner inconsistent with any provision of the Bill of Rights." S. AFR. CONST. 1996 §§ 30, 31(2).
[53] *See, e.g.*, CONST. OF MALAWI, *supra* note 46, § 44(2); CONST. OF THE REPUBLIC OF UGANDA, *supra* note 47, § 43.
[54] *See, e.g.*, ZAMBIA CONST. (Constitution Act 1991) art. 112(g): "The State shall take measures to promote the practice, enjoyment and development by any person of that person's culture, tradition,

have ratified relevant international human rights instruments that carry provisions on cultural rights.[55] Hence, they provide some protection for cultural rights as well.

In our view, these guarantees of cultural rights require the courts to apply the living customary law of the people subject to customary law to their disputes arising under customary law.[56] In this respect, it has been argued elsewhere[57] that the right to culture obligates courts to consider the views of the customary communities on the content of their customary laws. This is so whether the court is developing customary law according to prescribed constitutional mechanisms[58] or merely applying customary law.[59] Otherwise, constitutional recognition of the right to culture and customary law generally would be a mere sham.[60] Thus, living customary law, as opposed to official customary law, is the object of the cultural rights provisions and other constitutional provisions recognizing customary law.

Should this view be accepted, the constitutional incorporation of cultural rights and the recognition of customary law generally by African constitutions has raised the status of living customary law so that it is included as part of the relevant legal systems. Stronger support for this view may be sought from the way living customary law is dealt with in the context of dispute resolution, which is addressed in the next section.

2.3.2.2. Manifestation of Living Customary Law in South African Court Decisions

Selected cases decided under the new South African constitutional dispensation illustrate the contribution of the courts to the recognition of living customary as part of the legal system.

Mthembu v Litesela[61] was one of the early cases decided under the interim Constitution of 1993. It was concerned with the constitutionality of the customary law principle of male primogeniture that, among other things, preferred males over females in inheritance. The Supreme Court of Appeal declined to invalidate the principle on the ground that it possessed certain features that saved it from

---

custom or language insofar as these are not inconsistent with this Constitution." *See also id.* at Part XIII, which recognizes the institution of chief and its support by the State.

[55] See, in relation to the human rights of women, FAREDA BANDA, WOMEN, LAW AND HUMAN RIGHTS: AN AFRICAN PERSPECTIVE chs. 3, 4 & 7 (Hart Publishing 2005).

[56] *See also* T. W. BENNETT, HUMAN RIGHTS AND AFRICAN CUSTOMARY LAW UNDER THE SOUTH AFRICAN CONSTITUTION 23–24 (Juta & Co. 1995).

[57] Himonga & Bosch, *supra* note 17, at 334.

[58] See, e.g., the mechanism afforded by S. AFR. CONST. 1996 § 39(2), which states that: "When interpreting any legislation, and when *developing* the common law or *customary law*, every court, tribunal or forum *must promote the spirit, purport and objects of the Bill of Rights.*" (emphasis added).

[59] Himonga & Bosch, *supra* note 17, at 334.

[60] *Id.* at 331.

[61] 2000 (3) SA 867 (SCA).

invalidation.[62] Our interest is in the constitutional recognition of customary law and the role this played in the judgment. The Court stated that:

> In view of the manifest acknowledgment of customary law as a system of law exist-
> ing parallel to the common law by the Constitution ... and the freedom granted
> to persons to choose this system as governing their relations (as implied in s 31), I
> cannot accept the submission that the succession rule [in question] is necessarily
> in conflict with s 8 [i.e. the right to equality provision in the interim Constitution].
> Neither is it contrary to public policy or natural justice....[63]

Thus, the Court partly relied, albeit uncritically,[64] on the guarantee of the right to culture to justify the continued existence of customary law. The customary rule in question was contained in an old statute and was thus, potentially, official customary law. But the Court would probably have taken the same stance if the rule had been a part of living customary law. Its reference to the right to culture in the quoted passage seems to support this proposition.

Mabena v Letsoala[65] was heard before the High Court. It concerned, among other things, the right and capacity of a mother to negotiate lobolo (bridewealth) for the marriage of her daughter and to consent to such marriage. According to the official customary law that was pleaded, the conclusion of a valid customary marriage required the consent of the bride's and groom's guardians. A woman could neither be guardian of her child nor could she negotiate the lobolo agreement. These were entitlements and capacities reserved to the bride's father or other relevant male guardian. However, the court received evidence of a (gender-neutral) rule of living customary law,[66] which it applied to the case.

In its judgment, the Court held that there were two forms of customary law, official and living customary law, and that a principle of living, actually observed, law had to be recognized by the Court as it would constitute a development in accordance with the spirit, purport, and objects of the Bill of Rights contained in the Constitution.[67]

---

[62] The decision has since been overruled. *See Bhe v Magistrate Khayelitsha* 2005 (1) SA 580 (CC), 2005 (1) BCLR 10. This case is, however, not alone in relying on the right to culture and other constitutional provisions recognizing customary law as a basis of its decision. This stance is also evident in *Mabuza v Mbatha* 2003 (4) SA 218 (C), especially ¶29, and *Thembisile and Another v Thembisile and Another* 2002 (2) SA 209 (T), ¶25.

[63] *Mthembu*, (3) SA at 945.

[64] For a comment on this decision, see Chuma Himonga, *Implementing the Rights of the Child in African Legal Systems: The Mthembu Journey in Search of Justice, in* 9 INTERNATIONAL JOURNAL OF CHILDREN'S RIGHTS 89 (2001).

[65] 1998 (2) SA 1068 (T).

[66] *Mabena* has been criticized on this account. *See Alastair J. Kerr, The Role of Courts in developing Customary Law*, 20 OBITER 41–51 (1999).

[67] *Mabena* (2) SA at 1074.

The Constitutional Court's contribution to the recognition of living customary may be illustrated by three cases. The first one is the *Certification*[68] judgment, which, as already noted, implicitly adjudged living customary law to be the legitimate system of law. Furthermore, the Court considered objections to the text of the final Constitution on the grounds that the horizontal application of the Bill of Rights and the subjection of the constitutional recognition of customary law to legislation would result in the annihilation of customary law and institutions. The Court held that "the feared destructive confrontation between the Bill of Rights and legislation on the one side and indigenous law on the other need not take place in the manner that the objectors observed."[69]

It is submitted that if courts remain alive to this pronouncement of the Constitutional Court in their interpretation of the Bill of Rights and application of customary law, then living customary law stands a good chance of not being readily abolished by courts in the process of reconciling it with the Constitution. Presumably, courts will make every effort to find, appreciate, and adopt interpretations of the Constitution or legislation that avoid destructive confrontations between these laws and living customary law in specific cases before them. And there is reason to believe the courts will do this. In this respect it may be observed that in all the cases where the Constitutional Court has found customary law to be invalid, the customary law in question was official rather than living customary law.[70]

This non-confrontational and non-destructive approach will greatly enhance the future of living customary law considering that human rights pose the greatest challenge to the existence of customary law owing to the latter's potential to conflict with the former.

The next two cases are *Bhe v Magistrate Khayelitsha*[71] and *S v Makwanyane*.[72] *Bhe* led to the abolition of the male primogeniture principle of succession in official customary law contained in § 23 of the Black Administration Act[73] on the grounds that it violated the constitutional principle of equality. Because it has involved official customary law, the decision is not relevant to our argument, except to confirm the perception that official customary law embodies gender discrimination, as discussed in the next section.

---

[68] *Exparte Chairperson of the Constitutional Assembly: In re Certification of the Constitution of the Republic of South Africa*, 1996 (4) SA 744, 1996 (10) BCLR 1253.

[69] *Id.* ¶ 201.

[70] *See Bhe v Magistrate Khayelitsha* 2005 (1) SA 580 (CC), 2005 (1) BCLR 10; *Moseneke and Others v The Master and Another* 2001 (2) SA 18 (CC) (2001 (2) BCLR 103); *Gumede v President of the Republic of South Africa* 2009 (3) BCLR 243 (CC).

[71] (1) SA 580.

[72] 1995 (3) SA 391 (CC) at ¶ 225.

[73] Act 38 of 1927 (repealed).

However, there are two aspects of the decision that are directly relevant to the present discussion. Firstly, the Court made pronouncements affirming the recognition of living customary law as discussed earlier.[74] Secondly, the Court left a window for the development and evolvement of living customary law through family agreements. After abolishing the principle of male primogeniture, the Court filled the gap in the law by applying the Intestate Succession Act and holding that this Act would apply to all estates previously regulated by § 23 of the Black Administration until Parliament enacted a law to regulate the customary law of succession. However, it left open the possibility of the deceased's family reaching an agreement to have the estate administered in a manner that does not exclude the application of customary law subject to certain conditions.[75] By so doing, the Constitutional Court created the opportunity for the living customary law of inheritance to evolve from the practices of families within the confines of its decision and the Constitution.

S v Makwanyane[76] is famous not only for its abolition of the death sentence but also for introducing the concept of *ubuntu* into the South African constitutional jurisprudence. *Ubuntu*, described by the majority in *Bhe* as a "healthy communitarian tradition,"[77] and by some scholars as "one of the leading concepts in recent currents of African philosophy,"[78] played a significant role in the abolition of the death penalty by *Makwanyane*. The concept is translated literally in Zulu as *Umuntu ngumuntu ngabantu* (the human being is a human being because of other human beings). Although there is no claim to this concept being exclusively African,[79] it is widely acknowledged as a part of the African legal tradition[80] and, therefore, of living customary law.

The idea of *ubuntu* was introduced into South African constitutional law through the interim Constitution. In a bid to address the South African history of segregation, violence, and gross violation of human rights, this Constitution included a provision called the Epilogue.[81] This provision, which included the word *ubuntu*,

---

74 *See supra* Section 2.2.
75 *See Bhe* (1) SA ¶ 130.
76 (3) SA 391.
77 *Bhe* (1) SA ¶ 45.
78 *See* Hinz, *supra* note 4, at 273.
79 *See* Helen Keep & Robert Midgley, *The Emerging Role of Ubuntu-Botho in Developing a Consensual South African Legal Culture, in* EXPLORATIONS IN LEGAL CULTURES 29, 33 (Fred Bruinsma & David Nelken eds., Elsevier 2007).
80 *See* Sachs J's judgment in *Makwanyane* (3) SA 391
81 *See* S. AFR. (Interim) CONST. 1993. This provision, known as the epilogue or post-amble, stated: "The adoption of this Constitution lays the secure foundation for the people of South Africa to transcend the divisions and strife of the past, which generated gross violations of human rights, the transgression of humanitarian principles in violent conflicts and a legacy of hatred, fear, guilt, and revenge. These can now be addressed on the basis that there is a need for understanding but not for vengeance, a need for reparation but not for retaliation, a need for *ubuntu* but not for victimisation." *Id.*

would act as the country's bridge toward the reconciliation of the people (previously divided by race, gender, class, etc., under colonialism and apartheid) across the whole country.

Though not precisely defined in legal contexts, the concept of *ubuntu* is said to encompass communality and the interdependence of the members of the community, a respect for life and human dignity, humaneness, social justice and fairness, and an emphasis on reconciliation rather than confrontation.[82] The concept rose to prominence when the Constitutional Court in S v *Makwanyane* linked it to the right to dignity with reference to the abolition of the death penalty. The Court held that the right to dignity was an integral part of *ubuntu*.[83] Since then, the concept has influenced the dignity jurisprudence in several high-profile cases in South Africa.[84] In one such case, the concept has been said to suffuse "the whole constitutional order."[85]

There are other ways of assessing the impact of *ubuntu* on the recognition of living customary law. An interesting example is a statistical study conducted in 2007,[86] which considers how the concept has been employed in litigation. The study shows that since 1993, the reference to the word *ubuntu* has appeared in thirty-one cases and thirty-eight separate judgments. In seven of these, the reference was peripheral to the argument and outcome of the case, but it was central to the reasoning and outcome of the case in nine instances. In five other cases where the concept did not form a central part of the court's reasoning, it nevertheless played some contextual role. Further, the study shows that the concept has been used at all levels of superior courts – the Constitutional Court, Supreme Court of Appeal, and High Court. And in eight Constitutional Court cases in which it was referenced, it resulted in fifteen separate judgments in which the concept was used explicitly.[87] The study further shows that, in terms of the specific categories of law, the concept has been used in, for example, criminal law, administrative law (specifically socio-economic rights), and delict.[88] The concept has also been employed "where there is a need to emphasise the Constitution's transformative role – reforming the sentencing and compensation systems by making them more restorative; requiring government to take active steps in providing housing; and integrating customary law into the mainstream legal system."[89]

---

[82] See *Makwanyane*, (3) SA ¶¶ 223–225, 237, 250, 263, 300, 308, 309.
[83] *Id.* ¶ 225.
[84] For an analysis of the cases in which *ubuntu* has been employed by the Courts, see Keep & Midgley, *supra* note 79.
[85] *Port Elizabeth Municipality v Various Occupiers* 2005 (1) SA 217 (CC); (2204) 12 BCLR 1268 (CC), ¶ 37.
[86] See Keep & Midgley, *supra* note 79, at 37.
[87] *Id.*
[88] In general, delict is a civil law concept where an act of negligence or a willful wrong may give rise to a legal obligation.
[89] See Keep & Midgley, *supra* note 79, at 37.

Thus, *ubuntu* as an African legal and philosophical concept seems to permeate a considerable area of the South African legal order.

From the preceding discussion, it is important to emphasize that the authority and legitimacy of living customary law is firmly rooted in the Constitution and constitutional jurisprudence. Further, court decisions project living customary law as a potentially human-rights-friendly system. This proposition is expanded in the next section.

2.3.3. *Living Customary Law's Potential to Protect Human Rights*

Propositions to the effect that official customary law is the embodiment of institutionalized gender inequality are not uncommon in African customary law literature.[90] In contrast, living customary law is increasingly projected as a potentially human-rights-friendly system.[91] For example, with regard to inheritance, studies by WLSA based on empirical research in seven countries in Southern Africa – Botswana, Lesotho, Malawi, Mozambique, Swaziland, Zambia, and Zimbabwe – show a remarkable flexibility in the living customary law in which women inherit alongside with men, contrary to what was projected by the official version of the male primogeniture rule. They found, among other things, that in all the six countries included in the inheritance research, "no one person ... was to take over all the property [of the deceased] to the exclusion of other family members," and that in some of the countries, "all children of the deceased, including females are given a share of the property."[92] This proposition has been vindicated by South African case law since the new constitutional dispensation. Selected decisions are used to illustrate this point further in this chapter, though space does not permit their detailed discussion.

[90] *See, e.g.,* Martin Chanock, *Neotraditionalism and the Customary Law in Malawi*, 16 AFRICAN LAW STUDIES 80–91 (1978); Banda, *supra* note 55, at 17–19; ANNE HELLUM ET AL., HUMAN RIGHTS, PLURAL LEGALITIES AND GENDERED REALITIES: PATHS ARE MADE BY WALKING 416–421 (University of Zimbabwe & Weaver Press 2007); Welshman Ncube, *Muddling in the Quicksands of Tradition and Custom and Skating Down the Slippery Slopes of Modernity: The Reform of Marriage and Inheritance Laws in Zimbabwe*, 13 ZIMBABWE L.REV. 1, 13 (1996); Alice Armstrong et al., *Uncovering Reality: Excavating Women's Rights in African Family Law*, 7 INTERNATIONAL JOURNAL OF LAW, POLICY AND THE FAMILY 314, 327 (1993); Himonga, *supra* note 64, at 107–108.

[91] *See* Lisa Fishbayn, *Litigating the Right to Culture: Family Law in the New South Africa*, 13 (2) INTERNATIONAL JOURNAL OF LAW, POLICY AND THE FAMILY 147 (1999).

[92] *See* WIDOWHOOD, INHERITANCE LAWS, CUSTOMS, AND PRACTICES IN SOUTHERN AFRICA 53 (Welshman Ncube & Julie Stewart eds., Women and Law in Southern Africa 1995). *See also id.* at 54–57. Other studies have similarly shown that the lowest courts in Zambia are likely to apply living rather than official customary law (see Himonga, *supra* note 10), and distribute matrimonial property to divorced women contrary to rules of official customary law that deny them such rights (see Chuma Himonga, *Property Disputes in Law and Practice: Dissolution of Marriage in Zambia, in* WOMEN AND LAW IN SOUTHERN AFRICA 56 (Alice K. Armstrong ed., Zimbabwe Publishing House 1987).

Latching on to the adaptability and evolving features of living customary law as confirmed by the *Certification* judgment, the Constitutional Court in *Alexkor Ltd and Another v Richersvelt Community and Others*[93] expressed optimism that customary law would develop in line with the Constitution. It stated:

> In applying indigenous law, it is important to bear in mind that, unlike common law, indigenous law is not written. It is a system of law that has its own values and norms. Throughout its history it has evolved and developed to meet the changing needs of the community. *It will continue to evolve within the context of its values and norms consistently with the Constitution* [presumably, including the Bill of Rights].'[94]

Thus, the Court linked the conceptualization of living customary law, and the ability of living customary law to evolve and develop, to the protection of rights within the framework of the Constitution.

The Constitutional Court's optimism was subsequently somewhat vindicated in *Shilubana*, where the Court found that the Valoyi community had – through the decision of its royal family to install a female as a traditional leader (hosi) – developed its customary law in accordance with the Constitution.[95] Previously, the customary law of this community denied women the right to succeed to this office. Thus, living customary law had adapted to the demands of the constitutional principle of equality in relation to traditional leadership.

The contributions of *Mabena* and *Makwanyane* to the protection of rights should also not be overlooked. As already stated, in *Mabena*, the High Court preferred a rule of living customary law over official customary law and, in the specific circumstances of the case, pronounced its application of the former to "constitute a development [of customary law] in accordance with the spirit, purport and objects of the Bill of Rights' as mandated by the Constitution."[96] On the other hand, *Makwanyane* has brought the idea of *ubuntu* into the arena of the human right to dignity in a positive way.

A consideration of the potential of living customary law to protect human rights would, however, be incomplete without addressing the critical question of how to ensure that this system of law develops in line with constitutional rights and other human rights. Again, the courts have pointed the way toward a resolution of this problem.

---

[93] 2003 (12) BCLR 1301 (CC).

[94] *Id.* ¶ 153. This statement is also interesting from another point of view. It shows how enduring the flexibility attribute of living customary law is, in the sense that a court in 2003 said exactly the same thing as a court in 1908. *Lewis v Bankole*, [1908] 1 N.L.R. 81.

[95] *See Shilubana and Others v Nwamitwa and Other* 2009 (2) SA 66 (CC) ¶¶ 49, 55, 73, & 75.

[96] S. AFR. (Interim) CONST. 1993 § 35(3), S. AFR. CONST. 1996 § 39(2).

Where the living customary law concerned is not incompatible with constitutional rights, the solution is easy and uncontroversial. All that is necessary on the part of the court is to acknowledge and recognize the status quo. This is essentially what happened in *Mabena*,[97] where the court found that the rule of the community as pleaded by the witnesses was compatible with human rights. Some scholars have called this method passive development of customary law.[98] The notion of passive development of customary law is also prominent in *Shilubana*, especially in its elaboration of the third factor for the determination of customary,[99] discussed in the next section. This notion of passive development led the Court to recognize the change made to customary law by the Valoyi traditional authority as having been developed by the community.[100] We will come back to this aspect of the decision.

The more problematic situation, however, is where the living customary law conflicts with human rights and there is, therefore, a need to reconcile it with the human rights in conflict. A solution proposed by some scholars – active development – is entirely appropriate in such a case.[101] For our purposes, the most important feature of this method is that it facilitates the alignment of customary law with human rights while preserving, as far as possible, the values and fundamental features of customary law.[102] Equally important, this method permits input by outsiders, including judges, on issues of customary law for purposes of its alignment with human rights. Thus, it has an objective element that informs the determination of whether and, if so, how living customary law should be aligned with the Constitution. In other words, the decision on this critical question is not left solely to the community whose customary law is under consideration; the courts whose duty it is to uphold the Constitution must participate in the decision. And if the court finds it necessary to overrule the community decisions on these questions – after having taken all the factors, as well as the caution about avoiding destructive confrontations into account – then it must do so. Again, *Shilubana* recognizes this notion of active development in its discussion of the third factor for ascertaining the content of customary law discussed in the next section.

The minority in *Bhe* seems to introduce another element to the methods of ensuring that customary law develops in line with constitutional rights and other human rights. This consists of a community-oriented framework for dealing with the development of living customary law in conflict with human rights. The minority in that

[97] See Wieland Lehnert, *The Role of the Courts in the Conflict between African Customary Law and Human Rights*, 21 SAJHR 241 (2005); Chuma Himonga, *Taking Stock of Changes to Customary Law in a New South Africa, in* ESSAYS IN HONOUR OF AJ KERR 230 (Graham Glover ed., LexisNexis & Butterworths 2006).
[98] See Lehnert, *supra* note 97.
[99] See *infra* Section 4.4.
[100] This may be controversial (see *infra* Section 4.5).
[101] See Lehnert, *supra* note 97; Himonga, *supra* note 97.
[102] See *id.*

case held that the adaptation of living customary law to changed circumstances within the framework of the Constitution required the Court to apply the law actually lived by the people – what people are actually doing. It continued to say:

> That is not to say that in this process courts should not have regard to the Constitution. Of course, in the process of developing indigenous law and adapting it to the ever-changing circumstances, courts are required by s 39(2) of the Constitution to do so in a manner that promotes the spirit, purport and objects of the Bill of Rights.[103]

Thus, the minority judgment envisages a court actually engaging with living customary law in the process of aligning it with the constitution or human rights. *Shilubana* adds to this view by equally emphasizing the role of the community in the development of its customary law. In this respect, the Court stated:

> It is true that Ms Shilubana's installation leaves unanswered some questions relating to how the Valoyi succession will operate in the future. However, customary law is living law and will in future inevitably be interpreted, applied and, when necessary, amended or developed by the community itself or by the courts. This will be done in view of existing customs and traditions, previous circumstances and practical needs, and of course the demands of the Constitution as the supreme law.[104]

It is clear from the discussion in this section that the ability of living customary law to protect human rights is now no longer just a perception of, and speculation by, scholars; it has been tested and confirmed by the courts. Moreover, there are emerging frameworks from case law for dealing with conflicts between this system of law and human rights. Hopefully, scholars and judges will continue to develop and refine these frameworks, with a view to solving some of the challenges discussed in Section 2.4 of this chapter.

In concluding this section, it is observed that the association of living customary law with protection of human rights places this system of law in a favorable position. This is profound in African contexts where the search for ways of protecting human rights, especially of women and children, under African customary law continues to elude judges, legislators, and academics alike. It may be noted in this respect that there is a proliferation of human rights protection provisions in national constitutions, international human rights instruments, court decisions, and the legislative reforms of customary law aimed at enhancing the protection of women's rights. However, these provisions and strategies have not gone very far in achieving their intentions in practice. This is mainly due to implementation problems.[105]

---

[103] *Bhe v Magistrate Khayelitsha* 2005 (1) SA 580 (CC), 2005 (1) BCLR 10.

[104] *Shilubana and Others v Nwamitwa and Other* 2009 (2) SA 66 (CC) ¶ 81.

[105] *See* Chuma Himonga, *Law and Gender in Southern Africa Human Rights and Family Law, in* THE UNCERTAIN PROMISE OF SOUTHERN AFRICA 275 (York W. Bradshaw & Stephen N. Ndegwa eds., Indiana University Press 2000); Himonga, *supra* note 11.

Protection of human rights through the evolvement of human-rights-friendly norms of living customary law, developed by the communities themselves (with or without the active intervention of outsiders), may offer an additional, if not a more promising alternative, form of protection of human rights.

2.4. JUDICIAL ENGAGEMENT WITH THE ASCERTAINMENT AND PROOF OF LIVING CUSTOMARY LAW

One of the most endemic problems concerning the application of living customary law is how to ascertain its content and prove it before the courts. It has both taxed the minds of scholars[106] and prevented courts from playing their constitutional role to develop customary law.[107] It is also this same problem that is responsible for the continued application by the courts of the official version of customary law.[108]

The merits of its decision apart,[109] the Constitutional Court underscored this point in *Bhe*:

> The question whether the Court was in a position to develop that rule [of male primogeniture] in a manner which would 'promote the spirit, purport and objects of the Bill of Rights' evoked considerable discussion during argument. In order to do so, the court would first have to determine the true content of customary law as it is today and to give effect to it in its order. *There is however insufficient evidence and material to enable the court to do this. The difficulty lies not so much in the acceptance of the notion of "living" customary law, as distinct from official law, but in determining its content and testing it, as the court should, against the provisions of the Bill of Rights.*[110]

The minority Court shares the view of the majority on this issue, as evident from the following statement:

> *The evolving nature of indigenous law and the fact that it is unwritten have resulted in the difficulty of ascertaining the true indigenous law as practised in the community.* This law is sometimes referred to as living indigenous law. Statutes, textbooks and case law, as a result, may no longer reflect the living law. *What is more, abuses of indigenous law are at times construed as a true reflection of indigenous law, and these abuses tend to distort the law and undermine its value. The difficulty is one of identifying the living indigenous law and separating it from its distorted version....*

---

[106] *See, e.g.,* Bennett, *supra* note 34 (2004), at 44; Himonga & Bosch, *supra* note 17, at 336; Kerr, *supra* note 66.

[107] *See Bhe* (1) SA 580.

[108] *See* Bennett, *supra* note 34 (2004), at 49; Himonga & Bosch, *supra* note 17, at 329–331.

[109] For a discussion of the merits of the decision on this and other aspects of the case, see Himonga, *supra* note 11 (2005).

[110] *Bhe* (1) SA ¶ 109 (emphasis added).

In these cases [i.e., the cases before the Court], no attempt was made to ascertain the living indigenous law of succession. *These matters were approached on the footing that indigenous law of succession is that which is described in the textbooks and case law. Whether that is the proper approach to a system of law that is dynamic and evolving is not free from doubt.*[111]

It is against this backdrop that the contribution of the Constitutional Court's guidelines on the ascertainment of customary law set out in *Shilubana* must be considered and appreciated. The Court set out three main factors for determining the content of customary law.[112]

The matter before the Court concerned the right to succeed as hosi (chief) of the Valoyi traditional community in Limpopo. The dispute was between the daughter of Hosi Fofoza Nwamitwa (Fofoza), Shilubana, and the son of Hosi Malathini Richard (Richard), Nwamitwa. Fofoza died in 1968 without a male heir. At that time, succession to hosi was governed by the principle of male primogeniture. Consequently, Shilubana, being a woman, was not considered for the position, despite being of age in 1968. Instead, Fofoza's younger brother, Richard, succeeded him as hosi of the Valoyi. The current dispute between Shilubana and Nwamitwa arose following the death of Richard in 2001.

In 1996, during the reign and with the participation of Richard, the royal family of the Valoyi met and unanimously resolved to confer chieftainship on Shilubana. The resolution noted:

[T]hough in the past it was not permissible by the Valoyis that a female child be heir, in terms of democracy and the new Republic of South African Constitution it is now permissible that a female child be heir since she is also equal to a male child.... The matter of chieftainship and regency would be conducted according to the Constitution of the Republic of South Africa.[113]

Shilubana did not want Hosi Richard replaced; as a result, the royal council resolved that Hosi Richard would continue in his position for an unspecified period of time. On February 25, 1999, Richard wrote a letter that, though not unequivocal, was accepted by the High Court and the Supreme Court of Appeal as a withdrawal of his support for Shilubana's chieftainship. The royal family met again on November 4, 2001, after Richard had died, and confirmed that Shilubana would become hosi. On November 25, 2001, at a meeting of the royal family, Tribal Council, representatives of local government, civic structures, and stakeholders of various organizations, Shilubana was again pronounced hosi. However, groups of community members

---

[111] *Id.* ¶¶ 154–155 (emphasis added).
[112] *See Shilubana and Others v Nwamitwa and Other* 2009 (2) SA 66 (CC) ¶¶ 42–52.
[113] *Id.* ¶ 4.

at the meetings in November and December 2001 and January 2002 voiced support for Nwamitwa to succeed as hosi. On September 16, 2002, Nwamitwa instituted proceedings in the High Court seeking a declaratory order, *inter alia*, that he, and not Shilubana, was heir to the chieftainship of the Valoyi and thus entitled to succeed Richard. The High Court and thereafter the Supreme Court of Appeal held in Nwamitwa's favor. Both courts took the view that even if the traditions and customary law of the Valoyi currently permit women to succeed as hosi, Nwamitwa, as the eldest child of Hosi Richard, was entitled to succeed him.

On appeal to the Constitutional Court by Shilubana, the Court held in her favor on the basis, among others, that the royal family had, through its resolution, exercised its constitutional right to develop the customary law of the Valoyi. A considerable section of the judgment concerned the factors to be taken into account when ascertaining customary law within a constitutional framework. A careful study of the judgment shows that the Court did not make specific reference to living customary law in its formulation of these factors. However, it is clear from the context that the factors in question contemplate this system of customary law. These factors may now be discussed.

2.4.1. *The Traditions and Past Practices of the Community Concerned*

According to this factor, the traditions and practices of the community whose customary law is in issue must be considered. A consideration of these matters takes account of the development of the customary law as a body of rules and norms over the centuries. It also "focuses the enquiry on customary law in its own setting rather than in terms of the common-law paradigm,"[114] in line with its constitutional recognition. However, the inquiry into the content of customary law involving this factor "must be cautious of historical records, because of the distorting tendency of older authorities to view customary law through legal conceptions foreign to it."[115] Further, the element of "past practice" in respect of customary law is different from its counterpart under common law. In this regard, the Court rejected the classical test for the existence of custom as a source of law set out in *Van Breda v Jacobs*.[116] In that case, it was held that to be recognized as law, a practice must be certain, uniformly observed for a long period of time, and reasonable.

The reasons for rejecting the *Van Breda* test confirm and establish several aspects and features of living customary and, therefore, justify their detailed statement in the language of the Court, which said:

[114] *Id.* ¶ 44.
[115] *Id.*
[116] 1921 A.D. 330.

Van Breda dealt with proving custom as a source of law. It envisaged custom as an immemorial practice that could be regarded as filling in normative gaps in the common law. In that sense, custom no longer serves as an original source of law capable of independent development, but survives merely as a useful accessory. Its continued validity is rooted in and depends on its unbroken antiquity. By contrast, customary law is an independent and original source of law. Like the common law it is adaptive by its very nature. By definition, then, while change annihilates custom as a source of law, change is intrinsic to and can be invigorating of customary law.

Customary law must be permitted to develop, and the enquiry must be rooted in the contemporary practice of the community in question.[117] ... The legal status of customary-law norms cannot depend simply on their having been consistently applied in the past, because that is a test which any new development must necessarily fail. Development implies some departure from past practice. A rule that requires absolute consistency with past practice before a court will recognise the existence of a customary norm would therefore prevent the recognition of new developments as customary law. This would result in the courts applying laws which communities themselves no longer follow, and would stifle the recognition of the new rules adopted by the communities in response to the changing face of South African society. This result would be contrary to the Constitution and cannot be accepted.[118]

According to this statement, past practice (and tradition) may be relevant to the determination of the content of customary law. Within a constitutional framework, however, it is "but one important factor to be considered with other important factors."[119] Past practice will be sufficient to prove a norm of customary law "where a norm appears from tradition, and there is no indication that a contemporary development had occurred or is occurring,"[120] but it will not be sufficient "where the contemporary practice of the community suggests that change has occurred."[121] In the latter case, the first factor (i.e., the traditions and past practice of the community) has to be considered together with the other two factors. "Past practice will also not be decisive where the Constitution requires the development of the customary law in line with constitutional values."[122]

---

[117] The Court referred to S. Afr. Const. 1996 § 211(2) to support this proposition. *See Shilubana* (2) SA ¶ 55. S. Afr. Const. 1996 § 211(2) provides: "A traditional authority that observes a system of customary law may function subject to any applicable legislation and customs, which includes amendments to, or repeal of, that legislation or those customs." *Id.*

[118] *Shilubana* (2) SA ¶¶ 54–55.

[119] *Id.* ¶ 56.

[120] *Id.*

[121] *Id.*

[122] *Id.*

2.4.2. Respect for the Right of "Customary" Communities
to Develop Their Law

This factor requires the Court to take into consideration the right of communities to develop their own customary law as set out in the Constitution.[123] This right is derived from section 211(2) of the Constitution. The Court explains this at paragraph 73 as follows:

> Section 211(2) specifically provides for the right of traditional communities to function subject to their own system of customary law, including amendment or repeal of laws. A community must be empowered to itself act so as to bring its customs into line with the norms and values of the Constitution. Any other result would be contrary to s 211(2) and would be disrespectful of the close bonds between a customary community, its leaders and its laws.[124]

The right of the community to develop its own law is connected to the evolving nature of customary law, and the need of communities "to meet the needs of a rapidly changing society."[125] This brings into focus the practices of the customary community concerned, as well as the method for resolving intra-community disputes about the content of a customary law norm. Where such a dispute exists, "parties should strive to place evidence of the present practice of that community before the courts, and courts have a duty to examine the law in the context of a community and to acknowledge developments if they have occurred."[126]

2.4.3. Balancing Community Rights with Legal Certainty
and Protection of Rights

This factor entails a balancing act: The rights of communities to regulate their lives according to flexible norms (i.e., living customary law); their right to develop this system of law; and the duty of the courts to facilitate the development of this system of law must all "be balanced against the value of legal certainty, respect for vested rights, and the protection of constitutional rights."[127] Also to be considered are: "the nature of the law in question, in particular the implications of change for constitutional and other legal rights; the process by which the alleged change has occurred or is occurring; and the vulnerability of parties affected by the law."[128]

---

[123] If applied at a continental level, the nature or extent of the right that entitles the community to the development of its laws will not be the same in every African country; some countries do not have a constitutional provision requiring the development of customary law, in order to align it with the constitution.

[124] *Shilubana* (2) SA ¶ 73.

[125] *Id.* ¶ 45.

[126] *Id.* ¶ 46.

[127] *Id.* ¶ 47.

[128] *Id.*

Another, albeit less forceful, way of expressing this balancing process is to say that there is a need to distinguish between development of customary law by the courts and by a customary community. The essence of this distinction is two-fold: Firstly, "a court engaged in the adjudication of a customary-law matter must remain mindful of its obligations under s 39(2)[129] of the Constitution to promote the spirit, purport and objects of the Bill of Rights."[130] In other words, the court must remain aware of its broader obligations under the Constitution to uphold the principles of the Constitution and to develop customary law to bring it in line with the Constitution. Secondly, "[i]f development happens within the community, the court must strive to recognise and give effect to that development, to the extent consistent with adequately upholding the protection of rights."[131] According to the Court, the outcome of the balancing act will depend on the facts of each case.[132]

In concluding this section, three observations can be made about the Court's contribution to the development and future of living customary law through the factors it has established. Firstly, the guidelines represent the first comprehensive attempt by a superior court, let alone the highest court in the land, to provide solutions to the problems of ascertainment and proof of customary law in new contexts. Notably, these new contexts consist of demands for a sound balance between the application of a constitutionally protected authentic system of customary law and the protection of group and individual human rights.

Secondly, in establishing these factors, the Court responded to long-identified challenges "facing the courts in the application of customary law in accordance with constitutional imperatives within which this law has been recognised."[133] Further, the Court attempted to fill a critical gap in the application of customary law that the legislature has miserably failed to fill.[134]

Thirdly, the issue of ascertainment of customary law is critical to the survival of this system of law; it determines whether or not it will be applied by the courts. By tackling the issue of ascertainment, the Court has begun to cover the grave in which customary law should have been buried as anticipated by the metaphors about the demise of customary law with which we started this chapter!

Thus, in our view, the apparent shortcomings of the *Shilubana* judgment are mitigated by the benefits connected with the Court's attempt to make living customary law a viable and workable system through the guidelines it has introduced. However,

---

[129] *See* S. AFR. CONST. 1996, *supra* note 58.
[130] *Shilubana* (2) SA ¶ 48.
[131] *Id.* ¶ 49.
[132] *Id.* ¶ 47.
[133] Himonga & Bosch, *supra* note 17, at 340.
[134] *See* SA Law Commission Report Project 90 The Harmonisation of the Common Law and the Indigenous Law: Conflicts of Law (Sept. 1999).

there is still a need to identify the challenges of this decision, and the prominence of living customary law in legal systems shown by this chapter raise. This leads us to the issues highlighted in the conclusion to this chapter.

2.5. CONCLUSION: THE CHALLENGES ARISING FROM THE PROMINENCE OF LIVING CUSTOMARY LAW

This chapter has attempted to show that living customary law is poised to play a prominent role in African legal systems, as indicated by a number of factors and developments. However, the prominence of living customary law in African legal systems poses several challenges. Some of these challenges are directly connected to court decisions by which this system of law has risen to prominence. In this section, we highlight some of the pressing challenges that will need to be addressed to enhance living customary law's emerging status as part of national legal systems.

Firstly, though new foundations established by the Constitutional Court in *Shilubana* provide a base for fresh engagement, the issue of ascertainment and proof of living customary law will continue to be a challenge for some time. Among the pertinent questions is how to ensure that courts do not hastily sacrifice the idea of the community as a source of living customary law at the altar of gender equality, or at the altar of some other individual rights, in the process of ascertaining customary law. Related to this question is the issue of how to ensure that the colonial collusions between state institutions and traditional authorities, which resulted in the making of often oppressive and discriminatory customary law rules and norms, do not creep into the new contexts in which customary law is ascertained and applied. As already stated, these contexts require maintaining a healthy balance between competing rights and interests under the umbrellas of individual rights and group rights.

Secondly, giving back to customary law communities the right to develop their own customary laws and to align them with the Constitution is ideal to the notion of a living customary law. But who, it may be asked, is the community and who in the community should participate in the creation of constitutionally acceptable rules and norms? Do constitutional principles of equality and democracy enter the arena at this level as well? In short, what are the constitutional implications of the making and interpretation of rules and norms of living customary law at the local community level – given the power hierarchies and gender inequalities that may exist at this level, on the one hand, and human rights and the constitutional principles of democracy, on the other hand?

Stated differently, at the heart of this challenge is the question of how to guard against the undemocratic creation of rules and norms of living customary law by the powerful few in the community in the process of their court-confirmed right to develop their customary laws. This concern is especially acute if in a given country,

(a) the constitutional recognition of traditional governance under customary law is subjected to democratic principles underlying a country's constitution, and (b) the rules and norms created by the powerful within traditional leadership violate the individual rights of vulnerable members of the community, especially women and children.

Thirdly, the safeguards to the preceding challenges partly lie in the method of active development of living customary law that has now been confirmed by the Constitutional Court in *Shilubana*. However, the limitation of this solution has to be acknowledged as a challenge in itself: The solution is restricted to dispute resolution in superior courts, but access to these courts is a problem for the majority of people subject to customary law.

Fourthly, the challenge of ensuring that living customary law is not turned into official customary law is central to the survival of living customary law as a system of law. There are a number of ways in which courts can turn living customary law into official rules and norms. One example may be cited. This is the doctrine of precedent, where the courts apply their decision(s) on the customary law of one community to disputes arising under the customary law(s) of other ethnic groups.[135] This is based on the assumption of uniformity of the laws of the different ethnic groups in the country, an assumption that need not be true.[136] The temptation of using precedent in legal circles is particularly high in relation to Constitutional Court decisions. Legal professionals trained in western common law may find it very hard to resist this temptation.

But there is also another dilemma here: Although precedent is undesirable for the development of living customary law, it is the very means of its validation, as shown in this chapter. The development of various aspects of living customary law by the courts can only shape the future of living customary law if the court decisions concerned are followed as precedent.

It is clear that all the challenges identified in this section of the chapter relate to the methods of establishing the content of living customary law within constitutional and human rights frameworks in which this system of law must now be applied. In our view, this is the major area to which African customary law scholarship should be directed. Mapping the way forward may require a careful review of all the literature written on this subject to date, as a point of departure in the search for ways of strengthening existing methods for determining the validity and content of living customary law or for creating new ones.

---

[135] *See* Himonga, *supra* note 10, at 27; Woodman, *supra* note 10, at 148.
[136] *See* Woodman, *supra* note 10, at 148.

3

The Future of Customary Law in Africa

Abdulmumini A. Oba

3.1. INTRODUCTION

African customary law was the dominant legal system in much of pre-colonial sub-Saharan Africa. With the advent of colonialism in Africa in the middle of the nineteenth century, customary law gradually lost its primacy to the European-style legal systems and laws brought by the colonizing nations. The common law,[1] civil law,[2] and, to some extent, Roman-Dutch law[3] became the general law and the primary legal system in many African countries in the colonial and post-colonial eras.[4] In addition, Islamic law had emerged as the dominant law in some places in the continent prior to colonialism.[5] Islamic law is different from customary law, even though the British colonial authorities decreed in some of their colonies that Islamic law is

---

[1]   *See* Theirry Verhelst, *Safeguarding African Customary Law: Judicial and Legislative Processes for Its Adaptation and Integration* 8 (African Studies Center, University of California, Los Angeles, Occasional Paper No. 7, 1968), *available at* http://repositories.cdlib.org/international/asc/ops/verhelst ("The British brought with them the common law, the doctrines of equity, and the statutes of general application which were in force in England at a particular cut-off date. This body of law was made applicable in the colony as far as local conditions permitted."). These were applicable in the "British West, East, and Central Africa north of the Zambezi, and including Liberia and the Sudan." Antony N. Allott & Eugene Cotran, *A Background Paper on Restatement of Laws in Africa: The Need, Value and Methods of Such Restatement, in* INTEGRATION OF CUSTOMARY AND MODERN LEGAL SYSTEMS IN AFRICA 17, 23 (The Law Faculty, University of Ife ed., Africana Publishing Corporation and University of Ife Press, Ile-Ife 1971).
[2]   France, Belgium, Italy, Portugal, and Spain brought the civil law into their colonies. *See* Allott, *supra* note 1, at 23.
[3]   This family of laws was exported to South Africa, the former South Rhodesia, and the former High Commission Territories. *See id.*
[4]   *See* A. N. Allott, *Towards the Unification of Laws in Africa*, 14 INT'L & COMP. L. Q. 366, 371–372 (1965).
[5]   For an example in the Muslim part of northern Nigeria, see JAMES NORMAN DALRYMPLE ANDERSON, ISLAMIC LAW IN AFRICA 6 (Frank Cass 1978).

a customary law.[6] With these developments, customary law lost and never regained its status as a full-fledged legal system in modern African nation states.

Customary law has proved very resilient in a number of ways, however. As discussed in this chapter, customary law is still relevant in the lives of Africans. Many aspects of customary law have remained authoritative and some others are making comebacks. Customary law thinking was very prominent in the transitional justice programs that addressed the genocide in Rwanda and other gross violations of human rights that occurred in parts of Africa, such as Sierra Leone, Uganda, and Kenya, within the last few decades.

What does the future hold for customary law in Africa? This chapter considers the nature of African customary law, the position of customary law under colonial and post-colonial governments, and the major changes in the African society and the African worldview that have affected African customary law. The chapter also assesses the future prospects of African customary law.

3.2. THE NATURE OF CUSTOMARY LAW

African customary law has undergone a lot of changes since the colonial era. These changes are reflected in its definitions.[7] Law generally can be said to be "the body of rules which are recognized as obligatory by its members."[8] Looked at from its pristine pre-colonial perspective, African customary law could be described as "the organic or living law of the indigenous people" in Africa[9] or "that body of law deriving from local customs and usages of traditional Africa."[10] From the colonial era onward, African customary law has often been defined by taking into consideration the changes in the society.[11] Thus, customary law today as a source of law in Anglophone countries has been defined as "these rules of traditional customs which

---

[6] For an overview of the British policy in this regard, see *infra* pp. 2–6. For country-specific studies, see Adam Haji Bakari, *The Sharia Marriage Practices amongst the Islamic Communities in Tanzania*, 52 PUNJAB UNIV. L. J. 55, 57–62 (1995); Abdulmumini A. Oba, *Islamic Law as Customary Law: The Changing Perspective in Nigeria*, 51 INT'L COMP. L. Q. 817–850 (2002). Many judicial pronouncements challenged the idea of equating Islamic law with customary law because Islamic law is very different from African customary law. *See Khamis v. Ahmad* (1934) E.A.C.A 130, 133 (East African Court of Appeal); Bakari, *supra*, at 61 (citing *Mbuwana v. Chongwe* (Unreported) Appeal No. 67 of 1967) (Tanganyika); *Alkamawa v Bello* (1998) 6 S.C.N.J. 127 (Nigerian Supreme Court).

[7] *See* Abdulmumini A. Oba, *The Administration of Customary Law in the Post-Colonial Nigerian State*, 37 CAMBRIAN L. REV. 95, 95–96 (2006).

[8] TASLIM OLAWALE ELIAS, THE NATURE OF AFRICAN CUSTOMARY LAW 55 (Manchester University Press 1956).

[9] *Oyewunmi v Ogunsesan* (1990) 5 S.C.N.J. 33, 53 (Nigerian Supreme Court).

[10] Charles Ogwurike, *The Source and Authority of African Customary Law*, 3 UNIV. GHANA L. J. 11, 12 (1966).

[11] Alexander Nekam, Third Melville Memorial Lecture at the Centre of African Studies, Edinburgh University: Experiences in African Customary Law 2 (1966).

are discoverable by judicial inquiry and which are enforceable because they are acceptable as conforming to what ought to be the current values in the society."[12] Another modern contextual definition of customary law is proffered by Plateau State (Nigeria) as "the rule of conduct which governs legal relationships as established by custom and usage and not forming part of the common law of England nor formally enacted by the Plateau State House of Assembly but includes any declaration or modification of customary law but does not include Islamic personal law."[13]

Customary law in Africa is a diverse affair. In Africa, there are more than 800 ethnic/language groups, each with its own customary laws.[14] In spite of its diversity, the group of laws described as African customary law has some distinctive or common features in terms of content that makes it identifiable as a distinct family of laws.[15] Three such features include that customary law tends to be expressed communally; that customary law is more *concrete* than *abstract*; and that customary law involves the supernatural.[16] Other common traits of African indigenous jurisprudence include an emphasis on reconciliation and compromise;[17] an emphasis on general principles; group responsibility; and frequent use of informal enforcement procedures.[18]

The colonial courts and their successors in some African countries have identified some other characteristics of customary law.[19] For example, in Nigeria, the courts have held that customary law is unwritten;[20] that customary law depends on acceptance by the society;[21] that customary law is a "mirror of accepted usage";[22] and that the enforceable custom is "existing native law and custom and not that of bygone days."[23] Another characteristic of customary law identified by the courts is flexibility, that is, customary law adapts to changing times and circumstances.[24]

---

[12] Ogwurike, *supra* note 10, at 17.
[13] Plateau State Customary Court of Appeal Law, 1979, § 2.
[14] *See* VINCENT. B. KHAPOYA, THE AFRICAN EXPERIENCE: AN INTRODUCTION 14–15 (Prentice-Hall, Inc. 1998).
[15] *See* Eugene Cotran & Neville N. Rubin, *Introduction, in* 1 READINGS IN AFRICAN LAW xviii–xix (E. Cotran & N. N. Rubin eds., Frank Cass 1970); AFRICAN LAW AND LEGAL THEORY xv–xvi (Gordon Woodman & A. O. Obilade eds., Dartmouth Publishing Co., Ltd 1995).
[16] *See* John F. Holleman, *An Anthropological Approach to Bantu Law (With Special Reference to Shona Law)*, 10 RHODES – LIVINGSTONE J. 51–56 (1949). *See also* J.H. Driberg, *The African Conception of Law*, 34 J. AFR. SOC'Y 230, 239–240 (1955).
[17] *See* more on these *infra*.
[18] *See* J. M. ELEGIDO, JURISPRUDENCE 128–130 (Spectrum Books, Ltd. 1994).
[19] *See* Oba, *supra* note 7, at 96–97.
[20] *See Alfa v Arepo* (1963) W.N.L.R. 95, 97.
[21] *See Eleko v Government of Nigeria* (1931) A. C. 662, 673.
[22] *Owonyin v Omotosho* (1961) 1 All NLR 304, 309.
[23] *Lewis v Bankole* (1909) NLR 100.
[24] *See id.* at 100–101.

Today, legal pluralism is the most significant feature of law in Africa. Customary law is struggling not to be submerged by Islamic law and other European legal systems that came with the colonization of the continent.

3.3. CUSTOMARY LAW IN THE COLONIAL ERA

Colonialism had a great impact on the study, exposition, and judicial enforcement of customary law. Pre-colonial Africa neither had written records nor jurisprudential analysis of its laws. The study of customary law was pioneered by outsiders, that is, non-Africans, and by anthropologists and administrators rather than lawyers.[25] Anthropologists showed interest in customary law from the ethnographic perspective for the purpose of documenting it largely for official use. Colonial administrators studied customary law for administrative purposes. The results of these efforts proved inadequate from the legal point of view. They are considered generally "too fluid for purpose of legal analysis."[26] Lawyers came rather late into the field and the works of lawyers on customary law generally lack cultural content. Rather, the lawyer's approach to customary law generally centered on customary law that is enforceable in the courts without reference to customary law as it is with the people.[27]

Another important factor that affected the development of customary law was that the colonial authorities did not see customary law as a viable legal system. Rather, the general attitude of colonial authorities was that customary law would eventually whither away.[28] Others more charitably believed that some aspects of customary law would be integrated into the laws brought by colonialism; hence the huge scholarly interest in unification of laws projects in the latter part of the colonial era and the early independence period.

Colonialism impacted customary law in Africa in a number of other ways, some of which are examined further in this chapter.[29]

3.3.1. *Arbitrary Nature of Legal Jurisdictions*

Customary law in Africa is ethnic-based. Communities belonging to the same ethnic group usually have the same customary law. Colonialism brought into being

---

[25] *See* Cotran & Rubin, *supra* note 15, at xiv.
[26] Elias, *supra* note 8, at 2–3.
[27] *See* Gordon Woodman, *Some Realism about Customary Law – The West African Experience* 1969 WIS. L. REV. 128, 146 (1969).
[28] *See* Verhelst, *supra* note 1, at 34 n.83; ANDREW EDWARD WILSON PARK, THE SOURCES OF NIGERIAN LAW 142–143 (Sweet and Maxwell 1963); Hallie Ludsin, *Cultural Denial: What South Africa's Treatment of Witchcraft Says for the Future of Its Customary Law*, 21 BERKELEY J. INT'L L. 62, 70 (2003).
[29] *See generally* Carlson Anyangwe, *The Whittling Away of African Indigenous Legal and Judicial System*, (Special Issue) ZAMBIA L. J. 46, 51–56 (1998).

new territories, which disrupted the existing ethnic configurations.[30] All over the continent, ethnic groups were arbitrarily separated or merged to create new political entities and new legal jurisdictions.[31] The incoherent jurisdictions produced therefrom made the administration of customary laws rather complex.[32]

3.3.2. *Displacement and Relegation of Customary Law*

Colonialism established the law of the colonizing power as the general law of the land, and customary law became a "secondary" or "exceptional" law. Customary law was widely excluded from matters of public law such as constitutional law, administrative law, criminal law and procedure, labor law, commercial law, torts, and contract law.[33] Customary law became confined to civil matters and was limited to land law, chieftaincy matters, and personal law governing family matters.[34] Even in these matters, the colonial authorities abolished aspects they considered unacceptable or "repugnant to civilized ideas;"[35] the rest they permitted subject to the validity tests. In British colonies, in order to be enforceable in the courts, the customary law could not be "repugnant to natural justice, equity, and good conscience," incompatible with statute, or contrary to public policy.[36] In Francophone colonies, the tests varied. Generally, customary law could not be inconsistent with public policy and "*ordre public*";[37] or to the "general spirit of the legislation of the particular country; or to the fundamental rules concerning public order and the liberty of persons";[38] or it had to be *in accordance* with the statutes, public order, and morality.[39]

3.3.3. *Relegation of Traditional Adjudicating Bodies*

The colonial authorities relegated traditional African adjudicating bodies to mere informal methods of settling disputes instead of recognizing them as judicial

---

[30] *See* Adekunle Ajala, *The Origin of African Boundaries*, 1 NIGERIAN FORUM 243 (1981).
[31] *See* Allott, *supra* note 4, at 367, 371.
[32] *See id.*
[33] *See* Verhelst, *supra* note 1, at 20.
[34] *See id.* at 21.
[35] Antony N. Allott, *The Extent of the Operation of Native Customary Law: Applicability and Repugnancy*, 2 J. AFR. ADMIN. 4, 8–9 (1950); Michel Alliot, *The Role of Justice in the Application of the Law in Francophone States of Africa, in* INTEGRATION OF CUSTOMARY AND MODERN LEGAL SYSTEMS IN AFRICA, *supra* note 1, at 76.
[36] Verhelst, *supra* note 1, at 21; LAWRENCE C.B. GOWER, INDEPENDENT AFRICA: THE CHALLENGE TO THE LEGAL PROFESSION 26–28 (Harvard University Press 1967); Oba, *supra* note 7, at 98–100.
[37] Verhelst, *supra* note 1, at 22; Nelson Enonchong, *Public Policy and* Ordre Public: *The Exclusion of Customary Law in Cameroon*, 5 AFR. J. INT'L COMP. L. 503–523 (1993).
[38] Verhelst, *supra* note 1, at 22.
[39] *See id.* at 20–24.

bodies.⁴⁰ They also established a new court system that replaced the traditional system in the administration of customary law. Together, these developments seriously
undermined the traditional system. The new courts, whether manned by the colonialists or Africans, departed radically from the traditional system. Although they
administered customary law, the new courts were closer in terms of mode of proof,
formality, practice, and procedure to their European models than to the African
customary law dispute-resolving structures.⁴¹ In Anglophone Africa, the colonial
authorities also created separate courts to administer the "general" law consisting of
common law and statutory law. The parallel or dual system of courts that emerged
from this arrangement was a constant source of concern to colonial authorities.⁴²

3.3.4. Transformation or Invention of Customary Law

Colonialism transformed the normative content of customary law in many ways.
This was due mainly to the attempts at documenting customary law and also to the
activities of colonial courts and their successors.

Customary law is largely unwritten, so it is sometimes difficult to ascertain. To
address this difficulty, some countries have codified or attempted to codify customary law.⁴³ Others have argued that codification is inappropriate, however, as it will
lead to ossification of obsolete customs thereby stifling the development of customary law. Accordingly, some countries have instead created restatements of customary
law.⁴⁴ Such restatements avoid the criticism that codification ossifies as they merely
serve as guides rather than authoritative statements of customary law.

The administration of customary law by European-style courts brought many challenges to the application of customary law. One of these is the mode of ascertaining
customary laws before these courts. In many jurisdictions in Africa, customary law is

---

⁴⁰ See Anyangwe, supra note 29, at 60–64. For an overview of the indigenous African judicial system, see
   GEORGE B.N. AYITTEY, INDIGENOUS AFRICAN INSTITUTIONS 39–69 (Transnational Publishers, Inc.
   1991).
⁴¹ See Mike Imadun Isokun, How Customary Is the Customary Court System?, in TOWARDS A
   RESTATEMENT OF NIGERIAN CUSTOMARY LAW 204 (Yemi Osinbajo & Awa. U. Kalu eds., Nigerian
   Federal Ministry of Justice, 1991).
⁴² See R.E. Robinson, The Administration of African Customary Law, 1 J. AFR. ADMIN. 158 (1949); N.J.
   Brooke, The Changing Character of Customary Courts, 6 JOURNAL OF AFRICAN ADMINISTRATION 67,
   72 (1954).
⁴³ See Verhelst, supra note 1, at 34–47.
⁴⁴ See id. at 41; John Miles, Customary and Islamic Law and Its Development in Africa, 1 L. DEV. REV. 100,
   108–09 (2006), available at http://ssrn.com/abstract=1015783; Eugene Cotran, Restatement of African
   Law: Kenya I: The Law of Marriage and Divorce, in 1 RESTATEMENT OF AFRICAN LAW (A.N. Allott
   ed., Sweet & Maxwell 1968); Eugene Cotron, Kenya II: The Law of Succession, in 2 RESTATEMENT
   OF AFRICAN LAW (A.N. Allott ed., Sweet & Maxwell 1969); J.O. Ibik, Malawi I: The Law of Marriage
   and Divorce, in 3 RESTATEMENT OF AFRICAN LAW (A.N. Allott ed., Sweet & Maxwell 1970); J.O. Ibik,
   Malawi II: The Law of Succession, in 4 RESTATEMENT OF AFRICAN LAW (A.N. Allott ed., Sweet &
   Maxwell 1971).

not a question of law but one of fact.[45] This means that every norm of customary law that a litigant intends to rely on must be proven with reference to facts and evidence rather than allowing the court to take judicial notice of the existence of that particular norm.[46] This not only effectively has placed customary law on the same level with foreign law; it has serious implications for the normative content of customary law. Given the adversarial nature of litigation in the courts, the customary law "proved" is more likely to be the version alleged by the stronger party. Some have suggested that the patriarchal version of customary law – which puts women at a subservient position and which has become the dominant customary law in Africa – emerged from the colonial courts.[47] The status of chiefs in many communities also underwent a transformation in the colonial era, with the colonial authorities enhancing the powers of the chiefs.[48]

Thus, since the colonial era, customary law in Africa can be divided into "official" and "living" customary laws.[49] Official customary law is customary law that "has been recognized in anthropological studies, court judgments, restatements, and in legal codes."[50] Living customary law is "the practices and customs of the people in their day-to-day lives."[51] Official customary law is largely a creation of colonialism and of the nation states that emerged from colonialism. Restatements and the activities of the courts are increasingly transforming customary law into formal law.[52]

3.3.5. *Avenues for Opting Out of the Customary Law System*

The colonial authorities provided avenues by which the African could opt out of the customary law system whenever he or she so desired.[53] In many jurisdictions, Africans could expressly exclude the application of customary law from any of their transactions.[54] They also implied to have excluded the application of customary law

---

[45] See Verhelst, *supra* note 1, at 24–27; Antony N. Allott, *The Judicial Ascertainment of Customary Law in British Africa*, 20 MOD. L. REV. 244–63 (1957).

[46] See Verhelst, *supra* note 1, at 24–27; Allott, *supra* note 45, at 244–63.

[47] See Martin Channock, *Neither Customary nor Legal: African Customary Law in an Era of Family Reform*, 3 INT'L J. L. FAM. 72, 75–77 (1989).

[48] See Leila Chirayath, Caroline Sage & Michael Woolcock, *Customary Law and Policy Reform: Engaging with the Plurality of Justice Systems* 13–14 (World Development Report, Background Paper, 2005), *available at* http://siteresources.worldbank.org/ INTWDR2006/Resources/477383–1118673432908/ Customary_Law_and_Policy_Reform.pdf.

[49] See Ludsin, *supra* note 28, at 71–73. *See also* Alliot, *supra* note 35, at 77; Imadun Isokun, *supra* note 41, at 205–06.

[50] Ludsin, *supra* note 28, at 71 (citing C. Himonga & C. Bosch, *The Application of African Customary Law under the Constitution of South Africa*, 117 SALJ 308, 328–329 (2000)).

[51] Ludsin, *supra* note 28, at 71 (citing Himonga & Bosch, *supra* note 50, at 319).

[52] See Woodman, *supra* note 27, at 146, 169; Ogwurike, *supra* note 10, at 18.

[53] See Anyangwe, *supra* note 29, at 63–64.

[54] See *Griffin v Talabi* (1948) 12 W.A.C.A. 371.

to transactions which were unknown to customary law.[55] They could also be deemed by their lifestyle to have excluded customary law as their personal law.[56]

3.4. CUSTOMARY LAW IN THE POST-COLONIAL ERA

Post-colonial African states retained the colonial attitude toward, and structures impacting, customary law. Many other factors emerged in this period that have serious implications for the survival of customary law in these states. The more significant factors are those of legal pluralism, state control over customary courts, the attitude of lawyers and legal education, and the emergence of written constitutions.

3.4.1. *Legal Pluralism*

The legal terrain in modern African nation states is a pluralistic one. Apart from customary law, there are also Islamic laws and state laws.[57] Incidental to this is also the multiplicity of courts to handle each of these laws. As discussed earlier, Anglophone countries generally have a dual or parallel system (with separate lower courts hearing cases governed by customary law and other bodies of law) with a unified appellate courts system and a supreme court at the apex.[58] The parallel system has raised a lot of controversies. Some have argued that such multiplicity of laws and courts is neither convenient administratively nor conducive to national unity.[59] They have suggested that all these laws be harmonized or fused into one single law, and administered within a unified courts system. The problem of multiplicity of courts does not arise in Francophone countries where there is typically a unified courts system.[60]

Customary law itself is often a pluralistic matter even within particular nation states.[61] The plurality of customary laws has raised the question of national integration. Some have argued that a nation cannot remain united with such diversity

---

[55] *See, e.g., Bakare v Coker* (1935) 12 N.L.R. 31 (promissory notes); *Green v Owo* (1936) 13 N.L.R. 43 (conveyance in English law form); *Salau v Aderibigbe* (1963) W.N.L.R. 80 (hire purchase).

[56] *See infra* Section 3.4.4.

[57] There is even Hindu personal law in the eastern part of the continent. *See* Laurence Juma, *The Legitimacy of Indigenous Legal Institutions and Human Rights Practice in Kenya: An Old Debate Revisited*, 14 AFR. J. INT'L COMP. L. 176, 194–196 (2006).

[58] *See* Verhelst, *supra* note 1, at 13–18.

[59] *See* I.O. Agbede, *Legal Pluralism: The Symbiosis of Imported, Customary and Religious Laws: Problems and Prospects, in Fundamentals of Nigerian Law* 235, 236–241 (M.A. Ajomo ed., Nigerian Institute of Advanced Legal Studies 1989) 235. For the refutations of the arguments against legal pluralism, see Gordon Woodman, *Legal Pluralism and the Search for Justice*, 40 J. AFR. L. 152, 160–164 (1996); Anyangwe, *supra* note 29, at 47–49.

[60] *See* Anyangwe, *supra* note 29, at 58–59.

[61] *See* Khapoya, *supra* note 14, at 3–4.

in its customary laws and have suggested that the customary law be unified. As a result, some states have attempted to unify their customary laws, but with little or no success.[62] Divergence in customary law is not necessarily detrimental to national unity.[63] Unification of customary laws is not particularly desirable for it would in essence mean imposing another customary law on some communities.[64] Some have gone further with the unification-of-laws idea by proposing that *all* the laws in the state be unified.[65] This is an even more problematic venture.

Legal pluralism in Africa has brought with it conflict of law and the problem of choice of law. In some countries, a customary court is competent only where all the parties voluntarily submit to its jurisdiction.[66] In other countries, the descent and lifestyle of the person in question are important factors in determining whether customary law applies to that person.[67] The competition between the "descent" and the "manner of life" tests is well illustrated in the Kenyan case of *S. M. Otieno*.[68] The deceased, S. M. Otieno, a well-known lawyer belonging to the Luo ethnic community, married Wambui Otieno, a Kikuyu, in the early 1950s. The marriage was conducted according to Christian rites. Otieno died intestate in 1986. His widow applied for burial rights and administration of his estate under English law. The brother of the deceased opposed this saying that he was entitled to administer his brother's estate under Luo customary law. The High Court relied on the "manner of life" test and upheld the widow's contention. The court held that the deceased had by his westernized lifestyle brought his personal affairs out of the ambit of customary into English law. On appeal, however, the Court of Appeal reversed the decision of the High Court. The Court of Appeal held that because the deceased belonged to the Luo ethnic community by descent, the Luo customary law applied to his estate. This case attracted a barrage of criticisms, particularly from the human rights perspective.[69]

---

[62] See Antony N. Allott, *What Is to Be Done with African Customary Law: The Experience of Problems and Reforms in Anglophone Africa from 1950*, 28 J. AFR. L. 56, 70 (1984).

[63] See *id*. at 65.

[64] See *id*. at 66.

[65] See Taslim Olawale Elias, Inaugural Lecture at the University of Lagos: Law in a Developing Society 18–19 (1969); T. Akinola Aguda, *Towards a Nigerian Common Law, in* FUNDAMENTALS OF NIGERIAN LAW 249 (M.A. Ajomo ed., Nigerian Institute of Advanced Legal Studies 1989).

[66] See Verhelst, *supra* note 1, at 30.

[67] See *id*. at 18–20.

[68] SC No. 210–298 (Zimbabwe, Feb. 16, 1999).

[69] For discussions of the case, see John W. van Doren, *Death African Style: S. M. Otieno, Kenya's Unique Burial Saga*, 35 AM. J.COMP. L. 329–350 (1989); Adam H. Bakari, *African's Paradoxes of Legal Pluralism in Personal Law – A Comparative Study of Tanzania and Kenya*, 3 RADIC 545–557 (1991); Rebecca Farrar, *Addressing the Tension of Laws in Legal Pluralism: Women's Rights in Africa* 25–28 (Stetson University, Unpublished Paper, 2009), *available at* http://works.bepress.com/rebecca_farrar/2.

3.4.2. *State Control over Customary Courts*

Post-colonial states have retained control of customary courts as was the case under colonialism. In some countries, customary courts were integrated into the modern court system whereas in others, they were abolished and their jurisdiction transferred to modern courts.[70] These arrangements raise the question of authenticity. A major criticism of the "customary courts" established by the states is that they are patterned after foreign models and that they are more sympathetic to foreign values.[71] This could widen the gap between "official" customary law and "living" customary law.

3.4.3. *Attitude of Lawyers/Legal Education*

Legal education at university and law schools levels in most African countries ignores customary law.[72] The things lawyers typically know about customary law relate to the validity tests employed in the courts and which are no more than a catalogue of "repugnant" aspects of customary law. This creates an aversion to customary law in many lawyers who tend to see this body of law as primitive and backward.[73] Many such lawyers would gladly see customary law disappear.[74]

3.4.4. *Emergence of Written Constitutions in Most African Countries*

Many African countries now have written constitutions. These constitutions generally incorporate a bill of rights. The constitutions also affirm their supremacy over all other laws in the relevant states. The bills of rights could pose serious threats to the survival of customary law because certain areas of customary law may conflict with rights guaranteed by the written constitutions. The terms of these bills of rights vary from country to country, as demonstrated with respect to provisions addressing gender equality with different results for challenges brought to customary law rules. In South Africa, for example, the Constitution recognizes customary law but makes it subject to the Constitution and to statutes.[75] The South African

---

[70] *See* Anyangwe, *supra* note 29, at 52–53.

[71] *See* Gower, *supra* note 36, at 94; *see, e.g.,* Akilagpa Sawyerr, *Judicial Manipulation of Customary Family Law in Tanzania, in* LAW AND THE FAMILY IN AFRICA 115–128 (Simon A. Roberts ed., Moulton 1977).

[72] *See* Anyangwe, *supra* note 29, at 64–66.

[73] *See* John Bewaji, *Aspects of Legal Education and Socio-Political Order in Indigenous Yoruba Society,* 1 AFR. J. LEGAL THEORY 85, 86 (2007), *available at* http://www.afrilegstudies.com/legaltheory/docs/bewajiespaper2.doc.

[74] *See* Gower, *supra* note 36, at 93.

[75] *See* S. AFR. CONST. 1996 s. 211(3).

Constitution contains a bill of rights which, inter-alia, entrenches gender equality. The effect of this on customary law was brought to the fore in *Bhe v Magistrate, Khayalitsha*[76] where primogeniture[77] was declared unconstitutional on the basis that the exclusion of women from inheritance and the notion of male domination are incompatible with the gender equality and right to human dignity guaranteed in the South African Constitution.[78] In Nigeria, the Constitution does not expressly entrench gender equality but includes a provision on non-discrimination on the basis of "sex."[79] It has been held *obiter* that this does not create absolute gender equality in the country,[80] and Nigerian courts have found that primogeniture does not violate the constitution.[81] In Zimbabwe, the constitution exempts customary law from the gender equality provisions of its Constitution, and thus the Supreme Court in *Magaya v Magaya*[82] upheld the validity of primogeniture.

The bills of rights in national constitutions are now supplemented by international human rights law. The African regional human rights system, which is fast developing, presents additional challenges to customary law, particularly in the area of women rights.[83]

[76] *Bhe v Magistrate Khayalitsha; Shibi v. Sithole; South African Human Rights Commission v. President of the Republic of South Africa* 2005 (1) 580 (CC).

[77] Primogeniture is a system of inheritance whereby the estate passes to the eldest son.

[78] *Bhe v. Magistrate, Khayalitsha* paras. 89 and 91. See discussion of the case in M.C. Schoeman-Malan, *Recent Developments Regarding South African Common and Customary Law of Succession*, 1 POTCHEFSTROOM ELECTRONIC L. J. 1, 20 (2007). "As a direct result of *Bhe's* case the Repeal of the Black Administration Act and Amendment of Certain Laws Act 28 of 2005 [which inter-alia approved primogeniture] was promulgated on 12 April 2006". *Id.* at 24 n.139.

[79] Section 42 (1) of the 1999 Constitution provides that "A citizen of Nigeria of a particular ... sex ... shall not, by reason only that he is such a person be subjected either expressly by, or in the practical application of, any law in force in Nigeria or any executive or administrative action of the government to disabilities or restrictions ... [or] ... any privilege or advantage to which citizens of Nigeria of other ... sex ... are not made subject." It has been argued that "[t]he section only prohibits discrimination against an individual where other members of a class to which he belongs, e.g. religious class do not suffer the same. Hence where the discrimination is common to that class he cannot complain". Ayo Oyajobi, *Better Protection for Women and Children under the Law*, in WOMEN AND CHILDREN UNDER THE NIGERIAN LAW 34 (Awa U. Kalu & Yemi Osinbajo eds., Nigerian Federal Ministry of Justice, c. 1989).

[80] *See Mojekwu v Iwuchukwu* (2004) 4 S.C.N.J. 180, 193–194. The case is discussed critically in Abdulmumini A. Oba, *Broaching the Limits to Gender Equality in Nigeria*: Augustine Nwafor Mojekwu v Mrs. Theresa Iwuchukwu, 47 INDIAN J. INT'L L. 289–297 (2007).

[81] *See Idehen v Idehen* (1991) 7 S.C.NJ. 196.

[82] (Unreported) SC No. 210/98, Zimbabwean Supreme Court, decided on Feb. 16, 1999. The case has provoked a lot of criticism. *See* David M. Bigge & Amelie von Briesent, *Conflict in the Zimbabwean Courts: Women's Rights and Indigenous Self-Determination*, in *Magaya v Magaya*, 13 HARV. HUM. RTS. J. 289 (2000); Simon Coldham, *The Status of Women in Zimbabwe*: Veneria Magaya v Nakayi Shonhiwa Magaya SC No. 210/98, 43 J. AFR. L. 248–252 (1999).

[83] More relevant here is the Protocol to the African Charter on Human and Peoples' Rights on the Rights of Women in Africa, adopted on July 11, 2003, which came into force on November 25, 2005. The Protocol entrenches strict gender equality. See the discussion of some areas of conflict between

The result of all the factors examined earlier is that, in modern African nation states, the scope of customary law and customary law courts are being chiseled away. State law is now becoming the domineering influence on land law, and even chieftaincy matters. Apart from these and family law, which includes such matters as marriage, divorce, custody of children, and inheritance, very little remains of customary law.

3.5. FUNDAMENTAL CHANGES IN AFRICAN SOCIETY AND WORLDVIEWS

Pre-colonial African communities have been rightly described as "strong, tightly knit, homogeneous" communities.[84] In traditional Africa, law is not merely an abstract set of rules. Rather, law forms an integral part of the whole fabric of the society. In Africa, "Law is part of the whole cultural complex ..."[85] Or, stated more philosophically: "African laws are deeply rooted in African culture and tradition and are inseparable from the African ontology."[86] Once a part of the structure changes, the laws relevant thereto tend to become meaningless and in need of change as the law can never "survive the community which created it."[87] Many factors have radicalized African societies in a manner that challenges many aspects of customary law. The advent of colonialism, new religions – Islam and Christianity – western education and the resultant westernization, and changes in economic and social patterns have brought fundamental changes to the African way of life.[88] Many of these changes have been so radical that some have wondered whether customary law is still relevant at all. For example, there is a tendency to see customary law in Africa as the "law of small-scale communities"[89] or as the law of the rural or agrarian society of the "interior," as opposed to the modern law applicable in the elitist industrial and commercial centers or "economic enclaves" in the urban area.[90] However, this is an over-simplification because the urban in Africa is often sprawling cities that incorporate rural villages; Africans are usually a composite of the urban and rural; and customary law as a personal law attaches to the individual and goes with him

African customary law and international human rights norms in Kaniye S.A. Ebeku, *A New Hope for African Women: Overview of Africa's Protocol on Women's Rights*, 13 NORDIC J. AFR. STUD. 264 (2004); Farrar, *supra* note 69.

[84] Nekam, *supra* note 11, at 3.
[85] Driberg, *supra* note 16, at 230.
[86] Fidelis Okafor, *From Praxis to Theory: A Discourse on the Philosophy of African Law*, 37 CAMBRIAN L. REV. 37, 39 (2006). *See also* Alliot, *supra* note 35, at 76; Kojo Yelpaala, *Circular Arguments and Self-Fulfilling Definitions: 'Stateless' and the Dagaaba*, 10 HIST. IN AFR. 349, 377 (1983).
[87] Nekam, *supra* note 11, at 6.
[88] *See id.* at 12.
[89] Miles, *supra* note 44, at 102.
[90] Verhelst, *supra* note 1, at 6 n.2.

or her wherever he or she goes.[91] The urban/rural dichotomy is often no more than a shorthanded reference to degrees of acceptance of westernization among varying levels of elitist structures. It overlooks the resilience of customary law and the many Africans who – in spite of their education and exposure to the western civilization – still cling in varying degrees to aspects of their culture.

It is imperative that one understands the nature of some of these changes before one can venture into predicting the future of African customary law. Some of the changes are examined hereunder.

3.5.1. *Loss of Supremacy of the African Traditional Institutions*

African traditional institutions generally and their legal authorities in particular lost their supremacy first to the colonial powers and later to the nation-states that emerged from colonialism. As noted earlier, both authorities provided avenues for Africans to opt out of customary law at will. The authority of the personnel in charge of administering African customary law – chiefs, elders, and priests – was seriously weakened as a result.[92] They became answerable to these new authorities, which in some cases are administered by the new African elite.

3.5.2. *Social, Economic, and Political Changes*

There have been many social, economic, and political changes that have displaced the old premises upon which customary law was based. For example, the free mobility and urbanization that characterize the modern era have rendered traditional sanctions and means of social control – such as exile, ostracism, and disgrace – obsolete.[93] In the pre-colonial era, when individual protection depended on membership in a group (family, clan, community), forced exile was tantamount to capital punishment whereas boycott effectively paralyzed the social-economic life of the individual, and disgrace attached not only to the culprit but also to his or her social network such as family, age grade, and guilds as they all have solidarity with their members.[94] If the offense was particularly gross, they would take steps to expel the culprit from their fold.[95]

---

[91] See CHIDI ANSELM ODINKALU, PLURALISM AND THE FULFILLMENT OF JUSTICE NEEDS IN AFRICA 4 (Open Society Justice Initiative 2005).

[92] *See* Nekam, *supra* note 11, at 6.

[93] See description of these sanctions in Alan Milner, *The Sanctions of Customary Criminal Law: A Study in Social Control*, 1 NIGERIAN L. J. 173 (1964). Some of these methods still exist as private means of social control and to new situations even in western countries. *See* Bruce Benson, *Customary Law with Private Means of Resolving Disputes and Dispensing Justice: A Description of a Modern System of Law and Order without State Coercion*, 9 J. LIBERTARIAN STUD. 25, 37–39 (1990).

[94] *See* J. A. SOFOLA, AFRICAN CULTURE AND THE AFRICAN PERSONALITY 125–126 (African Resources Publishers 1973); Khapoya, *supra* note 14, at 40–45.

[95] *See* Khapoya, *supra* note 14, at 44–45.

The treatment of widows provides a good example of the impact of these changes.[96] In most of pre-colonial African communities, a widow could not inherit from her husband's estate but was provided for in number of ways. She could contract a levirate marriage (now often wrongly construed as "widow inheritance"), join the home of one of her adult sons, or return to her natal family.[97] These were adequate in those days given the traditional checks and balances that existed within communities. With the disappearance of these checks in modern times, however, these arrangements are easily exploited to the detriment of the widow.[98]

3.5.3. *Changes in the Magico-Religious Belief*

Magico-religious belief played an important role in the pre-colonial African customary law. In matters of evidence, juju oaths, divination, ordeals, and appeal to the ancestors were crucial and often final steps in the quest for truthful evidence, especially in matters that had defied human efforts.[99] In substantive matters, the gods and ancestors often defined the taboos while belief in reincarnation formulated many of the laws relating to inheritance. Western education and advancement in science have helped dispel many of the superstitious beliefs, but some still have a tenuous hold on the African mind, in spite of the relentless onslaught of Islam and Christianity. This is so with regard to belief in witchcraft and the use of juju oaths. State laws do not recognize witchcraft but belief in it persists.[100] Juju oaths too have proved resilient in the African psyche so much so that they are still a potent force in both the informal and formal systems of administration of justice.[101]

3.5.4. *The Rise of New African Elites*

The exposure of Africans to western education and western culture has led to the emergence of a new class of African elites who have replaced the colonial minority as the "dominant decisional force" in modern African nation states.[102] Many of these westernized indigenous elites reject the African way of life and are very critical of African customary law. They are largely inclined to the West in their tastes and aspirations. They see the salvation of Africa in replicating the West in all respects. Some

---

[96] *See* B.A. Rwezaura, *The Changing Role of the Extended Family in Providing Economic Support for an Individual in Africa, in* AFRICAN AND WESTERN LEGAL SYSTEMS IN CONTACT 57–89 (Eckhard Breitinger ed., Bayreuth African Studies Series 11 1989).

[97] *See id.* at 66.

[98] *See id.* at 58.

[99] *See* Elias, *supra* note 8, at 228–238.

[100] *See* Ludsin, *supra* note 28.

[101] *See* Abdulmumini A. Oba, *Juju Oaths in Customary Law Arbitration and Their Legal Validity in Nigerian Courts*, 52 J. AFR. L. 139–158 (2008).

[102] Odinkalu, *supra* note 91, at 4.

educated African elites are not like this. They are proud of their African heritage and want to give expression to its positive aspects. In recent times, Africans are showing more interest in the exposition of African customary law as the growing literature on the subject shows.[103] They are searching for positive aspects of African customary law that could be preserved or incorporated into modern law.

3.5.5. *External Socio-Cultural Influences*

Customary law thrives in homogenous communities with strong ethnic solidarity resulting in values easily shared by all.[104] What the foregoing shows is that Africa is gradually or steadily changing. The "strong, tightly knit, homogeneous" community that nurtured and created customary law is fast becoming a thing of the past. Globalization has brought into Africa an influx of foreign culture via satellite televisions, the Internet, films (widely available on pirated DVDs), and the mass media. These have even introduced a strong element of westernization into rural areas in Africa. The growing wave of Islamic revivalism among Muslims across the world is also felt in Africa. More and more Muslims are opting for Islamic law. The implication is that Islamic law is displacing customary law in the life of these Muslims and is re-emerging as state law in some countries.[105]

3.6. PROSPECTS OF CUSTOMARY LAW

With all the chiseling away of the substantive and procedural aspects of customary law, what then does the future hold for customary law? It is plain that customary law can no longer go back to its pre-colonial status as a full-fledged legal system. It is equally certain that, contrary to the colonial dream, customary law will not simply disappear or wither away.[106] Only a few countries shared the colonial vision

---

[103] For example, the literature on Yoruba customary law alone includes: O. Adewoye, *Proverbs as a Vehicle of Juristic Thought Among the Yoruba*, 3 OBAFEMI AWOLOWO UNIV. L.J. 1 (1987); A.T. OYEWO & O.B. OLAOBA, A SURVEY OF AFRICAN LAW AND CUSTOM WITH PARTICULAR REFERENCE TO THE YORUBA SPEAKING PEOPLES OF SOUTH-WESTERN NIGERIA (Jator Publishing Co. 1999); O.B. Olaoba, YORUBA LEGAL CULTURE (FOP Press 2002); John Bewaji, *Human Rights: A Philosophical Analysis of Yoruba Conceptions*, 37 CAMBRIAN L. REV. 49–72 (2006); O.A. Balogun, *A Jurisprudential Analysis of Yoruba Proverbs*, 37 CAMBRIAN L. REV. 85–94 (2006); W. Idowu, *Law, Morality, and the African Heritage: The Jurisprudential Significance of the 'Ogboni' Institution*, 14 NORDIC J. AFR. STUD. (2005).

[104] *See* Nekam, *supra* note 11, at 12.

[105] *See, e.g.*, Abdulmumini A. Oba, The Impact of Customs on Islamic Family Law in Northern Nigeria (July 13, 2009) (Paper presented at the Sixth ILS Conference, "Islamic Law and Custom," University of Exeter, United Kingdom, July 13–16, 2009) (on file with author).

[106] *See* Allott, *supra* note 62, at 67.

of gradual withering away and eventual disappearance of customary law.[107] Again, customary law cannot be legislated away as some failed attempts in this direction have shown.

The future of customary law formed the focus of papers written in the 1960s by two distinguished scholars, A.N. Allott and Thierry Verhelst. Allott argued that customary law now forms only a part of African law, which encompasses all the laws in Africa. The origin of the laws no longer matters because the governments of African nations now have the sovereignty to decide which laws they accept and which ones they want to reject. To him, African governments must (1) modernize their legal systems in line with prevailing social and economic realties, (2) unify their legal systems, and (3) Africanize their legal systems.[108] Two decades later, Allott examined unification, integration, and restatements of customary law as options.[109] He ultimately preferred harmonization, arguing that what is of benefit in African customary law should be extracted and merged with the modern law.[110] Verhelst argued that customary law "should be *retained* in a number of fields because it is the body of law best suited to the African society."[111] This is also because, unlike foreign law, it "reflects the cultural and societal patterns of the population to which it applies."[112]

The main problem, however, is who does the adaptation of customary law? Should it be the legislature or the courts through creative judicial interpretations?[113] In traditional Africa, legislative power resided in the people[114] or in the traditional ruler who makes law either *suo motu* or by proclamation after consultation with the chiefs and various bodies in the community.[115] Creation of customary laws by the courts or by the

[107] *See* Verhelst, *supra* note 1, at 52 (for example, such countries as Uganda and Cote D'Ivoire). Although Uganda, which abolished customary courts in 1966, has subsequently rejected the policy by re-establishing them in 1986. *See* M. Kane, J. Oloka-Onyango, & Abdul Tejan-Cole, Reassessing Customary Law Systems As A Vehicle For Providing Equitable Access To Justice For The Poor 6 (Dec. 12, 2005) (draft working paper produced for the World Bank conference, "New Frontiers of Social Policy: Development in a Globalizing World," December 12–15, 2005, Arusha), *available at* http://siteresources.worldbank.org/INTRANETSOCIALDEVELOPMENT/Resources/Kane.rev.pdf.

[108] *See* A.N. Allott, *The Future of African Law*, in AFRICAN LAW: ADAPTATION AND DEVELOPMENT 216, 223–240 (H. Kuper & L. Kuper eds., University of California Press 1965).

[109] *See* Allott, *supra* note 62. See Allott's definition of the terms "unification," "integration," and "harmonization" in A.N. Allott, *The Codification of the Law of Civil Wrongs in Common-Law African Countries*, in INTEGRATION OF CUSTOMARY AND MODERN LEGAL SYSTEMS IN AFRICA, *supra* note 1, at 175–176.

[110] *See* Allott, *supra* note 62, at 70–71.

[111] Verhelst, *supra* note 1, at 6.

[112] *Id.*

[113] *See id.* at 11.

[114] *See* A.N. Allott, *The People as Law-Makers: Custom, Practice, and Public Opinion as Sources of Law in Africa and England*, 1 J. AFR. L. 1 (1977).

[115] *See* I. Schapera, *The Sources of Law in Tswana*, 21 J. AFR. L. 150 (1977); N.A. FADIPE, THE SOCIOLOGY OF THE YORUBA 142–143 (University of Ibadan Press 1970).

government through legislative intervention would be liable to the criticism that these bodies have usurped the legislative power of the people or the traditional ruler.[116]

This chapter maintains that customary law should be relevant in five main respects:

3.6.1. *Survival of Some Customary Law Norms as Unofficial Law*

Some norms and concepts under customary law will continue to influence the lives of Africans even if these are not consistent with state law.[117] Such concepts include ethnic vicarious liability, collective responsibility, and solidarity.[118] A person looks up to one's ethnic community for protection against "outsiders." The extension of this principle vests this person with a vicarious and collective responsibility for the acts perpetuated against outsiders by the members of his or her group. For example, if a member of a community kills an outsider, although the primary liability rests with the individual culprit, the victim's community will consider the culprit's community as being collectively answerable (and every member as being vicariously liable) for the act. Where the murder is not redressed to its satisfaction, the victim's community would feel that they are at liberty to kill at random a person of similar status with the victim from the culprit's community in retaliation. Although this approach is inconsistent with some notions of "justice," it is consistent with the African notion of justice.

The idea of collective responsibility is a prominent feature of pre-colonial African customary law.[119] This principle was invoked by the British in the colonial era in matters relating to riots and communal conflicts. The application of collective punishment on communities by imposing huge fines on the offending community has been found to have some merits in resolving and preventing communal conflicts as communities did their best to prevent the commission of offenses by erring members and, when they failed, they promptly identified the offenders.[120] These concepts perhaps hold the keys to understanding and resolving the many ethnic conflicts that have continued to plague post-colonial Africa.[121]

---

[116] *See* Woodman, *supra* note 27, at 146, 169; Ogwurike, *supra* note 10, at 17.

[117] *See* Nekam, *supra* note 11, at 8; Simon Roberts, *Some Notes on* "African Customary Law," 28 J. Afr. L. 1, 1 (1984).

[118] *See* the discussion of how these concepts operate in African communities in Driberg, *supra* note 16, at 238–39; Ian Milner, *The Sanctions of Customary Criminal Law: A Study in Social Control*, 1 Nigerian L. J. 173, 181–82 (1964); E.V. Mittlebeeler, *Collective Punishment*, 8 J. Islamic & Comp. L. 27 (1983); Elias, *supra* note 8, at 87–92; Taslim Olawale Elias, Judicial Process in the Newer Commonwealth 252–253 (University of Lagos 1990).

[119] *See supra* note 118.

[120] *Id.*

[121] *See generally* Crawford Young, *The Politics of Cultural Pluralism* (Madison: University of Wisconsin Press, 1979).

3.6.2. *Survival of Some Customary Law Norms as Official Law*

Some norms of customary law will continue to survive particularly in the realms of land law and family law (marriage, divorce, and inheritance).[122] Customary law regulates the lives of most Africans in these matters.[123] The issue of wills illustrates vividly the attachment of Africans to their customary family laws. Under the Wills Act 1837 applicable in England and imported into some parts of Anglophone Africa, any person of full capacity can make a will. However, will making has not proven popular in Africa. This indicates "how deep is the distrust of the will as a threat to family solidarity" in Africa.[124] The import of the Wills Act was brought vividly and forcibly to Nigerians in *Yunusa v Adesubokun*,[125] where a Muslim made a will and the terms of the will were inconsistent with the Islamic law of inheritance. It was contended that the testator, being a Muslim (to whom Islamic law applied as personal law), could not do this. The trial court upheld this contention and set aside the will. On appeal, the Supreme Court reversed the decision on the basis that the testamentary freedom granted by the Wills Act cannot be limited by such considerations.[126] Much criticism followed this decision and within a few years virtually all the states in the country amended their Wills Laws by making these laws *subject* to customary law.[127] Thus, a person subject to Islamic law or customary law can no longer make a will depriving his or her heirs of what they are entitled to under these laws. This amendment has been applied to protect primogeniture under customary law even in the face of testamentary disposition to the contrary.[128]

3.6.3. *Introduction of Customary Law Norms and Concepts into Modern Legal Systems*

Some African customary law norms and concepts could be profitably introduced into the modern law and court systems in Africa.[129] There are two methods to do this. First, there is "a growing category of statutory law that shows an admittedly remote yet definite relation to customary law. Strictly speaking, it has nothing in common with customary law and yet is indebted to it."[130]

---

[122] *See* Verhelst, *supra* note 1, at 55; Allott, *supra* note 62, at 67.
[123] *See* Miles, *supra* note 44, at 103.
[124] Allott, *supra* note 109, at 235.
[125] (1968) N.N.L.R. 97.
[126] *See Adesubokan v. Yinusa* (1971) N.N.L.R. 77.
[127] *See, e.g.,* Wills Law, Cap. 168 of Laws of Kwara State, 1994, § 3(1). *See also* Oba, *supra* note 6, at 848.
[128] *See Lawal-Osula v Lawal-Osula* (1995) 10 S.C.N.J. 84.
[129] *See* Allott, *supra* note 109, at 227–240.
[130] The oft-cited examples in this regard are the various land reform laws in many African countries which, while modernizing the administration of land, vest the ownership of land in the community or the state with the individual having the right of usage only. *See* Verhelst, *supra* note 1, at 47–51.

Second, Allot envisages a more direct influence through a process of Africanization of African law.[131] African customary law has some undeniable positive features, including its popularity with the people, its speed, simplicity, flexibility, and absence of technicalities.[132] These contrast favorably with the delay, huge expenses, and technicalities usually involved in the European-inspired legal systems.[133]

Customary law norms and concepts are also now finding relevance in Alternative Dispute Resolution ("ADR") measures such as commercial arbitration,[134] the creation of family courts – which are official courts vested with jurisdiction in matrimonial matters – and simplified court procedures. Modern family courts are a testimony to Allott's commendation of methods of settling family and matrimonial disputes in the traditional African setup.[135] The problem, however, is that the some family courts tend to be too legalistic and formal as some of the failed experiments showed.[136] This is because lawyers are considered indispensable to administration of "justice" and thus dominate as judges and lawyers in these family courts.[137]

Modern legal systems can be Africanized by incorporating African legal concepts and other concepts depicting African values. For example, in determining negligence in the Law of Torts, the "reasonable man of ordinary prudence" test, which reflects "community standards," is usually applied.[138] Across the Commonwealth, the reasonable man is often construed in relation to the "man on the Clapham omnibus" and other similar hypothetical men.[139] Indigenous "reasonable man" tests have been found to exist too among segmented peoples in Africa such the Lozi (Barotse) of western Zambia,[140] Nuer of southern Sudan, Tiv of central Nigeria, and Masai of East Africa.[141] These standards are equally found among centralized peoples in Africa. Among the Hausa of northern Nigeria, the well-behaved person is said to have *kirki*.[142] Among the Yoruba of southern Nigeria, the *Omoluabi* (well-

[131] *See* Allott, *supra* note 109, at 227–240.
[132] *See id. See also* Kane, *supra* note 107, at 9–11.
[133] *See* T.A. AGUDA, THE CRISIS OF JUSTICE 12–14 (Eresu Publishers 1976).
[134] For the possibilities in this regard, see Andrew Chukwuemerie, *The Internationalization of African Customary Law Arbitration*, 14 AFR. J. INT'L & COMP. L. 143 (2006).
[135] *See* Allott, *supra* note 109, at 233.
[136] The proposed Matrimonial Arbitration Court in Kano State (Nigeria) is one such example. Auwalu Hamisu Yadudu, *What Became of the Kano Social Policy*, 19 J. ISLAMIC & COMP. L. 55, 59 (1993).
[137] *See id.*
[138] *See* JOHN FLEMING, THE LAW OF TORTS 107 (5th ed., The Law Book Co., Ltd, 1977).
[139] In *Hall v Brooklands Club* (1933) 1 K. B. 205, 224, the court described this man as "the man in the street" or "the man on the Clapham" or as "the man who takes the magazines at home, and in the evening pushes the lawn mover in his shirt sleeves."
[140] *See* Max Gluckman, *The Reasonable Man in Barotse Law*, 8 J. AFR. ADMIN. 101–105 (1956).
[141] *See* Max Gluckman, *Reasonableness and Responsibility in the Law of Segmentary Societies, in* AFRICAN LAW: ADAPTATION AND DEVELOPMENT 121–146 (H. Kuper & L. Kuper eds., University of California Press 1965).
[142] *See* Frank A. Salamone, *The Waziri and the Thief: Hausa Islamic Law in a Yoruba City: A Case Study from Ibadan, Nigeria*, 42 J. LEGAL PLURALISM 139 (1998).

behaved person, that is the person who lives in a manner consistent with the community's norms and culture and is extremely caring about the well-being of others) is the quintessential reasonable man.[143] In contrast to the *Omoluabi* is the *A lai loju ti* (the shameless or remorseless) and the *Odaju* (the reckless or callous). Thus, it would be more African if the courts use the *Omoluabi* and other similar standards rooted in Africa rather than the English "man on the Clapham omnibus" test. The African, whose conduct the law is to shape, would more readily identify with the *Omoluabi* than this strange Englishman.

A good example of the practical possibilities of the African value system described above is the invocation of the Xhosa concept of *ubuntu* in the transitional justice process of the post-apartheid South Africa.[144] *Ubuntu* says that "I am because you are," which derives from a Xhosa saying that "a person is a person through other persons."[145] Among the Xhosa, a person with *ubuntu* is the *Omoluabi*. According to Archbishop Desmond Tutu, "When we want to give high praise to someone we say, '*Yu, U nobuntu*'; 'Hey, he or she has *ubuntu*.' This means they are generous, hospitable, friendly, caring and compassionate. They share what they have.... We belong in a bundle of life."[146]

Ubuntu is fundamental to the African value system and is therefore indispensable to African law.[147] It can be harnessed for positive social control.[148] It could also "promote ethically sound interpretations" of difficult aspects of the law.[149] Even though some have pointed out the problems and difficulties in adopting a "fluid" idea such as *ubuntu* as a legal concept,[150] it nonetheless remains valid as an ideal which mankind should strive to attain.

3.6.4. *Revival of African Jurisprudence as Supplement to the Official Law*

Traditional African legal concepts can be and are often invoked when state law proves inadequate. This phenomenon is again well illustrated in the impact of African jurisprudence on transitional justice in the continent. The invocation of *ubuntu* in

---

[143] *See* Sofola, *supra* note 94, at 152–156.
[144] *See generally* DESMOND TUTU, NO FUTURE WITHOUT FORGIVENESS (Doubleday 1999).
[145] Frank Haldemann, *Another Kind of Justice: Transitional Justice as Recognition* 4 (University of Berne, Unpublished Paper, 2008), *available at* http://works.bepress.com/frank_haldemann/1; Nkiruka Ahiauzu, *Ubuntu and the Obligation to Obey Law*, 37 CAMBRIAN L. REV. 17, 32 (2006); Lorna McGregor, *Reconciliation: I Know It When I See It*, 9 CONTEMP. JUST. REV. 155, 160 (2006).
[146] Ahiauzu, *supra* note 145, at 32–33 (quoting Archbishop Desmond Tutu).
[147] *See* Drucilla Cornell & Karin van Marle, *Exploring Ubuntu: Tentative Reflections*, 5 AFR. HUM. RTS. L. J. 195, 205–207, 211–219 (2005).
[148] *See* Ahiauzu, *supra* note 145, at 33–35.
[149] Cornell & Marle, *supra* note 147, at 219; Y. Mokgoro, *Ubuntu and the Law in South Africa*, 1 POTCHEFSTROOM ELECTRONIC L. J. 15 (1998).
[150] *See* McGregor, *supra* note 145, at 160–161.

the South African transitional justice program discussed earlier is one example and there are other examples. First, there is the appropriation of a traditional African justice system to meet the challenges of transitional justice. The best known example of this is the Gacaca system ("the adaptation of local indigenous traditions by the national government to process lower-level perpetrators of genocide"[151]) established in Rwanda when it became apparent that the formal courts could not cope with the deluge of cases arising from the genocide in the country.[152] Although these courts do not conform to the strict legalism of international standards of transitional justice, they are largely in conformity with the sense of justice of most Rwandans.[153]

Secondly, the African concept of justice with its emphasis on reconciliation (which frequently involved ritual cleansing) found expression in the transitional justice programs in many countries in Africa.[154] For example, the *mato oput* ceremony used by the Acholi people of northern Uganda requires a wrongdoer to acknowledge the wrong and ask for forgiveness. This is followed by a ceremony wherein a bull or goat is slaughtered and its meat is eaten by all the parties and other members of the community.[155]

Thirdly, holistic traditional spiritual purification and cleansing rituals have been invoked following conflict in a number of places, including Angola, Mozambique, western Kenya, Uganda, and Sierra Leone.[156] In Sierra Leone, water is used to cleanse "ex-soldiers" and to give them "a cool heart." The ceremony turns them into a new person and they are accepted back into the community.[157]

3.6.5. *Evolvement of New Customs*

As previously discussed, one of the well-known features of customary law is its ability to respond to changing conditions. Customs have evolved either as a response to changing conditions or simply as a reaction to the failure of the imported models or structures. One such response is the rise of vigilante groups. The rising crime

---

[151] Kieran McEvoy, *Beyond Legalism: Towards a Thicker Understanding of Transitional Justice*, 34 J. L. & SOC'Y 411, 435 (2007).

[152] *See* Amaka Megwalu & Neophytos Loizides, *Dilemmas of Justice and Reconciliation: Rwandans and the Gacaca Courts*, AFR. J. INT'L & COMP. L. 1, 1–4 (forthcoming 2010), *available at* http://ssrn.com/abstract=1406863.

[153] See the evaluation of the Gacaca courts, *id.* at 9–31.

[154] *See* EMILY FARELL & KATHY SEIPP, THE ROAD TO PEACE: A TEACHING GUIDE ON LOCAL AND GLOBAL TRANSITIONAL JUSTICE 71 (The Advocates of Human Rights 2008).

[155] See accounts of the *mato oput* in Joanna R. Quinn, *Social Reconstruction in Uganda: The Role of Customary Mechanisms in Transitional Justice*, 8 HUM. RTS. REV. 389, 394 (2007); Linda M. Keller, *Achieving Peace with Justice: The International Criminal Court and Ugandan Alternative Justice Mechanisms*, 23 CONN. J. INT'L L. 209, 223–224 (2008).

[156] *See* Quinn, *supra* note 155, at 397–398.

[157] *See* Farell & Seipp, *supra* note 154, at 71.

wave and the apparent impotence of the authorities to curtail the same have led to the emergence in Africa of vigilante groups organized along traditional patterns. These include the *Sungusungu* (based on traditional Sukuma and Nyamwezi organizations)[158] created in rural Tanzania in the 1980s,[159] the *Makgotla* (sing. *Lekgotla*) in South Africa,[160] the Bakassi Boys in eastern Nigeria, and ethnic-based Oduduwa Peoples' Congress (OPC) in southwestern Nigeria.[161] These groups do not always follow the due process of law and are thus often at loggerheads with the official authorities.[162] Without doubt, "jungle justice" is objectionable. An effective state police is preferable to these vigilantes. But where there are communities terrorized by gangs of armed robbers who invade and occupy the community for hours, looting, raping, and committing other atrocities with impunity, and the state law enforcement agents are unable to check them, it is only natural that the communities form or turn to vigilante groups for protection. Until the state's agents are able to provide effective security, it would be appropriate for the state to support the vigilante groups and to provide an appropriate regulatory framework for their activities.

3.7. CONCLUSION

The days of African customary law as a full-fledged legal system are gone. However, customary law is still very strong in the realm of family law. It would not be wise for the State to interfere too much in this. Customary law is also still very relevant in land and chieftaincy matters. Admittedly, modern living presents many challenges to which customary law has no ready answers. Yet, some norms of customary law are positive, beneficial, and relevant even in modern times. These norms should be incorporated into modern laws.

There is a need for an expanded understanding of African jurisprudence. The Gacaca courts, reconciliation, and cleansing rituals are African attempts to move beyond what has rightly described as "an immediate past saturated with unspeakable cruelty."[163] Although these traditional African concepts of justice may face serious objections from the legalistic perspective, their contextual usefulness cannot be denied. As has been wisely pointed out, "Lawyers would do well in such

---

[158] *See* Sufian Hemed Bukurura, *The Maintenance of Order in Rural Tanzania: The Case of Sungusungu*, 34 J. LEGAL PLURALISM 1, 1–29 (1984).

[159] *See id.* for the analysis of the activities of the *Sungusungu. See also* Chirayath, *supra* note 48, at 6, 16–17.

[160] *See* Bukurura, *supra* note 158, at 23–24.

[161] *See* OSITA AGBU, ETHNIC MILITIAS AND THE THREAT TO DEMOCRACY IN POST-TRANSITION NIGERIA (Nordiska Afrikainstitutet 2004), *available at* http://130.238.24.99/webbshop/epubl/rr/rr.127.pdf.

[162] *See* Chirayath, *supra* note 48, at 16–17.

[163] Haldemann, *supra* note 145, at 2.

contexts to keep their discussions and analysis more measured and grounded in local realities."[164]

Harnessing customary law concepts for use in the modern era needs some caution, however, considering that not all traditional concepts are positive. The customary methods of adjudication are problematic in certain respects,[165] and customary law is not free from gender prejudices.

The preceding discussion makes a case for Africanization of laws and legal systems in Africa. However, one major obstacle is that the affairs of many African countries are in the hands of westernized Africans who are often averse to anything customary. Lawyers and judges are more so in this respect than others. Perhaps, this is because they hardly learned anything of customary law during their training. There is therefore an urgent need to integrate the study of customary law into the mainstream of legal education in African countries.[166]

---

[164] McEvoy, *supra* note 151, at 427.
[165] See the detailed consideration of the merits and demerits of the customary law system of adjudication in Kane, *supra* note 107, at 9–15.
[166] See proposals on how this can achieved in Abdulmumini A. Oba, *Towards Rethinking Legal Education in Nigeria*, 6 J. COMMONWEALTH L. & LEGAL EDUC. 97 (2008).

PART TWO

Ascertainment, Application, and Codification of Customary Law

4

The Quest for Customary Law in African State Courts

Janine Ubink

4.1. INTRODUCTION

Customary law is a distinguishing feature in the landscape of contemporary Africa. In many countries, it continues to regulate people's access to land, labor, and capital and to form the main normative system for dispute settlement. In recognition of the importance of customary law in the regulation of people's lives, but also in an attempt to control the customary sphere to a certain extent, many African governments have granted state courts jurisdiction to decide cases on the basis of customary law. It is, however, not easy for a judge to ascertain the customary law applicable to a particular case. This difficulty flows partly from the multiplicity of different customary laws – varying widely from community to community, but also within communities – and partly from the fluid nature of customary law itself.

Scholars and administrators have grappled with the study of customary law since the beginning of the colonial period. This chapter will first discuss the scholarly debate about the study of customary law and show that most legal anthropologists share an orientation to studying dispute processing and regularized conduct to ascertain rules of customary law.[1] They emphasize the negotiability of customary rules and the discretion with which they are applied. A discussion of a case study of customary land law in Ghana shows that in circumstances of change, conflict, and imposition, anthropological descriptions demonstrate that a generally acceptable customary rule has not yet crystallized. In such circumstances, customary norms are still in formation or highly contested, and both statements and practice will display various customary norms.

The extensive knowledge gathered by anthropologists about customary law and its functioning in the localities is most often not very useful for judges who have to apply customary law in a court case. The legal system simply does not allow them

---

[1] See *infra* section 2 Part II for a detailed discussion of these and other methodologies relied on by anthropologists to determine rules of customary law.

to conclude a case with the statement that a generally acceptable customary rule has not yet crystallized in the locality. In such cases, judges are expected to select and apply one of the local versions. Since the colonial period, several devices have been developed that can aid judges in their search for knowledge. These include codifications, restatements, the gradual creation of a body of case law, and the use of witnesses and assessors.

These devices have met with various objections. Discussion of the three main objections – the difficulty of capturing the variation as well as the fluidity of customary law and the problem of limited reliability of informants – demonstrates that, regardless of the method of ascertainment, inevitably a gap will develop between local customary practices and judicial customary law. Does this gap, this inevitable alteration of the nature and content of customary law, mean that state courts should not apply customary law at all, and that states should rather leave customary law completely up to the locality? Some authors are of the opinion that the importance of ensuring that "the law" reflects the relevant customary law of the people cannot be overemphasized. Otherwise, "the law will be honored by the people rather more in the breach than in the observance."[2] Others rather ignore this argument – and with it the question of the impact of judicial decision making on local practices – and categorically state that courts are empowered to play a creative role in the declaration and development of new rules designed to attune the contents of customary law to "the social necessities of contemporary life."[3] We can cut this debate short, however, as the simple reality of current African countries is that they have already decided that their courts will apply customary law. This enables these states, on the one hand, to protect the rights of people under customary systems through the enforcement of locally valid rules and the provision of authoritative decisions in disputes about these rules.[4] This allows for the preservation of customary law in cases where decisions of local dispute arbiters cannot be enforced without state interference and, at the same time, offers the possibility to check abuse of power by customary authorities. On the other hand, the application of customary law by state courts provides judges with the opportunity to test whether customary laws violate human rights or are contrary to other standards, such as public policy, legislation, or

---

[2] Mudiaga Odje, *The Repugnancy Doctrine and the Proper Development of Customary Law in Nigeria*, *in* TOWARDS A RESTATEMENT OF CUSTOMARY LAW IN NIGERIA 37 (Yemi Osinbajo & Awa U. Kalu eds., Nigeria Federal Ministry of Justice 1991).

[3] F.A. Ajayi, *The Judicial Development of Customary Law in Nigeria*, *in* INTEGRATION OF CUSTOMARY AND MODERN LEGAL SYSTEMS IN AFRICA: A CONFERENCE HELD AT IBADAN ON 24TH–29TH AUGUST 1964 128–130 (A.N. Allott ed., Univ. Ife Press 1971).

[4] The main reasons for Ghanaian litigants to bring their case to a state court were the perceived need for authority and certainty and the lack of enforceability of arbitration. Richard C. Crook et al., The Law, Legal Institutions and the Protection of Land Rights in Ghana and Cote D'ivoire: Developing a More Effective and Equitable System 30, Final Report SSRU Project R 7993 (2005).

"natural justice" (repugnancy clause). Furthermore, judges' frequent contact with customary law makes it possible for them to signal where the lawmaker might want to initiate new legislation to alter, unify, or overrule certain parts of customary law.

Despite the inevitability of a gap between locally practiced and judicial customary law, many African countries have thus opted for a legal system in which state courts have the jurisdiction to decide cases on the basis of customary law. In many such cases, ascertainment of a customary rule is not the issue or not a very complicated activity. There remain, however, quite some cases in which the customary rules are heavily contested, and the ascertainment of customary rules poses serious problems for judges.[5] So, how are judges in these cases supposed to decide which of the versions presented by the litigants they will apply? How much discretion do judges have in this decision, and can all local practices qualify as customary law? As discussed later in the chapter, jurisprudence defines two requirements for a practice to constitute a rule of customary law: a "fixed line of behavior" and "normative moment."[6] However, rules of customary law that are still in their formation stage and that are heavily contested in the locality are precisely characterized by an absence of these two qualities. This chapter argues that in such cases, judges need to take into account the wider customary normative framework, and be informed by the fixed line of behavior and normative moment with regard to related customary rules. This is again demonstrated on the basis of a case study of customary land law in Ghana.

By combining an overview of relevant literature with reference to an example of the difficulties surrounding the quest for customary law in Ghana, this chapter brings to the fore the fact that the old discussions regarding judicial ascertainment of customary law have lost nothing of their relevance for contemporary African judges, and thus hopes to contribute to taking these discussions one step further.

4.2. THE SCHOLARLY DEBATE

Customary law is a much debated and not unproblematic phenomenon that has troubled researchers, administrators, lawyers, and judges alike, from the colonial

---

5 *See, e.g.,* Barbara Oomen, Chiefs! Law, Power and Culture in Contemporary South Africa (2002) (unpublished dissertation Leiden University); JANINE M. UBINK, IN THE LAND OF THE CHIEFS: CUSTOMARY LAW, LAND CONFLICTS, AND THE ROLE OF THE STATE IN PERI-URBAN GHANA: LAW, GOVERNANCE AND DEVELOPMENT (Leiden Univ. Press 2008).

6 A.N. ALLOTT, NEW ESSAYS IN AFRICAN LAW 147 (Butterworths 1970); T.W. Bennett & T. Vermeulen, *Codification of Customary Law*, 24 J. AFR. L. 206, 215 (1980); T.O. Elias, *The Problem of Reducing Customary Laws to Writing, in* LEGAL PAPERS PRESENTED TO THE FIFTH INTERNATIONAL CONGRESS OF COMPARATIVE LAW, BRUSSELS, 4–9 AUGUST, 1958 (Stevens & Sons 1958); JOHN MENSAH SARBAH, FANTI CUSTOMARY LAWS: A BRIEF INTRODUCTION TO THE PRINCIPLES OF THE NATIVE LAWS AND CUSTOMS OF THE FANTI AND AKAN SECTIONS OF THE GOLD COAST WITH A SELECTION OF CASES THEREON DECIDED IN THE LAW COURTS 4–6 (London, Clowes 1897); MARTIN CHUKWUKA OKANY, THE ROLE OF CUSTOMARY COURTS IN NIGERIA 39 (Fourth Dimension 1985).

period until the present. What is customary law? Where can we find it? How to study it? How to bring it into the state realm? Even the term itself is ambiguous, as it evokes an image of an unchanging, antiquarian, and immutable normative system, whereas historical and anthropological research has revealed that customary law is dynamic and the historical result of interaction between local actors and state intervention.[7]

The "quest for customary law" has aroused considerable scholarly debate. How to "find" the unwritten – tribal, customary – law of a society? Early legal anthropologists and colonial administrators had tried to ascertain rules of customary law through conversations with traditional leaders and other "experts," to be conserved in textbooks and codifications. Danquah's *Gold Coast: Akan Laws and Customs and the Akim Abuakwa Constitution*[8] and Shapera's *A Handbook of Tswana Law and Custom*[9] are well-known African examples. In 1941, legal realist Llewellyn and anthropologist Hoebel published their joint work, *The Cheyenne Way*.[10] The authors were of the opinion that "the safest main road into the discovery of law" was through the study of disputes or "trouble-cases," because "not only the making of new law and the effect of old, but the hold and the thrust of all other vital aspects of the culture, shine clear in the crucible of conflict."[11] This book was a response to the case-law method for teaching law at American law schools, which stressed the order and logic in the law. Legal realists criticized this view for severing the ties between the study of law and everyday life.[12] By studying the law of the Cheyenne Indians mainly through an investigation of disputes, Llewellyn and Hoebel tried to show that "law is not an autonomous phenomenon separated from its cultural matrix,"[13] and that the study of trouble cases "offers a possibility of study of a culture at work on and through its people, for which no schematization of 'norms' can substitute."[14] They acknowledged that the study of disputes could not be fully understood without reference to abstract norms or rules and to actual behavior of members of a society.[15]

[7] Shem E. Migot-Adholla & John W. Bruce, *Introduction: Are Indigenous African Tenure Systems Insecure?, in* SEARCHING FOR LAND TENURE SECURITY IN AFRICA 3–4 (John W. Bruce & Shem E. Migot-Adholla, eds., Kendall/Hunt 1994).

[8] J.B. DANQUAH, GOLD COAST: AKAN LAWS AND CUSTOMS AND THE AKIM ABUAKWA CONSTITUTION (Routledge 1928).

[9] ISAAC SCHAPERA, A HANDBOOK OF TSWANA LAW AND CUSTOM: COMPILED FOR THE BECHUANALAND PROTECTORATE ADMINISTRATION (Oxford Univ. Press 1938).

[10] KARL N. LLEWELLYN & E. ADAMSON HOEBEL, THE CHEYENNE WAY: CONFLICT AND CASE LAW IN PRIMITIVE JURISPRUDENCE (Univ. Oklahoma 1941).

[11] *Id.* at 29.

[12] *See* LAURA NADER, THE LIFE OF THE LAW: ANTHROPOLOGICAL PROJECTS 89 (Univ. California 2002).

[13] Leopold Pospisil, *E. Adamson Hoebel and the Anthropology of Law*, 7 L. & SOC'Y REV. 537, 539 (1973).

[14] Llewellyn & Hoebel, *supra* note 10, at 28.

[15] *See id.* at 21.

Still, their arguments were largely based on fifty-three trouble cases, and their work induced a generation of legal anthropologists to concentrate almost exclusively on conflict and its resolution.[16]

In the 1950s and 1960s, several major works were produced in this field that advocated the study of customary law through an analysis of actual processes of adjudication, mostly restricted to public forums.[17] Pospisil, for instance, restricted the field of law to the bedrock of legal decisions and such principles as could be abstracted from them, thus excluding stated rules not confirmed by such decisions.[18] These studies challenged the older approach of ascertaining customary law through conversation with experts. Although the older approach lost considerable ground, it did not fully disappear. It was, for instance, still followed in the *Restatement of African Law* project of the London School of Oriental and African Studies, which aimed to abstract and systematize the unwritten rules of African customary substantive law.[19]

Some scholars have criticized the case-method approach as unduly restrictive, complicating the necessary analysis of the full range of socio-legal occurrences.[20] A well-known proponent of this view is Holleman, who proposes a move away from an exclusive focus on situations of dispute to an analysis of ordering in non-dispute situations.[21] He observes that "in the study of the substantive law and its practice, and in a field of law in which litigation is rare, a fieldworker relying mainly on a case-method focused upon actual trouble-cases may get a skewed idea of the accepted principles and regularities in this particular field.… The trouble-less case then

---

[16] *See, e.g.,* PAUL BOHANNAN, JUSTICE AND JUDGEMENT AMONG THE TIV (Oxford Univ. Press 1957); MAX GLUCKMAN, THE JUDICIAL PROCESS AMONG THE BAROTSE OF NORTHERN RHODESIA (Manchester Univ. Press 1955); P.H. Gulliver, *Social Control in an African Society: A Study of the Arusha: Agricultural Masai of Northern Tanganyika, in* INTERNATIONAL LIBRARY OF SOCIOLOGY AND SOCIAL RECONSTRUCTION (W.J.H. Sprott ed., Routledge & Kegan Paul 1963); LAW IN CULTURE AND SOCIETY (Laura Nader ed., Aldine 1969); LEOPOLD POSPISIL, KAPAUKU PAPUANS AND THEIR LAW (Yale Univ. Press 1958).

[17] *See* sources cited *supra* note 16.

[18] *See* Pospisil, *supra* note 16, at 256–57.

[19] *See* EUGENE COTRAN, RESTATEMENT OF AFRICAN LAW VOL. 1 KENYA I: THE LAW OF MARRIAGE AND DIVORCE (Sweet & Maxwell 1968), and VOL. 2 KENYA II: THE LAW OF SUCCESSION (1969); J.O. IBIK, RESTATEMENT OF AFRICAN LAW VOL. 3 MALAWI I: THE LAW OF MARRIAGE AND DIVORCE (1970), and VOL. 4 MALAWI II: THE LAW OF LAND, SUCCESSION, MOVABLE PROPERTY, AGREEMENTS AND CIVIL WRONGS (1971); A.K.P. KLUDZE, RESTATEMENT OF AFRICAN LAW VOL. 6 GHANA I: EWE LAW OF PROPERTY (1973); SIMON ROBERTS, RESTATEMENT OF AFRICAN LAW VOL. 5 BOTSWANA I: TSWANA FAMILY LAW (1972); N.N. Rubin, *The Swazi Law of Succession: A Restatement,* 9 J. AFR. L. 90 (1965).

[20] *See* Bronislaw Malinowski, *A New Instrument for the Interpretation of Law – Especially Primitive,* 51 YALE L.J. 1237, 1252 (1942); Sally F. Moore, *Law and Anthropology, in* BIENNIAL REVIEW OF ANTHROPOLOGY 270 (B.J. Siegel ed., Stanford Univ. Press 1970); Nader, *supra* note 12, at 97.

[21] *See* Sally Engle Merry, *Legal Pluralism,* 22 L. & SOC'Y REV. 869, 890 (1988).

becomes a necessary check on the trouble-case, rather than the other way around."[22] He therefore pleads for a much closer integration of, and equal emphasis on, all components of the "methodological triad of legal anthropological approach": normative statements (rules/norms), practice (troubleless cases), and disputes (trouble cases).[23] Holleman's position was that through a combination of these methodologies, the customary rules – valid in a certain locality at a certain period of time – could be ascertained.

Also from within the group of scholars focusing on disputes, criticism was heard. By the 1970s, a crucial move was underway to shift the focus from the description and analysis of dispute-settlement institutions to the description and analysis of behavior connected with disputing.[24] The "processualists," represented by legal anthropologists such as Nader and Todd Jr.,[25] Starr,[26] and Gulliver,[27] analyzed the entire process of conflicts in their total social context, thereby effecting a shift away from judge- and judgment-oriented accounts of dispute settlement that see customary rules as having the capacity to determine the outcome of disputes in a straightforward fashion, toward analyses that see customary rules as objects of negotiation and a resource to be managed advantageously.[28]

In the next decade, scholars studying disputing made an effort to synthesize the rule-centered approach and the processual approach.[29] Comaroff and Roberts, in their study on disputing in Tswana society, show that rules governing conflict behavior were not internally consistent codes of action analogous to western written law but were instead negotiable and internally contradictory repertoires that were

[22] J.F. Holleman, *Trouble-Cases and Trouble-Less Cases in the Study of Customary Law and Legal Reform*, 7 L. & Soc'y Rev. 585, 599 (1973). Holleman discusses the difficulty of abstracting rules focused on single interests or actions from decisions in conflict situations involving a plurality of these. Real-life disputes, he observes, often present a much more complex set of issues than can be covered by a single rule, and circumstantial factors can play a role and lead to an outcome that is not strictly in accordance with the rules. Furthermore, the rule-finding exercise is complicated by the fact that conflict resolution often seeks a feasible compromise rather than the enforcement of a rule of conduct. See *id.* at 590.

[23] *Id.* at 606–607.

[24] See Peter Just, *History, Power, Ideology, and Culture: Current Directions in the Anthropology of Law*, 26 L. & Soc'y Rev. 373, 373–74 (1992).

[25] See Laura Nader & Harry F. Todd, Jr., The Disputing Process: Law in Ten Societies (Columbia Univ. Press 1978).

[26] See June Starr, Dispute and Settlement in Rural Turkey: An Ethnography of Law (Brill 1978).

[27] See P.H. Gulliver, Disputes and Negotiations: A Cross-Cultural Perspective (Academic Press 1979).

[28] J.L. Comaroff & Simon Roberts, Rules and Processes: The Cultural Logic of Dispute in an African Context 14 (Univ. Chicago Press 1981). *Cf.* Just, *supra* note 24, at 374.

[29] Comaroff & Roberts, *supra* note 28; Sally F. Moore, Law as Process: An Anthropological Approach (Routledge and Kegan Paul 1978); Sally F. Moore, Social Facts and Fabrications: "Customary" Law on Kilimanjaro, 1880–1980 (Cambridge Univ. Press 1986).

applied with discretion.[30] With this conclusion, the authors challenge the existence of one set of ascertainable, valid rules, as the processualists had done before them. Another scholar who has questioned the possibility of finding the valid customary rules of a certain group of people is Martin Chanock, who observes in his work, *Neither customary nor legal: African customary law in an era of family law reform*, that within each group there will be variations within and conflicts about customary rules, which find expression both in normative statements of group members and in their actual actions.[31]

In the 1980s and 1990s, research showed an increasing attention to how legal institutions and actors created and transformed meanings, and a greater concern with the ways law both reflected and constructed and deconstructed power relations.[32] This research reinforced the insight that there was no such thing – and never had been such a thing – as a fixed body of customary law ready to be ascertained, but that customary law was fluid, relational, negotiable, and intimately tied to fluctuating social and political relations.[33] With regard to official versions of customary law, this insight led to the conclusion that what had been portrayed as the ascertainment of valid rules of customary law by colonial administrators and judges often entailed a political choice and was, at least partly, an invention of tradition.[34] Revisionist scholars displayed how official interventions, such as codification and judicial applications, created a customary law changed in form, content, and effect.[35] This was done in a dialogue – albeit within highly skewed power relations – between colonial administrators and African people.[36]

---

[30] *See* Sally Engle Merry, *Anthropology, Law and Transnational Processes*, 21 ANN. REV. ANTHROPOLOGY 357, 360 (1992).

[31] *See* Martin Chanock, *Neither Customary nor Legal: African Customary Law in an Era of Family Law Reform*, 3 INT'L J.L. & FAM. 72 (1989).

[32] *See* J.F. COLLIER, MARRIAGE AND INEQUALITY IN CLASSLESS SOCIETY (Stanford Univ. Press 1988); Merry, *supra* note 30, at 360.

[33] *See* Oomen, *supra* note 5, at 21.

[34] *See Cf.* MARTIN CHANOCK, LAW, CUSTOM AND SOCIAL ORDER: THE COLONIAL EXPERIENCE IN MALAWI AND ZAMBIA xi (Cambridge Univ. Press 1998).

[35] *See* Peter Fitzpatrick, *Traditionalism and Traditional Law*, 28 J. AFR. L. 20, 21–22 (1984).

[36] *See* Chanock, *supra* note 34; MAHMOOD MAMDANI, CITIZEN AND SUBJECT: CONTEMPORARY AFRICA AND THE LEGACY OF LATE COLONIALISM (Princeton Univ. Press 1996); LAW IN COLONIAL AFRICA (Kirstin Mann & Richard Roberts eds., Heinemann 1991); Merry, *supra* note 30, at 364; Moore, *supra* note 29; Terence Ranger, *The Invention of Tradition in Colonial Africa*, in THE INVENTION OF TRADITION (Eric Hobsbaum & Terence Ranger eds., Cambridge Univ. Press 1983); Francis G. Snyder, *Anthropology, Dispute Processes and Law: A Critical Introduction*, 8 BRIT. J.L. & SOC'Y 141 (1981). It is a different question whether such created customary law also existed out of the contexts in which it was produced, that is, to what extent this official customary law influenced local customary law. *See* KEEBET VON BENDA-BECKMANN, THE BROKEN STAIRWAYS TO CONSENSUS: VILLAGE JUSTICE AND STATE COURTS IN MINANGKABAU 29 (ICG Printing 1984). According to Shadle, in colonial Kenya, the official customary law had limited impact on local dispute settlements. Brett L. Shadle, *"Changing Traditions to Meet Current Altering Conditions": Customary Law, African Courts*

Whereas in the past, legal anthropologists mainly restricted the context of analysis to the local situation, there now came ample attention for the interaction between local, national, and global levels and the mutually constitutive nature between local customary law on the one hand and official customary law, national law, and international law on the other.[37] This has led to an increasing awareness and often condemnation of the gap between local customary law – sometimes termed "living law"[38] or "sociologists customary law"[39]– and official customary law as pronounced in court judgments, textbooks, and codifications.[40]

4.3. THE CUSTOMARY NORM IN CIRCUMSTANCES OF CHANGE, CONFLICT, AND IMPOSITION

Most legal anthropologists studying customary law share an orientation to the observation of patterns of actual behavior. For some scholars, the relevant behavior was that of people within the community or social group,[41] whereas for others, the relevant behavior was that of the disputing actors or institutions themselves.[42] The first category focused on regularized conduct or actual patterns of behavior; the second, on dispute processing. Both methodologies, however, are complicated in circumstances of change, conflict, and imposition when customary norms are contested.

---

and the Rejection of Codification in Kenya, 1930–60, 40 J. AFR. HIST. 411, 413 (1999) ("[I]n practice it was usually Africans in African courts, not administrators, who determined the real context and interpretation of customary law.").

[37] See PEOPLE'S LAW AND STATE LAW: THE BELLAGIO PAPERS (A.N. Allott & G.R. Woodman eds., Foris 1985); B. De Sousa Santos, Law: A Map of Misreading: Towards a Postmodern Conception of Law, 14 J.L. & SOC'Y 279 (1987); John Griffiths, What Is Legal Pluralism?, 24 J. LEGAL PLURALISM 1 (1986); Moore, supra note 29; Oomen, supra note 5; J. Vanderlinden, Return to Legal Pluralism: Twenty Years Later, 28 J. LEGAL PLURALISM 149 (1989); Von Benda-Beckmann, supra note 36; ANTHROPOLOGY OF LAW IN THE NETHERLANDS (Keebet Von Benda-Beckmann & Fons Strijbosch eds., Foris 1985); Gordon R. Woodman, How State Courts Create Customary Law in Ghana and Nigeria, in INDIGENOUS LAW AND THE STATE (Bradford W. Morse & Gordon R. Woodman eds., Foris 1988). For an overview of the literature, see Merry, supra note 30, at 363. Some work in this field was already published in the 1970s. See, e.g., Sally F. Moore, Law and Social Change: The Semi-Autonomous Social Field as an Appropriate Subject of Study, 7 L. & SOC'Y REV. 719 (1973); Gordon R. Woodman, Judicial Development of Customary Law: The Case of Marriage Law in Ghana and Nigeria, 14 U. GHANA L.J. 115 (1977).

[38] E. EHRLICH, FUNDAMENTAL PRINCIPLES OF THE SOCIOLOGY OF LAW (Walter L. Moll trans., Harvard Univ. Press 1936); Moore, supra note 37.

[39] Woodman, supra note 37.

[40] Brian Z. Tamanaha, REALISTIC SOCIO-LEGAL THEORY (Oxford Univ. Press 1997).

[41] See, e.g., BRONISLAW MALINOWSKI, CRIME AND CUSTOM IN SAVAGE SOCIETY (Kegan Paul, Trench, Trubner 1926); Ehrlich, supra note 38; Moore, LAW AS PROCESS, supra note 29; Marc Galanter, Justice in Many Rooms: Courts, Private Ordering, and Indigenous Law, 19 J. LEGAL PLURALISM 1 (1981).

[42] See, e.g., E. ADAMSON HOEBEL, THE LAW OF PRIMITIVE MAN (Harvard Univ. Press 1954); Paul Bohannan, The Differing Realms of the Law, in LAW AND WARFARE (P. Bohannan ed., Natural History Press 1967); Tamanaha, supra note 40, at 101.

This is especially the case when the rights and duties of traditional leaders are part of the debate.

Let us illustrate this briefly with a case study that deals with customary land management in peri-urban[43] Kumasi, Ghana, more specifically with the customary norm around allocation of residential land.[44] Kumasi is a bustling city and an important transportation hub. Due to the expansion of the city as well as population growth, peri-urban Kumasi witnesses a high demand for residential and sometimes commercial land. In this geographic area, customary land is managed by chiefs on the basis of customary law. Increasing land values are leading to widespread disputes over the powers to allocate rights in customary land and entitlements to the proceeds of these land allocations. Like other peri-urban areas, peri-urban Kumasi witnesses severe struggles between farmers and families on the one hand and chiefs on the other hand over the right to convert farmland into residential land.[45] Three main claims can be painted with a broad brush. Some people claim that, according to customary law, it is the farmers or families who have had secure use rights – often called customary freeholds – in the land for generations who can decide to convert and sell their farmland, with a marginal administrative role for the chiefs for the sake of land-use planning and central management. Chiefs thus have no right to alienate farmland. Others claim that this power customarily does lie with the chiefs, as they are in the best position to take care of communal matters, with the implicit or explicit condition that the chief should act in the best interest of the community. This setup requires a well-functioning system of chiefly accountability, with deposition as the ultimate sanction. A third group of people also claims that, according to customary law, this power lies with the chiefs. They see a different base for this power, however. They claim that chiefs are the owners of the land and can thus use it any way they please, although they should be constrained by the moral but unenforceable obligation to take care of communal interests.[46]

Just as the interpretations of customary law with regard to the conversion of communal farmland to residential land are highly varied, so are the outcomes of the various actions, struggles, and negotiations surrounding it. When three chiefs convert land in peri-urban Kumasi, one might get away with it, one might be deposed, and

---

[43] Peri-urban refers to areas immediately adjoining an urban area.

[44] For a detailed study, see Ubink, *supra* note 5.

[45] *See* Sulemana Abudulai, *Land Rights, Land-Use Dynamics & Policy in Peri-Urban Tamale, Ghana, in* THE DYNAMICS OF RESOURCE TENURE IN WEST AFRICA (Camilla Toulmin, Philippe Lavigne Delville, & Samba Traoré eds., IIED 2002); Liz Alden Wily & Daniel N.A. Hammond, Dep't for Int'l Dev., Ghana Rural Livelihoods Program, *Land Security and the Poor in Ghana: Is There a Way Forward?* (2001); Kasim Kasanga et al., Land Markets and Legal Contradictions in the Peri-Urban Area of Accra Ghana: Informant Interviews and Secondary Data Investigations, Land Tenure Center Research Paper no. 127 (Univ. Wisconsin 1996); Ubink, *supra* note 5.

[46] Ubink, *supra* note 5, at 219.

one might be able to push through some of the leases while having to return other plots to their previous usufructuary owners. In a similar vein, when community members try to convert the land themselves, some might get away with it unchallenged, others might be challenged by the chief but reach a revenue-sharing compromise, and again others might come out empty-handed. These outcomes depend on an array of circumstances, including the personalities of the chief and his opponents and the power configuration of the local arena in which these struggles are taking place.[47] For instance, does the village have one or more chiefs and if a village has several chiefs, do these chiefs collaborate or compete with each other? Other determining factors are whether there is strife or unity within the royal family, whether the chief or his opponents have a good relationship with the paramount chief or the *Asantehene*,[48] and whether powerful people, for instance members of parliament, come from the village. A chief's position within and outside the community and his ability to build coalitions with his elders, his family, and other powerful people within the community are crucial for creating room for maneuver with regard to land conversions.[49]

The preceding discussion raises questions regarding how an investigator looking for the customary norm on allocation of residential land in peri-urban Kumasi should go about his quest to "distinguish the *real* law from that which merely was claimed to be law,"[50] or whether he should abandon any such attempt as futile?[51] Both preferred methodologies of legal anthropologists – a focus on dispute processing or on regularized conduct – offer difficulties for the study of customary norms regarding residential land in peri-urban Kumasi. Disputes over residential land in peri-urban Kumasi are mostly not dealt with in local dispute institutions, that is, chiefs' courts, which are generally regarded as the main arena for the study of dispute processing, because those who would adjudicate – the chiefs – are a party in most disputes. The study of *regularized* conduct or *patterns* of behavior also runs into difficulties, because practices in peri-urban Kumasi show as much variation as the normative statements by the various actors. Holleman's term "troubleless cases" seems anyhow misplaced in peri-urban Kumasi, as almost every case of allocation of residential land encountered seems to be contested.[52]

"Direct observation of the rules of custom as they function in actual life"[53] thus is a complicated activity in circumstances of change, conflict, and imposition, when

[47] *See id.*
[48] The *Asantehene* is the king of Asante and as such is the highest traditional leader in the area.
[49] For some illustrations of this issue, *see* Ubink, *supra* note 5, at 88–89.
[50] Tamanaha, *supra* note 40, at 102.
[51] *See* Franz Von Benda-Beckmann, *Law out of Context: A Comment on the Creation of Traditional Law Discussion*, 28 J. AFR. L. 28, 30 (1984).
[52] *See* Ubink, *supra* note 5.
[53] Malinowski, *supra* note 41, at 125.

customary norms are contested and the rights and duties of chiefs are part of the debate.[54] When few legal transactions are "troubleless," all that can readily be studied are instances of struggles and negotiations. Outcomes of these contestations are determined by the various resources at the disposal of the parties, of which customary norms are only one. To further complicate things, these norms are often not explicitly referred to and, as mentioned earlier, ideas about them will differ between various groups.[55] An anthropological description of customary law in peri-urban Kumasi thus reads that there are various customary norms, both in statements and in practice, regarding the allocation of residential land, and that not one customary rule has crystallized as generally acceptable.

4.4. JUDICIAL ASCERTAINMENT OF CUSTOMARY LAW

The considerable knowledge that has been gathered over the decades by legal anthropologists is not very useful for judges confronted with problems of ascertainment of customary law.[56] Judges instructed to decide cases on the basis of customary law simply do not have the option to "shift the analytical focus from rules and outcomes to on-going negotiation and debate."[57] Whereas Von Benda-Beckmann rightly criticizes the search for "the" customary law as a futile venture, an idea that "can only come up in the confinement of legalistic doctrines,"[58] judges are expected to either apply *the* local customary rule or select and apply one of the existing rules.[59] Over the years, several devices have been developed that assist judges with determining the customary law. These devices display various ways to ascertain rules of customary law – either in a more or less comprehensive effort or on a case-by-case basis – and/or methods to record the outcomes. They include codifications, restatements,[60] the gradual recording of customary law through the development of case law, and the use of witnesses and assessors.[61] The first three of these "knowledge devices" are

---

[54] *Cf.* Chanock, *supra* note 34, at 17.

[55] *Cf.* Chanock, *supra* note 31; Chanock, *supra* note 34.

[56] *Cf.* A.N. Allott & E. Cotran, *A Background Paper on Restatement of Laws in Africa: The Need, Value and Value of Such Restatement, in* INTEGRATION OF CUSTOMARY AND MODERN LEGAL SYSTEMS IN AFRICA, *supra* note 3, at 21, 31.

[57] Sara Berry, *Tomatoes, Land and Hearsay: Property and History in Asante in the Time of Structural Adjustment*, 25 WORLD DEV. 1225, 1229 (1997).

[58] Von Benda-Beckmann, *supra* note 51, at 30.

[59] *See* Robert B. Seidman, *Rules of Recognition in the Primary Courts of Zimbabwe: On Lawyers' Reasoning and Customary Law*, 1 & 2 ZIMBABWE L. REV. 47 (1983–1984).

[60] Whereas a codification lays down customary law in a binding code, a restatement leads to an authoritative but non-binding document.

[61] Another method of making customary law accessible is through declarations by native authorities; but where this power has been given by statute, such as in Ghana, it has rarely been used. It should be mentioned that grounded research is increasingly undertaken with the specific aim of providing judges with information in specific court cases.

thought to increase the certainty in the application of customary law as they would make the customary law generally known, not so much among the "subjects" of the law, who in Africa are supposed to be quite cognizant of their customary laws,[62] but especially among "users" such as judges and legislators.[63] This should prevent judges from disregarding customary law in cases where they would otherwise have had difficulty ascertaining the content of customary law. It should also diminish the discretion of judges through the use of the repugnancy clause and other general tests of validity. Furthermore, it should protect the population against often unscrupulous individual interpretations of traditional authorities or other locally powerful people.[64] These devices have met with various objections, however, of which the three main ones will be discussed further in this chapter.

4.4.1. *Objections to "Knowledge Devices": Variation, Fluidity, and Reliability of Informants*

The first criticism reads that there are so many variations in the customary law, both between and within communities, that it will be almost impossible to record them all and highly difficult to record one customary law that all communities would have to follow. This would mean that large amounts of observed customary law would have to be cut out of the unified edition and thereby made illegal. As a result, the recording is faced with grave problems of credibility and acceptability, and might be completely ignored by many people as not reflecting their rules of customary law.[65] In fact, this is exactly what happened with Tanzania's experiment with codification of customary laws in the 1960s. In Tanzania, they more or less adopted one set of customary laws, practiced by one group of people, to the exclusion of others. By and large, the groups whose customary laws were not reflected in the codification ignored the codified law and continued quietly to apply their own customary laws in their dealings with each other.[66] According to Bennett and Vermeulen, however,

---

[62] See Bennett & Vermeulen, *supra* note 6, at 209–210.

[63] See Allott & Cotran, *supra* note 56, at 18–19; Epiphany C.J. Azinge, *Codification of Customary Law: A Mission Impossible?*, in TOWARDS A RESTATEMENT OF CUSTOMARY LAW IN NIGERIA, *supra* note 2, at 285–286; Darbo Narebo, *Codification of Customary Law*, in TOWARDS A RESTATEMENT OF CUSTOMARY LAW IN NIGERIA, *supra* note 2, at 310–312. Other reasons for recording customary law include unification, simplification, and modernization. Azinge, *supra*, at 285–286; M.I. Ojo, *Codification of Customary Law in Nigeria*, in TOWARDS A RESTATEMENT OF CUSTOMARY LAW IN NIGERIA, *supra* note 2, at 316; Yemi Osinbajo, *Proof of Customary Law in Non-Customary Courts*, in TOWARDS A RESTATEMENT OF CUSTOMARY LAW IN NIGERIA, *supra* note 2, at 264.

[64] See Azinge, *supra* note 63, at 287; Narebo, *supra* note 63, at 301–302; Ojo, *supra* note 63, at 313; Osinbajo, *supra* note 63, at 265.

[65] Cf. Odje, *supra* note 2, at 36; Bennett & Vermeulen, *supra* note 6, at 209.

[66] See Eugene Cotran, *Some Recent Developments in the Tanganyika Judicial System*, 6 J. AFR. L. 19 (1962); Osinbajo, *supra* note 63, at 265; Azinge, *supra* note 63, at 287.

almost any codification will suffer from problems of credibility and acceptability, "because (customary law) is a system of law evolved by the people themselves, any code will quite possibly seem to be an imposition by outsiders."[67] The same could be said for other devices of recording, such as restatements and the creation of a system of case law.

The second objection points to the fact that customary law is in a fluid state and constantly changes. To record customary law, it is argued, would mean freezing it at a premature stage and hindering its future developments, in fact "creating a road block to modernity."[68] A number of authors suggest that the recording of law cannot take place in a speedily developing society. It may be "too early"[69] or "premature"[70] and "may easily result in extensive discrepancies between law and practice and in the creation of the undesirable situation of the law becoming obsolescent in comparison with the evolution of legal concepts among a society subject to social and economic change."[71] Perhaps it would be "wiser to let it evolve its own way, adapting spontaneously to its new socio-economic context, and coming eventually to maturity in the new society it is called upon to reflect and serve."[72] However, the fact that the "not now" argument has been made by scholars and administrators ever since independence made some conclude in the 1990s that the phase of maturity might never come.[73]

The risk of freezing an evolving system will be largest in the case of a binding codification. Although a code can be kept up to date by amendment, experience shows that changes that have to be introduced by legislative process are long delayed.[74] A code need not be seen as a complete statement of a particular set of laws, not capable of being added to without the intervention of the legislature, however.[75] A code may contain inclusionary provisions that may allow for greater flexibility in the use of the code. Some claim that the risk of freezing hardly exists in the case of non-binding restatements, which are used as a guide only, with provisions for regular revision of rules when social circumstances have changed or when there are overreaching policy reasons why the restatement rule should not be applied in a particular

---

[67] Bennett & Vermeulen, *supra* note 6, at 219.

[68] Shadle, *supra* note 36, at 416. *Cf.* Ajayi, *supra* note 3, at 124; Osinbajo, *supra* note 63, at 261.

[69] Shadle, *supra* note 36, at 421.

[70] Odje, *supra* note 2, at 36.

[71] R.J.H. Pogucki, *A Note on the Codification of Customary Law on the Gold Coast*, 8 J. AFR. ADMIN. 192, 193 (1954).

[72] Theirry Verhelst, Safeguarding African Customary Law: Judicial and Legislative Processes for Its Adaptation and Integration 41, UCLA Int'l Institute, James C. Coleman African Studies Center, Occasional Papers Series no. 7 (1970).

[73] *See* Azinge, *supra* note 63, at 286.

[74] *Cf.* A.J. Kerr, *The Reception and Codification of Systems of Law in Southern Africa*, 2 J. AFR. L. 82, 96 (1958).

[75] *See* Osinbajo, *supra* note 63, at 265.

case.[76] This ignores the fact that the whole reason for a restatement project is to address the difficulty judges face in determining the local customary law. As a consequence of this difficulty, they might not be easily persuaded that customary law has changed. The restatements might thus not be a code de jure, but might in time become one de facto, as has happened to the restatement of civil customary laws in Kenya.[77] In the case of judicially recognized custom, it is also open to a party to show that this custom is no longer supported by established usage. Although courts will allow evidence in support of changes in judicially noticed custom, again it should be stressed that in reality such a change is hard to prove and most judges prefer to simply rely on earlier decisions.

A third criticism of knowledge devices is that there is no way of ensuring that informants – whether members of a restatement panel, local experts in codification programs, or assessors and witnesses in court proceedings – are reliable informants on the customary law. Authors question the reliability of expert statements about customary law largely for three reasons. First, local people are asked to translate their flexible, negotiable norms into hard rules, something we have seen anthropologists were unable to do. When people are asked to engage in such an exercise, they are invariably led to invent rules or to make inaccurate statements or subjective interpretations.[78] For instance Allott, discussing this issue with regard to expert witnesses in court, states that once one has discarded possible misrepresentations of the law due to the ignorance, bias, or corruption of the expert, there may be other causes for a variation between the actual customary law and the law as presented by the expert.[79] Two of these are "a tendency to idealise the law, to present what it ought to be instead of what it is; and a failure to appreciate that the ancient, traditional law has been modified."[80] This clearly comes to the fore in an article about colonial Kenya, which shows that what African court elders who served as law panel members in a restatement project represented as customary law in the panel minutes differed from the customary law they used in actual court cases.[81] In these courts, presiding elders remained committed to a fluid and situational customary law rather than the more fixed rules in the law panels.[82] Secondly, experts tend to present the customary law in such a way as to favor their personal and group interests. The information the elders in colonial Kenya provided on the expert panels led to the institution of rules that

---

[76] *See* Allott & Cotran, *supra* note 56, at 32–33.

[77] *See* Shadle, *supra* note 36, at 430.

[78] *See* Verhelst, *supra* note 72, at 42.

[79] *See* A.N. Allott, *The Judicial Ascertainment of Customary Law in Africa*, 20 MOD. L. REV. 244, 248 (1957).

[80] *Id.*

[81] *See* Shadle, *supra* note 36, at 424.

[82] *See id.*

permanently favored elders to the disadvantage of women and junior men.[83] It thus matters which people are able to present themselves as experts of customary law on restatement projects, codification programs, or in court. It is common knowledge that colonial as well as post-colonial policy shows a male elderly bias in this respect. Chanock, for instance, explicitly claims that colonial officers thought that "the *real* customary law was in the minds of the oldest men."[84] Thirdly, experts hardly testify against the interests of persons at whose instance they are in court to testify.[85] They can therefore not be expected to give evidence devoid of any particular interest. In the same vein, a Nigerian Attorney General comments:

> Experience has shown that this necessity for proof of customary law by evidence usually gives rise to litigants ranging respectable witnesses on their side to put forward a version of the customary law on the subject matter in issue to bolster up their claims or defences. The magistrate or the judge on the bench therefore, has the unpleasant task of choosing one of the other of the contradictory versions of the customary law.[86]

Other authors have criticized the knowledge devices for different reasons. For instance, the fact that the use of language, legal categories, and terminology alien to custom – most recordings were made in English – inevitably alters the nature of customary law.[87] Furthermore, anthropologists claim that it is both a mistaken and an unrealistic objective to try and mold customary law into a set of legal rules, as these rules have little meaning outside of the social context that explains and supports them.[88] In the case of codification, some authors mention the challenge to find able drafters that will carry out their drafting duties without errors and omissions in an unbiased, professional manner, with an open and positive attitude to customary law.[89] There is also a serious danger of those assigned with the task of codification coloring their findings with their pre-conceived ideas about a particular customary law.[90]

4.5. THE QUEST FOR CUSTOMARY LAW

Both the limited reliability of evidence by experts, witnesses, and assessors, as well as the recording of customary law through codification, restatement, or case law, in

---

[83] *See id.* at 413.
[84] Chanock, *supra* note 34, at 53.
[85] *See* Osinbajo, *supra* note 63, at 257.
[86] Azinge, *supra* note 63, at 289.
[87] *See* Verhelst, *supra* note 72, at 39.
[88] *See id.*
[89] *See* Kerr, *supra* note 74, at 97; R.E.S. Tanner, *The Codification of Customary Law in Tanzania*, 2 E. AFR. L.J. 105, 106–107 (1966).
[90] *See* Narebo, *supra* note 63, at 305.

effect changes the content and nature of customary law and creates a gap between what is locally practiced and what the state courts declare customary law, that is, judicial customary law. In fact, recording customary law will always change its content and nature, independent of the way in which this is done. The manner of recording merely determines the size of the gap, depending on the extent to which the recordings freeze customary law and the space they allow, both de jure and de facto, for revision. The methods of case law, restatement, and codification form a gliding scale from less to more change.

Not only the recording of customary law but even the mere imposition of a state court, with the power to impose rules and to enforce decisions in disputes, already transforms the nature of customary law. Whereas in local dispute settlements customary rules set the "parameters of the dispute" and the "guidelines for decisions," in state courts these rules will be strictly applied and imposed.[91]

Despite the inevitable gap between locally practiced and judicial customary law, many African countries have given their state courts jurisdiction to decide cases on the basis of customary law. In many cases, ascertainment of a customary rule does not present a challenge to the court. Litigants may, for instance, disagree about the facts instead of about the rules. Or the disagreement is not about rules or facts, but a court decision is sought to ensure that the defendant complies with certain customary rules. In other cases, the dispute is about the rule, but this rule is not heavily disputed in the locality and can fairly easily be ascertained by the court through the provision of evidence or with reference to authoritative texts or reference to case law. There remain, however, a number of cases that revolve around the ascertainment of a customary rule that is heavily contested between the litigants, and the applicable "customary community" also does not display "regularized conduct" or "consistent disputing behavior." It is these cases that pose serious problems of ascertainment of customary rules for judges.

When a rule of customary law is contested, judges have to select one of the versions presented by the litigants. But how are they supposed to make this choice? Do they have almost unlimited discretion to choose whatever version? Or, to put it differently, can any rule claimed to be in existence by a litigant qualify as customary law? Many African countries have not defined customary law. Others have provided a definition,[92] but their definitions do not "in any way describe any phenomenon of

---

[91] A.N. ALLOTT, ESSAYS IN AFRICAN LAW: WITH SPECIAL REFERENCE TO THE LAW OF GHANA 73 (Greenwood Press 2d ed. 1975); Chanock, *supra* note 31 at 80; Keebet Von Benda-Beckmann, *The Use of Folk Law in West Sumatran State Courts, in* PEOPLE'S LAW AND STATE LAW: THE BELLAGIO PAPERS, *supra* note 37, at 78, 87.

[92] Article 11(3) of the Ghanaian Constitution, for instance, states that customary law consists of "the rules of law which by custom are applicable to particular communities." GHANA CONST. 1992 Art. 11(3). In Tanzania, customary law is defined as the "rules established by usage in a community and accepted by such community in general." Interpretation of Laws and General Clauses Act, 1972 (Act No. 30/72) § 3(1) (Tanz.).

any kind."[93] However, for rules to qualify as customary law, it is generally accepted that they "must spring from the practices of a particular ethnic community."[94] But when there are competing practices, which of these practices constitute customary law? To deal with this problem, we will turn to jurisprudence. There we find an approach to customary law that is based on two concepts: a "fixed line of behavior" (*usus*) and "normative moment" (*opinio necessitatis*).[95] A practice can only constitute a rule of customary law when it fulfills these two requirements.

The first requirement reads that a customary rule can only exist when a fixed line of behavior is followed by a more or less constant group of persons for a certain period. This raises the dilemma of how long certain practices need to be repeated to be able to speak of a fixed line of behavior. When very little time is needed to establish it, change becomes an intrinsic feature of customary law. This not only creates problems for examining processes of change as a product of struggle between different social forces,[96] but it would also mean that any substantial group, by diverging from a customary rule, can abolish the rule and create a new one. This would make it impossible to evaluate whether changed behavior of a majority group is right or legal according to customary law. This would in fact deny customary law any normative character. On the other hand, when the establishment of a fixed line of behavior requires long periods of repetition, adaptations of customary norms to changing circumstances becomes difficult.

The second requirement holds that a custom, in order to be law, must be commonly believed to be obligatory. These include rules of behavior that are not only followed as a matter of practice, but *must* be followed as a matter of law.[97]

A practice can only constitute customary law when it fulfills these two requirements. Can they be helpful for judges attempting to determine which of the rules mentioned by the litigants qualifies as a rule of customary law? At first glance, the answer to this question would seem to be negative, as rules of customary law that are still in their formation stage are exactly characterized by the absence of fixed behavior and normative moment. This chapter argues, however, that in such cases, judges need to take into account the wider customary normative framework and be informed by the *usus* and *opinio necessitatis* with regard to related customary rules. This will be demonstrated on the basis of the Ghana case regarding leases of residential land in peri-urban areas.

---

[93] H.J.A.N. Mensa-Bonsu, *Of "Nuts in the Ground Not Being Groundnuts": The Current State of Customary Law in Ghana*, 22 Univ. Ghana L.J. 1, 3 (2002–2004).

[94] *Id.*

[95] *See* Allott, *supra* note 6, at 147; Bennett & Vermeulen, *supra* note 6, at 215; Elias, *supra* note 6; Mensah Sarbah, *supra* note 6, at 4–6; Okany, *supra* note 6, at 39.

[96] *See* Kojo Sebastian Amanor, Land, Labour and the Family in Southern Ghana: A Critique of Land Policy under Neo-Liberalisation 16 (Nordiska Afrikainstitutet 2001).

[97] *See* Allott, *supra* note 6, at 147; Elias, *supra* note 6; Llewellyn & Hoebel, *supra* note 10, at 283–284; Okany, *supra* note 6, at 39.

We have seen that at present, there is no fixed line of behavior in peri-urban Kumasi with regard to the conversion and allocation of residential land. The area displays a kaleidoscope of actions, struggles, and negotiations, with highly varied outcomes. Throughout history, however, there has been a more or less fixed line of behavior with regard to the security of indigenous farmers' usufructuary rights. The literature tells ample stories of chiefs profiting from customary land, but rarely at the expense of the customary freehold of indigenous community members.[98] In this regard, a rule that a chief can at his own discretion at any moment decide to terminate a customary freehold and sell the land in question does not square with the historical practice of secure customary freeholds. Such a rule would rather be in keeping with a strongly feudal system where chiefs can rule arbitrarily.

With regard to the conversion and allocation of residential land, there is also no normative moment in peri-urban Kumasi. The currently claimed interpretations of customary law with regard to these issues are highly varied. Customary land management in general, however, seems to be based on the shared opinion that a chief should act in the interest of his community. We can find this norm in various written sources, such as the Constitution,[99] case law,[100] and certain literature including that by writers closely related to chiefs.[101] This norm is also often prevalent in local discourse, not in the least by chiefs and elders themselves, who use it as legitimation

---

[98] They tell, for instance, of chiefs selling unused land at the expense of expansion of land by current farmers and future generations, with much of the profits flowing to the chiefs; of chiefs posing conditions such as fees and tribute systems on the use of land for market crop production; and of chiefs reclaiming land sold to foreigners. *See* Berry, *supra* note 57; Kathryn Firmin-Sellers, *The Politics of Property Rights*, 89 Am. Pol. Sci. Rev. 867 (1995); Ben Kwame Fred-Mensah, Changes, Ambiguities and Conflicts: Negotiating Land Rights in Buem-Kator, Ghana (Johns Hopkins Univ. 2000). Although these actions can have serious consequences for indigenous and stranger farmers, mostly they do not tamper with the customary freehold itself. *See also* Janine M. Ubink, *Customary Tenure Security: Wishful Policy Thinking or Reality? A Case from Peri-Urban Ghana*, 51 J. Afr. L. 215 (2007).

[99] *See* Ghana Const. 1992 Art. 267(1).

[100] *See* Janine M. Ubink, *Courts and Peri-Urban Practice: Customary Land Law in Ghana*, 22 Univ. Ghana L.J. 25 (2002–2004).

[101] *See* K.A. Busia, The Position of the Chief in the Modern Political System of Ashanti: A Study of the Influence of Contemporary Social Changes on Ashanti Political Institutions (Oxford Univ. Press 1951); Danquah, *supra* note 8; John Dunn & A.F. Robertson, Dependence and Opportunity: Political Change in Ahafo 53 (African Studies Series 9, J.R. Goody ed., Cambridge Univ. Press 1973); J.E.C. Hayford, Gold Coast Native Institutions: With Thoughts Upon a Healthy Imperial Policy for the Gold Coast and Ashanti (Frank Cass & Co. 1970); Kasim Kasanga, *Land Tenure, Resource Access & Decentralisation in Ghana, in* The Dynamics of Resource Tenure in West Africa, *supra* note 45; Osei Kwadwo, An Outline of Asante History (O. Kwadwo Enter. 1994); N.A. Ollennu, Principles of Customary Land Law in Ghana (Sweet & Maxwell 1962); R.J.H. Pogucki, *The Main Principles of Rural Land Tenure, in* Agriculture and Land Use in Ghana (Brian Wills ed., Oxford Univ. Press 1962); John Mensah Sarbah, Fanti Customary Laws: A Brief Introduction to the Principles of the Native Laws and Customs of the Fanti and Akan Districts of the Gold Coast with a Report of Some Cases Thereon Decided in the Law Courts (Frank Cass 3d ed. 1968).

of their power.[102] Their reference to this norm does not mean that chiefs always comply with it.[103] The ideal system of traditional checks and balances with its option to depose malfunctioning chiefs also underpins a general norm that chiefs should act in the communal interest. Also here, however, practice sometimes differs from the norm. Nevertheless, it seems to be widely believed that chiefs are obliged to act in the best interest of their community.

The three rules found in peri-urban Kumasi with regard to the allocation of residential land vary from much (1) to some (2) to little (3) recognition of the interests of the indigenous farmers. The third rule, placing full unrestrained power in the hands of the chiefs, clearly violates the earlier *usus* of secure customary freeholds and the *opinio necessitatis* that chiefs act in the interest of their communities. This rule tries to form new customary law contrary to the time-honored principles of customary law. The first and second rules, depending on their specific workings, could fit with these principles of customary law while also offering space for social evolution and the demands of modernity. The selection of one of these two rules would thus be in accordance with the wider framework of customary law.

Judges thus do not have complete discretion in choosing just any of the versions of customary law presented by litigants. In cases where a new rule of customary law is in its formation stage – and a fixed line of behavior and a normative moment will necessarily be absent – they need to be informed by fixed lines of behavior and normative moments with regard to related issues, as new rules are path-dependent and not isolated from the wider customary normative framework. This limits the discretion of judges and therefore leaves less room for following personal or political interests, or for being pressured to uphold the version of the most powerful (group of) litigants.

4.6. CONCLUSION

In this chapter we have discussed the difficulty judges meet when they have to decide cases on the basis of customary law. The considerable knowledge of customary law amassed by anthropologists is often not usable for rule-seeking judges or requires

---

[102] *See* Ubink, *supra* note 98.

[103] For notable examples of chiefs ignoring the needs of their people out of self-interest, see Wily & Hammond, *supra* note 45; KOJO SEBASTIAN AMANOR, GLOBAL RESTRUCTURING AND LAND RIGHTS IN GHANA: FOREST FOOD CHAINS, TIMBER AND RURAL LIVELIHOODS, Research Report No. 108 (Nordiska Afrikainstitutet 1999); Berry, *supra* note 57; Dep't for Int'l Dev., Further Knowledge of Livelihoods Affected by Urban Transition, Kumasi, Ghana, Natural Resources Systems Programme, Final Technical Report (2001); Dunn & Robertson, *supra* note 101; Firmin-Sellers, *supra* note 98; T C. MCCASKIE, ASANTE IDENTITIES: HISTORY AND MODERNITY IN AN AFRICAN VILLAGE 1850–1950 (Edinburgh Univ. Press 2000); Richard Rathbone, *Defining Akyemfo: The Construction of Citizenship in Akyem Abuakwa, Ghana, 1700–1939*, 66 AFR. 506 (1996); Ubink, *supra* note 5.

qualification or interpretation into legal terms. This applies even more in circumstances of change, conflict, and imposition when customary norms are contested.

Over the years, a number of devices have developed that provide judges with information about rules of customary law and that should thus bring more certainty for the "subjects" of the law. These knowledge devices have met with various objections, including that customary laws are too diverse to record, that their flexibility will be halted and their development hampered when they are recorded and thus fixed at a certain stage, and that the reliability of informants of customary rules cannot be guaranteed and their ability to truthfully present customary law is questionable. Regardless of the method of ascertainment, inevitably a gap will develop between local customary practices and judicial customary law. Despite this, many African countries have opted for a legal system in which state courts have the jurisdiction to decide cases on the basis of customary law. In some of these cases, the rule of customary law is heavily contested and none of the devices offers an acceptable authority. This chapter argues that in such cases, judges cannot freely choose between one of the stated versions. Not every rule claimed to be in existence by a litigant qualifies as customary law. In cases where a new rule of customary law is in its formation stage – and the two requirements of a fixed line of behavior and normative moment will necessarily be absent – judges need to consider the path-dependency of rules and take into account the wider customary normative framework and fixed lines of behavior and normative moment with regard to related issues. This limits the opportunity of powerful actors and groups to claim that their practice forms a new rule of customary law when this practice is in clear contradiction with earlier practices and normative beliefs. Or at least it limits the discretion of judges to accept such claims, and as such, protects the rights of weaker persons and groups under customary law.

The fact that many African countries, fully aware of the inevitable gap between local customary practices and judicial customary law, have nevertheless designed a legal system in which state courts apply customary law does not mean that this gap does not merit rethinking. We have seen that courts are expected to attune contents of customary law to "the social necessities of contemporary life." At the same time, it is obvious that when judicial pronouncements of customary law are too much out of tune with local practices, the locality will disregard judicial development of customary law, at least outside the decided cases. Judges are imbued with the difficult task of operating within this limited space for judicial activism. Various methods, including legal empowerment programs and the provisioning of wide media attention to watershed judgments, could enhance the impact of judicial decisions on local practices and thus enlarge judges' room for maneuver. These and other methods deserve careful attention from African governments and donor institutions.

5

The Withering Province of Customary Law in Kenya

A Case of Design or Indifference?

George Otieno Ochich

5.1. INTRODUCTION

Customary law is recognized as one of the sources of Kenya's laws where it is designated "African customary law."[1] Custom is the oldest source of law in Africa. It generated the body of law that governed the native African communities in precolonial Africa. The scope of customary law in the traditional African society was all-encompassing. The advent of colonial administration in Kenya in the latter part of the nineteenth century was to change that broad scope and status of customary law forever, and that regime of law has remained entangled in controversy since. The colonial administration considered customary law to be inferior to English law and initiated deliberate moves toward formalizing that perceived inferiority. So intense was that colonial influence that even later attempts at restoring the respectability of customary law in Kenya after independence have largely relegated it to further inferiority.

Contrary to reasonable expectations, Kenya's independence since 1963 has not instituted meaningful benefits for customary law. Customary law has had to contend with multifaceted assaults over the years, the consequence of which has been to considerably reduce its respectability and the scope of its application. The application of customary law in Kenya today is governed by the Judicature Act,[2] section

An earlier version of this paper was prepared for and presented at a conference on "African Customary Law Revisited: The Role of Customary Law in the 21st Century," University of Botswana, Gaborone, Botswana, October 22–25, 2008. The author is grateful to the Leitner Center for International Law and Justice at Fordham Law School in New York and the Department of Law at the University of Botswana for the opportunity to prepare this paper and for organizing the conference. The author is solely responsible for all the views expressed herein.

[1] See Judicature Act, (1967) Cap. 8 § 3(2). (Kenya). The expressions "African customary law" and "customary law" are used interchangeably herein to refer to one and the same regime of law.

[2] *See id.*

3(2) of which sets out the circumstances and conditions of application of customary law in Kenya. By dint of that statutory provision, customary law is no longer all-encompassing but may only be applied in certain cases if it meets certain conditions. The scope of that provision has been considerably reduced by statutory and judicial interventions, the sum effect of which has been to wither the scope of customary law to mere necessary evil in Kenya's legal system.

This chapter analyzes that withered place that customary law today occupies in Kenya's legal system. The analysis draws from certain historical developments that have attended customary law and attempts a forecast into the future of customary law. This analysis underlines the continued relevance of customary law and makes proposals for enhancing its place in the legal system.

5.2. HISTORICAL CONTEXTUALIZATION

Before the dawn of colonialism in Kenya, the various ethnic communities of Kenya had their own customary laws regulating their lives and social order.[3] African customary law was an expansive and all-encompassing regime. Such expansive scope was necessary because, in the absence of a centralized system, customary law had to extend to all spheres of life within the respective communities. The absence of such expansive scope would have given way to the emergence of a vacuum in the social order. As noted elsewhere, "customary law is necessarily a point of convergence for legal rules, social norms, moral principles, values and belief systems.... Outside the scheme, or in the absence of, the centralised control system, *custom* crystallises as the immanent regime of law."[4]

The content and scope of customary law changed forever upon the advent of colonial rule in Africa. The scope of customary law has consistently withered, and what remains of it today is a mere faint shadow of what that regime of law used to be in pre-colonial Africa. From the very early days of colonial rule, the colonial government embarked on deliberate steps toward phasing out customary law but soon realized that customary law was not easy to phase out. The government then grudgingly began to permit the application of customary law in the courts of law. But even then, in the early days, customary law could not rise to the upper echelons

---

[3] For detailed accounts of the pre-colonial systems of law in Kenya and elsewhere in Africa, see G.S. WERE & D. WILSON, EAST AFRICA THROUGH A THOUSAND YEARS: A HISTORY OF THE YEARS AD 1000 TO THE PRESENT DAY (3d ed., Evans Bros. 1984); KENYA BEFORE 1900 (B. A. Ogot ed., East Africa Publishing House 1984); B. DAVIDSON & J. E. F. MHINA, THE GROWTH OF AFRICAN CIVILIZATION: EAST AND CENTRAL AFRICA TO THE LATE NINETEENTH CENTURY (Longmans 1967); R. A. OLIVER ET AL., A HISTORY OF EAST AFRICA (Clarendon Press 1963).

[4] J. B. Ojwang, *Death and Burial in Modern Kenya: An Introduction, in* THE SM OTIENO CASE: DEATH AND BURIAL IN MODERN KENYA 8 (J. B. Ojwang & J. N. K. Mugambi eds., Nairobi University Press 1989).

in the judicial hierarchy; its application was restricted within the native courts and tribunals.[5] Appeals from the Native Tribunals led to the Native Court of Appeal and then to the District Commissioner and finally to the Provincial Commissioner. It was only much later that customary laws could be applied in the magistrate's courts. The judicial attitude toward customary law right from the earliest days of the colonial administration was that, though accepted as being applicable in courts of law, it was inferior to English law.[6]

The first formal colonial assault on customary law came through the East Africa Order in Council 1897,[7] which conferred on the Commissioner of the Protectorate[8] powers to legislate through the Queen's Regulations, including powers to legislate on matters relating to customs. Like other colonial officers of English origin and background, the Commissioner had little understanding of African customs and undoubted bias against the African customary ways of life. Moreover, the Commissioner's legislative powers were subject to the proviso requiring him to respect native law and customs only to the extent to which they were not opposed to justice or morality. Upon that background, it would have been unrealistic to expect the Commissioner to legislate for the progressive development of customary law. The Commissioner's subjective notions of justice and morality undoubtedly influenced the exercise of his legislative powers over native customs. Indeed, the regulations and orders that were made pursuant to the Commissioner's legislative powers turned out to be quite unfavorable to customary law. Although most of these regulations were later repealed, they formed the basis of subsequent legislation and set the tone for the subsequent development of customary law in Kenya. Their impact has persisted to date and the substance of some of those regulations still form the conditions upon which customary law is today applicable in the Kenyan courts.

The East Africa Order in Council 1897 and the Native Courts Regulations 1897[9] in effect established a two-court system, one for the native Africans and another for non-Africans. That two-court system remained in place until it was replaced at independence with a single-court system. The East Africa Order in Council 1897 was followed closely by the East African Native Courts (Amendment) Ordinance 1902,[10] which introduced special courts having full criminal and civil jurisdiction over natives in the district. These courts were to exercise their jurisdiction in accordance

[5] See YASH PAL GHAI & J. P. W. B. McAUSLAN, PUBLIC LAW AND POLITICAL CHANGE IN KENYA 359–380 (Oxford University Press 1970).
[6] An expression of that attitude may be discerned from the judges' views in *R v Amkeyo*, (1917) 17 E.A.C.A. 14 (Kenya). *See also Gwao bin Kilimo v Kisunda bin Ifuta*, (1938) 1 T.L.R. 403 (Kenya).
[7] East African Order in Council, 1897.
[8] The Commissioner was the British officer in charge of the administration of the East Africa Protectorate, which later became the colony of Kenya.
[9] Native Courts Regulations, 1897.
[10] East African Native Courts (Amendment) Ordinance, No. 31 of 1902.

with the laws in force in the Protectorate, including native (customary) law. Section 20 of the East African Native Courts (Amendment) Ordinance 1902 directed that:

> In all cases civil and criminal to which natives are parties, every court (a) shall be guided by native law so far as it is applicable and is not repugnant to justice and morality or inconsistent with any Order in Council, Ordinance or any Regulation or Rule made under any Order in Council or Ordinance; and (b) shall decide all such cases according to substantive justice without undue regard to technicalities of procedure and without undue delay.

The foregoing provision marked one of the earliest steps at subjecting the application of customary law to express legislative conditions. The substance of that provision was later reproduced in the Kenya Colony Order in Council 1921[11] in a more refined form: "In all cases to which natives are parties, every court shall be guided by native law so far as it is applicable and not repugnant to justice or morality or inconsistent with the provisions of any Order of the King in Council or with any other law in force in the colony."[12]

By providing that customary law was applicable only if it was not "inconsistent with the provisions of any Order of the King in Council or with any other law in force in the colony,"[13] the Kenya Colony Order in Council 1921 effectively subordinated customary law to all received law that was then applicable in Kenya, including the substance of the common law of England and doctrines of equity that had already been applied into Kenya through the East Africa Order in Council 1897. The substance of the provisions of Article 7 of the Kenya Colony Order in Council 1921 remained part of the laws of Kenya from that time onward and underpinned the trend of development of customary law from thenceforth.

The 1950s saw more attention being given to customary laws relating to land. The Native Lands Registration Ordinance 1959 sought to facilitate the registration of individual titles over land previously held under customary tenure.[14] The Ordinance established a committee to adjudicate on land claims in accordance with customary law. Although that was packaged as a recognition of customary land rights, it was actually yet another form of assault on customary law as it sought to transform customary land rights into an entirely different crop of rights, namely modern land tenure based on principles of English property ownership.

Implicit in the foregoing developments and reforms regarding customary law and its administration, including restricting the administration of customary law to the

[11]   Kenya Colony Order in Council, 1921.
[12]   *Id.* art. 7.
[13]   *Id.*
[14]   Native Lands Registration Ordinance, No. 2 of 1959.

lowest echelons in the judicial ranks, were broader designs by the colonial administration to trivialize and relegate customary law to the periphery.

5.2.1. *Has Independence Brought Any Difference?*

The attainment of independence presented an opportune moment for Kenya to uplift the status of customary law and place it in its deserved place in the legal system, taking into account the core position of customs in the social life of Kenyans. Unfortunately the government did not go far enough in re-affirming the fundamental place of customary law, instead beginning with a modest compromise position. The Lancaster Conferences,[15] which led to independence for Kenya, agreed on an Independence Constitution based on the Westminster model with the compromise that the colonial legislation was to be retained and preserved to the extent that was necessary to protect and facilitate continued British investment in the country.[16] The resolutions of the Conferences on a draft Independence Constitution were enacted as a schedule to the Kenyan Independence Order in Council 1963.[17]

Pursuant to those provisions of the Kenya Independence Order in Council 1963, the entire body of colonial legislation was retained and re-enacted verbatim by the independence constitutional order and restyled "Acts" rather than "Ordinances." The retention of English law in Kenya at independence was intended, in part, to take care of the lacuna then existing in Kenya's legal sphere. The level of development of the law in Kenya was relatively behind that of the United Kingdom, and there were many areas to which Kenyan law had not been extended. It was also designed to secure the gains that the colonial administration had achieved in protecting English investments and population in Kenya.

The retention of English law was meant to be a stop-gap measure as it was intended that Kenyan law would ultimately extend to all the areas to totally phase out imported English law. That phasing out is far from beginning. In fact, more than four decades after Kenya attained her independence, the bulk of Kenya's legislation is still replete with English law values and notions. The extent to which the Kenyan legal system is dependent on English law is so high that one may argue that Kenya's juridical autonomy and sovereignty has been compromised by English law.

Kenya's legislature has continued the colonial legacy by extending the scope of English law principles at the expense of local values. A majority of Kenyan statutes

---

[15] The Lancaster House Conferences consisted of three meetings in 1960, 1962, and 1963, where the independence of Kenya (after more than seventy years of colonial rule) and its new constitutional framework were negotiated.

[16] See REPORT OF THE KENYA CONSTITUTIONAL CONFERENCE (London 1960).

[17] SI 1963/1968 (UK).

have incorporated English law in general terms without any limitations. For example, the Registered Land Act[18] applies English law in these terms:

> Subject to the provisions of this Act and save as may be provided by any written law for the time being in force, the common law of England, as modified by the doctrines of equity, shall extend and apply to Kenya in relation to land, leases and charges registered under this Act and interests therein, but without prejudice to the rights, liabilities and remedies of the parties under any instrument subsisting immediately before such application.[19]

English law has been applied in many other areas, including in respect of contracts,[20] sale of goods,[21] partnerships,[22] admiralty jurisdiction,[23] and the administrative power of the High Court to grant the prerogative orders of certiorari and mandamus.[24]

5.3. THE PLACE OF CUSTOMARY LAW IN KENYA'S LEGAL SYSTEM TODAY

Previous developments notwithstanding, customary law remains recognized in Kenya's legal system right from the highest hierarchy of Kenya's legislative instruments. Kenya's supreme law, the Constitution of Kenya, sanctions the existence, validity, and application of customary law on matters of personal law, including adoption, marriage, divorce, burial, and devolution of property on death.[25] In a more explicit manner, the Constitution also sanctions the validity of customary laws that are exclusively applicable to members of a particular race or tribe to the exclusion of any law with respect to that matter which is applicable in the case of other persons.[26] Thus, the Constitution allows a broad area within which customary law can operate without having to be declared inconsistent with the Constitution. The Constitutional provisions on customary law, however, are very brief and have not been adequately reinforced by further statutory provisions. Neither have they been adequately consolidated by judicial practice. Such brief treatment reinforces

---

[18] (1963) Cap. 300. (Kenya).
[19] Id. § 163.
[20] *See* Law of Contract Act, (1961) Cap. 23 § 2(1). (Kenya).
[21] *See* Sale of Goods Act, (1981) Cap. 31 § 59(2). (Kenya).
[22] *See* Partnership Act, (1934) Cap. 29 § 49. (Kenya); *see also* Limited Partnerships Act, (1934) Cap. 30 § 6. (Kenya).
[23] *See* Judicature Act, (1967) Cap. 8 § 10 rules 4(1) and 7(1) of the High Court (Admiralty) Rules, No 8 (1979). (Kenya).
[24] *See* Law Reform Act, (1956) Cap. 26 § 8(2). (Kenya).
[25] *See Constitution*, § 82(4)(b) (2008) (Kenya). The current Constitution of Kenya was enacted on December 12, 1963, and has been amended several times since then.
[26] *See Id.* § 82(4)(c).

the structural and attitudinal biases against customary law that had been built into Kenya's legal system by the colonial administration.

The more substantive rules governing the application of customary law in Kenya today are contained in the Judicature Act.[27] Section 3(2) of the Act provides that the High Court and all subordinate courts are to be guided by African customary law in civil cases in which one or more of the parties is subject to it or affected by it, so far as it is applicable and not repugnant to justice and morality or inconsistent with any written law. In a nutshell, that provision confines the application of customary law to the following specific circumstances and conditions:

(a) Customary law is applicable only in civil cases.
(b) Customary law can be applied only if it is not repugnant to justice and morality.
(c) Customary law can be applied as a guide to the courts.
(d) Customary law can be applied only in respect of cases to which one or more parties are either subject to or affected by the customary law.
(e) Customary law can be applied only if it is not inconsistent with written law.

The bulk of these strenuous conditions governing the applicability of customary law – with the exception of (a) and (d) above – were carried over from the colonial legislative instruments, principally section 20 of the East African Native Courts (Amendment) Ordinance 1902 and Article 7 of the Kenya Colony Order in Council 1921.

A critical examination of these circumstances and conditions confirms that the independent Kenyan government has continued the colonial trend that has trivialized, relegated, and fundamentally withered the scope of customary law.

5.3.1. *Confinement to Civil Cases*

African customary law is applicable in Kenya only in civil cases. Such express statements of the law leave no doubt that customary law is not applicable in criminal cases or any other cases that are not of a civil nature. The Judicature Act talks of "civil cases" without defining any particular category of civil cases to which customary law may be applied, thus leaving the scope of customary law fairly open-ended. Furthermore, the Judicature Act gives both the High Court and the subordinate courts unlimited original jurisdiction in respect of civil cases under customary law. That wide and open-ended tenor of the subsection notwithstanding, its scope has been limited by judicial decisions and legislative enactments that have both

---

[27] *See* Judicature Act, (1967) Cap. 8. (Kenya). That is the Act of Parliament that defines the jurisdiction of both the High Court and the subordinate courts.

expressly and impliedly excluded the application of customary law to certain categories of civil cases. In so far as judicial decisions are concerned, the courts have moved to limit the scope by holding that customary law is not applicable in cases founded on torts and contracts.[28]

Regarding legislative enactments, the Magistrates' Courts Act,[29] which defines the jurisdiction of the magistrates' courts, has further limited the scope of the application of customary law by defining the category of civil cases to which the law may apply. Section 2 of the Act declares that "claim under customary law means a claim concerning any of the following matters under African customary law":

(i) land held under customary tenure;
(ii) marriage, divorce, maintenance or dowry;
(iii) seduction or pregnancy of an unmarried woman or girl;
(iv) enticement of or adultery with a married woman;
(v) matters affecting status, and in particular the status of women, widows and children, including guardianship, custody, adoption, and legitimacy.
(vi) intestate succession and administration of estates, so far as not governed by any written law.[30]

The wording and spirit of that list seems to have sealed the fate of customary law insofar as litigation in the subordinate courts is concerned. It means that customary law rules that govern any matters not included in the list cannot be entertained in the magistrates' courts. Thus, the Magistrates Courts Act unnecessarily limits the progressive development of customary law into new horizons. The High Court also found that section 2 of the Magistrates' Courts Act provides an exhaustive list of the category of cases in respect of which customary law may be applied.[31]

The nature of the matters to which customary law is confined by the Magistrates' Courts Act may prompt an argument that the legal system accords customary law a rather inferior position. Although the listed matters may not necessarily be termed inferior or less important, they, by any standard, are not matters that attract as much litigation or juridical interest as matters that are expressly or impliedly excluded. Considering that customary law is arguably closer to the people than statutory law, its relevance to commercial and criminal transactions that arise in the day-to-day lives of the people, especially in the remote rural areas, cannot be challenged. Customary law may present a desirable, less costly, informal, and speedy framework

---

[28] *See Kamanza Chiwaya v Tsuma*, (1970) Civil Appeal No. 6 (H.C.K., Mombasa) (unreported) (Kenya).

[29] (1989) Cap. 10. (Kenya).

[30] *See id.* § 2.

[31] *See Joseph Mwangi Wainaina v Gathoni Wainaina*, (1970) Civil Appeal No. 119 (H.C.K., Nairobi) (unreported) (Kenya).

for such transactions and a medium for the resolution of disputes that may arise out of such transactions.

Until the 1960s, customary law applied to crimes as well. This was to change soon after independence. Even before independence, customary criminal law seemed to have fallen out of favor with the government's trend of thinking. The colonial government had argued that customary criminal law was abused as the authorities used it to punish any act or omission that was not approved of by the colonial administrative officers, and that the courts had difficulties administering it.[32] These same arguments may have later influenced the thinking in the independent Kenya not to bother with retaining customary offenses, leading to their subsequent demise.

The Independence Constitution had provided that all criminal offenses should be part of written law within three years after independence. Upon the expiry of the three-year period, nothing had been done about the customary criminal offenses and, as a result, they disappeared through operation of the law. It has been noted that "[o]ne would have thought that with the initial enthusiasm, steps would have been taken to ensure that customary criminal offenses would be made part of the written law before 12 December 1966. But alas, that date arrived. Nothing was done and customary criminal law became no more."[33]

The fate of customary criminal law stands sealed by section 77(8) of the Constitution of Kenya, which provides that "[n]o person shall be convicted of a criminal offense unless that offense is defined, and the penalty thereof prescribed, in a written law." Similarly, the traditional courts that had tried customary law offenders before the dawn of colonialism were abolished by section 77 of the Constitution, which now recognizes that a criminal trial may only be conducted by a "court established by law."[34]

---

[32] *See* PHILLIPS, REPORT ON THE NATIVE TRIBUNALS IN THE COLONY AND PROTECTORATE OF KENYA ¶¶ 777, 794, 799 (Government Printer 1945).

[33] Eugene Cotran, *The Future of Customary Law in Kenya*, in THE SM OTIENO CASE: DEATH AND BURIAL IN MODERN KENYA, *supra* note 4, at 155..

[34] The term "law" as used here, though not defined, clearly does not contemplate customary law. Thus, the Constitution of Kenya recognizes only those courts that are established by written law. The written laws that establish courts in Kenya are the CONSTITUTION, §§ 60, 64 & 66 (2008) (Kenya), which establish the High Court, Court of Appeal, and the Kadhis Courts, respectively, and the Magistrates' Courts Act, (1989) Cap. 10 §§ 3 & 7 (Kenya), which establish the Resident Magistrates' Court and the District Magistrates' Court, respectively. Sections 4 and 8 of the Magistrates' Courts Act direct the Resident and District Magistrates' Courts to exercise their criminal jurisdiction in accordance with the Criminal Procedure Code and any other written law. As if in a rush to seal the fate of customary criminal law, the Judicature Act, (1967) Cap. 8 (Kenya) and Magistrates' Courts Act were enacted in quick succession as Acts No 16 and 17 of 1967, respectively.

Mere difficulties in the administration of customary criminal law could not reasonably suffice to justify a total abolition of customary criminal law. Replacing customary law on the basis of such an argument merely confirms the zeal with which the government has pursued its negative attitude toward customary law. Indeed, there are many other laws whose application and administration have occasioned difficulties and abuse, yet they have remained in existence, sometimes with improvements. Like all other social phenomena, customary law is a function of the social dynamics in the society in which it operates, and it is unreasonably pessimistic to assume that customary law is incapable of adjusting to changing or emerging trends.

It is noteworthy that the matters to which customary law is applied by virtue of section 2 of the Magistrates' Courts Act are not a preserve of customary law. Many aspects of those matters have been expressly or technically removed from the realm of customary law and are now also governed by statutes.[35] Because customary law applies only if it is not inconsistent with a written law,[36] the simultaneous application of written laws to these matters has the effect of invalidating any customary law provisions that are inconsistent with the statutory provisions. This has had the effect of fundamentally limiting the scope of customary law by further reducing the province of its application.

In respect of land tenure, the process of modernization of tenure that was begun in the latter part of the 1950s has continued. It culminated with the enactment of the Registered Land Act, which now recognizes private property rights over land. Despite its operation since 1963, the modern land tenure has continued to exist side by side with customary land tenure. In fact, even those who have secured registration of titles to land have continued sub-dividing and dealing with the parcels of land essentially in ways reminiscent of customary tenure principles.[37] Clearly, in this

[35] For example, the relevance of customary law to land disputes is being compromised as land held under customary tenure is progressively converted from customary tenure system to private tenure system through adjudication and registration. This has the effect of reducing land held under customary tenure, as the procedure sees the conversion of land into individual tenure system tailored around the English land tenure system as legislated in the Registered Land Act, (1963) Cap. 300. (Kenya). In addition, not all marriages are governed by customary law because certain matters of marriage and divorce are governed by the Marriage Act, (1902) Cap 150. (Kenya).; African Christian Marriage and Divorce Act, (1931) Cap. 151. (Kenya).; and Matrimonial Causes Act, (1941) Cap. 152. (Kenya).; succession matters are also governed by the Law of Succession Act, (1981) Cap. 160. (Kenya).; and matters affecting status of children (including maintenance, custody and adoption) are now governed by the Children Act, (2001) Cap. 8. (Kenya).

[36] See discussion on "consistency with written law," *infra*.

[37] The overriding intention of the modernization of land tenure was to consolidate the small and scattered parcels of land that had dotted the traditional Kenyan landscape into larger and more agriculturally productive parcels that could accommodate modern mechanized farming. That is far from achieved, as many landowners have continued to sub-divide their registered parcels of land into smaller parcels to accommodate the land requirements of their children and other dependants – a practice reflective of the traditional African society where a successful individual is expected to provide for his children

area, the urge to modernize has caused the written law to leap ahead of the realities in the Kenyan society.

5.3.2. *Repugnancy to Justice and Morality*

African customary law may apply only if it is not repugnant to justice and morality. This condition, popularly referred to as the "repugnancy clause," is intended to exclude the applicability of customary norms that are contrary to the principles of justice and standards of morality. The clause has, however, stirred difficulties and controversy. The concepts of justice and morality beg certain not-easy-to-answer questions: What and whose standards of justice and morality should be used to measure whether a custom is repugnant or otherwise? Is the standard to be found within the customary law itself or within the community applying that customary law? Or is it some constant standard external to customary law? The Judicature Act gives no clear guidelines on how these questions may be resolved.

The notion of repugnancy may be understood in two senses. In the first sense, repugnancy describes a situation of unbearability, distastefulness, disgust, and revulsion. In this sense, a custom is repugnant – and therefore inapplicable – if it is unbearable, distasteful, repulsive, or revolting to justice and morality. In this first sense, the test of repugnancy is entirely subjective, depending on individual perception as shaped consciously or subconsciously by the individual's culture and socialization. It is through such socialization that human beings learn and may develop their perceptions of what is repugnant or acceptable. It is also noteworthy that repugnancy is a function of social changes and what may be repugnant at one time may not be so at another time, and vice versa. Even within the same ethnic community, what is repugnant to one generation may not be repugnant to a later generation. In this sense, the repugnancy of a custom may only be fairly determined by a person who shares the perceptions, convictions, values, expectations, attitudes, and fears of those who subscribe to the custom in question. In other words, this is an internal standard by which the repugnancy of a custom can only be fairly determined by an "insider"[38] of the community that practices the custom. Each community, depending on its history, experiences, and level of socio-economic development, will have its own notions of what constitutes justice and morality.

In the second sense, repugnancy describes a situation of incompatibility or inconsistency with some accepted standard. In this sense, the test of repugnancy is an

---

and other relatives – much within the context of the extended African family system. The traditional systems determine the success of an individual by, among other factors, considering whether or not the individual owns a piece of land in his own right.

[38] As distinct from an outsider, this refers to either a member of the ethnic community that practices the custom or one who has been fully socialized into the ways of that community.

external objective standard. In this sense, therefore, a custom would be repugnant if, in the objective judgment of a reasonable man, it is inconsistent or incompatible with principles of justice and good morality.[39]

Throughout the colonial period, the courts used justice and morality standards imported from England as the determinants of the repugnancy or otherwise of African customs, thus disregarding the standards extant in the local communities in which the customs were practiced. That which was repugnant in England was rejected in Kenya too. Such application of English standards of repugnancy placed whole communities at the mercy of the subjectivity of the colonial courts. The repugnancy clause served as a tool through which the colonial administration rejected and condemned many African customary norms. That saw many African customs failing the repugnancy test, and precipitated deliberate moves through legislation, policy, and judicial decisions toward replacing the customs. In this regard, for example, the colonial courts declared as being repugnant to natural justice the Kisii custom that recognizes the paternity and child custody claims of a deserted husband in respect of any children born to the wife before the final dissolution of the marriage – irrespective of the identity of the child's biological father.[40] Similarly, customary polygamous marriages were characterized as being closer to "wife purchase" than to marriage, and children born in those marriages were described as issues of "concubinage or adulterous connections." In 1917, the Court of Appeal in *R v Amkeyo* had this to say:

> In my opinion, the use of the word "marriage" to describe the relationship entered into by an African native with a woman of his tribe according to tribal custom is a misnomer which has led in the past to considerable confusion of ideas. I know of no word that correctly describes it; 'wife-purchase' is not altogether satisfactory but

[39] It is prudent to expect that the repugnancy to justice of a custom should be determined in terms of the well-established principles of natural justice, whereas repugnancy to morality should be determined by the objective test of the reasonable man. In both cases, therefore, the standard should be external to the customary law itself. The reasonable man, however, should be a reasonable man from, or one who clearly appreciates the values of, the community practicing the custom. It would appear, however, that, in certain cases the repugnancy clause has been interpreted in the first sense. This is reflected in the judicial attitudes implicit in, for example, *Omwoyo Mairura v Bosire Angide*, (1958) 6 C.R.R. 4 (Kenya) and *Maurono Onchoke v Kerebi d/o Ondieki*, (1958) 6 C.R.R. 2 (Kenya). As already stated, in that sense, the determination of what is or is not repugnant to an individual or community depends on how the individual or community has been socialized. In the other cases where the objective test of the reasonable man has been used, the reasonable man has not been drawn from the community that practices the custom.

[40] This was the holding in, for example, the cases of *Omwoyo Mairura*, 6 C.R.R. 4, and *Maurono Onchoke*, 6 C.R.R. 2. Contrast with the decision in *Timina Olenja v Elam Kaya*, (1961) 10 C.R.R 8 (Kenya) where, although custody was granted to the mother, the court was prepared to recognize the husband's claim as entitling him to legal custody of the child.

it comes much nearer to the idea than that of "marriage" as generally understood among civilized people.[41]

Judicial decisions interpreting the repugnancy test during the colonial era reflect little empirical investigation of the origins, purposes, or effects of the customary norms in question, and they present little discussion of the processes by which the repugnancy or otherwise of the customs were assessed. The western socialization, education, and orientation of the European judges naturally steered them toward a bias against customary law. It is for that reason that the colonial judges' decisions on the repugnancy clause were mostly conclusory – as if to reflect pronouncements of pre-formed opinions without consideration of the possible effects of those decisions.[42] The judicial officers in the African courts and the native tribunals were not any different as they were concerned with pleasing their colonial superiors or masters. Furthermore, their objectivity was compromised by the administrative pressure under which they operated.[43] The African courts and native tribunals fitted into the wider colonial scheme of maintaining the unity of the common law throughout the British Empire.[44]

The colonial attitude toward the standard of repugnancy is best reflected by the following dictum in the Tanganyika[45] case of *Gwao bin Kilimo v Kisunda bin Ifuta*:

> Morality and justice are abstract conceptions and every community probably has an absolute standard of its own by which to decide what is justice and what is morality ... To what standard then does [the law] refer – the African standard ... or the British standard? *I have no doubt whatever that the only standard of justice and morality which a British court in Africa can apply is its own British standard* ... On this basis, then, the justice of applying to the present circumstances the native "law" which has been postulated in this case must be decided. Is it just *according to our ideas* to take away a man's property in order to compensate a party who has suffered injury at the hands of a man's son, the son being of full age and fully responsible for his own actions? I hold strongly the opinion that it is not just.[46]

That attitude persisted throughout the colonial period, and *R v Amkeyo* was cited with approval by Sir Ronald Sinclair, then-President of the Court of Appeal for East

---

[41] (1917) 17 E.A.C.A. 14 (C.A.) (Kenya).

[42] *See, e.g., Omwoyo Mairura*, 6 C.R.R. 4; *Maurono Onchoke*, 6 C.R.R. 2; *Timina Olenja*, 10 C.R.R. 8.

[43] In criminal cases, that pressure required them to convict or punish for any conduct which the administrators did not approve of. The reality of such pressure has been confirmed by a report on the operations of the tribunals. *See* Phillips, *supra* note 32, ¶ 792.

[44] See discussion on the historical contextualization, *ante*.

[45] Tanganyika was an East African Territory that was its own country from December 1961 to April 1964. It consisted of the countries that are now Rwanda, Burundi, and Tanzania (excluding Zanzibar).

[46] (1938) 1 T.L.R. 403 (emphasis added) (Kenya).

Africa, shortly before independence in 1963 in an appeal from Zanzibar.[47] Perhaps it is not surprising then that it has been argued that "[t]he repugnancy clause quite clearly was an engine of cultural imperialism."[48]

The influence of the colonial standard of repugnancy persists to date as the determination of the repugnancy or otherwise of customary law is today still influenced significantly by the notions inherent in the principles of English law. The failure by the Judicature Act to prescribe guidelines on how the repugnancy clause may be administered has not helped matters. The judicial trend after independence, just as in the colonial era, has not established any consistency in the interpretation and application of the repugnancy clause. In fact, certain judicial decisions in independent Kenya have tended to pursue the old colonial policy toward replacing customary law through the conclusory application of the repugnancy clause. For example, the custom in many Kenyan communities recognizing "woman to woman marriage"[49] has at certain times been judicially upheld and has at other times been declared to be repugnant to justice and morality;[50] and these have been done rather casually without sound jurisprudential analysis required of such a problematic legal concept as the repugnancy clause.[51]

The repugnancy clause has been administered in such a way that the repugnancy or otherwise of a custom does not necessarily depend on the utility of that custom

---

[47]   See *Abdulrahman bin Mohammed v Republic*, (1963) E.A. 188 (C.A.) (Tanzania).

[48]   H. W. O. Okoth-Ogendo, *Customary Law in the Kenyan Legal System – An Old Debate Revived*, in THE SM OTIENO CASE: DEATH AND BURIAL IN MODERN KENYA, *supra* note 4, at 143.

[49]   Such as the Kisii, Kuria, Kamba, Kalenjin, and so on. For a discussion of the practice of woman-to-woman marriages, see Babere Kerata Chacha, *Customary Law and Resource Struggle in Kenya: Implications on Woman to Woman Marriages, 1890–1990*, for the Leitner Center Conference on African Customary Law Revisited: The Role of Customary Law in the 21st Century, Botswana, October 23–24, 2008, this book.

[50]   See *Maria Gisese Angoi v Marcelia Nyomemenda*, (1982) Civil Appeal No. 1 (H.C.K., Kisii) (unreported) (Kenya). The High Court rejected the custom as practiced by the Kisii. An earlier decision of a subordinate court had found nothing wrong with the custom as practiced by the Nandi community. See *Esther Chepkurui v Chepngeno Chebet & Another*, (1980) Divorce Cause No. 16 (Resident Magistrate's Court, Kapsabet) (unreported) (Kenya).

[51]   See also *Kamau v Wanja & Another*, (1974) E.A. 348 (Kenya). The High Court, overturning an earlier decision of the subordinate court, found nothing offensive to justice and morality in the Kikuyu custom that recognized that a widow who returned with her children to her parents and had all the marriage consideration returned effectively severed the relationship between herself (and her family) and her late husband's family, and thereby disinherited herself and the children of the estate of the deceased. The court arrived at a largely conclusory decision without an analysis of certain valid questions into the justice and morality of that Kikuyu custom. For example, is it fair to disinherit the widow and the children merely because the widow decides to return to her parents? What of the intangible resources such as time that the widow may have invested into the marriage? Should the innocent children lose their inheritance rights merely because of their mother's unilateral decision? This decision may no longer be valid in the light provisions of the Law of Succession Act, Cap. 160. (Kenya).

to the community in question. The judicial tendency to interpret the repugnancy clause without adequate empirical investigation has attracted the criticism of the highest court in the land. Perhaps alarmed by the judicial bias against customary law, the Court of Appeal warned against the judicial tendency of condemning people's customs as being repugnant to justice and morality without adequate empirical investigation.[52] In *Otieno v Ougo & another*, the Court of Appeal was presented with an opportunity to determine the acceptability or otherwise of certain customs of the Luo community.[53] The Court of Appeal found nothing repugnant about those customs relating to the Luo ancestral funeral rites. The Court of Appeal departed from the old colonial approach through which the repugnancy clause was administered on the basis of English standard of justice and morality, and instead attempted to formulate a new formula of determining the repugnancy clause. The court determined the repugnancy of the Luo customary practices in question using the standard of an "insider," stating: "There is nothing repugnant or immoral about any of the above customary laws ... We are persuaded from our perusal of the evidence from a summary of the ebb and flow of the argument ... that there is nothing in the Luo customary law which *a reasonable man in Kenya would find repugnant to justice and morality*."[54]

Unfortunately, that opportunity which the Court of Appeal could have seized to authoritatively guide the interpretation of the repugnancy clause was largely squandered. That celebrated case did no more than declare the applicability of the Luo customary law on burial in that particular set of facts and circumstances. The court did not go as far as to lay down a universal guideline that could be used to interpret and administer the repugnancy clause generally.[55] The interpretation of the clause is still left to the discretion of the courts, with the consequence that the jurisprudence in this area remains as uncertain as ever. It is partly for that reason that we do not share the view advanced by others that the *SM Otieno* case has given customary law its real place – a place of prominence – in Kenya's legal system.[56]

In the face of these difficulties and controversy in the administration of the repugnancy clause right through the colonial era to independent Kenya, one could

---

[52] *See Hassan v Nathu Mwangi Transporters & Others*, (1986) 1 K.A.R. 946, 954–955 (C.A.) (Kenya).

[53] Popularly known as the *SM Otieno* case and hereinafter also referred to as the *Otieno* case *or SM Otieno* case: *Otieno v Ougo & another*, (1987) K.L.R. 371 (H.C.) (Kenya); also *Otieno v Ougo & another*, (1987) 4 K.L.R. 407 (C.A.) (Kenya).

[54] *Otieno v. Ougo & another*, (1987) 4 K.L.R. 407, 424–425 (C.A.) (per Platt, Nyarangi & Gachuhi JJA) (emphasis added) (Kenya).

[55] We are of the view that despite the elusiveness of the repugnancy test, some general guidance by the courts is still a possibility, and would not be unlawful. Whereas the repugnancy of a custom should still be determined by reference to the ethnic community concerned, it is prudent to set general beacons to guide judicial discretion in the interpretation of the repugnancy clause.

[56] *See* Cotran, *supra* note 33, at 159–161.

reasonably expect its repeal or amendment. Other former British colonies like
Ghana and Tanzania did repeal their equivalents of the repugnancy clause upon
independence. Kenya, however, has retained the clause in the form in which it
was inherited from the old colonial legislative instruments without even taking the
pains to adapt it to suit African values. Retaining the clause upon the attainment of
independence was a mistake, and its continued existence four decades after independence witnesses some stagnation and indifference in Kenya's juridical philosophy. The repugnancy clause is incompatible with a rational legal order, and as one
academic put it, "whichever way one looks at it, the 'repugnancy clause' is, in and
of itself, a most repugnant provision in our law."[57] The history and colonial origin
of this clause "remind one of those days when a judge had always to be on the look
out for the immorality or injustice 'inherent' in the customary laws of the colonized
peoples."[58]

The repugnancy clause gives the courts a discretion that is too wide and suscep-
tible to grave abuse. Judicial discretion is permissible in legal theory, but the trend
that the discretion has taken with regard to the repugnancy clause is particularly
indicative. Rather than let the society develop at its own pace – shedding negative
values and retaining the values it holds dear – there has been a deliberate policy
toward using the repugnancy clause to force "modernity" down the throats of the
society through the judicial process. This is out of tune with the modern trend,
which emphasizes the popular involvement of the people in upholding their needs
and aspirations, as opposed to the old process through which change was imposed.

5.3.3. *Customary Law as a Guide*

This condition, which may be referred to as the "guided by" clause of the Judicature
Act, provides that "[t]he High Court, the Court of Appeal and all subordinate courts
shall be guided by African customary law…."[59] The "guided by" clause has brewed
considerable controversy regarding its meaning and effect. The Judicature Act neither presents a definition nor prescribes the effect of the clause. It has been suggested that the word "guided" could have any of the following three meanings:

   (i) that the courts have an unfettered discretion on whether or not to apply cus-
       tomary law and, if they decide to apply customary law, they still have an
       unfettered discretion as to which customary rules to apply, and with whatever
       qualifications they think fit; or

---

[57] Okoth-Ogendo, *supra* note 48, at 144.
[58] S. C. Wanjala, *Conflicts of Law and Burial in Modern Kenya: An Introduction, in* THE SM OTIENO
CASE: DEATH AND BURIAL IN MODERN KENYA, *supra* note 4, at 105.
[59] Judicature Act, (1967) Cap. 8 § 3(2) (emphasis added). (Kenya).

   (ii) that the courts have no discretion whether or not to apply customary law, but they are bound to apply it, although they do not need to apply it in all its rigor and detail; or

  (iii) that the courts have no discretion; the courts must apply customary law in the prescribed cases, and they must apply it in full detail, save for that which is excluded by the repugnancy and inconsistency provisions.[60]

In our view, the third meaning is the more tenable one.

The Court of Appeal has interpreted the word "guided" as used in the clause to mean being "led by something,"[61] so that the courts must have in mind African customary law as the guiding light or principal law.[62]

The Court of Appeal's interpretation suggests a slightly higher status for customary law than has previously been thought. As guiding light or principal law, customary law should be considered superior to other laws. Unfortunately, that suggested supremacy in status of customary law has not been consolidated as it has not received subsequent adequate legislative or judicial backing. Instead, the guided-by clause has been interpreted as granting courts the discretion of determining whether or not to apply customary law in any particular case – even in respect of the category of cases to which it is applicable by virtue of the Judicature Act and the Magistrates' Courts Act.

In our view, the controversy around the guided by clause is rather superfluous, for all laws, written or unwritten, that are recognized in any legal system perform the function of guiding the courts in arriving at decisions one way or the other. The term "guide" and the phrase "guided by" are so plain and straightforward that they should simply be accorded equally plain and straightforward interpretation. The simple dictionary definition of the term "guide" is "a directing principle or standard."[63] Thus, a guide is simply a principle that directs or provides a basis for action in given circumstances. By providing that the courts shall be guided by customary law, the Judicature Act directs the courts to seek guidance from customary law and rely on it for direction and a basis of action. The clause uses the term "shall," which gives it a mandatory tone and suggests a firm instruction to the courts to apply customary law in appropriate cases. In this sense, customary law is no less than any other law, for, as previously stated, all laws provide a basis of decision making by the courts.

The apparent interpretation problem that has attended the meaning of this clause derives essentially from the misplaced perception that customary law should be

---

[60] A. N. ALLOTT, NEW ESSAYS IN AFRICAN LAW 133 (Butterworth 1970).

[61] Phillips, *supra* note 32, ¶ 792.

[62] *See id.*

[63] THE CONCISE OXFORD DICTIONARY OF CURRENT ENGLISH 525 (R. E. Allen ed., Clarendon Press 8th ed. 1990).

treated differently – a perception that owes its origin to the colonial administration. Indeed, the colonial judges had a reason for treating customary law differently for they were on a mission to relegate it to an inferior status, if not into extinction. The independent Kenyan judiciary should have avoided that line of thinking and taken the clause for what it is, namely for providing that customary law should direct the courts and be used as a basis of decision making. It is, undoubtedly, this status of customary law that the Court of Appeal in the *SM Otieno* case sought to assert when it interpreted the term "guided" as requiring the courts to use customary law as "the guiding light, as the principle law."[64]

Besides the colonial misconception, the order of arrangement and phrasing of section 3 of the Judicature Act may also have contributed to the difficulties in readily accepting that the guided-by clause was intended to accord a supremacy status upon customary law. Whereas subsection 1 of that section directs that "[t]he jurisdiction of the High Court, the Court of Appeal and all subordinate courts *shall be exercised in conformity* with" the Constitution, written laws, and received English law, sub-section 2 curiously changes the tone by adopting the "guided by" phrase. This has tempted some to think that the requirement to apply customary law as a guide was merely intended to allow the courts the discretion rather than require the application of customary law as a *mandatory* system of law.[65] Thus, according to this view, the courts are not bound to apply customary law.

In this sense, the guided-by clause has also had a downgrading effect on the status of customary law in the hierarchy of laws in Kenya's legal system. The discretion granted by this clause "confers the same discretion on all courts to depart from the rules of customary law as was formerly conferred only on courts in the British colonial system."[66] The discretion is so wide as to justify the court's departure from customary law even on flimsy grounds, including a departure on the ground that the court considers the particular rule to be "old-fashioned or out of date."[67]

5.3.4. *One or More Parties Must be Subject to or Affected by the Customary Law*

African customary law may be applied in Kenya only in cases in which one or more of the parties is either "subject to or affected by" the customary law. Thus, before the court can decide to be guided by customary law in any particular case or proceed to consider the substance or content of the customary law in question, the court

---

[64] Phillips, *supra* note 32.
[65] *See, e.g.,* Okoth-Okombo, *Semantic Issues, in* THE SM OTIENO CASE: DEATH AND BURIAL IN MODERN KENYA, *supra* note 4, at 96–97.
[66] *See* Ghai & McAuslan, *supra* note 5, at 375.
[67] *Id.; Talibu v. Executors of Siwa Haji,* (1907) 2 E.A.L.R. 33, 38 (Kenya).

must first determine this preliminary issue of whether at least one of the parties is either subject to or affected by the custom. The Judicature Act does not define these phrases, nor does it explain how one can become subject to or affected by a custom. It is apparent, however, that these phrases are intended to require some connection between the parties and the custom in question. It is such a connection that makes the person owe allegiance to the custom. The connecting factors can take various forms, principally birth, naturalization, or marriage. Thus, the test for applying customary law to any person is that person's membership or other connection with the ethnic community in which that custom obtains.

Being subject to customary law is a question of origin, affiliation, or descent, and it is patrilineal. A person becomes subject to customary law by reason of having been born into the community that recognizes that custom. In the *SM Otieno* case, the Court of Appeal held that a person becomes subject to customary law by virtue of birth. In explaining the deceased's connection with the customary law of his Luo ethnic community, the court stated that "Mr. Otieno [the deceased] having been born and bred a Luo remained a member of the Luo tribe and subject to the customary law of the Luo people."[68] Allegiance to customary law is patrilineal, so a person becomes subject to the customs of the ethnic community of his/her father. A child of an inter-ethnic marriage becomes subject to the customs of his/her father. A person can also become affected by customary law by reason of having some other connection, other than by birth, with that customary law. That connection often comes through marriage or naturalization into the community that recognizes the custom. Thus, a woman becomes affected by the custom of her husband even though she is not originally a member of his ethnic community. The Court of Appeal, in the *SM Otieno* case,[69] held that the appellant widow was affected by the Luo customary law despite her being of Kikuyu decent. This was because on marrying willingly into the Luo community, she submitted to the ways and customs of those people.

The provisions of both Article 7 of the East African Native Courts (Amendment) Ordinance 1902 and Article 20 of the Kenya Colony Order in Council 1921, which were the precursors to section 3(2) of the Judicature Act, applied customary law to cases in which both parties were natives. A non-African could be bound by customary law only if he chose to be so bound and that choice had to be signified in each particular case. Accordingly, where the rights of a native were affected by another party who was not a native, the native's rights and liabilities may have had to be determined by alien principles.[70] Through the affected-by clause, the Judicature Act has changed that position so that even a non-African may now become affected – and

---

[68] Phillips, *supra* note 32, at 415.
[69] *See id.*
[70] *See id.* ¶ 813.

therefore bound – by African customary law. It is no longer necessary to require the non-African to specifically consent in each case for him to be bound by the customary law. Such was the position, in *Case v Ruguru*,[71] where Mr. Case, a Briton, was held bound to comply with the Embu customary law on marriage when he purported to contract an Embu customary marriage with a woman of Embu ethnic origin. The court rejected the validity of the purported marriage for not having fulfilled the Embu customary requirement of the *ngurario* ceremony. According to the court, "[i]t is enough to say that, as there can be no valid marriage under [Embu] customary law if among other things this vital ceremony has not been performed, the court finds that ... a marriage between the plaintiff and the defendant under the custom never took place."[72]

5.3.5. *Consistency with Written Law*

Pursuant to the inconsistency clause, African customary law in Kenya can be applied only if it is not inconsistent with any written law. In this way, the inconsistency clause renders customary law inferior rather than complimentary to written law. Thus, the court can apply customary law in respect of any matter only after the court has taken into account the entire body of written law applicable in Kenya and concluded that the customary law is not contrary to any written law on the matter. The expression "written law" refers to the whole body of written law applicable in Kenya, namely the Constitution of Kenya, statutes enacted by the National Assembly of Kenya, by-laws, statutes of general application,[73] and other applicable Acts of parliament of the United Kingdom.[74] Once the court finds that the customary rule in question is inconsistent with any written law, the court will not hesitate to refuse to follow the rule of custom; the court will instead go by the provision of the written law.[75]

The inconsistency clause, by declaring inapplicable all customary laws inconsistent with written law, has had a further downgrading effect on the position of customary law in the hierarchy of Kenya's laws. The clause has considerably reduced

---

[71] (1970) E.A. 55 (Kenya).

[72] *Id.* at 59 (per Miller, J.).

[73] These are English statutes that were deemed to be of general applicability within the British Empire and that were, therefore, exported and applied in the colonies. They were exported into Kenya through the East Africa Order in Council, 1897.

[74] *See* Judicature Act, (1967) Cap. 8 § 3(1). (Kenya).

[75] For example, in *Wambua v Okumu*, (1970) E.A. 578 (Kenya), the High Court had no difficulty rejecting the Bagishu customary law on the basis of which the custody of a four-year-old girl had been awarded to her father on payment by him of cattle valued at Kshs 200 to the other party. The principle of the Bagishu custom was inconsistent with the principle of written law as contained in the then-Guardianship of Infants Act, Cap. 144 § 17 (Kenya), which required determinations of questions of custody to uphold the welfare and best interest of the child. The Guardianship of Infants Act was repealed and replaced by the Children Act in 2001.

the body of customary law that remains available for possible application by the courts.[76] As many statutes enacted by the National Assembly of Kenya or the concepts therein are essentially enactments of English law, such local statutes are no more than embodiments of imported law.[77] In the ultimate analysis, therefore, the inconsistency clause subordinates customary law to English law and a body of local statutes that are essentially premised on English law principles. It is, indeed, absurd that local law[78] remains subordinate to imported law[79] more than four decades after Kenya's independence merely because that foreign law is packaged in written form.

5.3.6. *Customary Law as Fact, Not Law*

Besides the continuing intrusion of English law, the status of customary law has been further compromised by the judiciary that, like the legislature, is bent on continuing the colonial legacy. In 1965, even after all the East African countries had attained independence from the colonial administration, the then-Court of Appeal for Eastern Africa still held that customary law is not law to be applied as such, but rather that customary law is a fact that must be pleaded and proved afresh in each particular case by the party who seeks to rely on it, and that, unlike other laws, customary law cannot be taken judicial notice of.[80]

In reliance on that landmark decision, which remains an authority in Kenya, the Kenyan courts have rejected the taking of judicial notice of customary law. That judicial position is actually contrary to the express provisions of the Evidence Act,[81] which requires the courts to take judicial notice of all laws, "written and unwritten."[82] The continued insistence on that position merely confirms the

---

[76] On the dimensions and effects of this, see discussion on the confinement of customary law to civil cases, *supra* Section 5.3.1.

[77] A good example is the written law on contracts, the Law of Contract Act, (1961) Cap. 23 (Kenya), the principal section of which merely provides as follows:

   Save as may be provided by any written law for the time being in force, the common law of England relating to contract, as modified by the doctrines of equity, by the Acts of Parliament of the United Kingdom applicable by virtue of subsection (2) of this section and by the Acts of Parliament of the United Kingdom specified in the Schedule to this Act, to the extent and subject to the modifications mentioned in the said Schedule, shall extend and apply to Kenya. *Id.* § 2(1).

[78] Namely, African customary law.

[79] Namely, the statutes of general application, the applicable statutes of the United Kingdom legislature, and English law principles embodied in local statutes.

[80] See *Kimani v Gikanga*, (1965) E.A. 753 (H.C.) (Kenya).

[81] Cap. 80. (Kenya).

[82] *Id.*

   § 60. (1) The courts shall take judicial notice of the following facts -
   (a) all written laws, and all laws, rules and principles, written or unwritten, having the force of law, whether in force or having such force as aforesaid before, at or after the commencement of this Act, in any part of Kenya. *Id.*

judicial inclination toward continuing the old colonial policy of trivializing and relegating customary law.

It is instructive to note that while the courts will take judicial notice of statutory law and such unwritten body of laws as "substance of the common law and doctrines of equity"[83] in keeping with the tenor of the provisions of the Evidence Act,[84] the same courts have refused to take judicial notice of customary law. Thus, whereas the sources of law prescribed in section 3(1) of the Judicature Act, including the "substance of the common law and doctrines of equity," are regarded as an authoritative body of law of which the court may take judicial notice, customary law is treated as though it were not law in the strict sense of the concept. This judicial practice is rather contemptuous and discriminatory of customary law.

Certain jurisdictions, however, have taken judicial notice of those customary laws that have become notorious by reason of repeated judicial proof. For example, in *Augu v Attah*,[85] the Privy Council accepted that customary law must be proved by expert evidence except in situations where a particular rule had "by proof in the courts, become so notorious that the courts take judicial notice of [it]."

5.3.7. *The Problem of Conflict and Ranking*

The question of rank is pertinent in resolving the riddle of the place of customary law in Kenya's legal system. Section 3 of the Judicature Act prescribes a hierarchical order in the binding force of Kenya's sources of law. The hierarchical supremacy of the Constitution of Kenya is clear,[86] and other written laws[87] rank immediately after the Constitution. The substance of the common law, doctrines of equity, and statutes of general application are then made subject to the Constitution and other written laws, in that order. African customary law is then detached and provided for in a different subsection. That customary law is confined to the detached subsection 2 suggests that the legislature intended that customary law should be the last in that hierarchy. It is inferior to all written laws as well as the other unwritten laws applicable in Kenya, including the English common law and doctrines of equity.

The courts have, indeed, interpreted section 3 of the Judicature Act in such a way as to give all body of received English law supremacy over African customary law.

[83] These are among the sources of Kenya's law. *See* Judicature Act, (1967) Cap. 8 § 3(1). (Kenya).
[84] *See* Evidence Act, Cap. 80 § 60. (Kenya).
[85] (1916) P.C. 43 (Kenya).
[86] Section 3 of the Constitution of Kenya declares the supremacy of the Constitution thus:
    This Constitution is the Constitution of the Republic of Kenya and shall have the force of law throughout Kenya and, subject to section 47, if any other law is inconsistent with this Constitution, this Constitution shall prevail and the other law shall, to the extent of the inconsistency, be void.
[87] With the exception of the statutes of general application, which are provided for differently. *See* CONSTITUTION, § 3 (2008) (Kenya).

That was the implicit view of the High Court in the *SM Otieno* case: "I researched on English authorities based on the common law, which deal with burial, but was unable to find any, nor were any referred to me … *That then leaves us with personal law which in this case, is the customary law*."[88]

The judge was clearly suggesting that his first option was English law and that had he found the English law dealing with the subject then he could have applied it, and that he applied customary law only because neither the common law nor other laws provided for the subject of the dispute. The High Court had earlier put it even more bluntly in *I v I*: "sub-s. (2) [of section 3 of the Judicature Act] is but a gloss upon sub-s. (1) [thereof] and that in any case it shows that a written law is to be preferred to customary law even where the parties or one of them is subject thereto."[89]

Perhaps what is most unfortunate is that customary law remains inferior to the common law of England and doctrines of equity.[90] Considering that English common law, doctrines of equity, and African customary law are all unwritten bodies of law, African customary law – being the indigenous law – should have been afforded superiority over the common law. The common law of England is itself an embodiment of the laws that the English judges have recognized and declared from time to time out of the habits, practices, and customs of the English people.[91] Thus, the common law is derived from the customs of the English people, just as African customary law in Kenya is derived from the customs of the people of Kenya. Subordinating customary law to the English common law epitomizes a mixture of legislative neo-imperialism and indifference considering that, by so doing, the legislature has limited the people's enjoyment of their indigenous customs while promoting foreign customs.

5.4. A QUESTION OF DESIGN OR INDIFFERENCE?

Customary law has remained under siege since the colonial times. It has found itself in a fierce conflict of laws in which it has emerged as the sacrificial lamb at the altar of what appears to be a government policy of modernization of the legal system. Customary law has been perceived as the stumbling block to the pursuit of that modernization. The present siege of customary law is the crystallization of that deliberate sacrifice.

---

[88] (1987) K.L.R. 371(H.C.) (emphasis added) (Kenya).
[89] (1971) E.A. 278 (H.C.) (Kenya).
[90] *See* J. W. Van Doren, *African Tradition and Western Common Law: A Study in Contradiction, in* THE SM OTIENO CASE: DEATH AND BURIAL IN MODERN KENYA, *supra* note 4, at 127 n.2.
[91] *See* W. B. ODGERS, THE COMMON LAW OF ENGLAND (Sweet & Maxwell 1920). *See also* J. INDERMAUR, PRINCIPLES OF THE COMMON LAW (Stevens & Heynes 1901).

The continued existence of customary law in Kenya's legal system is based on factors that scarcely involve any direct government interventions. Customary law is sustained mainly by its own resilience that derives from its deep roots within the Kenyan society, its closeness to the local populations, and the society's uncertainty about what might happen if customary laws were to be phased out entirely. Alongside the foregoing is the spirit and tendency of the local populations to fight back against moves aimed at disturbing that which they are accustomed to and that they trust. That was the spirit and tendency that underpinned the struggle for independence and the subsequent public rejection of government initiatives against customary law that came in the late 1960s when the president of Kenya appointed the Commission of Inquiry into Marriage and Divorce 1967[92] and the Commission of Inquiry into Succession Laws 1967.[93]

The appointment of those two commissions of inquiry marked the most deliberate step in the post-colonial era towards a total phasing out of customary law. The two commissions of inquiry were given specific terms of reference to inquire into the marriage and divorce and succession laws of Kenya with a view to drafting a unified comprehensive code that would apply to all persons in Kenya in the spheres of marriage, divorce, and succession and replace the customary laws and special religious laws that have been operating in those fields. The government's real intention was to come up with statutory laws on those subjects – the only remaining substantive subjects of customary law – thereby extinguishing the applicable customary laws.

The inquiries encountered serious resistance, especially from the Kenyan Muslims. The report and recommendations of the two inquiries were criticized for being biased in favor of women and for negating African customary values. As a result of that public opposition, the many attempts to enact the marriage and divorce recommendations through the Marriage Bill have not seen the light of day, and the Marriage Bill has remained on the shelf since 1970. Similarly, the recommendations of the inquiry on the law of succession never had a smooth sailing, as the Succession Bill failed to pass through parliament when it was first tabled in 1970. Although the Succession Bill was passed as the Law of Succession Act[94] upon its second tabling in the National Assembly in 1971, its coming into force was delayed until 1981 due to persistent public opposition that saw the Muslim community lead a delegation to petition the president of Kenya. As a result, the Kenyan president directed the attorney-general to consult the Muslims to see if a solution to their grievances could

---

[92] This Commission of Inquiry was appointed on March 17, 1967. Gazette Notice No. 1261, *The Kenya Gazette*, Vol. 74, No. 18 (Government Printer).

[93] This Commission of Inquiry was appointed on March 17, 1967. Gazette Notice No. 1095, *The Kenya Gazette*, Vol. 74, No. 18 (Government Printer).

[94] (1981) Cap. 160. (Kenya).

be found. No solution has been found so far, and the Act has remained in operation since its commencement in 1981.

The real place of customary law in Kenya's legal system remains unresolved – a situation that smacks of underdevelopment in Kenya's juridical philosophy and signifies an indifference toward the development of customary law in Kenya. The apparent indifference is sustained by a careful design through which the government is either unwilling or is apprehensive to take any substantive action on customary law. One gets the impression that there is a freeze on the development of customary law. Since the enactment of the Judicature Act in 1967, followed closely by the unpopular moves of creating the inquiries of 1967, the government has not taken any real initiatives to signal a policy on customary law. In fact, nothing visible is being done about customary law today.

The public rejection of the work and recommendations of the commissions of inquiry of 1967 seems to have cowed the government into reluctance about taking critical steps on matters of customary law, lest it evokes a repeat of public censure. One is tempted, however, to argue that the government policy manifested in the establishment of the two inquiries still reigns supreme. That apparent indifference is not by accident; rather, it is itself part of a wider government design of pursuing that policy toward phasing out customary law and replacing it with what it perceives to be "modernly" acceptable. The government looks forward to the day when customary law will fizzle away without triggering another public controversy, or the day when customary law will have been completely phased out through the ongoing legislative initiatives that constantly supplant rules of customary law.

In the meantime, the government pays lip service to customary law by purporting to be pursuing a policy of "Africanization" of the legal system; yet all overt acts by the government point toward a policy of modernization. These realities render the future of customary law highly unpredictable.

With the constant increase in legislative intervention in virtually all spheres and the absence of meaningful government initiatives on improving the status of customary law, customary law is being boxed into a tight and rather barren corner where it is limited to civil matters of limited significance. Failure to promulgate any comprehensive rules on customary law since the Judicature Act in 1967 has led to a stagnation in the development of customary law. The hostile and unsupportive government policy, which favors the more liberal and western-styled law, poses considerable challenges to the competitiveness of customary law.

On the face of it, one gets the impression that either the government means well for customary law or that the government does not want to disturb the regime of customary law. Far from it. All that the government has done is to change its tactic in the deliberate campaign against customary law – a well-designed campaign that traces its roots to the beginning of the colonial administration in Kenya in the nineteenth century. One of the lessons that the government learned out of the protests to the findings and recommendations of the Marriage and Divorce and Succession laws Commissions of Inquiry of 1967 was the risk in initiating an overt and substantive campaign against customary law. The new tactic is slow and tacit but systematic as customary law is progressively ousted from the spheres in which it previously reigned. Customary law is facing a silent extinction. As of today, the customary law that remains applicable is a rather faint shadow of what existed in pre-colonial Kenya. The future is even more uncertain.

5.5. CONCLUSIONS

That the Constitution of Kenya and the Judicature recognize the validity of customary law gives customary law the right of place in Kenya's legal system. It should be at par with the other regimes of law applicable in the country. The apparent stagnation that has characterized the development of customary law since the 1960s is deceptive as the government perpetuates the anti–customary law bias that was inherited from the colonial administration amidst a citizenry that still embraces customary law to a great extent. That apparent freeze is concealing very deliberate government designs against customary law and it ought to be disturbed so that the government is stirred into action.

The legislature ought to properly direct the path of the future development of customary law by reaffirming the place of customary law and legislating proper guidelines for its progressive application. The Judicature Act should be amended to place customary law at par with the other regimes of law and superior to the English common law. Such initiative by the legislature will send a signal to the judiciary too and, possibly, re-orient the negative judicial tendency.

Clearly, customary law is still determined to fight on. That customary law has survived so many odds since the colonial times gives one confidence in predicting that that African customary law will remain a feature in Kenya's legal system into the unforeseeable future.

6

Putting Old Wine in New Wine Skins

The Customary Code of Lerotholi and Justice Administration in Lesotho

Laurence Juma

6.1. INTRODUCTION

Although the interaction between the western colonizers and the African indigenous populations in the early eighteenth and nineteenth centuries produced responses that were mostly inimical to the development of African customary law, the thrust of the onslaught against its principles was somewhat diminished by political considerations. Undoubtedly, the significance that African customary law acquired during this period was a measure of the purpose that the colonial project found in it. In the British-controlled areas especially, such a purpose was coterminous with the demands of indirect rule that saw the native administrators, mainly the chiefs, being coopted into the colonial civil service, and dualism being entrenched into the legal system. Nonetheless, the colonial project, based on racist and pluralistic foundations, still manifested clear goals of civilizing the "native" and gradually phasing out what it perceived to be "primitive" law.[1] To achieve the dual purpose of civilizing the native and, at the same time, maintaining the political hold on the territories, the colonial project adopted an approach that sought a reinvention of African customary law so that its principles could support the smooth operation of the colonial justice systems. In some countries, this necessitated the codification or restatement of customary laws.[2]

---

[1] See, e.g., Laurence Juma, *From Repugnancy to Bill of Rights: African Customary Law and Human Rights in Lesotho and South Africa*, 21 SPECULUM JURIS 88, 88–112 (2007); Dani Nabudere, *Towards the Study of Post Traditional Systems of Justice in the Great Lakes Region of Africa*, E. AFR. J. PEACE & HUM. RTS 1 (2002).

[2] Codification here is used to refer to the inclusion of customary rules in the judicial code, and not the haphazard collection of rules or the documentation of court rules relating to matters of custom. *See* M. CHANOCK, LAW CUSTOM AND SOCIAL ORDER (1985). The examples of codification projects include the Natal Code of Zulu Law contained in Rule 151 of October 9, 1987, *Reg Gaz* 4136. In Act 6 of 1981, Kwa Zulu issued its own code of Zulu law, amended by Act 13 of 1984 and then revised and reissued in KwaZulu GN 36 of 1985. On the origins of the Code, see T. McClendon, *Tradition and Domestic Struggle in the Courtroom: Customary Law and Control of Women in Segregation-era Natal*, 28 INT'L J.

That codification and restatement did not fair well is not in doubt.[3] Even in terms of numbers, there were far too few countries where codification was carried to completion. In a majority of African states, customary law remains largely unwritten, informal, and often difficult to ascertain.[4] In other cases, the attempts were wrought with contradictions and difficulties and even abandoned altogether.[5] In those few cases where codification was completed, lasting legacies of strict traditional edicts were created and these have become permanent features of the legal systems in these countries. But what has been the effect of such codified law on the general development of African customary law? Alternatively, can one safely argue

AFR. HIST. STUD. 527 (1995); THE LAWS OF LEROTHOLI (Basotho National Council ed., 1903) [which is the subject of discussion here]. For the self-stated legal texts produced by traditional authorities in northern Namibia, see V.V. PALMER & S.M. POULTER, THE LEGAL SYSTEMS OF SESOTHO 101–127 (Michie Charlottesville 1972); MANFRED O. HINZ, CUSTOMARY LAW IN NAMIBIA: DEVELOPMENT AND PERSPECTIVE 91 (Centre for Applied Social Sciences 1996). There are several examples of restatement projects. These include, E. Cotran, *Kenya I: The Law of Marriage and Divorce, in* 1 RESTATEMENT OF AFRICAN LAW (A.N. Allott ed., Sweet & Maxwell 1968); E. Cotran, *Kenya II: The Law of Succession, in* 2 RESTATEMENT OF AFRICAN LAW (A.N. Allott ed., Sweet & Maxwell 1969); J.O. Ibik, *Malawi I: The Law of Marriage and Divorce, in* 3 RESTATEMENT OF AFRICAN LAW (A.N. Allott ed., Sweet & Maxwell 1970); J.O. Ibik, *Malawi II: The Law of Succession, in* 4 RESTATEMENT OF AFRICAN LAW (A.N. Allott ed., Sweet & Maxwell 1971); A.C. MYBURGH, INDIGENOUS CRIMINAL LAW IN BOPHUTHATSWANA (J.L. Van Schaik 1980); M.W. PRINSLOO, INHEEMSE PUBLIEKREG IN LEBOWA (J.L. Van Schaik 1983); A.C. MYBURGH & M.W. PRINSLOO, INDIGENOUS PUBLIC LAW IN KWA NDEBELE (J.L. Van Schaik 1985); N.N. Rubin, *The Swazi Law of Succession* 9 J. AFR. L. 90 (1965); A.P.K. Kludze, *Ghana I: Ewe Law of Property, in* 6 RESTATEMENT OF AFRICAN LAW (A.N. Allott ed., Sweet & Maxwell 1973). Apart from codification and restatements, there were also commissions instituted to gather pieces of traditional rules and compile them for use by the colonial administrators. *See, e.g.,* ISAAC SCHAPERA, A HANDBOOK OF TSWANA LAW AND CUSTOM (Oxford University Press 1938); ISAAC SCHAPERA, THE CAPE COMMISSION ON THE LAWS AND CUSTOMS OF THE BASOTHOS (1873).

[3] *See, e.g.,* T.W. Bennett & T. Vermeulen, *Codification of African Law,* 24 J. AFR. L. 206 (1980); W. Twinning, *The Restatement of African Customary Law: A Comment,* 1 J. MOD. AFR. STUD. 221, 228 (1963); WILLIAM L. TWINNING, THE PLACE OF CUSTOMARY LAW IN THE NATIONAL LEGAL SYSTEMS OF EAST AFRICA (University of Chicago School of Law 1964); Brett L. Shadle, *Changing Traditions to Meet Current Altering Conditions: Customary Law, African Courts and the Rejection of Codification in Kenya 1930–60,* 40 J. AFR. HIST. 411 (1999).

[4] *See* A.N. Allot, *The Judicial Ascertainment of Customary Law in British Africa,* 20 MOD. L. REV. 244, (1957). Because of this difficulty, some countries have enacted legislation to assist the court in ascertaining customary law. In Botswana, for example, the Common Law and Customary Law Act, c. 16:01, § 7(2) provides that: "If any court entertains any doubt as to the existence or content of a rule of customary law relevant to any proceedings, after having considered such submissions thereon as may be made by or on behalf of the parties, it may consult reported cases, text books and other sources, and may receive opinions either orally or in writing to enable it to arrive at a decision in the matter." The two South African cases of *Maqovuka v Madidi,* 1911 NHC 132, and *Nomantunga v Ngangana,* 1951 NAC 342, established the principle that the burden of proving customary law was on the person who sought to rely on it. The courts, however, seemed to prefer expert opinion of traditional rulers, those on whom the task of administering traditional rules was bestowed.

[5] *See generally,* E. Azinge, *Codification of Customary Law: A Mission Impossible, in* TOWARDS RESTATEMENT OF NIGERIA CUSTOMARY LAW (Yemi Osibajo & Kalu Awa eds., Lagos, Ministry of Justice 1991).

that codification has brought some coherency in the application of customary law in situations where codified law exists? This chapter attempts to answer these concerns by examining the experiences in the Kingdom of Lesotho, a small landlocked country completely surrounded by South Africa. In Lesotho, the essence of customary law is often projected as the sum total of the Basotho Code of customary law known as the Code of Lerotholi or Laws of Lerotholi.[6] The Code was promulgated in 1903 and has survived the various political changes that the country has experienced. Throughout this period, however, it has suffered alterations and erosion of its rules, as statutes and other governmental legislation came into being, especially in the period after independence. But this notwithstanding, the Code still commands a reasonable political and social constituency. It is also constantly used by the courts to decide matters of customary law even though its legal status is somewhat ambiguous.

Based on the hypothesis that codification has created an imbalance between what is generally perceived as modern and progressive legal institutions and the domain of traditional rules and custom, this chapter will examine how the system of codified law emerged in Lesotho by mapping out the path of the evolution of customary law from the colonial era to present day. It will seek to isolate the composite factors that led to codification and to analyze the content of the laws themselves and the variations and alterations that they have suffered in the evolution of common law and statutes since independence. Finally, this chapter will attempt to critically evaluate the relative importance of the Code to the development of political and legal institutions in Lesotho as a lesson to other plural societies in Africa.

6.2. CUSTOMARY LAW IN A CONTESTED POLITICAL SPACE: A HISTORICAL PERSPECTIVE

The origin of a unified Basotho nation is often associated with rise of King Moshoeshoe, who in the 1800s gathered the various groups fleeing Amazulu invaders and transformed them into a mighty kingdom.[7] After Moshoeshoe's death in

---

[6] The *Code of Lerotholi* is used here interchangeably with *Laws of Lerotholi*, but they both mean the same thing. In the current written version of the customs and laws of Basotho, the word "Code" has been dropped.

[7] *See generally*, E. ELDRIDGE, A SOUTH AFRICAN KINGDOM: THE PURSUIT OF SECURITY IN THE 19TH CENTURY LESOTHO (Cambridge University Press 1993); THE MFECANE, RECONSTRUCTIVE DEBATES IN SOUTHERN AFRICAN HISTORY (C. Hamilton ed., Witwatersrand University Press 1995). There is some controversy on whether the Sotho as a group, or a people, existed as such before Moshoeshoe. Ellenberger and MacGregor argue that the word "Basotho" comes from the nickname "Abashunto" (a Swazi word) given to the people of the Highveld who looked different from the lowlanders. It was King Moshoeshoe who used the word as a unifying term for his new kingdom. *See* ELLENBERGER & J.T. MCGREGOR, HISTORY OF THE BASOTHO: ANCIENT AND MODERN (1912).

1870, the Territory of Basutoland was annexed by the Cape Colony[8] in 1871 and then became a British Crown Colony in 1884. Basutoland became the Kingdom of Lesotho upon independence from the United Kingdom on October 4, 1966.

The significance of Moshoeshoe goes beyond his achievements in creating the Basotho nation. Recent accounts idolize him as the most vivid symbol of national unity.[9] This symbolism has survived in institutions that were associated with his rise to power. During his reign, traditional institutions of judicial and political governance were reinvented and elevated to acquire a national character. The Chieftaincy (*Borena*), for example, became institutionalized into a state system. And from it, tangible forms of authority became explicit.[10] Also, the traditional court system, the *Khotla* (or the chief's court) and *Pitsos* (the general council of the people), became intimate to the whole community and formed an integral part of the society's political and social structure.[11] These courts administered the law of custom that found legitimacy in the exercise of chieftain authority, although its application was still as variegated as the courts themselves. However, as the nation's administration became more centralized, so did its judicial structure. Thus, a legal system predicated upon loose forms of social organization and applied haphazardly throughout the nation became anathema to sustained leadership of the *Borena*. In the post-Moshoeshoe days, there were changed political and social conditions rendered by the arrival and accommodation of the missionaries, the colonial hegemony, and the contest within the traditional ruling elite. As a result, a systematic approach to defining the limits

---

[8] The Cape Colony was established in part of what is now South Africa by the Dutch East India Company in 1652. It became a British colony in the 1800s.

[9] A considerable amount of literature on King Moshoeshoe now exists. This includes, for example, L. THOMPSON, SURVIVAL IN TWO WORLDS: MOSHOESHOE OF LESOTHO 1786–1870 (Clarendon Press 1975); P. SANDERS, MOSHOESHOE, CHIEF OF THE SOTHO (Heinemann 1975); S. J. JINGOES, A CHIEF IS A CHIEF BY THE PEOPLE (Oxford University Press 1975); I. HAMNETT, CHIEFTAINSHIP AND LEGITIMACY (Routledge & Kegan Paul 1975). *See also* L.B.B.J. MACHOBANE, GOVERNMENT AND CHANGE IN LESOTHO 1800–1966: A STUDY OF POLITICAL INSTITUTIONS (Palgrave Macmillan 1990).

[10] *See, e.g.*, Ian Hamnett, *Koena Chieftainship Seniority in Basutoland*, 35 (3) J. INT'L AFR. INST. 241 (1965).

[11] *Khotla* proceedings were conducted in the chief's court. The crimes were tried in a traditional setting characterised by popular participation. Although it was the chief's prerogative to impose sentence, the process allowed parties to call witnesses, lead evidence, and cross-examine witnesses. *See* EUGENE CASALIS, THE BASUTOS 226 (1992). The noun *Pitso* is taken from the verb *ho bitsa*, which means "to call." The *Pitsos* conducted its affairs in a traditional fashion. Usually, the agenda at *Pitso* would be presented by one of the counselors and all other members would be invited to voice their opinion. The discussions were carried in the "spirit of freedom of speech and openness." After the deliberations, the chief would offer his deciding opinion, which would then be adopted as the position of the *Pitso* on the matter. Voting was not permitted and no system of checks and balances existed to contest the chief's views or moderate his opinion. *See* Sandra Wallman, *Pitso: Traditional Meetings in a Modern Setting*, 2 CAN. J. AFR. STUD. 167 (1968).

of customary authority and law became a project of immense interest to the various constituencies that competed for power.

It is useful to situate the discourse on codification of Basotho customary law within the historical development of traditional and political institutions. This is because normative activity, even within the context of a traditional society, is a product of intense competition among institutions of power. In the case of Lesotho, the competition began at the formative days of the nation but intensified with the establishment of colonial rule. In the trajectory, three levels of contests became manifest. The first was the competition between traditional institutions and the colonial authority, where the shift in power from the traditional chiefs to the agents of British colonial authority put strain on traditional institutions and sought to diminish their normative roles. The contests at this level invariably defined the contours of Lesotho's political history and were very much the force behind the colonial legal reform agenda. The second level of contest consisted of the many scrambles among the chiefs themselves for control of territory and population.[12] The policies of indirect rule introduced by the British abetted the abrupt usurpation of the authority of smaller chiefs in favor of *Morena e Moholo*, the Paramount Chief, thereby disturbing the balance of power in the hierarchy of traditional leadership and precipitating some discontent.[13] The third level of contest arose from the political challenges coming from the commoners. The greatest complaint was against corruption and uneven application of the law by the chiefs.[14] Although the last two levels are less canvassed in most historical accounts, they also affected normative developments during this period.

Given the nature of these contests, one might argue that traditional institutions, which had been the pillars of the Basuto nation before the British arrived, now constituted a field of contestation that later yielded to reorganization and reform. But the contests must be located within the larger historical framework that recognizes the contribution of all sectors of society toward the events that shaped the nation's destiny. Often, African social history of the nineteenth and twentieth centuries focuses on slavery and liberation struggles to give it a lineament of bitterness and human suffering emitted through the agency of colonialism.[15] No wonder that

[12] See Tim Quinlan & Malcolm Wallis, *Local Governance in Lesotho: The Central Role of Chiefs, in* Grassroots Governance? Chiefs in Africa and Afro-Caribbean 145 (Donald I. Ray & P. S. Reddy eds., University of Calgary Press 2003).
[13] *Morena* comes from the Sotho word *rena*, which means tranquil or prosperity. Thus, *Morena* signifies the responsibility of ensuring peace and public safety. See Eugene Casalis, The Basothos or Twenty Three Years in South Africa 228 (James Nisbet & Co. 1861).
[14] S. Rugege, *The Struggle over the Restructuring of the Basotho or Chiefs Courts in Lesotho: 1903–1950,* 3 Lesotho L.J. 159, 163 (1987).
[15] *See, e.g.,* the much publicized work by Eugene Genovese, Roll, Jordan, Roll: The World the Slaves Made (Pantheon Books 1974). *See also* Klaas van Walraven et al., *Rethinking Resistance in African History: An Introduction, in* Rethinking Resistance: Revolt and Violence in African History 1–40 (Jon Abbink, Mirjam de Bruijn & Klaas van Walraven eds., Koninklijke Brill 2003).

most studies that have sought to discover and interpret African experience during the colonial period have been based on a "resistance paradigm," thus magnifying the role of the European in shaping culture, politics, and law. Although it could be true that colonialism with all its injustices, racism, oppression, and genocide lends itself to this paradigm, the discourse on African experience and institutional development is incomplete without bringing into the fold broader themes of societal change predicated on class struggles, the participation of the so-called faceless masses, and competing economic forces.[16] Indigenous resistance to colonial rule would then be located within the broader understanding of societies embroiled in multi-layered contests of a socio-political and economic nature. Realizing as we do that Africans under the yoke of colonialism had nuanced experiences that shaped their attitudes and actions, internal African politics emerging at the time should be viewed, not a separate paradigm, but as an inclusive one that takes on board complex strategies of negotiations, resistance, and even collaboration. Although a full range of human action could have spanned the distance between resistance and domination, in between the poles, there were indeed "a very crowded spectrum of human interests, goals and needs."[17] In the context of normative action, such interests, goals, and needs did occasionally overlap to support the production of rules that were of benefit to both spectrums. The codification agenda in Lesotho was brought forth by such a combination of interests, manifest in the interaction of the various forces competing for hegemony within the narrow political space. Whereas mapping out these interactions and the forces that spawned then may be a lengthy undertaking, far exceeding the limits of this chapter, an attempt will be made, nevertheless, to highlight those features in the trajectory of events that had relevance to the development of codified customary law.

6.2.1. *Emergence of a Legal System and the Recognition of Customary Law*

When Basutoland was declared a British Crown colony in 1884, the colonial administration took steps to create what may be regarded as the first legal system in the country. This was done through the General Law Proclamation of May 29, 1884. It provided for the retention of the general common law of the Cape Colony that had been applicable in Basutoland since 1871 and "customary law as administered" by

---

[16] For a more expanded discussion of the class divisions in the colonial era, see J. Lewis, *The Rise and Fall of the South African Peasantry: A Critique and Reassessment*, 11 J. S. AFR. STUD. 1 (1984); Fredrick Cooper, *Peasants Capitalists and Historians: A Review Article*, 7 J. S. AFR. STUD. 284 (1981). *See also* A. Isaacman & B. Isaacman, *Resistance and Collaboration in Southern and Central Africa 1850–1920*, 10 INT'L J. AFR. HIST. STUD. 31 (1977).

[17] Eric Allina-Pisano, *Resistance and the Social History of Africa*, 37 J. SOC. HIST. 187, 193 (2003).

the chiefs.[18] Section 2 of the proclamation made minor amendments to the existing law as follows:

> In all suits, actions, or proceedings, civil or criminal the law to be administered shall as nearly as the circumstances of the country will permit be the same as the law for the time being in force in the Colony of the Cape of Good Hope: Provided however, that in all suits, actions or proceedings in any court to which all of the parties are Africans, and in all suits, actions or proceedings whatsoever before any Basuto court, African law may be administered.[19]

It also provided that no Acts passed by the Cape parliament after its date were to become part of the law of Basutoland. The idea was that, henceforth, Basutoland was to be administered as a separate entity, its historical connection to the Cape notwithstanding.

By virtue of regulations 1, 2, 4, and 12, the Proclamation created a dual court structure in which the imported law was to be administered by the courts of the Resident Commissioner, whereas customary law was left in the domain of traditional chief's courts. Section 4, which established the chief's courts, stated as follows: "It shall be lawful for any native chief ... appointed by the Resident Commissioner to adjudicate upon and try such cases, criminal or civil and to exercise jurisdiction in such manner and within such limits as may be defined by any rules established by the authority of the Resident Commissioner." Thus, the chief's courts were authorized to apply African customary law on all matters, subject only to the limits placed on them by the British colonial authority. Appeals from the chief's court lay to the combined court of the Chief and the Assistant Commissioner, and then to the Resident Commissioner.[20]

The recognition of customary law and the chiefs' authority to administer it was a marked departure from the earlier colonial policy of complete disregard for traditional authority manifest in the period prior to 1881. Indeed, the proclamation indicated a new path in the British approach to dealing with Basuto chiefs. The

---

[18] Regulation 12 of Proclamation No. 2B (promulgated under cape proclamation No. 412 of 1877).

[19] See the current provision in Law Revision Proclamation, No. 12 of 1960, section 7(2).

[20] Section 8 provided in part that, "It shall be lawful for any person, a party to any suit or proceeding before any Native Chief ... to appeal from the decision of such Chief, in the first instance to a court composed of an Assistant Commissioner and of such chief and in the event of their disagreeing the Resident Commissioner shall decide the matter in dispute." *See also* Crawford, *History and Nature of the Judicial System of Botswana, Lesotho and Swaziland*, 86 SALJ 476–479 (1969); Crawford, *History and Nature of the Judicial System of Botswana, Lesotho*, 87 SALJ 76 (1970). In 1938, the Resident Commissioners courts were replaced by the High Court, and the Assistant Commissioners courts by the Magistrates Courts. Also in 1938, the Chief's Courts were to be replaced by the Central and Local Courts (Basotho Courts) after the enactment of the Native Courts Proclamation 62 of 1938. This law was also later amended by Native Courts Proclamation and Rules (Amendment) Regulation No. 12 of 1965 and the Central and Local Courts Proclamation 1965.

colonial authority "showed maximum regard for customary authority of chiefs, and restricted intervention to such measures as were necessary to satisfy the more simple requirements of local rule, such as collection of tax or preservation of order."[21] Apparently, the British realized that to achieve total subjugation of the Basuto people, the chiefs needed to be fully incorporated into colonial service.[22] In the same vein, the new colonial legal order sought to utilize customary law as a tool for social and political control – an "instrument of the power of an alien state and part of the process of coercion."[23] To be successful in this endeavor, African custom and tradition had to be reinvented, drained of all the regenerative and adaptive qualities, and reduced to rigid concepts and rules capable of being administered by the colonial judicial system. Thus, the colonial administration became privy to a process that has since been referred to as the "invention of tradition."[24] The enactment of the Code of Lerotholi was part of the reinvention process and must be understood in this way to engender a more accurate assessment of what its role has been in the Basotho society.

6.3. THE LAWS OF LEROTHOLI

What are the Laws of Lerotholi and how did they come about? This section will begin with the latter part of this question to provide context for the overall discussion here. Two rather complementary developments paved the way for reducing the whole morass of customary law into a single code. The first related to the overall weakness of the colonial administrative structure, evident in its inability to completely harness the authority of the chiefs.[25] In this regard, the British system of indirect rule that had been so successful in parts of East and West Africa was faulted for limiting intrusion by the British administrator into the native affairs while giving the Chiefs almost unfettered control over people and territory. One British report characterized the colonial administration in Lesotho as falling short of the indirect rule standards and constituting instead "a policy of non-interference, of proffering alliance, of leaving

---

[21] *See* M. Hailey, An African Survey Revised 1956: A Study of Problems Arising in Africa South of the Sahara 272 (Oxford University Press 1957).

[22] *See* Richard F. Weisfelder, *The Basuto Monarchy, in* African Kingdoms in Perspective 160 (Réne Lemarchand ed., Clarke, Doble & Brendon 1977).

[23] *See* Chanock, *supra* note 2, at 4.

[24] *See* T. Ranger, *The Invention of Tradition in Colonial Africa, in* The Invention of Tradition 211, 251 (E. Hobsbawm & T. Ranger eds., Cambridge University Press 1983).

[25] One will remember that the collapse of the first British administration in Lesotho after the Gun Wars of 1880–1881 was precisely because of the same reason. *See* S. Gill, A Short History of Lesotho 128–130 (National University of Lesotho 1993); Richard Welsfelder, Defining National Purpose: The Roots of Factionalism in Lesotho (1974) (unpublished Ph.D. dissertation, Harvard University) (on file with author).

two parallel Governments to work in a state of detachment unknown in tropical Africa."[26] Whether diminished control by the British colonial officers was due to apathy or sheer incompetence, it allowed for a greater influence of traditional legal institutions such as the *Pitsos* and *Khotla* on the management of native affairs, and thus greater authority for the chiefs.

The second factor is connected to the first. As Basutoland entered a phase in its legal and judicial history where the chiefs became the cornerstone of justice administration and the bulk of disputes among natives were dealt with by the chief's courts established under section 4 of the Proclamation, cracks began to emerge on the role of customary law in the overall maintenance of public order. This was because the chiefs applied the law inconsistently and corruptly. The problem was compounded by the fact that the chiefs were also colonial civil servants. This being the case, there was no clear-cut difference between the exercise of judicial and political functions. This allowed the chiefs to grossly mismanage their judicial prerogatives and thus evoked much criticism and dissent from the commoners.[27] There was also a worrisome trend of smaller chiefs supporting the commoners against the principal chiefs.[28] Combined with the ambiguity of customary succession procedures, the whole institution of chieftaincy became a chaotic one, incapable of furthering the colonial interests in the country. At the same time, the British, who themselves came from a judicial tradition in which veritable distinctions existed between judicial and political organs, found the chiefs' powers to be unwieldy and in need of streamlining. With an arbitrary traditional governing class, a growing political awareness among commoners, and a very uneasy colonial administration, the future of a Basuto nation seemed threatened.[29]

To restore faith in the colonial administration and ensure its continuity, the traditional justice system had to be reformed. This could only be feasible in a context in which the social and political institutions of a traditional character had hitherto exercised their authority. No wonder then that the British sought to establish a traditional authority (a Council of sorts) akin to the *Pitsos* but with a national character in the period after 1884. The need arose from the combined interest of the British and the chiefs to maintain their positions amid the rising tensions and contests emanating from below. From the chiefs' perspective, such a body was seen to carry the

---

[26] *See* Sir Alan Pim, Report on Financial and Economic Position of Basutoland 48–49 (1935).

[27] *See* Rugege, *supra* note 14, at 160–168.

[28] *See* Richard Weisfelder, *Early Voices of Protest in Basutoland: The Progressive Association and Lekhotla La Bafo*, 17 Afr. Stud. Rev. 397 (1974).

[29] There were also rivalries among the competing Christian religious groups. *See* D. Khama, *Reinterpretation of the Historical Development of the Church and State in Lesotho's Education Partnership*, 16 Lesotho L.J. 152, 152–155 (2006). This is quite apart from the contests between religion and tradition, which occurred at almost every level of society.

promise of evolving norms and structures of justice administration that would reflect their true way of life and set them apart from the western influence. This would also allow them some autonomy in the exercise of judicial and legislative functions. The British, on the other hand, supported the formation of the Council because they thought it would perform advisory functions only. This divergence of opinion was to be the Council's greatest challenge.

6.3.1. *The Basutoland National Council* (Lekhotla La Lesotho La Sechaba)

The initial overtures to establish such a council came from the British but got immediate support from the paramount chief. In 1884, the newly appointed Resident Commissioner of Basutoland asked the High Commissioner for authority to establish a Council of Advice that would be comprised of chiefs and headmen. His initial recommendation was that the chiefs be nominated by the paramount chief, who was Letsie at the time, upon recommendation by the Resident Commissioner. Letsie accepted the idea in March 1886, but the Council was not established immediately due to the disagreements within the monarchy. In 1889, the Resident Commissioner again revived the discussion by suggesting a different composition of the council. It was proposed that the council would meet once every year to: consider any fresh laws submitted to it in so far as it would affect the Basotho; consider questions connected with local affairs; receive account of the hut tax expenditures; and deliberate on serious national cases. Although Letsie accepted the proposal, several contentious issues arose to delay its official inauguration. The first related to the issue of appellate jurisdiction. The Resident Commissioner had suggested that he and the paramount chief should retain powers to appoint from the members of the council to act as a Court of Appeal. Letsie was not happy with this arrangement because he was disinclined to share his powers with the Resident Commissioner. Secondly, the paramount chief felt slighted because his demand to be allowed unfettered discretion in nominating members of the council had been ignored.

Letsie died in 1891 and his son Lerotholi took over. The intervening period saw great unrest in the territory, with several attempts made to overthrow Lerotholi; an outbreak of rinderpest disease that devastated the cattle economy;[30] and the Anglo-Boer war in Orange Free State diverting the attention of the British. Thus, attempts to establish the Council were delayed for another eight years.[31] Having consolidated his position, and convinced by the missionaries that a Council would strengthen

---

[30] *See generally* Pule Phoofolo, *Face to Face with Famine: The Basotho and the Rinderpest 1897–1899*, 29 J, S. AFR. STUD. 503 (2003).

[31] *See* Palmer & Poulter, *supra* note 2.

his leadership, Lerotholi again revived the debate. His request was acceded to by the Colonial administration in 1903, and a Council was duly established under the name Basutoland National Council (BNC). It was this Council that eventually prepared the first text of the Laws of Lerotholi.

The BNC operated without any legislative force until 1910, when requisite regulations were made by the Resident Commissioner and later approved by the High Commissioner. According to these regulations, the Council was composed of 100 members, 5 to be appointed by the Resident Commissioner, 20 principal chiefs, and the rest would be appointed by the *Morena e Moholo* taking into account the fair share of representation of all sections of the Basoto society. In its first session in July 1903, a proposal was made to compile the Basotho traditional laws and reconcile them with the "laws of Moshoeshoe." Already, there were sets of laws believed to have been handed down by the great King Moshoeshoe that were different from the laws of the British, and that could be recollected and written down by his descendants (sons of Moshoeshoe).[32] Some of these laws had been published and distributed by the Resident Commissioner for use by the chief's courts. The proposal was accepted and as result, the members decided to form a committee consisting of six chiefs and eighteen councilors to undertake this task. The committee deliberated on proposals made in respect of the various rules to be included. These rules were meant to curb what was viewed as the rapacious decisions of the chiefs, provide greater security of property and land tenure, and synthesize the judgments and opinions of respected chiefs. The Committee came up with a set of twenty-one rules, which they presented before the council on July 20, 1903. A further deliberation by the Council reduced those rules to eighteen. There is little literature available on how actual deliberations took place, except that they were carried out in the Basotho tradition of openness and accommodation.[33] Also, the Council debated the rules that were already being applied and merely sought to streamline them so that the arbitrary powers of the chiefs could be curbed.

6.3.2. *The Structure of the Code*

The Code in its initial form covered the following areas:

- succession to chieftainship;
- the supremacy of the paramount chief;

---

[32] *See* HUGH ASHTON, THE BASUTO 196 (Oxford University Press 1952). An example of these laws that were published include the laws on liquor (1854), witchcraft (1855), and trade (1859) and can be found in 2 BASUTOLAND RECORDS 1833–1868 133 (G.M. Theal ed., 1964).

[33] The British Resident Commissioner at the time, Herbert Sloley described the Council's deliberations as guided by the Basotho rule of free speech. *See* Palmer & Poulter, *supra* note 2, at 151 (citing BASUTOLAND ANNUAL REPORT 12 [1902]).

- rights of appeal from the decisions of the chiefs;
- chiefs' access to free labor;[34]
- appeals from the decision of paramount chief to the Resident Commissioner;
- application of due process to the custom of "eating up";[35]
- debtors rights;
- allocation of land;
- forfeiture of land use;
- procedure and summons to chief's courts;
- disposal of immovable property upon removal from a chief's jurisdiction;
- law on theft;
- seduction and abduction of unmarried women;
- limits, duties, and responsibilities of heirs;
- rights of widows and male children:
- compensation for physical injury;
- jurisdiction of Assistant Commissioners and Resident Commissioners Courts;
- use of firearms.

These laws, henceforth known as the Laws of Lerotholi, were printed and issued the following year. Since then, however, the laws have been significantly amended, while some portions have become obsolete with enactment of legislation.[36] The current version of it is, in substance, a merger of the original 1903 version with the subsequent amendments, rules, and orders made by the paramount chief;[37] together with the promulgated laws and revisions since 1922 on land tenure systems, chieftainship, administration of justice, family law, and customary delicts; and what was referred to as the "Native Court Rules" included in the English version by the colonial administration in 1946.[38]

---

[34] Failure to perform tribute labor (*letsema*) was made an offense. Law No. 4 provided as follows: "Be it enacted that the paramount chief or any chief may call the chiefs and sub-chiefs under them and their people, to take messages for them and to cultivate their lands. Any chief or man refusing such lawful summons shall be liable to a fine not exceeding ten shillings or in default two days work." But the laws also conferred to the citizens the right to be allocated land for cultivation and "safeguarded them from against unreasonable dispossession." *See* Palmer & Poulter, *supra* note 2, at 36.

[35] "Eating up" is an old custom where the chiefs could inflict the ultimate punishment of driving away an offender's animals and burning his huts. *See* P. DUNCAN, SOTHO LAW AND CUSTOM 70 (1960).

[36] For example, in 1922, revisions on the right of appeal from the chief's court, right of a maternal uncle to a portion of the *bohali* paid on marriage of his niece, elaboration on wills, and declaration of a public holiday on Moshoeshoe Day were made. *See* Palmer & Poulter, *supra* note 2, at 152; S. Rugege, *Chiefs Commoners and Land: Struggles over Control and Access to Land in Colonial Lesotho* 8 LESOTHO L.J. 33 (1992). Other significant revisions were done in 1938, 1946, and 1955.

[37] Pursuant to sections 8 and 15 of the Native Administration Proclamation No. 61 of 1938, the paramount chief was given authority to make rules necessary for "peace, good order and welfare" of his people. These rules were subject to approval by the High Commissioner. Native Administration Proclamation, No. 61 §§ 8, 15 (1938).

[38] *See* High Commissioners Notice No. 32 of 1946.

The Laws are in three parts. Part one is entitled "Declaration of Basuto Law and Custom" and consists of rules contained in the 1903 version together with the subsequent revisions. It contains provisions that relate to the authority of the paramount chief, succession to the chieftainship, land allocation, and inheritance. Succession is decreed to be by birth in accordance with age-long customary practice. Chieftainship devolves through the male lineage as in any other patriarchal society. One other provision in this part that draws a lot of discussion regarding land ownership and tenure is in Section 7. It gives the Chiefs the powers to allocate land in their area of jurisdiction to all their subjects "fairly and impartially."[39] The provision also places at the discretion of the chiefs the power to take away from such subjects land or lands that are not properly used.

Part two is basically the rules made subsequent to the 1938 Proclamation by the paramount chief with some sections taken from the 1903 version dealing with seduction and abduction. It deals with a number of unrelated issues that were thought to fall within the jurisdiction of the chief's courts under the 1938 Proclamation. These include issues of abduction; special grazing areas set aside by the chiefs (*Leboella*); payments of local rates; regulations relating to animals, sale of beer, use and cultivation of Dagga (Marijuana); circumcision and initiation schools; marriage; and defamation of character. The marriage rules are contained in Section 34 and affirm the requirement of *Bohali* (bride price) to be paid before a marriage can be completed. This and other requirements specified in this section are becoming very contentious, as revealed by jurisprudence discussed later. Part three of the Laws of Lerotholi contains orders by the paramount chief that relate to the maintenance of good order and welfare of subjects.[40] They cover a wide range of activities that in the past have created some friction and suspicion among the people such as the keeping of livestock and proper use of agricultural land.

6.3.3. *The Status of the Laws of Lerotholi*

The status of customary law in Lesotho has not been enhanced by the codified law. From the days of colonialism to the present, customary law has remained subordinate to the western law. One argument that could be made is that the codification process was never really complete. Had it been, the Laws of Lerotholi could have been reenacted as part of the Native Proclamation and affirmed by the colonial legislative authority. This could have raised its status in the hierarchy of norms to bring it on par with other colonial ordinances. Because this was not done, colonial courts treated these rules as nothing but a collection of customary rules that could only be

---

[39] The current modification to this rule occurred in response to the High Court decision in *Nkhasi v Shopane Nkhasi* 1955 HCTLR 39 (Lesotho).

[40] *See* S. POULTER, LEGAL DUALISM IN LESOTHO 6–7 (Morija Sesuto Book Depot 1979).

applied if they met the usual repugnancy tests. For example, in the famous case of
Bereng Griffith v Mantsebo Seeiso Griffith (The Regency Case)[41] decided in 1943, the
court described the Laws of Lerotholi as lacking "official recognition" but nevertheless helpful "on any question as to the existence or extent of any customary practice
amongst the Basuto people." In this decision, the court maintained that the Laws of
Lerotholi were not the equivalent of other written law but that their status remained
similar to that of any other unwritten customary law.[42] The matter involved a contest between a widow of the late Chief Seeiso and his brother over the position of
regency. If the court had applied the customary rules set out in part one of the Laws
of Lerotholi, it would have denied the widow the right to succeed. But the Court
relied on the standards set out in a South African case of *Van Breda v Jacob*[43] and
refused to accept customary rules on the grounds that they were not well and firmly
established and had no force of law, and therefore proceeded to pronounce in favor
of the widow.[44]

The effort to raise the status of Laws of Lerotholi became a matter of protracted
debate especially after the *Regency* case. In 1951, especially, the Council resolved
that they should recodify the *whole* of customary law and have it reenacted as
part of the colonial Proclamations. This move was quickly stifled by the Resident
Commissioner.[45] It was certainly not in the interest of the British that rules of custom should assume a status that was equal to other legislation passed by the colonial
legislative machinery. The colonial project could have been threatened if a set of
rules that contradicted its values were to become binding on all of its courts.

Ironically, independence did not change matters very much, and the debate on
the relevance and status of the Laws of Lerotholi is still vivid. Today, the debate can-
vasses a wide range of issues, from the mundane concerns on what constitutes custom in any particular circumstances to the more problematic choice of law issues.
However, the position of the Code in the hierarchy of norms has remained the same.
The Laws of Lerotholi are still regarded only as one of the sources of customary rules.
Invariably the courts have resorted to the Laws of Lerotholi to determine disputes
over inheritance, chiefly succession, seduction, marriage, and burial, which traditionally fall within the ambit of customary adjudication. Even so, the gap between
the applicable law and prevailing customary practices seems to be widening. For

[41] 1926–53 High Commission Territories L. Rep. (HCTLR) 50.
[42] The court stated: "No legislative authority or official recognition has been extended to this code;
nevertheless it is helpful, though not conclusive, on any question as to the existence or extent of any
customary practice among the Basuto people... It is in no sense written law. Its provisions though
reduced to print, do not emanate from any law giver." *Bereng Griffith v Mantšebo Seeiso Griffith (The
Regency case)* 1926–53 H.C.T.L.R. 50, 58.
[43] 1921 S. Afr. App. Division Rep. 330.
[44] *Bereng Griffith v Mantšebo Seeiso Griffith (The Regency case)* 1926–53 H.C.T.L.R. 50.
[45] *See* Palmer & Poulter *supra* note 2, 158.

example, Section 34 of the Laws of Lerotholi, which provides an entry point for any enquiry on the essentials and procedures for contracting customary marriage, has elicited unfavorable treatment from the courts.[46] For a customary marriage to be completed, the section requires three things: an agreement between the parties, an agreement between the parents, and payment of *bohali* in part or full. However, in the Basoto society like any other, men and women rarely feel constrained by such conditions in their relationships. Indeed, with the introduction of civil marriages under the *Marriage Act No. 10 of 1974*,[47] the respect for tradition among the younger educated couples is waning.[48] The courts have persistently shown reluctance to deny the existence of marriage simply because one of the customary law essentials has not been fulfilled. In *Manthabeleng Makara v Makoetla Makara & 3 Others*, for example, the *bohali* was discussed and not paid.[49] Yet the court still found that there was a valid marriage. In the court's view, a person could acquire the status of a wife under Basuto custom even without the fulfilling the requirements of the Laws of Lerotholi. What this means is that the tenets of a customary marriage today can not be defined through regimes of a codified customary law. Things have changed, and the limitations of these laws have become more than apparent. In an earlier decision of *Ramaisa v Mpholenyane*,[50] the court had made this observation: "I think a large part of the difficulties encountered in these cases have arisen because attempts have been made to reduce customs, but not all others, and in haphazard fashion, by a body lacking experience in the art of legislative drafting, into ink and paper with the result that the written words have assumed a quality of rigidity out of all proportion to their true meaning or significance."[51] Thus, it seems that the Laws of Lerotholi have been outpaced by the changes in the Basuto social life. This does not only affect marriage. Inheritance under the male primogeniture rule, which is sanctioned by the Laws of Lerotholi, is equally under threat. Claims based on human rights and gender equity have multiplied, and the legal system will be forced to respond. In all likelihood, it will follow the jurisprudence emerging from South Africa and other jurisdictions.[52]

---

[46] See Q. Letsika, *The Place of Sesotho Customary Law Marriage within Modern Lesotho Legal System* BOTSWANA L.J. 73, 77 (2005).

[47] The Marriage Act No. 10 of 1974, Section 42.

[48] The Courts have added to this conundrum by holding that customary marriages following a civil marriage will be null and void. See *Mokhutu v Manyaapelo* 1976 LLR 281 CA; *Makata v Makata* 1980–84 LAC 198; *Leoma v Leoma & Another* 2000–04 LAC 253; *Ntloana & Another v Rafiri* 2000–04 LAC 279.

[49] High Court Civ/App/471/2007 (Unreported).

[50] 1977 LR 138.

[51] *Id.* at 149. See also *Tseli Moeti v Tanki Lefalatsa & Another* 1991–2001 LLR 511, at 513 G & P, 514 D-H.

[52] See, e.g., *Bhe v Magistrate Khayelitsha* 1997 (2) SA 936 (1); *Shibi v Sithole* 1998 (2) SA 675 (2) and *South African Human Rights Commission v President of the Republic of South Africa* 2005 BCLR 1

Practice has also shown that the courts will only apply or refer to the Laws of Lerotholi when there is no legislation dealing with the issue before it. This confirms the earlier view that the Code has added no value to customary law rules in Lesotho. In the recent case of *Semahla v Lephole*, for example, the appellant in a dispute regarding customary succession to land alleged, *inter alia*, that since the nomination of heir to the deceased property had not been done in accordance with a 1992 statute, any rights to such property purportedly acquired under customary law as provided for in the Laws of Lerotholi, or any other rules, were invalid.[53] On this claim, the court avoided dealing with the more problematic question of which law to apply because it found an easier way of disposing of the matter. Apparently, the property that was the subject of dispute was in an urban area and thus fell outside the ambit of the statute, which only covered properties in rural areas.[54] Although the court upheld the rule of customary law in this instance, it was clear from the judgment that, had the land been in a rural area, the statute would have overridden the Laws of Lerotholi.[55]

In view of the foregoing, a few observations could be made regarding the status of the Laws of Lerotholi. First, they do not enjoy any preference above the informal rules of custom. Second, the court will only revert to them when there is no legislation or common law that is applicable. Third, nothing in the current legal system or practice seems to suggest that there might be any change toward enhancing the position of customary law. The current status of customary law, with hallmarks of informality and fluidity, seems to suit traditionalists and constitutionalists alike. Even outside the courts, the debate on status of the Laws of Lerotholi is muted. Not many voices are heard in support of the codified law. Moreover, those who live in urban areas and engage in modern commerce have no recourse in customary law and may not be unduly concerned about the future of the codified customary law. As discussed later in the chapter, despite these imperatives, the Laws of Lerotholi, and indeed other customary law rules, are unlikely to vanish anytime soon.

(CC); *Mthembu v Letsela* 2000 (3) SA 867 (SCA (3)). *See also* D. Ndima, The African Law of the 21st Century in South Africa 34 (2) CILSA 323 (2003); E. Knoetze, *Westernization or Promotion of African Women's Rights?*, Speculum Juris 105 (2006); W. Lehnert, *The Role of the Courts in the Conflict between African Customary Law and Human Rights*, 21 SAJHR 241 (2005); C.M.A. Nicholson, *The Realization of Human Rights within the Context of African Customary Marriages*, 2003 (3) Journal of Contemporary Roman-Dutch Law 373 (2003); Van der Meide, *Gender Equality v Right to Culture: Debunking the Perceived Conflicts Preventing the Reform of Marital Property Regime of the Official Version of Customary Law*, 116 SALJ 100–110 (1999).

53 *Semahla v Lephole*, 2000–04 LAC 69. The Statute in reference is Order 6 of 1992, which amends the Land Act 1979. Section 5 of the Order provides that such rights can only be acquired by persons designated by the deceased or his family.

54 This limitation is contained in section 7 of the Order.

55 *See Semahla v Lephole*, 2000–04 LAC 69, 75.

6.4. INFLUENCE OF THE LAWS OF LEROTHOLI ON GOVERNACE AND ADMINISTRATION OF JUSTICE

For the approximately one hundred years that the Laws of Lerotholi have existed, there has always been contest about its content – especially with regard to the powers that it conferred on some traditional institutions – and on its status in the hierarchy of norms. Ironically, it is these same contests that have ensured its survival. As protagonists fought against the excesses of the chiefs and their appropriation of powers derived from the Laws of Lerotholi, the same were amended or revised to further entrench its application. For this reason, the text of the Laws has invariably changed to accommodate the configuration of power and evolving administrative patterns. For example, Section 7, which deals with allocation of land and recognizes the power of the High Commissioner to ratify the appointment of chiefs and headmen, was adopted in 1938 to conform to the Native Administration Proclamation of the same year.[56] In the post-independence era, this power is now vested in the Minister in charge of chiefs (Home Affairs and Local Government) by the *Chieftainship Act*.[57] Though rarely acknowledged, these revisions/amendments have incrementally transfused custom into "modern" institutions of governance, to make tradition an integral part of the Basoto society. Thus, even without finding a direct reference to the Laws of Lerotholi in the new constitutional dispensation, its influence is felt through the application of a wider spectrum of customary jurisprudence. But this occurred irrespective of the status of the Laws of Lerotholi. In fact, as far as the agencies outside the court are concerned, the Laws of Lerotholi bear no distinct identity other than being part of the general customary law. The question then remains as to whether the Code is still influential. An examination of three aspects of Basuto society, namely the institution of chieftaincy, the structure of the legal system, and the practice of democracy, can help answer this question.

---

[56] Proclamation No. 61 of 1938 required that the chiefs and headmen be declared as such by the High Commissioner by notice in the Gazette. *See* Native Administration Proclamation, No. 61 (1938). In *Molapo v Molapao*, 1926–53 H.C.T.L.R. 210, the colonial courts considered the matter of assigning chiefs purely to be administrative. The consequence was that any chiefs not recognized by the High Commissioner could not exercise chiefly authority. *See Nkhasi v Nkhasi* quoted in J.C. 136/57. For a discussion of this case and others, see PATRICK DUNCAN, THE SOTHO LAWS AND CUSTOM 48–53 (Morija Publishers Lesotho 1960).

[57] Under section 14 of the Chieftainship Act 1968 (and as amended by section 2 of the Amendment Act No. 12 of 1984), the Minister has power to amend the names published through the High Commissioner's or government's notice immediately prior to the commencement of the Act. *See Maqetoane v Minister of Interior & Others*, 1985–89 LAC 71; *Ministry of Home Affairs and Local Government & Others v Sakoene*, 2000–04 LAC 332. In both cases, the Court of Appeal held that the omission of a person's name in the Gazette publishing his status as a chief did not hinder his assumption of office if there was evidence supporting his legitimate claim to the same.

6.4.1. *The Institution of Chieftancy* – Borena

As already stated, chieftaincy among the Basotho has been significant as the symbol of a nation's cohesion and identity from the days of Moshoeshoe. Moshoeshoe's chieftainship was a loose combination of individual leaders left alone to manage their affairs. In the subsequent years, the Basuto chieftaincy, like many others within the continent, succumbed to the demands of colonialism and European capitalism to become part of the colonial civil service. Despite its demonstrated propensity to embrace forces that protect its interests, and to vigorously fight those that threaten it, the chieftaincy was unable to withstand the colonial maneuvers, and thus lost the ability to assert its traditional authority over resources and subjects. The situation had become so bad that some scholars even predicted the extinction of chieftaincy institution in Africa by the turn of the century.[58] The institution reinvented itself, however, adapting to the new realities and renegotiating its role in a constantly changing cultural and political landscape. Today, chieftaincy in Lesotho could be considered as both traditional and modern, its power and relevance drawing from a cultural etiquette that has been hard to shake off. Its resilience, attributed by some to the "retraditionalization" of society and political manipulation, may have a deeper correlation with how nationalism and statehood have been constructed in the Basuto community.[59] For some, such resilience stems from the construction of national identity by the "conceptual unity of the chieftainship in Sotho consciousness."[60] For support, this argument draws on the practice of "placing," which ensured the spread of chiefs from lineage founders and later the maintenance of a leadership hierarchy in the colonial administration. From the chieftaincy, a political structure emerged that determined a national identity alongside the territorial boundaries of Basutoland. This engineering of national identity could not have been possible without drawing from a repertoire of acceptable traditional practices and custom, some of which were consolidated in the Laws of Lerotholi.

---

[58] *See, e.g.*, J.P. Warnier, *The King as a Container in Cameroon Grasslands*, 39 PAIDEUMA 303 (1993); A. Harriet-Sievers, *Igbo Traditional Rulers: Chieftaincy and the State in South Eastern Nigeria*, 33 AFRIKA SPECTRUM 57 (1998). For a discussion of contemporary theories on African chieftaincies, see Francis Nyamjoh, *Chieftaincy and Negotiation of Might and Right in Botswana Democracy*, 21 J. CONTEMP. AFR. STUD. 233 (2003); Comaroff, *Rules and Rulers: Political Processes in Tswana Chiefdom*, 13 MAN 1 (1978). *See also* D. LERNER, THE PASSING OF TRADITIONAL SOCIETY: MODERNISING THE MIDDLE EAST (Free Press 1958).

[59] *See, e.g.*, E. VAN ROUVEROY VAN NIEUWAAL, L'ÉTAT EN AFRIQUE FACE À LACHEFFERIE: LE CAS DU TOGO (2000); K. Linchwe II, *The Role of Chief can Play in Botswana's Democracy, in* DEMOCRACY IN BOTSWANA 99–102 (J. Holm & P. Molutsi eds., 1989). *See also* Quinlan & Wallis, *supra* note 12, at 146.

[60] Ian Hamnett, *supra* note 9, at 43.

The relationship between the chieftaincy and tradition has been a lopsided one, where the former only reverts to the latter when its position is threatened.[61] In the post-Moshoeshoe era, the chieftaincy position has manifested an enduring sense of disregard for fairness even within the confines of traditional law. The individual chiefs have constantly manipulated the rules to guarantee control and self-preservation. The 1903 version of the Laws of Lerotholi, for example, may have been seen as triumph of those who sought, so vigorously, the limitation and streamlining of the chiefs' powers and the succession procedures.[62] But even under the 1903 Laws, the commoners' grievances were moderated through a procedure in which the chiefs had enormous influence. The 1903 Laws also guaranteed for the chiefs free labor and complete control over resources. The chiefs continued to exercise judicial functions until 1938 when the chief's courts were abolished and local courts established in their stead.[63] Even then, however, the chiefs continued to wield tremendous influence over these courts as they were considered to be the custodian of customary rules. The subsequent amendments to the Laws of Lerotholi and the enactment of the Chieftainship Act 22 of 1968[64] may have curtailed some of these prerogatives, but they left intact the position of power and influence that the chiefs have continued to enjoy. This is partly because the chieftaincy structure established by the colonial administration was adopted by the post-independence government to a large measure. One could even argue that it is through the chieftaincy system that decentralized governance has been achieved in Lesotho. Moreover, both the Chieftainship Act of 1968 and the Constitution recognize hierarchical chieftaincy order and the chiefs' participation in executive and legislative organs of government. What is crucial to this discussion, however, is that so long as the chieftaincy maintains its prominence, the Laws of Lerotholi will continue to provide reference to the applicable custom and traditional rules.

---

[61]   In some instances, the chiefs even thought that they were above customary law. In the bizarre case of *Nkuebe* (J.C. 591/52), Chief Sempe claimed that he was not subject to the customary rule that requires the return of cattle upon divorce. D.M.L. Mojela rejected this claim and observed: "The custom means that which applies to the nation generally; it can not affect only a certain sector of it. . . . Law and custom should be the same throughout the nation." Although this might be the desirable position, it wasn't really the case. There were many privileges that exempted the chiefs from strict observance of the law.

[62]   The simple succession rule as stated by the LAWS OF LEROTHOLI (1903) was as follows: "The succession to chieftainship . . . shall be by right of birth. That is the first born male child of the first wife. If the first wife has no male issue, then the first born male child of the next wife in succession shall be heir to the chieftainship." See also *Khosi Molapo v Lepoqo Molapo*, 1973 High Court Civil Appeal No. 8 (discussed in Sebastian Poulter, *Marriage, Divorce and Legitimacy in Lesotho*, 1977 21 J. AFR. L. 66 [1977]). This rule was reenacted in section 10 of the Chieftainship Act of 1968. See Chieftainship Act (1968) (Lesotho).

[63]   The Native Courts Administration Proclamation, No. 62 (1938).

[64]   Chieftainship Act, No. 22 (1968) (Lesotho).

6.4.2. *Response of the Legal System*

As discussed earlier, the General Law Proclamation of 1884 that allowed for the application of customary law in Basutoland set the stage for the reinvention of custom by the colonial administration and their handmaidens, the Christian missionaries.[65] The introduction of customary law as a component of the colonial judicial enterprise and the sustenance of it at an inferior level arguably constitute evidence of its utility as a structure of extra economic and political coercion. Using the chieftaincy institution, the official customary law was nurtured and later codified. With codified law, the wieldy exercise of judicial powers by chiefs became moribund. The 1938 Native Courts Proclamation abolished the traditional chief's courts and placed the jurisdiction of administering customary law on statutory courts. In 1965, the Native Courts Proclamation was renamed Central and Local Courts Proclamation and the Native Courts became known as the Basotho Courts. Under Section 9 of this Proclamation, these courts were given jurisdiction to preside over all customary law matters and not the common law. However, the exercise of this jurisdiction was restricted by the repugnancy clause, a familiar pattern in most British colonies.[66] The law also prohibited legal practitioners from representing litigants in these courts.[67] The general import of this law was to provide a transitional mechanism to natives as they assimilate to the modern (western) legal system. That is why it deliberately kept customary law at an inferior position to all other written laws. These arrangements survived independence, and today the bulk of

---

[65] The thesis connecting the emergence of "customary law" with the establishment of colonial rule has been explored by many scholars. *See, e.g.,* MAHMOOD MAMDANI, CITIZEN AND SUBJECT (Princeton University Press 1996); T. Manuh, *The Women, Law and Development Movements in Africa and the Struggles for Customary Law Reform,* THIRD WORLD LEGAL STUD. 207, 211 (1994). Other writers have associated the development of customary law to the introduction of colonial capitalism. While tracing the "creation" of customary law among the Banjal Jola community of Senegal, Snyder has written: "Customary law was an ideology with real practical effects; it marked a specific phase in the development of capitalism in Senegal. At the same time it embodied the partial dissolution and transformation of Banjal conceptions and their subordination to legal ideologues and social relations through state." Francis Snyder, *Colonialism and Legal Form: The Creation of "Customary Law" in Senegal,* 19 J. LEGAL PLURALISM 49 (1981). *See also,* M. Chanock, *Making Customary Law: Men Women and Courts in Colonial Northern Rhodesia,* in AFRICAN WOMEN AND THE LAW: HISTORICAL PERSPECTIVES 53–67 (Margaret Jean Hay & Marcia Wright eds., Boston University Press 1982). Bennett advances the view that African traditions were exploited by the colonial authorities to stifle local development and perpetuate white domination. *See* T.W. BENNETT, HUMAN RIGHTS AND AFRICAN CUSTOMARY LAW 2 (Juta Legal and Academic Publishers 1995).

[66] The courts in Lesotho have always taken the view that customary law could be repugnant to justice and morality if it conflicted with any statute. *See Ramalapi v Letsie,* H.C. Civ./A/21/1971. Poulter, *supra* note 40, at 17–19.

[67] This position has only been recently changed by the Court of Appeal's decision in *Attorney General v Mopa* 2000–04 LAC 427. The justification for excluding legal practitioners from the courts, so amplified by the Court in *Mahloane v Letele,* (H.C.Civ/Apn/93/1974), was found to be contrary to the spirit of the 1993 Constitution.

customary law disputes are still being handled by the Local (Basuto) Courts, with the Subordinate Courts and the High Courts acting in a supervisory role.

It is interesting to note that not a single colonial statute mentioned the Laws of Lerotholi. The same is true today. Whereas the current 1993 Constitution refers to customary law in section 18, 45, and 154, it never in any section mentions the Laws of Lerotholi.[68] As to the content of customary law to be applied by the courts, there has never been any special province reserved for the Laws of Lerotholi. To the contrary, it seems that the courts are willing to look beyond the Code to find the "living law" in the current practice of the people. As discussed earlier, this has happened in several instances, especially with regard to marriage law. The Court of Appeal affirmed this position in *Ramaisa Mphulenyane* when it observed that Section 34 of the Laws of Lerotholi was "not a comprehensive statement of all Sotho customary Law."[69]

Whereas one might argue that the codified law provides easy access to customary rules for judges and Magistrates, most of whom may not be aware of Basoto customs, their general predisposition toward liberal understanding of concepts such as equality, justice, and human rights will still deter any meaningful engagement with the evolving nature of custom. Also, lack of proper reporting of cases in Lesotho and over-reliance on South African textbooks, case law, and judges make Basoto courts less attuned to developing their own jurisprudence, let alone developing customary law. One leading scholar has lamented thus:

> In Lesotho the problem is that the Court of Appeal is seldom in a position to discuss legal principles in a wholesome manner because previous decisions are not timeously reported or reported at all. The result of this is South African text books are used which are written by people who did not have Lesotho in mind and were not aware of difference between the ... law of Lesotho and that of the Republic of South Africa. The Court of Appeal becomes a victim of the unfavourable conditions under which it operates.[70]

6.4.3. *Customary Law and the Practice of Democracy*

Liberal elements within the Basuto body politic have always viewed tradition with scepticism. This is because they see in tradition the forces that undermine the efforts

---

[68] Under Section 154, Law is defined to include "customary law of Lesotho and any other unwritten rule of law." Customary law is then defined as the "customary law of Lesotho for the time being in force *subject to any modification or other provision made in respect thereof by any Act of Parliament.*" CONSTITUTION OF LESOTHO 1993 § 154 (emphasis added).

[69] *See Ramaisa v Mphulenyane*, 1977 LLR 138, at 149. *See also Matsepe Sejanamane v. Libenyane Ntlama* 1971–73 LLR 217. The judicial Commissioner in *Thejane v Tlali* (JC 68/1974) made similar observation: "It seems to this Court that section 34 of the *Laws of Lerotholi* when given strict interpretation can have results which do not apply in ordinary Basotho way of life."

[70] *See* W.C.M. MAQUTU, CONTEMPORARY FAMILY LAW 83 (2005).

to completely democratize the Basuto society. In the period leading up to independence, this fear was manifested in the demand to marginalize the monarchy and seek a complete break from the past. The Constitutional Reform Commission appointed in 1958 moderated these fears by relegating the position of the king (the former paramount chief under the British colonial rule) to that of a constitutional rather than an executive monarch. This was deeply opposed by those who saw in this arrangement the deliberate attempt to reduce the monarchy to a position of impotence. These fears and contests bubbled to the surface in the period immediately after the first post-independence elections in 1965,[71] leading to open political rivalry between the king (joined by the Marematlou Freedom Party – "MFP") and the ruling Basuto National Party ("BNP"). A settlement of sorts agreed on by both parties in January 1967 confirmed the acceptance of this constitutional arrangement by the King and set the country on the path to democratic consolidation. This, however, was not to be. A military coup a year later, successive riots, mutiny, and general violence have since been a common feature of Lesotho's political landscape.

It has been argued that the survival of the Basuto monarchy is largely due to the fracture of the Basuto political heritage.[72] Indeed, the violent contests between political parties that has characterized the political landscape since independence is in contrast to the cohesive political heritage bequeathed to the succeeding generations by the great King Moshoeshoe. These contests have also eroded the nations' ability to forge a workable democratic system and thereby allowed the King to retain a reasonable measure of political authority. This may be so, but in our view, the position of the monarchy in social and political realms is galvanized by Lesotho's attachment to tradition. This is more than evident in the manner in which the 1993 Constitution has treated the chieftaincy, the most vivid symbol of traditionalism. For example, although chapter 5 of the Constitution recognizes the role of the king as head of state, customary law dictates how he discharges his functions and the methods of succession. In Section 45, the Constitution provides that the king will be succeeded by a person "capable of succeeding under the customary law of Lesotho."[73] The source of the applicable customary law is the Laws of Lerotholi.[74] Thus, even though such appointment is to be done by the College of Chiefs, who

---

[71] *See* W. MAQUTU, CONTEMPORARY CONSTITUTIONAL HISTORY OF LESOTHO c. 2 (Mazenod Institute 1990).

[72] *See* R. Southall, *Between Competing Paradigms: Post-Colonial Legitimacy in Lesotho*, 21 J. CONTEMP. AFR. STUD. 251 (2003).

[73] CONSTITUTION OF LESOTHO 1993 § 45.

[74] The pertinent rule provides as follows: "The succession to chieftainship shall be by right of birth; that is, the first born male of the first wife married; if the first wife has no male issue then the first born male child of the next wife in succession shall be chief.... Provided that if a chief dies leaving no male issue, the chieftainship shall devolve upon the male following according to the succession houses."

are themselves subject to the rules of customary succession, the whole project is governed by customary law and not common law, save for the fact that the disputes arising from the appointments made under Section 45 are to be heard by the High Court and not the Local Courts.[75] The influence of the Laws of Lerotholi can also be seen in the composition of parliament, which, according to Section 54, is comprised of the king, the Senate and the National Assembly. The Senate is basically a traditional institution because it is composed of the twenty-two principal chiefs and eleven other persons nominated by the king. Undoubtedly, the state has found a way of meshing tradition with modern practice of government. This indicates the likelihood that the Laws of Lerotholi, despite their lack of statutory status, will endure for a long to come.

6.5. CONCLUSION

What seems certain is that the survival of the Code in Lesotho today is hinged on the political goodwill that customary law enjoys. This is not an entirely new phenomenon. As demonstrated earlier, the evolution of codified customary law is inevitably connected to the rise of Basotho nationalism that began in the early 1800s. Right from the days of the great King Moshoeshoe, the perpetuation of rules of custom had an ineluctable connection to the political demands of the day. For the most part, the relationship between politics and tradition was fostered by the application of customary rules as an ordering mechanism, but also as a source of legitimacy for the traditional rulership. In the post-independence era, this relationship has survived and its influence has been felt through the constitutional monarchical system and limitations on the exercise of liberal rights by the rules of custom. Today, the Laws of Lerotholi stand as a monolith of traditional symbolism that speaks to the legality of certain traditional aspects of people's lives and provides legitimacy to custom as an integral part of the country's legal system. The Laws of Lerotholi have also abetted the survival of traditional institutions of governance despite their flagrant discordance with most neo-liberal policies that Lesotho has sought to embrace after independence. So long as the relevancy of customary law is maintained by forces keen to perpetuate their hold on traditional privileges, and larger segments of rural populations remain outside the domain of state-engineered economic development programs, the force of change necessary to remodel rules of custom embodied in the Code will remain an illusion. As it is now, the government has far greater challenges in alleviating poverty, harmonizing its electoral procedures, and stamping out corruption, and may be less disposed to appropriate the little available resources in changing or modifying the law of custom.

---

[75] *See* CONSTITUTION OF LESOTHO 1993 § 45(5).

Unlike many African countries where institutions of African customary law created in the colonial era have been overthrown by the nascent epistemic constituencies, Lesotho presents an interesting variation where neo-traditionalism endures forty years after independence. The reasons could be found in the homogeneity of the *Basotho* community, the stagnation rendered in the wake of apartheid influence in the region, the establishment of a constitutional monarchy, and the relative poverty of its population. All these factors have conspired to give life to a Code of customary law that may have long have outlived its usefulness. As for lessons that others can learn from the Lesotho experience, not much can be said. In totality, Lesotho sails in the same boat as other African countries, and its attempt at codifying customary law could as well be classified as a wasted effort.

7

Traditional Authorities

Custodians of Customary Law Development?

Manfred O. Hinz

7.1. INTRODUCTION

Many lawyers still have difficulties accepting that customary law is not static, but changes, even *is* changed in the communities in which it is applied.[1] The widely made reference to the Roman law perception of customary law, according to which one criterion to distinguish customary law from customs is the continued observation of the first over time,[2] is unable to explain the dynamics inherent in customary law recorded by legal sociologists and anthropologists. It is only recently that South African courts have acknowledged that the *living law* of communities differs from what has been reported to be the *official customary law*.[3] These courts have opted to recognize the living law over the official version.[4]

When the original Namibian Traditional Authorities Act[5] was re-promulgated in 2000,[6] the new Act contained a provision that was not in the original version. Section 3(3)(c) of the 2000 Act authorizes traditional authorities to "make customary

---

A slightly amended and shortened version of this chapter appeared as *Phase 1 of the Namibian Ascertainment Project* in the 1 Namibia Law Journal 2 (2000) (reprinted with permission).

[1] *Cf* F.M. d'Engelbronner-Kloff, *The People as Law-Makers: The Judicial Foundation of the Legislative Power of Namibian Traditional Communities, in* TRADITIONAL AUTHORITY AND DEMOCRACY IN SOUTHERN AFRICA 62, 62f (F.M. d'Engelbronner, M.O. Hinz, J.L Sindano eds., New Namibia Books 1998) (on the concept of customary law). The term "community" is used to denote "traditional community" as defined in the law that governs traditional authorities in Namibia, the Traditional Authorities Act, 25 of 2000 and its predecessor, Act 17 of 1995 as amended.

[2] The usual reference in southern Africa is the case *Van Breda v Jacobs*, 1921 AD 330.

[3] *See, e.g.*, Chuma Himonga,*The Future of Living Customary Law in African Legal Sustems in the 21st Centure and Beyond with Special Reference to South Africa, supra*, Chapter 2.

[4] *Cf* C. Himonga & C. Bosch, *The Application of African Customary Law Under the Constitution of South Africa: Problems Solved or Just Beginning?*, 117 SALJ 306 (2000).

[5] Act 17, 1995.

[6] As Traditional Authorities Act, 25 of 2000.

law."[7] This provision has legal implications that have not been fully explored and interpreted yet, including potential conflict with the Namibian Constitution that suggests that parliament is to be the main, if not only, lawmaker.[8] Apart from the authority to make customary law, the Traditional Authorities Act expects the traditional authorities to "ascertain" the customary law applied in the various communities and also to "assist in its codification."[9]

No efforts have been undertaken to codify customary law in Namibia.[10] However, most traditional communities in Namibia have started a process of what has been called *self-stating* customary law.[11] Self-stating customary law refers to making and

[7] Traditional Authorities Act 25, 2000, § 3(3)(c).
[8] Article 44 of the Namibian Constitution says: "The legislative power of Namibia shall be vested in the National Assembly.…" THE CONSTITUTION OF THE REPUBLIC OF NAMIBIA art. 44. Does this mean that no other body than the national assembly has the power to enact law? What d'Engelbronner argued before the enactment of the 2000 Traditional Authorities Act, *see* d'Engelbronner, *supra* note 1, is still relevant, as the constitutional question on the authority of lawmaking has not been overtaken by the added provision in the 2000 Act. For those who follow the Kelsenian state-centered approach according to which all legal actions are eventually linked to the grundnorm, lawmaking by non-delegated authorities remains an unacceptable anomaly. Legal pluralism avoids the strictness of the state-centered approach by accepting societal forces to create and administer their own laws. For more on legal pluralism, compare M.O. Hinz, *Legal Pluralism in Jurisprudential Perspective, in* THE SHADE OF NEW LEAVES: GOVERNANCE IN TRADITIONAL AUTHORITY, A SOUTHERN AFRICAN PERSPECTIVE 29 (M.O. Hinz & H.K. Patemann eds., Lit Verlag 2006); W. MENSKI, COMPARATIVE LAW IN A GLOBAL CONTEXT: THE LEGAL SYSTEMS OF ASIA AND AFRICA 82 ff (2d ed., Cambridge University Press 2006).
[9] Traditional Authorities Act, 25, 2000, § 3(1)(a).
[10] The ascertainment of customary law was the topic of an international workshop organized by the Namibian Ministry of Justice in 1995. *See* THE ASCERTAINMENT OF CUSTOMARY LAW AND THE METHODOLOGICAL ASPECTS OF RESEARCH INTO CUSTOMARY LAW: PROCEEDINGS OF WORKSHOP (T.W. Bennett & M. Rünger eds., Law Reform and Development Commission 1996). Apart from the alternative of codifying customary law, its restatement as practiced in many African countries by the School of Oriental and African Studies of the University of London was debated. *Cf.* A.N. Allott, *The Restatement of the African Law Project and Thereafter, in* THE ASCERTAINMENT OF CUSTOMARY LAW AND THE METHODOLOGICAL ASPECTS OF RESEARCH INTO CUSTOMARY LAW: PROCEEDINGS OF WORKSHOP, *supra* at 31. The author of this article pleaded for law reform from within, including the need to link the various communities in Namibia with each other in order to create an interactive process of law reform. *See* H. Becker & M.O. Hinz, *Customary-Law Research in Namibia: Methodological Remarks, in* THE ASCERTAINMENT OF CUSTOMARY LAW AND THE METHODOLOGICAL ASPECTS OF RESEARCH INTO CUSTOMARY LAW: PROCEEDINGS OF WORKSHOP, *supra* at 77, 92.
[11] *See* M.O. HINZ, DEVELOPING CUSTOMARY LAW: SELF-STATED LAWS OF NAMIBIAN COMMUNITIES AND CUSTOMARY LAW CONSULTATIVE MEETINGS WITH TRADITIONAL LEADERS 3ff (Centre for Applied Social Sciences 1995) [hereinafter HINZ, DEVELOPING]; M.O. HINZ, CUSTOMARY LAW IN NAMIBIA: DEVELOPMENT AND PERSPECTIVE 41ff (8th ed., Centre for Applied Social Sciences 2003) [hereinafter HINZ, CUSTOMARY LAW]; M.O. Hinz, *Law Reform from Within. Improving the Legal Status of Women in Northern Namibia*, 39 J. LEGAL PLURALISM & UNOFFICIAL L. 69 (1997) [hereinafter Hinz, *Law Reform*]; M.O. Hinz & J.W. Kwenani, *The Ascertainment of Customary Law, in* THE SHADE OF NEW LEAVES: GOVERNANCE IN TRADITIONAL AUTHORITY, A SOUTHERN AFRICAN PERSPECTIVE, *supra* at 203.

ascertaining of customary law by the communities themselves.[12] Self-stating also encompasses the making of rules by the communities in accordance with their customary law. Although the process of self-stating results in written texts, self-stating is opposed to restating in the sense of the restatement project of the School of Oriental and African Studies of the University of London.[13] Ascertaining or self-stating customary law is also very different from codifying it. When, for example, criminal common law is being codified, this codification is meant to replace the common law in force before. The law in force before can still be used to interpret the codified law, but will otherwise cease to exist as law. Self-stating of customary law does not render the non-ascertained parts of the customary law obsolete. The non-ascertained part of the law still continues to exist; the ascertained part of it may even be revisited by the underlying customary law in existence before the ascertainment.[14]

The following observations are intended to give an account of the state of affairs of what has developed over the years into the *ascertainment of customary law project by self-stating* in Namibia. Some conclusions will be drawn to respond to the question of whether traditional authorities are not only the custodians of customary law, but also the custodians of customary law development.

7.2. FROM THE *ONGWEDIVA MEETING* TO THE NATIONWIDE PROJECT OF SELF-STATING CUSTOMARY LAW

7.2.1. *First Developments in Dealing with Customary Law after the Independence of Namibia*

At a conference on the administration of justice for magistrates, other judicial officers, and traditional authorities organized by the Namibian Ministry of Justice in

---

[12] To what extent communities develop their laws by themselves, that is by their members or, at least, in line with community-accepted rules, is a question to which this work will revert back at a later stage, although it will not be possible, on the basis of the available information, to provide the reader with a comprehensive answer.

[13] Allott, Professor of law at the School of Oriental and African Studies and in charge of the customary law restatement project, defines the restatement approach "borrowed from the American Restatements" as follows: Restatements "were authoritative, comprehensive, careful and systematic statements of common-law rules in such fields as torts, contracts and property. Necessarily cast in semi-codified form, they were still not codes, as they lacked the force of legislated law. Instead they were the most accurate and precise statements of what those producing them had concluded were the main principles and rules as evolved by the courts, and, as such, courts and practitioners alike could turn to them as guides." Allott, *supra* note 10.

[14] What has been said in this paragraph is still open for further consideration. However, the outlined principles are concluded from opinions held in comparative law about the European approaches to codification, *Cf.* K. Zweigert & H. Kötz, Einfühung in die Rechtsvergleichung auf dem Gebiete des Privatrechts 84ff (J.C.B. Mohr 1996), common sense, and observations of court traditional court practices.

April 1992,[15] one of the Namibian traditional communities – the Vakwangali, who live in the western part of the Kavango Region[16] – presented a document, titled *The Laws of Ukwangali*.[17] The Laws of Ukwangali deal with different wrongs (such as murder, robbery, rape, assault) and the legal consequences a traditional court may impose in the case of conviction.

The Laws of Ukwangali were presented at the conference in order to create awareness about the working of law at the very local level and by doing so to call on the meeting to take note of the traditional administration of justice as an integral part of the overall justice system of the country. With this, the conference became a challenge to all who thought that the traditional administration of justice was something of the past. In fact, the debate in the 1992 conference became the starting point of a long process to investigate the administration of justice under customary law, the inherited legal framework for this system of justice, and to set forth principles for the drafting of a new uniform piece of legislation that would provide for the operation of traditional courts in line with constitutional requirements.

Research following the 1992 conference and visits to various traditional communities[18] revealed that other communities had compiled documents similar to the Laws of Ukwangali. The first analysis of the documents showed that even communities belonging to the same language group and living close to each other provided for different consequences for the very same wrong. This led to several rounds of consultations in various parts of the country. The consultations were used to expose the communities to information about the legislative achievements of the other communities. The first consultation of this kind, the meeting with the Oshiwambo-speaking

[15] *Cf.* M.O. Hinz & M.F. Sichilongo, Seminar on the Administration of Justice for Judicial Officers, Police Officers, Regional Commissioners and Traditional Leaders Report (Apr. 4–5, 1992) (unpublished report, on file with the Namibia Ministry of Justice; M.O Hinz, *Traditional Governance and African Customary Law: Comparative Observations from a Namibian Perspective*, in HUMAN RIGHTS AND THE RULE OF LAW IN NAMIBIA 59, 71 (N. Horn & A. Bösl eds., Macmillan Namibia 2008) [hereinafter Hinz, *Traditional Governance*]; M.O. Hinz, *Traditional Courts in Namibia – Part of the Judiciary? Jurisprudential Challenges of Traditional Justice*, in THE INDEPENDENCE OF THE JUDICIARY IN NAMIBIA 149, 149ff (N. Horn, A Bösl eds., Macmillan Education Namibia 2008) [hereinafter Hinz, *Traditional Courts*].

[16] In accordance with article 102 of the Constitution of Namibia, the country is divided into thirteen regions with regional government structures. Apart from those, traditional structures of government are in place. In many parts of the country, traditional structures are the first (and sometimes only) governmental entry points for the people. I have dealt with this matter in Hinz, *Traditional Governance, supra* note 15, in general terms and in Hinz, *Traditional Courts, supra* note 15, with respect to the administration of justice. The Vakwangali (singular Mukwangali) are one of the five recognized traditional communities in the Kavango Region. They are recognized pursuant to the Traditional Authorities Act, which expected communities with the wish to be part of the official traditional setup of the country to go through the recognition process provided for in the Act. *See* Traditional Authorities Act 25, 2000.

[17] The laws of Ukwangali can be found in Hinz, DEVELOPING, *supra* note 11, at 119ff.

[18] Aspects of the research are summarized in Hinz, *Traditional Governance, supra* note 15, at 71ff.

communities,[19] was held in Ongwediva in May 1993 and became, in retrospective, the most prominent one as it set the tone for meetings in other parts of the country and eventually led to the birth of a nationwide project to ascertain customary law by self-stating in the various communities.[20]

The exchange of information, indeed, prompted the Oshiwambo-speaking communities, the communities of the Kavango region, and the Nama communities to consider the harmonization of certain parts of their customary laws.[21] Efforts to harmonize customary law applied in particular to the fines for wrongs committed, including the amount of compensation to be paid by guilty persons. Prior to harmonization, in the Oshiwambo-speaking communities, the amount of cattle to be paid as compensation in cases where someone was killed ranged from nine to fifteen heads of cattle. The Ongwediva meeting decided to standardize the fines for killing at ten heads of cattle.[22]

The customary law of inheritance was another matter of importance discussed in the consultative meetings of the Oshiwambo-speaking communities at Ongwediva and the communities of the Kavango in Rundu. Both groups of communities follow a matrilineal system of kinship, which had created serious problems in cases where men died leaving their wives and children behind. It was custom that in such cases, a widow would return to her family of origin because, in accordance with the matrilineal order in place, the wife did not legally become part of the husband's family by virtue of marriage.[23] Property (including rights to land under customary

---

[19] The Oshiwambo-speaking people, who comprise at least 50 percent of the total population of Namibia, have traditionally occupied the central part of Northern Namibia, now divided into four Regions. *Oshiwambo* is used to refer to the standardized language understood by all the members of the eight recognized Oshiwambo-speaking communities.

[20] The Ongwediva meeting and those who followed were organized by the Centre for Applied Social Sciences (an independent research institution later associated to the Faculty of Law of the University of Namibia) through its Customary Law Unit in co-operation with the Ministry of Justice. The Customary Law Unit is now under the jurisdiction of the Human Rights and Documentation Centre of the Faculty of Law of the University of Namibia. The work of the Customary Law Unit was supported by several foreign donors, SIDA of the Swedish government, and, in recent years, by the Mission of Finland in Namibia.

[21] After the Ongwediva meeting (May 25–26, 1993), the Kavango groups followed in Rundu in June 8–9, 1994; the Nama communities of central and southern Namibia had their first meeting in the Kai-Ganaxab Centre in December 1–2, 1994. The minutes of the meetings can be found in Hinz, DEVELOPING, *supra* note 11, at 119ff. The Ongwediva minutes were also included in ELELO, ELELO LYOPASHINGWANA LYOSHILONGO SHONDONGA – TRADITIONAL AUTHORITY OF ONDONGA. OOVETA (OOMPANGO) DHOSHILONGO SHONDONGA – THE LAWS OF ONDONGA 75ff (2d ed., Evangelican Lutheran Church in Namibia 1994).

[22] *See* Hinz, DEVELOPING, *supra* note 11, at 124ff; Elelo, *supra* note 21, at 88f.

[23] *Cf.* M. TUUPAINEN, MARRIAGE IN MATRILINEAL AFRICAN TRIBE. A SOCIAL; ANTHROPOLOGICAL STUDY OF MARRIAGE IN THE ONDOGA TRIBE IN OVAMBOLAND (The Academic Bookstore 1970); H. BECKER & M.O. HINZ, MARRIAGE AND CUSTOMARY LAW IN NAMIBIA 53ff (Centre for Applied Social Sciences 1995).

law) occupied by the family during the lifetime of the husband was understood to
have been the property of the deceased husband. This resulted in the family of the
deceased husband taking over the estate of the deceased, whereas the rights to land,
in accordance with Owambo customary law, reverted back to the authority in charge
of allocating land rights – the respective traditional authority.

Complaints about hardship and injustice arising from this matrilineal inheritance
system date far back.[24] They were caused by substantial socio-economic changes
in Namibia that drastically affected communities based on extended family structures for which cattle raising and small-scale, primarily subsistence agricultural production were essential. Where the accumulation of individual wealth was not the
prominent feature, the fact that the wife and the children were not legally kin to
the husband and his family was made up for by the relationship to the wife's family.
This compensation failed to work when the balances underpinning the network
of extended families ceased to exist. In many instances, the changed situation left
widows and their children stranded between the families from which the deceased
husbands emerged and the families from which the wives originated.

The need to effect substantial changes in the inherited customary law resulted
in customary law enactments aimed at remedying the situation of widows and children. The self-stated laws of the Aandonga and Ovakwanyama[25] reflect these enactments, which took place in the 1980s.

The first edition of the self-stated *Laws of Ondonga* was enacted in 1989.[26] The
Laws were published as a small pocket-size booklet and contained some thirty sections dealing with various aspects of the Ondonga customary law. Section 9 of the
1989 Laws contained a rule that can be seen to express the growing understanding
that widows and their children needed clear legal protection with respect to property
belonging to the household of the widow and her deceased husband. According to
section 9, the distribution of property was allowed to take place only after a period
determined by the amount of time needed to conduct the funeral pursuant to custom. This was an important change to the prior law, according to which the widow

---

[24] Cf. R. Gordon, *Widow "Dispossession" in Northern Namibian Inheritance, in* 31 ANTHROPOLOGY S.
AFR. 1 (2008); M.O. Hinz & P. Kauluma, *OoVeta dhOshilongo shOndonga _ Efalomo. The laws
of Ondonga – Introductory remarks, in* ELELO LYOPASHINGWANA LYOSHILONGO SHONDONGA –
TRADITIONAL AUTHORITY OF ONDONGA. OOVETA (OOMPANGO) DHOSHILONGO SHONDONGA –
THE LAWS OF ONDONGA 9, 33f (2d ed., Evangelican Lutheran Church in Namibia 1994).

[25] Aandonga (plural of Omundonga) mean the people of the Kingdom of Ondonga; Ovakwanyama
(plural of Omukwanyama) mean the people of the Kingdom of Oukwanyama. In terms of historical importance and also in terms of the numbers of their members, the two kingdoms represent the
most prominent communities among the Oshiwambo-speaking traditional communities in the north-
central part of the country. The Laws of Oukwnayama were issued after the Laws of Ondonga, i.e., in
1993. Cf. Hinz, DEVELOPING, *supra* note 11, at 11ff, 17ff. The following will concentrate on the Laws
of Ondonga reverting back to the Laws of Oukwanyama at later stage.

[26] See ELELO, ELELO LYOPASHINGWANA LYOSHILONGO SHONDONGA. OOVETA (OOMPANGO) DHO-
SHILONGO SHONDONGA (1st ed., Evangelican Lutheran Church in Namibia 1989).

was restricted to a determined area of the homestead during this period. This restriction in movement allowed the relatives the opportunity to search the homestead and carry away what they liked. The 1989 Laws granted the widow the right to move freely in and around the homestead and hence to secure its integrity until the end of the mourning period. As to the land occupied by the family of the deceased, the 1989 Laws stipulated that the widow could remain on the land subject to making payments to the deceased's family. Depending on the size of the land in question, the widow was expected to pay between R300 and 400.[27]

However, and in view of the fact that many widows did not have money to pay, the reported change of the inherited matrilineal inheritance law did not lead to a substantial improvement of the situation of widows. Many cases were reported of widows and children being chased away from the land after the death of the husband. The cases of evicted widows occupied the public discourse and even led to interventions in the Namibian parliament and calls to change the customary law of inheritance.[28]

The Ondonga community respected the call and amended the 1989 laws in 1993. The new Laws of Ondonga were enacted after several debates of and consultations with the king of Ondonga and his council. On November 16, 1992, a historic meeting of the Ondonga King's Council took place in which I had the privilege to participate. During this meeting, I was unexpectedly asked to give an opinion on land inheritance. In giving my opinion, I emphasized the fact that many women in rural areas had spent years cultivating the land during their years of marriage and raising children. Would it not be appropriate to recognize this human capital that was now part of the soil? After an intensive discussion, the Council decided to delete the provision dealing with payments for the land from the Laws of Ondonga. Widows and their children should not only be allowed to reside on the land after the death of their husbands, but also be allowed to remain there without any payment.[29]

The Women and Law Committee of the Namibian Law Reform and Development Commission in the Ministry of Justice[30] played an important role in facilitating the further process to implement the reported decision of the Ondonga King's Council. On May 19, 1993, the Committee paid an official visit to the Ondonga King's Council

---

[27] *See* Laws of Ondonga, 1989, § 9. Rand used to be the currency of South-West Africa and during the first years after independence of the Namibia. Rand is still an accepted currency in the country with 1 N$ being equivalent to 1 ZAR.

[28] *Cf.* Hinz & Kauluma, *supra* note 24, at 35.

[29] *See* Elelo, *supra* note 26.

[30] For information on the Women and Law Committee, see my remarks in M.O. Hinz, *Strengthening Women's Rights: The Need to Address the Gap Between Customary and Statutory Law in Namibia*, *in* WOMEN AND CUSTOM IN NAMIBIA. CULTURAL PRACTICE VERSUS GENDER EQUALITY? 93, 95ff (O.C. Ruppel, ed., Macmillan Education Namibia 2008). Otherwise, the technical task of amending the 1989 Laws of Ondonga on the basis of the Ongwediva meeting was given to me – a difficult task that took me and language assistants considerable time to complete.

during which the 1992 decision was confirmed. The consultations with the King's Council demonstrated contradictory interests in the leadership of the community, however. Removing the requirement of payment, indeed, had consequences on the income of traditional leaders at the village level who benefited from possible re-allocation of land after the land use rights reverted back to them.[31] Nevertheless, the voice of the king and the majority of the Council won. Invited by the Women and Law Committee, the king of Ondonga attended a press conference in Windhoek on July 12, 1993, and announced publicly the change in the Ondonga customary law.

The May 1993 meeting at Ongwediva – which took place after the historic meet-ing with the Ondonga King's Council but before the visit of the Woman and Law Committee – confirmed the Ondonga move in changing the customary law. The Ongwediva decision was that widows and their children should have the full right to remain on the land that they occupied during the lifetime of the husband without any payment by the widow. However, the Ongwediva decision was not understood as making law with immediate effect. The Ongwediva decisions were more under-stood to be obligations that had to be followed by community implementations.[32] Nonetheless, all Oshiwambo-speaking traditional authorities consented to follow the position of the Ondonga King's Council and to transform the position into their respective domestic laws. This was of particular importance for the Oukwanyama community, which had issued the Laws of Oukwanyama on February 9, 1993, and which basically followed the model of the Ondonga laws of 1989, including the provisions regarding payments for land by widows after the death of their husbands. A report in a Namibian newspaper of August 17, 1993, confirmed that the position reached at the Ongwediva meeting was adopted as the law of Oukwanyama.[33]

7.2.2. The Ascertainment of Customary Law – A Nationwide Project

By the end of 1995, about fifteen pieces of self-stated customary law could be col-lected.[34] Although there are many similarities among the documents, in many instances the documents differ in accordance with what the respective community

---

[31] Some relevant statements by traditional leaders are quoted in Hinz, *Law Reform, supra* note 11, at 73ff.

[32] *See* Hinz, DEVELOPING, *supra* note 11, at 123f.

[33] The amended version of the Laws of Oukwanyama (Eevetamango Doukwanyama 2007) reflects this. *See* Eevetamango Doukwanyama, EEVETAMANGO DOUKWANYAMA. THE LAWS OF OUKWANYAMA § 7 & fn (Northern Printing Press 2007). Section 7 of the Oukwnayama laws is almost identical to Section 9 of the Laws of Ondonga. The footnote to Section 7 informs that the earlier version of the law requir-ing payment had been deleted.

[34] *See* Hinz, DEVELOPING, *supra* note 11, at 9ff. The collection was done as part of the mentioned Customary Law Unit of the Centre for Applied Social Sciences. It was this collection that prompted the development of a project on its own: the ascertainment of customary law project.

finds important to put in writing. This can be demonstrated by what happened in the 1994 version of the Laws of Ondonga in comparison with the 1989 version. In the 1994 version, one can identify three types of changes effected in amendment: formal changes to clarify the language used in the 1989 version of the laws; insertions of new offenses reinforced by defined fines; and, most importantly, the already reported changes to strengthen the situation of widows.

Although more research is needed to establish details about what happened in the various traditional communities of Namibia with respect to the written ascertainment of their customary law, one can distinguish four phases of developments in the documenting of customary law:[35] *first*, the phase of pre-colonial documentation; *second*, the phase of colonially influenced statements of customary law; *third*, the phase of customary law statements around independence – including the phase of emerging awareness of the need to ascertain and develop customary law as response to the challenge of the new socio-political order after independence; and *fourth*, the current phase as guided by the ascertainment of customary law project.

Phase one: Although systematic research will most probably reveal more information about lawmaking and law-documenting processes in traditional communities, what we know allows us to state that both lawmaking decisions and their documentation have pre-colonial traditions. "Traditional laws and social norms of Owambo kingdoms" were documented in northern Namibia dating back to the nineteenth century.[36] King Mandume ya Ndemufayo of Oukwanyama enacted "new laws" when he came to power in 1917.[37] The seven sections of Mandume's laws contain the demand for peace with the tribes of the South, provide for the termination of cattle theft by nobles within Oukwanyama, the payment of fines in cases of assault where blood was drawn, the prohibition of killing a person who was accused of witchcraft, and the prohibition of abortion in the instance of a girl becoming pregnant before her initiation (*efundula* in Oshiwambo).[38] All of these provisions appear to have been necessary deviations from the order in existence before Mandume ascended to the throne.

Phase two: The German colonial government was interested in documenting customary law through empirical research with the possible aim of codifying the law. However, it took quite some time for the administration in Germany to agree on the way to achieve codification.[39] Several versions of a questionnaire were developed

---

[35] *Cf.* Hinz & Kwenani, *supra* note 11, at 206ff (distinguishing the four phases slightly differently also by concentrating on the recent developments).

[36] F.N. WILLIAMS, PRECOLONIAL COMMUNITIES OF SOUTHWESTERN AFRICA: A HISTORY OF OWAMBO KINGDOMS 1600–1900 187 (National Archives of Namibia 1991).

[37] E.M. LOEB, IN FEUDAL AFRICA 33 (Indiana University Press 1962).

[38] *See id.*

[39] M. BOIN, DIE ERFORSCHUNG DER RECHTSVERHÄLTNISSE IN DEN "SCHUTZGEBIETEN" DES DEUTSCHEN REICHS 33ff (Lit Verlag 1995) (providing a detailed overview about the history of the German inquiry about the law of the people in Germany's colonies).

and distributed to officials in the then-German colonies.[40] What eventually resulted
in several publications had no direct impact on the customary law of the former
colonies, however.[41]

The approach by the South African government and legal anthropological
scholars who worked on Namibian customary law during South African colonial
times was very different from what the Germans had started with.[42] In line with
the changed approaches in legal anthropology – away from the one-dimensional
evolutionist concepts to a functional understanding of law as part of the overall
social system – these scholars concentrated on the functioning of customary law.
The political understanding of separate development and apartheid called for the
focus on tribal entities and the law applied by them. The particular interest of the
South African colonial administration was on the communities in the North of the
country, the Oshiwambo-speaking communities, and the communities in the now
Kavango and Caprivi Regions as the most populated areas of the colony and, to a
high degree, under the jurisdiction of traditional governments. Apart from studies
on individually selected communities, three major research projects were set up and
aimed at compiling comprehensive records about the law in the three mentioned
areas.[43] Only one of the three projects was, at least partially, completed. The law of
the Kavango communities[44] contains the results of empirical research in the area
and refers, inter alia, to observed cases but does not attempt to generalize Kavango
customary law into a document of ascertained rules.[45]

There was a study on the socio-political system of the Aangandjera[46] conducted
within this greater research effort, however, that contains a document very relevant

---

[40] *Id.* at 57ff.
[41] *Cf.* S.R. STEINMETZ, RECHTSVERHÄLTNISSE VON EINGEBORENEN VÖLKERN IN AFRIKA UND
      OZEANIEN (Springer 1903); E. SCHULTZ-EWERTH & L. ADAM, 1 DAS EINGEBORENENRECHT
      (Strecker & Schröder 1929); E. SCHULTZ-EWERTH & L. ADAM, 2 DAS EINGEBORENENRECHT
      (Strecker & Schröder 1930). The questionnaires have remained of interest to legal anthropology.
      See E. OKUPA, INTERNATIONAL BIBLIOGRAPHY OF AFRICAN CUSTOMARY LAW: Ius non scriptum
      2f (Lit Verlag 1998). The JOURNAL OF AFRICAN LAW published an article on one of the question-
      naires only recently. *See* A. Lyall, *Early German Legal Anthropology: Albert Hermann Post and His
      Questionnaire*, 52 J. AFR. L. 114 (2008).
[42] Namibia became a German colony called German South-West Africa in 1884. Following World War
      I, South Africa administered the territory.
[43] According to oral information from academics involved in the three projects. Unfortunately, no
      research has been done on the background, implementation, and achievements of the projects.
[44] P.H. Van Rooyen, Die Inheemse Reg van die Kavango (1977) (unpublished M.A. dissertation) (on file
      with author). The study served as the author's M-thesis; one can, therefore, assume that other publica-
      tions were expected to appear, but, for whatever reasons, did not.
[45] *Id.* at 156ff.
[46] W. Louw, Die Socio-Politieke Stelsel van die Ngandjera van Ovamboland (1967) (unpublished M.A.
      dissertation) (on file with author). The Aangandjera (Omungandjera in singular) are one of the
      Oshiwambo-speaking communities in the central North of Namibia.

for the purpose of this article.[47] The author of the study attached a "code" with an introductory remark in which he notes that this code of the Ongandjera customary law was certainly prompted by white officials, but was nevertheless to be seen as the product of the secretary of the community established in co-operation with the king[48] of the community and his council, and also in line with practice in the traditional court of the community.[49] It is unclear whether there were similar initiatives in the other Oshiwambo-speaking communities or whether the 1989 version of the Laws of Ondonga, as referred to earlier, was related to a most probably standardized approach to ascertaining customary law in the area of the Oshiwambo-speaking communities.[50]

Phase three: The third phase fell, in broader political terms, into the period of the transition to independence of the country and the first attempts to cope with the new socio-political order of Namibia under the overall guidance of the Constitution of 1990. The Constitution re-confirmed the validity of customary law as part of the law of the land.[51] The institution of traditional leadership was more or less ignored, however, as many in the new political leadership held that traditional leadership was something of the past and rendered more unacceptable because of co-operation with the colonial administration.[52] As much as this understanding proved to be wrong as a general assessment, post-independence inquiries showed that despite unavoidable acts of co-operation with the colonial administration, the traditional leadership in the country enjoyed wide support by the people throughout the country.[53]

What we find in the self-stated laws of these years are responses of the traditional leaders to the challenges originating from the new political and legal (i.e., constitutional) order. The changes in the customary inheritance law discussed earlier can be seen in this respect. One interesting response to a constitutional controversy – about the relationship between the general law of the country, customary law, and article 12(2) of the Constitution (which guarantees that nobody should be convicted and

---

[47] *See id.* at 131ff.

[48] Louw uses the Afrikaans word: *Kaptein. See* Louw, *supra* note 46.

[49] *See id.* at 131.

[50] It is worthwhile to note that the current secretary of the Ongandjera traditional community requested the author of this article to provide him with a copy of the 1967 version of the Laws of Ongandjera after the author mentioned in one of his addresses to the Council of Traditional Leaders that the early Laws of Ongandjerato were one of the first pieces of self-stated customary law, apart from the self-stating of customary law as belonging to phase one.

[51] Article 66(1) of the Constitution says, "Both the customary law and the common law of Namibia in force on the date of Independence shall remain valid to the extent to which such customary law does not conflict with this Constitution or any other statutory law." THE CONSTITUTION OF THE REPUBLIC OF NAMIBIA art. 66(1).

[52] *Cf.* Hinz, *Traditional Governance, supra* note 15, at 68ff.

[53] *See* REPORT BY THE COMMISSION OF INQUIRY INTO MATTERS RELATING TO CHIEFS, HEADMEN AND OTHER TRADITIONAL AND TRIBAL LEADERS (Republic of Namibia 1991) [hereinafter COMMISSION OF INQUIRY REPORT].

punished again for any criminal offense for which conviction or acquittal had taken place) – can be found in the already mentioned Laws of Ukwangali. The constitutional controversy, which continues to occupy legal minds, developed around the different traditional and modern understandings about adequate legal consequences in serious criminal cases.[54] A widespread traditional understanding maintains that the appropriate penalty for murder is to sentence the murderer, or his/her family, to pay compensation to the family who lost a member. Modern understanding is based on the state monopoly in criminal law and expects a murderer to spend part of his or her life in prison. What is the legal position when a murderer is made subject to both the modern trial (resulting in imprisonment) and the traditional trial (resulting in compensation)?

The mentioned Laws of Ukwangali provide a very special answer to this question. Ukwangali law requires that the traditional court, which sits on the matter after the state court, consider a balance between the sentence of the state court and the expected sentence under customary law, thus allowing the traditional court to reduce the customary law compensation in accordance with the years spent in prison.[55]

It is also interesting to note that the scope of the self-stated laws changes. More recent versions of self-stated customary law have taken note of societal topics that we do not find regulated in the same manner in older documents. For example, environmental concerns have received a very prominent place in the Laws of Uukwambi, again an Oshiwambo-speaking community. The Laws of Uukwambi contain long sections on water, trees, wild animals, and grass.[56]

The interest of traditional communities to reposition themselves into the new social and political order led eventually to a process of, what I have called elsewhere, the "re-appropriation" of the tradition.[57] This re-appropriation has manifested itself in two directions. The first is state policy to accommodate parts of the tradition (its forms of governance and the customary law related to it) into acts of parliament. The second includes efforts by traditional leaders and traditional communities to re-discover the tradition after colonial distortions and oppressions.[58]

Traditional communities were certainly very able to understand that the legislative actions to re-regulate traditional governance and traditional courts would have

---

[54] *Cf.* Hinz, CUSTOMARY LAW, *supra* note 11, at 175ff.; *see also* N. Horn, *Criminal or Civil Procedure? The Possibility of a Plea of Autrefois in the Namibian Community Courts Act, in* THE SHADE OF NEW LEAVES: GOVERNANCE IN TRADITIONAL AUTHORITY, A SOUTHERN AFRICAN PERSPECTIVE, *supra* note 11, at 183.

[55] *See* Hinz, DEVELOPING, *supra* note 11, at 47.

[56] *See* Laws of Uukwambi (unpublished) (on file with the Customary Law Unit).

[57] *Cf.* Hinz, *Traditional Governance, supra* note 15.

[58] Such efforts certainly include the *invention* of traditions, as I also noted in Hinz, *Traditional Governance, supra* note 15, with reference to relevant anthropological sources.

impact on their authority. They learned about expected inroads into their authority from the work of the presidential commission of inquiry mentioned earlier,[59] the 1992 conference of the Ministry of Justice, and the subsequent consultative regional meetings. As a result, they prepared themselves to exercise influence on the legislative process, but also to react to the challenges expected by the new laws.

The legislation on traditional governance, specifically the Traditional Authorities Act that came into force in 1995,[60] and the envisaged act on traditional courts,[61] were particular challenges. The challenge of the Traditional Authorities Act prompted traditional communities to document their internal political setup – a matter that eventually led to chapters on the constitution of the community in self-stated pieces of customary law providing information about traditional hierarchies; the functions of the various traditional stakeholders; and organization division in traditional governance. The challenge of the traditional courts legislation led to an increasing readiness of traditional communities to undertake the drafting of the self-statements of customary law as such, the re-drafting of existing documents, and the extension to areas not covered in previous written versions of the customary law.[62]

Phase four: It was eventually the Council of Traditional Leaders[63] that elevated the project of ascertaining customary law by self-stating to a national project, that is a project of all the traditional communities represented in the Council.[64] The Council passed a resolution in 2001, according to which all traditional authorities were requested to embark on a project of self-stating customary law. The previously mentioned Customary Law Unit in the Faculty of Law of the University of Namibia assisted in conducting the project.[65] National and regional workshops were held to inform and guide the various communities in their task to ascertain their customary laws. The Council of Traditional Leaders was regularly informed about the progress made and also about obstacles encountered.

---

[59] *See* COMMISSION OF INQUIRY REPORT, *supra* note 53.

[60] Traditional Authorities Act 17, 1995.

[61] The 1992 conference resulted in substantial efforts to research the traditional administration of justice and to draft the necessary legislation. *Cf.* Hinz, *Traditional Governance, supra* note 15, at 70ff. However, it took until 2003 for the legislation to be adopted by the Namibian parliament. The Community Courts Act, 10 of 2003, is an act in force, but has not been implemented yet. *Cf.* Hinz, *supra* note 35, at 102f.

[62] All this will be further documented in the forthcoming first volume of the self-stated customary laws of Namibia. *See infra.*

[63] The Council of Traditional Leaders was established under the Council of Traditional Leaders Act, 13 of 1997, following the requirement set out in art 102(5) of the Constitution of Namibia.

[64] There are currently forty-nine traditional communities that have seats in the Council.

[65] The Customary Law Unit is now under the jurisdiction of the Human Rights and Documentation Centre of the Faculty of Law of the University of Namibia. The work of the Customary Law Unit was supported by several foreign donors, SIDA of the Swedish government, and, in recent years, by the Mission of Finland in Namibia.

Some of the Namibian communities are more advanced in stating their customary law than others. Meetings with the various communities in Namibia have shown that the communities in the northern part of the country are, in general, far ahead in their efforts to put customary law on paper. The reason is that the communities in the north, where the colonial administration practiced a system of indirect rule, were able to continue to operate their traditional courts during the time of colonialism despite inroads by the colonial administration. The communities in the central and southern parts of the country were exposed to direct colonial rule and are now in the difficult position of not only re-appropriating their traditions of governance and law, but also of re-establishing the necessary structures of traditional government and law.[66]

In view of this, at a meeting in 2008, the Council of Traditional Leaders was informed by the Customary Law Unit that the ascertainment project would be separated into two parts. The first part of the project would cover the seventeen communities in the central and northeastern parts of the country: the eight Oshiwambo-speaking communities, the five in the Kavango Region, and the four in the Caprive Region. The remaining thirty-two communities in the northwest and the central and southern parts will be left to a second part of the project.

The Council was also informed that at regional meetings with the seventeen communities in part one of the project, the communities resolved to have their laws published in two languages, English – the official language of Namibia – and the respective vernacular language. The laws of each community will be introduced by a community profile that would allow the reader to get at least some background information about the community.

At the same time, it was also repeated to the Council that it was not the role of the Customary Law Unit to work through the laws in detail. Rather, only obvious contraventions of constitutional provisions would be highlighted to the communities for respective change. It will be the sole responsibility of the communities to decide what they want to have in their laws and what not.

The work on part one of the project has been completed.[67] The publication of the laws for the relevant communities is expected to come out before the end of 2009. The second part of the project is scheduled to come to an end in 2011.

---

[66] This is a statement that needs amendments in view of some of the communities not covered in the part of the ascertainment project. The Batswana ba Namibia (see later in this chapter) had achieved a situation quite comparable to communities in the North. Communities that did not have any recognized structure until recently, such as the San communities, are very much at the beginning of organizing governance and law.

[67] Hinz, M. O., ed., assisted by N. E. Namwoonde. Customary law ascertained. Vol. 1. The customary law of the Owambo, Kavango and Caprivi communities of Namibia. Windhoek 2010: Namibia Scientific Society.

7.2.3. *Preliminary Assessment of the Ascertained Customary Law*

A few preliminary observations on some of the obvious features of the documents resulting from the self-stating of customary law project as it is in the fourth phase should conclude this sub-chapter.[68]

First: Some of the self-stating documents go beyond the field of law in the narrower sense. They also give the cultural background of the respective community, thus embedding the law of the community in the socio-economic environment of the community. Examples of this are the Laws of the Batswana ba Namibia and the Laws of the Mayouni Mafwe.[69] The Batswana ba Namibia are a small community of Setswana-speaking people in the east-central part of the country. The Mayouni Mafwe are a community in the Caprivi Region, which obtained its recognition under the Traditional Authorities Act only after the independence of Namibia. Communities have a special interest in stating important elements of history, language, and culture in order to express their identity. It will be seen whether examples of this kind will influence other communities to bring their rules on governance and law into such educative texts. Given that many mechanisms available in olden days to guarantee the transfer of wisdom and knowledge from one generation to the next have lost prominence against the exposure to modern forms of knowledge transfer, it might be advisable to consider the examples of those communities that have opted for the mentioned contextualization of their laws.

Second: There is an increasing readiness to assure certain rule of law principles in the self-statements. The Laws of Ondonga are relatively technical in the sense that they describe rules on access to the courts. For example, section 1 of the Laws of Ondonga informs potentially aggrieved persons that they have the right to launch a legal case, which must be done at the lowest level. Should a complainant or respondent not be satisfied with the decision at the level of the headman, he or she may request a letter from the headman that would be the procedural requirement to continue with the case at the level of the senior headman.[70] In case that decision is not to the satisfaction of one of the parties, the same procedure will be available to take the case up to the court of the king, the King's Council.[71] Recently received self-statements are more concerned with procedural matters to ensure the rights of the parties before the courts. The Laws of the Mayeyi community in the Caprivi

---

[68] The in-depth analysis of the seventeen submissions by the traditional communities in the central and northeastern parts of the country to the Customary Law Unit has not been completed yet.

[69] *See* Laws of the Batswana ba Namibia (on file with the Customary Law Unit); Laws of the Mayouni Mafwe (on file with the Customary law Unit).

[70] *See* Elelo, *supra* note 26, §§ 2.1, 2.2.

[71] *Id.* § 2.3.

Region have a special section on procedures,[72] which has ten sub-sections, namely on: how to submit a complaint; who may be accused of a crime; investigation; the decision to prosecute; issuing of warnings; how a case is conducted; who may appear before the court; rights of the accused; rights of victims and witnesses; and how a case is appealed.

Third: Developments in the Oshiwambo-speaking areas and the Kavango Region indicate that there is a growing tendency to achieve standardization and harmonization in the laws of the respective clusters of communities. Both clusters of communities have a working tradition of meeting regularly on legal issues and agreeing on rules applicable in all communities. The communities in the Kavango Region went one step further by drafting one document containing laws that would be applicable for four of the five Kavango communities, if not the whole of the Kavango Region.[73] The documents handed in to the Customary Law Unit differed only in the introductions, which contain different profiles of the respective communities.

Fourth: Some of the communities have adopted rules with respect to the conduct of the business in general in traditional offices, that is, rules not focusing on the administration of justice as such. The Laws of Ombadja,[74] for example, have a clause that expresses the expectation that the traditional leader be "friendly, tolerant, patient, humble and honest."[75] The Ondonga community has added to their laws regulations that contain information on the organization and structure of the Ondonga traditional office, as guidelines for community members in need of help, but also for the office bearers.[76]

7.3. CONCLUSION

Having been involved in the ascertainment of customary law project by self-stating since it started shortly after the independence of Namibia, I have no reason to change my assessment of the process of lawmaking in the communities. I wish to repeat what I have said in earlier writings:

> The exercise of self-stating customary law is an exercise of law reform from within. Law reform from within is a much better guarantee for the acceptance of legal changes than changes enacted by parliament. The experience with self-stating of customary law has shown that most traditional authorities have an underutilized

---

[72] Laws of the Mayeyi, § 3, (on file with the Customary Law Unit).

[73] From the document received by the co-ordinator of the Kavango cluster, it is not clear whether all the five Kavango communities have accepted the harmonized version of the Kavango laws.

[74] Again, one of the Oshiwambo-speaking communities in Namibia.

[75] Laws of Ombadja, § 3.2.7 (on file with the Customary Law Unit).

[76] *Cf.* J.S. Asino, Epukululo Lyowina Komuleli Gwopamuthigululwako (ELOC Printing Press 2007); The New Law of Ondonga (on file with the Customary Law Unit).

potential for law reform. The examples given prove that traditional authorities are not only the custodians of customary law as such, but also the custodians of customary law development.[77]

Special research of students in the Faculty of Law of the University of Namibia conducted over the last five years contributed to this statement but also demonstrated obstacles to the application and making of law at the local level. I refer here to research which was done in the field regarding the administration of natural resources under customary law.[78] The case studies on the law of grass, trees, plants, the administration of communal land in general, and the working of conservancies and community forests underscored the potential of customary law to deal with matters of protection and sustainability.[79] The case studies show that in many cases, the relevant customary law is more suitable to achieve community-accepted solutions compared to state law, which in many instances lacks respect for the local law and thus renders itself irrelevant to local communities. But the case studies show also that certain conflicts of interest, such as the interests of wealthy cattle farmers who may hold influential political offices, are difficult to handle under the jurisdiction of traditional leaders and customary law.

It will, therefore, be very important to observe the application of customary law by traditional courts and the further development of customary lawmaking. There are individuals or groups of individuals who take a prominent role in the writing up of customary law. Some communities have special committees tasked with drafting the laws. Many communities have advisory councils to the traditional leadership of the community. These councils are composed of retired politicians, civil servants, and church employees. Such individuals all hold views based on their respective experiences. The interest in some communities to get members of the ruling families into university education, or more specifically into legal education, will sooner or later result in new intellectualized blood flowing into the discourses at the traditional levels. The ascertainment of customary law project will certainly come to its envisaged end. The societal process of making customary law, however, will not end with the scheduled publication and will continue to stimulate political and academic discourses.[80]

---

[77] *See supra* note 9 and accompanying text.

[78] *Cf.* BIODIVERSITY AND THE ANCESTORS: CHALLENGES TO CUSTOMARY AND ENVIRONMENTAL LAW. CASE STUDIES FROM NAMIBIA (M.O. Hinz & O.C. Ruppel eds., Namibia Scientific Society 2008). *But see* M.O. HINZ, WITHOUT CHIEFS, THERE WOULD BE NO GAME: CUSTOMARY LAW AND NATURE CONSERVATION (Out of Africa 2003).

[79] M.O. Hinz, *Findings and the Way Forward, in* BIODIVERSITY AND THE ANCESTORS: CHALLENGES TO CUSTOMARY AND ENVIRONMENTAL LAW. CASE STUDIES FROM NAMIBIA (M.O. Hinz & O.C. Ruppel eds., Namibia Scientific Society 2008).

[80] Cf in this respect the review of Customary law ascertained by N Horn in Namibia Law Journal 2011 (3.1):133ff.

8

Engaging Legal Dualism

Paralegal Organizations and Customary Law in Sierra Leone and Liberia

Chi Mgbako and Kristina Scurry Baehr

8.1. INTRODUCTION

Paralegal organizations working in Africa are often comprised of non-lawyers who assist communities and individuals in the resolution of justice disputes. African paralegal organizations often operate in legal dualist systems in which both formal law and African customary law co-exist. Paralegals may be trained in formal law and frequently have intimate knowledge of customary law. Paralegals' backgrounds in both areas of law place them in a unique position to assist communities in navigating the formal and customary systems.

As in many African countries, a dualist structure characterizes both Sierra Leone's and Liberia's legal landscapes. Timap for Justice (Timap) in Sierra Leone and the Justice and Peace Commission's Community Legal Advisor Program (JPC) in Liberia are examples of two paralegal organizations dedicated to the legal empowerment of the poor within complex systems of legal dualism. Timap is comprised of twenty-seven paralegals supervised by two lawyers in thirteen paralegal offices throughout Sierra Leone. JPC receives financial, legal, and technical assistance from the Carter Center's Liberia office and employs thirty-five community monitors in two regional offices and eight county offices. Both Timap and JPC engage legal dualism by advocating for the positive development of customary law; confronting injustice within customary forums by appealing to the formal system when necessary; and developing sophisticated mediation practices to provide communities and individuals with viable alternatives to the formal and customary systems when desired.

The challenges and successes of Timap's and JPC's engagement with legal dualism provide illuminating examples for other African paralegal organizations operating within the legal dualist universe. Using the work of Timap and JPC as a roadmap, this article argues for a pragmatic approach to the engagement of legal dualism by paralegal organizations, one that is aimed at achieving the most just outcome for the clients and communities involved. Sometimes this will involve engaging customary forums on their own terms. Other times this will involve reaching out to traditional authorities and communities for the progressive evolution of customary law. This may also necessitate checking injustice in customary forums by appealing to the formal system. At still other times it will call for the mediation of disputes outside both the customary and formal realms.

Paralegal organizations working in legal dualist systems should neither demonize nor romanticize customary law. Instead, organizations should acknowledge the strengths and weaknesses of both the formal and customary systems and seek to overcome the dualist divide and meet the needs of their clients by engaging both systems, encouraging a working relationship between the two, and providing healthy competition for both systems through paralegal mediation.

This chapter is divided into two sections exploring the ways in which Timap and JPC pragmatically engage legal dualism in order to best meet the needs of clients in the communities where they work. Both sections describe the systems of legal dualism in Sierra Leone and Liberia, including the strengths and weaknesses of both the formal and customary systems. They explore Sierra Leoneans' and Liberians' relationship to customary law – its relevance, strengths, and shortcomings. The sections also explore how Timap and JPC engage customary law; challenge injustice in customary forums; wrestle with gender bias within the customary system; and develop mediations that provide healthy competition to both the formal and customary system. The conclusion presents lessons learned for African paralegal organizations operating in systems of legal dualism.

8.2. TIMAP FOR JUSTICE AND SIERRA LEONEAN CUSTOMARY LAW

8.2.1. *Legal Dualism in Sierra Leone*

The Sierra Leonean Constitution and relevant statutory law recognize both the formal and customary legal systems.[1] Although the formal legal system co-exists with traditional customary law, the two systems rarely interact. Most Sierra Leoneans rely on the customary system to resolve justice disputes, whereas the formal system remains foreign, inaccessible, and impractical. In a country with fewer than two hundred lawyers, most of whom are concentrated in the capital of Freetown, the formal system is out of reach for an overwhelming majority of Sierra Leone's five million citizens.[2]

---

[1] *See* SIERRA LEONE CONST. ch. XII (170)(2); Local Courts Act, 1963 (No. 20 of 1963).
[2] *See* Vivek Maru, *Between Law and Society: Paralegals and the Provision of Justice Services in Sierra Leone and Worldwide*, 31 YALE J. INT'L L. 427, 436 (2007).

The history of the dualist legal structure dates back to the creation of a British protectorate in Sierra Leone in 1896.[3] The 1896 ordinance that solidified Sierra Leone's status as a British protectorate also recognized that "courts of the native chiefs" would continue to administer customary law.[4] Present-day Sierra Leonean customary courts operate in accordance with the 1963 Local Courts Act, which give "local courts" and the local court chairmen who operate the courts formal legal recognition as adjudicators of customary law.[5] In addition, the Local Courts Act grants local courts the jurisdiction to preside over criminal matters punishable by up to six months imprisonment and civil matters involving small sums of money.[6]

The dominance of the customary law system is largely driven by its cultural relevance, which facilitates its wide acceptance in Sierra Leonean society. The customary law system, which varies by ethnic group, is based on the memory of elders, cultural practices, and traditional principles.[7] For most Sierra Leoneans, the customary system, with its focus on restitution and reconciliation, is the one they understand and can access. The Sierra Leonean formal legal system, in contrast, is based on a system of courts and codified law inherited from colonial British rule.[8] In substance, customary law in Sierra Leone can sometimes conflict with formal law and human rights principles.[9]

Local court chairmen have exclusive jurisdiction over matters of customary law in state-sponsored local customary courts.[10] However, individuals often circumvent the local court system and go directly to village and section chiefs who apply customary law and informally resolve disputes outside of the local court system.[11] Although chiefs are allowed to mediate disputes that community members voluntarily bring to them, chiefs who assume the role of local court chairmen by collecting fines, pronouncing judgments, presiding over hearings, and charging fees do so in violation of the Local Courts Act.[12]

[3]   See Allison D. Kent, *Custody, Maintenance, and Succession: The Internalization of Women's and Children's Rights under Customary Law in Africa*, 28 MICH. J. INT'L L. 507, 522 (2007).
[4]   *Id.*; Maru, *supra* note 2, at 436 (citing ARTHUR ABRAHAM, MENDE GOVERNMENT AND POLITICS UNDER COLONIAL RULE: A HISTORICAL STUDY OF POLITICAL CHANGE IN SIERRA LEONE 1890–1937 126 (1978)); Vivek Maru, *The Challenges of African Legal Dualism: An Experiment in Sierra Leone*, in HUMAN RIGHTS AND JUSTICE SECTOR REFORM IN AFRICA: CONTEMPORARY ISSUES AND RESPONSES 18 (Open Society Justice Initiative 2005), *available at* http://www.timapforjustice.org/file_download/3.
[5]   Kent, *supra* note 3, at 522.
[6]   See Maru, *supra* note 2, at 436.
[7]   See *id.*; interview with Vivek Maru in Bo, Sierra Leone (Nov. 13, 2005).
[8]   See interview with Vivek Maru, *supra* note 7.
[9]   See Maru, *supra* note 2, at 437.
[10] See *id.* at 523.
[11] See *id.* Each chiefdom consists of sections, which are further divided into villages. Village chiefs enjoy a local level of control over their respective villages, but they are subordinate to section chiefs who operate under the paramount chief that controls the entire chiefdom. *Id.* at 523 n.99.
[12] See *id.* at 524–525.

There are a number of weaknesses in both the customary and formal systems, which impede access to justice. A major problem with customary courts includes the excessive fines and other monetary charges associated with the adjudication of customary disputes.[13] One of the authors observed customary court proceedings in Bo Local Customary Court #1 in southern Sierra Leone and interviewed a woman who was about to be imprisoned for failure to pay a debt and fines imposed by the customary court. Her situation exemplified the astronomical fees often associated with local court proceedings. The customary court had ordered the woman to pay back a debt of 50,000 Leones ($13.12 USD) previously owed to the plaintiff in the case, as well as 42,000 Leones ($11.02) in additional court fees, almost doubling the total amount she owed. Before being placed in a cell where she would remain for fourteen days if no one paid the debt on her behalf, the debtor described the many monetary charges that had been associated with her case. If she did not pay the debt, the court would allow the creditor to make a "thunderbolt swearing," or curse, against her. The court required the debtor to obtain the thunderbolt swearing in the form of a signed document from a medicine man as security in the case. In order to obtain the thunderbolt swearing, the debtor paid 10,000 Leones ($2.62 USD) to the paramount chief, 5,000 Leones ($1.31) to the section chief, and 2,500 Leones ($.66 USD) to the village chief, all to secure a recommendation for a medicine man who would create the swearing for yet another fee. When asked if payment could be symbolic if one did not have the money, the debtor looked perplexed. "You do not go to the chief without money," she replied.[14] Excessive fines and other monetary charges in customary courts remain a serious challenge. The individual fined or jailed might be the family breadwinner, and thus the ramifications of excessive fines and fees may have debilitating effects on entire families.[15]

In addition to excessive fines and court fees, substantive and procedural unfairness is typical in the customary law system and stems from a lack of independent review. Although individuals have the right to appeal local court decisions to the District Appellate Court in the formal court system, such appeals are rare due to lack of resources and access to formal courts.[16] As Vivek Maru, co-founder of Timap, notes, "There is an oceanic divide between the customary and formal realms. If you're looking for rice for tomorrow then how do you have time to go and file an appeal in District Court?"[17] Customary law officers in the Attorney General's office serve as another avenue of potential review of local court decisions.[18]

---

[13]   *See* interview with Vivek Maru, *supra* note 7.
[14]   Interview with debtor in Bo, Sierra Leone (Nov. 14, 2005).
[15]   *See* interview with Marian Tibbie, paralegal, in Bumpeh, Sierra Leone (Nov. 15, 2005).
[16]   *See* Maru, *supra* note 2, at 437.
[17]   Interview with Vivek Maru, *supra* note 7.
[18]   Customary law officers are attorneys who double as public prosecutors in the formal courts in the countryside and reviewers of the decisions of local court chairmen in the local customary courts. Kent, *supra* note 3, at 524; Maru, *supra* note 2, at 437. The independence of customary law officers is

Parties who wish to contest local court decisions can submit their cases for review to customary law officers, who in turn can refer local court cases to the District Appellate Court for review. In practice this is rare and fraught with challenges.[19] There are only three customary law officers in the entire country.[20] In addition, most individuals lack information about how to engage customary law officers to review their cases.[21]

The formal legal system is also imperfect with a severely limited reach to the countryside. Concentrated in the nation's capital of Freetown, the formal legal system consists of a Supreme Court, Court of Appeals, High Courts, Magistrate Courts, and the District Court of Appeals. The Supreme Court consists of a chief justice and three other justices. As of 2006, there were only ten magistrates and twelve high court judges in the country. Five of the ten magistrates are located in Freetown whereas the remaining five rotate throughout the country's twelve provincial magistrate courts. Ten of the twelve high court judges sit in Freetown and the remaining two are assigned to provincial courts. Further impeding representation of ordinary citizens in Sierra Leone's formal courts is the fact that more than 90 percent of Sierra Leone's lawyers are based in Freetown.[22] The court system is incomprehensible, if entertaining, to the vast majority of people. As one of the authors observed magisterial court proceedings, Vivek Maru explained why the courtroom was packed with spectators curious about the peculiar proceedings underway:

> For many [the formal court system] is like a spectator sport. It's like theater but most people don't really understand what's going on.... The formal system here is more British than it is in Britain.... Everything is in code. However, wherever the [formal] law exists there is a mystique and people are drawn to it. It's like black magic to people. It has power but it is a power that most people do not understand.[23]

The formal system is also a time sink – cases move slowly through the system, and the proceedings are in English, with translations further slowing the process.[24]

Because the formal legal system is far removed from the average individual by distance and understanding, customary law assumes far more practical relevance in the everyday lives of Sierra Leoneans, the majority of whom are from rural

---

debated because they are members of the executive branch as opposed to the judicial branch. Maru, *supra* note 2, at 437.

[19] *See* Kent, *supra* note 3, at 524; Interview with Vivek Maru, *supra* note 7.

[20] Maru, *supra* note 2, at 437.

[21] *See* Kent, *supra* note 3, at 524.

[22] Maru, *supra* note 2, at 436.

[23] Interview with Vivek Maru, *supra* note 7.

[24] *See id.*

communities.[25] Far more than the formal courts, it is the system that engages (however imperfectly) their justice dilemmas.

The international development community has been ambivalent about engaging the customary system. Although this is changing in Sierra Leone, justice sector reform efforts have historically failed to pay significant attention to customary forums. The divide between the formal and customary realms in Sierra Leone may be attributable to the historic neglect of the countryside, which during colonialism was regarded as the domain of the "natives."[26] Instead of encouraging the divide between the capital and the countryside, Timap engages both the formal and customary realms, attempts to build bridges between them, advocates for their positive development, and continues to refine mediation techniques that serve as healthy competition to both systems.

8.2.2. *Engaging Legal Dualism*

Recognizing the strengths and weaknesses of both the formal and customary systems, Timap adopts a pragmatic approach to the dualist legal structure and engages both sets of legal institutions to best achieve the needs of its clients.[27] According to Vivek Maru, "There is a saying in Sierra Leone: 'Bear with it.' There is the idea that people must learn to live with arbitrary suffering – that the weak must bow to the powerful. Timap is trying to counter this notion."[28] Timap fulfills this vision by increasing access to justice and making the system work more effectively for ordinary citizens. This approach has also had an effect on the paralegals themselves. Marian Tibbie, a Timap paralegal from the Kaniya office, states: "The organization has given me a strong heart and mind to approach authorities. It has given me a power that I didn't have before on the grassroots level to approach authorities."[29]

Embracing the reality that traditional institutions, despite their limitations, often play a valuable role in the lives of Sierra Leoneans, Timap works to foster the internal positive development of customary law.[30] To curb excesses in the traditional realm, they use the formal system to check unjust decisions from local courts. Through their mediation activities they also provide an alternative route for resolving disputes. The idea is to offer access to the formal and customary systems as well as alternatives to both.

---

[25] *See* Maru, *supra* note 4, at 20.
[26] *See* interview with Vivek Maru, *supra* note 7.
[27] *See* Maru, *supra* note 2, at 460.
[28] Interview with Vivek Maru, *supra* note 7.
[29] Interview with Marian Tibbie, *supra* note 15.
[30] *See* Maru, *supra* note 2, at 460.

8.2.2.1. Engaging Customary Law from Within

Departing from law reform efforts that often focus solely on formal legal systems, Timap works to improve the customary law system from within.[31] Timap's engagement with customary law reflects the organization's respect for customary institutions' traditional origins, accessibility, and relevance to the majority of the population.[32] Distinguishing themselves from conventional "legal missionaries" who work to "banish customary darkness with formal legal light," Timap engages customary law by advocating a positive evolution of traditional institutions.[33] According to Vivek Maru, Timap embraces a delicate, gradual approach to the development of customary law:

> There is a lot of skepticism [in Sierra Leone] with regard to radicalism – the RUF was talking in terms of social transformation and this talk ended up in war. There is a saying in Sierra Leonean culture: 'small-small.' Things can't happen overnight. But change is in the conversations that are started. There is not a lot of institutional imagination, not a lot of rethinking of the social fabric in Sierra Leone. Dialogue is a larger, slower process. But people don't want to just talk about rights. They want to see justice being done. The bread and butter of our work is dealing with people's everyday justice problems. This is what gives us the legitimacy to talk about and encourage dialogue regarding community level problems and change from within.[34]

Relationship building lies at the core of the organization's efforts to support the evolution of customary law. Paralegals identify progressive chiefs and elders who can serve as allies and assist with internal advocacy efforts. They also hold community meetings to foster dialogue on justice issues relevant to a particular chiefdom.[35]

Timap successfully utilized creative thinking and customary law to challenge an age-old practice in its approach to sassywood in Binkolo chiefdom. Sassywood is a potentially lethal concoction made out of tree bark and used as a mystical "judge" to render decisions. Sassywood is most commonly used in customary courts where the accused party is forced to drink the sassywood potion in order to determine his guilt or innocence. The accused is found guilty if he becomes ill after ingesting the sassywood. This can result in the impairment or death of the accused. With the goal of curtailing the practice of sassywood in Binkolo, Timap paralegals worked with local community members to modify the practice so that *both* the accuser and the accused would have to drink the potion if either party insisted on using sassywood in a given

---

[31] See id.
[32] See Maru, *supra* note 4, at 21–22.
[33] See Maru, *supra* note 2, at 461–462.
[34] Interview with Vivek Maru, *supra* note 7.
[35] See Maru, *supra* note 4, at 22.

case. The change in the practice requirements resulted in a dramatic reduction of its use in Binkolo. Armed with an understanding of community dynamics, Timap collaborated with community members to provide a local solution that was accepted by all.[36] These cases exemplify the way in which Timap engages with customary law on its own terms in order to reach the best outcome for a particular client.

In some cases, Timap does not directly challenge the customary law but rather shifts attention away from it onto the problem at hand. In a case of alleged witchcraft, Timap paralegals did not attack the community's belief in witchcraft itself, which customary law acknowledges, but instead intervened and turned the community's attention to the medical causes of the situation. In a village in the Gbonkolenken chiefdom, the parents of a sick child named Lasa accused an elderly woman named Maktaba[37] of being a witch and causing Lasa's serious illness. Lasa had been in Maktaba's care for many years. Even though Maktaba vehemently denied the allegations, the entire village became convinced that Maktaba's witchery was the cause of Lasa's illness and reported the case to the chief for adjudication. The villagers and Lasa's parents did not provide her with western medicine because they were convinced that Maktaba, as the alleged source of the child's illness, was the only individual who could reverse the spell. They called on diviners to identify Maktaba as a witch.[38]

Maktaba appealed to Timap's office for help with her desperate situation. Timap's paralegals, working in partnership with elders and chiefs in the community, approached Lasa's parents and convinced them to suspend fixation on the witchcraft accusations and instead to take Lasa to a health center in the chiefdom's town headquarters. Within a few days of treatment, Lasa's condition rapidly improved. Because the child fully regained her health after treatment, the villagers and Lasa's parents did not pursue the witchcraft charges against Maktaba, and the chiefs did not adjudicate the issue. Maktaba now lives in peace with the villagers. The paralegals, believers in witchcraft themselves, made the calculated decision that directly attacking the villagers' and parents' belief in the possibility of witchcraft as the source of the child's illness would not relieve Maktaba of the allegation. Instead, they focused on convincing the parents, villagers, and chiefs to concentrate on accessing medical intervention for the child.[39] The paralegals' focus on medical intervention in this case undermined the claim of witchcraft in such a way that going forward, villagers may be more prone to seek medical treatment for a sick child rather than accusing a community member of witchcraft.

---

[36] *See* Heather Sensibaugh, *Legality and Localism*, 30 HARV. INT'L REV. (2009).
[37] The authors have changed all client names in the chapter in order to protect confidentiality.
[38] *See* Daniel Sesay, Lead Paralegal, Report on Timap's Customary Law Cases (unpublished report) (on file with author).
[39] *See id.*

8.2.2.2. Using the Formal Legal System as a Check
on the Customary System

Although, as demonstrated earlier, Timap engages customary law when it best suits
the needs of its clients, there are other times when outcomes in customary forums
are unjust. In these cases, Timap may use the formal legal system as a "check"
on excesses within traditional forums.[40] Timap's use of the formal system to check
unfairness and exploitation arising in the customary system provides some of the
most compelling examples of its work.

The case of "Pa Lansana" illustrates Timap's success in its use of the formal system to regulate corruption that is common in the customary system. Pa Lansana, a
farmer in his sixties, brought his case to Timap after he had gone bankrupt by trying to resolve a land dispute in a local court. Although private ownership of land is
impossible under customary land tenure in Pa Lansana's chiefdom, families have a
right to the land that they possess and cultivate based on historic allocation by chiefs.
Pa Lansana's family had enjoyed entitlement to a large fertile plot of land for several
generations. Throughout the course of their land entitlement, the Lansanas had
allowed other local farmers to cultivate palm trees for free on sections of their land.[41]
When a series of family tragedies left the Lansanas in a dire financial situation, Pa
Lansana asked the local farmers who used his family's land for a contribution of
palm oil. The dispute arose when two families refused to contribute.[42]

Pa Lansana initially brought the dispute to his village chief and later filed the case
in his local customary court. After doing so, he discovered that both men involved in
the dispute were related to the paramount chief. He received a letter from the paramount chief informing him that the paramount chief was removing his case from
the local court and would settle the matter personally. Pa Lansana appealed to the
local court chairman to protest the removal of his case, but the local court chairman,
pressured by the paramount chief, instructed Pa Lansana to follow the direction
of the paramount chief.[43] The paramount chief compiled a series of fines against

[40] In its approach to the formal system, Timap uses various avenues in order to bridge the dualist divide.
In some cases, Timap's paralegals assist community members to engage the formal system in fighting
abuses that stem from other organs of the formal system. For example, in 2007, Timap engaged in
advocacy with the Education Ministry to assist a group of education workers to recover two years' worth
of unpaid wages. In support of broader community campaigns and departing from the more common
tactic of responding to a particular abuse, Timap extends access to formal structures so that poor
people can participate and use formal structures to address issues of concern. Examples of Timap's
work in this area include assisting a farmers' cooperative in applying for support from the Ministry of
Agriculture or alerting the Education Ministry to the need for school renovations in rural areas. Maru,
supra note 2, at 461.

[41] *See id.* at 430–431, 443.

[42] *See id.* at 431.

[43] *See id.*

Lansana amounting to 67,000 Leones (USD $25.28) for incidents such as speaking out of turn and for disputing the paramount chief's right to hear the case.[44]

With little hope and no money left, Pa Lansana brought his case to Timap. A Timap paralegal informed him that the paramount chief's actions violated the Local Courts Act and that the law provided him with avenues for redress such as the customary law officer, a government lawyer charged with reviewing contested local court cases. Pa Lansana had never heard of the institution of the customary law officer and was unaware of his right to appeal. With support and advice from the Timap paralegal, Pa Lansana decided to approach the customary law officer to review the paramount chief's actions. After reviewing the case, the customary law officer confronted the paramount chief who reversed his position after facing pressure from the government lawyer and agreed to return Pa Lansana's case back to the local court. He also refunded a portion of the fines paid by Pa Lansana.[45] Timap was able to use the formal legal institution of the customary law officer to check the paramount chief's abuses of the customary law process and help Lansana achieve justice in his case.

In another strategic use of the formal system, one of the co-authors observed Timap appeal to the Customary Law Office to help enforce a local court debt judgment that had been in its client's favor. In a rare move, the debtor in the case had appealed the local court decision to the Bo district appellate court. Simeon Koroma, Timap's co-director and a Sierra Leonean lawyer, represented the creditor in the district appellate court proceedings. The district appellate court judge dismissed the case and held that the local court judgment still stood. Timap believed the debtor used the appellate process as a way to delay the enforcement of the local court judgment. Following the dismissal of the case in district appellate court, one of the co-authors accompanied Timap's co-directors to the Customary Law Office where Timap sought to obtain assistance in enforcing the local court judgment. Fearing that corruption at the local court level would impede enforcement of the judgment, Timap secured an assurance from the customary law officer that he would write a formal letter to the local court chairman instructing him to enforce the judgment.

8.2.2.3. Mediation

In addition to working within the customary law system and using the formal system to challenge unjust outcomes in customary forums, Timap also offers mediation as an alternative to the dualist structure. Timap's approach to mediation is consistent with the best aspects of Sierra Leone's traditional restorative legal tradition

---

[44] *Id.* at 431–432.
[45] *See id.* at 443.

and emphasizes negotiated, peaceful resolutions.[46] In a World Bank report assessing Timap's work, respondents familiar with its mediation process found that Timap sought the most beneficial outcome for all parties and resolved disputes with cultural sensitivity.[47] With the majority of Timap paralegals born and raised in the areas where they work, their approach to mediating disputes is married to an understanding of local dynamics and traditions.[48]

Where appropriate, Timap mediations can engage both modern and traditional approaches, and Timap relies on local, national, and international laws and principles.[49] For example, a Timap paralegal mediating between a misbehaved child and a father who uses a physical method of punishment may begin the mediation by discussing the Convention on the Rights of the Child and end with a traditional ritual where the child places his head on his father's feet.[50]

Timap's staff builds and maintains relationships with traditional leaders, elected officials, the police, and religious officials whom they may involve in mediations where appropriate.[51] The presence of traditional authorities at mediations, for instance, can at times further legitimize the process and help with enforcing mediation agreements.[52] In addition, Timap established Community Oversight Boards (COBs) comprised of local community members and leaders, who oversee paralegals' work, ensure they are serving the community's needs, and provide valuable insights that assist with Timap's mediations.[53]

In some cases, chiefs and police officials have recognized that Timap was better positioned to resolve disputes in a given case, and have called on the organization for advice or have referred cases directly to Timap for dispute resolution. Such collaboration reflects the positive headway that Timap has made in gaining the trust and credibility of community members and leaders alike. These collaborations are not without their tensions, however. Although Timap mostly enjoys support from traditional leaders, some have expressed their frustration and desire for a clearer delineation of dispute resolution roles. Timap's partnership with traditional leaders depends largely on its paralegals respecting the authority of traditional leaders without overstepping boundaries. Several chiefs have requested clarity from Timap regarding the proper dispute resolution roles for chiefs and Timap's paralegals.

---

[46] *See* Pamela Dale, World Bank Justice for the Poor, Delivering Justice to Sierra Leone's Poor: An Analysis of the Work of Timap for Justice 20 (2009).

[47] *See id.*

[48] *See* Chi Mgbako, International Crisis Group, Liberia: Resurrecting the Justice System 12 (Africa Report No. 107, 2006).

[49] *Id.* at 21.

[50] Maru, *supra* note 4, at 22.

[51] *See* Dale, *supra* note 46, at 22.

[52] *See id.*

[53] *See id.* at 23; Maru, *supra* note 2, at 442.

Chiefs were especially concerned that Timap would engage in disputes regulated by chiefdom bylaws, which set out clear fines. They feared this type of interference would impact the chiefdom budget and encourage disrespect for tradition.[54] Timap will mediate a dispute when they believe it is in the best interest of the individuals involved and has the greatest chance of leading to a just outcome. They greatly respect the role of the chiefs and continue to monitor and nurture relationships with traditional authorities to decrease tensions wherever they arise.

8.2.2.4. Confronting Gender Bias in Customary Law

Timap's engagement with customary law presents unique challenges in relation to gender issues where conflicts between customary legal rights and international human rights are often most evident and outcomes for women often unjust. Although Timap accommodates customary law when it is in the best interest of its clients, the organization maintains a hard-line stance with respect to gender-based violence, specifically domestic violence and rape.[55] In its mediation practice, the organization will not accept an agreement between a couple that would allow the husband to beat his wife, even though wife beating is allowed under some forms of customary law. The traditional approach to dealing with rape is through mediation conducted by families or village chiefs, but Timap refuses to mediate rape cases and insists on criminal prosecution for cases involving sexual violence[56] – a stance that may eventually influence customary law in the areas where Timap operates.

Timap also strongly advocates for its female clients' inheritance rights. Under customary law, women are generally prohibited from inheriting family property.[57] In the case of Sadiwa, Timap successfully conducted a mediation that resulted in their client's realization of her property rights. Sadiwa and her husband had purchased land prior to his death. Following her husband's death, Sadiwa's in-laws refused to hand over the deed to the land. Sadiwa had hoped to sell the land so she could support herself and her one-year-old child.

After many fruitless attempts to convince her in-laws to transfer the land deed or sell the property and share the proceeds, Sadiwa approached Timap's office for assistance. The Timap paralegal assigned to the case knew that appealing to customary law would lead to an unjust outcome for Sadiwa. According to Temne customary law, a woman has no rights over her deceased husband's property and is in fact herself considered property. Instead, the paralegal conducted a mediation in which he

[54] *See* Dale, *supra* note 46, at 23.
[55] *See* Maru, *supra* note 2, at 443.
[56] *See id.*
[57] *See id.* at 437.

invited Sadiwa, her in-laws, and Sadiwa's relatives to participate. During the mediation, the paralegal stressed Sadiwa's contribution to the procurement and maintenance of the property. The mediation was successful, and the family agreed to sell
the land and share the proceeds with Sadiwa. An elder later revealed to the Timap
paralegal that it was the first time that a widow in the village had received proceeds
from the sale of her deceased husband's property.

In its handling of family law cases such as child and spousal maintenance, child
protection, and family disagreements, Timap addresses gender bias by utilizing all of
the tools in its arsenal including traditional dispute resolution methods and the evo-
cation of human rights principles and progressive gender-sensitive national law.[58]

8.3. THE JUSTICE AND PEACE COMMISSION
AND LIBERIAN CUSTOMARY LAW

8.3.1. *Legal Dualism in Liberia*

As in Sierra Leone, Liberia's dual legal system is rooted in a history of inequities.
African-American settlers who colonized the region established the Republic of
Liberia in 1843.[59] The colonists, or "Americo-Liberians" as they came to be called,
settled among people whose ancestors had inhabited the region for generations.[60]
Despite their own African descent, they ruled over this "native" local population just
as their European counterparts had in other colonies. They created two legal systems: a western-style formal system for Americo-Liberians and a customary system
for indigenous Liberians in the hinterland.[61] The "natives" could not access formal
courts, and the chiefs who adjudicated customary law had no jurisdiction over "civilized" parties, which included Americo-Liberians and Europeans.[62] Today, customary and formal courts continue to constitute parallel legal structures. In the formal
system, magistrate courts and circuit courts hear both civil and criminal cases. In
the customary system, clan chiefs, town chiefs, and paramount chiefs have original
jurisdiction over civil cases but have no authority over criminal cases.[63]

---

[58] *See* Lotta Teale, Timap for Justice, An Evaluation of the Way that Paralegals at the
Timap Programme in Magburaka, Sierra Leone, Deal with Family Cases 10–13 (2007).

[59] *See* Stephen Ellis, The Mask of Anarchy 192 (2007).

[60] *See id.* at 193.

[61] *See* Jallah A. Barbu, United States Institute for Peace, An Analysis of the Formal Legal
Framework Governing Customary Law in the Republic of Liberia 33 (2009).

[62] *See* Mgbako, *supra* note 48, at 8.

[63] According to the Revised Rules and Regulations of the Hinterland, which delineates the jurisdiction
of customary courts, the Circuit Court of the Assize has original jurisdiction over criminal offenses.
This court of "Assiz," here included in the customary framework, is the same Circuit Court in the
statutory framework. In other words, only formal courts can preside over criminal offenses. Revised
Rules and Regulations Governing the Hinterland of Liberia Art. 38 (2000).

Chiefs are quasi-executive and quasi-judicial figures. They are employed by the executive Ministry of Internal Affairs but their judicial decisions are subject to judicial review by the Circuit Court and Supreme Court.[64] Although they are free to adjudicate cases under customary law, they are bound by constitutional and formal limitations. Where customary and formal laws conflict, the Supreme Court has held that formal law prevails.[65] Although the customary system is subject to formal law, in practice it has generally operated separately and virtually unchecked by formal authority.[66]

Each system has its strengths and weaknesses. Customary forums, despite the limitations discussed later, meet Liberians' now well-documented desire for justice that is efficient, culturally relevant, and reconciliatory.[67] Traditional authorities attempt to get to the "root cause" of a problem, addressing not only the symptom or offense, but also the underlying tensions and relationships.[68] Customary law is mostly reconciliatory, unlike western notions of justice in which one party wins and one party loses. The parties share the kola nut after the dispute – a tradition rooted in forgiveness.[69] Reconciliation is often deemed more important than the finding of right or wrong of one party or another.

Notwithstanding the positive aspects of the customary system, as in Sierra Leone, customary justice in Liberia is expensive and at times incompetent. Liberian customary forums can impose excessive fees and misuse or abuse their authority. Although chiefs are technically employed by the state, they are often unpaid and earn their livelihood through fines and fees.[70] Chiefs are largely untrained in the law – or in any adjudication methods – and may incorrectly apply both customary and formal law alike.[71] Many do not know, do not understand, or choose to ignore formal limitations on their jurisdiction. They tend to apply customary law even when it infringes on constitutional or formal rights.[72]

---

[64] See Barbu, *supra* note 61, at 28.

[65] See Tenteah v. Republic of Liberia, 7 L.L.R. 63 (1940).

[66] In addition to the state-sponsored customary and formal courts, informal justice mechanisms have emerged in the form of secret societies. The Poro and the Sande secret societies adjudicate disputes without formal authority. For further review of the Poro and Sande, see INTERNATIONAL CRISIS GROUP, LIBERIA AND SIERRA LEONE: REBUILDING FAILED STATES (Africa Report No. 87, 2004). *See also* DEBORAH H. ISSER ET AL., UNITED STATES INSTITUTE OF PEACE, LOOKING FOR JUSTICE: LIBERIAN EXPERIENCES WITH AND PERCEPTIONS OF LOCAL JUSTICE OPTIONS 23 (2009).

[67] See Isser et al., *supra* note 66, at 3–4.

[68] See *id.* at 27.

[69] See EZEKIEL PAJIBO, INSTITUTE FOR DEMOCRACY AND ELECTORAL ASSISTANCE, TRADITIONAL JUSTICE MECHANISMS: THE LIBERIAN CASE 17 (2008).

[70] See Mgbako, *supra* note 48, at 8.

[71] See *id.* at 8. Note that the Carter Center has been partnering with the Ministry of Internal Affairs and is beginning to provide training to traditional leaders on rule of law.

[72] See Telephone interview with Raymond Chie, JPC Lead Monitor, in Grand Kru, Liber. (Feb. 15 2010).

Chiefs continue to illegally preside over criminal cases and apply customary law often to the detriment of the accused.[73] Chiefs throughout Liberia practice a type of magic called Trial by Ordeal to determine the guilt of an accused party. They administer some form of potential harm to the accused, and he is deemed innocent only if he is able to withstand that harm.[74] There are various forms of this practice. Some, like forcing the accused to eat dirt, are relatively harmless. Others, such as sassywood, also practiced in Sierra Leone, where the accused must drink from a poisonous tree bark, can be deadly. Sassywood is explicitly forbidden by the Rules and Regulations Governing the Hinterland and has been found to be unconstitutional by the Supreme Court, but other forms of trial by ordeal are also illegal to the extent that the chief is exercising jurisdiction over criminal offenses.[75]

As in Sierra Leone and other parts of Africa, customary forums in Liberia can be particularly unjust to women. Under customary law, women are property to be bought with a dowry. Because they are property, they cannot buy, inherit, or own property.[76] Women are also often left without recourse from physical or sexual violence in the home.[77] Although customary forums are traditionally inclusive, bringing interested parties together under the "palava hut," women are rarely represented in important deliberations.

Despite these flaws, the vast majority of Liberians adjudicate their legal issues in the customary realm. The formal system is literally and figuratively far from their reality. Courts are inaccessible, expensive, corrupt, and incomprehensible. The fees and abuse of authority prevalent in customary justice are equally as prevalent in the formal justice system. Liberians overwhelmingly lack confidence in justice institutions, including the police, magistrate courts, circuit courts, and administrative bodies.[78] A recent cross-county survey by Oxford CSAE found that 89 percent of disputes that were taken to a third party for resolution were taken to a customary authority, compared to eleven percent taken to a formal institution.[79] The international community has focused on the inequities and generally failed to embrace the positive aspects and traditions within customary law.[80]

---

[73] *See* Mgbako, *supra* note 48, at 8.

[74] *See* Isser et al., *supra* note 66, at 58.

[75] *See* Rules and Regulations Governing the Hinterland Art. 73 (2000); Jedah v. Horace, 2 L.L.R. 26 (1916).

[76] *See* When the Carter Center initially conducted rule of law education, Liberian men were surprised to learn that their wives would inherit one-third of their property. Some men asked, "How can property own property?" *See* THE CARTER CENTER, REPORT ON PROJECT ACTIVITIES FOR THE MINISTRY OF JUSTICE 15 (2007) (on file with author).

[77] *See* Telephone interview with Raymond Chie, *supra* note 72.

[78] *See* Mgbako, *supra* note 48, at 1.

[79] *See id.* at 25.

[80] *See* Isser et al., *supra* note 66, at 6.

8.3.2. *Engaging Legal Dualism*

Like Timap for Justice, the Justice and Peace Commission (JPC) works with ordinary people in rural areas for whom both the formal and customary systems are flawed. JPC monitors help clients navigate traditional and formal forums or opt out of both and mediate the case instead. In whichever forum, JPC promotes access to justice for a given client by ensuring that the client understands the law and processes, plays an active role in the legal or quasi-legal process, that her voice is heard, and that her case is fairly adjudicated.

JPC dwells at the crossroads, striving to harness the good in both the customary and formal realms while discouraging the corruption and injustices that plague both systems. It embraces the Liberian values of peace and reconciliation and believes that the inequities within customary forums can be overcome. JPC hopes to infuse customary law with principles of equal rights by working alongside traditional authorities as cultural leaders. Quietly and respectfully, JPC uses the legal authority of formal law to check customary courts. Finally, like Timap, JPC offers mediation as an alternative, adding healthy competition to the justice marketplace and promoting transparency and fairness from the outside.

While JPC's greatest challenges arise when formal law clashes with customary law, JPC monitors can navigate the dual landscape because they are members of the communities they serve. Yet in a culture that so values maintaining relationships, it is taxing to challenge community norms, especially when JPC monitors may harbor some of the biases the program is designed to contest. Women's rights cases illustrate this internal predicament.

8.3.2.1. Empowering Traditional Authorities with Formal Law

JPC monitors approach customary law with the utmost respect but seek to infuse it with principles of fairness and equality. They hope that continual exposure to formal law and personal relationships will influence traditional authorities to internalize the law as their own but must directly challenge traditional authorities when they violate formal law or abuse their authority. JPC monitors also have to maintain relationships with both customary and formal officials even when they challenge abuses of power.[81]

---

[81] *See* telephone interview with John Hummel, TCC Project Manager, in Monrovia, Liber. (Feb. 12, 2010). JPC monitors are constantly working with both formal and customary authorities, but they tend to engage customary authorities more often. Mobile monitors, or those monitors who travel from rural village to village, engage customary authorities three times as often as formal authorities. *See* The Carter Center, Community Legal Advisor Program Case Data Analysis 2008–2009 Preliminary Draft 29 (2010). These statistics reflect JPC's pragmatic approach to customary institutions, given their dominance in rural communities.

In their quest to bridge the gap between customary and formal law, JPC enlists traditional leaders. As JPC monitor Eleane Keamue describes, "The good aspects of the customary law are that the chiefs are there and they know the people well, they are respected among their people. They are real leaders."[82] Effecting change in the community, then, must be done through the chiefs. JPC's Regional Coordinator in the Southeast, Thomas Mawolo, points out, "If you leave the chief out or the community out of the process, you will not really achieve the goal. So in everything we are doing, we have to have them involved."[83]

JPC's work begins with community education. Monitors conduct workshops with a dual purpose: 1) to educate communities about formal laws and human rights; and 2) to advertise the services that they provide. The majority of JPC's cases arise out of these education efforts. The outreach begins with the chiefs.[84] The monitor approaches the chief and introduces himself. He states his full name, explains who he works for and what his goals are, and then finally asks permission to speak with the community. He asks that the chief be present during the education to provide his symbolic approval.[85]

For the most part, the chiefs warmly receive the JPC monitors. They benefit politically from "inviting" legal specialists to share knowledge with their constituents, and many chiefs appreciate the legal education themselves.[86] Some have told the monitors, "This law that you are talking about, this is the first time we are hearing it. If you continue to do this, it will help us."[87] These trainings are not one-off drop-ins. Monitors go back to the communities and establish a presence there as they begin to take cases. The education is ongoing and becomes a dialogue.[88] Yet the people do not always – and are not expected to – immediately accept the human rights concepts or new formal laws on equal rights, rape, or inheritance. They ask questions over time and wrestle with these new concepts.

JPC is primarily "training" on formal law, but it also often appeals to customary law and culture. As the Carter Center trains JPC monitors, they suggest, "Don't

---

[82]   Telephone interview with Eleane Keamue, JPC Monitor, in Ganta, Liber. (Feb. 15, 2010).

[83]   Telephone interview with Thomas Mawolo, JPC Regional Coordinator, in Harper, Liber. (Feb. 9, 2010).

[84]   *See* telephone interview with Bindu Kromah, TCC Project Officer, The Carter Center, in Gbarnga, Liber. (Feb. 12, 2010); telephone interview with Nyan Flomo, TCC Project Officer, in Gbarnga, Liber. (Feb. 12, 2010); telephone interview with Eleane Keamue, *supra* note 82; telephone interview with Thomas Mawolo, *supra* note 83.

[85]   *See* telephone interview with Thomas Mawolo, *supra* note 83; The Carter Center & Ministry of Justice, Handbook for Civil Society Partners, Community Education and Awareness Program on the Rule of Law 5 (2008) (on file with author).

[86]   *See* telephone interview with John Hummel, *supra* note 81.

[87]   Telephone interview with Thomas Mawolo, *supra* note 83.

[88]   *See* telephone interview with A.B. Wleemogar Tyler II, JPC Monitor, in Maryland, Liber. (Feb. 9, 2010).

think of your work as always imposing something new upon the people. Instead, look for the ways they are already demonstrating the values we are trying to share.... Enter communities with an open mind, remembering that none of us has all the answers."[89] When monitors teach on sassywood, for example, they remind that the "Liberian way" of resolving problems is to bring people together and to sit and talk openly. Sassywood is against this culture because it is secretive.[90]

JPC monitors ask the community to consider their traditions in a fresh light. JPC monitor Wleemogar Tyler explains, "In the past, if I have my wife and I die, my wife will go in the middle of the family to make relation for new family. She is grieving for past husband. This is the way we put it to the traditional people to get their own point of view. We are always forcing the woman to do something she does not want to do.... And people tell me, 'I know it is true.'"[91] The principles of equality on which formal law is based resonate with people. Those in power have historically driven the inequities in customary law, whereas the historically disempowered have longed for the articulation of these rights.[92]

Even chiefs may see tradition differently when they consider its implications for their own families. Wleemogar Tyler continues, "People don't believe that woman is entitled to property. But today, the inheritance law says that women are entitled to the property of their parents. And if you ask the chief, 'Who will take control of *your* property?' he will say, 'I prefer my own child to have my property.' So I tell them, 'Try the new law and see.'"[93] Because JPC monitors are members of the communities they serve, they are able to challenge these norms personally and persuasively.

JPC hopes that chiefs will eventually internalize the formal law in such a way that the chief and the community come to "own" the law.[94] If a widow comes to a chief because her husband's family tries to take her property, a chief might tell the family that she has the right to own the property under the new Inheritance Law.[95] Yet, The Carter Center (TCC) and JPC are realistic. TCC Project Manager John Hummel says, "There are some ways that they'll change and some ways they won't. But at least they'll know the law."[96]

Remarkably, chiefs have ceded some of their own authority to seek out JPC's advice. For example, a chief recently invited JPC to take part in a case where the

[89] THE CARTER CENTER & MINISTRY OF JUSTICE, *supra* note 85, at 11.
[90] *See* telephone interview with Jeffrey Austin, former TCC Project Officer, in Atlanta, Ga. (Feb. 6, 2010).
[91] Telephone interview with A.B. Wleemogar Tyler II, *supra* note 88.
[92] *See* Mgbako, *supra* note 48, at 9.
[93] Telephone interview with A.B. Wleemogar Tyler II, *supra* note 88.
[94] *See* telephone interview with Laurie Reyman, TCC Project Officer, in Harper, Liber. (Feb. 12, 2010).
[95] The "Inheritance Law" or the Equal Rights of the Customary Marriage Law of 2003 provides that a woman has the right to own property and a woman whose husband dies intestate inherits one-third of his property. *See* Equal Rights of Customary Marriage Law §§ 2.6, 3.2 (2003).
[96] Telephone interview with John Hummel, *supra* note 81.

husband was trying to disown his wife. The chief called JPC as an expert to explain the law to the husband.[97] In some cases, chiefs have turned over their adjudication entirely to JPC. A chief in Baila, Bong County, came to JPC monitor George Mulbah with a dispute between community members and the community leaders. The community felt that the leaders had misused funds entrusted to them for communal projects. JPC facilitated a large mediation session for the community members, leaders, and the chief. During mediation, the accused leaders admitted their wrongdoing and begged the community to forgive them. In the end, the group created financial policies to prevent fiscal abuse in the future. Afterward they all shared the kola nut.[98] As a neutral outsider, Mulbah was able to guide the parties toward resolution and reconciliation. The mediation was both fair and culturally sensitive.

8.3.2.2. Appealing Customary Court Decisions

Of course there are also times when chiefs perceive JPC as a threat to their autonomy. Where a traditional authority violates formal law or abuses their authority, JPC monitors, like Timap paralegals, serve as watchdogs and advocates.

Clients approach JPC when they are dissatisfied with the way a chief has handled a particular case.[99] Most chiefs encourage parties to go to another forum if they are not satisfied with the holding.[100] Clients may choose to take the case to mediation, to formal court, or appeal the case within the customary framework, but the appeal is rarely as linear as the pathway provided by law.

Clients who wish to appeal the chief's decision to a higher authority may use JPC as the first step of the appellate process.[101] If the chief has violated formal law, the JPC monitor will first delicately and respectfully approach the chief and explain the law in question. She will then explain that the Supreme Court has held that where the formal law and customary law conflict, the formal law rules.[102] If advocacy at the local level is not successful, the JPC monitor can help the client appeal to the County Commissioner, the Ministry of Internal Affairs representative who presides over customary authorities.[103]

---

[97] *See* telephone interview with David K. Zaza, Jr., JPC Lead Monitor, in Zorzor, Liber. (Feb. 18, 2010).
[98] *See* telephone interview with George P. Mulbah, JPC Monitor, in Gbarnga, Liber. (Feb. 15, 2010).
[99] *See* telephone interview with Nyan Flomo, *supra* note 84; telephone interview with Laurie Reyman, *supra* note 94.
[100] *See* Isser et al., *supra* note 66, at 33.
[101] *See* Cases heard in the Court of the Clan Chief, or by village chiefs, may be appealed to the Paramount Chief and then to the Court of the District Commissioner. *See* Revised Rules and Regulations Governing the Hinterland of Liberia Art. 38 (2001).
[102] *See* Tenteah v. Republic of Liberia, 7 L.L.R. 63 (1940).
[103] *See* Isser et al., *supra* note 66, at 33. The County Commissioner is an executive officer under the Ministry of Internal Affairs with administrative duties in the county. Interestingly, he also has appellate

JPC may use both formal law and culture to challenge customary law in a particular case, but might not prevail even when the law is clear. For example, JPC client,
Susan Cooper, was accused of witchcraft. The community wanted to perform Trial
by Ordeal, or force her to drink from a poisonous tree to determine if she was guilty.
JPC explained to the elders that this practice is unconstitutional and when they
insisted, JPC involved state authorities. The community eventually hired an herb-
alist/healer instead of performing Trial by Ordeal, and the healer determined that
Susan was indeed a witch. They then attempted to charge Susan for the herbalist's
expense. Susan decided that to pay this money would be to admit her "guilt" and
declined. The community in turn forbade her from working on the farm and virtually banished her from the community.

JPC then changed tactics and appealed to culture. They pleaded that according
to its own values, the community takes care of its people and ensures that no member goes hungry. It was wrongly punishing Susan's innocent husband, children, and
other relatives for her alleged "transgression." The community never acquiesced,
and Susan was banned from the farm. The case was not resolved until two years
later when her husband's family paid the fee to the community. JPC's success in this
case was mixed: They did succeed in saving Susan from Trial by Ordeal but were
not able to convince the community to accept her. Traditional leaders are not always
receptive to direct challenges to their authority.

8.3.2.3. Enforcing Jurisdiction

In the chaos that came with Liberia's long civil wars, state and non-state actors alike
assumed extraordinary judicial authority and "presided" over criminal and civil
cases. The United States Institute for Peace (USIP) recently conducted an extensive national qualitative survey on Liberian experiences with and perceptions of
justice. The USIP report found that there is still a "remarkable degree to which a
broad range of actors who have no legally or socially recognized roles in any forum
become involved in … cases ranging from the most trivial to the most serious."[104]
Many traditional leaders, like state officials, took advantage of the lawless state to
abuse their authority. Chiefs acted as police officers, judges, and even wardens, forcing "prisoners" to work in their fields.[105]

JPC intervenes in cases where traditional authorities preside over criminal cases.
Where a chief attempts to adjudicate a crime, JPC gently reminds him that he is

---

adjudicatory power as the "Court of the District Commissioner," according to the Revised Rules and
Regulations Governing the Hinterland of Liberia Art. 38 (2001). In practice, the Commissioner informally hears appeals or complaints in his office.

[104] Isser et al., *supra* note 66, at 24.

[105] *See* Mgbako, *supra* note 48, at 8.

acting outside his jurisdiction. If he persists, JPC will report him to the Commissioner or even the County Attorney, the county prosecutor responsible for felonies.

Again this task is not easy. TCC Project Officer, Nyan Flomo, states, "The challenges have been very real from the traditional people *and* from the court system because [JPC] might be stopping them from what they were previously doing.... They think JPC is coming to do away with their job."[106] Traditional authorities and formal authorities acting outside of their jurisdiction collect fees to preside over these matters, and JPC interference is perceived to be taking away their livelihood.

JPC faces an even greater concern: While customary forums may be inappropriate for criminal proceedings, the formal system in its current form may not be any better. When Liberians have obeyed the law and followed the government's repeated requests to direct criminal cases to formal courts, they have been appalled by the results.[107] A victim may be asked to pay fees for gas money for the police, the writ of arrest, the detainee's food in prison, the suspect's transportation to court, bribes for the clerk and warden, and lawyers' fees.[108] Suspects are often released because the single prosecutor in the county has not been able to bring charges within the statutory window.

Traditional authorities are not only embarrassed by jurisdictional limits but also frustrated with the lack of a viable alternative. The government in Monrovia has forbidden traditional authorities from practicing Trial by Ordeal, a ritual that traditional authorities believe deters crime and successfully identifies perpetrators, but the state's own attempts to combat crime have been deficient at best.[109] The withdrawal of criminal jurisdiction from the customary courts combined with the inadequacy of the formal courts has simply resulted in less justice.[110] The USIP survey found that "various forms of crime, social conflict, and acrimony are perceived to be flourishing, unchecked by either the debilitated and discredited formal court system, or by customary institutions perceived to have been hobbled by government policies that undermine their effectiveness."[111] Liberians blame the State for the mounting insecurity and perceived lawlessness in their communities.

In this regard, JPC is stuck between a rock and a hard place. JPC may lose credibility in traditional communities by directing criminal cases to a formal system that is not functioning. As Laurie Reyman, TCC Project Officer and primary liaison to the JPC Program, explains, "Justice vacuum is a great term. People look at us and we all know that if you indeed go to the police, there's a good chance they'll be

---

[106] Telephone interview with Nyan Flomo, *supra* note 84.
[107] *See* Isser et al., *supra* note 66, at 3.
[108] *See id.* at 3.
[109] *See id.* at 53.
[110] *See id.*
[111] *See id.* at 77.

corrupt or inept and nothing will actually happen to resolve your problem. No good answer yet, except 'we're trying.'"[112] TCC Project Manager John Hummel similarly admits, "This is a risk that's developing. We started the messaging before we had the resources."[113] In other words, the State passed the new limits and the Ministry of Justice worked with their partners to spread the word long before the formal system had the capacity to try these cases effectively. On the other hand, customary authorities practicing sassywood, presiding over criminal cases without real legal training, and detaining prisoners with forced labor in their fields is not a good alternative either.[114] Real reform in the formal system will take decades. It is in this transitional period that a program like JPC can be most fruitful.

8.3.2.4. Mediation as a Third Alternative

Perhaps JPC's greatest contribution to the dual legal system is the provision of mediation as a free and fair alternative. It is now well documented that Liberians are dissatisfied with the formal justice system.[115] Even if the formal system functioned as it should, the western-style justice model where one party wins and one party loses would not meet the justice need in rural Liberian communities.[116] Liberians prefer justice mechanisms that allow them to resolve the dispute while maintaining their relationships.

JPC's mediation models the reconciliation, speed, proximity, and cultural relevance of the customary system, and is fully informed by the rights that the formal law is meant to protect. Unlike both the formal and customary systems, it is free, fair, and voluntary. Mediation comes naturally to Liberians. It parallels the tradition of the palava hut, where parties sit and speak openly to address problems.[117] After a successful JPC mediation, the parties often share the kola nut or prepare a feast to celebrate the resolution of the dispute.[118]

Like Sierra Leone, Liberia's dual legal system is a marketplace for justice, and JPC adds some healthy competition. To the extent that JPC offers a free, fair, culturally relevant alternative down the road, traditional authorities might improve their own forums. As John Hummel explains, "It keeps customary leaders on their toes. If you're the only game in town, you're charging fees. If not, you might have to improve the way you dispense justice."[119]

[112] Telephone interview with Laurie Reyman, *supra* note 94.
[113] Telephone interview with John Hummel, *supra* note 81.
[114] *See* Mgbako, *supra* note 48, at 10.
[115] *See* Isser et al., *supra* note 66, at 3–4; Mgbako, *supra* note 48, at 8.
[116] *See* Isser et al., *supra* note 66, at 4.
[117] *See* telephone interview with Jeffrey Austin, *supra* note 90; *see also* Pajibo, *supra* note 69, at 18.
[118] JPC monitor David Zaza said, "At the end of mediation, we often drink kola nut together. People believe it." Telephone interview, *supra* note 97.
[119] Telephone interview with John Hummel, *supra* note 81.

8.3.2.5. At the Crossroads: Gender Issues

JPC is playing many roles in Liberia's justice marketplace: Monitors can be neutral mediators, advocates, educators, watchdogs, or all of the above in a single case. They have a delicate position in the community. They respect cultural and formal authorities even as they challenge them; they seek to build and maintain relationships in the community even as they question community norms. Monitors struggle in the balance. Interviews reveal their deep concerns for their reputations and perceptions of them in the community. Monitors indicated, for example, that they often mediate a dispute instead of advocating for a client because they are afraid of alienating the community even when the law or "justice" is on the client's side.[120] They want to be seen as neutral.

This advocate-mediator dilemma is particularly acute in areas where the formal law clashes with customary law or community norms, and there is no greater clash than in the area of women's rights. Raymond Chie, lead monitor in Barclayville describes:

> There are many ways the formal law conflicts with custom and the customs will always be there. For example, the woman will not be able to report the husband when the husband does something to [her], when the woman's rights have been violated. They have been denied decision-making in the communities because a customary woman belongs to the kitchen or to the farm or to take care of the home. These are customs that were handed down by our people. The new statutes are saying that all are equal before the law. All have equal rights. And a woman is not just a housekeeper.... Under customary law, if a woman has money, she is supposed to give her money to her uncle or brother to buy things for her. Even if she wanted to take a cow, she must go through this man. But right now everyone has the right to own property. So property ownership, customarily, that belongs to the man.[121]

These "rights" are new, or newly protected, under formal law: that a woman has the right to own and inherit property, that she has the right to decide whom she will marry, that her husband cannot beat or rape her.[122] There is great resistance to the new laws in communities that have valued a different tradition for generations; and some traditional authorities cling fast to the customary norms they feel

---

[120] *See* interview with Raymond Chie, Gabriel Nimely, & Thomas Mawolo in Barclayville, Liber. (Oct. 23, 2008).

[121] Telephone interview with Raymond Chie, *supra* note 72.

[122] In the last ten years, Liberia has passed significant legislation protecting women's rights. The Equal Rights of Customary Marriage Law of 2003 protects customary wives' rights before, within, and after marriage. Shortly thereafter, the amended Rape Law of 2005 withdrew the spousal exemption for rape, under which marriage was an affirmative defense to sex by force without consent. *See* Act to Amend the New Penal Code Chapter 14 Sections 14.70 and 14.71 and to Provide for Gang Rape § 5(b) (2005).

are under siege by the people in Monrovia. If monitors are so concerned with their perception in the community, how will they handle the advocate-mediator dilemma in these cases? It turns out that their approach depends on the type of gender issue. Monitors take a firm stand against customary law in forced marriage, dowry, and inheritance cases, but they often cling to neutrality in domestic violence and rape cases.

MARRIAGE AND PROPERTY. Monitors overwhelmingly choose to be advocates in inheritance, forced marriage, or dowry cases. Each monitor reports that formal law trumps customary law according to the Supreme Court, and the law is clear. The Equal Rights of the Customary Marriage Law 2003 provides that: 1) a woman has the right to own property; 2) no woman shall be forced to marry a husband not of her choosing, including her husband's kin should he die; 3) a woman whose husband dies intestate inherits one-third of his property; 4) dowry is considered a gift; it may not be required to be returned in case of separation or divorce.[123] Monitors discourage clients from going to traditional authorities in these cases and instead advocate on the woman's behalf. JPC Lead Monitor Raymond Chie explains, "If the woman goes to the chief, the chief may use the traditional law. But under the [formal] law, the woman owns the property. We give education on these new laws. We call the family of that man. And we try to advocate for the woman. Strictly advocate because the law is on the books."[124] For example, when client Emily Post separated from her husband, he asked her family for the dowry back. The JPC monitor approached him and explained that not only could he not get the money back, but he could be fined if he attempted to force her to return it. The monitor also explained the law to the chief and elders and successfully recruited them to confront the husband.[125]

Monitors advocate for these rights even when the community and traditional authorities object and express their displeasure with the monitor. When JPC client Elizabeth Sampson's husband died, her husband's family tried to force her to marry his brother. JPC Southeast Coordinator Thomas Mawolo went to the chief to explain that under the law, she did not have to marry anyone. The chief became angry with JPC and yelled, "You people are causing problems!"[126] Here, Thomas Mawolo's reputation and relationship with the traditional authorities in this village were at risk, but he chose to continue to advocate on her behalf, taking the case to the Commissioner. In both of these cases, the monitors took a strong advocacy role.

---

[123] *See* Equal Rights of Customary Marriage Law §§ 2.6, 2.10, 3.2, 2.2 (2003).
[124] Telephone interview with Raymond Chie, *supra* note 72.
[125] *See* telephone interview with Helen Kieh, JPC Monitor, in Sinoe, Liber. (Feb. 15, 2010).
[126] Telephone interview with Thomas Mawolo, *supra* note 83.

DOMESTIC VIOLENCE. Paradoxically, JPC monitors have historically taken the opposite approach in domestic violence cases, remaining neutral as they emphasized reconciliation, thus erring on the side of Liberian tradition and culture. Although domestic violence is a crime under formal law in Liberia, it is generally mediated in customary and formal forums alike.[127] Under customary law, women are generally not to report their spouses for what happens behind closed doors.[128] But if particularly severe or public, a woman might bring the problem to the chief. The chief will hear both sides and bring the families together. He might tell the husband not to beat his wife, but he will surely remind the wife to respect her husband. Community-based women's rights groups, like SEWODA, take a similar approach, telling an abusive spouse not to beat his wife and encouraging the wife not to do things that irritate her husband.[129] Indeed, most mediations in domestic violence are more like marriage counseling. Thunder Tikklo, a Women and Children Protection police officer in Harper, explains that violence is against the law, but then he asks abusers to make a list of all the things that bother him in their marriage. The parties sign an agreement in which the wife promises not to do those things, and the husband promises not to beat her.[130]

JPC's current approach to domestic violence is not unlike these other forums.[131] Consider Elizabeth Smith's case: By the time Elizabeth came to JPC, she had had enough of her husband's physical abuse. Visibly injured, she traveled by foot several miles to JPC's office in Harper. JPC monitors greeted her warmly, listened to her story, and sympathized as she told them that she wanted a divorce. Then they sent her home. Alone. They convinced her that she should not leave the household and instead she should apologize and reconcile with her husband. They promised that they would follow up and conduct mediation later. The following week, a monitor went to Elizabeth's home and guided her and her husband through mediation; they signed a mediation agreement in which she promised to respect him and he promised not to beat her.[132]

---

[127] There is no explicit "Domestic Violence" statute in Liberia, but spousal violence is generally accepted to constitute assault and battery. *See* Ministry of Justice, Standard Operating Procedures for GBV: Justice Sector Response 2 (2009) (on file with author).

[128] *See* telephone interview with Raymond Chie, *supra* note 72.

[129] *See* interview with SEWODA members Marie C. Tobey, Valeria B. Samalee, Marah A. Suku, Comfort B. Hinneh, Cecilia M. Williams & Regina W. Jarpee, in Harper, Liber. (Oct. 21, 2008).

[130] *See* interview with Thunder Tikklo, Police Officer, Women and Children Protection Section, in Harper, Liber. (Oct. 20, 2008).

[131] Note that JPC is in the process of creating Domestic Violence protocols. Their new approach will be discussed later in the chapter.

[132] *See* interview with JPC Monitors Caroline Doe, Benetta Sebo & A.B. Wleemogar Tyler, JPC Coordinator Thomas Mawolo, Attorney John Gbesioh & TCC's Bindu A. Kromah, in Harper, Liber. (Oct. 20, 2008).

Elizabeth's case is not uncommon, and the human rights implications are troubling. JPC monitors always discourage separation and divorce because it is against their culture. In one isolated case, JPC even represented an abusive husband and helped him beg his wife to return to him.[133] Monitors expressed that even though they sympathize with victims, they do not want to be seen as breaking up families.[134] Monitors emphasize reconciliation at all costs, even at the expense of a client's safety or stated desire, as in Elizabeth's case.

The written resolutions are also troublesome. In one mediation agreement, the wife promised to cook for her husband and he promised not to beat her.[135] In another case, where the man would get drunk and beat up his girlfriend to the extent that she became unconscious, the man promised not to beat his girlfriend and she promised to respect him.[136] Indeed, the bargains for respect in exchange for non-violence appear to be common. Rather than staying "neutral," JPC may actually be doing harm in these cases. The agreements reinforce the message that the husband has permission to beat the wife if she "disrespects" him in some way. JPC implies that safety is something for which one must bargain, rather than a basic human right.

RAPE. Monitors expressed that rape cases are particularly challenging. Under customary law, rape has traditionally been handled "the family way," where the family of the accused pays the family of the victim to make restitution for the offense.[137] To take the offender to court or send him to prison is interpreted as a slight to his family. In contrast, the state has taken a firm stance that rape is a crime reserved for the formal system. Liberia passed a robust Rape Law in 2005, followed by advocacy campaigns that broadcast that rape must be prosecuted and encouraged communities to report rape to the police.[138] The problem is that rape is subject to the justice vacuum discussed earlier.[139] Most Liberians have heard the message that rape must be referred to formal courts, but few Liberians are satisfied with the way police or courts handle these cases.[140]

The formal law is virtually impossible to enforce. Lead monitor Raymond Chie notes the problems at all levels: Rape cases are "very difficult to handle because of all the actors from the survivor or survivor's family and the police. There is always

[133] *See* telephone interview with Jeffrey Austin, *supra* note 90.
[134] *See* interview with Caroline Doe et al., *supra* note 132.
[135] *See id.*
[136] *See* telephone interview with George P. Mulbah, *supra* note 98.
[137] *See* interview with Caroline Doe et al., *supra* note 132.
[138] *See* Act to Amend the New Penal Code chapter 14 Sections 14.70 and 14.71, and to Provide for Gang Rape (2005).
[139] *See* Isser et al., *supra* note 66, at 70.
[140] *See id.*

the issue of money. If you get all of these documents, sometimes the survivor's family will not appear in court.... Survivors are not willing to go to court."[141]

Monitors' responses to rape cases appear to be mixed. Some play an active role. JPC monitor Helen Kieh, for example, describes the importance of helping the survivor's family understand the legal process: "JPC tells them not to wash the clothes and keep everything that they have from the rape so that it may be evidence. Some people are not aware that they need to keep the evidence.... [Sometimes] the girl's family members destroy evidence because they do not want the girl to go to court. That's why the education is so important." Other monitors, however, simply refer cases to the police since "[rape] goes to the criminal justice system."[142]

JPC's approach to rape actually seems to be shifting away from advocacy toward neutrality. Previously, JPC seemed comfortable in the role of advocate for a rape survivor. JPC would never mediate a rape case, but they could help a client through the medico-legal process. JPC monitor Caroline Doe in particular demonstrated exemplary practices: She told a survivor and her family that the rape was not her fault, went with her to the hospital to ensure that she got proper specialized care, accompanied her to the police station to make the report, and helped her throughout the prosecution.[143] When one of the authors followed up with telephone interviews in February 2010, however, JPC and TCC staff indicated that monitors' approach to rape had changed. Monitors no longer accompany a rape survivor to the hospital or police station. They might follow up after her, but they do not want to be seen walking alongside her.[144]

This new hesitancy to accompany a rape survivor to the police or court is another manifestation of fear of their perception in the community. Monitors are, perhaps legitimately, concerned for their safety. If tradition suggests that the survivor is slighting the offender's family by reporting the case to the police, then the monitor will also be seen as "taking sides." It is interesting, however, that monitors do not share this concern in other types of cases, where they clearly advocate for one particular party against another who has violated their rights.

8.4. TOWARD AN ADVOCACY APPROACH TO GENDER-BASED VIOLENCE

JPC's emphasis on neutrality in gender-based violence cases stands in stark contrast to the unequivocal advocacy in marriage, inheritance, and right-to-property cases.

---

[141] Telephone interview with Raymond Chie, *supra* note 72.
[142] Telephone interview with Michael Biddle, JPC Lead Monitor, in Gbarnga, Liber. (Feb. 18, 2010).
[143] *See* interview with Caroline Doe et al., *supra* note 132.
[144] *See* telephone interview with Laurie Reyman, *supra* note 94; telephone interview with Bindu Kromah, *supra* note 84.

This dichotomy illuminates the challenges of community legal advisors in a dual legal system where formal and constitutional rights sometimes conflict with customary norms and practices. The dilemmas are exacerbated when the paralegals themselves are part of the tradition that they are in the position to challenge. The same monitor who unequivocally advocates for a woman's right to property – even at the risk of his own reputation in the community – emphasizes neutrality in the case of domestic violence. Laurie Reyman at the Carter Center explains: "Some monitors are more easily removed from some customs like sassywood ... or inheritance. It's clear cut. But DV and rape are different. Those issues are more tied to them personally."

Liberian communities are collectively renegotiating what it means to be a man and a woman in Liberia. Monitors are members of these communities and part of the dialogue at a very personal level. They may themselves harbor their own biases toward a traditional understanding of how marital problems should be adjudicated. Violence against women in Liberia is unfortunate but common. Perhaps monitors, like most Liberians, have yet to buy into the notion that this type of violence is truly criminal.

Another explanation for JPC's divergent approaches to the two types of gender issues is the relative clarity of the law or policy. The Equal Rights of the Customary Marriage Law that protects women's right to own and inherit property is clearly written and easy to follow. The preamble specifically states that it is meant to supplant the customary law in the area of equal rights.[145] Each monitor has a copy of the law.[146] It is easier for them, therefore, to stand firm in a community on a woman's behalf and point to the law. In contrast, there exists no explicit domestic violence statute, nor has there been real community education on the subject. There is a rape law, but monitors may be confused about their role as non-lawyers when cases are required to be referred to formal forums. As Raymond Chie has articulated, the combination of survivors' or their families recanting and the failures of the police and court system render these cases particularly murky.

In the absence of clear laws, it may help to have clear JPC policies in these difficult areas where formal rights (or human rights) conflict so strongly with customary law and cultural norms. The Carter Center has been helping JPC wrestle through

---

[145] "Whereas, according to law extent, the customary wife is considered a chattel, the property of her husband, which doctrine is repugnant not only to the Universal Declaration of Human Rights, but also the Liberian Constitution which provides that 'No person shall be held in slavery or forced labor within this Republic, nor shall any citizen of Liberia or any person resident therein deal in slaves or subject any other person to forced labor, debt, bondage or personage.'" Equal Rights of the Customary Marriage Law pmbl. (2003).

[146] Each monitor has a copy of the TCC / Ministry of Justice Handbook for Civil Society Partners, which includes the Equal Rights of the Customary Marriage Law in its appendix. *See* THE CARTER CENTER & MINISTRY OF JUSTICE, *supra* note 85.

the issues and devise a standard approach to domestic violence cases in line with JPC's values. JPC posits that they always empower their clients to make their *own* justice decisions about the type of forum, whether and when to mediate, whether to sign an agreement, whether to report a case to the police or pursue legal action in court. JPC's current approach to domestic violence fails in this regard. When JPC monitors encourage a visibly injured woman to return to her husband, they are not empowering her to make her own choice.

This month, JPC is rolling out a new domestic violence protocol based on empowerment principles; they believe that a survivor knows what is best for her safety and should make her own choice. Following a standard "DV Checklist," the monitor will provide survivors with the following choices:

1. Go to the clinic or hospital for treatment (Monitor offers to accompany client).
2. Talk to the client's family (Monitor offers to help negotiate).
3. Mediation (Monitor serves as mediator of a dispute using a non-violence agreement form).
4. Pursue promissory note in Magistrate Court (Monitor offers to refer to JPC attorney and follow up the case at the court).
5. Go to police station to report the case (Monitor offers to follow up the case with the police).
6. Divorce/separation/continue relationship (Monitor offers to refer to JPC attorney, follow up the case at the court or any other assistance the client requests).
7. Traditional justice system (If appropriate, Monitor offers to accompany client).[147]

Monitors will not pressure DV survivors to remain in the relationship *or* to leave. The survivor makes her choice, and the monitor assists.

Again, their approach is pragmatic. JPC and The Carter Center realize that many women will continue to choose mediation. Given the current culture, many women *want* to mediate with their spouses and maintain their relationships, but clients will no longer sign mediation agreements bargaining for their safety. Instead, the parties will sign a "Non-Violence Agreement" in which both parties agree not to partake in violence, including emotional or financial abuse. The mediation will look more like advocacy, as monitors are instructed to explain that spousal violence is against the law and subject to criminal sanction were the perpetrator to be prosecuted. JPC may also consider creating a specific policy for rape cases that again errs on the side of advocacy for the survivor whose rights have been violated.

[147] Justice and Peace Commission, Domestic Violence Checklist (2010) (on file with author).

Shifting from neutrality to advocacy in gender violence cases may take time. The Carter Center hopes that continual dialogue regarding women's equality, human rights, and the cycle of violence will help shift JPC monitors' and staff members' own understandings of gender violence; they hope that monitors might eventually embrace an advocacy role in all women's rights cases.[48] Here, the relationship between the Carter Center and JPC is not unlike the relationship between JPC and traditional communities. The hope is that exposure, education, patience, listening, and time to wrestle with the issues will first shift attitudes and then affect practice in real cases.

Gender-based violence illuminates harsh realities in post-conflict settings; cultural norms, inept police, inadequate courts, and the resulting justice vacuum can be virtually debilitating for those seeking justice and for those attempting to provide access to justice. During this transitional period, John Hummel sums up a paralegal program's approach to survivors: "You do what you need to do. If you're there, you help them. You come up with some way to help them.... And you do no harm." Indeed, in this transitional period, scrappy and creative access to justice strategies may be the best approach for all clients.

8.5. LESSONS LEARNED

Timap and JPC have an intensely pragmatic approach to the dualist legal systems in Sierra Leone and Liberia. In individual cases, they empower clients to choose a forum where they will be heard and their claim adjudicated fairly. Paralegals embrace customary law and traditional authorities when appropriate for a given client. Where clients cannot access fair justice in the customary realm, paralegals help clients challenge traditional authorities or take their claim elsewhere. They offer mediation as an alternative to both the customary and formal forums, adding healthy competition to the justice marketplaces in Sierra Leone and Liberia.

Timap and JPC's successes and challenges present several lessons for other African paralegal programs engaging customary law:

1. *Embrace the reality of customary forums.* The customary realm will remain the forum of choice for the vast majority of Sierra Leoneans and Liberians to adjudicate civil disputes. These forums are culturally relevant and geographically desirable for most people. Although customary forums may be expensive and at times corrupt, the formal court system is expensive and incompetent as well. Timap and JPC have been most effective when they pragmatically help their clients access justice through customary forums as well as more formal legal institutions.

---

[48] *See* telephone interview with Laurie Reyman, *supra* note 94.

2. *Develop customary law from within.* Timap and JPC appeal to customary law and tradition to achieve justice in individual cases. Both organizations have challenged sassywood *within* the customary realm. Timap adapted the practice to require both the accuser and accused to drink the potion, and JPC appealed to the principles of transparency and inclusivity in customary law to challenge the secrecy of sassywood. Here, the organizations have embraced the flexibility of the customary realm; its institutions and leaders can and will adapt and change over time.

3. *Empower traditional authorities with formal law and human rights.* Timap and JPC relentlessly build relationships with traditional authorities. As they develop a presence and trust in rural communities, their education efforts go beyond formal outreach workshops to individual conversations about justice. With continual exposure to equal rights and formal law, traditional authorities in many cases have come to "own" these values and apply them in their adjudication. Timap and JPC hope to quietly infuse customary law with equal rights principles.

4. *Use formal law and institutions to challenge inequities in customary law.* Timap and JPC have helped clients appeal customary law decisions where traditional authorities have reached an unjust result in a particular case or exceeded their authority.

5. *Present mediation as an alternative.* In a dualist setting where both customary and formal legal institutions are flawed, mediation offers a free and fair alternative. The paralegal mediation model complements the reconciliation, speed, proximity, and cultural relevance of the customary system with the rights that the formal law is meant to protect. Perhaps most importantly, third-party mediation offers healthy competition for chiefs in the justice marketplace. Chiefs may improve their own adjudication to attract individuals to bring their disputes to their tribunals. Or they may improve by observing paralegals who exemplify good practices in dispute resolution.

6. *Be mindful of the justice vacuum.* Both organizations recognize that neither mediation nor informal adjudication in customary tribunals is appropriate in criminal cases. In Liberia, the government and their partners have succeeded in spreading the message that chiefs may not preside over criminal matters. Even where chiefs accept these limits, they are frustrated by the lack of a viable alternative. The formal court system is barely functioning, and Liberians fear the resulting "justice vacuum" where crime is simply not addressed. The Carter Center recognizes that perhaps the messaging came too early; the government encouraged people to refer all criminal matters to the police and the courts before the police or courts were equipped to handle them. Communities have rightly been disappointed with the results. Paralegal

organizations should be mindful of this reality; they risk contributing to the public distrust of government if they blindly refer victims to formal institutions without carefully monitoring the rest of the process.

7. *Develop clear policies in those areas where formal and customary law clash.* JPC's experiences with gender-based violence illustrate the conundrum for paralegals when formal law conflicts with the customary law. Paralegal organizations should recognize that their staff members are part of the communities and traditions that they are sometimes asked to challenge. They should create space for continual dialogue about gender or other areas where human rights might clash with paralegals' own traditional backgrounds. Through these discussions, organizations should develop clear guidelines for these types of cases. The JPC experience has shown that paralegals are able to withstand community pressure and advocate strongly for clients when they understand the law or are able to point to a clear policy.

8. *Empower clients to make their own justice decisions.* The greatest lesson in Timap and JPC's work arises out of their relentless empowerment of individual clients. In every case, paralegals should see their role as helping their client make his or her own decision about the choice of forum or pathway to justice. In domestic violence cases, for example, they can present clients with a range of choices. JPC's new "Domestic Violence Checklist" is a fantastic example of individual empowerment. Once a client has made her choice, the paralegal can support her unequivocally in the manner that she has chosen. In dualist legal systems, where justice forums are flawed and societal norms are in flux, the best contribution that paralegals can make is to help the client in front of them.

9

The Future of Customary Law in Ghana

Joseph B. Akamba and Isidore Kwadwo Tufuor

9.1. INTRODUCTION

Customary law in contemporary Ghanaian society has undergone tremendous transformation. Its evolution has been necessitated by the need to adapt to modern development trends and join in the globalization movement. The Ghanaian legal system is characterized by the duality of applicable norms: It straddles customary law on the one side and statutory and common law on the other. The system has witnessed a sort of friction between these operative sources in the bid to institutionalize a single and coherent framework of law. The consequential exchanges thereof have been targeted at the attainment and configuration of a comprehensive system of law within Ghana and a refinement of the customary rules and practices in their adaptation to and participation in the concept of law in aid of the country's development.

Subchapter 9.2 considers the sources and scope of customary law in Ghana. Subchapter 9.3 addresses the role of customary law in the administration of justice. Subchapter 9.4 discusses the question of ascertainment of customary law in Ghana. Subchapter 9.5 then analyzes related selected decisions of courts applying customary law. The manner in which courts have transformed and developed customary law will also be examined in this part. Subchapter 9.6 briefly examines the concept of living customary law versus official customary law. The chapter concludes with a discussion on the future of customary law in Ghana in Subchapter 9.7.

9.2. SOURCES AND SCOPE OF CUSTOMARY LAW IN GHANA

The legal systems of most countries of Anglophone Africa are generally founded on laws derived from three major sources[1]: legislation, judicial decisions, and customary

---

[1] These sources are divisible into two main categories. The first two may be referred to as the "formal sources" of law constituting the realm of laws technically posited by competent constitutional bodies, whereas customary law reflects the usages and practices inherent in the traditions of the

laws as recognized by most Constitutions of these countries.[2] Ghana, like most of these nations, hosts a number of ethnic communities, each with its own deep-rooted customary practices, handed down from generation to generation and reflecting the unique cultural identities of these communities.

Built from a conglomeration of traditional ancient states,[3] mostly resulting from ethnic migration, trade, and ethnic warfare, Ghana witnessed a settlement process that trailed with it traces of customary laws, the sources of which were as diverse as the different peoples who founded the country. The existing customs in Ghana are as many and varied as there are communities,[4] and generally embody the history and traditions of these particular communities. Some of these communities by their appurtenance to a larger group defined on the basis of tribe share many similarities.

Customary law in simple terms refers to the body of law deriving from the local customs and usages of the various traditional communities in Ghana.[5] It is also defined as a set of established norms, practices, and usages derived from the lives of people.[6] It manifests the communities' general acceptance of these norms as governing rules, and brandishes the character of law. Though the phrase is singular, it is used in generic terms and refers to the entire collection of these peculiar and assorted customs. This feature of customary law depicts a picture of it as a mosaic of customs differing, either substantially or otherwise, from community to community, tribe to tribe, and even ethnic group to ethnic group.[7]

Customary law in this definitional concept has permeated the Ghanaian legal system and has been applied by the courts since the implementation of the Supreme

local communities. This division underlies the dual system of law, as will be seen in our subsequent paragraphs.

[2] *See* Charles Ogwurike, *The Source and Authority of African Customary Law*, 3 U. GHANA L.J. 11, 11 (1966).

[3] Historians suggest that the Mole-Dagbane states of Mamprusi, Dagomba, and Gonja, and the Mossi states of Yatenga and Wagadugu, were among the earliest of the kingdoms to emerge in Northern Ghana. The area below Northern Ghana or the middle belt of Ghana saw the founding of such ethnic groups as the Banda, Adansi, Denkyira, Fante, Akyem, and Asante, collectively described as the Akan people. The western coast consisted of the Guan and the eastern coast comprised the Ga, the Adangbe, the Shai, Krobo, and the Ewe. *See* W.C. Ekow-Daniels, *Development of Customary Law*, 18 REV. GHANA L. 68, 69 (1991–92).

[4] *See* G.K. Acquah, *Customary Offences and the Courts*, 18 REV. GHANA L. 36, 36 (1991–92) (stating that "[w]ithin a particular tribe, there are as many varied customs as there are communities").

[5] *See* GHANA CONST. art 11(3) (1992).

[6] *See* Julie A. Davies & Dominic N. Dagbanja, *The Role and Future of Customary Tort Law in Ghana: A Cross Cultural Perspective*, 26 ARIZ. J. INT'L & COMP. L. 303, 303 (2009).

[7] *See* Lord Denning, *Foreword*, 1 J. AFR. L. 1 (1957). In his foreword to the first issue of the *Journal of African Law*, Denning described the variety of laws prevailing on the African continent by referring to the legal system as a "jumble of pieces much like a jig-saw. One group of pieces is founded on the customs of the African peoples, which vary from territory to territory and from tribe to tribe...." *Id.*

Court Ordinance of 1876 (No.4 of 1876) to the present.[8] The 1992 Constitution, in force today, recognizes customary law as one of the primary sources of law in Ghana and defines it as "rules of law which by custom are applicable to particular communities in Ghana."[9]

In terms of scope, customary law operates on a very broad range, thus making it highly impracticable to set a fine line around its contours and give it a specific delimitation. As noted by a Chief Justice of the Republic of Ghana, "some of the customary practices and offences are related to the history of the founding fathers of the community, others to particular incidents in the lifetime of the people, others to marriage and puberty rites of the women, and others to the day to day life in the community."[10] A leading scholar in Ghana defines the scope of customary law as coterminous with "the living embodiment of the country's cultural heritage,"[11] with allusion to such matters as "acquisition of rights in land; matters involving the family relationship: husband and wife, child and parent, marriage and divorce and chieftaincy,"[12] among others.

If at a point in time in the history of customary law, the consensus among writers on customary law was that customary law was law par-excellence, this simply was based on the fact that it derived from the local customs and usages, found its roots in the people, and reflected their common consciousness.[13] This is, however, only a manifestation of the nature of customary law as originally configured in its pristine form, and current realities as we will address later put this view far from truism.

In effect, when the Gold Coast was proclaimed a British colony on July 24, 1874, it was given its own colonial executive and legislative council body and a Supreme Court. The colonial legislature passed the Supreme Court Ordinance of 1876, which introduced the dual system of law in the country, a system that still persists today under the current constitutional regime.[14] The ordinance entrenched a

---

[8] The Supreme Court Ordinance of 1876 established the Supreme Court of Judicature for the Gold Coast colony. It was established after the English pattern and introduced in the colony a Court of Appeal, a High Court of Justice, and a Magistrate's Court, which were charged to observe and enforce the customary law in civil disputes. Section 19 of the Act reads, in part, as follows: "Nothing in this Ordinance shall deprive the Supreme Court of the right to observe and enforce the observance, or shall deprive any person of the benefit of any law or custom existing in the said colony and territories subject to its jurisdiction, such law or custom not being repugnant to natural justice, equity and good conscience, nor incompatible either directly or by necessary implication with any enactment of the Colonial legislature."

[9] GHANA CONST. art 11(3).

[10] G. K. Acquah, *Customary Offences and the Courts*, 18. REV. GHANA L. 36, 36 (1991–1992).

[11] Seth Yeboa Bimpong-Buta, *Sources of Law in Ghana*, 15 REV. GHANA L. 129, 129 (1983–1986).

[12] *See id.*

[13] *See* Ogwurike, *supra* note 2.

[14] Section 14 of the said Ordinance stipulated that: "The Common law, the doctrines of equity, and the statutes of general application which were in force in England at the date when the colony obtained a local legislature, that is to say, on the 24th day of July, 1874, shall be in force within the jurisdiction of the Court." Supreme Court Ordinance of 1876 § 14.

citizen's right to be governed by his or her own native law by guaranteeing the right of the Supreme Court to observe and enforce the observance of any law or custom existing in the colony.[15]

Thus, what today has come to constitute the body of laws operating the legal system in Ghana is nothing more than the product of a confrontation between – and later of a synthesis of – the received English law and the indigenous customary law. Within the operation of the legal system, a relationship developed between the two parallel systems of law, and the status of customary law as a binding set of rules came to depend largely on the fulfillment of certain conditions laid down by the received English law as a condition for their recognition. In other words, the legitimacy of the indigenous customary traditions depended on a validation by the imported endogenous English law.

9.3. THE ROLE OF CUSTOMARY LAW IN THE ADMINISTRATION OF JUSTICE

The Ghanaian legal system, as earlier mentioned, is characteristically a dual system of law. Customary law, obviously the first of these two systems and drawing directly from the customs of the peoples, remains the first procedure of administration of justice dating long before the official receipt of English law in Ghana in 1876. As an integral part of the legal system, it remains an important tool for the dispensation of justice, being at the core of the traditional legal system and reflecting a purely traditional practice.

The preservation of customary law and its recognition over time through the various Ghanaian constitutions, proclamations, and statutes since the application of the Supreme Court Ordinance, and especially amid the numerous criticisms and attacks founded on modern ideas of development, testifies to the role of customary law in the administration of justice in Ghana. Its constitutional institutionalization as a source of law operating within the legal system,[16] its administration by the courts and traditional bodies, and the detailed elaboration of its mode of ascertainment and application provided for under the Courts Act of 1993, Act 459[17] ("Courts Act of 1993"), depict the significance of its contribution to the solidification of the Ghanaian legal system.

The administration of customary law in the Ghanaian legal system has basically taken two main approaches, the first being an infusion of customary law matters in the jurisdiction of the courts of competent jurisdiction[18] established under the

[15] *See id.* § 19.
[16] *See* GHANA CONST. art. 11(2)-(3).
[17] Courts Act, 1993, Act 459 §§ 54–55 (Ghana).
[18] Here we are referring to customary law as administered by the courts of competent jurisdiction, which we term "formal administration" of customary law.

Courts Act of 1993, and the second reflective of a more informal system of adjudication of customary law in the form of customary arbitration.

The formal administration of customary law in the Ghanaian judicial system
by the competent courts has had a checkered history. Suffice it to say, however,
that since the promulgation of the 1966 Courts Decree,[19] which came with the first
revolution,[20] customary law has come to be administered by the formal courts without
any specialty, and this practice and procedure has been followed and maintained by
the Ghanaian legal system to date.[21] Today, customary law remains officially administered by the courts as established under the current Courts Act of 1993.[22]

One area of customary law, however, that has been taken out of the jurisdiction of these regular courts is the entire set of chieftaincy matters. The Courts Act
of 1993 reserves all "cause or matter affecting chieftaincy"[23] to the determination
by the traditional adjudicatory bodies, in particular the National House of Chiefs,
Regional Houses of Chiefs, and Traditional Councils (ranking from the highest
body to the lowest). With final judicial power vested in the judiciary,[24] however,
the 1992 Constitution grants a final right of appeal in all chieftaincy matters from a
decision of the national houses of chiefs to the Supreme Court of Ghana.[25] These
institutions have been attached in parallel to the formal administrative courts system
and classified as part of the lower courts of the country,[26] but remain wholly separate
and independent bodies.

As mentioned earlier, customary law is also applied in a second manner, that
is, the informal procedure of administration of customary law through customary

[19] National Liberation Council Decree, N.L.C.D. 84 (Ghana).
[20] This refers to the 1966 military coup led by army officers including Colonel E.K. Kotoka, Major A.A.
Afrifa, Lieutenant General (Rtd) J.A. Ankrah, and the Inspector General of Police J.W.K. Harley, who
accused the then-ruling Convention People's Party of abusive and corrupt administration, among
other charges. The new military government that took over was the National Liberation Council,
which repealed the 1960 Courts Act (C.A.9) and promulgated the N.L.C.D. 84.
[21] It is to be noted, however, that the 1969 Constitution had made provision for traditional courts to be
established under Article 102(4), which provided that "The Judiciary shall consist of the Supreme
Court of Ghana, the Court of Appeal and the High Court of Justice which shall be superior courts
of record and which shall constitute one Superior Court of Judicature, and *such other inferior and
traditional courts as Parliament may by law establish*." (emphasis added). These courts, however, were
not established until the Constitution was suspended. The provision was not re-enacted by subsequent legislations.
[22] Courts Act, 1993, Act 459, pts. I-II (Ghana).
[23] *Id.* § 39(d) (Ghana).
[24] *See* GHANA CONST. art. 125(3) (stipulating that "the judicial power of Ghana shall be vested in the
Judiciary, accordingly, neither the President nor Parliament nor any organ or agency of the President
or Parliament shall have or be given final judicial power").
[25] *See id.* art. 131(4) ("An appeal from a decision of the Judicial Committee of the National House of
Chiefs shall lie to the Supreme Court with the leave of that Judicial Committee or the Supreme
Court"). *See also* Courts Act, 1993, Act 459 § 4(4) (Ghana).
[26] *See* Courts Act, 1993, Act 459 pt. II (Ghana).

arbitration. Customary arbitration has been generally adopted as a mode of adjudication of conflicts and disputes in civil matters. Customary arbitration has been recognized by the courts, which have laid down certain principles of law aimed at regulating the procedure to promote justice in the customary sense. This mechanism finds necessity in the fact that the majority of Ghanaian people live in rural areas, where procedures founded on English Common Law and Acts of Parliament are generally unknown.[27]

In the various native communities, the chiefs administer the law and sit as customary arbitrators in the resolution of disputes, because customary law in essence endorses settlements rather than promotes litigations. The power of chiefs to act as customary arbitrators is preserved today under the Chieftaincy Act, 2008, Act 759, which stipulates that "the power of a chief to act as an arbitrator in customary arbitration in any dispute where the parties consent to the arbitration is guaranteed."[28]

Customary arbitration is a judicially controlled process that becomes enforceable in a formal court of law only if it meets the specific requirements of validity as laid down in the High Court case of *Budu II v. Caesar*.[29] In this case, sometime in 1946, Gotfried Tetteh Caesar (head of the Caesar family) commenced in the Native Court an action in trespass against Nana Budu, with respect to three pieces of land. While the case was still pending, Nana Asare Akoto, Omanhene (chief) of Akwamu at that time, intervened and tried to settle the dispute between the two parties. He solicited, and obtained, the assistance of some of his divisional chiefs, sub-chiefs, and other persons in that effort. According to Nana Budu's subsequent evidence, this settlement or arbitration was concluded but the opposite view was held by the Caesar family. In a subsequent land litigation commenced in 1955 by Nana Budu against certain members of the Caesar family, one of the issues that arose for determination by the court was whether the 1946 attempt at settlement was a valid customary arbitration.

Justice Ollennu, in addressing the issue, laid down for the first time the basic ingredients of a valid customary arbitration as applied today as follows:

(1) It is a voluntary submission of the disputes by the parties to arbitrators for the purpose of having the dispute decided informally but on the merits.

(2) There is prior agreement by both parties to accept the award of the arbitrators.

(3) The award must not be arbitrary, but must have been arrived at after the hearing of both sides in a judicial manner.

---

[27] *See* Enoch D. Kom, *Customary Arbitration*, 16 Rev. Ghana L. 148, 150 (1987–88).
[28] Chieftaincy Act, 2008, Act 759 § 30 (Ghana).
[29] G.L.R. 410 (1959).

(4) The practice and procedure for the time being followed in the Native Court or tribunal of an area must be followed as nearly as possible.

(5) There must be publication of the award.[30]

Parties to a valid customary arbitration cannot resile from it.[31] It is binding on them and estops a losing party from bringing an action in court against his or her opponent in respect of the same subject matter or issue that was arbitrated on.[32] The successful party reserves the right to bring an action in court to enforce the award.[33]

9.4. ASCERTAINMENT OF CUSTOMARY LAW

The recognition of customary law as a subset of the body of laws operating within the Ghanaian legal system brought with it the question of ascertainment of its content. Such question is closely linked with the legal development, in the history of the Ghanaian legal system, from the Supreme Court Ordinance of 1876 to the coming into force of the 1960 Republican Constitution, which saw the transformation of customary law from a question of fact to its current settlement as a question of law.

The legal status of the customary rules and practices, as distinct from the received English law, was determined by the Supreme Court Ordinance that made elaborate provisions as to the terms and conditions by which "native law and custom" should be observed and enforced by the court. According to the Ordinance, these customary rules and practices were to be applied and enforced by the courts only if they were not "repugnant to natural justice, equity and good conscience."[34] Flowing therefrom, the quantum of enforceable customary laws was found limited to the class of such laws that satisfied the following criteria:

---

[30] *Id.* at 412.

[31] *See Aniamoah v. Otwiraah*, 1 G.L.R. 405, (1961) SC.

[32] *See Saasu v. Temabi*, 1 G.L.R. 439, 442 (1962); *Asano v. Taku*, 2 G.L.R. 312, 319 (1963).

[33] Native Ordinance, Cap 76, § 58 (Ghana), which expressly prohibited the enforcement of customary arbitration awards by providing that "resort shall not be had, for the purpose of enforcing the award to the powers and facilities provided by this ordinance," was replaced by the State Council Ordinance 1952 without repeating the prohibition on enforcement. *See Osae v. Apenteng*, 2 G.L.R. 615, 618 (1968) (J. Ollennu holding that "there was no machinery by which arbitrators could enforce an award they made and that the only process to enforce an award was an action in a court of competent jurisdiction").

[34] Section 19 of the Ordinance provided that "[N]othing in this Ordinance shall deprive the Courts of the right to observe and enforce the observance, or shall deprive any person of the benefit, of any native *law* or custom *not* being repugnant to natural justice, equity, and good conscience." This was re-enacted as Section 87 of the Courts Ordinance, Cap 4 (1951 Rev), which provided for the continued application of customary law where such law was not "repugnant to natural justice, equity and good conscience nor incompatible either directly or by necessary implication with any ordinance for the time being in force."

(1) The law or custom was to be proved to have existed in the said colony at the date of the passing of the Supreme Court Ordinance of 1876.[35]

(2) It was not to be repugnant to natural justice, equity, and good conscience.

(3) It ought not to be incompatible directly or by implication with any law for the time being in force.

(4) These customs must not to be contrary to public policy.[36]

Moreover, the mode of ascertainment of any such customary law was provided under the Supreme (High) Court (Civil Procedure) 1954, which provided that customary law had to be pleaded and proved as a question of fact by evidence of witnesses.[37] The judgment in the Privy Council[38] case of *Angu v. Atta*[39] stipulated that customary law had "to be proved in the first instances by calling witnesses acquainted with the native customs until the particular custom has, by frequent proof in the courts become so notorious that the courts take judicial notice of them."[40]

The advent of the first Republican Constitution[41] in 1960, alongside the enactment of the Courts Act, 1960 (C.A.9) marked a turning point. Section 67(1) of this Courts Act made the existence and content of any rule of existing customary law a question of law for the courts and no longer one of fact. This reverse of the trend was clearly affirmed in the landmark High Court case of *Ibrahim v. Amalibini*,[42] in which Justice Taylor in unequivocal terms held:

> [T]he yardsticks of equity, natural justice and good conscience used in the colonial and pre-Republican days for measuring their validity were not re-enacted after their repeal. Obviously our Republican legislature must have considered these colonial

---

[35] *See Welbeck v. Brown* (1884) Sar. FCL, 185 at 187 (C.J. H. Lesingham Bailey submitting that a custom could not actually date from a time that is in the memory of men now living, and that effect could only be given to native law and custom as it existed at the date of the passing of the Supreme Court Ordinance of 1876).

[36] The criterion of public policy was usually seen as synonymous with the repugnancy test.

[37] Order 19, rule 31, provided that in all cases in which the party pleading relies on native law and custom, the native law or custom relied on shall be stated in the pleadings with sufficient particulars to show the nature and effect of the native law or custom in question and the geographical area and the tribe, or tribes, to which it relates.

[38] The Supreme Court was established by the Supreme Court ordinance of 1876 as the highest court in the Gold Coast during the colonial era. Appeals from the Supreme Court went the West African Court of Appeal established in 1866. The Privy Council constituted the final court of appeal. Ghana withdrew from W.A.C.A following independence. The Constitution of the First Republic (1960) declared the Supreme Court the final court of appeal and abolished the appellate jurisdiction of the Privy Council.

[39] P.C. 74–28, 43 (1916).

[40] *Id.* at 44. *See also Amissah v. Krabah*, 2 W.A.C.A. 30, 31 (1931).

[41] Article 126(1).

[42] G.L.R. 368 (1978).

yardsticks as an affront to the integrity of our customary law and not in keeping with the dignity of a modern sovereign state....[43]

This new conception of customary law in force as of July 1, 1960, has permeated the Ghanaian legal system and is still reflective of the character of customary law today. The 1992 Constitution endorsed the position with the enactment of the present Courts Act of 1993, section 55(1) of which establishes customary law as a question of law.[44] Courts are deemed to have judicial knowledge of all customary laws applicable in the country.[45] For that reason, a well-established rule of custom applicable within a particular community did not have to be specifically pleaded. One exception to this principle, as admitted by the courts, has been the establishment of the "lesser or abstruse" rules of customary law applicable to certain localities.[46] In such instance, a court could resort to the powers given in section 67 of the Courts Act, 1960, which provided for an inquiry for the purpose of ascertaining a customary law of a particular tribe or locality.[47] The current Courts Act[48] replicated the same provision. Section 55 thereof provides guidance as to the question and mode of ascertainment of these lesser or abstruse customary law and states in its following subsections that:

(1) Any question as to existence or content of a rule of customary law is a question of law for the court and not a question of fact.

(2) If there is doubt as to the existence or content of a rule of customary law relevant in any proceedings before a court, the court may adjourn the proceedings to enable an enquiry to be made under subsection (3) of this section after the

---

[43] *Id.* at 397.

[44] *See* Act 459 § 55(1) (stipulating that "any question as to the existence or content of customary law is a question of law for the court and not a question of fact.").

[45] *See Ibrahim*, G.L.R. at 396.

[46] See, e.g., the High Court case of *Badu v. Boakye*, G.L.R. 283, 288–89 (1975), where the court entertaining doubt about the meaning of a custom called "akotoagyan," practiced by the people of Berekum in the Brong Ahafo region of Ghana, required the Brong Ahafo Regional House of Chiefs to supply to the court their written opinion on whether the "akotoagyan" is a marriage custom at all and if it is, what its content is. See also the High Court case of *Billa v. Salifu*, 2 G.L.R 87, 91–92 (1971), where in order to inform himself of the nature of the Dagomba (a tribe in the north of Ghana) customary law on relating to adultery and the resultant rights and remedies of an injured husband in cases of adultery, the learned Justice Taylor, heard the testimony of two witnesses: the Wula-Na who was the chief linguist of the Dagomba chief and the Zobogu-Na, a Dagomba sectional chief of the Tamale traditional area, and afterwards sought the written opinion of the Dagomba traditional council on the matter.

[47] *See Attah Yaw and ors v. Awuah*, G.L.R. 128, 131 (1964), also affirmed by *Assiamah & ors v. adjabeng*, 2 G.L.R. 171, 184 (1971). Both cases also affirmed an implied repeal of Order 19 rule 31 of the Supreme (High) Court (Civil Procedure) Rules that remained in the statute book still after 1960 and continued to subject customary law to proof as a question of fact. *See supra* note 39.

[48] Act 459 (1993) (Ghana).

court has considered reported cases textbooks and other sources that may be appropriate to the proceedings.

(3) The enquiry shall be held as part of the proceedings in such manner as the court considers expedient, and the provisions of this Act relating to the attendance and testimony of witnesses shall apply with such modifications as may appear to the court to be necessary.

(4) The decision as to the persons who are to be heard at the inquiry shall be one for the court, after hearing the submissions on it made by or on behalf of the parties.

(5) The court may require the House of Chiefs, Divisional, or Traditional Council or other body with knowledge of the customary law in question to state its opinion that may be laid before the inquiry in written form.[49]

Issues of internal conflict of laws arising when determining the applicable law (whether customary law or English common law) to apply to an issue are governed by the choice of law rules as laid down in section 54 of the Courts Act, 459.[50]

Despite these legislative developments, the question of ascertainment of customary law remains far from being fully and satisfactorily addressed. In effect, even though the 1992 Constitution makes customary law part of the laws of Ghana, the age-old problem of tribal variety remains. With the presumption of judicial knowledge on behalf of the courts, the question is that of the feasibility of the assumption of adequate grasp and understanding of these multitude of existing customary laws by judges for the purposes of adjudication. Knowledge of the judges who sit on cases involving customary law issues may be limited in reference to particular customs. Also, despite the legislative intervention in the establishment of the abstruse customs, the question of ascertainment of customary law is not made any easier for the courts, which continue to face challenges such as dealing with sometimes very

---

[49] *See Billa v. Salifu*, 2 G.L.R. 87 (1971). *See also Badu v. Boakye*, 1 G.L.R. 283 (1975) (referring to certain points of customary law to these traditional authorities for the court's opinion); *see supra* note 46.

[50] Section 54 deals within issues of internal conflict of law within the dual legal system. It stipulates clear rules defining the applicable laws in particular situations. It stipulates that where the parties intend a particular system of law to govern a transaction, the applicable law will be that intended by the parties, irrespective of their governing personal (customary) law (rule 1); absent any contrary intention of the parties issues arising out of the devolution of a person's estate shall his personal law (rule 2); where the parties involved are subject to the same customary law, issues as to title traceable to people who had the same customary law shall governed by that customary law (rule 3); where the parties belong to different customary groups applying different laws, the court will apply both laws in such as a way as to "achieve a result that conforms to natural justice, equity and good conscience" (rule 5); in a case where no customary law applies, the court may apply either customary law or the common law or both as "will do substantial justice between the parties, having regard to equity and good conscience" (rule 6); the court may also adopt, develop, and apply such remedies from any system of law (whether Ghanaian or non-Ghanaian) as appear to the court to be efficacious and to meet the requirements of justice, equity, and good conscience (rule 7).

old and sometimes inaudible witnesses who may remain the only vivid and credible authorities on particular issues of customary law.[51]

One important provision that is worth the deepest consideration in an attempt to simplify, if not solve, the problems associated with the ascertainment of customary law is section 55 (5) of the Courts Act of 1993.[52] This provision seeks to reserve the question of establishment of customary laws to the various House of Chiefs, Divisional, or Traditional Councils of those customs. This, of course, is a more appropriate and effective procedure in guaranteeing the existence and accuracy of the various customs from the very traditional root of those in whose bosoms lies customary law.

9.5. DEVELOPMENT OF CUSTOMARY LAW THROUGH COURT DECISIONS

One remarkable fact of legal importance in the administration of customary law is that it has, over the last quarter of the nineteenth century, undergone tremendous change. In effect, modernism and globalization have had a crucial impact on traditional customary laws and practices, which continue to face the pressure of reform from the legislature and the courts.

As noted earlier, before the introduction of the First Republican Constitution in 1960, the ascertainment of customary law was a question of fact, and the validity or otherwise of a custom depended on its satisfaction of the repugnancy test.[53] The resulting effect was that many of these customary rules came to be declared invalid and illegitimate once they were found by the courts to be "repugnant to natural justice, equity, and good conscience." This standard continued to be applied by the courts even after its official repeal by the 1960 Courts Act.[54]

Some courts' decisions that applied the repugnancy standard and shaped the form of some customary practices are worth considering. In the High Court case of *Foli and 7 others v. the Republic*,[55] the appellants were charged before the circuit

---

[51] It is generally allowed as an exception to the hearsay rule for witnesses to establish the existence of some customary rules by recounting community and family histories. *See* Evidence Act (1975), N.R.C.D. 323 §§ 128–129.

[52] *See supra* note 50.

[53] *See supra* note 34.

[54] Courts Act 1960 (C.A.4), § 67 (1).

[55] G.L.R. 768 (1968). See also *Abangana v. Akologo* G.L.R. 382, 385 (1976), where his Lordship Justice Taylor explicitly held that merely seeking the opinion of an expert on a matter of customary law and abiding by it as a particular customary rule of practice was insufficient "without the consideration of the impact of present social, political and economic changes in our society." (Later disapproved by *Ibrahim v. Amalibini*, G.L.R. 368 (1978), on the continued use of the repugnancy test, which had long been repealed).

court with two counts: (a) conspiracy to commit a crime contrary to sections 23(1) and 24(1) of Act 29,[56] and (b) causing harm to a corpse they had cremated contrary to section 53(1) of Cap. 80.[57] It was found that it was an established and long-standing custom in their locality that any person, such as the deceased, who was not purified before dying should not be accorded a decent burial but should be cremated. The appellants' defense was that by cremating the corpse they genuinely believed that they were acting in consonance with an accepted custom and did not know that they were offending against any law of the land. On their conviction on both counts, they appealed to the High Court. In rejecting this Akrofu[58] traditional custom, the High Court held that even though it was an established and long-standing custom in the area, it was one the continuance and performance of which was to cease immediately because it was repugnant and obnoxious. The court stated:

> Although native custom is recognized by our laws, our courts have always discountenanced and refused to give support to any custom which is obnoxious, repugnant and contrary to good conscience and natural justice. The custom which all the appellants so heartily upheld at the trial is one such custom and I fully support the learned trial circuit judge's outright condemnation and rejection thereof.[59]

With the abolition of the repugnancy test in 1960,[60] the question remains as to whether the courts' approach to dealing with customs unsuitable with modern socio-

---

[56] According to section 23 (1) of the criminal code, 1960, Act 29, "if two or more persons agree or act together with a common purpose for or in committing or abetting a crime, whether with or without any previous concert or deliberation, each of them is guilty of conspiracy to commit or abet that crime, as the case may be."

[57] Section 53 (1) of the Births, Deaths and Burials Ordinance, Cap. 80 (1951 Rev.) provides that "No person shall cremate or be concerned in the cremation of a corpse except such cremation is carried out with the consent in writing of the Medical Officer of Health and in accordance with such directions as he may see fit to give and subject to such regulations as may be prescribed." Section 285 of the criminal code, Act 29, prohibiting the hindering of the burial of a dead body under the general heading of Public Nuisances similarly provides that "whoever unlawfully hinders the burial of the dead body of any person, or without lawful authority in that behalf disinters, dissects, or harms the dead body of any person, or being under a duty to cause the dead body of any person to be buried, fails to perform that duty, is guilty of a misdemeanor."

[58] A tribe in the Volta Region of Ghana.

[59] *See supra* note 55, at 771.

[60] With the repugnancy rule, customary law remained subordinated and subject to English law, with the ensuing consequence that customary law was denied its legitimate right and status as law. This galvanized, after the declaration of independence in 1957, a spirit of nationalism against the repugnancy rule, inflamed by what was perceived as an "inane treatment of Ghanaians' own cherished customary law as foreign law while treating the received English law as rather being the common law in Ghana." This led to the abolition of the repugnancy rule by the First Republican Parliament of 1960. Dr. Kwame Nkrumah, first President of the Republic, also resounded this nationalist indignation at the formal opening of the Accra Conference of Legal Education and of the Ghana Law School on January 1963 as follows: "African law in Africa was declared foreign law for the convenience of colonial administration which found the administration of justice cumbersome by reason of the vast

economic standards has materially changed. The answer forcefully stands in the negative, because the courts today continue to apply emerging principles of social development and public policy to shape the application of customary-law principles and rules. Customary law today remains purely a question of law for the judges to decide and ascertainable through judicial enquiry. The courts' duty remains technically to determine whether or not a community holds a particular custom as binding. It does not extend to giving validity to customary laws.[61] However, the emphasis of the courts has shifted from the consensus of the community as to the mere existence of a customary rule to an attitude of the court to pick and choose, alongside socio-economic considerations and public policy, between enforceable customary rules and those they deem unenforceable. Thus, the courts proceed on the basis of according enforceability to traditional customary rules that are acceptable and conforming to modern societal values.[62] As succinctly captured by Justice Taylor of the Supreme Court of Ghana,

> If customary laws are to develop to meet the demands of a civilized populace and if they are to play any meaningful role in a concerted national effort to clean our country of corruption and unsavory practices, then we must endeavor to remove these artificial barriers that tend to block away and disable us from carrying out our functions.[63]

The Court of Appeal's decision in the case of *Attah v. Esson*[64] illustrates this point. In this case, the plaintiff's family was the tenants in perpetuity of the first defendant's family in respect of a large piece of land. The defendants entered the land and felled a large number of palm trees admittedly cultivated by the plaintiff's family. The plaintiff therefore sued for damages for trespass and perpetual injunction. The defendants contended that under an existing customary law rule as was stated by Sarbah[65] and which had not, by then, been declared unreasonable by any court, the

---

variations in local and tribal customs. African law had to be proved by experts. But no law can be foreign in its own land and country and African lawyers, particularly in the independent African States, must quickly find a way to reverse this judicial travesty." *See* David A Nii-Aponsah, *The Rule in 'Angu v. Attah Revisited*, 16 REV. GHANA L. 281 (1987–88).

[61] *See* Courts Act, 1993, Act 459 § 55.

[62] The courts proceed on the very nature of adaptability of customary law to change. It is admitted that customary law possesses the distinguishing feature of flexibility and changeability and has the potential to adapt to developing socio-economic conditions. *See Lewis v. Bankole* 1 N.L.R. 81, 100–101 (1909) (CJ Osborne notes: "[O]ne of the most striking features of west African native-custom is its flexibility; it appears to have been always subject to motives of expediency and its shows unquestionable adaptability to altered circumstances without entirely losing its individual characteristics.")

[63] *Sarkodie I v. Boateng II*, Supreme Court, Accra, 18 May 1983, digested in G.L.R.D. 73 (1982–83).

[64] 1 G.L.R. 128 (1976).

[65] John Mensah Sarbah was a lawyer, political leader, and writer on the Gold Coast, now Ghana. He authored a book titled FANTI CUSTOMARY LAWS, A BRIEF INTRODUCTION TO THE PRINCIPLES OF

first defendant's family were entitled as the landlords to enter the land at any time to fell the palm trees – being economic trees – and enjoy the fruits thereof whether or not the palm trees were already on the land before the tenancy or were planted by the tenant after the creation of the tenancy. The trial judge held that the defendants were not entitled to cut down the palm trees. General damages for trespass were subsequently assessed. Damages against the defendants and an order for perpetual injunction were also made against the defendants. On appeal by the defendants, Justice Amissah, delivering the judgment of the court and castigating this alleged custom in the central region of Ghana as bound to stifle initiative and impede the economic well-being of the nation, held:

> Customary law must develop and change with the changing times. What was reasonable in the social condition of the 19th century must not necessarily be reasonable today.... No proposition would be more out of accord with the hopes and aspirations of Ghanaians today than that a landlord who has spent no effort whatsoever towards that end should enter and collect at will the fruits of the labor of his tenant.... We cannot imagine an arrangement more ruinous of agricultural enterprise of subversive of expansion and consequently prejudicial to national development.[66]

The Court gave the final proposition of the law as follows: "We think that the customary law as stated by Sarbah became outdated and ceased to be law as soon as conditions in society changed so as to make it unreasonable for persons to conduct themselves by it."[67] Thus customary rules derive their final recognition and enforcement, at least officially, not from the assent of the community but from their recognition by the court in the light of the development policies and existing laws in the country.

The impact of the courts on the development and transformation of customary law is quite remarkable in the area of criminal law. Judicial intervention in Ghanaian criminal law established a principle that all customs must comply with the requirements of the criminal statute in force in their definition of criminal offenses. One case in point is the High Court decision in *Debrah v. The Republic*.[68] The accused in this case, a mason, was seen collecting some stone particles on the road in front of the palace of the chief of Kadjebi[69] one early morning in July 1990. A complaint was lodged with the linguist to the chief Nana Ogyeabour Akopim Finam II,

---

THE NATIVE LAWS AND CUSTOMS OF THE FANTI AND AKAN DISTRICTS OF THE GOLD COAST, with a report of some cases thereon decided in the Law Courts (1904). He is renowned for his critiques of the British rule and his call for the preservation of Africa's traditional communal virtues.

[66] See Taylor, *supra* note 64, at 132.

[67] *Id.* at 133.

[68] 2 G.L.R. 517 (1991).

[69] Kadjebi is a traditional area in the Volta region of Ghana.

regarding the conduct of the accused, which was allegedly against Kadjebi custom. The linguist in turn reported the matter to the chief of Kadjebi, who together with some elders held an arbitration over the complaint. At the arbitration, the accused explained that he intended to use the stone particles to manufacture grinding stones as a means of earning his livelihood. The accused was nevertheless found liable and ordered by the chief and elders to pay four bottles of schnapps, one live sheep, and a pot of palm wine. The accused, without speaking through the linguist, announced directly to the chief and elders that he would not pay the fine and thereafter was said to have left the palace without permission. In consequence, the linguist to the chief of Kadjebi reported the conduct of the accused to the police who investigated the matter and subsequently arraigned the accused before the district magistrate court on a charge of insult to the chief of Kadjebi by way of conduct. At the trial, the linguist, as the first prosecution witness, testified that the offense of the accused consisted in his (1) refusing to talk through the linguist but speaking to the chief directly; (2) leaving the palace without asking for leave from the linguist as custom demanded; and (3) picking stones in front of the chief's palace without permission. The trial court found the accused guilty. On appeal, the High Court dismissed the custom that made it an offense to talk directly to the chief and not through a linguist and to leave the palace without leave from the linguist in the Kadjebi traditional area. The High Court noted that "no citizen can be subjected to violation of vague, undefined and uncodified offences alleged to be against custom. The individual is entitled to know what the offense is and the punishment for it."[70] This legal principle is founded on section 8 of the Ghanaian criminal code, 1960, Act 29, which provides that "no person shall be liable to punishment by the common law for any act."[71] The court found that it was the right of every citizen not to be punished for any offense that had not been directly set out and the punishment thereon equally laid down in the relevant statutory instrument. Hence, for any customary offense to be criminally punishable, the particulars of such an offense together with the appropriate punishment should have been clearly and statutorily spelled out. This was to ensure that individuals were not subject to capricious and sometimes outmoded, unintelligible, and undefined offenses alleged to be against custom.

The court in this case, however, made room for the recognition of a limited number of offenses peculiar to particular customs. It held that whenever a traditional community is of the view that certain particular conducts should constitute

---

[70] *See* Debrah, *supra* note 68, at 534.

[71] The term "common law" is defined in section 17(1) of the Interpretation Act, 1960 (C.A.4) (Ghana) as consisting "[I]n addition to the rules of law generally known as the common law, of the rules generally known as the doctrines of equity and of the rules of customary law included in the common law under any enactment providing for the assimilation of such rules of customary law as are suitable for general application."

customary criminal offenses against their customs and tradition, and that such offenses ought to be punished, the traditional area in question should take steps in accordance with the procedure laid down in sections 41–46 of the Chieftaincy Act, 1960, Act 370[72] (now sections 49–56 of the new Chieftaincy Act, 2008, Act 759) to have those offenses, together with the appropriate sanctions, formalized.

The impact of the courts in the civil aspect of customary law remains principally an application of the statutory provisions on rules of choice of law in claims or suits as laid down in section 54 of the Courts Act of 1993.[73] In customary civil cases, the courts will only apply and give such remedies as are available under and according to particular customs. Thus, in the High Court case of *Billa v. Salifu*[74] where the respondent wanted his claim for damages against the appellant for adultery to be decided according to Dagomba Customary law, in accordance with the then-rule 6 of paragraph 64(1)[75] of the Courts Decree 1966 (NLCD 84), the court held that adultery per se does not give rise under Dagomba custom to civil claim for damages, that is, compensation for the violation of the husband's marital rights. The court held that the idea of claiming monetary compensation for adultery was foreign to the Dagombas unless the husband was divorcing the wife as a result of the adultery. The learned judge therefore concluded that the action was misconceived as it was unknown to Dagomba custom.

In any case, the determination of these customary law issues by the courts reinforces their supervisory powers over customary practices. This has led to a remarkable judicial modification of otherwise enforceable customary rules and practices so as to ensure their adaptation to modern trends of social development and influenced by the adopted social policies of western culture that have permeated the legal system since the reception of English law in the country.

In this context, one of the areas of customary law that has incited a stern interest of the courts to streamline customary practices and adapt them to modernism and ensure social equity is the domain of customary family law, and in particular its subset of customary law marriages. Issues of succession and inheritance at customary law obviously depend on the validity of the marriage under a particular custom, and the unsatisfactory nature of the traditional method of proof of the existence of valid customary law marriages invariably called for the courts' modification of the interpretation of the so-called essentials of a valid customary marriage.

---

[72] Looking principally at the assimilation of customary law rules into common law.
[73] *See supra* note 50.
[74] 2 G.L.R. 87 (1971).
[75] The rule stipulated: "[S]ubject to the foregoing rules, an issue should be determined according to the Common Law unless the plaintiff is subject to any system of customary law and claims to have the issue determined according to that system when it should be so determined." Courts Decree of 1966, N.L.C.D 84, ¶ 64(1) (Ghana).

The conventionally called essentials of a valid customary law marriage were first gleaned from the multitude of the varying customary marriage practices in Ghana by Justice Ollennu in the locus classicus High Court case of *Yaotey v. Quaye*[76] as follows:

(1) agreement by the parties to live together as man and wife;
(2) consent of the family of the man that he should have the woman to be his wife; that consent may be indicated by the man's family acknowledging the woman as wife of the man;
(3) consent of the family of the woman that she should be joined in marriage to the man; that consent is indicated by the acceptance of drink from the man or his family, or merely by the family of the woman acknowledging the man as the husband of the woman; and
(4) consummation of the marriage, that is, that the man and woman are living together in the sight of all the world as man and wife.

The mechanical elevation of these essentials into rigid requirements, against which customary law marriages were legally tested, was already seen by some writers[77] as being obsolete in modern circumstances. A call was thus made for a more liberal assumption of marriage, essentially based on the society's recognition of the union of the parties to the claimed marriage and on the parties' performance of customary spousal duties.[78] The courts, in effect, were already witnessing the hardship instituted by the strict and formal compliance of these essentials, which resulted most often in the denial of the marriage status to couples who had otherwise lived as spouses. This denial usually resulted in the deprivation of property rights to the surviving partner on the death intestate of his or her "all along assumed" spouse by the family of the deceased. The deceased's family was often swift to refute the existence of mar- riage between the parties in the absence of specific show of compliance with these requirements, with the failure of any of them rendering any purported marriage ineffectual.[79] Thus, some early cases had already expressed the courts' tendency to soften the stance and to infer those requirements of customary marriage from the realities of the couple's lives rather than an explicit fulfillment of formalities. One

---

[76] G.L.R. 573, 578–579 (1961). *See also* Nil Aman Ollennu, The Law of Testate and Intestate Succession in Ghana 224 (1966).

[77] *See* Adinkrah Kofi Oti, *Essentials of a Customary Marriage: A New Approach*, 12 Rev. Ghana. L. 40 (1980).

[78] *See id.*

[79] *See Badu v. Boakye*, 1 G.L.R. 283 (1975). *See also* holding (2) of the Court of Appeal case of *Asumah v. Khair*, G.L.R. 353 (1959) (insisting that there can be a valid customary marriage only where drinks and/or presents are sent to the girl's family and accepted by them). Judgment of J. Ollennu.

such case is the High Court case of *Essilfie and Another v. Quarcoo*,[80] decided by Justice Lutterodt.[81]

In this case, following the death intestate of Theophillia Alaba Codjoe, on November 28, 1986, her mother in her capacity as the head of her immediate family and her sister as her customary successor jointly applied for letters of administration to administer her estate. The estate comprised of an uncompleted house, personal effects, savings, and building materials. The defendant, claiming to be the husband of the deceased and the father of her two infant children, caveated. The plaintiffs claimed that as the head of family and the customary successor respectively of the deceased, her whole estate devolved on them, and that the defendant was only the deceased's concubine and not husband, and therefore had no interest in her estate. The defendant claimed that he was the husband of the deceased because he had married her under Fanti customary law; furthermore, because he had two children with her, even if he was held not to have any personal interest in the estate, as the father of the children he was entitled to the grant. Evidence established that after the defendant had impregnated the deceased, his family sent drinks to the family of the deceased to acknowledge his responsibility for the pregnancy and thereafter the deceased and the defendant lived in the defendant's house for seven years until she died at childbirth, survived by the two minor children she had had with the defendant. The court further found on the evidence that (a) the first plaintiff had been visiting the couple in their house; (b) on the death of the deceased's father, the defendant at the request of the plaintiffs' family performed the custom required of a son-in-law; (c) forms the deceased had filed with her employers indicated that she was married; and (d) the defendant at the request of the plaintiffs' family, provided the shroud and the grave used in burying the deceased.

In the determination of the controversy before her, the court came to address one of the most serious and controversial issues as to whether or not the defendant was married to the deceased under Fanti customary law. The court discerned two forms of valid marriages known to the Ghanaian customary law.[82] It first referred to the ordinary case, "where a man seeks the hand of a woman from her family and with their consent, the necessary ceremonies of the payment of drinks, customary fees, dowry, etc. are performed."[83] This appears to be the form of customary marriage that fully complies with the requirements as enunciated in *Yaotey v. Quaye*. She then addressed this other form of a valid marriage "where though the above customary

---

[80] 2 G.L.R. 180 (1992).
[81] Currently the chief Justice of the Republic of Ghana and today known as Mrs. Justice Georgina Theodora Wood.
[82] See *Essilfie and Another*, 2 G.L.R. at 183.
[83] *Id.*

marital rites have not been performed, the parties have consented to live in the eyes of the world as man and wife and their families have consented that they so do and the parties actually live as such man and wife in the eyes of the whole world."[84] Applying this second test, which seems to be a substantial modification of the customary law by expansion of the laid down essentials, rather than a total invention of the courts, the court paved the way for the judicial recognition of valid customary-law marriage by implied satisfaction of the customary essentials. It held that:

> The evidence overwhelmingly shows that thereafter they lived as man and wife in the sight of the whole world, the first plaintiff (the deceased's mother) having frequently gone to them sometime during their cohabitation, when one of her daughters who had a baby went to stay with them in their house. Furthermore, the evidence of the defendant and his witnesses showed that at the death of the first plaintiff's husband, i.e. the deceased's father, the defendant performed the necessary customary funeral rites of a son-in-law.... The evidence also shows the defendant's family, including his mother, attended the funeral to perform the custom. Would the defendant's family go that far if he were not a husband and was performing something on behalf of the infant children? I think all the ingredients essential to a customary law marriage have been proved by the defendant. These are that (a) the parties agreed to live together as man and wife and they did in fact so live; and (b) they obtained the consent of their two families to the marriage.[85]

These are but a few of the decided cases illustrating the role of the courts in the development of customary law as a tool for social development. Customary law must develop as society follows a universal paradigm of growth, and the role of the courts in promoting its adaptation to modern practices of socio-economic development has been pertinent.

9.6. OFFICIAL CUSTOMARY LAW VERSUS LIVING CUSTOMARY LAW

One question that remains is whether the statutory and judicial modifications of customary law rules automatically affect their practice by members of the affected communities. The issue becomes more difficult when the members of particular communities, in blatant disregard and breach of the legal pronouncements on particular rules, continue to observe certain customary practices abrogated by the courts with a consensual sense of obligation. Generally, the effect of judicial decisions on the ascertainment and determination of validity of customary law rules as practiced by the various communities has been to "fine tune and filter them through

---

[84] *Id.*
[85] *Id.* at 187–188.

a prism of refinement, in which the opinion of scholars, various judicial rules and precedents have been critical."[86] What remains undeniable is that though the courts find themselves transforming the rules of customary law into formal law, this judicial practice has not prevented some communities from regarding customary rules as their living law even when prohibited by legislation or rejected by the court.[87] Thus the conservative respecter of his or her custom sees the authority and source of rules of customary law as something lying beyond the determination and qualification by statutes and judicial decisions. This attitude has led to the discernment by some authors of a distinction between "judicial customary law" on the one hand and "practiced customary law" on the other hand.[88] So long as society continues to be the field of emergence of customary law rules, the customary law actually administered by the court may differ from the practice of the people in the community, and the very customary practices in the societies will constitute the living force at the basis of the customary law.

Inevitably and naturally, the new shape given by the courts to customary law, generally imbued with modern principles of socio-economic values, will meet a somewhat insidious resistance of any conservative society with cherished values for its customary glories of the past.[89]

9.7. THE FUTURE OF CUSTOMARY LAW AND THE COURTS

The demands of social, economic, and political changes in the face of globalization and vis-à-vis the national developmental policies and goals have tremendously influenced the courts in the application and administration of customary law rules in Ghana as we have developed in the previous parts of this paper. Today, the need for tribal unities to enhance nation building principally calls for an attempt to draw up a common set of applicable customary law. The courts and the legislature have responded in various ways to achieve this uniformity. The area of criminal law seems to have chalked up some notable success in the pursuit of this venture, with section 8 of the criminal code setting a standard of criminality for all across the nation.

---

[86] Nii Armah Josiah-Aryeh, *Customary Law's Unsteady Strides Forward*, U. GHANA L.J. (1996–99).
[87] *See* Ogwurike, *supra* note 2.
[88] *See* Josiah-Aryeh, *supra* note 86.
[89] As noted by the Court in *Eshun v. Johnfia*, "The duty of a court is to endeavor always to ascertain and apply the customary rules and usages in force at any particular time in the community. Since customary law is elastic and progressive, our people who live in the modern world should be credited with the capability to adapt their customs and usages to modern situations without any coercion from external authority. Once external coercion, judicial or legislature, is brought to bear on the customs and usages of the people, there is bound to be polarization of what is actually preached by the people in their day-to-day lives on the one hand, and parallelism between the law making process and the advancement of the practices, customs and usages of the people to avoid frustrations." *See Eshun v. Johnfia*, High Court, Sekondi, 8 June 1981; digested in [1982–83] G.L.R.D. 45.

Obviously, the courts will also continue in their mandate to prune customary law and streamline it in its adaption to modernism and values of development, in line with the 1992 Constitutional mandate to prohibit "[a]ll customary practices which dehumanize or are injurious to the physical and mental well-being of a person...."[90] Much of the enterprise however, seems to have officially fallen to the National House of Chiefs rather than the courts.

In effect, the 1992 Constitution of Ghana establishes the National House of Chiefs and the Regional House of Chiefs and requires these institutions to "undertake an evaluation of the traditional customs and usages with the view to eliminating those customs and usages that are outmoded and socially harmful."[91] It also engages the Houses with the task of undertaking "a progressive study, interpretation and codification of customary law with a view to evolving, in appropriate cases, a unified system of rules of customary law, and compiling the customary laws and lines of succession applicable to each stool or skin."[92] In addition, the new Chieftaincy Act 759 of 2008 empowers the National House of Chiefs to promote the development of the customary law by undertaking the progressive study, interpretation, and codification of customary law in order to evolve a unified system of rules of customary law, where appropriate. In appropriate circumstances, the House of Chiefs may recommend to the Minister that a customary law be assimilated by the common law.[93] These progressive developments are aimed at making customary law ascertainment and dispute resolution much easier and more straightforward.

Though these provisions were lying in our statute books for years,[94] it was not until 2008 that the customary law ascertainment and codification exercise staggeringly took off. The project, in its pilot phase, is being jointly undertaken by the National House of Chiefs and the Law Reform Commission under the chairmanship of Professor Justice Kodzo Parku Kludze[95] in twenty traditional areas with funding from the German Technical Co-operation (GTZ). It is aimed at initially covering two main aspects of customary law: family and customary land laws. The project is to proceed in phases. Several workshops are being organized, which are to be followed by data collection through questionnaire, after which the information gathered will be validated at the level of the traditional area, the regional level, and finally at the

---

[90] GHANA CONST. art. 26(2).
[91] *Id.* art. 272(c).
[92] *Id.* arts. 272(b), 274 (3)(f).
[93] *See* Chieftaincy Act, 2008, Act 759 § 49 (Ghana).
[94] Previous statutes have had the same provisions. *See* Chieftaincy Act of 1971, Act 370 § 40, *repealed by* Chieftaincy Act, 2008, Act 759 (Ghana) (stipulating that "The National House of Chiefs shall, subject to clause (2) of article 126 of the Constitution, undertake the progressive study, interpretation and codification of customary law with a view to evolving, in appropriate cases a unified system of rules of customary law").
[95] Former justice of the Supreme Court of Ghana.

national level before being codified. Assuredly, the benefits anticipated include not only a documentation of customary law for use by the courts, academic institutions, communities, and individuals, but also the institutionalization of a reference point for customary law issues that will consequentially solidify the Ghanaian legal system in terms of fixation, accuracy, and predictability. This customary law project is still in its preliminary stages and much of its anticipated successes and problems will for now be a matter of speculation.

It is also worthy to note that, since the grant of independence in March 1957, chiefs in Ghana have been pivotal to the development of customary law, which continues to be an important feature in the lives of most of the rural people. However, one principal scourge that has sneaked into this laudable endeavor has been the spate of chieftaincy disputes in the traditional communities in Ghana today. The various Houses of Chiefs have found themselves overwhelmed with protracted chieftaincy disputes resulting in the relegation of its proper functions assigned to them by the 1992 Constitution and section 49 of the Chieftaincy Act, 2008 to an almost forgotten background. Reducing the impact and quickly addressing such an issue are imperative to the success of the development of customary law. We believe that a restatement of the customary law project coupled with a compilation of chiefs' list and other data on chiefs is in the right direction in addressing the phenomenon.

Also, with the new policy of the judiciary to decongest the courts and reduce litigation in view of the overwhelming number of cases choking up the courts, the promotion of alternative dispute resolution mechanisms remains the available option. Customary arbitration certainly may regain its privilege of dispensing customary law, but a lot continues to depend on the confidence that the administrating customary institutions engender in the people. Where the customary adjudication is fair and equitable, citizens will patronize them in preference to the alternative of facing high legal fees charged by lawyers and undue delays caused by courts that are overwhelmed with cases. To ensure certainty and avoid conflicting claims as to what was agreed at arbitrations, customary arbitration awards and negotiated settlements that have been accepted by the parties should be registered with the nearest District or Circuit Courts, as it is presently the case with court-connected mediation settlements.

9.8. CONCLUSION

Customary law is not just a system of law but the manifestation of the identity of a people. Its preservation is thus in keeping with the exercise of cultural values as a community right and demonstrate its importance in the foundation of the Ghanaian legal system. The courts have had a great impact in the development and transformation of customary law through its embedded qualities of adaptability and growth.

We must note, however, that though the challenge of meeting the requirements of the new development order would seem, on its face, to be an ordinary task, the living customary law appears to diverge from its delineation by the courts and statutes. The Constitution's involvement of the traditional authorities in the task of developing of customary law is a step in the right direction to ensure compliance by the traditional community. If customary law is to be properly determined, both in form and content, its ascertainment and codification should remain the preserve of those who know, understand, practice, and live those customs. The empowerment of the Houses of Chiefs, among others, to further the promotion and development of customary law is a worthy challenge to the holders of such high customary office to continue to lead the way. Section 49 of Act 759[96] appears to be a powerful tool in the hands of our chiefs and other customary office holders in evolving an enduring system of customary law that will stand the test of time. The question remains, however, as to when customary law will grow on its own without statutory interventions.

[96] Chieftaincy Act, 2008, Act 759 (Ghana).

PART THREE

The Role and Power of Traditional Authorities

10

Traditional Courts in South Africa in the Twenty-First Century

Digby Sqhelo Koyana

10.1. INTRODUCTION

This chapter analyzes the evolution, features, function, and future of traditional (or customary law) courts in South Africa. It begins by examining, and ultimately discarding, the critique that traditional courts are not "real" courts of law. It then outlines the main features of traditional courts that differentiate them from common and civil law courts. The third section of the chapter acknowledges and responds to some of the major criticisms of the customary legal system in South Africa. The final part of the chapter is devoted to the future of traditional courts.

10.2. ARE TRADITIONAL COURTS REAL COURTS OF LAW?

A court has been aptly described as a body of persons duly assembled under the authority of law for the administration of justice.[1] Courts applying customary law in Africa fit this description because the persons concerned derive their authority from customary law. This then raises the further question whether customary law itself is really law.

For a long time after the advent of colonization in Africa, customary law was referred to as "native law," "local law," or "African law," both in statutes and in the writings of anthropologists.[2] From that description the fallacy arose that customary law is not really law. In Central Africa, that fallacy was expressed in the dicta of judges in court decisions. Thus in the Rhodesian[3] case of *Chitambala v. R*, the court

---

[1] *See* WILLIAM BENTON, WEBSTER'S THIRD NEW INTERNATIONAL DICTIONARY (1768). The writer says further that in England, the word is also used in several different contexts *inter alia*: the meeting place of a sovereign and his retinue of officers or councilors.

[2] *See* Eugene Cotran, *The Place and Future of Customary Law in East Africa* 72, *in* EAST AFRICAN LAW TODAY (British Institute of International and Comparative Law 1966).

[3] When this case was decided, the term "Rhodesia" referred to the British colony occupying the territory of modern Zambia and Zimbabwe.

stated: "Native customary law ... is more or less in the same position as foreign law and it must be established by an expert before courts other than the Native Courts."[4] However, the validity of customary law has since been defended by scholars and practitioners. For example, Judge Eugene Cotran[5] wrote, "there is no doubt that when one speaks of customary law, one is referring to law which, though based on custom must have the force of law. To isolate law from custom, as the term 'native law and custom' or 'African law and custom' suggests, would imply recognition of customs that do not have the force of law."[6] Cotran emphasized that English common law itself is derived from traditions, customs, and precedent dating back to the Norman Conquest, though no one today questions the authority of common law. Whereas scholars may continue to debate the efficacy and place of customary law in the constitutional and legal structure of modern African states,[7] the reality is that customary law governs at least some aspects of life for the vast majority of Southern and Eastern Africans.[8] Furthermore, at independence, many East African governments expressed great interest in the study, unification, and recording of customary law.[9] Thus, the status of customary law as a legitimate source of legal authority is no longer seriously contested.

In South Africa, recognition of customary law and of the customary courts began as early as 1927 with the passage of the Black Administration Act.[10] This opened the door to state-recognized judicial activity among the traditional authorities, from whose judgments appeals lay to the magistrate's courts. Any doubts about whether these courts are courts in any real sense were shattered as early as 1948 by the case

---

[4] (1957) 6 NLR 29. *See also Mbowela v R* 1962 R&N 112 FSC where Briggs, Federal Judge of the then Rhodesias and Nyasaland, said that the definition of law is not wide enough to include unwritten native customary law, which is not law in the strict sense.

[5] Eugene Cotran is an expert on Middle Eastern and African law. He has taught at the School of Oriental and African Studies at the University of London, and served as an appellate judge in Kenya and England.

[6] Cotran, *supra* note 2, at 73. *See also* N.A. ALLOT, NEW ESSAYS IN AFRICAN LAW 148 (1970).

[7] *See* Gordon R. Woodman, *A Survey of Customary Law in Africa in Search of Lessons for the Future*, opening essay (Chapter 1) of this book.

[8] *See* Cotran, *supra* note 2, at 74.

[9] *See id.* at 79.

[10] Act 38 of 1927. "The Black Administration Act of 1927 did not codify or define African customary law. It simply singled out Africans as a separate segment of society, subject to a different, discriminatory set of rules and laws, under the apartheid system. It provided that all Africans were subject to African customary law." Media Statement by the South African Law Reform Commission on its Investigation into Customary Law of Succession (Project 90). Section 11 of the Black Administration Act gave magistrates' courts the power to apply customary law in cases between blacks. Section 12 authorized chiefs and headmen on whom jurisdiction had been conferred to hear and determine any civil claims arising out of customary law. Section 20, in turn, authorized chiefs and headmen to try and punish persons who had committed offenses at common law and under statutory law, provided such offenses were not listed in the Third Schedule to the Act.

of *Mdumane v. Mtshakule*.[11] In that case, it was stated that the judgments of the traditional courts are binding on the parties, and would be given effect by the highest courts of the country. The active participation of traditional courts as arms of the justice system of the country continued through the dark days of racial discrimination in South Africa, and not infrequently the judgments of these courts were upheld by the Supreme Court of Appeal.[12] At the advent of democracy in South Africa, in 1994, there were 1,500 traditional courts.[13] Their continued existence and operation is guaranteed by the new Constitution[14] and legislation that is presently before Parliament,[15] and they continue to function to date as ever before.[16]

Traditional courts have unique structures, rules, procedures, and jurisdiction that distinguish them from the rest of the South African court system. The Black Administration Act allocates both civil[17] and criminal[18] jurisdiction to customary law courts, though with certain limitations. Only chiefs and deputies who have been specially appointed under provisions of the Black Administration Act can preside over official courts.[19] Civil jurisdiction is limited to matters governed by customary law, though excluding questions of nullity and divorce.[20] Traditional courts have criminal jurisdiction over all matters under customary or common law, except those offenses listed in the Third Schedule of the Black Administration Act.[21] Chiefs' criminal jurisdiction is further limited in two ways. First, traditional courts have no jurisdiction where the defendant or victim is *not* "black,"[22] as that term is defined in the Act.[23] Second, the array of punishments available to a chief is strictly circumscribed.[24]

---

[11] 1948 N.A.C. (C&O) 28 (Bizana).
[12] *See, e.g., Nombona v Mzileni & Another* 1961 N.A.C. (S). On appeal to the magistrate, the judgment of the Chief was overturned, but on further appeal to the Appeal Court, the judgment was reinstated as correct.
[13] T. W. BENNETT, A SOURCEBOOK OF AFRICAN CUSTOMARY LAW FOR SOUTHERN AFRICA 63 (Juta & Co. 1991).
[14] S. AFR. CONST. 1996 Item 16(1) of Schedule 6.
[15] *See* Traditional Courts Bill, Govt. Gazette No. 30902, March 27, 2008.
[16] For an example of the huge workload that is carried and disposed of by the traditional courts in South Africa, see KOYANA & BEKKER, THE JUDICIAL PROCESS IN THE CUSTOMARY COURTS OF SOUTHERN AFRICA (Unitra 1998). The writers show that, for instance, whereas there is one magistrate's court for each of the 37 districts of the Eastern Cape Province, there are no less than 250 traditional courts dispensing justice on a daily basis in that province. Bigger districts like St. Marks have eleven traditional courts; Mthatha and Gatyana have ten each, whereas smaller districts Libode, Tsomo, and Mzimvubu have three each.
[17] *See* Black Administration Act 38 of 1927 § 12(1).
[18] *See id.* § 20.
[19] *See* Bennett, *supra* note 13, at 64.
[20] *See id.* at 65–66.
[21] *See id.* at 64.
[22] *See id.*
[23] *See* Black Administration Act 38 of 1927 § 35.
[24] *See* Bennett, *supra* note 13, at 64.

Structurally and procedurally, customary law courts are marked by their informality. Proceedings generally take place outdoors at whatever time the chief or headman prefers.[25] There are no set rules for presenting evidence or for the kind of evidence that may be admitted.[26] The procedure for who can be called as a witness, who can question the witness, and what questions are permissible is similarly flexible.[27] In theory, all adult male members of the village can participate in the discussion of a case.[28] Finally, the form and substance of a decision by a headman or chief, if one is given, is completely at his discretion.[29] The procedural preoccupation of western jurisprudence has no place in traditional South African courts.

The entire system of customary law in South Africa is set to be reformed by the Traditional Courts Bill[30] now making its way through the National Assembly. The goal of the Bill is to update and bring the organs of traditional justice into line with the human rights and equality provisions of the 1996 Constitution.[31] The draft Bill now before the legislature governs nearly every aspect of customary law courts: training of traditional leaders, civil and criminal jurisdiction, procedure, sanctions that may be given, enforcement of those sanctions, appeals, recording of proceedings, misconduct of presiding officers, and punishable offenses, among others. If passed, the Traditional Courts Bill would be the most extensive statutory attempt to govern and regulate the system of traditional justice in South Africa.

10.3. MAIN ADVANTAGES OF TRADITIONAL COURTS

Traditional or customary law courts in South Africa are distinguished from magistrates' courts in several ways. First, they are eminently accessible, both socially and geographically.[32] Traditional courts exist in almost every village, so those seeking justice do not have to travel long distances to district headquarters like they would in order to be heard by a magistrate.[33] Additionally, similarities in social status, wealth, and education between the chief presiding over a traditional court and the disputants dispel the intimidation such litigants might feel when appearing in a western-type court.[34] Second, customary law courts provide affordable access to

---

[25] *See id.* at 70.

[26] *See id.*

[27] *See id.*

[28] *See id.* at 71.

[29] *See id.*

[30] Traditional Courts Bill, Govt. Gazette No. 30902, March 27, 2008.

[31] *See id.* at Preamble.

[32] *See* South African Law Commission, *The Harmonisation of the Common Law and Indigenous Law: Traditional Courts and the Judicial Function of Traditional Leaders* 2, Discussion Paper 82 (May 1999). *See also* Bennett, *supra* note 13, at 57.

[33] *See* SA Law Commission, *supra* note 32.

[34] *See id.*

justice. Transportation costs are negligible, fees levied are often payable in kind, and the absence of lawyers further reduces cost.[35] Third, because customary law derives from the rules and practices of a particular community, all parties appearing in traditional courts are assumed to have a great familiarity with the law. Unlike common or statutory law, which is often viewed as imported and confusing, customary law has remained simple enough for ordinary people to participate in traditional law proceedings without requiring the assistance of trained counsel.[36] Fourth, like customary law itself, the procedure utilized in traditional courts remains simple, flexible, and user-friendly, thus increasing popular participation and legitimacy.[37] Finally, customary courts conduct their proceedings in the local language of the parties, facilitating access and eliminating translation errors.[38]

10.4. CRITICISMS OF TRADITIONAL COURTS

Despite the previously noted advantages over magistrates' courts, some features of traditional courts have also been criticized. The next three subsections of this paper respond in depth to three of the major criticisms leveled against customary courts, whereas the fourth examines an often overlooked benefit. This section will briefly note a few of the other critiques of the traditional court system in South Africa. However, given space constraints, this chapter will not address these critiques in detail.

Many of the criticisms of traditional courts in South Africa, though extant during the Apartheid era, have been brought to the forefront by the passage of the new Constitution in 1996. On the one hand, the Constitutional Court of South Africa has held[39] that the Constitution explicitly recognizes and legitimizes traditional courts in section 166(e)[40] and 16(1) of Schedule 6.[41] On the other hand, various rights and protections enshrined in the Constitution raise their own concerns when it comes to customary courts. The first of these deals with the composition of traditional courts.

---

[35] *See id.*
[36] *See id. See also* Bennett, *supra* note 13, at 63.
[37] *See* SA Law Commission, *supra* note 32, at 2–3.
[38] *See id.* at 3.
[39] *See Ex Parte Chairperson of the Constitutional Assembly: In re Certification of the Constitution of the Republic of South Africa* 1996 (4) SA 744, 835 (CC).
[40] "The courts are any other court established or recognised in terms of an Act of Parliament, including any court of a status similar to either the High Courts or the Magistrates' Courts." S. AFR. CONST. 1996 § 166(e).
[41] "Every court, including courts of traditional leaders, existing when the new Constitution took effect, continues to function and to exercise jurisdiction in terms of the legislation applicable to it, and anyone holding office as a judicial officer continues to hold office in terms of the legislation applicable to that office, subject to (a) any amendment or repeal of that legislation; and (b) consistency with the new Constitution." S. AFR. CONST. 1996 § 16(1) of Schedule 6.

Traditional courts are presided over by chiefs or headmen, often assisted by a group of counselors. The constitutional criticism offered is that chiefs and headmen, who are usually uneducated and sometimes illiterate, do not meet the qualifications set out in section 174(1) of the Constitution: "Any appropriately qualified woman or man who is a fit and proper person, may be appointed a judicial officer."[42] Even assuming that chiefs and headmen are well versed in the customary law that they apply, they are not qualified to adjudicate in matters involving common law or statutory law where they lack expertise.[43]

A second critique of the composition of traditional courts is the lack of a role for women.[44] Female litigants are prohibited from making their own case before customary courts and must rely on a male relative to represent them.[45] In traditionally patriarchal South African society, women do not succeed to chieftainship, and therefore are unable to preside over traditional courts, though some evidence suggests that this practice is changing.[46] It has been argued that women's roles, or lack thereof, in customary courts violate principles of non-discrimination and equality set down by the Constitution.[47] The draft version of the Traditional Courts Bill, which seeks to harmonize traditional courts with the requirements and protections set out in the South African Constitution, addresses the role of women. Section nine, which deals with procedure, mandates that the presiding officer must ensure "[t]hat women are afforded full and equal participation in the proceedings, as men are."[48]

A third concern is that the procedure utilized in customary courts leaves no room for a presumption of innocence for an accused person. Generally, a chief and/or his counselors will question the accused who must then convince the court of his innocence through his answers.[49] This procedure, which necessitates a vocal defense, eliminates an accused person's constitutionally protected right to remain silent[50] and can prejudice the nervous or the inarticulate, not to mention women who are prohibited from presenting their own cases.[51] However, other experts argue that it is a fundamental misinterpretation of customary procedure, based on a common law-centric worldview, to claim that accused persons lack a presumption of innocence.[52]

---

[42] *See* SA Law Commission, *supra* note 32, at 5.

[43] *See id.* at 4–5.

[44] For a more general feminist critique of South African customary law, see Christina Murray and Felicity Kaganas, *Law and Women's Rights in South Africa: An Overview, in* GENDER AND THE NEW SOUTH AFRICAN LEGAL ORDER (Christina Murray ed., Juta & Co. 1994).

[45] *See* SA Law Commission, *supra* note 32, at 4; Murray and Kaganas, *supra* note 44, at 17.

[46] *See, e.g., Shilubana and Others v. Nwamitwa* CCT 03/07, 2008 (9) BCLR 914 (CC).

[47] *See* SA Law Commission, *supra* note 32, at 4.

[48] Traditional Courts Bill, Govt. Gazette No. 30902, March 27, 2008, § 9(2)(a)(i).

[49] *See* SA Law Commission, *supra* note 32, at 4.

[50] S. AFR. CONST. 1996 § 35(3)(h).

[51] *See* SA Law Commission, *supra* note 32, at 4.

[52] "Questions in cross-examination are generally framed on the assumption that a person is lying, and it has therefore been incorrectly alleged that in African courts an accused is assumed by the judges to

Instead, it has been suggested that chiefs and headmen in South African customary law courts function more like civil law judges who must discover the truth for themselves through cross-examination.[53]

A fourth argument leveled against traditional courts, and those who preside over them, is that they do not respect the constitutional principle of separation of powers.[54] Village chiefs and headmen are, first and foremost, executive officials. However, they also fulfill a judicial function when they preside over customary courts. When a chief or headman wears two hats – executive and judicial – concurrently, he violates the independence and impartiality required of the judiciary.[55] One response to this criticism is that separation of powers is a western legal/constitutional concept and should not be imposed on a traditional system with no similar notion.[56] In fact, some colonial powers hoped that the familiar combination of administrative and judicial functions in the person of the chief would lend greater legitimacy to the traditional court system in the eyes of ordinary Africans.[57]

Finally, some commentators have questioned the unlimited monetary jurisdiction of traditional courts. They argue that customary courts, which are simple by design and run by men with no legal training, are ill equipped to decide complex legal questions involving thousands of Rand.[58] There is concern that traditional court verdicts, which have historically been small, will increase as South Africa's economy continues to open to the outside world.[59] Other Southern African countries, including Zimbabwe and Botswana, have placed monetary caps on traditional court awards, and some argue that South Africa should do the same.[60] The most recent version of the proposed Traditional Courts Bill addresses this concern. Section 5 prohibits customary courts from hearing civil cases where "the claim or value of the property in dispute" exceeds an amount determined and modifiable by the Minister for Justice and Constitutional Development.[61]

This chapter will now consider four of the prominent features of traditional courts that differ from those of magistrate's courts: legal representation, record keeping and codification, the distinction between civil and criminal cases, and the conciliatory rather than retributive nature of customary courts.

be guilty and must prove his innocence. In fact, in Barotse and all other African courts I know, guilt must be demonstrated." Bennett, *supra* note 13, at 74.
[53] *See id.*
[54] *See* S. AFR. CONST. 1996, Constitutional Principle VI and § 165.
[55] *See Bangindawo and Others v. Head of Nyanda Regional Authority and Another; Hlantlalala v. Head of the Western Tembuland Regional Authority and Others*, 1998 (3) SA 262 (TK).
[56] *See* SA Law Commission, *supra* note 32, at 13–15. *See also Bangindawo* 1998 (3) SA at 272–274.
[57] Bennett, *supra* note 13, at 56.
[58] *See* SA Law Commission, *supra* note 32, at 25–26.
[59] *See id.* at 25–26.
[60] *See id.* at 25.
[61] Traditional Courts Bill, Govt. Gazette No. 30903, March 27, 2008, § 5(2)(e).

10.5. THE ISSUE OF LEGAL REPRESENTATION

A prominent feature of traditional courts is that they do not allow legal representation. Some African scholars have argued that these courts should be abolished
because of this deficiency or, alternatively, that they should be required to allow
legal representation. However, in this regard, it has been pointed out that a presiding traditional courts' chief is not a trained judicial officer. Indeed many chiefs have
no formal education at all.[62] One concern with allowing attorneys and advocates to
participate in customary court proceedings is that it would introduce the element of
litigation costs that are unknown to these courts. Justice is ensured to the parties by
the fact that an appeal lies from these courts to the magistrates' courts of the district
in which they are situated.

It is noteworthy that lawyers and lawyers' associations typically have not come
out and demanded audience in traditional courts. We could trace one case, from
neighboring Lesotho, in which such demand was made. In *Mahloane v. Letele*,[63]
the defendants asked for the case to be transferred from a traditional court to a
magistrate's court so that they could be legally represented. This request was turned
down by the magistrate, and on appeal the High Court confirmed the magistrate's
decision.[64] The Court declared:

> The legislature, in its wisdom, decided that legal practitioners are barred from
> appearing in these courts.... If one considers the matter closely one finds many
> good reasons why legal practitioners are not allowed. They [traditional courts] are
> accessible to most people, and at little expense. The nature of the disputes is simple
> and can adequately be dealt with by those courts.[65]

In any event, if one looks at a traditional court for what it is, and not as a court of the
western legal tradition, one finds that there is a very effective system of representation in place. In general, procedure is not fixed and may vary from day to day, and
even from case to case.[66] The key feature of customary procedure is its informality
and malleability rather than the uniformity prized by common and civil law courts.[67]
All men are entitled to attend court and to put questions to the parties and to their
witnesses.[68] The men from party A's ward, having gathered facts of the case, which
would be common talk in the village, put questions that favor A, whereas the men

---

[62] *See* Civil Practice and Procedure in All Bantu Courts in Southern Africa (Juta & Co.,
   2d ed. 1970).
[63] H.C. Civ/App./93/1974.
[64] *See id.*
[65] *Id.*
[66] *See* Bennett, *supra* note 13, at 71.
[67] *See id.* at 70–71.
[68] *See id.*

from party B's ward put questions that favor B. At the end, the presiding chief is able to weigh the evidence and give a verdict. The Black Administration Act followed the practice of the traditional courts and prohibited representation by advocates and attorneys.[69]

In South Africa, the most recent challenge[70] to traditional courts based on their prohibition of legal representation was triggered by the advent of the interim Constitution in 1993[71] and the new Constitution of 1996.[72] The thrust of the challenge in *Bangindawo and Others v. Head of Nyanda Regional Authority and Another* and *Mhlekwa v. Head of the Western Tembuland Regional Authority and Another* was directed at five recently created, statutory regional authority courts (a.k.a., Courts of Paramount Chiefs), which had been given increased powers by the Regional Authority Courts Act (RACA).[73] However, one of the constitutional complaints raised by the applicants in *Bangindawo* and *Mhlekwa* was the same as that which had been raised against the traditional authority courts over the years, *inter alia*, that they do not allow legal representation.[74]

The *Bangindawo* and *Mhlekwa* applicants challenged the fairness of trials in the regional authority courts. More specifically, the applicants attacked section 7(1) of the RACA, which prohibited legal representation in proceedings before regional authority courts, as inconsistent with the interim and current Constitutions of South Africa.[75] Lack of legal representation is of far greater concern in regional authority courts because these courts, unlike traditional courts, have concurrent jurisdiction with magistrate's courts. That is, they have full statutory and common-law jurisdiction, including over criminal matters, in addition to customary-law jurisdiction. The *Bangindawo* court found the prohibition on legal representation codified in section 7(1) of RACA, when considered in the far more serious context of complex civil and criminal cases handled by the regional authority courts, simply could not be justified on the same grounds as such a ban in the realm of ordinary traditional courts.[76] The *Mhlekwa* court determined that preventing an accused from utilizing legal representation in a regional authority court case violated the general right to a

---

[69] See Act 38 of 1927 § 5 of the Regulations governing procedure in the traditional courts.

[70] See *Bangindawo and Others v. Head of Nyanda Regional Authority and Another; Hlantlalala v. Head of the Western Tembuland Regional Authority and Others*, 1998 (3) SA 262 (TK); *Mhlekwa v. Head of the Western Tembuland Regional Authority and Another; Feni v. Head of the Western Tembuland Regional Authority and Another* 2001 (1) SA 574 (TK).

[71] S. Afr. (Interim) Const. 1993.

[72] S. Afr. Const. 1996.

[73] Act No. 13 of 1982 of the Transkei National Assembly.

[74] Further that they place the onus of proof on the accused/defendant in civil and criminal cases, that they do not give a right to call for further particulars, or to apply for the discharge of the accused at the end of the state's case. See *Bangindawo* 1998 (3) SA 262 (Tk); *Mhlekwa* 2001 (1) SA 574 (Tk).

[75] See *Bangindawo* 1998 (3) SA at 275; *Mhlekwa* 2001 (1) SA at 618.

[76] *Bangindawo* 1998 (3) SA at 276.

fair trial set out in section 35(3) of the South African Constitution.[77] In both cases, the courts struck down the prohibition on legal representation contained in section 7(1) of RACA as inconsistent with South Africa's constitutional requirements.[78] The *Bangindawo* and *Mhlekwa* decisions apply only to the regional authority courts, however, not to the thousands of ordinary customary law courts operating across the country.

The continued existence of the prohibition of legal representation in traditional courts would be ensured by the passage of the Traditional Courts Bill, once again before parliament in South Africa.[79] Section 9 of the Bill states bluntly that legal representation by attorneys will not be allowed in the customary law courts, thereby codifying the traditional absence of legal representation.[80] However, a party may be represented by a family member, neighbor, or member of the community, so long as such representation conforms to customary law and practice.[81]

10.6. RECORDING AND CODIFICATION

Traditional courts are not courts of record as such. All proceedings are conducted orally in the language most widely spoken in the area of jurisdiction of the court.[82] However, the provisions of the Black Administration Act governing their functioning require each traditional court to lodge with the clerk of the magistrate's court of the district in which the traditional court is situated, a summary of the case on a prescribed form, showing:

- the name of the plaintiff;
- the name of the defendant;
- particulars of the claim;[83]
- particulars of the defense;[84] and
- the judgment.[85]

---

[77] *Mhlekwa*, 2001 (1) SA at 617–18; S. AFR. CONST. 1996 § 35(3), specifically §§ 35(3)(f)-(g).
[78] *See Bangindawo* 1998 (3) SA at 277; *Mhlekwa* 2001 (1) SA at 619.
[79] Traditional Courts Bill, 2008, Bill 15 in GG30902 of 27 March 2008.
[80] *See id.* § 9(3)(a).
[81] *See id.* § 9(3)(b).
[82] Xhosa, Zulu, Sotho, Tswana, Pedi, etc., as the case may be in the South African context.
[83] For example, plaintiff claims five heads of cattle or their value; R 7,200.00 being damages for seduction of plaintiff's daughter Nondwebi by defendant.
[84] For example, defendant denies liability.
[85] For example, decision for plaintiff as claimed with costs or for defendant with costs. In this way the judgment of the traditional court is registered and attains the status of a judgment of the magistrate's court. The unsuccessful party is able to file a notice of appeal through the clerk of the magistrate's court, with the requirement that it serve a copy of the notice of appeal against the opponent. The necessary steps will then be taken to secure a date of hearing of the appeal.

This basic recording is done by the clerk of the traditional court who need not have a high standard of education. Some clerks merely have a Standard Six Certificate[86] and that is quite adequate for the tasks. It is not difficult to find a young person with such a certificate in the rural areas of South Africa.

Despite the record-keeping requirements set out by the Black Administration Act, "the keeping of proper records in the lower courts was a continual problem."[87] The low status of traditional courts in the judicial scheme of South Africa meant that their decisions, even when properly recorded, were rarely reported.[88] Although litigants in customary law courts had the right of appeal to magistrate's courts, considerations of cost, distance, and unfamiliarity with South Africa's hybrid civil/common law system effectively precluded most from taking an appeal.[89] These factors, taken together, ensured that traditional courts evolved nearly independently from South Africa's parallel system of magistrates' courts and prevented the High Court or the department of justice from regulating or supervising traditional courts or their presiding officers.[90] Uniformity and the quality of justice dispensed in customary law courts suffered as a result, and led to criticism by the legal profession, progressive politicians, and eventually African nationalists.[91]

The current draft of the Traditional Courts Bill attempts to remedy some of these problems by enhancing recording requirements.[92] According to an earlier draft Bill, these records would be sent to the Registrar of Customary Courts for the province. That was going to entail a measure of re-organization. Many chiefs who preside at these courts do not have a formal education, or education that is sufficient to enable them to make satisfactory recordings of proceedings. The Transkei Regional Authority Courts for Paramount Chiefs, created under Act 13 of 1982 (Transkei), were courts of record, and this problem was overcome by having officers of magisterial rank doing all the recording (and also assisting the presiding officers when intricate points of law arose). Only five courts of Paramount Chiefs were created by the Regional Authority Courts Act of 1982, and it was thus fairly easy to overcome the problem posed by the recording requirement. It would be difficult to overcome the same problem with respect to more than 1,000 traditional courts.

The idea of formal recording, favored by common law and civil law courts, and the creation of a Registrar of Customary Courts for the Province has been abandoned.

---

[86] The Standard Six School Leaving Examination is taken by students at the end of their primary education. The examination is offered in seven subjects, and those who pass achieve a Standard Six Certificate.

[87] Bennett, *supra* note 13, at 58.

[88] *See id.*

[89] *See* Section 10.3 on Main Features of Traditional Courts, *supra*.

[90] *See* Bennett, *supra* note 13, at 58.

[91] *See id.* at 57.

[92] *See* Traditional Courts Bill, 2008, Bill 15 in GG30902 of 27 March 2008 § 18.

Section 18 of the revised Bill now before Parliament retains a simple kind of recording very similar to what was in place under the Black Administration Act.[93] It requires traditional courts to record the nature of each charge, a summary of the facts of the case, and the decision of the court.[94] The legislature realized that traditional court authorities are not ready to engage in the kind of recording done by a learned and legally trained magistrate. The new version of the Bill also provides for a course of training for traditional leaders.[95] The nature and content of such training will be detailed in regulations to be made by the Minister for Justice and Constitutional Development.[96]

Closely related to the issue of the traditional court being or not being a court of record is the question of codification of the legal system itself. This question arose when the Cape of Good Hope Government Commission on Native Laws and Customs was considering whether or not to recommend a codification of customary law.[97] The chief proponent of codification was Mr. Ayliff, a member of the Cape Government Commission on Native Laws and Customs 1883, and the strong stance he maintained in support of his recommendation was the knowledge he had gathered on the nature and functioning of the traditional courts. He urged that the "kafir"[98] law did exist after all, so why not codify it? The power of the chief was subject to checks and balances, and councilors maintained equipoise between the authority of the chiefs and the rights of the tribesmen. Lawsuits were conducted under the supervision of the chiefs assisted by their councilors "as decorously as any I have seen in our courts, and disturbances are not tolerated."[99] Regrettably, Ayliff's recommendations for a codification of customary criminal law were rejected by the majority of the commissioners. What was agreed on was a criminal code for the native territories.[100] It codified rules of English law with some elements of Roman Dutch Law grafted into it. There were also a few traces of rules of customary criminal law that showed up in the code. Thus, the Native Territories Penal Code created the possibility for magistrates who were trying criminal cases to give liberal compensation to complainants out of the fines payable as sentences by convicted persons.[101] This provision was enacted in response to the prevailing procedures of the traditional courts and was an entrenchment thereof.

[93] *See id.*
[94] *See id.*
[95] *See id.* §4(5).
[96] *See id.* § 21(1)(b).
[97] REPORT AND PROCEEDINGS, WITH APPENDICES, OF THE GOVERNMENT COMMISSION ON NATIVE LAWS AND CUSTOMS (W. A. Richards & Sons 1883) [hereinafter COMMISSIONS REPORT].
[98] Alternately, "kaffir" is a term used disparagingly in South Africa to mean black African, particularly someone of Xhosa descent. *See* Merriam-Webster's Online Dictionary; Dictionary.com.
[99] COMMISSIONS REPORT, *supra* note 97.
[100] The Native Territories Penal Code of 1886, this being the year it was eventually enacted by the Parliament of the Cape of Good Hope as Act 24 of 1886.
[101] *See id.* § 18.

10.7. DISTINCTION BETWEEN CIVIL AND CRIMINAL CASES

The traditional courts deal with every case that comes before them in the same proceeding, without formally declaring it to be a civil case or a criminal case. The difference between civil and criminal cases is therefore not a pronounced one, inasmuch as there are no separate civil courts and criminal courts, and there are not separate days designated for civil cases or for criminal cases. That notwithstanding, we must not go so far as to say that customary law and, accordingly, the customary courts do not distinguish between civil and criminal cases.[102]

There are clear indications that a distinction has always been drawn between civil and criminal cases. Before the advent of colonization, each person was regarded as "the child of the chief" (*umntwana wenkosi*). Consequently, an injury to an individual that was criminal in nature was regarded as punishable by the chief. The overriding principle was that "a man cannot eat his own blood" (i.e., if a person was injured, the right to take action for that lay with the chief and the fine accrued to the chief), unlike in civil cases where the fine accrues to the individual bringing suit. This rule was recognized in the Native Appeal Court case of *Nkwana v. Nonqanaba*[103] where the Court declared:

> According to Native Custom in force in the Thembu and Gcaleka Government (of the Eastern Cape Province of South Africa) the person of each individual of a tribe was the property of the Chief and any injury to the person or character of such individual was an offence against the chief punishable as a crime by fine.[104]

Yet countless cases of seduction and pregnancy, adultery, divorce, cases arising out of *lobola* (dowry) transactions, and out of contracts and quasi-contracts were civil cases wherein A sued B before the chief and obtained judgment as claimed, whenever successful.

After the Union of South Africa was formed, cohesion and uniformity between the four provinces and between the various non-white ethnic groups of South Africa was reached via the Black Administration Act of 1927.[105] That legislation dealt with several aspects of so-called native administration, including the governance of the traditional courts. A clear distinction in the legislation was made between civil cases[106] and criminal cases.[107] Traditional courts were given the power to try criminal

---

[102] *See, e.g., Traditional Authority Courts, in* INTRODUCTION TO LEGAL PLURALISM IN SOUTH AFRICA 144 (J. C. Bekker, C. Rautenbach & N. M. I. Goolam eds., LexisNexis/Butterworths 2006). The preferred formulation there reads: "From early until now, traditional courts have never had a clear distinction between civil and criminal matters."

[103] 1904 (1) N.A.C. 79 (ex-Mqanduli district) (S. Afr.).

[104] *Id.*

[105] Act 38 of 1927.

[106] These were governed by §12 of the Act.

[107] These were governed by §20 of the Act.

offenses at common law, statutory law, or under customary law, with the exclusion of offenses listed in Schedule 3 of the Act.[108] The traditional courts have since then functioned in terms of this statute or similar statutes passed by self-governing states within South Africa.

A recent investigation into the functioning of the traditional courts shows that the traditional judicial authorities do observe the distinction between civil and criminal cases. That investigation report[109] has section 1 devoted to civil cases[110] and section 2 devoted to criminal cases.[111] The cases reported on here relate to bodily injury, disobedience to authorities, abusive language, and cases relating to witchcraft. For instance, a case from the St. Marks district, duly registered at the Magistrate's Office, Cofimvaba, reads as follows:

> Plaintiff: Notozamile Sibango
> Defendant: Nomhlutulu Qolintaba
> Offence: Defendant severely assaulted the plaintiff
> Judgment: Found guilty and fined R100.00

In the South African court terminology, of course, the titles "plaintiff" and "defendant" are reserved for civil cases. In criminal cases, we invariably speak of the "complainant" and the "accused." As pointed out earlier, there are also no separate courts for criminal and for civil cases in the traditional courts, no judicial officers who specialize in civil or criminal cases, and no days set aside for the hearing of civil and criminal cases. All that notwithstanding, and in view of the aforementioned exposition, we would contend that the traditional courts do distinguish between civil and criminal cases.

The draft of the Traditional Courts Bill now before parliament further highlights the distinction. The Bill would give criminal jurisdiction to traditional courts,[112] and in its Schedule gives a list of the offenses that are within their jurisdiction: theft, malicious damage to property, *crimen injuria*, and assault of a minor nature.[113] The first three mentioned offenses were excluded from the jurisdiction of the traditional courts by the Black Administration Act.[114] The indications are

---

[108] These included treason, public violence, murder, robbery, rape, arson, perjury, bribery, etc. *See* Black Administration Act 38 of 1927 ch. IV §§ 12 & 20, Third Schedule.

[109] *See* D. S. KOYANA & J. C. BEKKER, *supra* note 16.

[110] *See id.* at 54–91. The cases reported on relate to the law of persons and family law, e.g., dissolution of marriage and return of the cattle that were paid as "dowry" (*lobola*), contracts, and delicts, e.g., claims for damages for adultery, animal trespass, and other damages related to animals, including the *actio de pauperie*.

[111] *See id.* at 92–116.

[112] *See* Traditional Courts Bill, 2008, Bill 15 in GG30902 of 27 March 2008 §§ 6, 10 & the Schedule.

[113] *Id.* at the Schedule.

[114] *See* Act 38 of 1927 at Third Schedule.

therefore that more and more powers are being given and will continue to be given to the traditional courts.

10.8. RECONCILIATION RATHER THAN RETRIBUTION

A differentiating feature of traditional courts is that, from pre-colonial societies to the present day, they evince an overall purpose of reconciling the parties so that they can live in peace with each other in the village. Taking Kenya as an example, the Kikuyu adjudicatory system was described as follows:

> The elders acted as arbitrators rather than judges, their duty was to point out the recognized tradition and custom of the family to be followed. The chief object in their deliberations was to find ways and means by which they could bring the disputing parties into mutual agreement and to avoid any act of vengeance which might result in breaking up the family group.[115]

The reconciliation feature of the traditional courts remains prominent to the present day. The previously mentioned investigation[116] reveals this. In some instances, a defendant in his response to a claim requests the matter to be sent back to the parties for further discussion and the court readily accepts that, with the recording "Judgment: Court accepted the application, matter to be discussed at home."[117] In a case from the Gatyana district relating to a break-up between husband and wife, the husband's reply was: "I never chased her away from the house, I need her now."[118] The recorded judgment stated: "Wife to go back to her husband and to report back to court should a misunderstanding crop up again."[119]

It should be noted that the reconciliation feature may be problematic in some instances. In certain cases, like domestic violence, it is not clear that a legal system premised on reconciliation, and in which parties are not treated equally, is the most desirable.

10.9. THE FUTURE OF TRADITIONAL COURTS

There have always been some strong challenges to the continued existence of the traditional courts of South Africa. The factors that have militated and continue to

---

[115] *See* JOMO KENYATA, FACING MOUNT KENYA 214 (1953), *quoted in* L. Juma, *Institutions of African Law and Justice Administration in Kenya,* 17 LESOTHO LAW JOURNAL 1, 33 (2007). *See also* R. B. MQEKE, CUSTOMARY LAW IN THE NEW MILLENNIUM 21 (Lovedale Press 2003). The writer says that reconciliation, together with the element of flexibility, features prominently in the sphere of dispute resolution and is expressive of the primary objective of African traditional systems of law.
[116] Koyana & Bekker, *supra* note 16.
[117] *Id.*
[118] *Id.*
[119] *Id.*

militate in favor of a bright future for these courts carry sufficient weight to be able to keep them on stage through the present century and without doubt into the next one and beyond.

As previously discussed, the early challenges were those brought against customary law itself, that it was not really law, from which it followed that traditional courts were themselves not courts in any real sense.[120] This argument was greatly weakened by the Black Administration Act,[121] which gave recognition to the courts and strengthened the distinction between civil and criminal cases.[122] Criticism against the procedure in the courts followed, especially the criticism arising from prohibition of legal representation.[123] The advent of the new Constitution in South Africa, with its emphasis on human rights, and especially its provision that every person shall be entitled to legal representation,[124] provided an opportunity for concerned lawyers to revive the issue of lack of legal representation in the traditional courts. However, as shown earlier in the chapter, the traditional courts as they have existed and functioned since the advent of colonization in South Africa survived this powerful constitutional onslaught.[125]

A more serious challenge faced by traditional courts as a result of the advent of democracy was posed by some of the people of South Africa through political activism. Apart from newspaper and radio reports about strong opposition to traditional courts, further and more direct evidence of such opposition was obtained from the traditional leaders of the affected area itself, the Ciskei Region of the Eastern Cape Province of South Africa. Thus Chief Justice Mabandla of Victoria East district went on record as saying:

> Ever since 1990, when rioting and the *toyi-toyi* dance[126] became the order of the day, the chiefs were unable to continue holding sittings of their courts in their areas. The South African National Civic Organisation (SANCO) is the organisation that now handles the cases of residents in rural areas. This is unconstitutional because the chiefs' courts used to function in terms of a law of Parliament, but the SANCO courts are functioning by force and not in terms of any law of Parliament.[127]

---

[120] *See* discussion *supra* section 1, 10.1.
[121] Act No. 38 of 1927.
[122] *See* discussion *supra* section 9.2, 10.2.
[123] *See* discussion *supra* section 9.2, 10.2.
[124] *See* S. AFR. CONST. 1996 § 35.
[125] *See* discussion *supra* section 9.2, 10.2, and the constitutional cases cited.
[126] Toyi-toyi, a protest dance of Zimbabwean origin, became popular in South Africa during the struggle against apartheid. The dance involves simultaneous stomping and chanting, often of political slogans. It was used effectively to intimidate South African troops during the street protests of the 1970s and 1980s.
[127] *See* Koyana & Bekker, *supra* note 16, at 232. Likewise, Chief S. M. Burns-Ncamashe of AmaGwali Traditional Authority indicated how political activists were openly preaching against the traditional authorities and, accordingly, their courts. In the Metropolitan area of East London, the judgments of

Fortunately for the traditional court system, this challenge was short-lived. Firstly, the affected area was the smaller section of the Eastern Cape Province. It comprises only nine out of the total thirty-seven districts of the Eastern Cape Province; the remaining twenty-eight provinces were not affected.[128] Secondly, the Constitution that was passed following the rioting and *toyi-toyi* dances, described by Chief Justice Mabandla as having heralded the dawn of democracy during the period 1990 to 1994, boldly gave recognition to and ensured the continued functioning of the traditional courts.[129] It provided that every court – including courts of traditional leaders – existing when the new Constitution took effect, continued to function and to exercise jurisdiction in terms of legislation applicable to it, and anyone holding office continues to hold office in terms of the legislation applicable to that office, subject to amendment or repeal of that legislation and consistency with the Constitution.[130] Thirdly, the government of the new South Africa, as soon as it took office after the coming into effect of the new Constitution, adopted a stance supportive of traditional leadership generally. This stance manifested itself in several legislative and policy mechanisms that were aimed at developing customary law and its concepts and institutions in order to harmonize them with mainstream socio-economic and legal practices.[131] Fourthly, Parliament now has before it the Traditional Courts Bill about which much has been said earlier, and which gives the surest guarantee of a bright future for traditional courts in South Africa.

Apart from legislative measures and policy mechanisms, the traditional courts have their own resources and built-in legal mechanisms which, in our view, guarantee them a bright future. For one thing, they remain suited to the needs of the African people – who form the vast majority of the population of South Africa – for resolving their disputes. Traditional courts have simple and convenient procedures. They remain unconcerned with the legal niceties and technicalities of the common law. Another factor that guarantees a good future for traditional courts is their ability to adapt to changes and thus be seen to be adaptable. The continued enchantment

---

traditional courts would be registered in the Magistrate's Office, as happens everywhere else. However, by letter dated October 31, 1996, S. A. Van Stander, Magistrate of East London, confirmed to the research team that there were no registered judgments of traditional courts. *See id.* This is despite the existence of rural areas with chiefs and headmen within the magisterial district of East London.

[128] The Province of Kwa-Zulu Natal alone has more than twice the number of traditional authorities that exist in the Eastern Cape Province.

[129] *See S. Afr. Const.* 1996 §§ 211–12.

[130] *See S. Afr.* (Interim) *Const.* 1993 §§ 229, 241–42.

[131] These include the establishment of the National House of Traditional Leaders in terms of Act 10 of 1997, a body set to advise the National Government and make recommendations on matters relating to customary law and customs of the various indigenous communities, the Recognition of Customary Marriage Act No. 120 of 1998, which for the first time in the long history of the Parliament of South Africa gives recognition to the customary marriage, and the Communal Land Rights Act No. 11 of 2004, which defines the powers of traditional leaders regarding land control and distribution.

of the populace with these traditional courts is proved by the fact that so very few out of the huge volume of cases heard by them ever go on appeal to the magistrate's courts.[132] The courts bring the legal machine within easy reach of the members of the communities and retain to date the flexibility and informality which were their distinguishing features from pre-colonial times.[133]

The preference for the traditional courts as the fora for resolving the disputes of the majority of the people of South Africa has been observed and highlighted by the judges of the High Court of South Africa in cases that have come before them. Thus in *S v. Kwinana*, the court expressed approval of the procedure adopted in the traditional courts in these words: "It brooks no doubt that the old tribal court, being part of the people's traditions, is best understood by them, and hence best respected, and it is thus proper that the authority and techniques of such courts should be maintained as far as possible."[134]

This statement was quoted with approval by the court in the case of *Bangindawo and Others v. Head of the Nyanda Regional Authority and Another*.[135] The accused was charged with contempt of court for failing to appear before the Nyanda Regional Authority Court (Paramount Chief's Court) though duly summoned to do so.[136] He was found guilty and he applied to the High Court for the conviction to be set aside because, *inter alia*, presiding officers in the five Regional Authority Courts are neither independent nor impartial because they are an arm of the government from which they earn salaries.[137] This criticism of course applies equally to all presiding officers in all the traditional courts of South Africa who similarly lay charges of contempt of court when people fail to appear though duly summoned. Dismissing that criticism, the court ruled that "the embodiment of all these powers in a judicial officer ... is not a thing of the past; it continues to thrive and is believed in and accepted by the vast majority of those ... who continue to adhere to African customary law."[138] They "believe in the impartiality of the chief or king when he exercises his judicial functions."[139] Therefore the court concluded there was no reason for the imposition of the western concept of judicial impartiality and independence in the African customary legal system, especially the judicial facet thereof.[140]

[132] *See* Bennett, *supra* note 13, at 58. But see the critique of traditional courts in Section 10.6 on Recording and Codification, *supra*, arguing that most litigants do not take appeals to the magistrate's courts because of cost concerns, great distances to travel, language barriers, or unfamiliarity with South Africa's hybrid common/civil law system.

[133] South African writers on customary law would not quarrel with this contention. *See, e.g.,* T. W. BENNETT, CUSTOMARY LAW IN SOUTH AFRICA 140 (Juta & Co. 2004).

[134] 1985 (3) SA 369 (TK).

[135] 1998 (3) SA 262, 273 (TK).

[136] *See id.*

[137] *See id.* at 271.

[138] *Id.* at 272.

[139] *Id.* at 273.

[140] *See id.* at 272–273.

Traditional law and traditional courts respond positively to the recipe for survival of a legal system and its courts that was laid down by the court in *O'Callaghan NO v. Chaplin*.[141] The court noted, having in mind the Roman Dutch law, "It is the duty of a court … so to administer a living system of law as to ensure without the sacrifice of fundamental principles, that it shall adapt itself to the changing conditions of the time. And it may be necessary sometimes to modify, or even to discard doctrines which have become outworn."[142] The same is true for traditional courts applying customary law.

The last issue to be dealt with is the dual court system (i.e., separate state and traditional courts) that the continued existence of the traditional courts perpetuates. There is indeed a body of opinion that favors a unified legal system as against a plural type. In some countries, the tendency on attainment of independence was to unify the judicial systems. An example is Ghana where all "native" courts were abolished in 1960. All courts were to apply western law unless the parties affected could show the propriety of applying customary law in the remaining courts.[143]

On the other hand, some countries generally favored a separation of customary law and statutory law, with traditional courts applying customary law and non-African courts applying English or English-based law. In South Africa, the Black Administration Act created parallel court systems at the trial and primary appellate levels designed principally for indigenous (courts of chiefs and headmen) and non-indigenous (magistrates' courts) communities.[144] Appeals from the African courts lay to officers (known as native commissioners) well versed in traditional law but not being the judges of the High Court of the country.[145] Further appeals, from decisions of the commissioners' courts, were routed back to the Appellate Division of the Supreme Court, thus reconnecting the parallel court systems at the secondary appellate level.[146] This approach was prevalent in East Africa.[147]

As previously shown, South Africa has taken the path of a dual court system. South African jurists have also directly or by implication voiced their support for the dualism entrenched by the traditional courts system. Thus, Professor Van Der Vyver, discussing the issue of human rights vis-a-vis customary law, points out that where a foundation for distinct differentiation is found to be present, justice will not in fact be satisfied by absolute uniformity in the arithmetical sense.[148] Likewise, Professor

---

[141] 1927 AD 310.
[142] *Id.* at 327.
[143] *See* Thierry Verhelst, African Studies Center, Safeguarding African Customary Law (University of California, Los Angeles 1968).
[144] *See* Bennett, *supra* note 13, at 62.
[145] *See id.* at 62–63.
[146] *See id.*
[147] *See* Cotran, *supra* note 2.
[148] *See* Van Der Vyver, *Human Rights and the Dual System Applying to Blacks in South Africa*, 1982 CILSA 306, 315.

Bennett pleads for the legal endorsement of cultural differences, "where the society in question is in fact culturally plural, as South Africa still is."[149] There is, therefore, some consensus in South African legal circles on the correctness of the continued existence of a dual court system incorporating both state and traditional courts.

Traditional courts have been the principal venue for the majority of South Africans to seek justice since well before the arrival of Europeans. They continue to function today because of the many benefits they have over the state court system for average citizens. Customary law courts are inexpensive, uncomplicated, and ubiquitous throughout the country. Cases are heard in the litigants' own language before local leaders. Traditional courts have seen their credibility affirmed by the Constitution and numerous statutes and regulations. Valid criticisms of the customary law court system remain, and further harmonization with the Constitution and prevailing human rights norms seem inevitable. However, for the foreseeable future, traditional courts will continue to play a major role in South Africa's justice system.

---

[149] T. W. Bennett, *The Compatibility of African Customary Law and Human Rights, in* ACTA JURISDICA 3 (1991). Fortunately for South Africa, the judicial system no longer exists in watertight compartments since the passing of the special courts for Blacks Abolition Act no. 34 of 1986, which abolished the old Native Commissioners' Courts, the Native Appeal Courts, and the Native Divorce Courts that were created by the Black Administration Act No. 38 of 1927. The Judges of the High Court therefore do participate, in the normal course of business, in cases on customary law.

11

Customary Law and Chieftainship in Twenty-First-Century Botswana

Wazha G. Morapedi

TRANSLATIONS OF SETSWANA TERMS

Setswana – Language of the people of Botswana. It can also be used to mean the norms, practices and customs of Batswana.

Kgosi – Chief (pl. *dikgosi*)

Morafe – Tribe (pl. *Merafe*)

Bogosi – Chieftainship

Kgosikgolo – Paramount Chief

Kgotla – Village Assembly. It can also mean the court where cases are heard.

11.1. INTRODUCTION

Independence and the rise of multi-party politics in sub-Saharan Africa in the 1990s have seen a remarkable resurgence of the institution of chieftainship. In some countries, chieftainship was abolished by revolutionary movements immediately after independence because chiefs were regarded as puppets of minority oppressive white governments. These chiefs were intermediaries between the colonial governments and the people. The chiefs implemented directives from the government and were closely supervised by organs of the colonial state.[1] As such, "traditional leaders played a central role as bureaucratised representatives of forcibly created tribes, enjoying more legitimacy within the state than with the people they claimed to represent."[2] In Pondoland under apartheid South Africa, for example, migrants had a variety of grievances ranging from increased taxes to land reclamation and cattle culling. The wrath of the migrants was directed at chiefs, who were regarded as "bearers of apartheid reforms – indirect

---

[1] *See* BARBARA OOMEN, CHIEFS IN SOUTH AFRICA: LAW POWER AND CULTURE IN THE POST APARTHEID ERA 11, 104 (Palgrave Macmillan 2005).

[2] *Id.* at 4.

rule – and who stood to benefit from these directly."[3] Chiefs were also seen as symbols of the influx control, and revolts became an anti-chief phenomenon.[4]

It is in view of such scenarios that researchers on the institution of chieftainship have emphasized the amazing resurgence of this institution after independence, especially in recent times with the rise of multi-party politics in Africa. Monarchies have been revived and restored where they were banned, and traditional leaders have been restored and strengthened.[5] As noted earlier, during the struggle against apartheid in South Africa, revolutionaries regarded chiefs as collaborators who deserved no place in a democratic free South Africa. In Mozambique, the Front for the Liberation of Mozambique ("FRELIMO") detested chiefs during the liberation struggle against Portugal, branded them reactionaries, and banned the institution upon attainment of independence in 1975. In Uganda, the government of Milton Obote abolished the institution and exiled the Baganda monarchy, and in Zimbabwe, the liberation movements regarded chiefs as stooges of the minority settler regime and saw no role for them in independent Zimbabwe. In all these countries, however, chieftainship has made a remarkable resurgence. In Mozambique, it was revived after FRELIMO suffered the loss of rural support. In Uganda, the Buganda monarchy has been officially restored and recognized. In Zimbabwe, traditional leaders have been welcomed to parliament and customary courts reinstated, whereas in South Africa, the collapse of apartheid and the beginning of a multi-party democratic political system saw the resurgence and consolidation of chieftainship.[6]

Botswana is an interesting case in Africa because during the colonial period, there were instances where the *dikgosi* (chiefs) collaborated with the colonial government and oppressed their own people. There were also instances when the colonial government targeted *dikgosi* and reduced their powers and on such occasions, *dikgosi* received support from their subjects. When Botswana became independent in 1966, a Westminster liberal multi-party democratic state was established, and *dikgosi* were not treated with hostility, as was the case in some other countries. Some of the politicians who assumed power were aristocrats and others had aristocratic backgrounds. Although these new political leaders did not ban chieftainship, they set out to systematically curtail the powers of *dikgosi*. The newly elected government introduced legislation that reduced the powers of *dikgosi*, but the institution proved resilient and, because of the flexibility and adaptability of customary law, *bogosi* (chieftainship) has remained at the core of the political, administrative, and social center of Botswana's society.

---

[3] MAHMOOD MAMDANI, CITIZEN AND SUBJECT: CONTEMPORARY AFRICA AND THE LEGACY OF LATE COLONIALISM 195–196 (James Currey 1996).

[4] *See id.*

[5] *See* Oomen, *supra* note 1, at 11, 104.

[6] *See id.* at 11.

It has been argued that the core aspects of the 1990s global order – the changing role of the nation state and the elevation of culture as a way of dealing with modernity – have facilitated the surprise resurgence of traditional leaders.[7] African states had attempted to destroy chieftainship in the 1950s with the aim of building a common nationhood, but in the 1990s, chieftaincies were back with vigor. During the latter period, two conditions seem to have determined the resurgence of traditional leadership in sub-Saharan Africa. These were (1) a weak or collapsed state such as Angola, Somalia, and Congo, where government institutions were not working and had been replaced by traditional authorities; and (2) relatively strong states reacting to global and local conditions and aiming at attaining extra legitimacy, "by recognising traditional structures of rule."[8] Examples of the latter condition are Zimbabwe, Uganda, Nigeria, and Ghana. In the former British colonies that experienced indirect rule, nation-states embarked on an increased official recognition of traditional leaders, their structures of governance, and their representative bodies. However, the resurgence of traditional leaders also occurred in countries that were not British colonies such as Togo, Mozambique, and Niger.[9]

There are three empirical and normative reasons why states decided to recognize traditional leadership: Firstly, African leaders believed that traditional institutions should be recognized and play some role in governance. Secondly, in some cases, it was believed that traditional leadership could add legitimacy to the ailing nation state. Lastly, state governments determined that traditional authority could not be wished away in any event.[10]

Although it was not an ailing state at independence, and has not been so far, Botswana also recognized and upheld chieftainship for these reasons. As stated earlier, in Botswana, the political leaders who took over at independence recognized traditional leadership and its structures of governance and representative bodies. However, the state promulgated legislation that stripped *dikgosi* of their powers and progressively subordinated traditional leadership to the state.[11] Simultaneously, as

---

[7]   *See id.*
[8]   *Id.*
[9]   *See id.*
[10] *See id.*
[11] The struggles between the colonial state and *dikgosi* in Botswana have been a subject of numerous studies. *See, e.g.,* G. Sekgoma, The Nature, Structure and Functions of Chieftainship in Contemporary Botswana: Possibilities for Democratisation? (1994) (unpublished paper); M. Lekorwe & G. Somolekae, *The Chieftaincy System and Politics in Botswana, 1966–1995, in* BOTSWANA: POLITICS AND SOCIETY (M. Lekorwe & W. Edge eds., J. L. van Schaik 1998); N. Seretse, et al., Chieftainship in Botswana: Pre Colonial, Colonial and Post Independence (1983) (unpublished customary law research paper, Gaborone). These studies have demonstrated that the colonial state passed legislation that was designed to undermine the powers, duties, and influence of *dikgosi*. However, *dikgosi* succeeded in watering down the effectiveness of this legislation and compelled the colonial government to accommodate some of their interests.

discussed later in the chapter, *dikgosi* assumed more administrative functions and the state also recognized them as core pillars of the country's administrative, social, and political landscape. As the state wrested more powers from *dikgosi*, the latter acquired more roles that were not necessarily customary, but which have since become customary. This was due to the flexibility and adaptability of customary law, which ensured that chiefs were accorded legitimacy and voluntary support by their subjects.[12] The viability of customary law from the colonial period to the present has also been noted elsewhere.[13]

This chapter presents a brief overview of historical antecedents on the resilience of *bogosi*, but it largely focuses on the post-colonial period. Its point of departure from previous works is that it shall focus largely on the roles and duties of *dikgosi* and customary law in the political and social context of Botswana, and not on succession issues, which have received significant attention in studies of *bogosi* in post-colonial Botswana.[14] With this context, this chapter will consider how customary law regarding chieftainship has enabled the institution to remain relevant in modern Botswana.

11.2. CUSTOMARY LAW REGARDING CHIEFTAINSHIP IN BOTSWANA

Although there is no single universal definition of the concept of customary law, there are certain core features that are discernible in most of the definitions. Those include that customary law is not written and much of it has been passed on by word of mouth from generation to generation. Customary laws consist of norms, practices, and traditions that are binding on society. These are flexible, adaptable, and also evolutionary.[15] Customary law has different meanings to different people and should

---

[12] *See* Jean Comaroff, *Rules and Rulers in Political Processes in a Tswana Chiefdom*, 13 MAN 1, 4–6 (1998).

[13] *See* M. CHANOCK, LAW, CUSTOM AND SOCIAL ORDER: THE COLONIAL EXPERIENCE IN MALAWI AND ZAMBIA xi (Heinemann 1998). Writing on colonial Zambia and Malawi, Chanock posits a question that if customary law is strongly rooted in colonialism, why is it that ordinary people today invest so much in it? He answers the question by showing that, "custom is constantly recreated, re-imagined and re-invented." Chanock further emphasizes the fact that customary law is not in the past, but is part of the present systems of African polities and societies. *Id.*

[14] *See, e.g.*, F. Nyamnjoh, *Chieftainship and the Negotiation of Might and Right in Botswana Democracy*, 21 JOURNAL OF CONTEMPORARY AFRICAN STUDIES 2 (2003); Might and Right: Chieftainship and Democracy in Cameroon and Botswana (Dec. 8–12, 2002) (paper presented at the tenth General Assembly of the Council of Social Science Research in Africa, Kampala, Uganda); Yonah Matemba, *A Chief Called 'Woman': Historical Perspectives on the Changing Face of Bogosi (Chieftainship) in Botswana, 1834–2004*, 7 JOURNAL OF CULTURE AND AFRICAN WOMEN STUDIES 18 (2005).

[15] *See* IAN HAMNETT, CHIEFTAINSHIP AND LEGITIMACY: AN ANTHROPOLOGICAL STUDY OF EXECUTIVE LAW IN LESOTHO 16 (Routledge & Kegan Paul Books 1975); A. Molokomme, *Customary Law in Botswana: Past, Present and Future*, in BOTSWANA IN THE 21ST CENTURY 348–349 (Botswana Society

be understood in its cultural, political, and economic aspects. In Botswana, there is the "'Traditionalist's" customary law, which encompasses the values, traditional norms, habits, and other principles that have been linked with different Batswana[16] ethnic groups before contact with Europeans.[17] Used in this context, customary law is equated with traditional and cultural values as shown in setswana phrases *ngwao ya Setswana* (Setswana culture) *mekgwa le melao ya Setswana* (ways and laws of Setswana). This type of law is often employed by traditionalists in an effort to resist the introduction of new laws and policies.[18]

The other variant of customary law is the "Living Customary Law." This "describes a way of life based upon certain norms of behaviour which are based, in varying degrees, on tradition."[19] This "living" or "contemporary" customary law is shown by the way of life of many people in both rural and urban Botswana. This law is not static, but dynamic, negotiable, flexible, fluid, and is a reflection of the people's adaptation to socio-economic changes occurring in Botswana society. Although viewed by traditionalists as contaminated by modernization and other western ways and values, this customary law is often closer to the real lives of ordinary people.[20] This is the variant of customary law that largely enabled *bogosi* to adapt to changing situations and remain viable and relevant to present circumstances.

11.3. THE NATURE OF *BOGOSI*

In Botswana, the various pre-colonial Tswana states were autonomous or independent political entities. Each *Kgosikgolo* (Paramount Chief) was the head of his own tribe and did not owe allegiance to any other superior authority. In setswana customary law, a *kgosi* was (and still is, to a large extent) born. *Bogosi* was hereditary in the male line, passing normally from father to son, hence the saying, "A chief is never selected."[21] Upon the death or incapacitation of a *kgosi*, his eldest son from the senior wife would automatically accede to the throne. This rule appears to have been largely upheld during the pre-colonial period, although there were a few cases where *bogosi* was acquired through some unconventional methods such as trickery or force.

1994); J. Yakubu, Colonialism, Customary Law and the Post Colonial State in Africa (Dec. 8–12, 2002) (paper presented at the tenth General Assembly of the Council for the Development of Social Science and Research in Africa, Kampala, Uganda).

[16] "Batswana" is a term that refers to citizens of Botswana.

[17] *See* Molokomme, *supra* note 15, at 347–369.

[18] *See id.*

[19] *Id.* at 348–349.

[20] *See id.*

[21] ISSAC SCHAPERA, TRIBAL INNOVATORS: TSWANA CHIEFS AND SOCIAL CHANGE 52 (Athlone Press 1970).

If the eldest son was still too young to assume the reins of power, his uncle would rule as a *Motshwareledi* (regent). No woman could assume the position of *Kgosi*. The installation of a setswana *kgosi* was conducted by his subjects in a *kgotla* where his uncle draped him with a leopard skin.[22] Setswana customary law conferred immense powers and privileges on a *kgosi*. This is demonstrated by the fact that "[t]he Chief, as head of the tribe occupies a position of unique privilege and authority. He is a symbol of tribal unity, the central figure round which the tribal life revolves. He is at once ruler, judge, maker and guardian of the law, repository of wealth, dispenser of gifts, leader in war, priest and magician of the people."[23]

While the *kgosi* had great powers and commanded immense wealth, he also had duties and obligations to his subjects. In times of stress, such as drought, he would redistribute cattle or grain to his subjects, and he had an obligation to protect his people, take care of the needy in society, and be hospitable to visitors.[24] "He was supposed to be generous in return for the privileges accorded him, and use his wealth for the general welfare of the community."[25] The immense powers, prestige, and superior status of the *kgosi* did not mean that he was an autocrat who was above the law. There was a council of advisors, normally drawn from the *kgosi's* senior relatives, such as his uncles, that limited the manner in which the *kgosi* exercised his powers. A *kgosi* was obliged to cooperate with his subjects as symbolized by the setswana saying, *Kgosi ke kgosi ka morafe* (A chief is a chief by grace of his tribe). There were also some tribal mechanisms in place designed to act as checks on those leaders who tended to deviate from the norm. For instance, his *morafe* (tribe) could depose him in a *kgotla* if his conduct deserved that. The role of a chief and his relationship to the *morafe* have been described among the Tshidi Rolong of both Botswana and South Africa as a permanent dialogue between the chief and his people. The chief and his subjects are "thought to be involved in a permanent transactional process in which the former discharges obligations and, in return, receives the accepted right to influence policy and command people."[26] This is the situation that, to some extent, still characterizes chieftainship in Botswana and one which embodies the legitimacy of the institution.

11.4. HISTORICAL ANTECEDENTS

Botswana became a British Protectorate in 1885 and attained independence in 1966. Initially, some Batswana *dikgosi* opposed the declaration of a protectorate because

---

[22] See *id*.
[23] *Id*. at 62.
[24] See *id*. at 68.
[25] *Id*. at 68–69; *see also* Lekorwe & Somolekae, *supra* note 11, at 188.
[26] Comaroff, *supra* note 12, at 6.

they felt that there were no external threats to their independence. However, in the end, they reluctantly accepted British "protection." The British did not want to carry the burden of administering poor Botswana, hence the adoption of the "Parallel" and later "Indirect Rule" system that was viewed as cheaper and less disruptive to local political systems.[27] With a skeletal administration of a few Resident Magistrates, the Border Police, and other minor officials in Botswana, Britain started introducing laws (proclamations) and orders, some of which eroded the powers of *dikgosi*, contravening and undermining existing Tswana laws and customs in the process.

Realizing the impending threat to their authority, some Tswana *dikgosi* contested these measures, arguing that British actions amounted to interference in the affairs of their *merafe*. *Kgosi* Sebele II of Bakwena and Sekgoma Letsholathebe II of Batawana were some of the protectorate *dikgosi* who came into conflict with the colonial administration after the issuance of the 1891 proclamation, which gave the administration powers to interfere with the administrative and judicial functions and powers of *dikgosi*. The colonial administration wanted to depose these *dikgosi* and install those it regarded as loyal, but the *merafe* opposed these intentions and they were abandoned. During these early phases of colonial rule, the British were not well enough established to depose *dikgosi*, and in instances where there was no clear support from *merafe*, such moves had to be abandoned.[28]

The period between 1930 and 1943 was characterized by heightened tension between the administration and *dikgosi*. A new Resident Commissioner, Charles Rey, was appointed in 1929 to "facilitate" development in the country. It was argued that one of the hindrances to development was the autocratic nature of *dikgosi* rule. Popular resentment had mounted in the 1920s against the indirect rule system, and this led to the appointment of a commission that confirmed widespread abuses of powers by *dikgosi* and their headman.[29] To achieve his objectives, Rey promulgated two proclamations, the Native Administration Proclamation of 1934[30] and the Native Tribunal Proclamation of 1934,[31] to "tame" *dikgosi*.[32] These proclamations provided for the recognition, approval, dismissal, and suspension of *dikgosi* by the resident commissioner. They introduced Native Councils to assist *dikgosi* in tribal administration. The Native Tribunal Proclamation re-affirmed the dictates of the 1891 law that deprived *dikgosi* of the powers to try serious cases such as those involving

[27] *See* J. Makgala, The Policy of Indirect Rule in the Bechuanaland Protectorate, 1926–1957 2–4 (2001) (PhD thesis, Cambridge University).

[28] *See* P. Mgadla & A. Campbell, *Dikgotla, Dikgosi and the Protectorate Administration, in* DEMOCRACY IN BOTSWANA 50–51 (P. Molutsi & J. Holm eds., Macmillan 1989).

[29] *See* Mamdani, *supra* note 3, at 88.

[30] Native Administration Proclamation, No. 74 of 1934.

[31] Native Tribunal Proclamation, No. 75 of 1934.

[32] *See, e.g.*, Sekgoma, *supra* note 11, at 3–5; Lekorwe & Somolekae, *supra* note 11, at 189.

murder, rape, and treason, and transferred these powers to the magistrate courts and the high court. These laws seriously eroded the independence and powers of *bogosi* and changed Tswana law and custom regarding the institution.[33] However, *dikgosi* mounted intense pressure and opposition to these pieces of legislation, which resulted in some compromises when new legislation was promulgated in 1943 by the new resident commissioner, Arden Clarke. The new legislation watered down the earlier measures and reinstated some of the customary measures. In fact, customary law on *bogosi* remained resilient because in instances where the British fell out with a *kgosi*, they would "install" a royal who had some semblance of recognition and legitimacy from the *morafe*, and would not appoint a commoner or an outsider with no royal connection. In the main, the colonial rulers still recognized the vitality of the institution as the main link between these rulers and the populace. In this regard, Arden Clarke apparently realized that progress could only be attained with the support of *dikgosi*, especially the influential and articulate Bangwato Regent Tshekedi Khama.[34] Thus, in effect, from 1930s to the 1950s, indirect rule greatly empowered *dikgosi* against the peasantry in several ways.[35]

11.5. POST-1966 PRESSURES AND SURVIVAL OF *BOGOSI*

If *dikgosi* had entertained any hopes that their powers would be restored after independence by an African government, then those were dashed even during the transition period. The struggle between the young and educated politicians who led the country to independence and *dikgosi* started during the constitutional talks in

---

[33] See Sekgoma, *supra* note 11; Lekorwe & Somolekae, *supra* note 11. *See also* Mgadla & Campbell, *supra* note 28, at 54–55.

[34] See Makgala, *supra* note 27, at 174.

[35] See Mamdani, *supra* note 3, at 46. The *kgotla* had acted as a check on the authority of a *kgosi* before indirect rule. However, during the colonial period, the public assembly became a forum "where decisions were announced and not debated." *Id.* In the 1920s, the colonial government made some reforms that did not restore the powers of the *kgotla*, but rather reduced the powers in relation to the colonial state. Mamdani further writes that after reducing the powers of the *kgosi*, the state started to reinforce the powers of *dikgosi* over the populace in phases. This started with a law in 1938, which gave *dikgosi* powers to appoint finance committees and supervise local treasuries. The law accorded *dikgosi* powers to enact by-laws, "with the agreement of the kgotla." *Id.* In 1954, there was the African administration proclamation that gave *dikgosi* "legislative and executive authority as long as these were exercised with the consent of the kgotla." *Id.* At this stage, "the consent of the kgotla was just an euphemism for the veto power the colonial state exercised over all chiefly decisions, for it was the colonial authority that had the ultimate power to decide what the real interests of the *kgotla* (the people) were." *Id.* However, the chiefs remained all-powerful in relation to the peasant because they had, among others, the powers to allocate land and administer schools. They also had the powers to approve the appointment of clerks and police, as well as adjudicate cases. It should be noted that merely assigning the *kgotla* some role, however superficial, the British conferred upon *dikgosi* some measure of legitimacy. This was because the Tswana chiefship institution assigned the *kgotla* a prominent role in the administration of the *morafe* through consultations, deliberations, and the application of customary law in court cases.

1963.[36] At stake was the issue of the amount of power to be wielded by *dikgosi* in the new dispensation. Ultimately, while the new government accorded *dikgosi* some recognition, it further reduced their powers. Contrary to what transpired at independence in some African countries, *bogosi* was not abolished in Botswana.[37] Here, however, the government introduced a series of legislation that, as some analysts have observed, further reduced the powers of *dikgosi* and rendered the institution almost meaningless.[38] The party that emerged victorious from the first general elections of 1965, the Botswana Democratic Party (BDP), was led by a traditional chief and had amassed wide support from the rural areas where chieftainship had massive appeal. Unlike the radical Botswana Peoples Party (BPP), the BDP had realized the influence and grasp of *bogosi* on Batswana and hence its utility as a vote bank. This party has since treaded delicately on issues of *bogosi*, heaving off some crucial powers from *dikgosi* while also acceding *dikgosi* some crucial benefits and privileges because of their strategic position in society and the influence they wield. This scenario by the government can be said to have been influenced by factors noted earlier – that traditional institutions could not be wished away and were worthy of recognition. Also, although Botswana has not been a weak or collapsed state, the government still values the legitimacy conferred by customary law that *bogosi* added.

At independence in 1966, the new constitution that was adopted entailed separation of powers, with legislative powers being the preserve of parliament, policy-making powers falling under the executive, and judicial powers coming under the judiciary. The new system of government differed from the pre-colonial *bogosi* where judicial, executive, and legislative powers were vested in the *kgosi*.[39] But this superstructure operated alongside or above a tribal setswana customary system, which in fact continued to be the main judicial and administrative system in the rural areas where the majority of Batswana lived. The resilience of traditional leadership alongside the superstructure was due to the perceived legitimacy of *dikgosi* by the people, which implied acceptance of the "right to rule" and compliance that was more or less voluntary.[40]

11.6. THE CHIEFTAINSHIP ACT, CUSTOMARY LAW, AND LEGITIMACY

The first piece of legislation that indicated that the new government was intent on wresting some of the remaining powers from *dikgosi* and enhancing the earlier

[36] *See* T. TLOU & A. CAMPBELL, A HISTORY OF BOTSWANA 335 (Macmillan 1997).
[37] *See* Lekorwe & Somolekae, *supra* note 11, at 19.
[38] *See*, *e.g.*, Sekgoma, *supra* note 11, at 15; Lekorwe & Somolekae, *supra* note 11, at 190–197; Tlou & Campbell, *supra* note 36, at 335–337.
[39] *See* Lekorwe & Somolekae, *supra* note 11, at 190.
[40] *See* Oomen, *supra* note 1, at 167.

colonial legislation was the Chieftainship Act of 1965.[41] The Act recognized the institution of *bogosi*, but it explained the position of *dikgosi* in relation to the government by stating that:

> … no person shall hold or assume chieftainship of any tribe or exercise or perform any of the powers of a chief unless he has been recognised as chief of such a tribe under this Act. Such person shall have to be designated by a tribe assembled at a kgotla in the customary manner, and his name shall be sent to the president.… The president shall by notice in the Gazette, recognise the person so designated as chief of such tribe.[42]

It has been argued that this provision of the Chieftainship Act means that the president can choose not to recognize a *kgosi* for any reason known to him and that the president's decision to recognize a *kgosi* was similar to that of the colonial government – where a *kgosi* had to be loyal and subordinate to the central government.[43] In this regard, a *kgosi* was recognized for political reasons. However, with respect to the setswana-speaking groups, the government has not at any time refused to recognize a paramount chief who has been designated by a particular tribe to ascend to the throne. It should be noted that the Chieftainship Act of 1965 still emphasizes the customary law, which is essential for the continued legitimacy and resilience of chieftainship, by stipulating that "[s]*uch person shall have to be designated by a tribe assembled at a kgotla in the customary manner* …"[44] Thus, *this* customary manner empowers such a leader to rule and the assembled *kgotla* accedes to his right to rule. Thus, unlike elected politicians whose legitimacy to office emanates from elections, this customary practice legitimizes the position of a *kgosi*.

The Act of 1965 was further strengthened by the Chieftainship Amendment Act of 1970,[45] which placed *dikgosi* under closer control by the government. The amended Act accorded the president powers to unseat a *kgosi* without waiting first to receive complaints from his subjects. After consulting the *morafe*, the president could appoint a regent to rule a *morafe* if the rightful heir was not ready to assume office. This Act means that, "in Botswana the decision to recognize the appointment of a Chief is the prerogative of the President."[46] Although the state had armed itself with drastic powers such as the suspension or removal of a paramount chief, in practice such powers have been rarely evoked, and in instances where they have, the government has suffered political setbacks such as the loss of votes at elections and

---

[41] Chieftainship Act of 1965 (Government Printers 1965).
[42] *Id.*
[43] *See* Lekorwe & Somolekae, *supra* note 11, at 191.
[44] *Id.* (emphasis added).
[45] Chieftainship Amendment Act 26 of 1970.
[46] Sekgoma, *supra* note 11, at 8.

non-cooperation from the chief's subjects, as shall be seen with the Bangwaketse case discussed later.

In truth, the Botswana government has continued its further erosion of the powers of *dikgosi* in the past four decades. The Chieftainship Amendment Act of 1987[47] was a law that further subordinated the *dikgosi* to the government. This Act placed *dikgosi* under the minister of local government. The Act maintains that a Chief is an individual who "has been designated as a Chief in accordance with customary law by his tribe assembled in the kgotla; and has been recognized as a Chief by the Minister."[48] Accordingly, in independent Botswana, succession to *bogosi* is not based on the dictates of customary procedure in selecting the rightful heir, but rather on whether the selected heir is acceptable to the government. The 1987 Act empowers the minister to suspend a *kgosi* if he/she has valid reasons to believe that the *kgosi* of any *morafe* has abused his powers or is not capable of exercising them.[49] After this suspension, the minister can order an inquiry and consider representation from the chief's side. Following this inquiry, the minister can depose a *kgosi* from *bogosi* for a period of not more than five years.[50] This Act has, "therefore, continued to elevate the status of politicians at the expense of chiefs."[51] The intention of this Act was to obtain cooperation from *dikgosi*, denigrate their political influence, and restrict their ability to act freely. Exercising the powers given by the Act, the minister of local government can simply remove a *kgosi* from office just like a civil servant, although a *kgosi* comes from a royal house.[52]

Powers conferred on a minister to remove a *kgosi* should not be viewed as indicative of the demise of *bogosi* and customary law. In reality, it has proved difficult for ministers to exercise such powers, especially in instances where the *morafe* stood behind their *kgosi*. The massive support enjoyed by *dikgosi tse dikgolo* renders the exercise of draconian powers difficult as such action could be political suicide. The mere removal of a *kgosikgolo* by a minister does not appear to be as simple as the law seems to imply. It is an action that calls for full and unflinching tribal backing.

In some rare instances, the government has indeed invoked its powers under the 1987 Act. Testimony to this was a situation that pitted the government against Bangwaketse, a territory in Botswana, in 1994. In that year, the minister of local government suspended *Kgosi* Seepapitso for allegedly failing to cooperate with the government during a visit by the Zambian President to the Bangwaketse capital of Kanye. The minister proceeded to appoint Seepapitso's son to act as *kgosi* of

---

[47] Chieftainship Amendment Act 19 of 1987.
[48] *See id.* § 4(1). *See also* Lekorwe & Somolekae, *supra* note 11, at 191.
[49] *See* Chieftainship Amendment Act of 1987 § 12.
[50] *See id.* § 12(3).
[51] Lekorwe & Somolekae, *supra* note 11, at 191.
[52] *See* Sekgoma, *supra* note 11, at 8.

Bangwaketse. This matter was contested in the courts by the *morafe* and their *kgosi* against the government, and it ended up at the court of appeal, which ruled that the suspension was lawful but that the minister had made an error by not consulting the tribe before appointing the son. *Kgosi* Seepapitso was reinstated following this judgment.[53] In the aftermath of this saga, the ruling party lost the Kanye parliamentary seat to the opposition in the 1999 general elections. Although Kanye has been an opposition stronghold since 1965, some residents have argued that, in this case, Bangwaketse wanted to punish the ruling party for suspending their *kgosi*.[54] In this instance, the government had acted against custom and tradition. The appointment of Seepapitso's son to act as *kgosi* was regarded as an illegitimate move by the *morafe*; hence their overwhelming support for the substantive and legitimate leader. Support for *kgosi* Seepapitso was shown by the voluntary assistance by the *morafe* and their non-cooperation with the government in this area.

The government later appointed *Kgosi* Seepapitso as Botswana's Ambassador to the United States. Whereas this appointment has rightly been interpreted as a move aimed at removing an errant chief from the scene,[55] elsewhere it has been seen as an attempt to placate the *kgosi* and his *morafe* and thus gain political mileage.[56] The appointment of a *kgosi* to a diplomatic position ahead of career diplomats has also been seen by observers and the opposition as a political move designed to boost the image and revive the political fortunes of the ruling party in Ga-Ngwaketse. Here, the need by post-colonial African governments to gain legitimacy can be discerned in the case of Botswana. The ruling BDP has been in a weak position in this area for some time, and this move could have been aimed at adding this essential ingredient.

11.7. CUSTOMARY LAW AND THE FUTURE OF *BOGOSI*

This chapter maintains that the institution of *bogosi*, backed by customary law, shall continue to exist and, if its ability to adapt to the changing circumstances is anything to go by, it shall live for some time to come. Although it is true that some of the functions, powers, and privileges of *dikgosi* have continued to diminish in relation to those of politicians and top civil servants, the fact is that *dikgosi* have become a core pillar in the administrative and judicial spheres of this country. *Dikgosi* have already taken up new roles that do not necessarily accord with the traditionalist and ideal form of *bogosi*, such as taking up ambassadorial positions. These roles have so

---

[53] *See* Lekorwe & Somolekae, *supra* note 11, at 192–193.
[54] *See* interview with five Bangwaketse tribesmen (Oct. 21, 2002).
[55] *See* Nyamnjoh, *supra* note 14, at 192.
[56] *See* interviews with Montsho Seditse (73), Keto Matlhare (80), at Kanye (Oct. 21, 2002).

far proved to be in accordance with the existing social and political realities, hence affirming the concept of the living customary law.

In the judicial sphere, it was the Customary Court Act of 1966 that further whittled down the remaining judicial powers of *dikgosi*. In the pre-colonial period, *dikgosi* possessed unlimited jurisdiction, tried all types of cases, and determined criminal sentences. The Customary Court Act placed further limits on the powers of *dikgosi*. The district commissioners and the magistrates have since been armed with powers to revoke decisions of customary courts. In present-day Botswana, one can decide whether to be tried by a magistrate or customary court.[57] This was the development that undermined the role of *dikgosi* in today's legal system.

As already stated in the previous sections, the colonial and post-colonial state introduced measures that undermined traditional setswana *dikgotla* (courts) and the manner in which they dispensed justice. The introduction and superimposition of the district commissioner and magistrate courts over customary courts clearly shows diminution of customary law. However, the majority of Batswana live in the rural areas, and even those who stay in towns cannot afford the exorbitant fees and services of attorneys. Customary courts have been introduced in towns and, despite the transformations that have taken place, it is evident that many Batswana still seek, and shall continue to seek, recourse in the customary courts of the country. The vitality of customary law in Botswana's society has been highlighted by *Kgosi* Linchwe when he stated that, "There is growing recognition that customary law is here to stay. However, it is being called upon to be more innovative than has hitherto been the case."[58] Customary law has demonstrated its innovativeness because there is "living customary law" that does not depend on precedent as many of the judgments on cases, rules, and norms in the long past have been forgotten. This law is based on the prevailing circumstances (that is, it takes into account the changes that have taken place in society and the realities of today), and this is the customary law used in some of the customary courts in towns.[59] This attests to the flexibility of customary law, and hence the resilience of *bogosi*, which applies and enforces this law.

Bogosi plays a vital role in Botswana's judicial system, and the government has realized the important role of *dikgosi* in it. The importance that government attaches to customary law and the resilient nature of *bogosi* has been well stated as: "Notwithstanding its loss of power since independence, bogosi has proved to be resilient, especially in applying customary laws and custom in the settlement of

---

[57] *See* Sekgoma, *supra* note 11, at 10.

[58] Kgosi Linchwe, *Chieftainship in the 21st Century, in* BOTSWANA IN THE 21ST CENTURY, *supra* note 15, at 400.

[59] *See* Molokomme, *supra* note 15, at 350.

disputes. The government has recognised the importance of customary law by establishing the customary court of appeal. It is interesting that so far the government has appointed royals to be presidents of the court."[60] This indicates that customary law still commands respect from important quarters in Botswana, and that the *dikgosi* are still regarded as custodians of customary law. Although appeals from the customary court proceed to the customary court of appeal, which was established in 1986, and matters can be appealed to the high court and finally to the court of appeal, customary law and *dikgosi* would have played their role in the application of customary law. With the increase in criminal and civil cases, the role of customary courts in the future cannot be over-emphasized. The cardinal role played by *dikgosi* in Botswana's judicial system is shown by the fact that in 1978, officially recognized customary courts heard 8,759 cases. Between 1990 and 1992, magistrate courts heard 22,835 civil cases, whereas customary courts attended to 16,539. Between 1989 and 1991, 20,844 criminal cases were sent to and concluded by customary courts.[61] In 2006, customary courts in the country attended to 11,337 cases, whereas in 2007, they dealt with 12,089 cases.[62] Without customary courts, which are largely presided over by *dikgosi*, the Botswana judicial system would be overwhelmed by pending cases. Many cases resolved at customary courts have not been recorded. The fact that the overwhelming numbers of Batswana utilize customary courts shows that they have confidence in customary practices and law. Because *dikgosi* are custodians of cultural law, their subjects have shown tenacious voluntary support and accorded them legitimacy by continuing to rely on them to dispense customary justice. Immediately following is an example of how the customary court system works. This will help explain why Batswana use and support the system.

The setswana customary court system is hierarchical. It starts at the family level. From here, the next level is the ward and ultimately the *kgotla*. Usually, misunderstandings and other minor issues are first attended to by family members, especially the elders, and if they are not resolved, they then can be referred to the ward headman for arbitration. At this level, efforts would be geared toward *go letlanya* (reconciliation). It is only if a resolution is not found that the matter is referred to the *kgotla*. Here, efforts would again be made toward *go letlanya* and a case is only started if that is not possible.[63]

In a matter that is taken to the *kgotla*, a summons would be issued to the defendant and a date set for the hearing. On the day of the matter, the *kgosi* (who is usually assisted by his deputy and village headmen) together with village elders and

[60] Tlou & Campbell, *supra* note 36, at 337.
[61] Molokomme, *supra* note 15, at 359.
[62] Customary Court Statistics Office, Tribal Administration Headquarters, Gaborone.
[63] *See* interviews with Kenna Makepe (68) & Thabo Motlhabai (74), in Tlokweng (June 2006).

other villagers would be in attendance. The complainant(s) would present their case and the defendant(s) would then be allowed to present their side of the story. The two parties are allowed to speak freely and present their case. Witnesses are also called on to testify. Everyone in the *kgotla* is allowed to ask the two parties questions. In the end, the evidence is weighed and the judgment passed by the *kgosi* is based on the evidence presented. The *kgosi* also uses the penal code in trials and in determining judgments and sentences. The *kgosi* and those in attendance may decide to reconcile the two parties and not proceed with a trial, or the *kgosi* may pass judgment. If one party is not satisfied with the judgment, they are allowed to appeal to a higher court.

Batswana prefer customary courts over magistrate courts for a number of reasons. For one, in the customary court system, cases are heard immediately without unnecessary postponements unlike with magistrate courts where cases can be postponed for months. For cases brought before the customary court, no fees are charged whereas at magistrate courts, lawyers charge exorbitant fees that most Batswana cannot afford. Accordingly, at the magistrate courts, justice is the preserve of the rich, but at customary courts the poor and illiterate also get justice. Batswana believe that justice is, to a large extent, fairly delivered in the customary system because there are no lawyers who sometimes rely on technicalities to get their clients freed even though there is evidence to convict them. With the customary system, it is the evidence brought forth that is important. Customary courts are also preferable for many people because they use the setswana language, which is understood by all. In the magistrate courts, there is denial of justice because magistrates do not understand customary matters, such as cattle colors in dealing with stock theft, and this results in confusion and acquittal of guilty parties.[64] The customary court system is also crucial in *go letlanya*, which brings harmony and mutual understanding. Customary courts were set up in urban areas because the government realized that people in towns originate in rural areas and therefore they are used to the customary system, which they understand better. *Dikgosi* also call and preside over all matters affecting their *merafe* both within the court system and more broadly. If *bogosi* were to be abolished, there would be chaos.[65]

---

[64] There have been instances when complainants in stock theft cases have lost such cases because of the complexity of describing livestock colors in Setswana tradition. In such cases, the accused person's lawyer would use the English equivalents of the color/colors given by the complainant to argue that his/her client did not steal the livestock described. Because the Setswana descriptions would not necessarily be the same as the English ones, the magistrate ends up dismissing the complainant's evidence and acquitting the accused person. Even local magistrates do not have a good grasp of the complex Setswana description of livestock colors.

[65] *See* interviews with five Batlokwa tribesmen (June 11, 2006); interviews with eight Bangwato tribesmen (June 10 & 19–20, 2006).

It seems Botswana society has come to accept and expect the new roles and status of *dikgosi*, and this would accord well with the concept of the living customary law whereby new rules and practices, which are not necessarily customary in the traditionalist sense, come to be accepted as such. These new roles should not be viewed as insignificant. They indicate that *dikgosi* play, and shall continue to play, a pivotal role in national security and social mobilization for national development in the twenty-first century. For example, in the rural areas, *dikgosi* have effectively mobilized people against the rising crime rate.[66] The multiple roles of *dikgosi* are in accordance with Tswana tradition that *Kgosi ke Mmabatho* (A chief is mother of the people). Moreover, the cooperation from *merafe* shows support and legitimization for the varied duties and functions of chiefs and the adaptation of customary law.[67]

Recent political developments have demonstrated the viability and might of *bogosi* in Botswana. In fact, some *dikgosi* have manipulated Botswana's political landscape to their advantage. This is evidenced by two paramount *dikgosi* who have, in recent years, joined politics on the side of the ruling BDP. Just before the 1999 general elections, Bangwato paramount chief, Ian Khama Seretse Khama, retired from the army and joined the BDP where he was appointed Vice President after the elections. Khama was the Bangwato paramount chief while in the army, and today, he is president of Botswana and also the Bangwato paramount chief. Since his installation as *kgosikgolo* of Bangwato, Khama has been garbing other *dikgosi* with leopard skins at their coronations. He officiated at the coronation of both *dikgosi* Letlamoreng II of Barolong and Kgari Sechele II of Bakwena in 2001 and 2002 respectively. On September 20, 2008 he garbed *Kgosi* Kgafela Kgafela III of Bakgatla with a leopard's skin. The garbing of other *dikgosi* is important because it is supposed to be done by a paramount *kgosi*. Here, it buttresses Khama's position as paramount *kgosi* even though he was a vice president, and is currently president. This is indicative of the double role the president is enjoying – as both politician and chief. This means that "effectively, he enjoys the best of both worlds – having his cake and eating it."[68] Khama's double role has been criticized by a few, mainly opposition politicians and some academics. Many Batswana, especially his subjects in Ga-Mmangwato and

---

[66] *See* MIDWEEK SUN (Bots.), Aug. 15, 2001.

[67] In South Africa too there is a similar situation where chiefs advise and assist the government and territorial and regional authority in relation to national, moral, and social well-being of residents in their areas. They maintain law and order in their communities, report conditions of unrest and any other matter of serious import or concern to government. The chiefs attend to public health matters, registration of people in their areas, and the detection and punishment of crime. They convene meetings of their tribes and communities and endeavor to ensure maximum attendance by their tribes or communities. F. DE VILLIERS, SELECTED SOUTH AFRICAN LEGISLATION ON CUSTOMARY LAW AND TRADITIONAL AUTHORITIES (Occasional papers 1998).

[68] BOTSWANA GAZETTE, Aug. 21, 2002.

the larger central district, support Khama in both roles because he is traditionally a leader and, in addition to "having the right to rule," he is given extensive voluntary support. Customary law legitimizes this dual role that Khama continues to play because it regards him as a natural leader.

Just before the commencement of the BDP primary elections popularly known as *bulela ditswe* in 2003, Batawana paramount chief Tawana Moremi II declared that he was taking leave from *bogosi* to join politics and run for MP of the Maun West constituency on the ticket of the BDP. Kgosi Tawana was widely supported by his *morafe*, who were happy that he was emulating the Bangwato paramount. Tawana told his *morafe* in a *kgotla* meeting that he would be available when his services were needed in tribal matters. This statement is indicative of the fact that Tawana would still wield influence in the *kgotla* while he was also a politician, thus combining politics and civil service. It emerged that prior to the BDP primaries in 2003, both Tawana and Khama were to stand unopposed from within the BDP, unlike in other constituencies where there was stiff competition. In this regard, it has been observed that Tawana sought to "exploit his royalty for a smooth transition to politics."[69] Tawana had a lot of support from his subjects, who held that customarily Tawana was a traditional leader, and he deserved the right to be also a political leader.

The fact that no one dared oppose Khama and Tawana from within the BDP shows the massive political influence of these paramount chiefs, because likely contenders accepted the inevitable – defeat. In fact, since he joined politics in 1999 and stood for the Serowe constituency, no contender has emerged to face Ian Khama from the BDP in this constituency. In the general elections that followed in 2004, Khama was again unopposed in his constituency, because the opposition realized the futility of opposing the powerful chief, although they cited lack of resources as the reason for non-participation.

The political influence and potential voter utility of *dikgosi* have been shown by the reported attempts by an opposition political party to try and woo Tawana to stand for it in the Maun West constituency after his falling-out with the BDP. The party sought to exploit the *kgosi* for political expediency, a move that they have often condemned and associated with the ruling party. Thus, the utility of *dikgosi* as "vote banks" in the Botswana political scenario is undoubtedly immense. This has also been realized in South Africa where the chiefs are capable of delivering the rural vote to political groups. In fact, the African National Congress realized the utility of this aspect when earlier on its cadres had spurned chieftainship during the apartheid era.[70] In South Africa, chiefs have immense influence and powers. They have,

[69] MMEGI (Bots.), June 4–10, 2003.
[70] *See* Oomen, *supra* note 1, at 141–143.

on two occasions, caused postponement of local government elections, ignored laws that accorded them ceremonial duties, and have wrested from the president a guarantee that "powers and functions of traditional leaders in local government, will not be eroded, even if this means amendments to the Constitution."[71]

Although some *dikgosi* in Botswana have referred to *bogosi* as a toothless institution, with *kgosi* Tawana likening *dikgosi* to "surrogates of the government," "lame ducks," and reduced to "rubber stamps,"[72] *dikgosi* in fact still wield a lot of influence and support from their subjects, and politically, "sustenance of electoral support still rotate around the fulcrum of bogosi."[73] This is largely due to the adaptability of customary law which has made *bogosi* vital in changing environments.

In Botswana today, members of parliament, ministers, and civil servants understand that the success or failure of their *kgotla* meetings and their agendas to a large extent depend on the importance that a *kgosi* attaches to such visits and the vigor with which they mobilize the general populace. This situation accords well with the view that states could acquire additional legitimacy by associating with "that other traditional; moral and political order," which could enable them to overcome "their own administrative weaknesses and physical and emotional distance from their populations."[74]

The position concerning the relevance and adaptability of chieftainship in twenty-first-century Botswana has been well summed up as "chieftaincy remains … part of the cultural and political landscapes, but is constantly negotiating and renegotiating with the new encounters and changing material realities."[75] The new roles performed by *dikgosi* in modern Botswana and the adherence to some age-old customary practices, such as the non-election of chiefs and the ascendancy to chieftainship to be the preserve of royals, accord with a view that chieftainship has been able to adapt to changing realities by "marrying tradition with modernity."[76] *Bogosi* is a major component of Botswana's tradition and culture and, although some aspects of culture do change, others remain the same because they are a symbol of a people's identity. As argued elsewhere, "The way in which a society conceives its traditions is fundamental to its understanding of itself. Traditions symbolise continuity, cultural identity and orderly existence …"[77] Thus, in Botswana, *bogosi* still maintains some of its core features from the pre-colonial period and these appear to be well rooted into the future as they are part of Batswana identity.

---

[71] *Id.* at 85.
[72] MMEGI (Bots.), Jan. 21, 2004.
[73] BOTSWANA GAZETTE, May 1, 2002.
[74] *See* Oomen, *supra* note 1, at 12.
[75] Nyamnjoh, *supra* note 14, at 8.
[76] *Id.*
[77] *See* Chanock, *supra* note 13, at xi.

11.8. CONCLUSION

This chapter counters the conclusion that the institution of *bogosi* is bound to die a natural death or collapse under the weight of state legislation. Although the state has since independence progressively weakened the institution of *bogosi*, Batswana have upheld and clung to it, and the state has realized the crucial administrative link, indispensability, and vitality of *dikgosi* to successful governance. Despite its somewhat weakened status in modern Botswana, *bogosi* – backed by the flexibility of customary law, which enables it to adapt to new roles – continues to enjoy sizeable support, especially in the rural areas. *Bogosi* has maintained its strategic position, administrative muscle, and influence amid massive assault by the colonial and post-colonial state to emasculate and render it impotent. Chieftainship has been able to adapt to changing socio-economic and political landscapes and, whereas the institution's powers have been gradually eroded and undermined by the government after independence, chieftainship has remained resilient and seems set to play a crucial role in twenty-first-century Botswana. This chapter also concludes that society at large has accepted the new roles of the *dikgosi*, a situation made possible by the adaptability of customary law. *Dikgosi* have succeeded in their quest to play a crucial political and administrative role in the country, reaping substantial benefits and concessions from the state, which relies on them for political and administrative expediency. The conclusions drawn here are that despite assertions by some scholars and current opinions by some in Botswana that, chieftainship has been overtaken by events, in fact, the institution has become central to government and shall be difficult to discard. It is a powerful institution with immense social and political clout and appeal, and it will continue to play an indispensable role in Botswana's socio-political and economic system.

Traditional Institutions and Governance in Modern African Democracies

History, Challenges, and Opportunities in Ghana

Ernest Kofi Abotsi and Paolo Galizzi

12.1. INTRODUCTION

In most African countries, constitutionally established authorities exercise the power of government alongside traditional authorities.[1] Executive, legislative, and judicial functions are generally attributed by most modern African constitutions to presidents and prime ministers, parliaments, and modern judiciaries. However, almost invariably the same functions, whether or not formally defined and characterized in the same terms or exercised in the same manner, are also performed by traditional institutions and their leaders. Chiefs[2] administer land and people, contribute to the creation of rules that regulate the lives of those under their jurisdiction, and are called on to solve disputes among their subjects. The relationship between traditional leadership and inherited western-style governance institutions often generates tensions. In Ghana, for example, local governance is an area where traditional leadership and the constitutional government sometimes "lock horns." Traditional leaders often feel left out when the government takes decisions affecting their people and land without their consent or involvement. Chieftaincy is further plagued with its own internal problems, including issues of relevance, succession, patriarchy, jurisdiction, corruption and intra-tribal conflict. Challenges confronting the institution of chieftaincy have continued from the colonial era into recent times. The role of chieftaincy within

---

[1] The authors would like to thank Chris Yaw Nyinevi and Nelson Akondo, law students at the Faculty of Law of the Kwame Nkrumah University of Science and Technology, Kumasi, Ghana for their research assistance toward the preparation of this chapter.

[2] In Ghana, the word "chief" refers to a traditional leader who exercises legislative, executive, and adjudicatory functions at the traditional level. The term was a collective designation given to all traditional leaders by the colonial government to describe all such leaders because, at the inception of colonial rule, the various ethnic groups and communities had different designations for their traditional leaders.

post-colonial African countries continues to incite lively debates, as the case of Ghana exemplifies.[3]

This chapter examines traditional leadership within the context of the emerging constitutional democracy in Ghana.[4] After examining the history, challenges, and opportunities for the institution of traditional leadership within a modern democracy, the chapter considers the effect of the current constitutional guarantee for chieftaincy and evaluates its practical workability and structural efficiency under the current governance system. The chapter further examines the dabbling of traditional leaders in the political process in spite of the proscription of the institution from mainstream politics and, in this context, analyzes the policy rationale for attempting to detach chieftaincy from partisan politics. It then analyzes the implications of the dual allegiance of the citizenry to chiefs and the government. In this context the chapter further touches on the compatibility of the institution of chieftaincy with constitutional principles such as equality, accountability, natural justice, good governance, and respect for fundamental human rights. Finally, the chapter considers the future of the institution against the background of the many issues and challenges considered.

12.2. ANTHROPOLOGICAL OVERVIEW OF THE MAIN ETHNIC GROUPS IN GHANA

In Ghana, chieftaincy has a long history reaching back perhaps about 4,000 years, when scholars believe communal living, crop farming, and domestication of animals first began.[5] Anthropological studies in West Africa, including the geographical area occupied by present-day Ghana, reveal that early inhabitants of this region were "simple foragers, fishers and hunters"[6] who moved from one area to another, depending on wild fruits and animals for their sustenance. Under pressure to farm and domesticate animals for food, early West Africans became less mobile and began settling in groups (usually of the same kin) around water sources.[7] With the development of human communities, the need arose to have a leader (i.e., a chief) to manage the interactions between groups of households and individuals living as a community. Chiefs were thus the leaders who managed these communities,

---

[3]   The relevance of the institution of chieftaincy in constitutional and governance structure of contemporary Ghana is one of the issues being considered by the ongoing Constitutional Review Commission.

[4]   For a comprehensive discussion on the legal regulations on chieftaincy in Ghana, see STEPHEN A. BROBBEY, THE LAW OF CHIEFTAINCY IN GHANA (Accra: Advanced Legal Publications, 2008).

[5]   *See* Akan Chieftaincy, http://en.wikipedia.org/wiki/Akan_Chieftaincy (last visited Aug. 4, 2010).

[6]   EUGENE L. MENDONSA, WEST AFRICA: AN INTRODUCTION TO ITS HISTORY, CIVILIZATION AND CONTEMPORARY SITUATION 113 (2002).

[7]   *See Id.* at 214.

fulfilling legislative, executive, judicial, economic, religious, and cultural functions. Chieftaincy acted as the socio-political and military[8] unit around which local tribes were organized, and provided the requisite focal point for common action.

Chieftaincy is known to the different ethnic groups who make up Ghana's population.[9] According to the Statistical Services of Ghana, eight major categories of ethnic groups exist: Akan, Ga-Adangbe, Ewe, Guan, Gurma, Mole-Dagbon, Grusi, and Mande-Busanga.[10] Chieftaincy has common broad sociological elements in all these ethnic groups but differs according to structural organization and its significance in the socio-political context within each ethnic group.

For example, the Akans, who make up 49.1 percent of the national population and are the largest tribe in Ghana, are headed by the *Omanhene* (the paramount chief).[11] The traditional Akan state is further divided into smaller units headed by sub-chiefs who owe allegiance to the paramount chief. The office of the chief is symbolized by a stool[12] and a sword. Chiefs are chosen by a select group of kingmakers, made up of representatives of every clan within the stool's jurisdiction. Candidates for chiefs are nominated by the queen mother from royal lineages or families.[13] The queen mother is usually the mother of the reigning king and is also regarded as the mother of the royal lineage.[14] The role of the queen mother in the Akan chieftaincy setup cannot be underestimated: It is believed that the queen mother was originally and historically the overall leader of the tribe, but delegated a male member of the royal lineage to be the chief.[15] Interestingly, the most important positions within

---

[8] According to Elsa Redmond, warfare provided a means for aspiring community leaders to distinguish themselves and lay claim to leadership. This may explain why warfare was used both as a strategic means of expansion and also in the pursuit of personal and parochial interests. Elsa M. Redmond, *In War and Peace: Alternative Paths to Centralized Leadership, in* CHIEFDOMS AND CHIEFTAINCY IN THE AMERICAS 68 (Elsa M. Redmond ed., 1998).

[9] The population of Ghana has been variously estimated but is officially said to be 22 million. A population census is billed to take place in September 2010.

[10] STATISTICAL SERVS. OF GHANA, 2000 NATIONAL POPULATION AND HOUSING CENSUS (2002).

[11] The Akans are a tribe consisting of different ethnic groups speaking a similar language referred to as the Akan language. Among ethnic groups making up the Akan tribe are the Fantis, Ashantis, Gomoas, Denkyiras, and others. The Ashantis, however, are headed by the Asantehene.

[12] The stool is traditionally a chair-like object on which the chief sat. It represented his powers. Unlike many tribes, however, the Golden Stool of the Ashantis is merely symbolic and is not a stool on which the chief actually sits. Indeed, legend has it that anyone who physically touched the Golden Stool would become impotent.

[13] The Akans operate a matrilineal family system, which means that the lineage is traced to a female ancestor, as opposed to patrilineal communities, which trace their lineage to a male ancestor.

[14] The role of the queen mother has been the subject of some disagreement. Whereas in some societies she was the chief's mother, in others she was not necessarily so but played her own independent role. In nearly all societies, however, the queen mother played roles similar to the chief's, save that her role was mainly confined to issues that affected women and the election of a new king.

[15] *See* Irene K. Odotei, *Women in Male Corridors of Power, in* CHIEFTAINCY IN GHANA: CULTURE, GOVERNANCE AND DEVELOPMENT 81, 85 (Irene K. Odotei & Albert K. Awedoba eds., 2006).

Akan chieftaincy institutions are almost always divided between men (as chiefs) and women (as queen mothers).[16]

The structure of chieftaincy among the Ewes and Ga-Adangbes is similar to that of the Akans. The major difference lies in the organization of the family system; the Ewes and Ga-Adangbes follow a patrilineal family system whereas the Akan follow a matrilineal family system.[17] Among the Ewes, the highest political authority is the paramount stool occupied by the *fiaga* or "big chief." There are sub-divisional chiefs (*dufia*) who head areas known as the *du*. The smallest unit of the Ewe community is the clan (*fome*), each with its own head. Ewe chiefs are elected from royal clans. In certain areas where there is more than one royal clan, each clan forms a "gate" and the stool rotates among them. The election is done by kingmakers who may include the head of the royal clan, heads of other clans (or "gates"), the queen of the clan, and others directly related to the stool. The kingmakers vet and approve a candidate from the clan for subsequent enstoolment.[18]

The election of a chief among the Ga tribe is done through two elections. The first is the election of a nominee by the members of the stool house known as *dzase*. The dzase is analogous to the royal clans of other ethnic groups. The nominee is then presented to the group's military officers, called the *manbii*, who conduct the actual election. Only the manbii have the power to elect or reject a proposed candidate for chief.

The main ethnic groups in northern Ghana are the Mole-Dagbon, Grusi, Gurma, and Mande-Busanga. Among these groups, princes contesting the position of chief are required to appear individually before a college of kingmakers to make a claim to the "skin" office of chief. Factors considered by the kingmakers include seniority, character, and popularity of the candidate. Some groups also practice the gate system, alternating the selection of the chiefs between competing gates or eligible families of royal lineage.[19]

---

[16] *See id.*
[17] Inheritance under the traditional Ghanaian system was of two kinds. Under the patrilineal system, succession to a dead person's property or office was traced through persons related to him, like his son or daughter. Under the matrilineal system, succession was traced through the mother or person in maternal relationship. For a fuller discussion of the patrilineal and matrilineal inheritance systems in Ghana, see Jeanmarie Fenrich & Tracy Higgins, *Promise Unfulfilled: Law, Culture, and Women's Inheritance Rights in Ghana*, 25 Fordham Int'l L.J. 259 (2001).
[18] The concepts of enstoolment and destoolment are used to refer to the process of ascension and dethronement of a chief from office as such chief. The analogous concepts that are used among the northern tribes of Ghana are enskinment and deskinment. Chiefs who sit on stools (equivalence of the throne) are said to be enstooled just the same way those who sit on the skin of animals are said to be deskinned when they are removed from office.
[19] Among these groups are the tribes of the Dagbon people in northern Ghana, who are widely known to practice the gate system in Ghana, which unfortunately led to conflict in 2003 following the murder of the sitting paramount chief, who belonged to one of the two gates, namely the Abudu and Andani gates.

Within some ethnic groups in Ghana, the traditional power structure further divides authority between a chief and a high priest. For example, among ethnic groups in Northern Region, the earth priest, or *tengdana*, is the custodian of the land.[20] The tengdana is chosen by divination and consultation of a soothsayer, rather than by a group of kingmakers, because of his spiritual role.[21] Similar examples are found among the Ga-Adangbe people of the Greater Accra region and the southeastern part of the Eastern Region. Oral traditions confirm that initially the Ga and the Adangbe did not have chieftaincies and were instead ruled by priests, known as *wulomei*. Chieftaincy was introduced in these tribes through contact with other ethnic groups such as the Akans.

In contemporary Ghana, chiefs still play an important role in the governance of all ethnic groups. Their relevance and functions vary considerably throughout the country, depending on the different rules and tradition of each ethnic group. Overall, their influence in peoples' lives is still considerable. Chiefs' legitimacy rests on the strong support and loyalty to the institution found in many sections of Ghanaian society, particularly in rural areas. Such support is, however, not unanimous: Many have in fact questioned and denounced chieftaincy as an outdated and anachronistic institution.[22]

12.3. THE LEGAL REGULATION OF CHIEFTAINCY: A HISTORICAL PERSPECTIVE

From colonial Gold Coast[23] to modern independent Ghana, the regulation of chieftaincy by different successive constitutional regimes has been characterized by efforts to incorporate traditional leadership into their political structure and governance.[24] These attempts were partly due to the yearning by colonial and post-colonial governments to regulate chiefs' competences and modernize the institution, while creating a nation out of the plethora of traditional structures with largely sectarian orientations. Regulatory measures on chieftaincy have taken a variety of forms in the colonial and post-colonial state with at least two common characteristics: first,

---

[20] *See* F.M. BOURRET, GHANA: THE ROAD TO INDEPENDENCE 1919–1957 (1960).

[21] At times, females have also been chosen as tengdana. The position of chief, however, has always been reserved to males.

[22] *See, e.g.*, GhanaWeb.com, Pratt: Chieftaincy Institution Has No Relevance Today (May 16, 2010), http://www.ghanaweb.com/GhanaHomePage/NewsArchive/artikel.php?ID=182141.

[23] Ghana used to be called the Gold Coast during colonial rule, and it has been said that the name derived from the abundant gold found by the early Portuguese explorers who first visited the area during the fifteenth century.

[24] *See* Richard C. Crook, *Decolonization, The Colonial State, and Chieftaincy in the Gold Coast*, 85 AFR. AFF. 75, 84 (1986); DAVID APTER, THE GOLD COAST IN TRANSITION (1955).

an overarching prescription of conduct for chiefs; and, second, the proscription of customs, rules, and traditions deemed incompatible with the values of the colonial and, subsequently, independent state.

The legal evolution of chieftaincy can be broadly divided in three periods, namely the pre-colonial, colonial, and post-colonial.

12.3.1. *Chieftaincy in the Pre-Colonial Era*

Prior to contact with the Europeans, indigenous African states or communities had a well-structured system of governance constituted by a chief[25] and a council of elders.[26] In Ghana, although historians agree on the existence of ethno-political institutions of different character and arrangement,[27] the institution of chieftaincy was widespread[28] and represented the major political unit around which most ethnic groups were organized.[29]

The chief was the head or leader of the government of the indigenous African "state" or community. The pre-colonial institution of chieftaincy was usually segmented[30] and hierarchically patriarchal,[31] with males dominating offices in line with the overall cultural and socio-political demands of the time.

Broadly speaking, a person became a chief in pre-colonial times in one of three manners. Most commonly, the chief was the leader of the group of first settlers on a particular land. The area occupied was vested in the community with the

[25] "The Ghanaian chief emerged as a natural leader. He was essentially the founder and therefore the father of the traditional state over which he presides. The chief was highly respected because he was considered the most capable person to lead and speak on behalf of his people, based on his personal qualities as a man of valor and wisdom. He was not only the military leader and defender of his people against aggression; he was also the chief priest of the people.... Additionally the chief performed judicial, administrative, legislative, economic and cultural functions. On the basis of these functions the chief was the embodiment of the beliefs, hopes, fears and aspirations of his people." Chris Abotchie, *Has the Position of the Chief Become Anachronistic in Contemporary Ghanaian Politics?*, in CHIEFTAINCY IN GHANA: CULTURE GOVERNANCE AND DEVELOPMENT, *supra* note 15, at 170.

[26] *See* Justice G.K. Acquah, *The Judicial Role of the Chief in Democratic Governance*, in CHIEFTAINCY IN GHANA: CULTURE GOVERNANCE AND DEVELOPMENT, *supra* note 15, at 65.

[27] *See* L. GRAY COWAN, LOCAL GOVERNMENT IN WEST AFRICA (Columbia Univ. Press 1958); W.B. HARVEY, LAW AND SOCIAL CHANGE IN GHANA (Princeton Univ. Press 1966).

[28] A.K.P. KLUDZE, EWE LAW OF PROPERTY (Sweet & Maxwell 1973).

[29] *See* Though widespread, it is important to mention the fact that not all the tribes were organized around chiefs as titular political figures. For example, the Tellensi in the northern part of Ghana, were not organized around a centralized political figure. *See* AFRICAN POLITICAL SYSTEMS (Meyer Fortes & E.E. Evans-Pritchard eds. 1940).

[30] *See* C.E.K. Kumado, *Chieftaincy and the Law in Modern Ghana*, 18 U.G.L.J. 194 (1991–1992).

[31] *See* Odotei, *supra* note 15. Ghanaian tribes are mainly divided into matrilineal and patrilineal tribes on the basis of succession to property and office. Whereas succession under the matrilineal system is through the female line, succession to office or property under the patrilineal system is through the male progenitor.

chief as its custodian.[32] A second way by which a person could become a chief was through military invasion and conquest. A chief would impose his authority on the defeated people and exercise control over the land and its natural resources.[33] Thirdly, chiefs assumed power through military gallantry. Bravery and prowess were applauded in indigenous Ghanaian society, and those who distinguished themselves during wars or in perilous situations at peace were rewarded with the highest honor – chieftaincy.[34]

In pre-colonial times, the chief and his council of elders exercised legislative, administrative, adjudicatory, and military responsibilities.[35] With the discovery and use of metals such as iron and gold, the idea of power and use of military force built up the chieftaincy institution. Stronger tribes began expansionist activities to conquer weaker ones, control their resources, and develop trade routes. Chiefs provided leadership, mobilized support for their communities' development, and adopted laws by decree or proclamation. Chiefs' powers were kept in check by customary laws, including taboos to which they were subject. A council of elders also provided an institutional check on chiefs who sought absolute powers.[36] Chiefs acted as custodians, not personal owners, of the land and community's property. As such, chiefs could dispose of land or community property only with the consent of at least a majority of the council of elders.

Chiefs adjudicated disputes within a community, including offenses considered hateful to the ancestral spirits and other spiritual beings.[37] Judicial functions were exercised in three jurisdictional tiers: The village chief was subject to a senior or divisional chief, who in turn was subject to a paramount chief.[38] Village courts had original jurisdiction in petty civil and criminal offenses within their geographical limits. Divisional chiefs exercised appellate powers in disputes decided by the village or town courts within their jurisdiction. The paramount chief or king's court was at the apex of the system, with the greatest geographical jurisdiction and appellate powers. Significantly, chiefs also played vital magico-religious functions that sustained and reinforced their political power and respectability. Thus chiefs were the link between the living and the dead, leading the performance of sacrifices and rituals.

---

[32] *See* Abotchie, *supra* note 25, at 170. Indeed, an important symbol of chiefly authority was his dominant authority exercised over land.

[33] *See id.* This usually happened during those years of inter-tribal wars when stronger tribes fought and defeated weaker ones in order to expand their frontiers, area of authority and, importantly, sources of minerals like gold.

[34] *See id.*

[35] *See* Acquah, *supra* note 26.

[36] *See* ARHIN BREMPONG, TRANSFORMATIONS IN TRADITIONAL RULE IN GHANA (1951–1996) (Sedco Publ'g 2001).

[37] *See id.*

[38] *See* Acquah, *supra* note 26. G.K. Acquah is a former Chief Justice of Ghana.

12.3.2. *Chieftaincy during the Colonial Administration in the Gold Coast*

European expansion was facilitated by chiefs: Their political influence lessened the need for an open military campaign in the colonization of the Gold Coast.[39] The role of the chief as a titular political figure, coupled with the dynamic of inter-ethnic wars, gave the colonial power opportunities to annex large territories through protective agreements without openly waging wars of expansion. The Bond of 1844, a treaty of protection between the British and the coastal Fanti states, marked the first and most crucial step in establishing British colonial jurisdiction over the Gold Coast and set the stage for the subsequent interferences with native institutions including chieftaincy. Under the Bond of 1844, Fanti chiefs agreed to cede part of their jurisdiction to the British in return for protection against the Ashanti tribe.[40] The Bond of 1844 obliged local leaders to submit serious crimes, such as murder and robbery, to British jurisdiction. The subsequent Native Jurisdiction Ordinance (1878)[41] recognized and defined the jurisdiction and power of the chief.[42] It also gave the British governor power to sub-divide chiefs' territories and to depose them.[43]

Colonial efforts to delimit the sphere of chieftaincy's influence increased over the years, as chieftaincy's autonomous political power was inconsistent with the emerging colonial hegemony within the Gold Coast.[44] The Chiefs' Ordinance of 1904 was another landmark colonial legislation that interfered with chieftaincy as an institution in native administration.[45] The Ordinance was designed to facilitate the proof of election, installation, and deposition of chiefs and provided that chiefs could apply to the colonial governor for confirmation of their installation. The governor's confirmation was not mandatory and was merely designed to improve certainty in chiefs' interactions with the colonial government. Scholars have argued that this

---

[39] It is noteworthy that the British did not wage open war in bringing a large part of Ghana under colonial rule. This was due to the military threat posed by Ashanti to the other tribes, particularly those on the coast and to the northern part of Ghana prior to the arrival of the Europeans and the inception of colonial rule. By signing treaties of protection with the British, the colonial power was authorized to wage a military campaign against Ashanti in pursuance of its obligations of protection.

[40] The Ashanti tribe was arguably the most well organized and powerful tribal group in the area that subsequently became the Gold Coast and then Ghana. Indeed, many historians assert that its military dominance and influence extended beyond the boundaries of the Gold Coast. As a result of this, many of the smaller tribal states entered into treaties of protection with the British, and the Bond of 1844 was one of the major treaties signed between the British and some of the smaller southern states against Ashanti conquest.

[41] The Native Jurisdiction Ordinance, No. 8 of 1878.

[42] *See id.* §§ 3, 4, 10, 30.

[43] *See id.* §§ 4, 29.

[44] *See* Donald I. Ray, *Divided Sovereignty: Traditional Authority and the State in Ghana*, 37–38 J. LEGAL PLURALISM 181 (1996); Crook, *supra* note 24.

[45] Chief's Ordinance, No. 4 of 1904, Laws of the Gold Coast Colony, 1928, Cap. 21, at 151. *See also* Kumado, *supra* note 30.

requirement represented the formal introduction of governmental participation in the election and installation of chiefs.[46] Although the Ordinance allegedly intended only to solidify the legal basis for the exercise of traditional authority,[47] it had, in reality, an intrusive effect on chieftaincy's role.[48]

The nature of colonialism, coupled with the implantation of its political institutions, constituted an assault on the sphere of influence exercised by chiefs and traditional authorities. The colonial government shifted power from chiefs to colonial institutions[49] through legislation and other policy strategies, preserving chieftaincy's domain only when it served to promote colonial domination.[50] The colonial government actively asserted a policy of indirect rule,[51] a stratagem created by the British to co-opt chieftaincy as the ground structure for their administration, with chiefs acting as the official representatives of the colonial government in their areas of jurisdiction. This policy was designed to avoid the creation of parallel institutions at the local level and to eliminate potential resistance from indigenous people to colonial rule. Indirect rule led to the elevation, and in some cases creation, of chieftains[52] in areas where the institution did not previously exist or where it took some other form,[53] thus creating conflicts between "implanted" institutions and local customs and structures.[54] The British also wrongly relied on the assumption that the nature and anthropological dynamic of chieftaincy was identical across tribes.[55] They applied common standards across the country without regard to the

---

[46] *See* Harvey, *supra* note 27, at 220–221. *See also* Kumado, *supra* note 30.
[47] WILLIAM MALCOLM HAILEY, NATIVE ADMINISTRATION IN THE BRITISH AFRICAN TERRITORIES, Vol. III, at 202 (1951).
[48] *See* Kumado, *supra* note 30. *See also* Harvey, *supra* note 27.
[49] The economic independence of chiefs, for example, was undermined by the establishment of local authorities to whom local taxes previously paid to chiefs came to be paid. *See* Kwame Boafo-Arthur, *Chieftaincy and Politics In Ghana Since 1982*, 3 W. AFR. R. (2001), *available at* http://www.westafricareview.com/vol3.1/boafo.html.
[50] *See* Nana Arhin Brempong, *Chieftaincy, an Overview*, in CHIEFTAINCY IN GHANA: CULTURE, GOVERNANCE AND DEVELOPMENT, *supra* note 15, at 28.
[51] *See* L.P. MAIR, NATIVE POLICIES IN AFRICA (1936) (defining indirect rule as the "progressive adaptation of native institutions to modern conditions"). *See also* Kumado, *supra* note 30.
[52] As governor Sir Gordon Guggisberg declared in 1921: "Our policy must be to maintain any Paramount chiefs that exist and gradually absorb under these any small communities scattered about. What we should aim at is that some day the Dagombas, Gonjas and Mamprusi should become strong native states. Each will have its own little Public Works Department and carry on its business with the Political Officer as a Resident and Adviser. Each state will be more or less self-contained." MARTIN STANILAND, THE LIONS OF DAGBON: POLITICAL CHANGE IN NORTHERN GHANA 58 (1975).
[53] In Accra, for example, this led to the elevation of the Mantse, a traditionally religious position, to the status of paramount chief, with all the clout of politics that goes with it. *See* Hailey, *supra* note 47, pt. III, ch. VIII, at 194 (1951). *See also* Kumado, *supra* note 30.
[54] *See* Kumado, *supra* note 30.
[55] Note, however, a contrary conclusion by Harvey, *supra* note 27.

different traditions of the various ethnic groups, thus contributing to tensions when chiefs exercised powers in manners incompatible with specific traditions and rules of a given group. Indirect rule had a disruptive and, in many cases, distorted effect on chieftaincy, drawing a wedge between the people and their traditional rulers,[56] reinforcing instability, and causing rampant destoolments.[57]

The erosion of chiefs' authority and powers was furthered by a coordinated process designed to consolidate the structures of dependency.[58] One such structure was recognition. Through the mechanism of recognition, the colonial government undermined the source of chiefs' legitimacy.[59] The source of chiefs' power ceased to be rooted in the traditions and customs of their communities and became subject to the recognition and acceptance of the newly established foreign colonial hegemony.

The regulation of the chieftaincy came to a head with the passage of the 1944 Ordinances.[60] Under these laws, the colonial government regularized the appointment of chiefs, established treasuries with regular tax income, and rationalized native courts. Each of these carefully interwoven policies had fundamental effects on the overall influence and effectiveness of chiefs. Provincial councils were established by the colonial government with representation for chiefs.[61] Provincial councils played multiple roles for the colonial establishment and represented a strategic means of dealing with chieftaincy within a regulated structure.[62] The lines of

---

[56] In many places, chiefs were superimposed on the people and ruled arbitrarily, knowing that they were not accountable to the people but to the colonial government, which would support them so long as they did its bidding.

[57] Destoolment is a term that refers to the process of "removing" a chief from the throne, and it is called so because the chief is said to be symbolically an occupant of the stool. Similarly, the chief whose symbol of authority is the skin is said to be deskinned when he is removed from office.

[58] The mandate of the chief became re-oriented toward the colonial end from a monolithic function to a dual mandate. *See* The Native Jurisdiction Ordinance, No. 5 of 1883, as amended, Laws of the Gold Coast Colony, 1928, Cap. 113; FREDERICK JOHN DEALTRY LUGARD, THE DUAL MANDATE IN BRITISH TROPICAL AFRICA (Blackwood 1923). *See also* Chieftaincy (Amendment) Law, 1985, PNDCL 107; Harvey, *supra* note 27; DAVID KIMBLE, A POLITICAL HISTORY OF GHANA, 1850–1928 (Clarendon Press 1963).

[59] *See* The Chiefs Ordinance, No. 4 of 1904, Laws of the Gold Coast Colony, 1928, Cap. 21. *See also* Chieftaincy (Amendment) Law, *supra* note 58.

[60] Native Authority (Colony) Ordinance, No. 21 of 1944; Native Courts (Colony) Ordinance, No. 22 of 1944.

[61] The provincial councils were created under the 1925 Guggisberg Constitution, by which the British sought to institutionalise the indirect rule policy. The colony was divided into three provinces, namely the eastern, central and western provinces. The paramount chiefs in each of those provinces were constituted into the provincial councils to act as the local government structures for the British colonial administration.

[62] Hargreaves argues, for example, that the provincial councils were used by the colonial government as electoral collages. *See* John D. Hargreaves, *Decolonization and African Independence, in* THE TRANSFER OF POWER IN AFRICA: DECOLONIZATION, 1940–1960 (Prosser Gifford & Wm. Roger Louis eds., 1988).

demarcation between the colonial political hierarchy and the hitherto autonomous institution of chieftaincy were de facto erased and a new era in chieftaincy's "politicization" opened. Chiefs' quests for endorsement by the colonial government[63] as the overarching hegemonic political overlord in the Gold Coast increased.[64] Chiefs cooperated with the colonial government, often at the expense of their indigenous constituency and institutions. An enhanced level of instability within the institution followed, owing to the discontent and disenchantment of subjects with their chiefs at the perceived betrayals of the chiefs' customary oaths of allegiance.

The evolutionary trajectory of chieftaincy during the colonial era predisposed it toward gradual irrelevance as the colony headed for independence. Indeed, one author has argued that the institution was doomed because "it made sense only during the era of high colonialism, but had to go when colonialism itself, for whatever reason, came to an end."[65] This view is consistent with the rather hazy and convoluted role the institution assumed within the colonial political setup. Chiefs were not fully integrated within the institutional architecture of the colonial state, as the colonial government tried to maintain the appearance of independence of the institution. Chieftaincy's future was further challenged with the inception of independence. The decision to grant independence to the Gold Coast raised the issue of the form of government for the new country.[66] After a century of engagement with traditional institutions, the colonial government confirmed the opportunistic nature of its policy of indirect rule and relation with traditional leaders. The British government suddenly but tactically engaged the educated elites of the Gold Coast over issues of political succession at the expense of traditional rulers.

It has been argued[67] that the main reason for the colonial change of partnership, from the chiefs to the educated elites, was due to the desire to bequeath a democratic, Westminster-style government. In the view of the colonial government, the tenets of traditional leadership were anachronistic and outdated for the governance of a modern state.[68] Furthermore, in the absence of any chiefdom with a level of influence, political clout, and control cutting across the entire territory, it was hard to hand over the reins of power to chiefs.[69] A combination of variables built on

---

[63] *See* Harvey, *supra* note 27.

[64] *See* Ray, *supra* note 44.

[65] Crook, *supra* note 24, at 75–105.

[66] *See id.*

[67] *See id.*

[68] Governor Guggisberg, for example, urged the maintenance of the institution in its traditional forms, whereas authorities in London thought that these features of chieftaincy represented nothing more than museum artifacts. *See id.*

[69] Indeed, when Dr. Kwame Nkrumah tabled the motion in parliament asking independence, he requested that independence be granted to the chiefs and people of the Gold Coast.

social Darwinism[70] and a misapprehension about the internal workings of the institution led the colonial government to believe that chieftaincy was an autocratic
institution lacking the essential features of democracy and checks and balances.
The colonial administration did, however, recognize the factual resilience and per-
manence of the institution of chieftaincy in the Gold Coast.[71] Thus, the Coussey
report[72] noted that chieftaincy was so deeply rooted in the culture of the people
that its exclusion from the governance of the emerging nation would have been
disastrous.[73] This recognition led to the reintegration of chiefs into mainstream
politics and to a redefinition of their role within the context of the governance paradigm of the emerging nation. In this new position, chiefs were accorded a diminished role as political sub-actors.[74] Chiefs were not satisfied with their lesser role,
as was amply manifested in the struggles and clashes between the chiefs and the
new political elites to whom the reins of government were being handed. A compromise arrangement was arrived at in which the Independence Order-Council
"guaranteed" the institution of chieftaincy in accordance with customary law and
usage. The Order-Council also established regional assemblies vested with local
government functions and Houses of Chiefs in the regions.[75] In reality, however,
the regional assemblies effectively stripped away all the residual local government
functions chiefs had had,[76] and practically rendered them politically superfluous
and expendable.

12.3.3. *Chieftaincy in Post-Colonial Ghana*

Since independence, Ghana has witnessed four constitutional changes: 1960, 1969,
1979, and 1992. Each constitution was abrogated by military government following

---

[70] This is a concept employed to explain anthropological reactions to differences in cultures and their
   tendency to treat one culture as both functionally and innately superior to others.
[71] *See* Brempong, *supra* note 50.
[72] In 1948, there were riots throughout the Gold Coast after which the Watson Commission was set up to
   look into the cause of the riots. The Commission found that the riots were largely a result of dissatisfaction with colonial government and recommended that constitutional reforms be made. The Coussey
   Committee was subsequently set up to recommend necessary reforms.
[73] *See* Brempong, *supra* note 50. Prior to the granting of independence, the colonial government found
   itself in a dilemma in respect of whom to grant political power to, the choice being between the newly
   and emerging educated elites referred to as "intelligentsia" or the chiefs who claimed that, considering that political power was initially taken from them with the inception of colonialism, they were the
   rightful heirs to political power in an independent Ghana. The Coussey Commission's work was part
   of efforts aimed at verifying the feasibility of maintaining or abolishing the institution of chieftaincy
   in the governance structure to be bequeathed the Gold Coast upon the granting of independence.
[74] *See id.*
[75] *See id.*
[76] *See id.*

a military coup.[77] The immediate post-independence era saw a marked increase in political interferences in the chieftaincy institution. The 1960 constitution established a presidential system of government and vested great power in the first president, Kwame Nkrumah. His attitude to traditional rule appeared generally negative and cynical. Some have argued that Dr. Nkrumah's regime actively took steps to undermine the institution with laws and policies designed to render its position less important within the governance paradigm of Ghana.[78] For example, as far as the judicial power of chiefs was concerned, the Houses of Chiefs Act 1958 and its successor, the Chieftaincy Act 1961, abolished native courts and stripped chiefs of all their judicial powers in both criminal and civil matters, except for those relating to or affecting chieftaincy.[79] The 1961 Act further encroached on the institution's power by making the installation of chiefs subject to the government's recognition. Statutes such as the Constitution (Repeal of Chieftaincy Restriction Act) 1958,[80] the Ashanti Stool Lands Act (No. 28) 1958,[81] the Local Council Act 1958,[82] and the Akyem Abuakwa (Stool Revenue) Act 1958[83] also in one form or another impinged on the constitutional and monetary competencies of chiefs. For example, the Akyem Abuakwa (Stool Revenue) Act subjected the administration of the revenues and properties of Akyem Abuakwa to a receiver appointed by the minister for local government. The Local Courts Act, which abolished the Native Authority Tribunals, had a greater impact, effectively ending chiefs' formal exercise of judicial powers.[84] The collective effect of these statutes was to regulate the institution and subject it to the control or oversight of government.

As the boundaries of authority and exact relationship between chiefs and central government bodies continued to be redefined, constitutional challenges emerged.

---

[77] Indeed, there was an earlier constitution adopted in 1957, but that is not counted among the constitutional epochs due its enactment as an Act of the British Parliament. This constitution was repealed by the 1960 constitution.

[78] *See id.*

[79] "Cause or matter affecting chieftaincy" is defined as "a cause, matter, question or dispute relating to any of the following: (*a*) the nomination, election, selection or installation of a person as a chief or the claim of a person to be nominated, elected, selected or installed as a chief; (*b*) the deposition or abdication of a chief; (*c*) the right of a person to take part in the nomination, election, selection or installation of a person as a chief or in the deposition of a chief; (*d*) the recovery or delivery of stool property in connection with the nomination, election, selection, installation, deposition or abdication of a chief, and (*e*) the constitutional relations under customary law between chiefs." *See* The Chieftaincy Act, 2008, § 76. A "cause or matter affecting chieftaincy," as defined in the 1961 Chieftaincy Act and also the 1971 Act (cited below), was substantially similar in terms to the 2008 definition.

[80] Constitution (Repeal of Chieftaincy Restriction Act), No. 38 of 1958.

[81] Ashanti Stool Lands Act, No. 28 of 1958.

[82] Local Council Act, No. 6230 of 1958.

[83] Akyem Abuakwa (Stool Revenue) Act (1958), Act 8.

[84] From the very inception of colonialism, the judicial powers of chiefs were undermined. The Supreme Court Ordinance of 1876 introduced a court system based on western adjudicatory mechanisms and the common law. Customary law and native administration of justice were sidelined and, at best, made subservient to the system of justice introduced under colonial rule.

By guaranteeing the institution, the constitution sought to abstain from interfering with the customary bases of chiefly authority. Its failure to comprehensively deal with the institution, however, left many thorny issues outstanding and created the potential for disputes and uncertainty.[85]

The 1969 Constitution also guaranteed chieftaincy. It created National and Regional Houses of Chiefs tasked with new constitutional functions,[86] including the mandate to undertake a study of customary law "with a view to evolving a unified system of rules of customary law...."[87] Chiefs' judicial functions remained limited to matters affecting chieftaincy. Under the Chieftaincy Act 1971, chiefs did not have to be officially recognized by the government to perform the customary roles that had survived colonization, though the Act required official recognition of the minister for local government before a chief could perform any of the constitutional/statutory functions introduced by the Act and the 1969 Constitution.[88]

The overthrow of the 1969 constitutional regime ushered in a series of military governments, ultimately leading to the establishment of the third republic under the 1979 Constitution. The 1979 Constitution introduced landmark reforms insulating chieftaincy from the central government's interference and completely abolished the requirement of governmental recognition of chiefs. For the first time, the definition of "chief" was provided by the Constitution. According to Article 181, a chief is "*a person who hailing from the appropriate family and lineage has been validly nominated, elected and enstooled, enskinned or installed as a chief or queenmother in accordance with the requisite applicable customary law and usage.*"[89]

The newly accorded independence to chiefs was short-lived, however. With the overthrow of the constitutional order in 1981,[90] the ground was set again for government interference in chieftaincy matters. In 1985, Provisional National Defense Council (PNDC) Law 107 brought back the requirement of government recognition for chiefs before they could exercise any of the functions provided under statutes.[91]

---

[85] One recent example was a situation in Ghana when a woman was banished by a chief from her hometown for refusing to participate in community service. This generated heated constitutional debate nationwide, with some taking the view that the right of freedom of movement could only be constricted by the supreme court and not by any other authority, or person for that matter.

[86] These functions are substantially the same as those ones provided for in the 1979 and 1992 Constitutions. These are discussed later as part of the broader discussion of how the 1992 Constitution has impacted chieftaincy.

[87] GHANA CONST. (1969).

[88] Recognition, just as it was used during the colonial era, was exploited by post-colonial governments to control the behavior of chiefs vis-à-vis government and other political actors.

[89] GHANA CONST. (1979).

[90] The military government, led by Flt. Lt. Jerry John Rawlings, overthrew the government of Hilla Limann and the 1979 Constitution. This then brought to an abrupt end the governance system and the regulatory framework governing chieftaincy under that constitution.

[91] Chieftaincy (Amendment) Law, 1985, PNDCL 107.

The current constitutional provisions relating to chieftaincy are to be found in the 1992 Constitution that returned Ghana to civilian rule.[92] The 1992 Constitution guarantees the existence of the institution and defines a chief in very similar terms to the 1979 Constitution.[93] Article 270(1) specifies that: "The institution of chieftaincy, together with its traditional councils as established by customary law and usage, is hereby guaranteed."[94] Chapter XXII of the 1992 Constitution provides further guarantees for the institution of chieftaincy[95] and sets up a number of self-governance institutions for this purpose, including the National House of Chiefs[96] and Regional Houses of Chiefs.[97] The abolition of government recognition for chiefs is also reaffirmed.[98] To preserve the neutrality, independence, and integrity of chiefs, Article 276(1) proscribes their participation in political affairs: "[A] chief shall not take part in active party politics; and any chief wishing to do so and seeking to election to Parliament shall abdicate his stool or skin."[99] To ensure the integrity of the institution and chiefs' status as symbols of unity in communities that may be otherwise divided along political lines, those convicted for offenses "involving the security of the state, fraud, dishonesty or moral turpitude" are also prohibited from becoming chiefs.[100]

With respect to chiefs' powers and functions, the 1992 Constitution has not introduced substantial changes. Chiefs' judicial powers are still limited to causes or matters affecting chieftaincy, although they continue to act as arbitrators, as recognized by the Chieftaincy Act 2008.[101]

The Chieftaincy Act 2008 implementing the constitutional mandate, institutes specific measures aimed at ensuring that the institution and its role are respected.[102] For example, under the Act, the National House of Chiefs keeps a register of the

---

[92] The rule of the government of the PNDC that overthrew the 1979 Constitution ended in 1993 with the inception of the 1992 Constitution.

[93] The constitution defines a chief as "…a person, who, hailing from the appropriate family and lineage, has been validly nominated, elected or selected and enstooled, enskinned or installed as a chief or queenmother in accordance with the relevant customary law and usage." GHANA CONST. (1992).

[94] *See id.* art. 270(1) (1992).

[95] Article 270(2), for example, forbids Parliament from passing any law that confers on anyone a chiefly title, but permits the legislature to pass laws regulating succession so long as the same is in accordance with the relevant customary law and usage. The problem with this provision, as will be seen subsequently in this work, is the assumption of the ascertainment of customary law as a matter of course, in which case Parliament can merely perfect customary law through statutory codification. Regrettably that is not the situation. *See id.* art. 270(2) (1992).

[96] *See id.* art. 271 (1992).

[97] *See id.* art. 274 (1992).

[98] *See id.* art. 270 (1992).

[99] *See id.* art. 276(1) (1992).

[100] *See id.*

[101] *See* Chieftaincy Act 2008, § 30.

[102] *See generally id.*

chiefs duly elected or installed in accordance with customary law.[103] Entry into the register is evidence that a person has been duly installed as a chief and needs no further recognition from the government,[104] thus putting chiefs in charge of their own affairs, especially in matters relating to their own identity and recognition. Furthermore, under the Chieftaincy Act 2008, it is an offense punishable by a fine, a term of imprisonment not exceeding three months, or both to, for instance, knowingly use disrespectful or insulting language against a chief or otherwise insult him either by word or conduct, or to deliberately refuse to honor a call from a chief to attend to an issue.[105]

The constitutional guarantee for the institution of chieftaincy in the 1992 Constitution has not been without critics. Some have chastised the institution for failing to adapt to the historical and emerging changes and developments in the governance dynamics of Ghana.[106] Others have expressed concerns for its seeming inability to synchronize its roles and functions with the modern institutional arrangements and political setup. The institution has been further criticized for being anachronistic and lacking accountability, transparency, and democratic structures for succession, as well as mechanisms for grassroots participation in local governance.

The institutional regulation of chieftaincy under the 1992 Constitution has also reignited accusations of patriarchy. The Constitution provides for the establishment of houses of chiefs that invariably exclude females because the institution of chieftaincy is overwhelmingly male-dominated. Moreover, the continuing failure of queen mothers to gain representation in these institutions questions their representative and non-discriminatory character.[107] Others disagree with this assessment and argue that queen mothers continue to play pivotal functions and exercise significant political powers in the governance paradigm of traditional leadership, for example, by playing a crucial role in the selection of chiefs.[108] As Ghana strives to realign its developmental objectives in accordance with internationally recognized human

---

[103] *See id.* § 59.

[104] *See id.*

[105] *See id.* § 63. A person also commits an offence if he 1) acts or performs the functions of a chief when that person is not qualified to act; 2) being a chief, assumes a position that the person is not entitled to by custom; 3) refuses to undertake communal labor announced by a chief without reasonable cause; or 4) deliberately fails to follow the right procedures to destool a chief.

[106] For example, the institution has been criticized for failing to play a meaningful role in local governance but has, on the contrary, been a source of instability at the local level.

[107] *See* Odotei, *supra* note 15.

[108] *See id.* Indeed, it is instructive that some chieftains in Ghana oppose the representation of queen mothers (who were chiefs in their own right and not necessarily mother to any sitting chief) in formal institutions with chiefly representations on grounds that the position of the queen mother is not universal and is therefore limited to parts of the country. Others oppose it on grounds that any attempt to equate the position of the queen mother with that of the chief will violate the basic principles of traditional leadership.

rights standards, chieftaincy cannot continue to turn a blind eye to the accusations of patriarchy and male domination. Contemporary regulatory efforts[109] have essentially tried to modernize the institution and proceeded along the lines similar to those of the colonial government, even though the variables might have changed. Today the essential variables for consideration to ensure the institution complies with the 1992 Constitution are, *inter alia*, human rights,[110] good governance, and the rule of law.[111]

A major debate in the quest for regulation of chieftaincy in Ghana revolves around the political activities of chiefs. The current preferred option is for the insulation of chiefs from the mainstream political process, although such prohibition is not absolute. Chiefs are eligible for appointments to key national institutions such as the Council of State and other non-elective bodies or agencies. Whereas the Constitution has attempted to "institutionalize" chieftaincy, the current constitutional arrangement is unique in its exclusion of chiefs from local government administration.[112] The apparent goal here is to maintain and reinforce the political neutrality of chiefs while preserving the aura and dignity of the chief as a symbol of authority in the traditional state. Chiefs' insulation from active politics is generally accepted as functionally viable, although it has been questioned in some quarters as undermining the right of chiefs to fully participate in the democratic governance of Ghana in view of their wealth of experience in governance and administration, particularly at the local level. Allowing chiefs to partake in political activities would, however, open up the institution to partisan politics, potentially leading to division, de-legitimization, and factionalism within the spheres of traditional authorities, and the ultimate demise of the institution. Thus, the constitutional guarantee together with the proscription from participation in political activities represents a delicate balancing of interests in which chiefs' rights to political participation have been sacrificed for the overarching interest of preserving and promoting the institution's traditional profile.

[109] *See* GHANA CONST. (1992); Chieftaincy Act 2008.

[110] These are the main values championed by the Constitution. Under Article 106, all customary laws that are dehumanizing are to be deemed incompatible with the Constitution and, therefore, unenforceable. The Constitution does not provide a benchmark for the ascertainment of offending customs, however, generating tensions between government and chiefs anytime there are allegations of violations.

[111] The 1992 Constitution is shaped by these values, and, consequently, these have become standards for measuring the extent to which the conduct or actions of state and traditional institutions comply with the Constitution.

[112] *See* Joseph R.A. Ayee, *Some Thoughts on the Institutional Representation of Chiefs in the District Assemblies and the Sub-District Structure, in* CHIEFTAINCY IN GHANA: CULTURE, GOVERNANCE AND DEVELOPMENT, *supra* note 15, at 55. Note, however, that under Article 242 of the Constitution and Section 15 of the Local Government Act (Act 462), the government is allowed to appoint chiefs among its 30% appointees.

12.4. SUCCESSION, CONFLICT, AND INSTABILITY: CONTESTS AND CHAOS

Conflicts within the institution of chieftaincy provide a critical frame to examine the problems plaguing the evolution and adjustment of the institution within modern Ghana, in view of the inextricable link between chieftaincy, security, conflicts, and development.[113]

Chieftaincy has been associated with conflicts since time immemorial. As the basic political unit of the people during the pre-colonial era, chiefs were at the forefront of waging wars of expansion and providing defensive leadership whenever the "state" was under attack.[114] The conflicts associated with the institution in recent times are different both in character and in orientation.[115] Whereas pre-colonial chieftaincy conflicts were essentially oriented toward an external enemy in the character of another ethnic group or political organization and waged in the name of the state, contemporary conflicts are usually internal in character and, in many cases, challenge the legitimacy of existing chiefs or persons claiming entitlement to the throne. Since the attainment of independence, such chieftaincy conflicts have taken on a variety of forms, and have collectively served to augment public disenchantment with the institution. Although various studies have dissected the reasons and bases for these conflicts,[116] Ghana has yet to devise an effective model and strategy for dealing with threats posed by conflicts associated with the institution of chieftaincy and the peculiar developmental challenges they pose. Significantly, the nexus connecting chieftaincy and ethnic conflict is both complex and shifting, touching on issues of ethnic identity and changing constructions of ethnicity, group history, and rights. Conflicts are further accentuated by questions of access to land,[117] an issue intimately connected with status as well as economic opportunity. The causes of these conflicts are as numerous as they are complex. The following, however, could be identified as some of the main causes of chieftaincy conflicts in Ghana:[118] the absence of a codified body of rules on succession; historically diffuse lines of succession; and divisions based on identity, social constructs, or conflicts generated by feelings of ethnocentric superiority.

[113] *See* Julia Jönsson, *The Overwhelming Minority: Traditional Leadership and Ethnic Conflict in Ghana's Northern Region* (Oxford Univ. Dep't of Int'l Dev., Ctr. for Research on Inequality, Human Sec. and Ethnicity, Working Paper No. 30, Feb. 2007).

[114] *See* Odotei, *supra* note 15.

[115] *See* N.J.K. Brukum, *Chieftaincy and Ethnic Conflicts in Northern Ghana*, in CHIEFTAINCY IN GHANA: CULTURE, GOVERNANCE AND DEVELOPMENT, *supra* note 15, at 429.

[116] *See id.*

[117] *See id.* Land forms an essential resource, and a continuing incentive for the pursuit for inter-tribal wars in Ghana. Virtually all inter-tribal wars fought in Ghana revolved around land both as an economic resource and an exemplification of traditional political power.

[118] *See id.*

The failure of relevant statutory regimes to detail the modes and bases of succession unquestionably plays a role in chieftaincy's conflicts. The institution has substantially relied on non-documented traditions and customary rules of succession[119] under which proof is often difficult, creating conditions for disputes. The absence of rules on succession leads to doubts about the legitimacy of claims to succession whenever a particular claimant is challenged. Thus, persons put up for succession to thrones are often challenged on varying grounds.[120] The ensuing disputes are often violent.

In the Dagbon dispute of 2002, the paramount chief was beheaded and forty of his subjects were murdered in the chieftaincy conflict that arose due to lingering disagreements over the rotational system in place there.[121] In 2007, five people, including a police officer, were killed in Anlo as a result of a similar dispute. These incidents were preceded by other tragic events in Bimbilla in 1994–1995, when 2,000 people died and more than 200,000 people were displaced. Violent outbreaks as a result of chieftaincy succession disputes have taken place all over Ghana, and numerous chieftaincy disputes remain unresolved.

Royal lineage historically played a significant role in determining chieftaincy succession: The lineage provides the structure for selecting the heir apparent to the stool/skin. However, in many cases, non-royal members seek nominations due to the nobility, respect, and power associated with the institution. With no clearly defined records of succession, disputes often result from challenges to claims of membership of a particular royal lineage as well as claims to succession. In some instances, there are three or more contestants vying for the same stool or skin, leading to open conflicts and often loss of life.[122] Disagreements bordering on succession also occur when an alternate line of succession tries to monopolize the throne, or when attempts are made to bypass a line in the system.[123]

Historically diffuse lines of succession are another major factor in succession conflicts. Conflicts normally occur in areas with more than one line of succession from

[119] Succession rules are entirely steeped in customary law, which is essentially unwritten.

[120] For example, the chieftaincy conflict in the northern part of Ghana between the Abudus and Andanis stemmed from disputations of succession to the Yendi Stool. The conflict has led to numerous deaths and continues to fuel instability in the north as a trouble spot in Ghana. Some of the grounds on which a prospective candidate's nomination could be disputed are membership of the line of succession from which a chief is selected, or claim to succession by a gate when it is not its time to so inherit the throne.

[121] There are two gates or royal houses who ascend to throne in Dagbon, namely the Abudu and Andani groups. The system has not been without disputes and disagreements regarding which gate or royal house is entitled to the throne at any particular time.

[122] The Dagbon conflict is a classic illustration of an improperly managed succession dispute that has escalated into a continuing security nightmare for the entire northern region of Ghana.

[123] In the case of the Dagbon crisis, two gates succeed to the throne in alternation. The dispute arose out of disagreements over the rightful gate to succeed to the throne, leading ultimately to the murder of the sitting chief.

which a chief can be selected. This factor is itself the product of many connected variables: Some communities comprising settler and native communities have cohabited pursuant to well-understood and agreed terms of settlements. However, with time, different groups of settlers have laid claims to thrones, leading to conflicts of succession.[124] Multiple lines of succession created to settle past disputes or in appeasement to one royal line have also at times led to conflicts.[125] Furthermore, multiple lines of succession have arisen in some groups, in part because of colonial and post-colonial governments' meddling in the traditional government of local people. The policy of indirect rule led to colonial government intermeddling in the succession to thrones. Similarly, the creation of royal lineages in areas where none existed substantially undermined the stability of the institution, leading to the mushrooming of opportunistic claims to title in these areas.[126]

Another critical reason for conflicts arises from evolving ideas of identity and social constructions of divisions within the Ghanaian polity. Chieftaincy inspires pride, identity, and distinction in the people who identify with it. Conflicts associated with chieftaincy feed on these constructions and sometimes ethnocentric superiority. Particularly in the northern sector of Ghana, tensions still characterize the relationship between many ethnic groups, leading, in many instances, to inter-tribal conflicts. Significantly, chieftaincy provides both the fulcrum and point of identity to wage these conflicts.

Another important cause of chieftaincy conflict is the use of chiefs as proxies to incite conflicts for political goals.[127] The position occupied by chiefs at times disposes them toward political manipulation and exploitation by vested political interests. The 1992 Constitution's insulation of chiefs from the political process is precisely designed to avert this situation, but it continues to be undermined by the use of the institution in furtherance of parochial political ends.

A number of chieftaincy conflicts are fought over access to land.[128] The importance and value of land continues to appreciate in newly developing areas, and chieftaincy conflicts continue to increase and intensify. District and regional boundaries are drawn without reference to stool land boundaries, with fundamental repercussions

---

[124] A classic example of this is the Mampong-Mokwaa conflict in the Twifo-Hemang Lower Denkyira District, which lasted for decades.

[125] For example, among the Anlos of the Volta Region of Ghana, the lines of succession are diffused, which, according to legend, came about when the Ewes migrated from Notse in present day Republic of Benin, but left a stool behind, which had to be brought to Ghana by the King nephew after his son had refused to go for it. In appreciation, according to the legend, the King created another line of succession to operate in alternation to the regular line.

[126] See Brukum, *supra* note 115.

[127] See IRINNews.org, Ghana: Why is the North Blighted by Chieftaincy Disputes? (Feb. 1, 2006), http://www.irinnews.org/report.aspx?ReportId=58007. *See also* Kobina Kennedy, Chieftaincy Reform (Nov. 15, 2007), http://www.ghanaweb.com/GhanaHomePage/features/artikel.php?ID=133940.

[128] *See id.*

in recent times,[129] underscoring the dysfunctional cleavage between national planning and governance on the one hand and traditional authority and administration on the other.

The contributions of the institution of chieftaincy to conflicts and instability arguably undermine and endanger its continuing relevance and survival within modern Ghana. Chieftaincy conflicts exert enormous pressure on national resources and divert attention from other critical and functional issues. Succession is crucial for the survival of chieftaincy: Once a chief dies, a new one needs to be installed to continue the institution. However, continuing violent conflicts and disputes over succession may bring the institution to an end. In an attempt to address this endemic problem, the National House of Chiefs has undertaken a project to codify existing rules on succession.[130] Whatever the arguments in favor or against the maintenance of chieftaincy, and codification in general, the adoption of accepted rules on succession is crucial for chieftaincy and, more generally, for a peaceful Ghana, and should therefore be given priority. For such rules to be successfully implemented, they need to have broad support and legitimacy, starting at the grass root level where chieftaincy disputes often originate.

12.5. CURRENT PROBLEMS AND CHALLENGES

As the institution struggles to rediscover its position and role in contemporary Ghana, a number of hard issues need to be considered, including the role and place of chieftaincy; reform of customary law; and accountability and transparency. The challenges confronting the institution are many, as a few examples will demonstrate.

First, the role and place of the institution of chieftaincy vis-à-vis other governance institutions needs to be better defined and established. The constitutional guarantee of the institution per se, without more specific provisions, is both inadequate and unsatisfactory, as it fails to address the historically pervasive distortions and interferences with the operations of chieftaincy. Fuller statutory clarifications of issues connected with jurisdiction, powers, succession, and the relationship to constitutional bodies will situate the institution of chieftaincy within a governance context with functional roles and responsibilities. This will further reinforce the institution's legitimacy and clout in exacting respect and compliance from subjects. The present statutory position is both unsustainable and unproductive for at least two key

---

[129] For example, boundary disputes have occurred between chiefs in Accra and the Central region over lands lying between Kasoa and Weija. On January 18, 2008, there was a conflict over the sale of stool lands when the Asantehene destooled the Asomfohene after the Asomfohene sold large tracts of land disputed between the Asomfo and Atwima Agogo stools.

[130] This project is supported by donors, including the World Bank, and has been under implementation since 2007.

reasons: 1) legal rules promoting institutional insulation are often ignored as chiefs continue to partake in party political activities with divisive consequences; 2) given the fact that many people continue to live under customary law, the failure by existing statutory regimes to exploit the potential of the institution to act as a complementary agent in local administration and adjudication is unsatisfactory.

Second, the institution needs to reform customary law as well as reinforce its efficacy as a legal regime governing the affairs of a large number of people. The evolution and development of customary law since the inception of colonial rule has been checkered and stagnant. Colonial policies actively suppressed the development of customary law through the enactment of statutes inimical to its growth and development.[131] Quite apart from this, customary law itself possesses the attributes of conservatism and being non-written. While some critics exaggerate and sometimes confuse the essence and effect of these attributes, the regime needs to adapt in order to fit within the dynamic and evolving constitutional system presently prevailing in Ghana. Given the pivotal role played by the institution as the repository of traditional legal wisdom, and considering the constitutional and statutory roles assigned to the institution in this regard,[132] it is safe to assert that the institution is better placed than any other to lead in the ascertainment, reform, systematization, and overall development of customary law in Ghana. The constitutional role assigned to the institution in this regard is both pragmatic and functional.[133] The conventional fear of ossification of the law when codified should be given serious consideration but should not hold up codification. National reform of customary law could significantly aid in bridging the gap between the formal and informal systems of law, particularly at the local level, and potentially bolster access to justice and legal resources for local people, many of whom are indigent, illiterate, and detached from the formal legal system. Codification, however, should strive to ensure that the necessary flexibility and fluidity of customary rules is preserved and indeed guaranteed, allowing their natural evolution and adaptation to changing times and circumstances.

Connected to this issue is the near-complete demise of chiefs' judicial functions. Chiefs' powers to administer justice have been impliedly eroded by statutory provisions governing the institution. In the process, the exercise of the chiefs' judicial powers has been limited to matters connected with the enstoolment or destoolment

---

[131] *See* The Supreme Court Ordinance, No. 4 of 1876.

[132] *See generally* GHANA CONST. ch. 22 (1992); Chieftaincy Act 2008 (Act 759) §§ 49–56. Indeed, under Act 759, traditional councils have been empowered to determine that a particular rule of customary law is uncertain and should accordingly be revised. While the law may still fall short of establishing a systematic and sustainable mechanism of reviewing and updating customary law, it represents a step together with other initiatives in reforming customary law.

[133] GHANA CONST. (1992). *See also* Chieftaincy Act 2008 (Act 759), §§ 49–56.

of chiefs.[134] Any remnant of judicial power of chiefs is limited to "mediating" disputes, and their decisions are not enforceable at law. Given the enormous challenges facing the administration of justice in Ghana, particularly in the area of access to justice at the local level, empowering chiefs to administer justice could greatly benefit the state as well as keep the institution engaged in governance. Restoring the judicial powers of chiefs, however, will have to take account the institutional peculiarities associated with chieftaincy in its contemporary state. Particular attention should be paid to address issues of corruption, equality, and non-discrimination to ensure a fair exercise of judicial functions by traditional authorities.

Third, systems of accountability and transparency prevalent under traditional leadership structures including chieftaincy are in urgent need of review and reform. At the heart of many problems plaguing the institution is the lack of accountability for resource utilization and the collateral issue of the wanton dissipation and waste of such resources.[135] Supporters of traditional leadership point out that there exist sufficient and adequate safeguards under customary law to ensure accountability. Just as the customary law itself suffers from the problem of ascertainment, however, the issue of ascertainment of the rules on accountability remains both thorny and uncertain. Customary modes of accountability seem to limit accountability to other identifiable members and offices of the traditional leadership establishment and generally exclude subjects of the institution, both as an aggregate constituency and in their individual capacities, from directly holding chiefs to account.[136] The absence of effective systems of accountability for ensuring transparency in resource deployment and usage continues to undermine the credibility of chiefs as prudent and frugal public servants, leading to the popular impression that the institution is corrupt and wasteful. As the institution of chieftaincy strives to carve a new niche and image for itself within the current constitutional milieu, the issue of accountability cannot be overlooked and must be critically examined and reviewed. Furthermore, this situation might even arguably violate the constitutional requirement of accountability for the use and exploitation of stool properties.[137]

---

[134] *See* Acquah, *supra* note 26.

[135] *But see* Chieftaincy Act 2008 (Act 759), §§ 44–49 (discussing the accountability of chiefs for use of stool/skin property). The problem with the law lies in its failure to demand stringent accountability as well as spell out the consequences for misuse or misappropriation. *See also* Head of Family Accountability Law, 1985, PNDCL 114 (compelling all family heads to account for the use of family resources). The reality, however, is that chiefs and other heads of family continue to misuse family property without suffering any penalties.

[136] *But see* Alexander K.D. Frempong, *Chieftaincy, Democracy and Human Rights in Pre-colonial Africa: The Case of the Akan System in Ghana, in* CHIEFTAINCY IN GHANA: CULTURE, GOVERNANCE AND DEVELOPMENT, *supra* note 15, at 379. It is important, however, to stress in reaction that the institution as presently administered lacks the routine and open structures of public accountability accessible to all subjects of the respective stools/skins.

[137] *See* GHANA CONST. art. 267 (1992).

Chieftaincy needs to realign its internal workings to the core tenets of the constitution, particularly in the areas of human rights, good governance, and constitutionalism. Often criticized for being undemocratic,[138] chieftaincy has at times demonstrated its ability to operate an elaborate system of government with internal checks and balances. Chieftaincy needs to adapt its powers and operations to comply further with human rights and constitutionalism in traditional governance. The continuing prevalence of servitude[139] and other manifestations of slavery in the palaces of certain chiefs in Ghana, for example, remains a challenge, one the institution has to address within the context of provisions of the 1992 Constitution proscribing these practices. Similarly, the institution needs to confront and address accusations of patriarchy. The institution of chieftaincy has traditionally been male-dominated,[140] even though women play crucial roles in the selection, monitoring and supervision of the chief. Queen mothers have exercised critical roles in this respect and have represented the interest of women as a gendered group in state administration. Yet, the role played by women in chieftaincy affairs unquestionably smacks of patriarchy and male domination.[141] Mainstreaming gender in the affairs of chiefs and their representation will conduce to the contemporary evolution of the institution and further position it as a functional partner in the attainment of development in Ghana.

Finally, chiefs must demonstrate their utility in order to continue to be deemed important and relevant. As traditional leaders, chiefs are involved in community mobilization for socio-economic and political development. The institution must be seen to lead policy designs and implementation at the local and national levels, particularly in matters affecting chieftaincy and local government. The constitutional limitation prevalent in the meantime must not be a bar to chiefs leading local development in a non-partisan manner. This will not only reinforce their credibility as agents of development, but will also boost their functional significance within the constitutional scheme.

A broader criticism concerns the divisive nature of allegiance to traditional authorities. Ghanaian citizens, like those in other African countries, find themselves subject to the authority and rules of different chiefs. Ghanaians are divided among hundreds of ethnic groups, and their loyalty to the constitutional system

---

[138] *See* GHANA CONST. art. 267 (1992). *See also* R.S. RATTRAY, ASHANTI LAW AND CONSTITUTION 82 (Clarendon Press 1929); Kumado, *supra* note 30. It is wrong to reduce the definition of democracy in this context to the elective principle and thereby conclude that its absence makes the institution undemocratic without paying heed to the peculiar anthropological orientation of the institution and its internal structures of checks and consultations.

[139] *See* Akosua Perbi, *Servitude and Chieftaincy in Ghana, in* CHIEFTAINCY IN GHANA: CULTURE, GOVERNANCE AND DEVELOPMENT, *supra* note 15, at 375.

[140] *See* Odotei, *supra* note 15.

[141] *See id.*

may be challenged by that due to their closer and often more relevant traditional leader. Chieftaincy excludes those who are not within an ethnic group. Someone may reside in a particular area subject to the jurisdiction of a chief that he/she may not recognize. Different ethnic groups may compete for power, and this situation creates conflicts and tensions.

Nonetheless, in the midst of this quagmire, some chiefs have shown exemplary leadership, offering hope and providing arguments in support of the maintenance of the institution. These chiefs tend to be educated and better understand the dynamics of the modern world and how to position the institution of chieftaincy to meet the challenges of the present constitutional setting. For example, the Osagyefo Amoatia Ofori Panin, Paramount Chief of Akyem Abuakwa Traditional Area, has promoted environmental protection and actively campaigned to promote HIV/AIDS awareness.[142]

Otumfuo Osei Tutu II, the Asantehene, King of the Asante Kingdom, is another leading traditional leader at the forefront of promoting changes to modernize chieftaincy.[143] The Asantehene has promoted education campaigns, openly encouraged HIV/AIDS prevention and research, and encouraged discussions on the modernization of traditional rules and customs.[144]

[142] Since his ascension to the high position of Paramount chief of Akyem Abuakwa Traditional Area in the Eastern Region, Osagyefo Amoatia Ofori Panin has been at the forefront of the campaign for a better environment in Ghana. Through the Okyeman Environment Foundation, the Osagyefo has been waging a campaign against environmental degradation, pollution of water bodies, and the indiscriminate and illegal felling of trees. The Foundation operates through a task force known as the Okyeman Environment Brigade that, among other things, reports illegal chainsaw lumbering to the police or the Ghana Forestry Commission, and confiscates all illegal lumber and unregistered chainsaws and conveys these to the nearest Police Station or office of the Forestry Commission. It mobilizes the general public for tree planting and riverbank cleanup exercises, and also embark on educational campaigns teaching and encouraging best environmental practices. The objective of the campaign has been to "protect and conserve the environment for posterity and the survival of the human race."

In 2002, Osagyefo Amoatia Ofori Panin broke the taboo and stigma associated with the HIV/AIDS menace. In the attempt to promote HIV/AIDS awareness within his area of jurisdiction, he invited medical personnel to give talks, free voluntary counseling, and testing for the virus. The Osagyefo Amoatia Ofori Panin was the first to be tested on that occasion. Through such bold leadership, he encouraged other people to voluntarily come out to be tested.

[143] *See* Wilhelmina J. Donkoh, Ph.D., Dep't of General and African Studies, Kwame Nkrumah Univ. of Science and Technology, *Traditional Leadership, Human Rights & Development: The Asante Example* (Ghana), *available at* www.gpiatlantic.org/conference/reports/donkoh2215.pdf.

[144] Otumfuo Osei Tutu II was installed as King of the Asante Kingdom in April 1999. The office of the Asantehene (i.e. King of Asante) is a *sui generis* one. His jurisdiction extends over all paramount chiefs in the Ashanti Region of Ghana as well as others in the Brong Ahafo and Volta regions. This makes his office undoubtedly the biggest chieftaincy position in Ghana with the widest area of jurisdiction in terms of territory. Since his ascension to the high office in 1999, he has been at forefront of a campaign to provide better education and health for people within his jurisdiction and indeed in the whole of Ghana, and has established the Otumfuo Education Fund with the objective of supplementing the efforts of the central government in the provision of quality education for all. In 2003, the Asanteman

Togbui Afede XIV, Paramount Chief of the Asogli Traditional Area, is another dynamic traditional leader in Ghana. Togbui Afede has been particularly active in promoting investments in his region and throughout Ghana, and in mobilizing the population to promote measures aimed at poverty eradication.[145]

These traditional leaders, and several others, understand the importance of their role and are striving to ensure chieftaincy's future by bringing modernity into an often stagnant institution. By doing so, these leaders are the best guarantee for the survival and continuing relevance of chieftaincy in Ghana.

12.6. CONCLUSIONS

The institution of chieftaincy as presently regulated and administered in Ghana presents many contradictions,[146] largely similar to those found in other African countries. This chapter attempts a discussion of the many challenges confronting the

HIV/AIDS Control Project, which had been initiated by the Otumfuo as a research program to conduct studies on the prevalence of the disease in Ashanti and also to combat it, was turned into a foundation and registered as a Non-governmental Organization. The Serwah Ampem AIDS Foundation for Children, as it is called, has been engaged in providing support for children with HIV/AIDS in the areas of their educational and health needs, particularly those whose parents have died of the disease. The assistance provided by the Foundation comes in the form of the payment of their health insurance premium and also soliciting for and providing such children with anti-retroviral drugs where possible. The Foundation also bears the educational related cost of such children, which usually includes school fees, text books and clothing. During the tenth anniversary celebration of his installation as Asantehene earlier in 2009, Otumfuo Osei Tutu II announced yet again another ambitious developmental program of establishing a university to provide access to tertiary education for youths in the country. The Royal University of Excellence, as it would be known and called, is intended to promote the development of tourism, ICT, sports, culture and other disciplines in the country.

[145] Togbui Afede XIV has been at the forefront of using his unique position and influence as a chief to initiate some developmental projects, which stand to benefit all Ghanaians. In 2006 through 2007, Ghana was hit by a serious power crisis, which led to the rationing of electric power throughout the country. One of the areas government and energy experts thought the country should be looking to for long-term solution was the encouragement of private or independent power production. Togbui Afede, through the Strategic African Securities, owned by him, has entered into a joint venture with the Shenzhen Energy Group Company Limited of China and the China-Africa Development Fund Company Limited to form the Sunon Asogli Power (Ghana) Limited, which is putting up a gas-steam combined cycle power generation plant. This is expected to add 560 megawatts of power to the national power output. Again, through his initiative and leadership, chiefs in the Volta Region have come together to draw up a five-year Economic Development Plan for the Region. The plan, whose implementation is estimated to cost $250 million, is targeted at mobilizing the chiefs and people for a collective assault on poverty and deprivation. Within the framework of the plan, they expect to build new educational facilities, upgrade existing ones, as well as create job opportunities for the youth in the Region. *See* Wisdom Peter Awuku, Joseph Sempah, & Priscilla Gunn, Asogli Power Intact (July 14, 2008), http://www.modernghana.com/news2/174329/1/asogli-power-intact.html.

[146] Current regulatory orientations seem to promote both insulation and independence of the institution from political and other controls yet, as seen in statutes regulating the institution, define the functions and duties of the institution within the general governance paradigm.

institution as an inherited governance institution in modern Ghana. Chieftaincy remains resilient in the face of the sometimes daunting forces of modernity. As Ghana develops a system of government based on the concept of democracy, however, chieftaincy must not only discover its niche within the overall governance paradigm, but must strive to synchronize its rules, structures, and polity with core constitutional provisions and national visions if it is to prove functional in the Ghanaian democratic experiment.

Reform initiatives affecting the institution need to be reviewed and intensified. Issues related to ascertainment, codification, and systematization of customary law on chieftaincy, succession, and more generally need greater and critical attention. As the basic regulatory regime of the institution, chieftaincy cannot continue to treat the subject of customary law reform as ancillary and, indeed, secondary to institutional progress and development. While colonial and post-independence governments in Ghana have in diverse ways undermined the capacity of the institution to administer customary law toward national development, the time appears ripe for a revisitation of the subject of customary law reform as an inextricable component of the modernization process of chieftaincy.

A reformed, accountable, and transparent institution of chieftaincy could be further integrated in local government initiatives in Ghana. This could strengthen and adapt the capabilities of chiefs as well as reinforce their effectiveness and contribution to governance. The current national sentiment, as demonstrated by debates within the ongoing constitutional review discussion, seems largely against the abolish of the institution. The legitimacy of the institution and its survival largely relies on such popular support, but its growth and evolution depends on its institutional dynamism and embrace of modern values. Ghana, like other African countries, needs to devise an effective regulatory regime that harnesses the potential of the institution for national governance. Chiefs need to lead efforts to modernize the institution. Issues such as transparency, accountability, gender equality, and the institution's respect for and compliance with fundamental human rights can no longer be avoided. Until the institution adapts its workings to the dynamics of the modern state, its relationship with the state, and the issue of its own survival within contemporary governance system, will continue to be thorny.

PART FOUR

Customary Land, Property Rights, and Succession

13

Entrapment or Freedom

Enforcing Customary Property Rights Regimes in Common-Law Africa

Sandra F. Joireman

13.1. INTRODUCTION

Customary land tenure arrangements in Africa have enlivened and sustained the role of customary leaders and authority patterns in Sub-Saharan Africa long after they would have otherwise faded into disuse. Because the allocation and control of land has meaning that extends beyond the cultural realm and into the economic and political, those who control it are assured an important role in the social and political hierarchy of a community. The role of customary authority in Sub-Saharan Africa is tied to the colonial experience and to the decisions of colonial officials to create separate categories of land rights and authority structures for citizens and subjects. Where colonization did not occur, as in Ethiopia, we do not see the same significant role played by customary leaders in land administration systems or even in conflict resolution. Thus, property rights and authority are intimately connected throughout Sub-Saharan Africa.

This chapter examines customary property rights and the role of customary leaders in enforcing those property rights from an institutionalist perspective. The issue of societal benefit is at the forefront of this chapter, which proceeds in three parts. Subchapter 13.2 discusses the pervasiveness of customary tenure and customary authority structures throughout Sub-Saharan Africa and their genesis in the colonial era. Subchapter 13.3 notes the lack of consistency between statutory law and customary law, which leads to a pluralistic legal setting. This part also identifies the winners and losers within customary legal systems. Subchapter 13.4 discusses how we can evaluate customary land tenure patterns and customary authority. The chapter ends by suggesting ways in which customary property rights and customary authority might persevere with a positive benefit to the society.

13.2. CUSTOMARY LAND TENURE IN AFRICA

Prior to colonization, Africa was not a vast undifferentiated and ungoverned area. There were city-states and kingdoms, varying greatly in size and control of territory. These were scattered across the continent in the most habitable areas. Between the city-states were often large tracts of un-administered land, forests, and deserts. In the most politically organized societies, such as that of Abyssinia[1] or the Ashanti kingdom,[2] there was more resistance to colonization, which delayed or impeded foreign domination. In organized, pre-colonial political systems, law – what we now refer to as customary law – existed. However, there were also many areas of the continent untouched by customary law because the forms of political authority that existed were not as complex as the political kingdoms or were simply non-existent.

During the colonial era, "customary law" regulated access to land for Africans and continues to govern land tenure over approximately 75 percent of Sub-Saharan Africa.[3] However, "customary law" during the colonial period was substantially different from that in the pre-colonial period as it was no longer an instrument of organization, but a tool of domination – a fact that has led some scholars to assert that it was reconstructed as something new during the colonial era.[4] Virtually every colonized country in Africa had two systems of landholding in the colonial era, one that was regulated by the state and one by customary law and traditional leaders. The land regulated by the state was privately held by settlers and only infrequently by Africans. The rest of the land was governed by customary law. Although privately held land might have changed hands at independence, reflecting changes in population and political fortunes, customary land was largely left untouched, still regulated by and for the collective ethnic group. At independence, few countries had the capacity to embark on the herculean effort of unifying the disparate landholding institutions. Instead, an institutional lock-in occurred and the existing, bifurcated landholding system has remained intact to the present day with private and customary lands existing and administered separately in every country in Sub-Saharan Africa except Ethiopia.[5]

[1] Abyssinia was the political kingdom that was a precursor to modern-day Ethiopia.
[2] Located in what is currently Ghana, the Ashanti kingdom resisted British control and was not incorporated into the empire completely until 1902.
[3] *See* Interview with Clarissa Augustinus, Chief, Land and Tenure Section, Shelter Branch, UN Habitat, regarding her presentation Key Issues for Africa and Globally (2003), in Tororo, Uganda (Sept. 14, 2005).
[4] *See* Terence Ranger, *The Invention of Tradition in Colonial Africa, in* THE INVENTION OF TRADITION (T. Ranger & E. Hobsbawm eds., Cambridge University Press 1983); Martin Chanock, *Paradigms, Policies and Property: A Review of the Customary Law of Land Tenure, in* LAW IN COLONIAL AFRICA (K. Mann & R. Roberts eds., Heinemann Educational Books 1991).
[5] *See* Sandra F. Joireman, *The Mystery of Capital Formation in Sub-Saharan Africa: Women, Property Rights and Customary Law*, 36(7) WORLD DEV. 1233 (2008).

Private and customary land tenure institutions each articulate a very different bundle of rights to land, necessitating two different control and enforcement regimes. In the colonial era, this dual system followed racial lines; natives used land, white colonizers owned it. Because colonial governments did not find conceptions of land holding that were equivalent to that of fee simple or exclusive land ownership among colonized peoples, it was assumed that landholding was vested in the community. Africans maintained rights to land as groups and those groups were overseen by a chief who controlled land allocation. White colonizers had their property recorded in legal documents and their disputes heard in state courts, while Africans pursued conflict resolution through customary authority figures and rarely had written documentation of their land claims.

The belief in African communal land rights was supported by two linked administrative impulses of the colonial government: 1) the colonial administration's need to expropriate land and govern its occupation and exchange with some degree of legality; and 2) the necessity of space for the indigenous population to live and to farm.[6] The British and the French followed different systems of organization in their colonies with the French choosing to rule directly through colonial officials, and the British following a system of "indirect rule" in which British colonial officials exercised power through local leaders.[7] Under the system of indirect rule, the best type of arrangement to meet the indigenous population's need for space required no administrative oversight by colonial officials; hence the creation of native reserves, customary tenure areas, or tribal homelands. These areas could be administered by "traditional" leaders without requiring expatriate civil servants working in the adjudicative and administrative institutions of the colonial state. Where traditional rulers could not be found, they were created and empowered. Where their previous powers did not relate to the administration of land, they were given new powers.

The colonial state was complicit in supporting property rights claims proffered by traditional leaders when they served the goals of administration and control. In Ghana, for example, different versions of "customary law" were presented to colonial officials for their support by self-interested leaders, each of whom described a different version of the customary practices in their community.[8] Colonial officials were then left to decide which version they would recognize. At independence, the

---

[6] *See* Chanock, *supra* note 4; MARTIN CHANOCK, LAW, CUSTOM, AND SOCIAL ORDER: THE COLONIAL EXPERIENCE IN MALAWI AND ZAMBIA (Heinemann Educational Books 2d ed. 1998); MAHMOOD MAMDANI, CITIZEN AND SUBJECT: CONTEMPORARY AFRICA AND THE LEGACY OF LATE COLONIALISM (Princeton University Press 1996).

[7] *See* Sandra F. Joireman, *Colonization and the Rule of Law: Comparing the Effectiveness of Common Law and Civil Law Countries*, 15 (4) CONST. POL. ECON. 315 (2004).

[8] KATHRYN FIRMIN-SELLERS, THE TRANSFORMATION OF PROPERTY RIGHTS IN THE GOLD COAST (Cambridge University Press 1996).

enforcement of customary land rights typically remained with traditional leaders, although their role is increasingly under threat.

Customary law is, and has been, malleable and dynamic. It has changed over time and, in this regard, it is similar to common law that evolves in response to changing circumstances and customs. Customary law was both named and developed in the context of colonization and it became a mechanism for the assertion of power by dominated groups during the colonial era. Customary law is explicitly political and can also be an arena for the struggle for power within a society.[9] During the colonial era, customary law provided a way for older men within traditional societies to reclaim some of the independence and control that they lost due to colonization. They were able to use customary law to assert control over women, younger men, and children within their ethnic group – the limited realm over which they were given authority by the colonial power. It has been observed that "those who were doing economically well within the limits imposed by the colonial regime were those who had the most interest in promoting a 'customary' view of persons. A view that could be presented and validated in customary terms."[10] To some extent, it is still the case that customary law can be used as a tool for the promotion of the interests of certain individuals who are given responsibility for its definition.[11] In a 2002 interview, a senior chief in Kenya recognized that customary law in the current era is created and molded by contemporary traditional authorities, saying, "Customary law is what I describe."[12] The emphasis in this claim is on the control of the customary leader over what is defined as law. It is malleable and subject to the interpretation of leaders. Similarly, with respect to the nature of customary authority, "[m]any of the supposed central tenets of African land tenure, such as the idea of communal tenure, the hierarchy of recognized interests in land (ownership, usufructory rights and so on), or the place of chiefs and elders, have been shown to have been largely created and sustained by colonial policy and passed on to post-colonial states."[13]

In communal tenure areas, where an emergent land market developed, colonial officials suppressed it because a land market did not fit with ideas regarding the communal nature of African land tenure.[14] Colonial officials persisted in the belief

---

[9] See Pius S. Nyambara, *Immigrants, 'Traditional' Leaders and the Rhodesian State: The Power of 'Communal' Land Tenure and the Politics of Land Acquisition in Gokwe, Zimbabwe, 1963–1979*, 27(4) J. S. AFR. STUD. 771 (2001); SARA BERRY, NO CONDITION IS PERMANENT (University of Wisconsin Press 1992).

[10] Chanock, *supra* note 4, at 72.

[11] See FRANCOISE KI-ZERBO, LES FEMMES RURALES ET L'ACCESS A L'INFORMATION ET AUX INSTITUTIONS POR LA SECURISATION DES DROIT FONCIERS, ETUDE DE CAS AU BURKINA FASO (FAO 2004).

[12] Human Rights Watch, *Double Standards: Women's Property Rights Violations in Kenya*, in KENYA 11 (Human Rights Watch 2003).

[13] Ann Whitehead & Dzodzi Tsikata, *Policy Discourses on Women's Land Rights in Sub-Saharan Africa: The Implications of the Re-turn to the Customary*, 3 (1 & 2) J. AGRARIAN CHANGE 67, 75 (2003).

[14] Evidence of the rapid evolution of land markets in the work of Hill (1963) on cocoa farming and Budy (1979) on South Africa, also work in Zimbabwe by Cheater (1990). In Ethiopia, in traditional tenure

that Africans defined themselves only in terms of their group and kinship ties, even with regard to their economic behavior. This has led to criticism of the entrapment of Africans in the "world of the customary":

> European rule in Africa came to be defined by a single-minded and overriding emphasis on the customary. For in the development of a colonial customary law, India was really a halfway house. Whereas in India the core of the customary was limited to matters of personal law, in Africa it was stretched to include land. Unlike the variety of land settlements in India, whether in favor of landlords or of peasant proprietors, the thrust of colonial policy in Africa was to define land as a communal and customary possession. Just as matters of marriage and inheritance were said to be customarily governed, so procuring basic sustenance required getting access to communal land. With this development, there could be no exit for an African from the world of the customary.[15]

I argue that whether Africans are entrapped within customary law or freed by the ability to express their social and economic interests within it depends on which group of Africans we are discussing, as the legal recognition of customary law and tenure systems creates winners and losers with different interests. Because it applies to people as members of ethnic groups and not as citizens, customary law constructs a separate arena of authority beyond or outside of the state.

13.3. CUSTOMARY VERSUS STATUTORY LAW: THE WINNERS AND LOSERS

As in the colonial era, those who gain the most from customary systems of land tenure and authority are those who control it. Because customary law is unwritten and customary authority positions can be quite powerful and lucrative, they are sometimes the subject of dispute. In 2008, struggles over succession to a Ghanaian chieftainship resulted in twenty deaths as well as a greater number of wounded people.[16] The violence surrounding these struggles is evidence of the desirability of chieftainships. One of the reasons traditional leadership positions are sought after is the potential to gain from control over land. With the development of land markets within customary land systems, for example, those who gain the most from emergent markets in land are those with the most influence over its allocation.[17]

---

systems, there was evidence of land sales in communal tenure areas with the monetization of the economy. Sandra F. Joireman, *Contracting for Land: Lessons from Litigation in a Communal Tenure Area of Ethiopia*, 30 (3) CANADIAN J. AFR. STUD. 424 (1996).

[15] Mamdani, *supra* note 6, at 50.

[16] *See* International Committee of the Red Cross, *Ghana: Red Cross helps victims of fighting in north* (July 10, 2008), *available at* http://www.icrc.org/Web/Eng/siteengo.nsf/htmlall/ghana-news-100708?Open Document&style=custo_print.

[17] *See* Admos Chimhowu & Phil Woodhouse, *Customary vs Private Property Rights? Dynamics and Trajectories of Vernacular Land Markets in Sub-Saharan Africa*, 6 (3) J. AGRARIAN CHANGE 346 (2006).

It is evident that customary authority figures benefit from the recognition of customary law and land tenure. However, there are additional benefits that can accrue to a community from customary systems of property rights. There is a rich literature documenting the flexibility of customary land and resource arrangements. This sort of flexibility can be particularly helpful in controlling common property resources such as forests, pasture land, and water.[18] At the same time, the use of customary institutions to control these resources further accentuates the divide between those governed by customary and those governed by statutory law.[19]

Customary law was formed for ethnic groups and is used to control and organize ethnic groups. As such, it is very much rooted in place rather than ethos or ideology. Integrating or blending customary law with statutory law, which is based on notions of citizenship, poses tremendous problems. Customary law relates to groups of people in a place and only loosely to those people who live outside of that place. Customary law also differs between ethnic groups in the same country. Thus, conceptions of citizenship that bring with them ideas of equality across national space and territory are often at odds with customary law. Take, for example, the pernicious problem of land rights for migrants. Although virtually every constitution in Sub-Saharan Africa enshrines notions of citizenship that transcend ethnicity and region, migrants within a country who seek to settle in rural areas still face tremendous difficulties in either purchasing or renting land to farm, and on which to build housing.[20]

As citizens of a country, migrants should have the same rights to property all over the country. Yet, they do not, as customary land tenure systems by their nature exclude those who are not autochthones, or "sons of the soil."[21] This restriction on property ownership prevents entrepreneurial activity by nationals who might like to move into an area and acquire land. In fact, it may be easier for foreigners to access land for economic development than nationals in their own country who are not of the right ethnic group for a particular area; contrast this with the ease with which one

---

[18] See Tor A. Benjaminsen & Christian Lund, *Formalisation and Informalisation of Land and Water Rights in Africa: An Introduction*, 14 (2) Eur. J. Dev. Res. 1 (2002); Camila Toulmin, Philippe Lavigne Delville, & Samba Traore, The Dynamics of Resource Tenure in West Africa (Heinemann Educational Books 2002); Philip Woodhouse, *African Enclosures: A Default Mode of Development*, 31 (10) World Dev. 1705 (2003).

[19] See Jesse C. Ribot, *Decentralisation, Participation and Accountability in Sahelian Forestry: Legal Instruments of Political-Administrative Control*, 69 (1) Afr. 23 (1999).

[20] See V. Adefemi Isumonah, *Migration, Land Tenure, Citizenship and Communal Conflicts in Africa*, 9 (1) Nationalism and Ethnic Pol. 1 (2003); Ki-Zerbo, *supra* note 11; Integrated Regional Information Network, Cote D'Ivoire: Solving Conflict on a Smaller Scale (2006). Nyambara, *supra* note 9; Pauline E. Peters & Daimon Kambewa, *Whose Security? Deepening Social Conflict over 'Customary' Land in the Shadow of Land Tenure Reform in Malawi*, 45 J. Modern Afr. Stud. 447 (2007); Marja J. Spierenburg, Strangers, Spirits, and Land Reforms: Conflicts about Land in Dande, Northern Zimbabwe (Brill 2004).

[21] See Isumonah, *supra* note 20; Peters & Kambewa, *supra* note 20; Spierenburg, *supra* note 20.

can purchase a farm in any area of Australia, the United States, Canada, or Europe. Any list of losers from customary land tenure arrangements has to include migrants, whose right to own property and live anywhere within the territory is thwarted by customary land ownership patterns and customary authority.

The second, and larger, group of losers from customary land tenure systems and their corresponding authority structures are women. Women in Sub-Saharan Africa face a distinctive social dilemma. Because of their labor, they are the mainstay of agricultural economies; yet, married women in most African countries do not co-own marital property, do not have autonomous rights to lineage or family land, and do not have the ability to protect and retain their homes and movable possessions at the death of or divorce from a husband. There are some encouraging exceptions to these problems of property rights in West Africa where women are able to maintain some rights through their natal lineages.[22] There are also some countries, such as Ghana, Mozambique, Namibia, and Ethiopia, where efforts have been made to give women legal protection of property rights where they have not traditionally existed.[23] That said, in much of Southern and Eastern Sub-Saharan Africa, women have not traditionally or legally shared the same protections of their property and inheritance rights as men, or women in other parts of the world. They face difficulty in representing themselves economically and legally, for example in selling their own produce or in buying new fields on which to grow crops.[24] In Rwanda, women were not recognized as full citizens until the 1991 constitution.[25] Previous to that point they were legal minors. If a Rwandan woman wanted to buy a plot of land, a building, or even a home, she had to either do so in the name of a male relative or establish a corporation that could act as a legal person for her.[26] The position and status of women in Africa is so critical and so unusual that it needs to be taken into consideration, not just by feminist scholars, but by anyone wanting to write seriously about agricultural development, property rights, or capital formation.

---

[22] *See* N. Thomas Hakansson, *The Detachability of Women: Gender and Kinship in Processes of Socioeconomic Change among the Gusii of Kenya*, 21 (3) AM. ETHNOLOGIST 516 (1994); interview with Dzodzi Tsikata, in Accra, Ghana (July 6, 2007).

[23] *See* Married Persons Equality Act 1 of 1996 (Namib.); ASKALE TEKLU, LAND REGISTRATION AND WOMEN'S LAND RIGHTS IN AMHARA REGION, ETHIOPIA (International Institute for Environment and Development 2005); *Women Lawyers Demand Early Passage of Property Rights of Spouses Bill*, GHANAIAN NEWS AGENCY, 2009; INTEGRATED REGIONAL INFORMATION NETWORK, MOZAMBIQUE: WOMEN STILL STRUGGLE FOR LAND RIGHTS DESPITE NEW LAW, (2003).

[24] In Uganda, for example, while women grow food crops, many ethnic groups view it as the job of the husband to sell the agricultural produce at the market. Focus group interview with Women's Guild of Tororo, Tororo, Uganda (Sept. 14, 2005).

[25] *See* L. Muthoni Wanyeki, *Introduction, in* WOMEN AND LAND IN AFRICA: CULTURE, RELIGION AND REALIZING WOMEN'S LAND RIGHTS (L. M. Wanyeki ed., Zed Books Ltd. 2003).

[26] *See id.*

In most parts of Sub-Saharan Africa, the idea of co-ownership of marital property is an alien one. Women are not supposed to own property but rather, under customary law, they are (or were) property. The idea of a woman acquiring property in her own name during marriage is incendiary, as it implies that she is not committed to her husband or his family.[27] In the few African countries where there are laws providing for the co-ownership of marital property, such as the family home or other assets, these laws have proven very difficult to enforce because they are incompatible with cultural practices.[28]

Typically women have secondary rights to land access, meaning they can cultivate land because they have married a man who is of a particular kinship group or they have children who are seen as belonging to a particular kinship group.[29] In many places, once they marry and go to live with their husband's family, women are not viewed as having membership in their lineage, but are seen in some ethnic communities as a member of their husband's lineage and in others simply as a commodity.[30] One women's organization in Uganda developed the slogan "Women Have No Home" to illustrate the difficulty women face as they are not seen as belonging to any kinship group.[31]

[27] This point was driven home in conducting interviews on the new land law in Uganda in 2006. In an interview with a woman who was the regional gender officer for her part of the country, a fairly elevated position and one in which she was required to assist women in defending their property rights, the interviewee reported that "Women can't own land and have stable marriages." *See* interview with widow J., Mbarara, Uganda (2006). This is a sentiment that was repeated, albeit less vividly, in other interviews and contexts. *See also* Human Rights Watch, *supra* note 12.

[28] *See* Jeanmarie Fenrich & Tracy E. Higgens, *Promise Unfulfilled: Law, Culture and Women's Inheritance Rights in Ghana*, 25 FORDHAM INT'L L.J. 259 (2001); Susana Lastarria-Cornhiel, *Impact of Privatization on Gender and Property Rights in Africa*, 25 (8) WORLD DEV. 1317 (1997); INTEGRATED REGIONAL INFORMATION NETWORK, INHERITANCE RIGHTS STILL A THORNY ISSUE, Feb. 14, 2006.

[29] *See* Winnie Bikaako & John Ssenkumba, *Gender, Land and Rights: Contemporary Contestations in Law, Policy and Practice in Uganda, in* WOMEN AND LAND IN AFRICA (L. M. Wanyeki ed., Zed Books Ltd. 2003); Wanyeki, *supra* note 25; Ingrid Yngstrom, *Women, Wives and Land Rights in Africa: Situating Gender Beyond the Household in the Debate over Land Policy and Changing Tenure Systems*, 30 (1) OXFORD DEV. STUD. 21 (2002); Whitehead & Tsikata, *supra* note 13.

[30] This is true even in matrilineal societies where descent is traced through the female line. That said, it would be wrong to suggest that in all circumstances under customary tenure women have no access to land through their own kin group. In West Africa, women will have some residual claim to land in their natal kinship group or through wider social ties. However, this is more the exception than the rule. There is an anthropological framework for understanding the differences in lineage attachment for women in Africa. There is a bifurcation between lineage systems in which women maintain an identity in their natal lineage after marriage and those lineage systems in which they do not. If a woman maintains a social identity formed by her natal lineage after marriage, she is likely to have property rights associated with that lineage. However, if she is "detachable" and is identified with her husband's clan or lineage after marriage, then she is likely to have few, if any, socially recognized property claims in her natal lineage. Hakansson, *supra* note 22.

[31] This was articulated as a slogan by the Mifumi Project, a Ugandan NGO active in women's issues.

The fact that women have only secondary rights to land is inequitable, but the degree to which it becomes problematic depends on demand for land in a given area. Some anthropologists have praised the flexibility of traditional customary arrangements because they can adapt to changing family composition more readily than more formalized systems.[32] Where demand for land is low, this is almost certainly true. However, when the value of land becomes higher it is easier for traditional leaders to find themselves unable to accommodate all requests for land to farm. Where there is a high demand for land, migrants, divorced women, and women in general are most likely to face exclusion.[33]

Women's property rights and access to land are linked to inheritance patterns. Under customary law, daughters tend to inherit less than sons, and often nothing at all.[34] Inheritance can also be problematic for surviving spouses. Aili Tripp notes that in Uganda, "under customary law ... a woman may have jointly acquired land with her husband and may have spent her entire adult life cultivating land, but she cannot claim ownership of the property. If he dies, the land generally goes to the sons, but may also be left to the daughters. Nevertheless, [the husband] may still leave the wife with no land and therefore no source of subsistence."[35] With the mortality effects of AIDS, civil conflict in Africa, and decreasing life expectancies for men and women, institutionalized inheritance structures are of particular interest in understanding patterns of capital formation.

In many polygamous households, if the head of household dies, any childless wives will receive nothing and will have to return to their families.[36] Because these women have not provided the lineage with heirs, they have no status and no further link to any member of the lineage. Therefore, they can no longer expect to receive access to lineage land on which to farm or live. Women with children are in a slightly less precarious position. They are still not regarded as members of the

[32] *See* Angelique Haugerud, *Land Tenure and Agrarian Change in Kenya*, 59 (1) AFR. 61 (1989); Jean Ensminger, *Changing Property Rights: Reconciling Formal and Informal Rights to Land in Africa, in* THE FRONTIERS OF NEW INSTITUTIONAL ECONOMICS (J. N. Drobak & J. V. C. Nye eds., Academic Press 1997).

[33] *See* In Zimbabwe, land-allocating authorities viewed divorced women in particular as social misfits. Nyambara, *supra* note 9, at 777.

[34] This is true even in Islamic areas where sharia law controls inheritance for women. In Nigeria, in the northern states where sharia law is recognized, women still do not inherit as dictated by sharia law. The reason given is that according to the Maliki school of sharia law, Nigeria is an area in which Islam was imposed by conquest and therefore some allowance for pre-existing customs, *urf*, must be allowed. Hussaina J. Abdullah & Ibrahim Hamza, *Women and Land in Northern Nigeria: The Need for Independent Ownership Rights, in* WOMEN AND LAND IN AFRICA (L. M. Wanyeki ed., Zed Books, Ltd. 2003).

[35] Aili Mari Tripp, *Women's Movements, Customary Law, and Land Rights in Africa: The Case of Uganda*, 7 (4) AFR. STUD. Q. 1, 6 (2004).

[36] *See* Bikaako & Ssenkumba, *supra* note 29.

lineage, however, if they are taking care of minors, their property rights will sometimes be respected.[37]

Some studies have argued that inheritance rights for women are not a problem. In Kenya, for example, one study found that most women are able to hold onto their land after the death of a husband by turning to the community as a whole to gain support in legitimizing the wife's claim to the land.[38] In this study, a woman losing her home and land after a husband has died was the 304exception rather than the rule. This would be consistent with other studies in Malawi, Swaziland, and Uganda finding that women are able to negotiate customary law and maintain usufruct rights to land through social networking.[39] However, these studies contradict the weight of evidence emphasizing the vulnerability of women's property rights after the death of a spouse. Other studies in Kenya document that spousal loss of property is a frequent occurrence.[40] In Uganda in 1995, the Federation of Women Lawyers (FIDA) reported that 40 percent of the cases they handled were related to the harassment of widows and property grabbing by their husbands relatives.[41] Poverty and scarcity of resources can tax the goodwill of family members. If a woman has property left by her husband that is viewed as valuable, she may find herself cast off with no land to cultivate and her household goods appropriated by members of the lineage. In Uganda in the Luwero and Tororo areas, about 29 percent out of a total of 204 widows indicated that property was taken from them following the death of their husbands.[42] In Zambia, "[i]n an area where livestock represents one of the few reserves of asset wealth, it was found that in the preceding five years, 41% of female-headed households with orphans had lost all their cattle and 47% had lost all their pigs."[43]

Women's loss of property upon the death of their husband is a human rights issue, but it is also an economic problem. As women tend to be the ones cultivating the

[37] *See* Interview with B, Tororo, Uganda (Sept. 14, 2005); RICHARD S. STRICKLAND, TO HAVE AND TO HOLD: WOMEN'S PROPERTY AND INHERITANCE RIGHTS IN THE CONTEXT OF HIV/AIDS IN SUB-SAHARAN AFRICA (International Center for Research on Women 2004); Tripp, *supra* note 35.

[38] *See* M. Aliber, C. Walker, M. Machera, P. Kamau, C. Omondi, & K. Kanyinga, *Overview and Synthesis of Research Findings, in* THE IMPACT OF HIV/AIDS ON LAND RIGHTS: CASE STUDIES FROM KENYA (Human Sciences Research Council 2004).

[39] *See* Laurel L. Rose, *Women's Strategies for Customary Land Access in Swaziland and Malawi: A Comparative Study,* 49 (2) AFR. TODAY 123 (2002); Lynn S. Khadiagala, *Justice and Power in the Adjudication of Women's Property Rights in Uganda,* 49 (2) AFR. TODAY 101 (2002).

[40] *See* Human Rights Watch, *supra* note 12; RITU VERMA, GENDER, LAND AND LIVELIHOODS IN EAST AFRICA: THROUGH FARMER'S EYES (International Development Research Centre 2001).

[41] *See* Bikaako & Ssenkumba, *supra* note 29, at 250.

[42] *See* LAELIA ZOE GILBORN, REBECCA NYONYINTONO, ROBERT KABUMBULI, & GABRIEL JAGWE-WADDA, MAKING A DIFFERENCE FOR CHILDREN AFFECTED BY AIDS: BASELINE FINDINGS FROM OPERATIONS RESEARCH IN UGANDA 1 (Population Council 2001).

[43] Strickland, *supra* note 37, at 24. The study gave no indication of how this property was lost. *Id.*

land to provide food for their families, their loss of land, livestock, and moveable property has economic consequences for their children and for society as a whole.

13.4. EVALUATING SOCIAL WELFARE

In spite of these considerations of equity, strong arguments have been made for the benefits of customary land tenure systems and customary adjudicatory mechanisms. In areas where land is relatively abundant, customary law can effectively regulate the distribution of land in a manner that has fewer transaction costs than using a more bureaucratized registration system. In these settings, formal systems of property rights show few benefits over customary systems of land rights and, when new systems of property rights are adopted from the top down, they are unlikely to be implemented fully as the transaction costs of land registration are too high to make it worthwhile for people to register their land. After the Ugandan Land Act of 1998 made it possible for people on customary land to title their land and exchange it through governmentally recognized methods, individuals in land-abundant areas still chose to go through locally recognized institutions of exchange rather than the legal system to document land transfers.[44] These individuals felt their land was sufficiently secure to preclude any need to go beyond the recognition of members of their local government in a land exchange. Until the value of land or its attributes increases sufficiently to offset the transaction costs, titling and more formalized land transfers will not be embraced.[45] Moreover, rather than promoting security of tenure, titling efforts may lead to higher levels of conflict over land and thereby reduce productivity.[46]

Given the health and welfare demands on African states, there seems to be little reason to interfere with a customary law system that is working well in a land-abundant setting. In these areas, state mechanisms to regulate the registration and transfer of land are unlikely to be utilized or enforced because individuals feel their security in ownership or occupancy is sufficiently robust. However, no country has abundant land resources in all areas, especially not in capital cities, which invariably have shantytowns and slums that house people without the money or connections necessary for land access. Moreover, there is increasingly a mix between customary tenure arrangements and modern state-administered tenure systems, particularly in

---

[44] See Elin Henrysson & Sandra F. Joireman, On the Edge of the Law: The Cost of Informal Property Rights Adjudication in Kisii, Kenya, SSRN (2007).

[45] See YORAM BARZEL, A THEORY OF THE STATE: ECONOMIC RIGHTS, LEGAL RIGHTS AND THE SCOPE OF THE STATE (Cambridge University Press 2002); TERRY L. ANDERSON & PETER J. HILL, THE NOT SO WILD, WILD WEST (Stanford University Press 2004).

[46] See Klaus Deininger & Raffaelle Castagnini, Incidence and Impact of Land Conflict in Uganda, in THE WORLD BANK POLICY RESEARCH WORKING PAPER (The World Bank 2004).

peri-urban areas. It is in these areas where tenure systems and authority structures mix and demand for land tends to be high that the two systems clash most visibly.

Where land is scarce and population densities are higher, land allocation is contested, conflict over land is more frequent, and resort to the courts for dispute settlement and recognition of land transfer is more likely. Consistent with the economic literature on institutional change, ample evidence exists demonstrating the breakdown of institutions and the innovation of new ones when land values increase in Africa.[47] In areas where land has a higher value, customary land ownership patterns can empower and enrich those who make decisions regarding its allocation. "Authority in land whether vested in the chiefs, or in the government officials and political leaders, can in turn, lead directly to private economic benefits for these actors, derived from land accumulation, patronage and land transactions."[48] Traditional leaders can practice the politics of exclusion, denying resources to groups with less political power, such as divorced women and migrants, who are easily identified and denied access to land communally held.[49]

When and where is it appropriate to try to explicitly undermine customary leadership and customary tenure, with the huge social costs that are entailed in any such attempt? This is not a politically correct question to either ask or answer. Yet, given the push for economic growth and better macroeconomic policies, it is worth considering by what criteria we might judge the effectiveness of any land tenure system or customary authority structure. One approach would be to assess the customary land tenure institutions from the 3D perspective and examine the extent to which they are well-defined, divestible, and defendable. However, in this chapter I would like to avoid the question of whether and how customary land should be bought or sold. Literature from the new institutional economics, as well as my own interview data from studying property rights across Sub-Saharan Africa, point to a set of criteria that can help us evaluate the net social welfare resulting from any institutional

---

[47] *See* John Bruce, Land Reform Planning and Indigenous Communal Tenure (1976) (S.J.D. dissertation, School of Law, University of Wisconsin); Joireman, *supra* note 14; SANDRA F. JOIREMAN, PROPERTY RIGHTS AND POLITICAL DEVELOPMENT IN ETHIOPIA AND ERITREA: THE STATE AND LAND, 1941–1974 (Ohio University Press 2000).

[48] Camila Toulmin & Julian Quan, *Introduction*, in EVOLVING LAND RIGHTS, POLICY AND TENURE IN AFRICA (C. Toulmin & J. Quan eds., IIED 2000).

[49] *See* The Mid-Zambezi Rural Development Project in Zimbabwe illustrates this problem. In this case it was the government of Zimbabwe that in the 1990s recognized an area of communally held land in Dande. They sought to reallocate the land in a more ecologically sustainable way that would be conducive to agricultural development and the resettlement of families living on former European-owned land. In the process of doing so, they effectively stripped land rights from migrants who had been living in the area peacefully and cooperatively for years. Spierenburg, *supra* note 20. By not recognizing that migrants were part of this community, and instead adhering to the old idea of communally held lands belonging collectively to one people group, the government repeated the error of colonization. *Id.*

structure. Below, I develop a rubric that recognizes the joint nature of tenure systems and authority structures. As far as I am aware, there is no area on the continent where customary leaders are recognized but customary tenure is not, or vice versa. In this case, it is wholly appropriate to consider the definition and the defense of property systems as a unified social institution that includes the rules of customary land tenure and the authority structures that enforce it.[50] The criteria I use to assess customary institutions are: predictability, accessibility, equity, effectiveness, and restraint. A measurement rubric is included in the appendix to this chapter.

First, any social institution must be transparent and predictable in terms of access and structure. This should be the case whether it is a social norm or a statute. If I own a house and want to improve it, I would like to know that I will own the house in three years; otherwise my benefit might not be worth the costs of making any changes. A property rights enforcement regime such as a customary dispute resolution process should assist people in maximizing their well-being by enabling long-term investment.[51]

Second, social institutions must be accessible to function well. Courts, mediators, or mechanisms that are so far away as to be too costly to reach in terms of money, time, or both are ineffective in resolving problems.[52] With "simple, local mechanisms, to get conflicts aired immediately and resolutions that are generally known in the community, the number of conflicts that reduce trust can be reduced."[53] Economic historians have also observed the importance of accessible conflict resolution mechanisms in the development of markets. Where conflict resolution mechanisms exist, markets with impersonal exchange can develop and thrive.[54]

---

[50] In Botswana and Kenya, however, although traditional leaders and customary land tenure co-exist, the leaders have been legally stripped of any control over land. *See* The Chieftainship Act of 1987; Chiefs' Act of 1997.

[51] *See* Louis De Alessi, *Gains from Private Property: The Empirical Evidence, in* PROPERTY RIGHTS: COOPERATION, CONFLICT AND LAW (T. Anderson & F. McChesney eds., Princeton University Press 2003); Hernando De Soto, THE MYSTERY OF CAPITAL (Basic Books 2000); Douglass C. North & Robert Paul Thomas, *An Economic Theory of the Growth of the Western World*, XXIII, (1) THE ECON. HIST. REV. 1 (1970); WORLD BANK, WORLD DEVELOPMENT REPORT 1997: THE STATE IN A CHANGING WORLD (Oxford University Press 1997).

[52] *See* Brynna Connolly, *Non-State Justice Systems and the State: Proposals for a Recognition Typology*, 38 CONN. L. REV. 239 (2005); Henrysson & Joireman, *supra* note 44; Minneh J. Oloka-Onyango Kane & Abdul Tejan-Cole, *Reassessing Customary Law Systems as a Vehicle for Providing Equitable Access to Justice for the Poor*, World Bank (2005), *available at* http://siteresources.worldbank.org/ INTRANETSOCIALDEVELOPMENT/Resources/ Kane.rev.pdf; Celestine Nyamu-Musembi, *Review of Experience in Engaging with Non-State Justice Systems in East Africa, in* INSTITUTE OF DEVELOPMENT STUDIES, Sussex University (2003).

[53] Elinor Ostrom, *Collective Action and the Evolution of Social Norms*, 14 (3) J. ECON. PERSPECTIVES 137 (2000).

[54] *See* AVNER GREIF, INSTITUTIONS AND THE PATH TO THE MODERN ECONOMY: LESSONS FROM MEDIEVAL TRADE (R. Calvert & T. Eggertsson eds., Cambridge University Press 2006).

Third, social institutions must meet minimum standards of equity.[55] Those that work only for one ethnic group or exclude one segment of the society are undesirable. Institutions that solve problems based on the highest payment received from participants are also unacceptable (based on standards of equity). The less biased an institution, the better it will be able to serve everyone within a society regardless of their social location.

Fourth, any kind of allocation or enforcement regime must be able to serve its role authoritatively and completely. Resolutions that are temporary, transient, or must eventually involve another institution are disadvantageous.[56] Temporary solutions indicate the powerlessness or insignificance of the institution and may also identify a cumbersome extra step in attempting to achieve a goal, whether it be land access or the resolution of a land conflict.

Lastly, social institutions are desirable to the extent that they do not rely on unrestrained violence.[57] Private allocation or enforcement of property rights through violence can both consume valuable resources and undermine the potential for economic progress.[58] Additionally, conflict resolution that occurs through violence can exacerbate, rather than resolve, disputes.

Using these five criteria – (1) predictability, (2) accessibility, (3) equity, (4) effectiveness, and (5) restraint – we can assess the net benefit of different property rights regimes and customary authority structures. Traditional authority structures and conflict resolution mechanisms are strongest in the areas of accessibility, effectiveness, and restraint and weakest in terms of equity and predictability. Traditional leaders and conflict resolution mechanisms are often far more accessible than national courts (high, according to the rubric in the appendix). They are able to effectively adjudicate most property conflicts and only rarely lead to decisions that needed to be appealed to national court systems (medium high). Moreover, traditional leaders and conflict resolution systems seldom use violence (medium high). However, they are not equitable in their adjudication of disputes as they favor the interests of men over women and autochthones over migrants even though both are citizens of the

---

[55] See Gary D. Libecap, *Distributional Issues in Contracting for Property Rights*, in THE NEW INSTITUTIONAL ECONOMICS (E. G. Furubotn & R. Richter eds., Texas A&M University Press 1991); DOUGLASS C. NORTH, UNDERSTANDING THE PROCESS OF ECONOMIC CHANGE (Princeton University Press 2005).

[56] See TERRY ANDERSON & FRED MCCHESNEY, PROPERTY RIGHTS: COOPERATION, CONFLICT AND LAW (T. Anderson & F. McChesney eds., Princeton University Press 2003); North, *supra* note 55.

[57] See Fred S. McChesney, *Government As Definer of Property Rights: Tragedy Exiting the Commons?*, in PROPERTY RIGHTS: COOPERATION, CONFLICT AND LAW (T. Anderson & F. McChesney eds., Princeton University Press 2003); Barry Weingast, *Constitutions as Governance Structures: The Political Foundations of Secure Markets*, 149 (1) J. INSTITUTIONAL AND THEORETICAL ECON. 286 (1993).

[58] See TERRY L. ANDERSON & LAURA E. HUGGINS, PROPERTY RIGHTS: A PRACTICAL GUIDE TO FREEDOM AND PROSPERITY (Hoover Institution Press 2003).

same country (low). Additionally, traditional leaders and conflict resolution mechanisms tend to make decisions that are compromises rather than a clear victory of one party over another in a dispute. While this type of decision making can preserve the integrity of the community, it renders traditional conflict resolution systems unpredictable in terms of the kinds of decisions that are made and the factors that are taken into consideration.

Although it will not be attempted here because of space considerations, the land tenure and dispute resolution systems of the government in each country could also be subjected to the same set of assessment measures and these institutions would rank high in some areas and low in others. Differences in the traditional and state institutions would indicate the reasons why people would choose one over the other or "forum shop."

13.5. WHITHER TRADITIONAL AUTHORITY STRUCTURES?

What can we learn from the use of this assessment measure and the issues that have been raised earlier in the chapter to better understand the role of traditional leaders and customary law in the contemporary African setting? The first major lesson is that there are conflicting authority structures that are delivering different bundles of social goods. Increasingly, government officials are going to be implicitly doing what I am explicit about here – assessing the effectiveness of the different existing institutional systems. In this context, I would argue that if traditional leaders want to maintain any sort of legally recognized authority, they must consider their roles carefully. They must articulate an institutional identity that is not based on representing a single ethnic group or a geographically bounded set of interests, but instead a set of societal concerns that may have importance beyond the locality. For example, they need to articulate their roles not as leading or constructing the legal parameters for their ethnic group, but as preserving and protecting the land (or forests or water resources) as the patrimony of all citizens of the country.

In a similar way, traditional leaders must begin to articulate the interests of the whole society – not just the men. If traditional leaders do not begin protecting and advocating for the economic and social well-being of women and children in their communities, they will find themselves slowly sidelined by alternative sources of societal power as women's groups begin to challenge their authority through legal action and legislation.

This leads to the second major lesson, which is that constitutional standards of equity matter. If customary leaders and customary law are to remain relevant, they must align with constitutional standards of equity and citizenship. Increasingly around Sub-Saharan Africa, we are seeing constitutional challenges to customary authority based on citizenship rights. The Bhe case in South Africa is one example.[59] In Uganda, women have articulated their demand for land in terms of constitutional guarantees of equality of citizenship and equality of economic rights.[60]

Lastly, traditional leaders and customary dispute resolution systems have a clear advantage in their ability to provide a cheaper and more accessible source of land allocation and conflict resolution than the state institutions in most contexts. If they can allocate land and resolve conflicts in a manner that aligns with constitutional concerns for equity and citizenship rights, then they are likely to be accommodated rather than undermined in any reform of property rights and conflict resolution systems that occurs.

13.6. CONCLUSION

This chapter began by discussing the genesis of the customary land tenure systems and their endurance into the present era. It then addressed how customary law creates a bifurcation of winners and losers in the society. Those who benefit from customary law are traditional leaders, men and communities who are able to use customary law to protect important resources. Losers under customary systems are migrants, local entrepreneurs, and women. Given this split in the society between winners and losers under customary law, this chapter proposed a rubric to assist in assessing the overall impact of customary law on social welfare. Following this, I offered some suggestions for how customary law and customary authority structures might endure in their usefulness to society by playing to their advantages of local knowledge and accessibility and addressing the weakness of inequity.

---

[59] *See Bhe v. The Magistrate, Khayelitsha* 2004 (2) SA 544 (C) (S. Afr.). In South Africa, women are guaranteed equal rights under the law by a constitution that also recognizes the rights of traditional leaders to allocate land. Given that in customary tenure systems women do not have access to land in their own right, it was inevitable that a case would be brought on behalf of a woman denied access to land. In South Africa, the decision of the constitutional court in the *Bhe* case famously argued that a woman must be allocated land by a traditional leader. However, the reason given in the ruling was not that she had equal standing as a citizen of South Africa and a member of that kin group, but rather that she had children that were members of that kin group and their rights could not be denied. What was important in the *Bhe* case was that the children were girls. A decision that these girls deserve access to land because they are members of the kin group was an affirmation of their membership in the lineage – a membership that was not previously explicit in the case of girls or women. For a comprehensive discussion of the *Bhe* case, see Christa Rautenbach and Willemien du Plessis, *Reform of the South African Customary Law of Succession: Final Nails in the Customary Law Coffin?*, in this volume.

[60] *See* Interview with Carol Bunga Idembe, Kampala, Uganda (Sept. 12, 2005); interview with Atuki Turner, Kampala, Uganda (Sept. 16, 2005).

APPENDIX

Institutional Assessment Rubric

	Low	Medium	High
Predictability	Unclear what the cost will be to utilize the institution. Unclear whether the institution will work or how it will work.	Not entirely apparent why or how decisions are made. Costs, documentation, and other needs unspecified.	Costs and time frame are clear up front. Needed documentation obvious. Nature of decision-making process is clear.
Accessibility	Not affordable for the average person either due to fees or side payments demanded. Location requires a large sacrifice in terms of time or money to reach.	Affordable for some people in the society, although beyond the reach of others, proximate to some, limited need for side payments.	Fees are affordable for the average person, proximate venue to people who will be accessing.
Equity	Only serves the needs of some members of society. Discriminates on the basis of sex, ethnicity, or other trait.	Discriminates against some members of the society, serves the needs of others.	Serves the needs of all members of the community. No discernable discrimination based on individual traits.
Effectiveness	Unlikely to resolve problem. Will need to pursue some other parallel or competing process to achieve goal.	Can resolve conflicts in certain circumstances, although in others it is necessary to pursue other institutional remedies.	Will resolve problem and/or provide service finally and completely.
Restraint	Processes rely on violence or the threat of violence, intimidation, or other harm.	While generally free from violence or intimidation, at times these can enter into the process.	Completely free from unrestrained or illegal use of violence and threats.

14

Romancing Customary Tenure

Challenges and Prospects for the Neo-Liberal Suitor

Janet L. Banda

14.1. INTRODUCTION

The importance of land-based resources for developing nations cannot be over-emphasized. Much as development in the global North is mostly associated with free trade, privatization of state enterprises, and security of private property rights, for developing nations, in particular sub-Saharan Africa, the achievement of development depends substantially on access to land and the uses to which such land is put. Security of tenure is therefore central to these ends. By virtue of its potential to attract investment and enhance rural livelihoods, tenure security represents the key ingredient to achieve economic growth and poverty reduction for sub-Saharan Africa.

Not surprisingly, contemporary land reforms target customary tenure because it constitutes the bulk of landholding by the majority poor on the continent and is perceived as insecure. The approach to customary tenure reform has thus mostly focused on conversion and privatization through title registration. The poor performance of this approach has given rise to the emergence of numerous scholarly volumes debating its failure and ultimately the neo-liberal approach to customary tenure reform,[1] which has resulted in poor agricultural productivity and food insecurity across the continent. Broad consensus on two issues has emerged in the

---

[1] "Neoliberal land policies emerge from a pro-market critique of conventional (generally state-directed) land policies." SATURNINO M. BORRAS JR., THE UNDERLYING ASSUMPTIONS, THEORY, AND PRACTICE OF NEOLIBERAL LAND POLICIES (Land Research Action Network 2005), http://www.landaction.org/display.php?article=328. "They deal with both public and private lands, and have manifested in four broad policy types: i) privatization and individualization of public/communal lands, ii) privatization and individualization of property rights in state and collective farms in (ex-)socialist and capitalist settings, iii) promotion of land rental markets, and iv) land sales. These policies have been formulated by broadly pro-market scholars and policymakers, and have been aggressively promoted by the World Bank and other international development institutions as the solution to persistent landlessness and poverty in the countryside of most developing countries." *Id.*

academia. First, that colonial and post-colonial land policy has impacted negatively on contemporary land reform efforts on the continent. Second, that the neo-liberal approach to customary tenure reform has failed miserably insofar as the focus has been on conversion of customary tenure.

The World Bank,[2] however, considers that the informal nature of customary tenure and customary land institutions is to blame for the persistent failure of customary tenure reform efforts, and aggressively advocates De Soto's theory,[3] which holds that formalization of land rights is key to tenure security and poverty reduction leading to economic growth. This view has no qualms about context in implementing reforms and pushes titling programs in the belief that individualization and privatization of land rights motivates investment in agriculture and promotes the growth of land markets through commoditization of land, resulting in land transfers to more dynamic farmers. Customary tenure has no place here to the extent that it is considered vague, insecure, and inalienable and allegedly "tends to be both static in its technology and relatively insular."[4] Thus, the World Bank takes the "abolitionist"[5] approach to customary tenure reform.

While acknowledging the on-going debate, this chapter is more interested in emerging developments on the continent that have seen the strengthening of the "living customary tenure" (referring to contemporary customary landholding patterns and practices) and attempts to contribute to the debate by identifying two obvious but often neglected causes of the failure of the neo-liberal approach to customary tenure reform. The first is the continued presentation by African governments of the reconstructed customary tenure – aptly termed "the shadow"[6] – as an effective partner to neo-liberal land reforms. The chapter argues that this results in misrecognition of customary tenure and contributes to the lack of interest in emerging empirical evidence on the potentialities of the living customary tenure as an effective partner. The second factor, influenced by lack of understanding of customary tenure, is the World Bank's commitment to an inappropriate theoretical framework in marketing neo-liberal land reforms. This framework emphasizes transformation of existing indigenous tenure systems as opposed to affirmation of such systems. In contrasting the two approaches, I consider that "affirmation" approaches to tenure

---

[2] *See* THE WORLD BANK, LAND REFORM: A SECTOR POLICY PAPER (1975); THE WORLD BANK, SUB-SAHARAN AFRICA: FROM CRISIS TO SUSTAINABLE GROWTH (1989); THE WORLD BANK, LAND POLICIES FOR GROWTH AND POVERTY REDUCTION (2003).

[3] *See* HERNANDO DE SOTO, THE MYSTERY OF CAPITAL: WHY CAPITALISM TRIUMPHS IN THE WEST AND FAILS EVERYWHERE ELSE (Black Swan 2001).

[4] THE WORLD BANK, LAND REFORM: A SECTOR POLICY PAPER, *supra* note 2, at 19.

[5] Patrick McAuslan, Improving Tenure Security for the Poor in Africa: Framework Paper for the Legal Empowerment Workshop-Sub-Saharan Africa (2006) (unpublished manuscript).

[6] Martin Chanock, *Paradigms, Policies and Property: A Review of the Customary Law of Land Tenure, in* LAW IN COLONIAL AFRICA (K. Mann & R. Roberts eds., Heinemann 1991).

reform would refer to reforms that aim at recognizing and incorporating local tenure arrangements in a bid to correct inequitable access to land and enhance tenure security without disturbing the underlying framework that generates them. On the other hand, transformation approaches would be concerned with reforms that aim at replacing local tenure arrangements in a bid to correct inequitable access to land and enhance security of tenure by restructuring the underlying generative framework.[7] I argue that by seeking to transform and change the underlying generative framework of customary tenure, transformation approaches advocated by the Bank result in deconstruction and "non-recognition" of customary tenure and guarantee their inadequacy and failure. The issue therefore goes beyond mere efficacy and relevancy of the neo-liberal approach itself and questions the theoretical framework adopted by the World Bank in marketing neo-liberal land reforms. Hence, the totality of the argument in this chapter is that the combination of "mis-recognition" and "non-recognition" of customary tenure by African governments and the World Bank aggravates its oppression, which is the major hurdle to achieve effective customary tenure reform on the continent. As argued elsewhere, "[n]on-recognition or misrecognition ... can be a form of oppression imprisoning someone in a false, distorted, reduced mode of being. Beyond simple lack of respect, it can inflict a grievous wound.... Due recognition is not just a courtesy but a vital human need."[8] Applying this principle to approaches adopted in implementing customary tenure reform over the years exposes the extent of the grievous wound inflicted on customary tenure that has resulted in crippling its potential to adapt effectively to changing social and economic conditions.

Likewise, it has been argued that integrity requires approval or recognition from others[9] and, drawing an analogy, the integrity of customary tenure requires approval and recognition from its suitor, neo-liberalism, to result in an effective partnership. Denial of recognition amounts to disrespect and impairs the potential of customary tenure to adapt.

In discussing these issues, this chapter seeks to pose a number of pertinent questions. Why are contemporary land policies and statute books on the African continent still saddled with the shadow? More importantly, why do governments retain this shadow when it does not benefit the poor and it is generally accepted that it was a tool for control of indigenous communities during colonial times? What is

---

[7] I am indebted to Nancy Fraser for this understanding of these two concepts, which she uses in relation to politics of recognition. *See* Nancy Fraser, *From Redistribution to Recognition? Dilemmas of Justice in 'Post-Socialist' Age*, 212 New Left Rev.70 (1995).

[8] *Id.* at 71 (quoting CHARLES TAYLOR, MULTICULTURALISM AND THE POLITICS OF RECOGNITION 25 (Princeton 1992)).

[9] *See* AXEL HONNETH, THE STRUGGLE FOR RECOGNITION: THE MORAL GRAMMAR OF SOCIAL CONFLICTS (Polity Press 1996).

the motive behind the World Bank's continued commitment to the transformation approach to customary tenure reform despite its record of failure over half a century? What alternative theoretical framework may the World Bank explore in marketing neo-liberal approaches to customary tenure reform? The larger research project of which this chapter is a part seeks to engage with these questions and assess the strategies imposed in colonial, post-colonial, and contemporary land policies to effect customary tenure reform with particular reference to the impact of these strategies on the living customary tenure. This chapter then proposes a way forward.

In focusing on customary tenure and its potentialities, my perspective is one that sees the development of contemporary land policies and land relations in sub-Saharan Africa as shaped largely and regrettably by national choices and influences of international lending and development agencies, in particular the World Bank. It is indeed "regrettable that almost half a century after decoloni[z]ation, coloni[z]ation is still blamed as the culprit for the poor state of African economies and poor land relations in particular."[10] This chapter seeks to reflect the view that the substance and nature of contemporary land policies in sub-Saharan Africa rests on unreliable foundations due to poor policy choices, hence contributing to the problematic nature of customary tenure reform.

Let me enter two preliminary caveats. This chapter does not claim that customary tenure is uniform on the African continent; various studies have shown otherwise. The idea therefore is to zero in on the common and salient features of customary tenure in general. Further, the chapter does not claim that pre-colonial customary tenure was static but rather emphasizes the influence of colonial and post-colonial policies in shaping the path of evolution of present-day customary tenure, which has resulted in compromising its capabilities.

14.2. THE SHADOW FACTOR AND ITS IMPLICATIONS

Present-day customary tenure has both colonial and post-colonial tendencies culminating in the shadow. The shadow is the model of customary tenure constructed by colonial authorities and adopted by post-colonial states. It is based "on imperfect and muddled empirical evidence" and has had great influence on ideology about customary tenure shortcomings and tenure reform requirements on the continent.[11] The shadow exhibits three significant characteristics, which contribute to the failure of achieving effective customary tenure reform: the "communal" paradigm, which has done the greatest damage to the evolution of customary tenure; the exalted role

---

[10] McAuslan, *supra* note 5.
[11] Catherine Besteman, *Individualisation and the Assault on Customary Tenure in Africa: Title Registration Programmes and the Case of Somalia,* 64 J. INT'L AFR. INST. 484–515 (1994).

of chiefs in land management and allocation functions; and the alteration in the land rights of women. The combination of these three characteristics has resulted in mis-recognition of customary tenure and the focusing of land reform efforts on futile theoretical tenure arrangements.

14.2.1. *The Communal Paradigm*

In both colonial and post-colonial states, customary land was considered "occupied but not owned" based on the perception that it did not satisfy western concepts of ownership.[12] Additionally, customary land was declared inalienable due to its alleged communal nature. These notions about the nature of customary tenure were perpetuated by judicial decisions. For example, in 1919, Lord Sumner in the case of *In re Southern Rhodesia* condescendingly stated that:

> [t]he estimation of the rights of aboriginal tribes is always inherently difficult. Some tribes are so low in the scale of social organization that their usages and conceptions of rights and duties are not to be reconciled with the institutions or the legal ideas of civilized society.... It would be idle to impute to such people some shadow of the rights known to our law and then to transmute it into the substance of transferable rights of property as we know them.[13]

Likewise, in 1926, the Judicial Committee of the Privy Council, in the case of *Sobhuzan v Miller and others* stated that "[t]he notion of individual ownership is foreign to native ideas. Land belongs to the community not to the individual.... The title of the native community generally takes the form of a usufructuary right."[14] This narrow construction of customary tenure generally influenced economic policies involving customary land dealings. Consequently, land policies based on the premise that customary landholding patterns did not provide the necessary security to ensure agricultural investment and productive use of land, due to their communal nature, were aggressively pursued.[15] These policies encouraged and recognized a system of property rights based on western concepts of ownership as the only vehicle to the development of African nations.

The communal paradigm still reigns, but empirical evidence indicates that customary tenure is not exclusively communal. For example, studies have shown that

---

[12] *See* Liz A. Wily, *Land Rights Reform and Governance in Africa: How to make it work in the 21st Century*, (March 2006) (unpublished manuscript, on file with the United Nations Development Program), *available at* http://www.undp.org/oslocentre/docs07/Land_Rights_Reform_and_Governance_in_ Africa.pdf.

[13] (1919) AC 211, pp. 233–234.

[14] (1926) AC 518, p. 525.

[15] *See* Pauline Peters, *Challenges in Land Tenure and Land Reform in Africa: Anthropological Contributions*, 37 WORLD DEV. 1317–1325 (2009).

ownership rights under customary tenure exist in bundles and that these bundles are capable of disentanglement.[16] In conceptualizing the nature of customary tenure, one study from 1969 proposed a categorization of rights and interests in customary land to better understand customary tenure: "It is clear that there are two main sets of power which have to be distinguished, those to administer and control the [customary] land contingently, though the powers are concurrent, vested in superior positions, and the rights of beneficial enjoyment in particular items of land vested in these positions and in subordinates."[17]

Thus, the two main sets of powers are set forth as estates of administration and estates of production, with the former referring to rights of allocation, user control, and disposal restriction whereas the latter refers to the rights of beneficial use. Similarly, a recent discussion of the existence of the bundle of rights under customary tenure categorized these into two broad groups: "operational rights," covering those of access and use vested with individuals or small family units; and "management rights," covering allocation and transfer of land rights vested in the larger landholding group.[18] By categorizing the interests in customary land as such, one may begin to unbundle the rights to understand how concepts related to ownership of land under common law operate similarly under customary tenure, including the recognition of primary and lesser interests in land, which still amount to ownership.[19] Thus, operational rights or estates of production, which are, in a loose sense, "freeholds"[20] and "leaseholds,"[21] may be equated with those rights of beneficial use exercised by individuals or corporate bodies in western societies, whereas management rights or estates of administration would be congruent with those rights exercised by agents on behalf of the sovereign authority regarding granting of leases, freeholds, and user control.

It is therefore incorrect to conclude that mere existence of rules at the community level deprives individuals of ownership rights over allocated parcels of land and renders customary tenure exclusively communal. Further, the fact that customary tenure is unwritten and individual ownership rights exist within the context of a community does not render them any less secure. "[C]ustomary land law, being of local

---

[16] *See, e.g.,* MAX GLUCKMAN, IDEAS AND PROCEDURES IN AFRICAN CUSTOMARY LAW (Oxford University Press 1969).

[17] *Id.* at 55.

[18] *See* J. Chauveau & J. Colin, *Changes in Land Transfer Mechanisms: Evidence from West Africa, in* CHANGES IN CUSTOMARY LAND TENURE SYSTEMS IN AFRICA (Lorenzo Cotula ed., Int'l Inst. Envtl. Dev. 2007).

[19] *See infra* Part 3.2 (discussing relevant land rights under common law).

[20] A "freehold" is "[a]n estate in land or other real property, of uncertain duration; that is, either of inheritance or which may possibly last for the life of the tenant." *See* BLACK'S LAW DICTIONARY (6th ed. 1991).

[21] Broadly defined, a "leasehold" is a right to possess land for a fixed or ascertainable length of time. *See* RODGER SMITH, INTRODUCTION TO LAND LAW (Pearson 2007).

origin and application, is not uncertain in the eyes of the members of the community within which it operates."[22] Security of tenure in African societies is maintained through open-ended, on-going processes of negotiation, adjudication, and political maneuver as afforded by the customary norms of the community.[23] This is evidenced by findings from Botswana, for example, where registration certificates have made little impact, because customary landholders are assured of continuous and unchallenged use of their land based on customary tenure. Customary tenure alone has contributed more to the perception of a secure tenure than the certificates.[24]

The adoption of the concept of the communal by colonial authorities may be attributed to two factors: "misdirected paternalism and incomprehension of complex customary land ownership and land access norms"; and "political and administrative convenience."[25] The latter is associated with power motivations and culminated in political domination through a partnership between colonial authorities and chiefs, with colonial authorities giving chiefs control over the allocation of land through a system that insisted on communal land rights.[26] It was feared that granting individuals private property rights would disrupt the social fabric of rural communities and remove a privileged means of stabilizing the conquered country and consolidating colonial power.[27] This approach led to the imposition of the statutory principle of inalienability of customary land to achieve both the objective of preventing landlessness among indigenous communities and to control the key important resource. There is evidence that this principle was strongly opposed by indigenous communities in some parts of Africa, such as in Ghana, Uganda, Kenya, Malawi, and Tanzania, and people devised ways of circumventing it through pledges and other temporary transfers that were permanent in effect.[28]

One may then question the extent of inalienability of land held under customary tenure. Although customary tenure is not designed for western concepts of credit, empirical evidence has shown that customary land relations are dynamic. Simplified ways of accessing loans on security of land do exist, and temporary land transfers for rentals and pledges and even sales of part of family lands in times of need do occur.

---

[22] Frank Mifsud, Customary Land Law in Africa 45 (United Nations Food & Agriculture Organization 1967).

[23] See Sara Berry, No Condition is Permanent – the Social Dynamics of Agrarian Change in Sub-Saharan Africa (University of Wisconsin Press 1993).

[24] See Government of Botswana, Report of the Presidential Commission on Land Tenure, December (1983).

[25] Wily, *supra* note 12, at 8.

[26] See Robert Bates, *Some Conventional Orthodoxies in the Study of Agrarian Change*, 26 World Politics 234–254 (1984).

[27] See Jean-Philippe Platteau, *Land Reform and Structural Adjustment in sub-Saharan Africa: Controversies and Guidelines* (United Nations Food & Agriculture Organization, Economic and Social Development Paper 107, 1992).

[28] See Bates, *supra* note 26.

The growing body of evidence on the emergence of these "vernacular rural land sales and rental markets"[29] indicates the dynamics of customary land relations and unique ownership arrangements, and requires specific attention when implementing customary tenure reform. It also accentuates the potential of customary tenure to accommodate innovations due to the changing socio-political and economic landscape. With respect to the dynamism of customary tenure, the impact of growing population pressure and increasing commercialization of agriculture since colonialism has given rise "to gradual but meaningful changes in land tenure arrangements in the direction of enhanced individualization of tenure and larger incidence of land transactions."[30] Likewise, "corporate-tenure land is much less static and inalienable than the ideal model and western logic lead one to believe."[31] In fact, commoditization of land is not a new thing in African societies, even though it operates in a different context. This has led some commentators to observe that customary law merely discourages outright alienations of land as opposed to positively forbidding such transactions in its quest to conserve land resources for future generations.[32] The inalienability of customary tenure is thus exaggerated.

With this background in mind, one would then question why the communal paradigm still monopolizes contemporary land policies and statute books. Could this be attributed to "misdirected paternalism and incomprehension of complex customary land ownership and land access norms" on the part of most African governments? Is it a simple case of "political and administrative convenience" to facilitate control of rural communities? Or better still, is it a question of pure negligence or recklessness on the part of African leaders in view of growing empirical evidence suggesting a change of strategy is necessary?

14.2.2. *The Exalted Role of Chiefs in Land Management and Allocation Functions*

A number of scholars have written on how the role of chiefs regarding land matters changed during the colonial period and how this has affected security of tenure of

---

[29] Admos Chimhowu & Phil Woodhouse, *Customary vs. Private Property Rights? Dynamics and Trajectories of Vernacular Land Markets in Sub-Saharan Africa*, 6 J. AGRARIAN CHANGE 346–371 (2006) (arguing that recognition of the specific characteristics of "vernacular land markets" thus "commoditised land transfers within the framework of customary tenure is essential if state land policies are to promote the interest of the poor").

[30] *See generally*, Platteau *supra* note 27.

[31] John Cohen, *Land Tenure and Rural Development in Africa*, in AGRICULTURE DEVELOPMENT IN AFRICA: ISSUES OF PUBLIC POLICY 349–400 (R.H. Bates & M.F. Lofchie eds., Praeger 1980).

[32] *See* A. MULOLWA, APPROPRIATE TENURE MODEL FOR SUB-SAHARAN AFRICA (2002), http://www.fig. net/pub/fig_2002/Ts7-7/TS7_7_mulolwa.pdf; L. CAROLA, IS LAND INALIENABLE? HISTORICAL AND CURRENT DEBATES ON LAND TRANSFERS IN GHANA (2006), http://www.mpl.ird.fr/colloque_foncier/ communications/PDF/Lentz.pdf.

customary land. In describing the extent of the reconfiguration of custom in the
early colonial period, it has been noted that:

> There is a profound connection between the use of the chieftaincy as an institution
> of colonial government and the development of the customary law of land tenure.
> The development of the concept of a leading customary role for the chiefs with
> regard to ownership and allocation of land was fundamental to the evolution of
> the paradigm of customary tenure.... The chiefs were seen as the holders of land
> with rights of administration and allocation. Rights in land were seen as flowing
> downward.[33]

This exalted role of chiefs and elders under colonial governments in land allocation responsibilities and land management was in sharp contrast to their previous
role in pre-colonial societies. For example, this new role assumed customary land
ownership rights for the chiefs where previously only trusteeship rights existed.[34] A
chief's authority over a specific area previously represented a sphere of jurisdiction,
"not a property *per se*."[35] Thus the role of chiefs shifted from custodianship of customary land for the benefit of communities to landlordism. Anthropologists have
also written on a number of occasions that the responsibilities of the chiefs in land
management and allocation in pre-colonial times, where trusteeships existed, did
not extend to the power to alienate the land, which is congruent with ownership
rights. Not surprisingly, the Report of the Presidential Commission of Inquiry on
Land Policy Reform in Malawi, popularly known as the "Saidi Report," found that
when the chiefs gave concessions to white settlers in pre-colonial times, they did not
intend to alienate the land, as they were aware of their limited power regarding land
administration and allocation.[36] Arguably, the chiefs thought they were following
the usual system of allocating pieces of land to village groups in giving these concessions, albeit on a larger scale.

Findings from a study of Pondoland in South Africa support these sentiments.
It found that chiefs did not exercise power by controlling access to parcels of land
because distribution of land was left to homesteads. The chiefs only had control over
communal resources such as graveyards and forests.[37] Likewise, it has been argued that:

> In African property regimes the role of authority structures in relation to land was
> primarily to guarantee rights of access to productive resources, to regulate use of

---

[33] Chanock, *supra* note 6, at 64.

[34] *See* Ann Whitehead & Dzodzi Tsikata, *Policy Discourses on Womens' Land Rights in sub-Saharan
Africa: The Implications of the Return to the Customary*, 3 J. AGRARIAN CHANGE 67–112 (2003).

[35] Wily, *supra* note 12, at 20.

[36] *See* Malawi Government, Final Report of the Presidential Commission of Enquiry on Land Policy
Reform, Vol. 1 (March, 1999).

[37] *See* W. BEINART, THE POLITICAL ECONOMY OF PONDOLAND, 1860–1930 (Cambridge University
Press 1982).

common property resources and to help resolve disputes. Rights to land did not derive from an allocation by a land-owning political class, but from an entitlement of "citizenship." There was a relative balance of power between the leadership and rights holders, as well as between different levels of social political authority, which created a "downward accountability" of authority structure to commoners.[38]

The shift in the role of chiefs in land matters in colonial times therefore introduced a new paradigm in customary tenure, which persists to the present day and is a major problem for the African land question. It introduced "upward accountability" that left citizens in the cold and facilitated the "emergence of a (colonial) model of communal tenure premised on 'ownership' of land by chiefs" – a concept "at odds with indigenous notions of land rights."[39] This "feudal model" linked British land law and colonial contexts and fitted well with British ways of thinking about states and societies, and hence, served the interests of colonial administrators.[40]

In most post-colonial states, statutory law empowered chiefs to manage and administer customary land on behalf of governments for the benefit of communities. Contemporary land policies have mostly embraced this approach and perpetuate insecurity of customary tenure, because customary landholders are in effect tenants-at-will of both chiefs and governments. A pertinent question then becomes: Whose interest is this arrangement serving? Is it a strategy to control and govern rural communities through the use of chiefs? Or is it a strategy to consolidate power by rulers on the continent especially in this era of multiparty politics where evidence shows that chiefs are increasingly becoming agents of ruling parties (as in Malawi)? In view of the extent of evolution of customary tenure since colonial times, how relevant are chiefs in modern times as trustees of customary land, and how competent and effective is the institution of chieftaincy in land management and allocation functions to ensure equitable access to customary land in the twenty-first century?

14.2.3. *Altered Land Rights of Women*

The third paradigm shift in customary tenure relates to the land rights of women. The character of women's land rights was altered significantly during colonialism. As noted by one commentator, "[t]he ambivalence of the colonial regime towards recognition of male rights in land was not a problem when it came to women:

---

[38] Ben Cousins, Director, Programme for Land and Agrarian Studies, School of Government, University of the Western Cape, Aninka Claassens, *More Than Simply 'Socially Embedded': Recognizing the Distinctiveness of African Land Rights*, Address at International Symposium titled "At the Frontier of Land Issues: Social Embeddedness of Rights and Public Policy" 11 (May 17–19, 2006), *available at* http://www.landrightswatch.net/filestore/distinctiveness_of_african_land_rights.rtf.

[39] Wily, *supra* note 12.

[40] *See id.*

the customary regime of the colonial states did not accommodate at all the idea of women as landowners.... Claims by women, in the name of custom, were viewed with impatience as an impediment to the development process ..."[41]

Colonial authorities interpreted customary law with the purpose of strengthening patriarchal controls over women and encouraging a level of subordination to male kin that was new to customary law.[42] This project not only embraced the imposition of euro-centric views and prejudices but also involved the collusion of male patriarchs in African societies who were anxious to harness their diminishing control over female reproductive and productive power.[43] It is therefore not surprising that colonial legislation and policy regarding land rights of women resulted in denying women land rights – a situation that persists to the present day. Contemporary land policies have failed to address the issue of women's land rights, and titling and registration programs have aggravated insecurity of tenure and hindered access for women.[44]

Overall, adherence to the shadow has resulted in mis-recognition of customary tenure and is responsible for the gap between the lawyers' customary tenure found in land policies and statute books and the living customary tenure. This gives rise to tensions between the formal institutions that promote the shadow and the informal institutions that regulate practice. Customary tenure reform thus continues to be undermined through resistance in the form of local systems and social values.[45] With such tensions, it is indeed baffling why the shadow is still paraded as the ideal partner to neo-liberal land reform approaches.

14.3. THE NEO-LIBERAL APPROACH AND ITS SHORTCOMINGS

14.3.1. *Colonial, Post-Colonial, and World Bank Approaches*

During colonial times, customary tenure was ignored on the assumption that it was merely a stage in the historical evolution of societies and that it would wither away as western civilization introduced by colonial administrators became progressively

---

[41] Chanock, *supra* note 6.

[42] *See* C. WALKER, LAND REFORM IN SOUTHERN AND EASTERN AFRICA: KEY ISSUES FOR STRENGTHENING WOMENS ACCESS TO LAND (Food and Agricultural Organisation (March 2002) (unpublished report), http://info.worldbank.org/etools/docs/library/36270/WWalker-Land%20Reform %20and%20Gender.pdf.

[43] *See id.*

[44] *See* J. Asimwee, *Making Womens Land Rights a Reality in Uganda: Advocacy for Co-ownership by Spouses,* 4 YALE HUM. RTS. & DEV. L.J. 171 (2001); Celestine Nyamu-Musembi, *De Soto and Land Relations in Rurla Africa: Breathing Life Into Dead Theories About Property Rights,* Institute of Development Studies, Working Paper No. 272, 2006).

[45] *See* SECURING LAND RIGHTS IN AFRICA (Tor A. Benjaminsen & Christian Lund eds., Frank Kass 2003).

dominant in African societies.[46] This assumption influenced both the colonizers and post-independence states to adopt a transformation approach that ignored customary tenure and aggressively pursued policies that sought to replace it with new systems of land law based on western concepts. This approach was especially influenced by two key reports published toward the end of colonialism: the Report of the East Africa Royal Commission (1953–1955), and the 1954 Swynnerton *Plan to Intensify African Agriculture In Kenya*. Both of these reports emphasized the importance of replacing customary systems of landholding with modern systems through legal intervention and dictated the importance of individualization efforts for Africa. This influence carried into post-colonial Africa.[47]

With such propaganda against customary tenure, it is not surprising that no effort was made to interrogate the potentialities of customary tenure systems and identify key characteristics of such systems, despite the opportunity presented to new African leaders by the attainment of independence. This negligence, coupled with inadequate legislative assistance offered to the necessary process of modifying the indigenous systems of land tenure to enable such systems to cope with changing circumstances from colonial times, compounded the oppression of customary tenure.[48] The emphasis on a change of landholding patterns resulted in non-recognition of customary tenure and the valorizing of conversion and individualization of customary land rights to suit western ideals. The approach was concerned with the imposition of modernization on traditional systems through the transformation of the underlying cultural and socio-political structure of customary tenure systems. It was concerned also with integrating customary interests into the statutory system through title registration – an approach that leads to extinguishments of such interests.[49]

---

[46] *See* M.P.K. Sorreson, Land Reform in the Kikuyu Country: A Case Study in Government Policy (Oxford University Press 1967); G. Feder & R. Noronha, *Land Rights Systems and Agricultural Development in Sub-Saharan Africa*, 2 World Bank Res. Observer 143 (1987); Platteau, *supra* note 27; H.W.O. Okoth-Ogendo, *Legislative Approaches to Customary Tenure and Tenure Reform in East Africa*, in Evolving Land Rights, Policy and Tenure in Africa (C. Toulmin & J. Quan eds., International Institute for Environmental Development 2000).

[47] For example, Dr. Hastings Kamuzu Banda, the first President of Malawi, stated the following during a debate on land bills:

Under the present method of landholding and land tillage ... we can never hope to develop this country economically with agriculture as the backbone to our economic development ... the first thing we had to do to ameliorate the situation or to lessen the seriousness of the problem, was to change our methods of landholding or land tenure and the second was to change our methods of land cultivation or land tillage.

Fourth Session of Malawi Parliament 402 (April 4, 1967).

[48] *See* K. Bentsi-Enchill, *The Traditional Legal Systems of Africa*, in Property and Trust 68 (F.H. Lawson, International Encyclopedia of Comparative Law 1975).

[49] *See* Obiero v. Opiyo, (1972) E.A.L.R. 227 (Kenya); Esiroyo v. Esiroyo, (1972) E.A.L.R 388 (Kenya). In both cases it was found that title registration extinguishes customary interests in land.

The overall effect of the transformation approach in both colonial and post-colonial Africa has been manifold. The proper functioning of the customary tenure systems has been drastically affected. The effectiveness of customary institutions has been rendered inadequate to deal with land disputes in view of the emergence of new rules of customary tenure churned out by traditional courts established from colonial period. Furthermore, the legitimacy of customary systems and institutions has been undermined, which affects the integrity of such systems. These effects have resulted in further change to the nature and context of customary land rights and have important distributional consequences, typically eroding secondary rights, especially those of women.[50]

The World Bank, which has been the key international actor in setting the policy agenda on issues of land tenure, took over both colonial and post-colonial policies of land management in Africa without in-depth analysis of the African land question. Early World Bank studies and reports blamed customary tenure for the failure of agriculture in Africa. This is amply illustrated in the recommendations of the International Bank Missions to post-independence nations in the early 1960s and in later policy research reports such as the seminal World Bank *Land Reform: A Sector Policy Paper* (1975) and World Bank *Sub-Saharan Africa: From Crisis to Sustainable Growth* (1989). In these documents, the Bank encouraged a modern statutory system of registered title. In propagating for the redefinition of land rights in the 1989 report, the World Bank proclaimed: "One important incentive [to farmers] is the right to permanently cultivate land and bequeath it or sell it. Secure land rights also help rural credit markets to develop, because land is good collateral.... Traditional tenure systems need to be codified."[51]

The Bank's position has remained the same to date. This position embraces the transformation approach despite its failure to deliver in colonial and post-colonial states. Contemporary governments in developing nations have also largely embraced the World Bank's approach and thereby wittingly or unwittingly have contributed to non-recognition of customary tenure.

14.3.2. *Contemporary Land Policies: Basis and Principles*

Contemporary land policies and the new wave of land reform in sub-Saharan Africa are largely externally driven and based on the neo-liberal discourse. The neo-liberal model is rooted in the politico-economic structure of western societies and places emphasis on privatized and formalized land ownership rights. It is premised on two

---

[50] *See* L. Cotula & B. Neves, *The Drivers of Change, in* CHANGES IN CUSTOMARY LAND TENURE SYSTEMS IN AFRICA (L. Cotula ed., International Institute for Environmnet and Development 2007).
[51] WORLD BANK, SUB-SAHARAN AFRICA: FROM CRISIS TO SUSTAINABLE GROWTH 104 (1989).

basic principles of English common law: the separation of what is owned from the physical substance of the land itself, and the existence of divided rights of ownership.[52] According to the first principle, what is owned is not the land itself but an "estate" or "interest" in the land.[53] Thus, individuals' rights are limited to this interest rather than the physical substance of the land itself. The second principle, of divided rights of ownership, is equated with the "existence of a bundle of rights in each estate which at its highest confers on the owner of the estate all the powers over a piece of land which a lay person would associate with ownership."[54] This implies that there may be different degrees of ownership by various people in a piece of land. These may be interests such as freeholds, leaseholds, and mortgages. However, the existence of the bundle of rights under English common law does not automatically make such interests "communal" but rather merely gives recognition to other lesser interests in a piece of land, which still amount to ownership.

As a policy, neo-liberalism relies on "a market-oriented development model" and emphasizes free trade, privatization of state enterprises, and existence of secure property rights.[55] The essence of a neo-liberal position on land reform is therefore the proposition that individualized and privatized ownership of land fosters security of tenure, which in turn motivates investment in agriculture and promotes the growth of land markets. The resultant creation of economic opportunities then facilitates economic growth. This position has been reiterated in a number of policy documents of international lending and development agencies such as the World Bank,[56] United Nations Development Program,[57] Food and Agriculture Organization, United States Agency for International Development,[58] and the European Union.[59] However, the model has come under heavy criticism for its endorsement of the transformation approach to customary tenure reform, and its failure is attributed to attempts to transplant western concepts of land ownership without regard to context.[60] A common assumption of this approach is that unless property rights are

---

[52] *See* Patrick McAuslan, *Only the Name of the Country Changes: The Diaspora of European Land Law in Commonwealth Africa, in* EVOLVING LAND RIGHTS, POLICY AND TENURE IN AFRICA (C. Toulmin & J. Quan eds., International Institute for Environment and Development 2000).

[53] *See id.*

[54] *Id.* at 78.

[55] *See* AMBREENA MANJI, THE POLITICS OF LAND REFORM IN AFRICA: FROM COMMUNAL TENURE TO FREE MARKETS (Zed Books 2006).

[56] *See* WORLD BANK, LAND POLICY FOR GROWTH AND POVERTY REDUCTION (2003).

[57] *See* UNITED NATIONS DEVELOPMENT PROGRAM, ATTACKING POVERTY WHILE IMPROVING THE ENVIRONMENT INITIATIVE (1999).

[58] *See* UNITED STATES AGENCY FOR INTERNATIONAL DEVELOPMENT, NATURE, WEALTH AND POWER: EMERGING PRACTICE FOR REVITALIZING RURAL AFRICA (2002).

[59] *See* EUROPEAN UNION, LAND POLICY GUIDELINES (2004).

[60] *See* E.B. ZOOMERS & GEMMA VAN DER HAAR, CURRENT LAND POLICY IN LATIN AMERICA: REGULATING LAND TENURE UNDER NEO-LIBERALISM (KIT Publishers 2000).

transferable, both the magnitude and incidence of the benefits of secure tenure and land-related investment may be limited.[61] Privatization and markets are therefore considered key to efficient and equitable distribution of land and for creating a basis for sustainable use.[62]

The World Bank has consistently marketed the neo-liberal position on land reform together with the transformation theory despite its 2003 Land Policy Research Report: *Land Policy for Growth and Poverty Reduction*, which urged modification of this approach. The report emphasizes the need to "build on customary tenures and existing institutions" on the basis that these "systems have evolved over a long period of time, [and] they are often well adapted to specific conditions and needs."[63] It proclaims that "building on what already exists is in many cases easier and more appropriate than trying to re-invent the wheel, which can end up creating parallel institutions with all their disadvantages."[64] In this sense, the report advocates the adoption of affirmation (as opposed to transformation) approaches to customary tenure reform and considers recognition of existing local tenure systems central to the achievement of effective reform. Formal recognition of customary interests in land is seen as a means of ensuring that customary tenure becomes "more secure."[65] This is progressive and a shift from the abolitionist position, because such formal recognition of customary interests need not necessarily mean title registration as narrowly construed by the World Bank. Botswana typifies an African country that has successfully embraced a system of recording/registering of customary interests without necessarily resorting to title registration.[66]

Inasmuch as the neo-liberal model adopted by the Bank in practice advocates for title registration of customary interests in land, it effectively endorses the transformation and integration of customary interests into the statutory system, which results in the extinguishments of such interests.[67] It also endorses de Soto's assertion that unlocking the capital potential of assets held informally by poor people through formalization of land ownership rights is key to poverty reduction. According to de Soto, a nation cannot achieve meaningful economic growth if rural land remains a "dead asset," presumably because it is held under informal tenure.[68] In other words, informal tenure bleeds insecurity, and security lies in formalization. The

---

[61] *See, e.g.,* WORLD BANK, *supra* note 51.

[62] *See* O.E.G. Johnson, *Economic Analysis, the Legal Framework and Land Tenure Systems*, 15 J. L. & ECON. 259–276 (1972); Zoomers & van der Haar, *supra* note 60.

[63] *See* WORLD BANK, *supra* note 51, at 2.

[64] *Id.*

[65] *See id.*

[66] *See* B. Mathuba, *Reflecting on Customary Tenure Issues in Botswana* (National Land Tenure Conference: Finding Solutions, Securing Rights, Working Paper 2001); Mulolwa, *supra* note 32.

[67] *See* WORLD BANK, *supra* note 51.

[68] *See* De Soto, *supra* note 3.

World Bank aggressively pushes for titling and registration programs that more or less ignore existing local tenure systems on that basis. The gap between the report, which allegedly is not a policy document of the World Bank as it is merely a "Research Report," and what the Bank practices is glaring. The fact that the Bank has failed to adopt the findings and recommendations of a study it commissioned is baffling. It also makes mockery of the comprehensive process of consultations with stakeholders, which culminated in four Regional Workshops, including Africa and Latin America. Notwithstanding the Bank's stand regarding the report, policy makers in developing nations have embraced the report as the official policy position of the Bank on land reform and acclaim it, albeit erroneously, as a clear indication of the World Bank's effort to give a human face to development programs[69] and, hence, indicating a shift in policy.

14.3.2.1. Formalization of Customary Interests in Land

Customary tenure is considered uncertain and insecure for a number of reasons. It is alleged that boundaries to land parcels are unclear. Additionally, existence of individual ownership rights in land is challenged due to its alleged communal nature. It is also alleged that customary tenure provides unreliable and inadequate evidence of land dispositions and transactions due to its heavy reliance on oral accounts. It is thus argued that the aggregate of these factors compromises the full utilization of land by occupiers and users. The neo-liberal approach to land reform advocates for titling and registration of ownership rights to ensure clear boundaries and clear sets of interests to parcels of land. This is intended to promote security of tenure and facilitate the commoditization of such land, which should ultimately benefit the poor who are major beneficiaries of customary tenure. This approach calls for the replacement of existing customary tenure systems with western conceptions of land ownership rights consistent with the transformation theoretical approach. The weakness of this approach has already been illustrated in relation to colonial and post-colonial land policies.

Furthermore, empirical evidence has shown that formal title alone does not always guarantee security of tenure and new investment opportunities in the context of rural Africa. Across the continent, the direct benefits of land registration have been generally confined to local and national elites, and the introduction of formal systems of tenure has had little impact on customary practices of land allocation. Formalization in the form of title registration has also not led directly to improvements in supplies of rural credit, farm productivity, or overall growth. This has been amply illustrated by Kenya, a nation that embraced privatization and formalization of customary tenure

---

[69] *See* AMARTYA SEN, DEVELOPMENT AS FREEDOM (Oxford University Press 1999).

in the 1950s. Improvement to credit associated with land titling never materialized. A study of a sub-location of South Nyanza district in western Kenya illustrates the absence of a direct linkage between titling and credit. There, only 3 percent of the 896 titles had been used to secure loans, seven years after completion of the titling exercise.[70] The failure of titling of customary land in Kenya to lead to increased rural credit has been attributed to the absence of "other important economic or technological preconditions for the anticipated behaviour change ... and [to] farmers behaviour with regard to land [which] still reflected their adherence to the values of family and lineage."[71] In Bostwana, the lack of access to credit using rural land has been attributed to lack of infrastructure and other incentives to invest in the rural areas.[72] It has also been proven that improved access to credit markets is dependent on a number of factors such as: location, land use, creditworthiness of the applicant, the size of the landholding – with larger landholders accessing credit more easily than smaller ones – and existence of well-developed banking systems and formal credit markets.[73] Consequently, the relationship of formal title to effective credit markets and subsequent sustainable development has been seriously overstated.

In some cases, titling has resulted in increased landlessness and poverty by undermining livelihoods of those dependent on customary land rights "causing land insecurity for subsidiary claimants, especially women."[74] For example, a study of a title registration program carried out under the Customary Land Development Act in the peri-urban area of Chitipi in Lilongwe District of Malawi revealed that titles to land were mainly given to men as heads of households, despite the fact that the custom of the area required inheritance of land through the female child.[75] The men have sold most of this land without regard to the interests of women.

A household survey conducted in Ghana, Kenya, and Rwanda testing the allegation that indigenous land rights systems are a constraint on agricultural productivity has also revealed that formalized land rights are not significant in determining investments in land management, use of inputs, access to credit, or the productivity of land.[76] The researchers thus doubted the need for land registration and titling

[70] *See* Nyamu-Musembi, *supra* note 44.
[71] J.W. Bruce, *African Tenure Models at the Turn of the Century: Individual Property Models and Common Property Models, in* EVOLVING LAND RIGHTS, POLICY AND TENURE IN AFRICA (C. Toulmin & J. Quan eds., International Institute for Environment and Development 2000).
[72] *See* Government of Bostwana, *supra* note 24.
[73] *See* Mathuba, *supra* note 66.
[74] C. Toulmin & J. Quan, *Registering Customary Rights, in* EVOLVING LAND RIGHTS, POLICY AND TENURE IN AFRICA (C. Toulmin & J. Quan eds., International Institute for Environment and Development 2000).
[75] *See* C. Ngongola, *The Design and Implementation of Customary Land Reforms in Central Malawi*, 26 J. AFR. L. 115 (1982).
[76] *See* F. Place & P. Hazell, *Productivity Effects of Indigenous Land Tenure Systems in Sub-Saharan Africa*, 75 AM. J. AGIC. ECON. 10–19 (1993).

programs in sub-Saharan Africa. These experiences show that title has very little impact on farmers' investment behavior in rural Africa. Recent studies also show that most rural farmers do not care for title because they feel that they already own the land and consider the payment of registration fees an unnecessary burden.[77] Additionally, failure to pay taxes on registered rural land may result in higher insecurity. Furthermore, rural farmers, especially women, as a study in Tanzania revealed, have also shown a reluctance to use their parcels, where registered, as collateral to secure loans for fear of loosing their livelihood through foreclosure.[78] Research has also shown that issues of tenure insecurity on the African continent are mostly associated with predatory behavior of authorities whereby customary land is taken with little or no compensation. The deployment of the principle of eminent domain plays a major role in this behavior and facilitates the implementation of agricultural policies that favor export-crop estate farming at the expense of smallholder subsistence farming.[79] This mostly translates into "the rapid expansion of estate agriculture ... assisted by the availability of cheap labour, and land," made possible by "the ability to annex smallholder customary land."[80] This has led some to conclude that tenure insecurity is a possible consequence of registration programs rather than its absence.[81] Understanding behavioral patterns of governments in sub-Saharan Africa and assessing the extent of the perceived threat to customary tenure security is therefore vital.

Empirical evidence from Latin America indicates similar experience and show that existing titling programs have not met expectations. It has been found that titling increases social differentiation in that more often it is elites who register land due to the cost of the process. The assumption that land will be allocated to the most efficient users was also found to work very rarely because land passes in the hands of the well-to-do who are mostly interested in speculative aims rather than investing in the land.[82] In Honduras, experiments with titling did not coincide with the bundle of customary rights but resulted in complicating land ownership relationships.[83] This leads to insecurity of tenure and can increase disputes due to contestation of rights

---

[77] *See* B. Englert, *From a Gender Perspective: Notions of Land Tenure Security in the Uluguru Mountains, Tanzania*, 19 J. FUR ENTWICKLUNGSPOLITIK 75 (2003).

[78] *See id.*

[79] *See* Okoth-Ogendo, *supra* 46. He considers this a powerful instrument of public policy for sub-Saharan African governments.

[80] *See* J. Harrigan, *Malawi, in* AID AND POWER: THE WORLD BANK AND POLICY BASED LENDING (P. Mosley et al. eds., Routledge 1991).

[81] *See* Englert, *supra* note 77.

[82] *See* Zoomers & van der Haar, *supra* note 60.

[83] *See* Esther Roquas, *Muerte a los juices vendidos: Land Conflicts and the Paradox of Class Justice in Rural Honduras, in* CURRENT LAND POLICY IN LATIN AMERICA: REGULATING LAND TENURE UNDER NEO-LIBERALISM 177–200 (E.B. Zoomers & Gemma van der Haar, KIT Publishers 2000).

over land by individuals drawing from different sets of interacting legal rights.[84] It is therefore not surprising that a number of commentators drawing from previous experience with titling programs have cautioned against overstating the direct relationship of titling to productivity and economic empowerment for rural people, as insisted on by the World Bank and its partners. Further, others have argued that, in assessing the impact of formalization, it is important to re-assess the informal that needs to be formalized rather than generalizing the concept.[85] In this regard, de Soto may have been writing in the context of urban slums when he argued for formalization but mistakenly argued for formalization as generally applicable to rural land.[86] It is indeed true that the characteristics of customary landholding can seldom be equated with those of urban slums and, hence, demand a different approach.

Rather than adopting "the assumption that customary tenure is inherently insecure and that salvation lies in its replacement with a regime of individual property modelled on English tenure systems," policy makers should shift focus and interrogate and suggest policy and legal changes that may guarantee tenure regimes capable of conferring social security and equity and permit economic efficiency.[87] This position becomes poignant when one considers that in the African context, "formalization of title has become synonymous with transformation and increased visibility of men's control over land, and the simultaneous disappearance or invisibility of women's usage rights."[88] In this era, the question should therefore be how can growth and development be achieved within each and every tenure system, rather than which land tenure system is best.[89]

14.3.2.2. Creation of Land Markets

The neo-liberal approach to land tenure reform presumes that formalization of land rights is a pre-condition to the creation and operation of an effective land market. Land markets should in turn allocate land to efficient users and contribute to a more equal distribution of land, resulting in poverty reduction. These presumptions have not been supported by empirical evidence.

It has been shown that a market in land does exist in the absence of formal title, and that informal cash-based transactions in land do take place in the form of rentals, pledges, and land sales in spite of the existence of formal titles.[90] Informal social

---

[84] *See* J.D. Stansfield, *Projects that Title Land in Central and Latin America and the Caribbean: Expectations and Problems*, Land Tenure Centre, University of Wisconsin-Madison, Wisconsin, 1985.

[85] *See* Nyamu-Musembi, *supra* note 44.

[86] *See id.*

[87] *See* Okoth-Ogendo, *supra* note 46, at 129.

[88] Nyamu-Musembi, *supra* note 44, at 21.

[89] This was rightly observed in Land and Equity Movement in Uganda, "Does customary tenure have a role in modern economic development," *Discussion Paper* 4.

[90] *See* Nyamu-Musembi, *supra* note 44.

structures regulate this market.[91] Very simple procedures are followed in land sales, with chiefs or other traditional authorities witnessing transactions as official backing and informally recording land transactions on pieces of paper. The advantage of these practices is that they are locally owned, flexible, and do not involve a change in the nature of the customary interest as is occasioned by title registration. More importantly, the practices build on, rather than abolish, customary interests. In this sense, a recorded customary interest retains its existing integrity and mode of administration, thus resulting in affirmation of such interest. Affirmation of customary interests in this sense therefore promotes modernization of tradition as opposed to the imposing of modernization on tradition. These practices have been termed "informal formalisation," indicating that formalization processes are not the exclusive preserve of the state.[92] By increasingly blurring the distinction between the formal and the informal, such transactions expose a confluence between the two without necessarily resorting to titling programs. This casts doubt on the exaggerated relevance of titling programs to the development of rural land markets. Developing nations should pay attention to these evolving practices in considering tenure reforms rather than placing too much emphasis on foreign concepts.

Further, studies from Latin America have shown that rural elites who purchase land often bank such land for the next generation rather than use it as a productive asset.[93] Other commentators have also observed that land markets often result in land concentration and accelerated landlessness.[94] This puts the relationship of land markets to poverty alleviation on questionable footing. Nevertheless, it should not be assumed that all sales by the poor are distress sales.[95] Rather, operation of land markets requires a detailed analysis of the buyers and sellers and their motivation.[96]

14.4. TENURE SECURITY: NEO-LIBERAL–CUSTOMARY MODEL CONFLUENCES

The first point of reference in the seeming failure of a neo-liberal approach to customary tenure reform in sub-Saharan Africa is the unfortunate and misconceived pursuit of the objective of "development" in its narrowest sense, which has resulted

---

[91] See H.W.O. Okoth-Ogendo & W. Oluoch-Kosura, *Final Report on Land Tenure and Agriculture Development in Kenya, Nairobi* (Ministry of Agriculture, Livestock Development and Marketing 1995).

[92] Paul Mathieu, *Transactions informelles et marches fanciers emergents en Afrique, in* POLITICS, PROPERTY AND PRODUCTION IN THE WEST AFRICAN SAHEL: UNDERSTANDING NATURAL RESOURCES MANAGEMENT 22–29 (Tor A. Benjaminsen & Christian Lund eds., 2001).

[93] See Zoomers & van der Haar, *supra* note 60.

[94] See Platteau, *supra* note 27; M. Carter, *Old questions and new realities: land in post-liberal economies, in* CURRENT LAND POLICY IN LATIN AMERICA: REGULATING LAND TENURE UNDER NEO-LIBERALISM (A. Zoomers & G. van der Haar eds., KIT Publishers 2000).

[95] See Zoomers & van der Haar, *supra* note 60.

[96] See id.

in the oppression of customary tenure. To date, international development policy considers that only land reform that focuses on privatized/individualized and formalized tenure results in tenure security and subsequent development. Anything different is simply ignored, despite increasing evidence that this approach has not worked for developing nations in the last half century.

Despite the differences in approach between customary tenure and neo-liberalism, one may discern three synergies. First, individual tenure is recognized in both systems. What have been termed "user rights" under customary tenure are capable of being equated with interests under English common law because user rights entail long-term and exclusive rights regarding parcels of land allocated to individuals or families. Customary norms, which are well understood in the community, stipulate conditions for losing such rights. This arrangement ensures tenure security. Second, both tenure systems are rooted to some extent in processes and practices that systematically subject individual rights in land to external forces. Under English common law, individuals' rights are subject to external limitations in the public interest as may be determined by the sovereign, and are mostly implemented through planning authorities. Under customary tenure, individual interests in land are subject to the external limitation of community interest. Given these limitations under both systems, the pre-eminence of community interest in customary tenure has been overstated insofar as individual rights in customary land are concerned and confused with the "single powerful and immovable structural foundation" of customary land tenure systems, namely their communal basis in reference and adherence.[97] Third, dynamism is present in both tenure systems, and, as previously discussed, the inalienability of customary tenure has been exaggerated.

Consequently, the approach to rights over land in Africa and in the West is not dissimilar. The challenge lies in the different definitions of the concept of ownership in the two systems. Ownership of land in the West is defined with reference to alienation in pursuit of a market approach. Using this template for customary tenure is unsatisfactory, because access to resources is linked to the sovereign community or lineage. Hence, the major weakness of contemporary land policies in sub-Saharan Africa is that, in dealing with customary land, they have adopted a western approach that focuses on transformation of customary tenure. This exhibits a continuous failure to understand customary tenure systems and the misguided agenda of international lending and development agencies to fashion land relations on the continent according to their wishes.

Effective customary tenure reform requires adoption of affirmative approaches to allow the determination of the question of ownership to be based on the right to exclude others from the occupation and use of the land rather than the right

---

[97] *See* Wily, *supra* note 12.

to alienate. "[I]t is [indeed] arbitrary to use alienability as a test of the existence of ownership ... land cannot be said to belong less to someone, because he or they are unable to part with it."[98] Furthermore, ownership or user rights under customary tenure serves multiple objectives as opposed to mere economic efficiency. Customary land tenure systems are fundamentally of a socio-political nature, and land management institutions under customary law, in addition to regulating access to land and resources, manage the tension between land security as an individual good and land security as a common good.[99] Some commentators have argued that the management of the tension between the individual and the community allows flexible access to land in lineage holdings for all members.[100] This allegedly resolves the problems of access by the rural poor where there is no issue of land scarcity.

14.5. GENERAL CONCLUSIONS

This chapter has focused on the impact of the persistent mis-recognition and non-recognition of customary tenure in sub-Saharan Africa and on the need to reinterpret customary tenure to achieve effective tenure reforms. Several general conclusions can be drawn from the foregoing discussion to guide policy makers in suggesting effective neo-liberal customary tenure reform for sub-Saharan Africa.

There is need to seriously reflect on the appropriateness of the customary tenure systems that are adopted in contemporary land policies and consistently marketed as possible partners to neo-liberal land reforms. This is a crucial starting point in light of the gap that exists between the shadow and the living customary tenure. The continuous focus on the shadow from colonial times to the present date undermines customary tenure reforms and perpetuates the oppression of customary tenure. National governments in sub-Saharan Africa are therefore challenged to let go of the shadow if they are committed to reforms aimed at benefiting the poor.

Security of tenure does not depend on titling, as evidence from both Africa and Latin America has shown. Conversely, customary tenure is not insecure per se. However, the major threat to security of customary tenure on the continent seems to be the predatory behavior of land management authorities, including governments. This is in view of the downgrading of customary tenure as an ineffective system of landholding resulting in systematic customary land annexation. This exposes an urgent need for the establishment of management and allocation functions at

---

[98] Mifsud, *supra* note 22, at 45.
[99] See P.L. Delville, *Changes in Customary Land Management Institutions: Evidence from West Africa*, in CHANGES IN CUSTOMARY LAND TENURE SYSTEMS IN AFRICA (Cotula ed., International Institute for Environment and Development 2007).
[100] See M. BREUSERS, ON THE MOVE: MOBILITY, LAND USE AND LIVELIHOOD PRACTICES ON THE CENTRAL PLATEAU IN BURKINA FASO (LIT Verlag1998).

the local level to coincide with the prevailing informal formalization processes that are better adapted to protect the land rights of the most vulnerable. It is important to ensure that any institutional framework chosen at the local level enjoys a certain measure of autonomy from central government to prevent governments' undue influence and predatory tendencies.

Further, the neo-liberal approach to land reform is not inherently problematic, but rather the theoretical framework adopted by the World Bank and its partners in implementing those reforms is problematic. This approach judges customary tenure as inferior and promotes its transformation as opposed to its affirmation, thereby compromising any chance of recognizing customary tenure systems as viable systems of landholding that are capable of economic activity and full of potential. The Bank has blind faith in the effectiveness of western concepts of land. This results in the ignoring of evolving key aspects of existing local tenure systems and institutions by placing undue emphasis on title registration. The interrogation of customary tenure exposes synergies with neo-liberal approaches that can be built on in pursuit of a neo-liberal affirmation theoretical framework that may promote recognition of customary tenure. These synergies can be utilized to fashion effective customary tenure reforms, but they require contextual understanding of customary tenure concepts that should be embraced in contemporary land policies. More importantly, the concept of individual ownership under customary tenure should be recognized so as to pursue reforms that are consistent with this concept to preserve the objectives of customary tenure, which support individual rights concurrent with communal interests and promote food, social security, and dynamism. Governments should also capitalize on existent institutional innovations such as forms of recording land ownership rights and cash-based transactions, as well as forms of accessing cultivation rights such as sales, pledges, and rentals for effective reforms. Simple ways of documenting customary land resources and their use and location should be identified, influenced by such institutional innovations, without resorting to the cumbersome, costly, and not particularly useful process of titling.

Documentation of land rights in this way has several advantages and would be perceived as inevitable, because evidence on the continent indicates that people are institutionalizing land rights through the informal formalization processes. This ensures the preservation of a basic tenet of customary tenure (the unique concept of ownership) and incorporates a semblance of formality (a simple documentation system). The approach also has the advantage of guaranteeing acceptability of the reforms, because ownership rights under customary tenure shall not be disturbed unceremoniously but shall be allowed to evolve conditioned by economic, social, and cultural factors. Further, this shall guarantee ownership of the land tenure reform process by the people who matter – the poor – due to the shift from the exclusive focus on property rights. More importantly, the approach is congruent with neo-liberal aspirations characterized by affirmation approaches propagated by the 2003 World Bank Land Policy Research Report that emphasizes the importance of building on customary tenures and institutions. The approach also embraces the view that incorporating social conditions in development programs enhances people's sense of self and is key to their capability to function effectively.[101] The World Bank thus needs to reconsider its position and strategies and engage stakeholder governments more in order to preserve its credibility as a development partner in customary tenure reform efforts.

---

[101] *See* AMARTYA SEN, COMMODITIES AND CAPABILITIES (North-Holland 1985); AMARTYA SEN, DEVELOPMENT AS FREEDOM (Oxford University Press 1999).

15

Reform of the South African Customary Law of Succession

Final Nails in the Customary Law Coffin?

Christa Rautenbach and Willemien du Plessis

15.1. INTRODUCTION: NAILING THE ISSUES

The customary law of succession in South Africa is one area of customary law that has been subject to severe criticism over the years, and even more so since South Africa's new constitutional dispensation and people's growing awareness of human rights and freedoms.[1] It should therefore come as no surprise that this area of customary law has lately been subject to various judicial and legislative changes. In fact, there have been so many changes to the customary law of succession that one could easily argue that the contemporary customary law of succession is no longer customary law, but something totally different.

Before embarking on a discussion of the reform of the customary law of succession, there are a few issues that need to be addressed. The first issue concerns the use of the term "succession" in the title of this chapter. Laypersons and lawyers alike use succession as a synonym for "inheritance," and even the dictionary meanings of inheritance and succession are similar. According to some dictionaries, inheritance generally refers to the testate or intestate transfer of property rights to beneficiaries, but it might also include the transfer of rights, liabilities or title of the deceased.[2] Similarly, succession mainly includes "the order in which or the conditions under

---

[1]   It is trite that South Africa became a new democracy based on constitutionalism and the rule of law with the enactment of the two Constitutions: the Constitution of the Republic of South Africa Act 200 of 1993 (Interim Constitution), and the Constitution of the Republic of South Africa Act 108 of 1996. *See* S. AFR. (Interim) CONST. 1993; S. AFR. CONST. 1996.

[2]   *Merriam-Webster's Dictionary of Law* defines inheritance as "1: the act of inheriting: as a: the acquisition of real or personal property under the laws of intestacy or sometimes by will b: the succession upon the death of an owner either by will or by operation of law to all the estate, rights, and liabilities of the decendent 2 a: something that is or may be inherited b: something to which one is entitled as heir." MERRIAM-WEBSTER'S DICTIONARY OF LAW 245 (1996). In contrast, *Collins Online Dictionary* defines inheritance as "hereditary succession to an estate or title; the right of an heir to succeed on the death of an ancestor" or "something inherited or to be inherited," *at* http://www.collinslanguage.com/results.aspx?context=3&reversed=False&action=define&homonym=-1&text=inheritance.

which one person after another succeeds to a property, dignity, position, title, or throne."[3] Although the similarities between the two terms are especially prevalent in the South African common law of succession, where both terms are used indiscriminately to refer to the testate or intestate devolution of a testator's deceased estate, customary law knows only the term "succession," which is used mainly to describe the process whereby the successor steps into the shoes of the deceased with regard to the latter's property and his status.[4] In addition, the successor succeeds not only to the assets of the estate, but also to its liabilities.[5] As will be discussed below, the developments in the customary law of succession concern mainly succession rules applicable to the property of the deceased, whereas the rules about the status of the deceased have been left virtually untouched.[6]

Another area of customary law in which the term succession is used is in relation to succession to the throne of the king or to the position of traditional leader.[7] In general, it is traditional for the eldest son of the head wife, who is regarded as the mother of the community, to succeed to the position of the traditional leader.[8]

In both areas of customary law, succession to property and succession to traditional leadership, the rule of male primogeniture prevents females and other male children down the line from succeeding to property[9] and traditional leadership,[10] a fact that is regarded by many as against the values and rights contained in the Constitution. In this context, this chapter is concerned with the development of the customary rules regarding succession to property and succession to traditional leadership.

There are sometimes major differences between the "official" and "living" versions of customary law, as demonstrated in a number of empirical studies.[11] This

---

[3] MERRIAM-WEBSTER DICTIONARY OF LAW, *supra* note 2, at 480. Nevertheless, succession has a much wider meaning than inheritance. *See* Accurate and Reliable Dictionary, *at* http://ardictionary.com/ Succession (providing a numerous meanings for the word "succession").

[4] *See* N.J.J. OLIVIER & W.H. OLIVIER, DIE PRIVAATREG VAN DIE SUID-AFRIKAANSE BANTOETAALSPREKENDES 435 (Butterworths 1989); Brief of Amici Curiae Commission for Gender Equality, Bhe v. Magistrate, Khayelitsha, 2005 (1) BCLR 1 (CC) (2004) (S. Afr.); Shibi v. Sithole, et al., 2005 (1) SA 580 (CC) (S. Afr.). *See also* South African Human Rights Commission v. President of the Republic of South Africa, 2005 (1) SA 580 (CC) ¶ 76 (S. Afr.) [hereinafter *Bhe* or the *Bhe* case] (stating that "[t]he rules of the customary law of succession [are] mainly concerned with succession to the position and status of the deceased family head rather than the distribution of his personal assets.").

[5] This is referred to as universal succession. *See generally* C. Rautenbach et al., *Law of Succession and Inheritance*, *in* INTRODUCTION TO LEGAL PLURALISM IN SOUTH AFRICA 93 (LexisNexis South Africa 2006).

[6] *See infra* Section 15.2.

[7] *See infra* Section 15.3 (discussing the succession of a traditional leader).

[8] *See* Olivier & Oliver, *supra* note 4, at 497.

[9] *See infra* Section 15.2.

[10] *See infra* Section 15.3.

[11] *See* J.C. Bekker & I.P. Maithufi, *The Dichotomy between "Official Customary Law" and "Non-Official" Customary Law*, 1 J. OF JURIDICAL SCI. 1, 47–60 (1992); Mabena v. Letsoalo, (2) SA 1068 (T) (1998) (S. Afr.) (reiterating that the living version of customary law is actually the law observed by African

characteristic is also evident in the law of succession. Given that it would be difficult to discuss the official and living versions of the customary law of succession in one chapter, the focus here will be on the official version of the customary law of succession as found in textbooks, jurisprudence, and legislation, given that recent judicial and legislative developments concerned the official version of customary law and not the living version.

It is further important to note that the expression "customary law" refers to something that is not, in actual fact, a unified system of law. Customary law consists of the various "customs and usages traditionally observed among the indigenous African peoples of South Africa and form[s] part of the culture of those peoples."[12] This phenomenon is evident when one reads through the documented rules of succession of the various traditional communities of South Africa.[13] For that reason, this chapter focuses on customary law rules that can be identified as universal, for example, the rule of male primogeniture.[14]

A further issue worth raising is the place of customary law in the South African national legal system. Trying to explain the South African national legal system, and especially the place of the customary law within this system, is no easy matter. However, while keeping the dangers of generalization in mind, the situation can be summarized as follows.[15] Contemporary South African law is a mixed legal system comprising transplanted European laws (the core being Roman-Dutch law, subsequently influenced by English common law),[16] as well as indigenous laws, referred

---

communities). However, A.J. Kerr is of the opinion that "living law" is essentially "new particular customs," meaning that living law is different from the official law documented by writers. *See* A.J. Kerr, *My Lexis Nexis Family Law Service on "Customary Law"*, May 26, 2009, *at* http://www.lexisnexis.co.za/our-solutions/law/research-solutions/my-lexisnexis.aspx. The official customary law consists mainly of textbook versions, as well as jurisprudence and legislation, whereas the unofficial version comprises mostly unwritten customs and usages.

[12] Recognition of Customary Marriages Act 120 of 1998 § 1.

[13] *See* W. du Plessis & C. Rautenbach, *Law of Succession and Inheritance, in* INDIGENOUS LAW: LAW OF SOUTH AFRICA 215–23 (W.A. Joubert ed., LexisNexis 2004).

[14] One exception is the rules of succession to traditional leadership. *See infra* Section 15.3.

[15] For a more detailed discussion of the South African legal system, see C. Rautenbach, *South African Common and Customary Law of Intestate Succession: A Question of Harmonisation, Integration or Abolition*, 12 ELECTRONIC J. OF COMP. L. 1, 1–15 (2008).

[16] One of the features of the South African legal system is the fact that it is largely uncodified. Consequently, South African lawyers have to consult various sources to find out what the law is. Such sources include legislation, case law, old authorities (Roman-Dutch law), custom, customary law, modern legal textbooks, and the Constitution. According to Stephen Girvin, South Africa's mixed legal system largely stems from South Africa's earlier judges. *See* Stephen D. Girvin, *The Architects of the Mixed Legal System, in* SOUTHERN CROSS: CIVIL AND COMMON LAW IN SOUTH AFRICA 95 (Reinhard Zimmermann & Daniel Visser eds., Oxford University Press 1996). Historically, western culture generally refers to the lifestyle of early colonizers (mostly the United Kingdom and the Netherlands), whereas African culture refers broadly to the lifestyle of the traditional communities in Africa (mostly Sub-Saharan Africa). It may be argued that regarding Europeans as intruders in South Africa and Africans as indigenous to South Africa is erroneous, because the history books show us

to as customary law.[17] Together with the Constitution, which is supreme, the laws of these two systems form the modern South African legal system. After many years of being treated as the inferior body of South African law, there is now no doubt as to the place of customary law. It is part and parcel of modern South African law, equal to the Roman-Dutch law (referred to as the common law).[18] In *Mthembu v. Letsela*, the High Court of South Africa confirmed that "customary law has been accepted by the framers of the Constitution as a separate legal and cultural system which may be freely chosen by persons desiring to do so,"[19] and in *Alexkor Ltd v. Richtersveld Community*, the Constitutional Court confirmed the equal status of customary law by stating: "While in the past indigenous law was seen through the common law lens, it must now be seen as an integral part of our law. Like all law it depends for its ultimate force and validity on the Constitution. Its validity must now be determined by reference not to common-law, but to the Constitution."[20] This means that the South African court system, which is in essence a single unified system, has to apply more than one legal system, depending on the nature of a specific case before it. This could prove to be a challenging task, especially when one keeps in mind that not all law faculties at South African universities pay equal attention to customary law courses in their curricula.

that the original inhabitants of South Africa were Hottentots (Khoi) and Bushmen (San). Most other African people are immigrants from Northern Africa (at least north of the Zambezi River). After contact with European colonists, Africans migrated south, and Europeans migrated east and north. Both played a part in eradicating the Bushmen and Hottentots. The Africans and Europeans were more or less simultaneous immigrants, each occupying their respective tracts of land. They met and collided in the vicinity of the Kei- and Great Fish Rivers. Later, when the Europeans immigrated inland, north over the Orangeriver and across the Drakensberg and the Vaalriver, they fought each other in numerous wars for a long time to gain supremacy and territory. For a detailed discussion of the early history of South Africa, see generally C.F.J. MULLER, VYFHONDERD JAAR SUID-AFRIKAANSE GESKIEDENIS (Academica 1990) and A.J. KERR, THE NATIVE LAW OF SUCCESSION IN SOUTH AFRICA: WITH SPECIAL REFERENCE TO THE NGUNI TRIBES OF THE CISKEIAN AND TRANSKEIAN TERRITORIES AND NATAL 1–5 (Butterworths 1961).

[17] The Recognition of Customary Marriages Act 120 of 1988 defines "customary law" as the "customs and usages traditionally observed among the indigenous African people." Under the Black Administration Act 38 of 1927, "black" means "any person who is a member of any aboriginal race or tribe of Africa." The Law of Evidence Amendment Act 45 of 1988 defines "indigenous law" as the "[b]lack law or customs as applied by the [b]lack tribes in the Republic or in territories which formerly formed part of the Republic." The South African Law Reform Commission defines "customary law" as the "various laws observed by communities indigenous to the country." Although customary law and indigenous law are used as synonyms in South African law, the first is preferred because it is also the expression used in the Constitution.

[18] *See* T.W. BENNETT, CUSTOMARY LAW IN SOUTH AFRICA 43 (Juta 2004).

[19] 1997 (2) SA 936 (T) at 944B-C (S. Afr.).

[20] 2003 (12) BCLR 1301 (CC) ¶ 51 (S. Afr.). *See also* Pharmaceutical Manufacturers Association of SA: In re Ex Parte President of the Republic of South Africa, 2000 (2) SA 674 (CC) (S. Afr.); 2000 (3) BCLR 241 (CC) ¶ 44 (S. Afr.); Mabuza v. Mbatha 2003 (4) SA 218 (C) (S. Afr.); 2003 (7) BCLR 743 (C) ¶ 32 (S. Afr.); *Bhe, supra* note 4, ¶ 43.

While the common law operates in the private and public spheres, customary law generally deals with private relationships and thus mostly operates in the private sphere.[21] It pertains to limited areas of law, such as family law,[22] the law of property,[23] the law of delict,[24] traditional leadership and courts,[25] and, finally, succession laws, which are addressed in this chapter. Because there are no official statistics on point, it is difficult to estimate how many people still follow a traditional African lifestyle where customary law is the order of the day. Empirical research has been done from time to time in certain regional[26] or geographical rural areas,[27] but these research efforts normally do not reveal the population statistics. Nevertheless, it is estimated that almost half of the South African population live in rural areas, putting South Africa twenty-eighth in the ranking of countries with rural populations.[28] This estimate excludes people living in urban areas who still adhere to customary practices.[29] It can therefore be inferred that a large portion of the South African population still lives under a system of customary law.

The South African law of succession consists of two different systems of law: The common law of succession comprises testamentary[30] and intestate[31] succession,

---

[21]   The traditional public-private divide in western legal systems is unknown to customary law. The customary court system even deals with the relationship between the offender and his or her community. For a general discussion of the operation of customary courts in South Africa, see Christa Rautenbach, *Therapeutic Jurisprudence in the Customary Courts of South Africa: Traditional Authority Courts as Therapeutic Agents*, 21 SAJHR [first page], 323–35 (2005).

[22]   *See* R. M. Jansen, *Family Law, in* INTRODUCTION TO LEGAL PLURALISM IN SOUTH AFRICA, *supra* note 5, at 29–52 (discussing the legal principles applicable to marriage and the dissolution of marriage).

[23]   *See* J.C. Bekker & I.P. Maithufi, *Law of Property, in* INTRODUCTION TO LEGAL PLURALISM IN SOUTH AFRICA, *supra* note 5, at 53–77 (discussing the legal principles applicable to property rights).

[24]   *See* E. Knoetze et al., *Law of Delict, in* INTRODUCTION TO LEGAL PLURALISM IN SOUTH AFRICA, *supra* note 5, at 79–89 (discussing the legal principles applicable to delictual claims).

[25]   *See* J.C. Bekker & C.C. Boonzaaier, *Traditional Leadership and Governance, in* INTRODUCTION TO LEGAL PLURALISM IN SOUTH AFRICA, *supra* note 5, at 113–129 (discussing the characteristic indigenous authority system of the traditional communities, including the principles applicable to traditional leaders and traditional courts); D.S. Koyana et al., *Traditional Authority Courts, in* INTRODUCTION TO LEGAL PLURALISM IN SOUTH AFRICA, *supra* note 5, at 131–46.

[26]   For example, from 1995 to 1996, various South African universities, in collaboration with the University of Leiden of the Netherlands, conducted research in three provinces, namely the Northwest Province, the Northern Province, and KwaZulu-Natal, regarding the Administrative and Legal Position of Traditional Authorities in South Africa and their Contribution to the Implementation of the Reconstruction and Development Programme (unpublished research).

[27]   *See, e.g.,* BARBARA M. OOMEN, TRADITION ON THE MOVE: CHIEFS, DEMOCRACY AND CHANGE IN RURAL AREAS (Netherlands Institute for Southern Africa 2000).

[28]   *See* NationMaster, People Statistics: Rural Population (most recent) by Country, *at* http://www. nationmaster.com/graph/peo_rur_pop-people-rural-population.

[29]   *See, e.g.,* M.W. Prinsloo et al., *Knowledge and Experience of Lobolo in Mamelodi and Atteridgeville*, 30 DE JURE, 314–330 (1997).

[30]   Testamentary succession is regulated by common-law rules and the Wills Act 7 of 1953.

[31]   Intestate succession is regulated by common-law rules and the Intestate Succession Act 81 of 1987.

whereas the customary law of succession comprises intestate succession only. This discussion will focus only on the common and customary law of intestate succession.[32]

By now it should be evident that a discussion of customary law principles is no easy matter. Notwithstanding the magnitude of the task, this chapter will consider recent developments in the area of the customary law of succession to property[33] and to traditional leadership.[34] In doing so, the focus will be on the events leading up to these developments, including court decisions and legislative changes in these two areas of law. The main purpose of this analysis is to determine whether these new developments can be reconciled with the principles and values of customary law and/or the Constitution, or whether they amount to a total abolition of the customary law, thereby driving the final nails into the coffin of customary law of succession.

15.2. CUSTOMARY LAW OF SUCCESSION

15.2.1. *Background: Identifying the Nails*

This part considers the customary law of succession in the context of succession to the property of a deceased.[35] The common law does not distinguish between the beneficiaries on the grounds of gender (male or female) or status (legitimate, illegitimate, or first-born), whereas the customary law of succession applies the rule of male primogeniture[36] and excludes illegitimate children from inheritance under certain circumstances.[37]

The distinctive feature of male primogeniture in the customary law of succession does not conform to the notion of equality between the sexes or persons regardless of

---

[32] Unless indicated otherwise, all further references to the common and customary law of succession will be to intestate succession rules.

[33] *See infra* Section 15.2.

[34] *See infra* Section 15.3.

[35] As explained in Section 15.1, the terms "inheritance" and "succession" have been used interchangeably by legal scholars, courts, and the legislature. This chapter uses the latter. In this section, succession refers to the transfer of property, whereas succession in Section 15.3 refers to the transfer of status pertaining to traditional leadership.

[36] In monogamous traditional families, the eldest son or, failing him, the eldest male descendant of the eldest son inherits from the family head. Should the eldest son die without male issue, the second son becomes heir, and so it continues. If the family head dies without male issue, other male family members of the deceased inherit. Women (wives and daughters) generally do not inherit from the family head. *See* C. Rautenbach et al., *Is Primogeniture Extinct Like the Dodo, or Is There any Prospect of It Rising from the Ashes? Some Comments on the Evolution of Customary Succession Laws in South Africa,* 22 SAJHR. 99–118 (2006).

[37] For the position of illegitimate children, see *Bhe, supra* note 4, ¶ 79.

status, and it is thus not surprising that this aspect has, at regular intervals, been challenged in the courts[38] and in the literature,[39] especially on constitutional grounds. The matter has been more or less logically concluded with the recent decision of the Constitutional Court in the *Bhe* case[40] and the *Reform of Customary Law of Succession and Regulations of Related Matters Act* 11 of 2009 (hereinafter the *RCLSA*) that gives effect to this judgment.[41] The question is whether these developments, which seem to be in accordance with the constitutional imperative of equality between the sexes and persons regardless of status, can be seen as a necessary improvement to the customary law, or whether they amount to a total abolition of it.[42]

15.2.2. *From the First to the Last Nail*

Succession plays an important role in society. In 1980, an attorney from Lesotho observed as follows: "As we all know, the law of succession rarely changes because change might destabili[z]e society and its intimate family relationships."[43] It is probably too early to tell whether recent changes in the South African customary law of intestate succession will lead to such destabilization within the traditional communities living under a system of customary law.

[38] *See, e.g.*, Mthembu v. Letsela, 1997 (2) SA 936 (T); Mthembu v. Letsela, 1998 (2) SA 675 (T); Mthembu v. Letsela, 2000 (3) SA 867 (SCA); *Bhe, supra* note 4. In the *Mthembu* cases, the courts were reluctant to declare the rule unconstitutional. Their reasoning was based on, *inter alia*, the heir's maintenance duty and the non-applicability of the interim Constitution in horizontal matters.

[39] *See* R.B. MQEKE, CUSTOMARY LAW AND THE NEW MILLENNIUM 112–113 (Lovedale Press 2003); Bennett, *supra* note 18, at 337–362.

[40] *See supra* note 4. Three cases that came before the Constitutional Court of South Africa were heard together because they all concerned customary succession laws. The first two, Bhe v. The Magistrate, Khayelitsha, 2004 (2) SA 544 (C), and Shibi (7292/01 (T) November 19, 2003, unreported), came before the Court for confirmation whereas the third, an application for direct access, was brought jointly by the South African Human Rights Commission and the Women's Legal Centre Trust. The question in all three cases was whether male primogeniture was constitutional. The decision of the Constitutional Court and High Courts elicited numerous responses from legal writers. *See e.g.*, E. Knoetze, *End of the Road for the Customary Law of Succession?*, 67 J. CONTEMP. ROMAN-DUTCH L. 514–524 (2004); T. Banda, *The Constitutional Court's Approach to Customary Law in Bhe v Magistrate, Khayelitsha: Has the Baby Been Thrown Out with the Bath Water?*, 15 RESPONSA MERIDIANA, 5–18 (2005); I.P. Maithufi & G.M.B. Moloi, *Customary Law of Succession: Bhe v. Magistrate, Khayelitsha Case No 9489/02 (C)*, 67 J. CONTEMP. ROMAN-DUTCH L. 507–515 (2004).

[41] The Act was assented to on April 19, 2009, but its date of commencement has not yet been published.

[42] In *Issues Arising from a Challenge to the Constitutionality of the Customary Law of Intestate Succession – Mthembu v Letsela*, A.J. Kerr maintains that the commencement of the Act will probably lead to the customary law of succession ceasing to exist. *See* 64 J. CONTEMP. ROMAN-DUTCH L. 331–333 (2001). This might be true, but the same can be said about other aspects of the common law that have been changed over the years by legislation, such as the common law of intestate succession, which has been altered quite considerably by the Intestate Succession Act 81 of 1987.

[43] W.C.M. Maqutu, *Internal Conflicts in the Law of Succession of Lesotho, in* SOUTHERN AFRICA IN NEED OF LAW REFORM 53 (A.J.G.M. Sanders ed., Butterworths 1981).

The first codification of certain aspects of the customary law of succession was brought about by section 23 of the much criticized *Black Administration Act* 38 of 1927 (hereinafter the *Black Administration Act*),[44] which came into operation on January 1, 1929.[45] Section 23 has been regarded as the legislative endorsement of the customary rule of male primogeniture: It prohibited testamentary bequests by Africans in the case of house property and quitrent land[46] by providing that these properties had to devolve according to the customary law of succession. Whenever it was determined that the customary law of succession was applicable, the next step was to determine which community's succession rules were applicable. Whereas the succession rules of the Zulu community are largely codified, the succession rules of the various other communities in South Africa are uncodified and their content usually has to be determined by other means, such as precedent, Commission reports,[47] and expert evidence.[48]

Almost seventy-five years after its commencement, on October 15, 2004, section 23 was declared unconstitutional by the Constitutional Court in *Bhe v. Magistrate, Khayelitsha*,[49] but it remained on the statute books until its legislative repeal on April 12, 2006.[50]

The *Bhe* case had far-reaching implications for the existing customary rules of succession. The majority decision did not hesitate to strike down the rule of primogeniture in order to bring it in line with constitutional principles and values. According to the Court, male primogeniture excludes women and other male children (except the first-born) from inheritance. The rule is based on patriarchy, "which reserved for women a position of subservience and subordination and in which they were regarded as perpetual minors under the tutelage of fathers, husbands or the head of

---

[44] *See* Rautenbach, *supra* note 5, at 100–101 (discussing codified provisions of customary law).

[45] Section 23 was followed by the Regulations for the Administration and Distribution of the Estates of Deceased Blacks GN R200 of 1987, which also gave legislative recognition to the rule of male primogeniture and described how the estate of a deceased African had to devolve if section 23 of the Black Administration Act was not applicable and if the deceased did not dispose of his estate by means of a valid will.

[46] Quitrent land is land subject to a long-term lease contract instituted pursuant to legislation. The owner of land held under quitrent title has a limited real right; that is, he or she does not have full ownership of the land but only the right to lease the property from government for a certain period of time and against payment of a certain amount of money.

[47] These are reports from government-appointed commissions consisting of officials from government, judges, and other knowledgeable persons to investigate burning issues. *See e.g.*, SA Law Native Natal Commission Report (1881–1882); SA Law Native Laws and Customs Commission Report and Proceedings with Appendices (1883); SA Law South African Native Affairs Commission Report with Minutes of Evidence and Appendices (1903–1905).

[48] In KwaZulu-Natal, the Zulu customary law of succession has been codified. *See* KwaZulu Act on the Code of Zulu Law 16 of 1985; Natal Code of Zulu Law R151 of 1987.

[49] *See Bhe, supra* note 4.

[50] *See* Repeal of the Black Administration Act and Amendment of Certain Laws Act 28 of 2005.

the extended family."[51] The Court pointed out that the fundamental values of customary law were changing because of urbanization, individualization, the formation of nuclear families, poverty, unemployment, and the changing role of women in society.[52] However, the "rules of succession in customary law have not been given the space to adapt and to keep pace with changing conditions and values," and the application of customary law outside the traditional setting may cause severe hardship.[53]

The Court agreed that the legislature has a role to play, but found that the Court was obliged to forge innovative remedies if an urgent need exists and to "avoid an unacceptable lacuna which would be to the disadvantage of those subject to customary law."[54] The Court was not prepared to develop the rules of customary law or to allow them to develop on a case-by-case basis as that would not solve the uncertainties women and children currently experience under customary law.[55] Rather, it declared that the Court's task was "to facilitate the cleansing of the statute book of legislation so deeply rooted in our unjust past, while preventing undue hardship and dislocation,"[56] and that the Court was obliged to make an interim order. Accordingly, the rule of primogeniture (in customary law and as fossilized in section 23 of the *Black Administration Act*) was declared inconsistent with the Constitution as it excluded or hindered women and extra-marital children from inheriting; consequently, it was invalid.[57]

What does this judgment tell us about the Constitutional Court's approach when addressing customary law issues where constitutional guarantees are implicated? The Court's approach in the *Bhe* case is illustrative of the "transformative constitutionalism" followed by some South African courts.[58] According to this approach, the Constitution is a transformative document that must be interpreted with a view to transforming society into a just, democratic, and equal society. The Chief Justice of

---

[51] *Bhe, supra* note 4, ¶ 78.

[52] *See id.* ¶ 209.

[53] *Id.* ¶ 82–83.

[54] *Id.* ¶ 107.

[55] *See id.* at ¶109. The Court said that because of the gap between "official" and "living" customary law, it would not be possible to develop the customary law without determining its true content:

There is however insufficient evidence and material to enable the Court to do this [determine the true content of customary law]. The difficulty lies not so much in the acceptance of the notion of "living" customary law, as distinct from official customary law, but in determining its content and testing it, as the Court should, against the provisions of the Bill of Rights.

Id.

[56] *Id.* ¶ 116.

[57] *See id.* at ¶ 136.

[58] The expression "transformative constitutionalism" was the theme of an article published in the late 1990s. *See* K.E. Klare, *Legal Culture and Transformative Constitutionalism*, 14 SAJHR 146 (1998). Since then the expression has been embraced by various legal scholars and the judiciary. *See, e.g.,* Soobramoney v. Minister of Health, KwaZulu-Natal, 1998 (1) SA 765 (CC) ¶ 8 (S. Afr.); Rates Action Group v. City of Cape Town 2004 (12) BCLR 1328 (C) ¶ 100 (S. Afr.).

the South African Constitutional Court has expressed the view that the judiciary is responsible for achieving transformative goals: "A truly transformative South Africa requires a new approach that places the Constitutional dream at the very heart of legal education. It requires that we regard law as part of the social fabric and teach law students to see it as such. They should see law for what it is as an instrument that was used to oppress in the past but that has that immense power and capacity to transform our society."[59] In other words, law is seen as an instrument to bring about transformation in society, and this is how the law was used by the Constitutional Court when it abolished the customary rule of male primogeniture in the *Bhe* case. The Court hoped to transform society into a just society by applying constitutional values, such as human dignity, equality, and freedom, to discriminatory traditional customs.

In the minority decision, however, the opinion followed a more conciliatory approach. It found that the rule of male primogeniture was outdated in that it excluded women from succeeding as family head. The obligation in section 39(2) of the Constitution to develop the customary law, however, allowed the Court to adapt the rule of primogeniture to accommodate those observing the rule[60] by "removing the reference to male as to allow an eldest daughter to succeed to the deceased estate."[61]

Ad hoc applications to the high courts of South Africa were not the first and only attempts to have the customary law of succession changed. The South African Law Reform Commission launched its formal investigation into the matter on April 28, 1998, with the publication of Issue Paper 12, commenting on certain issues pertaining to the customary law of succession.[62] The Department of Justice and Constitutional Development drafted a Law of Succession Amendment Bill, which was introduced in Parliament as the Customary Law of Succession Amendment Bill 1998. The Bill was later discarded as a result *inter alia* of severe criticism from the House of Traditional Leaders.[63] The Law Reform Commission commenced with its investigation into the customary law of succession, and in August 2000, Discussion Paper 93 was issued for comments.[64] This was followed by the Commission's Final Report that included a draft Bill[65] that was submitted to the Minister of Justice and

---

[59] P. Langa, *Transformative Constitutionalism*, 17 STELLENBOSCH L. REV. 356 (2006).

[60] *See Bhe, supra* note 4, ¶ 215.

[61] *Id.* ¶ 222. Justice Ngcobo's argument is based on the fact that traditional living changed from agriculture to a cash-based economy, that there was an increase in poverty, urbanization, and migrant labor, resulting in women becoming the de facto heads of households, and contributing to the acquisition of family assets. *See id.* ¶ 221.

[62] SA Law Reform Commission, Issue Paper 12 Harmonization of Common Law and Indigenous Law (1998).

[63] *See* SA Law Reform Commission, Report Project 90: Customary Law of Succession (2004).

[64] SA Law Reform Commission, Discussion Paper 93 Project 90: Customary Law – Succession (2000).

[65] SA Law Reform Commission, *supra* note 63.

Constitutional Development in April 2004, where the matter dragged on for several years.[66] In 2008, the Reform of Customary Law of Succession and Regulation of Related Matters Bill[67] was published.[68] The Bill was finally transformed into an Act entitled the *Reform of Customary Law of Succession and Regulations of Related Matters Act* 11 of 2009 (hereinafter the *RCLSA*). As it now stands, the RCLSA has important implications for the customary law of succession to property, which will be discussed in more detail later in the chapter.[69] The question is not only whether this Act indeed abolished the customary law of succession by applying a "transformed" common law of intestate succession to customary intestate estates, but also whether the customary law of intestate succession influenced the common law of intestate succession, if at all. The basis for these questions will become evident in the following discussion.

15.2.3. *Reform of the Customary Law of Succession Act: A New Coffin?*

As already pointed out, the constitutionality of the rule of male primogeniture was challenged in the Constitutional Court in the *Bhe* case. The Court found that the rule conflicted with changing social conditions and values and the notion of equality, and it was accordingly struck down. But the Court went further than striking down the rule of male primogeniture; it swept aside the application of the customary law of intestate succession with one stroke of its pen, and replaced it with the *Intestate Succession Act* 81 of 1987 (hereinafter the *Intestate Succession Act*), which regulates the common law of succession. However, the Court instructed that this would be a temporary remedy until the RCLSA comes into operation. Though the Act is not in operation yet, it is a legislative endorsement of the findings in the *Bhe* case. These findings have far-reaching implications for the customary law of succession as we know it, and for that reason the Act is worthy of assessment.

One of the aims of the RCLSA is to adapt the customary law of succession to changing social circumstances because it appears that the traditional customary law of succession no longer provides adequately for the welfare of family members.[70]

---

[66] The Report was released by the Department of Justice and Constitutional Development only on March 6, 2008. *See* Parliamentary Monitoring Group, Black Administration Act: adoption; Reform of Customary Law of Succession Bill: briefing; Child Justice Bill: deliberations, *available at* http://www.pmg.org.za/print/12575 (2009).

[67] Reform of Customary Law of Succession and Regulation of Related Matters Bill B10 of 2008.

[68] *See* General Notice 309 of 2008, Government Gazette 30815 (Feb. 25, 2008).

[69] *See infra* Part 2.3.

[70] *See Preamble*, Reform of Customary Law of Succession and Regulations of Related Matters Act 11 of 2009. Chief Justice Langa also referred to these changes in *Bhe*.

"The setting has however changed. Modern urban communities and families are structured and organised differently and no longer purely along traditional lines. The customary law rules of

This aim is in accordance with the notion of transformative constitutionalism followed by the courts so far. The main provision responsible for far-reaching changes to the customary law of succession is section 2(1), which reads: "The estate or part of the estate of any person who is subject to customary law who dies after the commencement of this Act and whose estate does not devolve in terms of that person's will, must devolve in accordance with the law of intestate succession as regulated by the Intestate Succession Act...."[71]

At this stage, three points are of interest. Firstly, the *RCLSA* will not be retroactive and will thus apply only to estates where the deceased died after the commencement of the Act. Secondly, the Act will apply only to intestate customary estates. Lastly (also most importantly), the Act will alter the character of the customary law of succession by replacing it in essence with the *Intestate Succession Act*. The question that immediately comes to mind is whether this modification or replacement of the customary law of succession with an Act based on western principles[72] does not contradict the constitutional guarantee that both common law and customary law are legal systems that are equal to each other. A superficial perusal of the developments in question might create the impression that this is indeed the case; however, a careful analysis of some of the provisions of the *RCLSA* reveals another picture.

Firstly, we need to consider the definitions contained in the *RCLSA*. Section 1 defines the terms "customary law,"[73] "descendant,"[74] "house,"[75] "*Intestate Succession*

---

succession simply determine succession to the deceased's estate without the accompanying social implications which they traditionally had. Nuclear families have largely replaced traditional extended families. The heir does not necessarily live together with the whole extended family which would include the spouse of the deceased as well as other dependants and descendants. He often simply acquires the estate without assuming, or even being in a position to assume, any of the deceased's responsibilities. In the changed circumstances, therefore, the succession of the heir to the assets of the deceased does not necessarily correspond in practice with an enforceable responsibility to provide support and maintenance to the family and dependants of the deceased."*Bhe, supra* note 4, ¶ 80.

[71] Reform of Customary Law of Succession and Regulations of Related Matter Act 11 of 2009 § 2(1).

[72] In this context, "Western" refers to the legal systems of South Africa's colonizers in relation to the United Kingdom and the Netherlands. In this regard, the most obvious differences between common law and customary law have to do with the typical characteristics of the two succession systems. The common law of succession (embodied in the *Intestate Succession Act*) does not discriminate on the basis of gender and sex (male or female) or on the basis of status (marital or extra-marital children). In addition, the succession rules pertain to the nuclear family, which is rather a small family group, and polygyny is not tolerated. On the other hand, the characteristics of the customary law of succession include the rule of male primogeniture (preference of males), the extended family (which may include non-relations), and polygyny.

[73] Customary law is defined to mean "the customs and practices observed among the indigenous African people of South Africa which form part of the culture of those people." Reform of Customary Law of Succession and Regulations of Related Matters, Act 11 of 2009.§ 1.

[74] *See id.*

[75] A house is described as "the family, property, rights and status which arise out of the customary marriage of a woman." *See id.*

Act,"[76] "spouse,"[77] "traditional leader,"[78] and "will."[79] None of these definitions is contained in the *Intestate Succession Act*. However, in terms of the common law, some terms have been interpreted to mean something specific. In this regard, one can refer to the term "descendant," which is defined by the RCLSA to include: (a) a person who is a descendant in terms of the *Intestate Succession Act*;[80] (b) a person who was accepted by the deceased as his or her own child in terms of customary law; (c) a woman from an ancillary marriage;[81] and (d) a woman from a woman-to-woman marriage.[82] Given that the word descendant in the *Intestate Succession Act* usually refers to blood relations in the descending line (for example, the deceased's children, grandchildren, or great-grandchildren),[83] the customary law definition might sound unfamiliar. Nonetheless, in customary law, the circle of dependants is usually much wider than those of other legal systems and the RCLSA recognizes this.

As already pointed out, section 2(1) of the RCLSA modifies the customary law of succession by replacing it with the *Intestate Succession Act*. But section 2 also makes provision for additional forms of marriages, a situation that is not allowed in the common law of South Africa. The first category includes a customary union between a man and a woman who is not the spouse of that man, for the purpose of providing offspring for his house.[84] This kind of union is referred to as an ancillary marriage.

---

[76] This refers to Intestate Succession Act 81 of 1987 (applicable to all intestate estates except customary law estates).

[77] Spouse includes a partner in a customary marriage that is recognized in terms of section 2 of Recognition of Customary Marriages Act 120 of 1998. The Act provides for monogamous and polygamous customary marriages that were concluded before and after the Act. *See* Jansen, *supra* note 22, at 33–45. The meaning of "spouse" is further extended by section 2 of the Reform of Customary Law of Succession and Regulations of Related Matters, Act 11 of 2009 to include ancillary and woman-to-woman marriage. *See infra* notes 1573 and 1574.

[78] A traditional leader is one as defined by section 1 of the Traditional Leadership and Governance Framework Act 41 of 2004 (defining traditional leader as "any person who, in terms of customary law of the traditional community concerned, holds a traditional leadership position, and is recognised in terms of this Act.").

[79] A will is defined as meaning a will pursuant to the Wills Act 7 of 1953 § 1 (defining a will as "a codicil and any other testamentary writing.").

[80] The Intestate Succession Act does not define descendant, but the common law understanding of descendant is that descendants include the blood relations in the descending line. However, section 1 of the Intestate Succession Act extends the concept to adopted children who are regarded as the descendants of the adoptive parents.

[81] An ancillary marriage consists of a marriage between the deceased and another woman in accordance with customary law for the purpose of providing children on behalf of his wife. *See* Reform of Customary Law of Succession and Regulations of Related Matters, Act 11 of 2009 § 2(2)(b).

[82] A woman-to-woman marriage consists of a marriage between a deceased woman and another woman under customary law for the purpose of providing children for the deceased woman's house.

[83] *See* M.M. Corbett et al., THE LAW OF SUCCESSION IN SOUTH AFRICA 358 (Juta 2001).

[84] *See* Reform of Customary Law of Succession and Regulations of Related Matters, Act 11 of 2009 ("[A] woman, other than the spouse of the deceased, with whom he had entered into a union in accordance with customary law for the purpose of providing children for his spouse's house must, if she survives him, be regarded as a descendant of the deceased.").

The second category includes woman-to-woman marriages, where the purpose of the marriage was also to provide offspring on behalf of the deceased woman.[85]

Furthermore, section 3 of the *RCLSA* introduces special rules for interpreting certain provisions of the *Intestate Succession Act*. These rules include, firstly, that a wider meaning must be given to the term "spouse" when dealing with customary unions to include every spouse of the deceased and women in ancillary and woman-to-woman marriages with the deceased.[86] Secondly, a special circumstance prevails where the fixed amount is not enough to provide for all of the "spouses" of the deceased.[87]

Section 4 of the *RCLSA* introduces the common law concept of freedom of testation by giving women living under customary law the right to dispose of house property by means of a will.[88] The Act makes it clear that a customary law estate could be devolved in terms of a will, thus introducing the concept of freedom of testation into the customary law of succession.[89] Although customary family heads generally have the power to disinherit their customary heirs, this power is not comparable with freedom of testation in the common law.[90] The customary law of succession can now be applied only if it is chosen by a testator exercising his or her freedom of testation,[91] a freedom that is fairly unpopular and unknown to most indigenous communities.[92] If a deceased opts for the customary law of succession in his or her will, this could lead to interesting scenarios. According to customary law, the eldest male has the duty to support some of his family members. The inheritance that he receives is intended to help him in doing so. To date, the question of what would happen to his concomitant duty to support others if he does not receive his inheritance has not been sufficiently addressed by the legislature. The question remains whether the dependents would be able to compel him to support them on the basis of his customary duty, or

---

[85] *See id.* § 2(2)(c) ("[I]f the deceased was a woman who was married to another woman under customary law for the purpose of providing children for the deceased's house, that other woman must, if she survives the deceased, be regarded as a descendant of the deceased.").

[86] *See id.* § 3(1).

[87] *See id.* § 3(2)(iii). Normally, under the Intestate Succession Act, a descendant will be excluded by the spouse if the fixed amount exceeds the deceased's estate. However, under the Act, all spouses, including those regarded as descendants, will share the estate equally if the fixed amount is not enough to provide for each wife.

[88] *See id.* § 4(1).

[89] *See id.* § 2(1).

[90] *See* Bennett, *supra* note 18, at 350.

[91] This is also the option proposed by the Master of the High Court. *See* Department of Justice and Constitutional Development, Customary Law: The Way Forward. (unpublished information leaflet).

[92] It was accepted that a family head could make certain allocations of property to houses and individuals and that his deathbed wishes should be respected. These remarks serve to indicate that the idea of wills may well have been known to customary law, albeit not in the western legal sense. *See* Rautenbach et al., *supra* note 5, at 93.

whether they would have a common law claim for maintenance against the estate of the deceased.[93]

These are but a few of the modifications to and implications for the customary law of succession achieved by the proposed *RCLSA*. Although the Act might not be altogether reconcilable with traditional customary law principles, it is reconcilable with constitutional values and today's changed social circumstances. In addition, though the *Intestate Succession Act* was initially the product of modified Roman-Dutch law, it will now be infused with indigenous elements to apply to all South Africans. The new product will neither be a "pure" common law Act, nor will it be a "pure" customary law Act, but a new integrated and distinctly South African Act that applies to all South Africans irrespective of their race or color.

15.3. SUCCESSION TO TRADITIONAL LEADERSHIP

15.3.1. *Background: Identifying the Nails*

As already indicated, the customary rules of succession are also relevant in the context of succession to traditional leadership.[94] The well-known expression "Kgosi ke kgosi ka batho" (literally meaning "a traditional leader is a leader through his people") is illustrative of the importance of the traditional leader in South Africa. According to customary law, a traditional leader is born to the royal house and succession follows the rules of primogeniture as previously explained.[95] A child who will succeed to traditional leader is raised in a specific manner to gain knowledge of the ways of life of the particular community and its practices, and to interact with elders and institutions.[96] According to the decision in *Chief Pilane v. Chief Linchwe*, traditional leaders succeed in terms of the customs and practices of the *morafe* (indigenous community), and the *morafe* should be consulted at all times

[93] In terms of the common law, a needy child has a claim against a deceased parent's estate. *See* Corbett et al., *supra* note 83, at 41–42.
[94] *See generally* BARBARA M. OOMEN, CHIEFS IN SOUTH AFRICA: LAW, POWER AND CULTURE IN THE POST-APARTHEID ERA (Oxford 2005).
[95] *See supra* Section 15.2; D.S. KOYANA, CUSTOMARY LAW IN A CHANGING SOCIETY 80 (Juta, 1980); SA Law Reform Commission, *supra* note 64, ¶ 4.1.2. In a changing society, the customary law of primogeniture is only partially observed, and other children may also inherit. *See id.* ¶ 4.2.6. However, the eldest male still takes the largest share. *See id. See also* Department of Justice and Constitutional Development, *Draft Discussion Document towards a White Paper on Traditional Leadership and Institutions* 1–16 (April 26, 2000). The Swazi custom differs, as the royal family chooses a successor from the children of the different wives. The Swazis do not recognize a principal house. *See* L.P. Vorster, *Succession to bukHosi among the Swazi of Mpumalanga Province, South Africa*, 23 S. AFR. J. ETHNOLOGY, 143–149 (2000). An exception to the rule of male primogeniture is the Lovedu, who appoint a woman as Modjadji or Rain Queen. Women could act as regents for their heirs and in some areas women are already being appointed as traditional leaders. *See* Bennett, *supra* note 18, at 121–22; N.J.J. Olivier et al., *Indigenous Law, in* LAW OF SOUTH AFRICA ¶ 56 (W.A. Joubert et al. eds., LexisNexis 2004).
[96] *See* Bennett, *supra* note 18, at 222.

when the succession of traditional leadership is to be decided.[97] In some sources, it is stated that the royal family should be consulted, depending on the customs of the community.[98] A traditional leader is seen by the members of his community "as the embodiment of law and order, the upholder of values and the provider of the needs of the community. In some instances traditional leadership is even seen as an institution created by God."[99] A traditional leader is accordingly treated with respect.[100]

In 1927, the Governor General of the then Natal province[101] was given the authority to appoint and depose traditional leaders.[102] This authority passed subsequently to various authorities, such as the President of South Africa,[103] the former "homeland"[104] leaders, and, after the new constitutional dispensation, the premiers of the provinces.[105] During the apartheid years,[106] the various authorities – including those in the homelands – interfered with the institution of traditional leaders. If a traditional leader did not toe the line, his community was amalgamated with another community, and a new leader (not always one from the royal house) was appointed.[107] These appointments sometimes led to instability as the communities did not necessarily have respect for these leaders or the institution of traditional leadership. These leaders were regarded as allies of the previous colonial, apartheid, and homeland administrations.[108] Since then, numerous disputes regarding leadership have arisen,[109] and various commissions have been appointed in this regard.[110]

[97] 1995 (4) SA 686 (B) at 696F-G, 689G (S. Afr.).
[98] *See* Traditional Leadership and Governance Framework Act 41 of 2003 § 11(1)(i).
[99] *See* Traditional Authorities Research Group (TARG), *The Administrative and Legal Position of Traditional Authorities in South Africa and Their Contribution to the Implementation of the Reconstruction and Development Programme*, Volume XI: 1 (unpublished report 1997).
[100] *See* Bennett, *supra* note 18, at 103, 104.
[101] Now referred to as the KwaZulu-Natal province.
[102] *See* Black Administration Act 38 of 1927 § 7.
[103] Until 2005, the President of the Republic of South Africa was regarded as the "Supreme Chief of all Blacks in South Africa." Black Administration Act 38 of 1927 § 1.
[104] The homelands were semi-autonomous regions designated for Africans by the previous South African government under apartheid. These areas were incorporated into South Africa by the interim Constitution.
[105] South Africa is divided into nine provinces, each with its own provincial head referred to as a premier.
[106] The apartheid years include from approximately 1948 to 1994.
[107] *See* Black Administration Act 38 of 1927 §§ 5, 9. Some communities were divided and two new leaders were appointed. These leaders were sometimes headmen who did not have much authority. *See* Bennett, *supra* note 18, at 106–11.
[108] *See* S.F. Khunou, *A Legal History of Traditional Leadership in South Africa, Botswana and Lesotho* (2006) (unpublished thesis paper for North-West University, South Africa).
[109] *See, e.g.*, D. Balatseng & W. du Plessis, *Succession of Chieftaincy: Hereditary by Appointment or by Common Consent? – Chief Pilane v. Chief Linchwe* 1995 (4) SA 686 (B), 59 J. OF CONTEMP. ROMAN-DUTCH L. 349–355 (1996); J.S. Mohlamme, *Traditional Leaders of the Bakgatla-ba-ga-Kfagela and Their Succession Story*, 44 HISTORIA 328–344 (1999).
[110] *See* Traditional Leadership and Governance Framework Act 41 of 2003 §§ 21(1)(b), 25(2); MakHosini v. MEC for Local Housing and Traditional Affairs, ECJ 679/2006 (August 17, 2007) (unpublished decision).

Another factor that has led to disputes is paternity. During the apartheid regime, traditional leaders were sometimes forced to find work in the cities. Due to the application of the pass system,[111] their wives could not always accompany them, and some lived with women in the cities without marrying them. Once such a leader died, children unknown to the community arrived, claiming the position of traditional leadership.[112] Not surprisingly then, "[s]uccession to chieftaincy seldom went uncontested, and the death of a ruler often occasioned fierce disputes. As a result, the rules of succession were frequently manipulated or even ignored."[113]

15.3.2. *Constitutional Potential: A New Coffin?*

The new, post-1994 constitutional dispensation provided another opportunity for contenders to dispute succession to traditional leadership positions. Since 1994, the question has arisen why a first-born daughter, a mother, or an aunt may not inherit a leadership position in the absence of a male heir. According to custom, women generally cannot become traditional leaders, because once they marry they are considered to be part of their husbands' family:[114]

> [D]iscrimination against women with regard to succession is not aimed at excluding them from meaningful participation, but rather at preserving the lines of succession. When a woman from a royal family gets married, her children are not considered to be part of the royal family, but as part of her husband's family. Her children are therefore excluded from any rights accruing to members of their mother's family.[115]

---

[111] Pass laws restricted the movement of black Africans in predominantly white South African areas. Black Africans had to carry a passbook at all times in these areas to prove that they had the necessary authority to be there. The pass laws were repealed in the late 1980s.

[112] Between 2005 and 2008, for example, this situation occurred in a Batlhako community dispute in the North-West Province. *See* R.D. Coertze & F.C. de Beer, *Succession to Bogosi among the Batlhako ba Matutu in a Changing Dispensation*, 30 ANTHRO. S. AFR. 45 (2007). In regard to succession to traditional leadership by illegitimate children, see Olivier et al., *supra* note 95, ¶ 103 (stating that "[i]n the case of succession to the status of a traditional leader, a strong case for exclusion could be made as succession to the position of traditional leadership is determined on the basis of lineage, descent and bloodline."). According to the South African Law Reform Commission, "[t]he concept of illegitimacy was irrelevant to customary law ... a child's legitimacy was not defined simply by its parents' marriage but rather by payment of lobola." SA Law Reform Commission, *supra* note 63, ¶ 4.1.3. *See also supra* note 61; R.D. COERTZE, BAFOKENG FAMILY LAW AND LAW OF SUCCESSION 264 (SABRA 1990); J.C. BEKKER, SEYMOUR'S CUSTOMARY LAW 284 (Juta 1989); F.C. de Beer, *Succession to Traditional Venda Leadership in a Changing Constitutional Environment in South Africa*, 27 ANTHRO. S. AFR. 103–110 (2004).

[113] Bennett, *supra* note 18, at 120.

[114] *See* A DISCUSSION DOCUMENT TOWARDS A WHITE PAPER ON TRADITIONAL LEADERSHIP AND INSTITUTIONS 4 (Department of Provincial and Local Government, 2000), *available at* http://www.info.gov.za/view/DownloadFileAction?id=70345 [hereinafter TRADITIONAL LEADERSHIP AND INSTITUTIONS]. *See also* C. Rautenbach et al., *supra* note 5, at 117.

[115] TRADITIONAL LEADERSHIP AND INSTITUTIONS, *supra* note 114, at 33.

The interim and new Constitutions both provided for a right to equality and pro-hibited discrimination on the grounds of *inter alia* gender and sex.[116] The new Constitution also contains a right to culture.[117] The exercise of this right is, however, subject to the other rights in the Constitution such as the rights to equality and non-discrimination. Section 211(1) of the South African Constitution recognizes the insti-tution, role, and status of traditional leadership subject to the Constitution. Section 211(3) states that the courts must apply customary law when that law is applicable (for example, in the case of succession to traditional leadership) but subject to the Constitution and any other law dealing with customary law.

The *Promotion of Equality and Prevention of Unfair Discrimination Act* 4 of 2000 (hereinafter the *Promotion Act*) was promulgated to give effect to the guarantees of equality contained in section 9 of the Constitution. The *Promotion Act* provides that nobody may unfairly discriminate against any person, including on the basis of gender,[118] and lists as possible examples of unfair discrimination, among others, the system of preventing women from inheriting family property, the denial of opportu-nities, and the "systemic inequality of access to opportunities by women as a result of the sexual division of labour."[119]

To determine whether an action is fair or unfair, one must consider the context of the discrimination, certain factors as described in section 14(3),[120] and whether or not there is reasonable and justifiable differentiation intrinsic to the activity con-cerned.[121] In terms of the Constitution, the *Promotion Act*, and the *Bhe* case, no dis-crimination with regard to succession to property is allowed. As already stated, the rule of male primogeniture was abolished in the *Bhe* case, but only with regard to the inheritance of the estate of the deceased. The Constitutional Court did not dis-cuss succession to status and traditional leadership. It was just a matter of time before the customary rules about the succession of a traditional leader were challenged in

---

[116] *See* S. AFR. CONST. 1996, §§ 8, 9.
[117] *See* S. AFR. CONST. 1996, §§ 30, 31.
[118] *See* Promotion of Equality and Prevention of Unfair Discrimination Act 4 of 2000 § 6.
[119] *Id.* at § 8(c), 8(h), 8(i).
[120] Such factors include:

    (a) whether the discrimination impairs or is likely to impair human dignity;
    (b) the impact or likely impact of the discrimination;
    (c) the position of the person in society and whether he or she suffers from patterns of disadvantage or belongs to a group that suffers from such patterns of disadvantage;
    (d) the nature and extent of the discrimination;
    (e) whether the discrimination is systemic in nature;
    (f) whether the discrimination has a legitimate purpose;
    (g) whether and to what extent the discrimination achieves this purpose;
    (h) whether there are less restrictive and less disadvantageous means to achieve the purpose.

    Id. at § 14(3). *See also* INTRODUCTION TO LEGAL PLURALISM IN SOUTH AFRICA, *supra* note 5, at 129–132.
[121] *See* Promotion of Equality and Prevention of Unfair Discrimination Act 4 of 2000 § 14(2).

a court of law. In June 2008, the Constitutional Court was approached to determine whether or not a woman could become a traditional leader.

15.3.3. *Constitutional Court Has Spoken: Nailing Inequality*

The legal question before the Constitutional Court in *Shilubana v. Nwamitwa*[122] was whether a female could succeed as a *Hosi* (traditional leader) of the Valoyi Community in the Limpopo province. The applicant was the daughter of *Hosi* Fofoza Nwamitwa and the respondent was the son of *Hosi* Richard Nwamitwa. When *Hosi* Fofoza died in 1968, his younger brother Richard was appointed *Hosi* in terms of the rules of male primogeniture. The eldest daughter was not considered because of the same rule. In 2001, *Hosi* Richard died. The royal family decided to appoint the applicant in accordance with the principle of gender equality.[123] Usually, the royal family will identify a person to assume the position of traditional leader and inform the relevant customary structure to alert the premier of the province concerned.[124] If there is evidence or an allegation that the identified person was not identified in terms of customary law, customs, or processes, the case must be referred back to the specific province's House of Traditional Leaders for its recommendation.[125] The case may also be referred back to the royal family to reconsider.[126]

This appointment was approved by officials of the Limpopo Province. The respondent initially agreed to the applicant's appointment, but later contested her appointment.[127] The Pretoria High Court[128] issued a declaratory order that the male respondent was the rightful *Hosi* of the Valoyi community. According to the High Court, a woman could not be a *Hosi* prior to the interim Constitution,

---

[122] Shilubana v. Nwamitwa, 2008 (2) SA 66 (CC) (S. Afr.), *available at* http://www.saflii.org/za/cases/ZACC/2008/9.pdf [hereinafter *Shilubana 2*]; and Shilubana v. Nwamitwa 2007 (9) BCLR (919) (CC) (S. Afr.), *available at* http://www.saflii.org/za/cases/ZACC/2007/14.pdf [hereinafter *Shilubana*].

[123] *See Shilubana 2, supra* note 122, ¶ 4. The tribal resolution states: "though in the past it was not permissible by the Valoyis that a female child be heir, in terms of democracy and the new Republic of South African Constitution it is now permissible that a female child be heir since she is also equal to a male child." *See also* ¶ 4–7.

[124] *See* Traditional Leadership and Governance Framework Act 41 of 2003 § 11(1).

[125] *See id.* § 11(3). If there is still a dispute regarding customary law or customs within the traditional community, the community and traditional leaders must try to resolve the dispute internally. If the dispute cannot be resolved, it must be referred to a commission. *Id.* §§ 21–26; Houses of Traditional Leaders are established pursuant to the National House of Traditional Leaders Act 10 of 1997. *See generally* W. du Plessis & T. Scheepers, *Houses of Traditional Leaders: Role, Problems and Future*, 1 POTCHEFSTROOM ELECTRONIC L.J. (2000), *available at* http://www.puk.ac.za/fakulteite/regte/index.html.

[126] *See* Traditional Leadership and Governance Framework Act 41 of 2003 §§ 114(3)-(4).

[127] *See Shilubana, supra* note 122 ¶ 3.

[128] *See Nwamitwa v. Pillia*, 2005 (3) SA 536 (T) (S. Afr.).

the respondent had been appointed as *Hosi*, and the applicant was not appointed in terms of custom. The Court concluded that the royal family cannot change custom; "they can only recognise and confirm a *Hosi*."[129] The Court stated that the applicant's ineligibility was based on lineage and not gender, and she was therefore not discriminated against.[130] This ruling was subsequently confirmed by the Supreme Court of Appeal.[131]

The applicant was granted leave to appeal to the Constitutional Court. The Constitutional Court instructed the parties, as well as the National Movement of Rural Women (hereinafter "the Rural Women") and the Commission for Gender Equality as *amici curiae*, to address the Court on the following questions, among others:

(a) Does the royal family have the authority to develop the customs and traditions of the Valoyi community so as to outlaw gender discrimination in the succession to traditional leadership?

(b) In the course of developing the customs and traditions of a community, does the royal family have the authority to restore the position of traditional leadership to the house from which it was removed by reason of gender discrimination even if this discrimination occurred prior to the coming into the operation of the Constitution?[132]

The Court stated that this "matter appears to pose fundamental questions regarding the interplay between customary law and the Constitution and raise delicate issues regarding the relationship between traditional community structures and the courts of law."[133] The Congress of Traditional Leaders of South Africa (Contralesa)[134] was later admitted as *amicus curiae* as the Court decided it was in the interest of justice to be informed of Contralesa's views in this regard.[135]

The applicant argued that customary law is dynamic and adaptable, and that the Valoyi community acted within its power to amend its customs and traditions. The process of appointing the applicant was in accordance with tribal procedure, because both the royal council and the tribal council approved the decision.[136] In contrast, the respondent argued that lineage determines appointment to the position of *Hosi*.

---

[129] *Shilubana 2, supra* note 122, ¶¶ 20–22.

[130] *See id.* ¶ 23.

[131] *See* Brief of Amici Curiae Commission for Gender Equality, Shilubana v. Nwamitwa, 2007 (2) SA 432 (SCA) (S. Afr.).

[132] *Shilubana 2, supra* note 122, n.5.

[133] *Shilubana 2, supra* note 122, ¶ 5.

[134] The Congress of Traditional Leaders of South Africa.

[135] *See Shilubana 2, supra* note 122, ¶ 18.

[136] *See id.* ¶¶ 27–29.

The respondent further argued that the non-appointment of the applicant was not unconstitutional, based on the limitation in section 36[137] of the Constitution, which rendered the gender discrimination "acceptable, fair and reasonable."[138]

The Commission for Gender Equality argued that the courts should recognize the decisions of tribal communities to adapt customary law so as to reflect the values and spirit of the Constitution. The Commission stressed "that customary law should not be assessed through the lens of common law principles."[139] This argument was echoed by the Rural Women. They also indicated that customary law does not need to be "developed" because it is flexible.[140] Contralesa argued that a customary rule must be accepted by the whole community, which was not the case in this instance. The respondent's appointment as traditional leader was not unfair gender discrimination, because both younger sons and illegitimate sons also cannot succeed. Even in matrilineal communities, younger and illegitimate daughters cannot succeed.[141]

The Constitutional Court confirmed that customary law is part of South African law and that the courts should uphold these customs. The Court also emphasized that a cautious approach should be followed:

> [W]here there is a dispute over the legal position under customary law, a court must consider both the traditions and the present practice of the community. If development happens within the community, the court must strive to recognise and give effect to that development, to the extent consistent with adequately upholding the protection of rights. In addition, the imperative of section 39(2) must be acted on when necessary, and deference should be paid to the development by a customary community of its own laws and customs where this is possible, consistent with the continuing effective operation of the law.[142]

---

[137] Section 36 of the Constitution of the Republic of South Africa 108 of 1996 provides:

    1. The rights in the Bill of Rights may be limited only in terms of law of general application to the extent that the limitation is reasonable and justifiable in an open and democratic society based on human dignity, equality and freedom, taking into account all relevant factors, including
      1. the nature of the right;
      2. the importance of the purpose of the limitation;
      3. the nature and extent of the limitation;
      4. the relation between the limitation and its purpose; and
      5. less restrictive means to achieve the purpose.
    2. Except as provided in subsection (1) or in any other provision of the Constitution, no law may limit any right entrenched in the Bill of Rights.

    S. Afr. Const. 1996.

[138] *Shilubana 2, supra* note 122, ¶ 31.

[139] *Id.* ¶ 33.

[140] *See id.* ¶ 35.

[141] *See id.* ¶¶ 39–40.

[142] *Id.* ¶¶ 41–49.

This approach of the Court is similar to that of the minority decision in the *Bhe* case.[143]

The Court found that although the community's past practices with respect to male primogeniture were important, they were not "decisive where the Constitution requires the development of customary law with constitutional values."[144] The Court also considered the possibility that an amendment of customs may lead to uncertainty, and distinguished the case before it from the judgment of the *Bhe* case. Where the latter ruling of the Court affected the lives of many South African families, the appointment of a traditional leader affects one community: "[T]he change is not one that must be inferred from uneven changes in practice across the country, but appears from written solutions. Vulnerable persons are not denied the protection of the law as a result of the measure."[145]

The Court also considered and rejected the argument that the next traditional leader would not be fathered by a male *Hosi*. The Court stated that if the rules pertaining to the appointment of a traditional leader had changed, the customary law regarding who would be the next heir could also change. According to the Court, "[t]he actions of a traditional community cannot be illegitimate just because they involve a departure from past practice."[146] The Court indicated that although the traditional community had changed the practice of not appointing a woman as *Hosi*, other practices were not affected. The community still respected the fact that a *Hosi* was born and not elected and that the royal family has the authority to decide who the next traditional leader should be.[147] The Court accordingly found that the traditional authority acted in accordance with the Constitution.[148]

The cornerstones of the South African constitutional order, namely democracy, dignity, and equality,[149] have brought a new feature to the institution of traditional leadership. Women may no longer be denied the right to assume traditional leadership or leadership in the customary structures of governance. They now enjoy equal status with their first-born brothers. This means that they may now be appointed in terms of custom and tradition as queens and regents of their own communities.

Many may argue that this decision is another nail in the coffin of customary law. However, as the Court pointed out, it is but one deviation from the original position, which was not forced on the community but chosen by them. The royal family and council decided to adapt the customary law to changing circumstances, as

---

[143] *See supra* Section 15.2.2.
[144] *Shilubana 2, supra* note 122, ¶ 56, 51–57.
[145] *Id.* ¶ 77.
[146] *Id.* ¶ 79.
[147] *See id.* ¶¶ 82–85.
[148] *See id.* ¶ 91.
[149] *See* S. Afr. Const. § 1

has been done over many centuries. In this case, the impetus was the Constitution, while over the centuries, cultural practices, contact with other communities, religion, and modern influences have also ensured that customary law remained flexible and adaptable.

15.4. CONCLUSION: BURIAL OF THE CUSTOMARY LAW OF SUCCESSION?

Customary law used to be the inferior body of South African law: It was altered, fixed, modified, and changed by judging it against common law principles, and it was thereby constantly marginalized. It is no wonder that all new developments were viewed with suspicion and anger. However, this situation has changed dramatically. Customary law has an equal place in the new constitutional dispensation of South Africa. Like the common law, it is subject to the Constitution and has to develop to promote the spirit, purport, and objects of the Bill of Rights. Customary law must be judged through a constitutional lens and not through a common law lens.[150] Nevertheless, as clearly illustrated by the *Bhe* and *Shilubana* cases, customary law cannot escape constitutional transformation, and the Courts will not hesitate to develop customary law in order to ensure that it accords with constitutional values.

For many years, customary law has been largely ignored by legal reformers, and it therefore could never develop into a sophisticated system that is duly documented and acknowledged by the legal fraternity, unlike the common law, which received the most attention, and thus developed constantly. In *Alexkor Ltd v. Richtersveld Community*,[151] the Constitutional Court noted that "indigenous law is not a fixed body of formally classified and easily ascertainable rules. By its very nature it evolves as the people who live by its norms change their patterns of life."[152] It has now indeed "evolved and developed to meet the changing needs of the community."[153]

Two approaches were followed by the courts, namely transformative constitutionalism and cultural relativism. Transformative constitutionalism was applied where the customary law of succession in relation to the property of a deceased urgently needed reform. In the *Bhe* case, the Court pointed out that:

> The rules of succession in customary law have not been given the space to adapt and to keep pace with changing social conditions and values. One reason for this is the fact that they were captured in legislation, in text books, in the writings of experts and in court decisions without allowing for the dynamism of customary

---

[150] *See Alexkor Ltd v. Richtersveld Community*, 2003 (5) SA 460 (CC).
[151] *Id.*
[152] *Id.* ¶ 52.
[153] *Id.* ¶ 53.

law in the face of changing circumstances. Instead, they have over time become increasingly out of step with the real values and circumstances of the societies they are meant to serve and particularly the people who live in urban areas.[154]

Recent developments should therefore not be seen as the final nails in the coffin of customary law of succession rules. They should rather be seen as necessary within South Africa's new constitutional dispensation, where everyone is equal before the law, irrespective of whether that law is the common law or customary law. Bringing the developments to the attention of indigenous communities in the rural areas is of course another challenge that will not be discussed here. In other words, instead of remaining the inferior body of South African law, unacknowledged and unchanging, customary law is now transforming. It is encouraging that the common law is no longer the barometer against which customary law is measured; instead, customary law is measured against the values of the Constitution. This reality should still the voices of those who argue that the judiciary and legislature regard customary law as inferior to common law.

Nevertheless, in the area of the customary law of intestate succession, the situation is unique. It has been developed to the extent that it does not exist in its "old" form anymore, because its rules have been "merged" with the rules of the common law of intestate succession and a "new" system of intestate succession, as embodied in the *Intestate Succession Act* and as modified by the RCLSA. The "new" law of intestate succession will be applicable to everybody in South Africa, although different rules might be applicable, depending on the lifestyle of a deceased. In a sense then, the new system of intestate law of succession can be described as a unified system.

Against this background, one has to agree with the viewpoint of the late Chief Justice Mahomed that the common law (Roman-Dutch law) and the customary law influence each other.[155] This has been clearly illustrated by the developments in intestate succession: The common law of intestate succession has been influenced by customary law principles, and vice versa. We can still hope for a truly integrated system of law that retains the "good" values of both systems of law, and perhaps the developments in the law of succession will bring us one step closer to reaching a truly integrated legal system applicable to all South Africans irrespective of race or culture.

Unlike the unified customary law of succession rules, the rules pertaining to succession in the context of traditional leadership are restricted to the relevant indigenous community (the Valoyi community) that was the subject matter of the court application in *Shilubana v. Nwamitwa*. The approach of the Constitutional Court

---

[154] *Id.* ¶ 82.
[155] *See* I. Mahomed, *The Future of Roman-Dutch Law in Southern Africa, Particularly in Lesotho,* 1 Lesotho L.J. 1, 363 (1985).

in this regard was one of cultural relativism. Instead of judging the behavior of the community by the Court's own views on cultural and human rights issues, the Court left it to the community to adapt to changing circumstances and to uphold the right to equality. The decision of the Court does not drive the final nails into the coffin of succession laws about traditional leadership; rather, it is envisaged that women in other communities (if they qualify) will use the decision to establish their right to become community leaders.

The *Shilubana* approach correlates with the minority decision in *Bhe* where it was argued that customary law should be allowed to adapt and should not be abolished. In *Bhe*, however, the minority opinion adapted customary law rather than trying to change the community itself. This approach embraces both transformative constitutionalism and cultural relativism.

Whether the courts apply transformative constitutionalism or cultural relativism, customary law is finally "on the move,"[156] and as one writer has said, "customary law, which has inhabited some of the darker corners of the apartheid state, must now be thought of in relation to mainstream legal issues such as human rights, courts, procedures, legal formalism, the make-up of the judiciary, and of meaningful access to law."[157]

[156] Oomen, *supra* note 94, at 77.
[157] M. Chanock, *Law, State and Culture Thinking about "Customary Law" after Apartheid*, 10 CILSA 53 (1991).

PART FIVE

Customary Criminal Law

16

Customary Criminal Law in the South African Legal System

Thomas W. Bennett

16.1. INTRODUCTION

The occasion for writing this chapter is a long-overdue bill that has been proposed by the South African government to reconstitute the country's system of traditional courts.[1] Under the apartheid regime, the state had given these tribunals its full support, but since the new democratic Constitution of 1996,[2] their status – and, more generally, that of traditional rulers – has been uncertain. Eventually, on April 9, 2008, the government tabled a Traditional Courts Bill, confirming, although in modified terms, the courts' civil and criminal jurisdiction.

Strongly voiced protests immediately appeared in the liberal press. All criticized the wide powers given to traditional rulers to enforce customary law within areas of jurisdiction that correspond to the bantustans of the apartheid era.[3] Anyone who, when duly summoned, fails to appear before a traditional court commits an offense.[4] Rural South Africans are thereby confined to their former "tribal" homelands, even those who may have lost all connection with these areas. No provision is made for opting out of the system. Thus, "[i]nstead of focusing on what unites people, it reinforces the constructs of ethnic difference and insider-outsider status, which are at the heart of the violence gripping our country."[5]

---

[1] *See* Traditional Courts Bill, B15–2008.

[2] S. AFR. CONST. 1996. It is noteworthy, however, that traditional courts are given no mention in section 166 of the Constitution, which lists the tribunals constituting the judicial system.

[3] The bantustans were areas (comprising 13 percent of South Africa's land mass) reserved for occupation by Africans. Later, under the Promotion of Bantu Self-Government Act 46 of 1959, these areas became the basis for establishing independent territories known as the "homelands."

[4] *See* Traditional Courts Bill, B15–2008 § 20(c).

[5] Editorial, BUSINESS DAY (S. Afr.), June 2, 2008. The editorial goes on to point out that, in its present form, the bill will trap almost half of the country's population – those living in rural areas – under the authority of unelected traditional leaders (whose judgments will carry the same weight as those issued by magistrates' courts).

This chapter is concerned with an issue that is given only small mention in the Bill, namely customary "criminal law."[6] Even though the recognition of indigenous systems of "civil" law has long been settled, the position of criminal law has not been properly debated since the colonial conquest.[7] This is a curious omission in view of the fact that criminal justice is intimately concerned with matters of state, given that recognition of indigenous forms of crime implies recognition of indigenous sovereignty,[8] and sovereignty, in turn, implies recognition of the governmental powers of the guardians of the indigenous order – traditional rulers.

Although I will be approaching this inquiry on a purely theoretical basis, fieldwork in Africa makes it abundantly clear that formal state institutions have little to do with day-to-day matters of law and order.[9] As far as "civil" matters are concerned, various traditional and other fora now cater to the vast majority of the population's legal needs. Data on what could be thought of as criminal matters are scarcer,[10] but

---

[6] Although it must be appreciated that this term is a construct of western jurisprudence, and not necessarily of customary law, its use is essential if we are to pursue a debate in South Africa's dominant legal discourse.

[7] When the Cape annexed the Transkeian territories in the last quarter of the nineteenth century, it convened a Commission to consider the law to be applied in the courts. Legal certainty was a major problem, because magistrates did not know when to apply which law, and, of course, the people did not know which law to obey. The Commission was specially concerned to recommend codification of the criminal law, but there was a marked difference of opinion about whether to codify the common law, customary law, or a mixture of the two. *See* D. KOYANA, THE INFLUENCE OF THE TRANSKEI PENAL CODE ON SOUTH AFRICAN CRIMINAL LAW 27 (Lovedale Press 1992) (citing REPORT AND PROCEEDINGS, WITH APPENDICES, OF THE GOVERNMENT COMMISSION ON NATIVE LAWS AND CUSTOMS § 35 (W. A. Richards & Sons 1883)) [hereinafter REPORT AND PROCEEDINGS]. Customary law was thought to be inherently problematic because its provisions on crime were too vague, as was the distinction between crime and delict. *See id.* at 28 (citing REPORT AND PROCEEDINGS, *supra,* § 22). *Cf.* Jonathan Ayliff, *Minority Report, in* REPORT AND PROCEEDINGS, *supra,* at 45–50 (dissenting report urging the adoption of a code derived purely from customary law). The final product was, in fact, based squarely on the Indian Penal Code of 1860, together with a code drafted for England (although not accepted by Parliament).

[8] For that reason, Britain usually imposed a single system of criminal justice in its southern African colonies. See, for instance, Ciskei, where, in 1835, customary criminal law was formally abolished by treaty. *See* R. Mqeke, *The History of Recognition and Application of Indigenous Law in the Ciskei,* TRANSKEI L.J. 77, 79 (1986).

[9] *Cf.* the proceedings of a conference on *Human Rights and Traditional and Informal Justice Systems in Africa* organized by the U.N. Office of the High Commissioner for Human Rights, Windhoek, Namibia (June 20, 2007). *See also* Ewa Wojkowska, *Doing Justice: How Informal Justice Systems Can Contribute,* U.N. Development Programme: Oslo Governance Centre Report 5 (2006) ("Informal justice systems are often more accessible to poor and disadvantaged people and may have the potential to provide quick, cheap and culturally relevant remedies. Informal justice systems are prevalent throughout the world, especially in developing countries. They are the cornerstone of dispute resolution and access to justice for the majority of populations, especially the poor and disadvantaged in many countries, where informal systems usually resolve between 80 and 90 percent of disputes.").

[10] Even in the 1960s, however, it was estimated that probably 90 percent of criminal cases in Africa were tried by chiefs. *See* J.S. Read, *Criminal Law in the Africa of Today and Tomorrow,* 7 J. AFR. L. 5, 16 (1963).

a recent work on sub-Saharan Africa shows that a diverse range of non-state agents have taken over responsibility for maintaining communal order, peace, and security. These agents now exercise an extensive range of powers of prevention, deterrence, investigation, and punishment.[11]

Unlike many other African states, South Africa has the benefit of what is probably the best developed security and justice infrastructure on the continent. It is therefore a sad irony that the country is nevertheless notorious for its levels of crime and violence. Empirical research on the contribution of traditional law and institutions to solving this problem is minimal,[12] but this is the background against which policy makers must decide on the advisability of giving customary systems of criminal law full recognition.

16.2. THE AMBIGUOUS POSITION OF CUSTOMARY CRIMINAL LAW

Throughout Africa, the colonial powers imposed their own systems of law as the general laws of the land. Although they were prepared to make an exception for indigenous systems of customary civil law, the terms of recognition were usually not intended to supplant the metropolitan criminal law.[13] This was regarded as an overriding system, applicable to all subjects of the state, settlers and Africans alike.[14] The position of customary-law crimes was undecided.[15]

South Africa is a case in point. Today, the status of customary law in the legal system is determined, in the first instance, by § 211(3) of the 1996 Constitution:

---

[11] *See* B. BAKER, MULTI-CHOICE POLICING IN AFRICA 29 (Nordiska Afrikainstitutet 2008).

[12] *See* J. Hund & M. Kotu-Rammopu, *Justice in a South African Township: The Sociology of Makgotla*, 16 CILSA 179 (1983) (early study of Mamelodi). *See also* D. Nina, *Popular Justice and the "Appropriation" of the State Monopoly on the Definition of Justice and Order: The Case of Anti-Crime Communities, in* OTHER LAW: NON-STATE ORDERING IN SOUTH AFRICA ch. 5 (W. Schärf & D. Nina, eds., Juta 2001); A.M. Mangokwana, *Makgotla in Rural and Urban Contexts, in* OTHER LAW: NON-STATE ORDERING IN SOUTH AFRICA, *supra*, ch. 7.

[13] To have recognized the indigenous systems of criminal law would have contradicted a basic function of the judicial system, which was to proclaim the values of British civilization and the reach of state power. *See* M. CHANOCK, THE MAKING OF SOUTH AFRICAN LEGAL CULTURE 1902–1936: FEAR, FAVOUR AND PREJUDICE 48 (Cambridge Univ. Press 2000).

[14] *See* T.W. BENNETT, THE APPLICATION OF CUSTOMARY LAW IN SOUTHERN AFRICA: THE CONFLICT OF PERSONAL LAWS 40 (Juta 1985).

[15] Policy in the post-colonial era has been ambivalent. For example, section 3(3)(b) of the Namibian Traditional Authorities Act 25 of 2000 gives no indication whether these authorities may apply customary criminal law, whereas the Zimbabwe Customary Law and Local Courts Act (Chapter 7:05) allows local courts (i.e., courts of traditional rulers) no criminal jurisdiction. Sections 11 and 17 of the Laws of Botswana (Customary Courts) (Chapter 04:05) and section 12 of the Swazi Courts Act 80 of 1950, on the other hand, give traditional rulers fairly extensive criminal jurisdiction. *See* C. Anyangwe, *The Whittling Away of African Indigenous Legal and Judicial System*, 30 ZAMBIA L.J. 46, 52–53 (1998).

"The courts must apply customary law when that law is applicable, subject to the Constitution and any legislation that specifically deals with customary law."[16] In the second instance, the place of customary law is governed by a statute inherited from the apartheid era: "Any court may take judicial notice of . . . indigenous law in so far as such law can be ascertained readily and with sufficient certainty: Provided that indigenous law shall not be opposed to the principles of public policy or natural justice. . . ."[17] The term "indigenous law" in this section (which may be understood to mean the same as "customary law") is defined broadly to mean the "Black law or customs as applied by the Black tribes in the Republic or in territories which formerly formed part of the Republic."[18] The generality of this definition, when read with § 211(3) of the Constitution, clearly allows the inclusion of both customary criminal and civil laws. In consequence, not only are traditional courts allowed to enforce customary crimes, but also magistrates' courts and the High Court – which represents a marked break with an unspoken policy of the past.

Policy in the case of traditional courts, however, has always been quite different. Generally speaking, the colonial venture throughout sub-Saharan Africa ran on the basis of an uneasy coalition between settlers and traditional authorities.[19] Whenever government called on the services of the latter, however, the usual quid pro quo was recognition of their courts and customary laws.

In South Africa, modern policy can most conveniently be dated from 1927, when, plagued by a constant shortage of resources, and concerned to segregate and "retribalize" the African population, the government promulgated the Native Administration Act.[20] This enactment abolished differences between the earlier British colonies, the Cape,[21] Natal,[22] and the independent Boer republic of the Transvaal[23] in order to

---

[16] When section 211 is read in conjunction with other provisions in the Constitution, notably section 39(2), it can be taken to mean that customary and Roman-Dutch law have become equal partners as the general law of the land. *See S v Makwanyane & Another* 1995 (3) SA 391 (CC) ¶ 365.

[17] Law of Evidence Amendment Act 45 of 1988 § 1(1).

[18] *Id.* § 1(4).

[19] *See* WILLIAM MALCOLM HAILEY, AN AFRICAN SURVEY: A STUDY OF PROBLEMS ARISING IN AFRICA SOUTH OF THE SAHARA 527–529 (Oxford Univ. Press 2d ed. 1945).

[20] Native Administration Act 38 of 1927. One of the principal aims of this Act was to settle the position of traditional rulers in the administration of justice. *See* S. Dubow, *Holding "A Just Balance Between White and Black": The Native Affairs Department in South Africa c.* 1920–33, 12 J. S. AFR. STUD. 217, 230–234 (1986).

[21] The Cape, apart from the Transkeian territories, had refused to recognize the authority of traditional rulers or to allow any courts to apply customary law. *See* Bennett, *supra* note 14, at 540. In Southern Bechuanaland, a dependency of the Cape, however, sections 31 and 32 of Proclamation 2 of 1885 gave traditional rulers exclusive civil and (apart from certain serious crimes) criminal jurisdiction over their subjects.

[22] Under Ordinance 3 of 1849, traditional rulers had fairly generous powers to adjudicate disputes and apply customary law.

[23] Law 4 of 1885 enacted a policy similar to that in Natal.

establish a new, national system of courts with jurisdiction to deal exclusively with the African population. Thereafter the fate of customary criminal law was tied to traditional courts and, in turn, to traditional rulers.

Under the Native Administration Act, approved chiefs or headmen[24] could be authorized to hear both civil and criminal disputes arising among "blacks" within their areas of jurisdiction according to customary law.[25] These courts were not allowed to impose punishments involving death, mutilation, grievous bodily harm, imprisonment, corporal punishment or the imposition of fines in excess of R100 (or two heads of large stock or ten heads of small stock).[26] This system persisted for the next seventy years, until 1994, when a new democratic government came to power.

As in other parts of post-colonial Africa, the incoming government's attitude toward traditional rulers was ambivalent. On the one hand, chiefs were seen as inefficient and backward, as stooges of the apartheid regime and, more generally, as ethnically divisive. For ordinary people, on the other hand, their rulers were a "legal and constitutional horizon," a "personification of the moral and political order, protection against injustice, unseemly behaviour, evil and calamity."[27] Whatever the truth of these perceptions, administration of the rural areas was impossible without traditional leaders.[28]

Following intense political bargaining, South Africa's final, 1996 Constitution made provision for the retention of traditional rulers,[29] but no agreement could be reached on what role they were to play in the new constitutional order. After seven years of uncertainty, legislation was eventually passed to regulate these matters: the Traditional Leadership and Governance Framework Act.[30]

Customary courts, however, were a different matter. Because they provided the principal means for meeting the legal needs of litigants in rural areas, there was no question of shutting down the courts already in operation.[31] Notwithstanding

---

[24] Native Administration Act 38 of 1927 § 12(1).

[25] *See* Section 20(1) governed criminal jurisdiction. *Id.* § 20(1). Chiefs could try certain minor offenses at common or customary law. All major offenses, which were specified in the Third Schedule, had to be tried in the magistrates' courts or the Supreme Court.

[26] *See id.* § 20(2).

[27] E.A.B. van Rouveroy van Nieuwaal, *Chiefs and African States: Some Introductory Notes and an Extensive Bibliography on African Chieftaincy*, 25–26 J. LEGAL PLURALISM & UNOFFICIAL L. 1, 23 (1987).

[28] *See* T.W. BENNETT, HUMAN RIGHTS AND AFRICAN CUSTOMARY LAW 69–70 (Juta 1999). *Cf.* J.C. Bekker, *Rol van die Regsprekende Gesag in 'n Plurale Samelewing*, HSRC Reports, Pol. 21 (1983).

[29] Section 211(1) therefore provides that "[t]he institution, status and role of traditional leadership, according to customary law, are recognized, subject to the Constitution." S. AFR. CONST. 1996 § 211(1).

[30] Traditional Leadership and Governance Framework Act 41 of 2003.

[31] They were therefore included in section 16(1) of Schedule 6 (Transitional Arrangements) of the Constitution, 1996. Traditional courts included all those established by the various homeland governments before the reintegration of South Africa. D.S. KOYANA & J.C. BEKKER, JUDICIAL PROCESS IN THE CUSTOMARY COURTS OF SOUTHERN AFRICA 19 (Univ. of Transkei 1998). *See also Mhlekwa*

their accessibility, however, it seemed doubtful whether these courts could meet the requirements of the new Bill of Rights. Hence, to prepare the way for legislation redefining their powers and composition, the Department of Justice gave the South African Law Reform Commission the task of instituting a thorough inquiry.

In 1999, a Special Project Committee of the Commission published a *Discussion Paper* on Traditional Courts,[32] in which it recommended retention of the existing courts.[33] Although it noted certain problems – notably exclusion of legal practitioners, a tendency to presume guilt, sexism, and a lack of formal legal training[34] – the advantages of these courts clearly outweighed their disadvantages: They were simple, informal, cheap, accessible, and familiar with the laws and affairs of their communities.[35] Of course, traditional leaders themselves presented a strong lobby in favor of their own courts, but, even so, members of the public voiced no major objections.[36]

In 2005, most of the Black Administration Act[37] was repealed, along with the provisions constituting the traditional courts and defining their areas of jurisdiction.[38] Implementation of this measure was delayed, however, by a provision declaring that certain key sections[39] would remain in force until September 30, 2007, or until such date as national legislation was passed to regulate these matters, whichever occurred first.[40] This time period had to be extended to allow for the production of the Traditional Courts Bill, which finally appeared on April 9, 2008.[41]

& *Feni v Head of the Western Tembuland Regional Authority & Another*, 2001 (1) SA 574 (Tk) at 588, 596–598, 617–618, 2000 (9) BCLR 979 at 999–1001, 1019–1020.

[32] SA Law Commission Discussion Paper 82 The Harmonisation of the Common Law and Indigenous Law: Traditional Courts and the Judicial Function of Traditional Leaders (May 1999). A separate study was conducted on community forums, which were proposed for areas not serviced by traditional courts. SA Law Commission Discussion Paper 87 Community Dispute Resolution Structures (August 1999).

[33] As far as jurisdiction was concerned, however, the Commission recommended abolition of all racial criteria. Instead, it felt that jurisdiction should be determined by residence, nature of the claim, and applicability of customary law. *See* Discussion Paper 82, *supra* note 32, ¶ 6.6.2. Most of these recommendations were repeated in the Committee's final report. *See* SA Law Commission Project 90 Customary Law Report: Report on Traditional Courts and the Judicial Function of Traditional Leaders (January 2003).

[34] *See* Discussion Paper 82, *supra* note 32, ¶ 2.2.

[35] *See id.* ¶ 2.1.

[36] *See id.* ¶ 3.4.1. Objections to the Regional Authority Courts in Transkei constituted the major exception. *See id.* ¶ 3.4.1.

[37] Black Administration Act 38 of 1927 (formerly the Native Administration Act). The Constitutional Court had long called for repeal of this relic of the apartheid years. *See Moseneke & Others v The Master & Another* 2001 (2) SA 18 (CC) ¶ 21, 2001 (2) BCLR 103; *Bhe v Magistrate, Khayelitsha* 2005 (1) SA 580 (CC) ¶¶ 62–64; 2005 (1) BCLR 1.

[38] Repeal of the Black Administration Act and Amendment of Certain Laws Act 28 of 2005.

[39] *See id.* §§ 12, 20 and Third Schedule.

[40] *See id.* § 1(3).

[41] Traditional Courts Bill, B15–2008.

The bill sets out to "affirm the values of the traditional justice system, based on restorative justice and reconciliation and to align them with the Constitution."[42] The newly constituted traditional courts are designed to encourage "social cohesion, co-existence and peace and harmony in traditional communities"[43] by "enhancing access to justice [and] by providing a speedier, less formal and less expensive resolution of disputes."[44] Together with their usual civil jurisdiction, the courts will be entitled to "hear and determine offen[s]es brought before [them] if the offen[s]e occurred within the area of jurisdiction of the traditional court in question and if such offen[s]e is listed in Schedule 1."[45] The offenses in question are defined in typically common-law terms: assault (provided that grievous bodily harm was not inflicted), theft (whether under the common law or a statutory provision, including stock theft), malicious injury to property and *crimen injuria* (provided, in the latter three instances, that the amount involved does not exceed whatever is determined by the Minister by notice in the *Gazette*). Finally, the courts' penal jurisdiction may not involve:

(a) any punishment that is inhumane, cruel, or degrading, or which involves any form of detention, including imprisonment;
(b) banishment from the traditional community;
(c) a fine in excess of the amount determined by the Minister from time to time by notice in the Gazette; or
(d) corporal punishment.[46]

Clause 3, entitled "Guiding Principles," indicates that the system contemplated in the Bill is predicated on a popularly conceived dichotomy between common- and customary-law ideas of justice. The common-law system is stigmatized as "retributive," whereas the indigenous system is said to be "restorative" (i.e., designed to promote social cohesion and reconciliation).[47]

---

[42] *Id.* § 2(a).
[43] *Id.* § 2(b)(i).
[44] *Id.* § 2(b)(ii).
[45] *Id.* § 6. Conversely, the South African Law Reform Commission's proposal to establish community tribunals in the townships refused to stipulate a rule on criminal jurisdiction. Instead, it said that:

As soon as one labels an act as a crime, it shunts the processing into a "guilty" or "not guilty" mindframe. Community forums focus far more on the relationship between the disputants, and what [a] wrongful act has done to the relationship or to peaceful co-existence in the community.... The danger of splitting civil cases from criminal cases is that the community forums might lose their power and legitimacy (and therefore their effectiveness) if their role in deterring criminal behaviour is drastically restricted.

Discussion Paper 82, *supra* note 32, ¶ 4.3.5.
[46] Traditional Courts Bill, B15–2008 § 10(1). In any event, the whippings formerly imposed by certain traditional courts were prohibited by section 1 of the Abolition of Corporal Punishment Act 33 of 1997.
[47] Traditional Courts Bill, B15–2008 § 3(2). On the aim of reconciliation in traditional courts, see C.R.M. Dlamini, *Whither Lay Justice in South Africa?*, 14 SPECULUM JURIS 3, 6 (1985); M. GLUCKMAN, THE

In drawing up the bill, the Portfolio Committee for Justice and Constitutional Development evidently paid no attention to the Law Reform Commission's *Report on Traditional Courts*, in spite of the carefully considered recommendations and a lengthy process of consultation.[48] Although the time has now passed for lodging objections to the bill, it remains to be seen whether Parliament will accept it in its present form.

16.3. PROBLEMS WITH THE RECOGNITION OF CUSTOMARY CRIMES

Although customary criminal law is part of the national legal system, there are, nevertheless, cogent reasons for reconsidering its scope and position. The reasons can be classified into two groups: those of substance, involving issues of constitutional law and political structure, and those of procedure, involving issues of human rights.

16.3.1. *The State's Monopoly on the Use of Force*

The administration of criminal justice is closely linked to a state's monopoly of the use of force, a power that is in turn associated with state sovereignty.[49] This power has two aspects. First, only the state can force those under its jurisdiction to submit to its judicial process. Thus, an individual's resort to self-help in order to settle a dispute may be deemed vigilantism and punished as a usurpation of state power.[50] Secondly, only the state is entitled to inflict punishment for the commission of offenses.[51] If an unauthorized individual were to deprive another individual of life, liberty, or property, the act would *prima facie* be deemed a criminal (and probably also civil) offense.

Although recognition of customary criminal law might seem to infringe the state's monopoly on force, because it involves traditional rulers and their way of dispensing

---

IDEAS IN BAROTSE JURISPRUDENCE 94–97 (Manchester Univ. Press 1972). Although the concept of restorative justice is often used in relation to indigenous and non-state legal orders, it is far from being properly defined. It implies, however, negotiation among all interested parties and a consensus about the final settlement, which is ideally some form of reintegration of the offender, victim, and community. *See* A. Ashworth, *Responsibilities, Rights and Restorative Justice*, 42 BRIT. J. CRIMINOLOGY 578 (2002). The claims about restorative justice are more fully examined later in the chapter.

[48] *See Editorial*, BUSINESS DAY (S. Afr.), June 2, 2008.

[49] *See* J.E. Thomson, *State Sovereignty in International Relations: Bridging the Gap Between Theory and Empirical Research*, 39 INT'L STUD. Q. 213, 219 (1995) (providing a working definition of sovereignty, one which is firmly established in international law: "recognition by internal and external actors that the state has the exclusive authority to intervene coercively in activities within its territory").

[50] A dramatic example of this proposition occurred in South Africa during the 1980s, when anti-apartheid forces set up people's courts as a direct challenge to state authority. *See S v Mayekiso* 1988 (4) SA 738 (W). *See also S v Makwanyane* 1995 (3) SA 391 (CC) ¶ 168, 1995 (6) BCLR 665 (commenting on section 34 of the Constitution).

[51] *See* J. BURCHELL, PRINCIPLES OF CRIMINAL LAW 68 (Juta 3d ed. 2006).

justice, the contravention is relatively unimportant. At the outset, we can dispose of the question quite simply by noting that if traditional rulers have the necessary statutory authority to enforce customary-law crimes, they are acting as agents of the state, and hence are not violating its sovereign powers. Thus, although we have a legally anomalous situation, whereby sovereignty is divided between the central state and traditional rulers, the division is the result of a specific political compromise.[52]

In addition, we might note the frequent claim that customary law favors conciliation rather than punishment. If traditional courts can be compared with arbitral tribunals, consent becomes the basis of their jurisdiction, not force, and it then follows that they do not violate the state's monopoly on coercion. Indeed, as we have seen earlier, with respect to the Traditional Courts Bill, much has been made of the fact that customary law aims at restorative justice, not retribution.[53]

Perceptions of traditional justice, however, have been clouded by two extreme visions of its overall purpose. On the one hand, we still seem to be in a state of reaction to the evolutionist idea, popularized by Sir Henry Maine, that pre-state societies knew only retribution.[54] In this regard, he relied heavily on evidence from early Roman law, which could hardly support a global generalization. As later functionalist anthropology was at pains to demonstrate, pre-state societies lacked the physical infrastructure to inflict the type of punishments considered usual in a modern criminal justice system.[55]

On the other hand, for various reasons of criminal justice policy, we now have an overemphasis on the principle of restorative justice in customary law.[56] This principle is not an unvarying aim of traditional courts. Much depends on the nature of

---

[52] *See* T. Maloka & D. Gordon, *Chieftainship, Civil Society, and the Political Transition in South Africa*, 22 CRITICAL SOC. 37, 44 (1996).

[53] *See* A.L. Epstein, *Injury and Liability in African Customary Law in Zambia*, in IDEAS AND PROCEDURES IN AFRICAN CUSTOMARY LAW 292, 300 (M. Gluckman ed., Oxford Univ. Press 1969). *Cf.* further discussion, *infra*.

[54] *See* SIR HENRY MAINE, ANCIENT LAW ch. 10 (John Murray 1861) (stating that torts carrying penalties rather than mere compensation typified "primitive" law). For evolutionist anthropology, the blood feud was considered characteristic of politically decentralized societies. *See* E. EVANS PRITCHARD, THE NUER: A DESCRIPTION OF THE MODES OF LIVELIHOOD AND POLITICAL INSTITUTIONS OF A NILOTIC PEOPLE 150 (Clarendon 1940) (providing a classic account).

[55] Imprisonment, in particular, was unknown. Hence, any resort to punishment would have involved the infliction of immediate forms of physical suffering, whether loss of life, beatings, banishment, confiscation of property, reprimands, or fines of livestock. *See* M.W. Prinsloo, *Die Inheemse Strafreg van die Noord-Sotho*, 2 TYDSKRIF VIR DIE SUID-AFRIKAANSE REG [J. S. AFR. L.] 102, 107 (1979); A.C. Myburgh, *Punishment*, in INDIGENOUS CRIMINAL LAW IN BOPHUTHATSWANA 48–51 (A.C. Myburgh ed., UNISA 1980); M.W. PRINSLOO, INHEEMSE PUBLIEKREG IN LEBOWA 177 (Van Schaik 1983). This topic is summarized in G.J. van Niekerk, Comparative Study of the Application of Indigenous Law in the Administration of Criminal Justice in Southern Africa 34 (1986) (unpublished LL.M. dissertation University of South Africa).

[56] *See* Ashworth, *Responsibilities*, *supra* note 47; K. Daly, *Restorative Justice: The Real Story*, 4 PUNISHMENT & SOC'Y 55, 61–64 (2002) (questioning the claim that restorative justice is typical of indigenous and pre-state social orders).

a dispute, the parties' relationship, and the social and political structure of a particular society.[57] Where kin and neighbors are concerned, it is true that compromise
settlements might be preferred in order to preserve long-term relationships. Even
so, traditional courts are quite prepared to punish certain offenses, such as theft, for
the offender is thought to jeopardize the security of the community as a whole.[58] For
similar reasons, public defilement, such as incest, demands a retributive response,[59]
because social harmony requires living in accord with ancestors' will, and violation
of that will affects everyone.[60]

Finally, it should be noted that the normative status of the monopoly on the
use of force is not altogether clear. The idea obviously originated with the central-
ization of political power, prior to which law enforcement depended on various
species of self-help. However, the claim that only the state has the right to exert
force appeared quite late in European history, at the time of the eighteenth-century
Enlightenment.[61] Thereafter the monopoly on force, whether exercised internally or
externally, was taken to be definitive of the nation state.[62]

Weber therefore declared that an entity could be deemed a state only "if and insofar
as its administrative staff successfully upholds a claim on the monopoly of the legitimate
use of violence in the enforcement of its order."[63] Significantly, however, he did not claim
normative value for this proposition, nor did he say that people necessarily accepted its
legitimacy. He put it forward simply as a description of statehood, and, in this regard, he
seems to have been correct, for it is difficult to fix the proposition as a legal rule.

Moreover, it would be stretching the facts to say that it was descriptive even of the
modern state, because analysis of state-building indicates that central control varies
over time and place. In Africa, especially, there are few, if any, states with sole power to

---

[57] *See* S. ROBERTS, ORDER AND DISPUTE: AN INTRODUCTION TO LEGAL ANTHROPOLOGY 167 (Penguin
      1979).
[58] *See, e.g.,* P.A.W. COOK, SOCIAL ORGANISATION AND CEREMONIAL INSTITUTIONS OF THE BOMVANA
      151 (Jute 1931); C.L. HARRIES, THE LAWS AND CUSTOMS OF THE BAPEDI AND COGNATE TRIBES OF
      THE TRANSVAAL 109 (Hortors Ltd. 1929); H.O. MÖNNIG, THE PEDI 305–306 (Van Schaik 1967).
[59] *See* Myburgh, *Punishment, supra* note 55, at 43–48. A purification or conciliatory meal, however,
      might also suffice. M. HUNTER, REACTION TO CONQUEST 148–149, 184–186 (Oxford Univ. Press 2d
      ed. 1961).
[60] *See, e.g.,* H.A. JUNOD, THE LIFE OF A SOUTH AFRICAN TRIBE 446 (Attinger 2d ed., vol. 1 1927);
      Hunter, *supra* note 59, at 234; W.D. HAMMOND-TOOKE, THE BHACA SOCIETY: A PEOPLE OF THE
      TRANSKEIAN UPLANDS, SOUTH AFRICA 236–237, 242–243 (Oxford Univ. Press 1962).
[61] *See* E. Bittner & A. Platt, *The Right of the State to Punish, in* CONTEMPORARY PUNISHMENT: VIEWS,
      EXPLANATIONS, AND JUSTIFICATIONS 24, 28 (R.J. Gerber & P.D. McAnany eds., Univ. of Notre Dame
      1972) (quoting Bittner and Platt, *The Meaning of Punishment,* 2 ISSUES IN CRIMINOLOGY 79, 82
      [1966]).
[62] *See* Thomson, *supra* note 49, at 219. In reality, however, governments had no absolute control over
      their citizens until the late nineteenth century. *See* Baker, *supra* note 11, at 14, 18 (noting that, even
      then, policing was largely in the hands of civil society).
[63] M. WEBER, THE THEORY OF SOCIAL AND ECONOMIC ORGANIZATION 141–143 (A.R. Mendelson &
      Talcott Parsons trans., William Hodge 1947).

command force.[64] Thus, the state's monopoly on force seems to function as a statement of political theory and ideology rather than a strictly normative or factual proposition.

This is the precisely the type of situation addressed by legal pluralism, which demands that we take cognizance of facts rather than rules (or ideologies) proclaimed by states.[65] Indeed, research into social control shows that even in the developed world, policing and surveillance are being rapidly privatized, with or without state consent.[66] Viewed in these terms, we have what is probably the most powerful reason to enforce customary systems of crime.

16.3.2. *The Principle of Certainty*

This principle – also expressed as the legality principle – is a more serious obstacle to formal recognition of customary criminal law. In its modern form, legal certainty is associated with a movement to unify and codify national laws in eighteenth- and nineteenth-century Europe in order to resist autocratic rule.[67] Later, it gained a more utilitarian rationale through its connection with the deterrent theory of punishment: If punishment, as an evil in itself, is justified on the ground that it averts an even greater evil, then any penalty prescribed after the commission of an offense will not prevent the harm.[68] In these terms, the legality principle means that crimes and their corresponding punishments must be clearly stipulated before the commission of offenses.[69]

The principle is now encoded in all international human rights instruments.[70] In South Africa, it appears in § 35(3) of the 1996 Constitution:

Everyone who is arrested for allegedly committing an offen[s]e has the right – ...

(l) not to be convicted for an act or omission that was not an offen[s]e either under national or international law at the time it was committed or omitted; ...

---

[64] See Baker, *supra* note 11, at 181–183 (commenting on the western model of policing in Africa).
[65] See J. Griffiths, *What Is Legal Pluralism?*, 24 J. LEGAL PLURALISM & UNOFFICIAL L. 1, 12 (1986).
[66] See Baker, *supra* note 11, at 17–18.
[67] See STANISLAW POMORSKI, AMERICAN COMMON LAW AND THE PRINCIPLE NULLUM CRIMEN SINE LEGE 10–11 (Mouton 1975).
[68] J.P.A. Feuerbach in LEHRBUCH DES PEINLICHEN RECHTS (1801), therefore, advocated *nulla poena, sine lege*, and gave the legality principle its present formulation. See Pomorski, *supra* note 67, at 14. See also Burchell, *supra* note 51, at 95 n.8; J. HALL, GENERAL PRINCIPLES OF CRIMINAL LAW 34–35 (Bobbs Merril 2d ed. 1960). The modern rationale relates to fairness and the theory of "just deserts." See Burchell, *supra* note 51, at 104.
[69] See Hall, *supra* note 68, at 27–28; Burchell, *supra* note 51, at 94. Usually the principle is confined to defining the nature of the punishment, together with its upper and sometimes lower limits. Burchell, *supra* note 51, at 96. See generally J.M.T. Labuschagne, *Die sekerheidsbasis van die strafreg*, 1 S. AFR. J. CRIM. JUST. 52 (1988).
[70] See Universal Declaration of Human Rights art. 11(2), G.A. Res. 217A III, U.N. Doc A/810 (Dec. 12, 1948) [hereinafter UDHR]; International Covenant on Civil and Political Rights art. 15(1), *adopted* Dec. 19, 1966, *entered into force* March 23, 1976, U.N. Doc. A/6316, 999 U.N.T.S. 177 [hereinafter ICCPR]; African Charter on Human and People's Rights art. 7, *adopted* June 27, 1981, *entered into force* Oct. 21, 1986, OAU Doc. CAB/LEG/67/3 Rev. 5, 21 I.L.M. 58 [hereinafter African Charter].

(n) to the benefit of the least severe of the prescribed punishments if the prescribed punishment for the offen[s]e has been changed between the time that the offen[s]e was committed and the time of sentencing.

Although this provision does not say explicitly that vagueness in the definition of criminal conduct will infringe the Bill of Rights, vagueness might well run foul of § 35(3)(a) of the Constitution. This section provides that "[e]very accused person has the right to a fair trial, which includes the right (a) to be informed of the charge with sufficient detail to answer it."[71] Burchell says that the principle of legality functions, in the context of criminal law, as "the juristic kernel of the rule of law."[72] He therefore argues that any aspects of the principle not specified in the Bill of Rights can be supplied from a purposive interpretation of the rule of law, which is a founding value of the Constitution.[73]

While the legality principle is especially suited to systems of civil law, which lay down closed lists of crimes, it poses obvious problems for systems of common law. These allow a limited but nevertheless creative role for both custom and the judiciary in formulating new rules. Even so, the common law accepts the legality principle, which is said to mean that the courts may convict only for acts already recognized by the law as criminal (*ius acceptum*), and only if they are considered offenses at the time of their commission (*ius praevium*).[74] Furthermore, statutory crimes must be strictly construed (*ius strictum*), and common-law definitions of crimes must be reasonably fixed and certain (*ius certum*).[75]

All too easily, however, the process of interpreting rules may lead to the creation of new offenses,[76] and several early South African cases pointed to this danger.[77]

---

[71] *S v Friedman* (1) 1996 (1) SACR 181 (W).

[72] Burchell, *supra* note 51, at 106. In *President of the Republic of South Africa v Hugo*, Mokgoro J summed the matter up in the following words: "The need for accessibility, precision and general application flow from the concept of the rule of law. A person should be able to know the law, and be able to conform his or her conduct to the law." 1997 (4) SA 1 (CC) ¶ 102.

[73] *See* S. AFR. CONST. 1996 § 1(c). *See also* S. Hoctor, *Rape and the Principle of Legality*, 20 S. AFR. J. CRIM. JUST. 78, 79 (2007).

[74] *See R v Sibiyia* 1955 (4) SA 247 (A) at 256. The difference between the creation and the adaptation or extension of existing crimes, however, is problematic especially in view of the requirement under section 39(2) of the Constitution that, "when developing the common law or customary law, every court … must promote the spirit, purport and objects of the Bill of Rights." S. AFR. CONST. 1996 § 39(2). *See* Burchell, *supra* note 51, at 100–101. *See also Masiya v Director of Public Prosecution* 2007 (5) SA 30 (CC), in which the court a quo held that the common-law definition of rape as vaginal penetration was unconstitutional and required development under section 39(2). On appeal, however, the Constitutional Court refused to deal with the constitutionality of the existing definition of rape, instead allowing for the incremental development of the law according to the common-law tradition. *See* K. Phelps & S. Kazee, *The Constitutional Court Gets Anal About Rape – Gender Neutrality and the Principle of Legality in* Masiya v DPP, 20 S. AFR. J. CRIM. JUST. 341 (2007).

[75] *See* Hoctor, *supra* note 73, at 81; Burchell, *supra* note 51, at 96–104; *Masiya* 2007 (5) SA 30 ¶ 19.

[76] *See* Pomorski, *supra* note 67, at 25 & n.49.

[77] *See R v Robinson* 1911 C.P.D. 319 at 327. *See also R v Mhlongo* 1910 31 N.L.R. 271; *R v Maruba* 1942 O.P.D. 51; *S v Solomon* 1973 (4) SA 644 (C) at 647–648.

Conversely, however, the exact formulation of crimes is impossible: Finding the meaning of words always involves some degree of interpretive discretion.[78] Thus, the legality principle is phrased in terms of a maximum, not an absolute, certainty, which indicates a degree of compromise.[79] Any sense of unfairness for the offender may be offset by the fair trial requirement of access to legal representation to assist in determining the exact scope of a rule.[80]

To some extent, of course, problems with the legality principle may be resolved when crime and morality coincide. As far as the average person is concerned, major crimes are considered immoral, and so no advance warning is needed. Hence, "[t]he layman does not need to learn the difference between murder and manslaughter in order to understand that he must not kill others."[81] On this understanding, it is possible to allay concerns about the legality principle (together with the rule *ignorantia juris haud excusat*).[82]

Whereas the courts have devised a working relationship between common-law crimes and the legality principle, the same is not true of customary law.[83] In one of the rare cases in point, *R v Dumezweni*,[84] the Appellate division was squarely confronted with this problem. Here it was alleged that a person leaving the court of a traditional ruler without permission showed contempt amounting to criminal conduct. The court held that the criminal nature of the act had not been proven because it did not meet the demand for exact definition of the offense and all its elements.[85]

Such a requirement, however, seems unrealistic in the case of customary law. South Africans now enjoy a constitutional freedom to practice a culture of choice,[86] and one aspect of this guarantee is a right to live by the system of the law that gives the culture its distinctive quality.[87] Thus, courts and academics have been at pains

---

[78] *See* A. ASHWORTH, PRINCIPLES OF CRIMINAL LAW 74–75 (Oxford Univ. Press 5th ed. 2006) (citing *Kokkinakis v. Greece*, 17 Eur. Ct. H.R. 397 ¶ 40 (1994)).

[79] *See id.* at 77.

[80] *See Sunday Times v. UK*, 2 Eur. Ct. H.R. 245 ¶ 49 (1979). The standard set in the latter case has been applied in a number of subsequent decisions. *See, e.g., Hashman and Harrup v. UK*, 30 Eur. Ct. H.R. 241 (2000).

[81] G. WILLIAMS, CRIMINAL LAW: THE GENERAL PART 582 (Stevens 2d ed. 1961).

[82] *See* Ashworth, PRINCIPLES, *supra* note 78, at 76–77 (citing J. Gardner, *Rationality and the Rule of Law in Offences Against the Person*, 53 CAMBRIDGE L.J. 502 [1994]).

[83] One of the issues that troubled colonial policy makers was the vagueness and uncertainty of customary law. *See supra* note 7. Hence, one of the primary objects of the Natal Code of Zulu law had been to impose uniformity on the administration of justice. *See* A.J. Kerr, *The Reception and Codification of Systems of Law in Southern Africa*, 2 J. AFR. L. 92 (1958).

[84] 1962 (2) SA 751 (A) at 757.

[85] *See also* FUTURE OF LAW IN AFRICA: RECORD OF PROCEEDINGS OF THE LONDON CONFERENCE 1959–1960 36–37 (A.N. Allott ed., Butterworths 1960).

[86] *See* S. AFR. CONST. 1996 §§ 30, 31.

[87] *See* C. Himonga & C. Bosch, *The Application of African Customary Law under the Constitution of South Africa: Problem Solved or Just Beginning?*, 117 SALJ 306, 330–31 (2000). *See also* M. Pieterse, *It's*

to stress that customary law should be understood to be the law currently being lived by the community, not the "official" law as documented in codes, precedents, and textbooks.[88] Yet the variability of the law from time to time and from culture to culture would suggest that there are no uniform standards.[89]

Indeed, the very nature of customary law confounds the principle of legal certainty. The rules of such systems are captured in oral traditions, and, as a result, they are porous and malleable.[90] Because customary laws have none of the systemic coherence of written legal systems, they are best described as repertoires of rules from which discerning judges select whichever rule suits the needs of a case.[91] When functioning in its proper context, this flexible approach poses few, if any, problems: The law is derived from community practice, and is therefore known by everyone in the group concerned.

The rules are, nonetheless, almost infinitely variable: Not only can they change through the ineluctable processes of social practice, but also through particular acts of lawmaking by traditional authorities.[92] In the settled communities of the past, people could reasonably be expected to be aware of these changes, but can we impose the same demands today, when social and geographic mobility is more common? Can we expect migrant workers, for instance, or urban dwellers to keep constantly in touch with the laws governing their families in rural areas?

16.3.3. *Guarantees of the Defendant's Procedural Rights*

Writing about the history of legal institutions, Seagle said that at the time of the Enlightenment, a system of public criminal law subject to adversarial adjudication became "a sort of secular High Mass of advanced civilization."[93] He claimed that the primitive notion of vengeance in earlier forms of law was transformed into public punishment, based on deterrence as well as repression. To ensure that this state-imposed "peace" would not seem arbitrary or inhumane, the law emphasized due process. The further development of the common law was then a tug-of-war between state control and due process.

---

a *"Black Thing": Upholding Culture and Customary Law in a Society Founded on Non-Racialism*, 17 SAJHR 364, 377 (2001).

[88] *See, e.g.,* Langa DCJ in *Bhe & Others v Magistrate Khayelitsha & Others* 2005 (1) SA 580 (CC) ¶¶ 44, 81, 153; *Alexkor Ltd & Another v Richtersveld Community & Others* 2003 (12) BCLR 1301 (CC) ¶ 53; *Mabuza v Mbatha* 2003 (4) SA 218 (C) ¶ 25.

[89] *See* I. Hamnett, Chieftainship and Legitimacy, an Anthropological Study of Executive Law in Lesotho 9–10 (Routledge & Kegan Paul 1975).

[90] *See, e.g.,* J.F. Holleman, Issues in African Law 13 (Mouton 1974).

[91] *See* J. Comaroff & S. Roberts, Rules and Processes 70 (Chicago Univ. Press 1981).

[92] The legislative powers of traditional authorities were recently endorsed by the Constitutional Court in *Shilubana & Others v Nwamitwa* 2007 (5) SA 620 (CC) ¶ 70, 2007 (9) BCLR 919.

[93] W. Seagle, The Quest for Law 227–228 (Knopf 1941).

Seagle's account of the development of criminal justice proposes an opposition between interests of state and human rights that is typical of western thinking, and now provides the basis for considering enforcement of customary criminal law. If only the state is entitled to use force, then only the state can exact penalties for wrongful behavior. The severity of this process demands special protections for the accused, all of which have been encoded in human rights instruments. Customary law appears to conflict with several of these protections, all of which have been the subject of litigation in South Africa.

16.3.3.1. Legal Representation

In a complex and, for the layperson, inaccessible legal system, the assistance of an attorney may be critical to successfully defending against a criminal charge.[94] Section 35(3) of the South African Constitution thus provides that:

> Every accused person has a right to a fair trial, which includes that right –
>
> (f) to choose, and be represented by, a legal practitioner, and to be informed of this right promptly;
>
> (g) to have a legal practitioner assigned to the accused person by the state and at state expense, if substantial injustice would otherwise result, and to be informed of this right promptly....[95]

Unlike their western counterparts, however, traditional courts are non-professional in the sense that they are not monopolized by specially qualified practitioners. Instead, they operate on the understanding that all adults know the law and the judicial procedures of their people. To preserve an atmosphere of informality and to prevent wealthy litigants from enjoying an undue advantage, legislation then extended what is probably best considered an indifference to legal representation into a prohibition.[96]

When this prohibition was challenged in *Bangindawo & others v Head of the Nyanda Regional Authority & another*,[97] the Transkei High Court court held that exclusion of lawyers was permissible in civil claims.[98] On the one hand, there is no constitutional right to representation in such matters, and, on the other, both parties can be fairly presumed to know the law and procedures of customary courts. In criminal matters, however, the court could find no justification (under § 36 of the

---

[94] *See Yates v University of Bophuthatswana & Others* 1994 (3) SA 815 (BGD) at 846.

[95] *See also* ICCPR, *supra* note 70, arts. 14(3)(b), (d); African Charter, *supra* note 70, art. 7(1)(c).

[96] *See* Rule 5 of Chiefs and Headmen's Civil Courts Rules, No R2082 of 1967 Government Gazette Extraordinary No 1929.

[97] 1998 (3) SA 262 (Tk), 1998 (3) BCLR 314. The applicants based their argument on section 25(3)(e) of the 1993 Interim Constitution (now section 35(3)(f) of the 1996 Constitution). S. AFR. (Interim) CONST. 1993 § 25(3)(e); S. AFR. CONST. 1996 § 35(3)(f).

[98] Small claims courts also prohibit legal representation. Small Claims Courts Act 61 of 1984 § 7(2).

Constitution) for dispensing with the right to legal representation, given that crimes could involve complex legal issues and potentially severe penalties.[99]

Although the court in *Bangindawo's* case held that representation was necessary if litigants were to exercise their right of access to court in a meaningful way,[100] the South African Law Reform Commission's Special Project Committee on Customary Law felt that the prohibition should be retained,[101] and, evidently, the drafters of the Traditional Courts Bill did so too (thereby rendering an enactment of the Bill liable to constitutional review). Thus Clause 9(3) of the Bill provides that

(a) No party to any proceedings before a traditional court may be represented by a legal representative.

(b) A party to proceedings before a traditional court may be represented by his or her wife or husband, family member, neighbour or member of the community, in accordance with customary law and custom.

The justification for this provision would appear to be the minor nature of the offenses falling within the jurisdiction of traditional courts, such that they do not warrant professional assistance.[102]

16.3.3.2. The Presumption of Innocence and the Related Rules

Under the common law, conviction for an offense may carry severe consequences. Thus, in criminal cases, accused persons are offered a cluster of interrelated procedural rights that provide some counterweight to the enormous power wielded by the state[103] and ensure a measure of protection against mistakes in the process.[104]

The most basic of these rules is probably a presumption of the accused's innocence, which implies that the prosecution bears the onus of proving its case. Hence

---

[99] This part of the judgment was confirmed by *Mhlekwa & Feni v Head of the Western Tembuland Regional Authority & Another* 2001 (1) SA 574 (Tk) at 631–632. *See* R.B. Mqeke, *The Rule of Law and African Traditional Courts in the New Dispensation*, 22 OBITER 416, 416 (2001); Koyana & Bekker, *supra* note 31, at 223–227.

[100] The Court's comment in this regard, however, that the right to representation "applies with more force in respect of the vast numbers of uneducated and illiterate people" of South Africa, 1998 (3) SA at 277, 1998 (3) BCLR at 331, is best confined to the courts that were under consideration *in casu*, namely, the Transkeian Regional Authority Courts. These courts, although established by statute, were closely modeled on traditional courts. *See* Transkei Act 13 of 1982.

[101] *See* Discussion Paper 82, *supra* note 32, ¶ 7.5. It should be noted that the Commission had also recommended retention of the courts' criminal jurisdiction. *See* Project 90 Customary Law Report, *supra* note 33, at xii, 12 and draft bill attached at cl. 6.

[102] Another reason could be the customary practice of bringing *amici curiae* to court, which is alluded to in paragraph (b) of the Bill.

[103] *See* Ashworth, *supra* note 78, at 83.

[104] *See In re Winship*, 397 U.S. 358 (1970) (Brennan, J.). This right does not extend to civil matters. *Prinsloo v Van der Linde* (1997) 3 SA 1012 (CC).

the famous dictum in *Woolmington v DPP*[105] that, "throughout the web of the English criminal law one golden thread is always to be seen – that is the duty of the prosecution to prove the prisoner's guilt." This presumption is, in turn, related to the standard of proof required in criminal trials: Guilt must be established beyond a reasonable doubt.[106] What is more, during the process, accused persons have a right to remain silent,[107] and the right not to be compelled to make admissions or confessions that can be used in evidence against them.

The presumption of innocence is now enshrined in all major international human rights instruments.[108] In § 35(3)(h) of the South African Constitution, which prescribes the fair trial provisions for accused persons, the presumption is combined with the right to remain silent in the following terms: "every accused person has a right to a fair trial, which includes the right – ... to be presumed innocent, to remain silent, and not to testify during the proceedings." In addition, § 35(3)(j) provides that an accused may "not be compelled to give self-incriminating evidence."

Under customary law, these requirements would not be considered essential to protect offenders. In the proceedings of traditional courts, the rules of evidence are not nearly as strict as under the common law: There are no hard and fast rules about the burden of proof – although it generally rests with the person alleging guilt[109] – or about the standard of proof – although that is generally on a balance of probabilities.[110] Considerable weight is attached to confessions and admissions, with none of the safeguards thought essential under the common law.[111]

In general terms, customary law emphasises duty rather than right.[112] Given this perspective, and the principle that people must avoid harming others, once the fact of damage is established, offenders have to convince the court that they had no

---

[105] [1935] A.C. 462, 481–482 (H.L.) (U.K.). *See also* I. CURRIE & J. DE WAAL, THE BILL OF RIGHTS HANDBOOK 745 (Juta 5th ed. 2005).

[106] *See* P.J. SCHWIKKARD, PRESUMPTION OF INNOCENCE 35 (Juta 1999).

[107] *See S v Manamela & Another* 2000 (3) SA 1 (CC) ¶¶ 24–26; *S v Singo* 2002 (4) SA 858 (CC) ¶ 28.

[108] *See* UDHR, *supra* note 70, art. 11(1); ICCPR, *supra* note 70, art. 14(2); African Charter, *supra* note 70, art. 7(1)(b).

[109] There may, however, be exceptions, where an accused must prove innocence. *See* G.J. van Niekerk, *Principles of the Indigenous Law of Procedure and Evidence as Exhibited in Tswana Law, in* SOUTHERN AFRICA IN NEED OF LAW REFORM 138 (A.J.G.M. Sanders ed., Butterworths 1981); A.C. MYBURGH, PAPERS ON INDIGENOUS LAW IN SOUTHERN AFRICA 109 (Van Schaik 1985).

[110] *See* van Niekerk, Comparative Study, *supra* note 55, at 43.

[111] Hence a confession may result in the instant closing of a case. J.F. Holleman, *Law and Anthropology: A Necessary Partnership for the Study of Legal Change in Plural Systems*, 23 J. AFR. L. 117, 123, 126 (1979); van Niekerk, *supra* note 109, at 138; Prinsloo, *supra* note 55, at 284–285.

[112] Hence, article 27 of the African Charter, *supra* note 70, provides that individuals have duties to their families and society.

responsibility for the cause.[113] It follows that the person who remains silent may be taken to have something to hide. Guilt may therefore be presumed, and judges may question the accused on an understanding that s/he is lying.[114]

Even so, we should not jump to a conclusion that traditional courts are violating constitutional rights. In the first place, where the principal aim of a trial is to reconcile the parties, the procedural guarantees of the Constitution – which are aimed at protecting an accused against harsh penalties – become redundant. Even so, reconciliation is not the invariable aim of a traditional court. It depends on the nature of the parties' relationship: The more distant the relationship, the less likely the need for reconciliation and the more likely a presumption of guilt and culpability.[115]

In the second place, although it could be said that customary procedures are inquisitorial,[116] this term does no more than describe a technique used to test an accused or witness's credibility. It should not be taken to denote an overbearing exercise of state power. Indeed, the very term "inquisitorial" is a product of western jurisprudence, and is therefore to be used with reservation in the context of customary law.[117]

16.4. DISTINGUISHING CRIME

All of the problems about recognizing customary criminal law hinge on there being a clear category of law concerned only with crime.[118] Customary law, however, has no such precise distinctions. Traditional courts readily differentiate between offenses harming the individual and those harming the wider community,[119]

---

[113] In any event, alleged offenders are not necessarily required to plead. See van Niekerk, *supra* note 55, at 43.

[114] See Gluckman, *supra* note 47, at 231.

[115] See *id.* at 10–11; M. GLUCKMAN, THE JUDICIAL PROCESS AMONG THE BAROTSE OF NORTHERN RHODESIA 94–97 (1967).

[116] See S.E. Van der Merwe, *Accusatorial and Inquisitorial Procedures and Restricted and Free Systems of Evidence, in* SOUTHERN AFRICA IN NEED OF LAW REFORM, *supra* note 109, at 141–142; van Niekerk, *supra* note 109, at 130.

[117] Customary procedures are best compared with the domestic inquiries conducted by a parent. See Van der Merwe, *supra* note 116, at 146.

[118] Certain writers, however, claimed that customary law knew of no difference at all between crime and tort. See P. BOHANNAN, JUSTICE AND JUDGEMENT AMONG THE TIV 116. (Oxford Univ. Press 1957). Indeed, the lack of differentiation was taken as a mark of the backwardness of customary law. van Niekerk, *supra* note 55, at 25 (citing L.T. Hobhouse, *Development of Justice, in* PRIMITIVE AND ANCIENT LEGAL INSTITUTIONS 120–128 (A. Kocourek & J.H. Wigmore eds., Colorado 1979) (1915)). See also J.M.T. Labuschagne, *Die Oorsprong van die Onderskeid Tussen die Fenomene Misdaad en Delik in Primigene Regstelsels*, 12 OBITER 83 (1991).

[119] See generally Isaac Schapera, *Law and Justice, in* THE BANTU-SPEAKING TRIBES OF SOUTH AFRICA 197, 198–200 (I. Schapera ed., Maskew Miller 1956); A.C. Myburgh, *Law and Justice, in* THE BANTU-SPEAKING PEOPLES OF SOUTHERN AFRICA 284, 295–297 (W.D. Hammond-Tooke ed., Routledge & Kegan Paul 2d ed. 1974).

but these categories are not absolute, nor are they identical to those in the common law.[120]

The problem of differentiation is compounded by traditional courts allowing penalties to be imposed for wrongs that would not be considered criminal in the common law. As we have seen, it is a cardinal rule of this system that only the state may exact punishment; individuals may do no more than claim compensation or restitution.[121] Although traditional courts loosely conform to a similar rule,[122] they may decide to permit compensation for a crime[123] or a penalty for a delict.[124]

The blurring of any distinction between crime and delict has the most immediate implications for procedure. Because traditional courts do not work within precise conceptual categories, they adjudicate all cases in more or less the same way (and, of course, they may apply the same corrective measures).[125] Thus, they would have no basic criterion for determining when to apply the special protections available to accused persons in criminal matters.

As we saw earlier, the retributive system of justice, which is regarded as a hallmark of the common-law regime, is based on the state's notionally exclusive responsibility to correct serious offenses,[126] which in turn gives rise to a set of special safeguards for the offenders. In close-knit communities, however, the courts may have less interest in the public implications of offensive acts and more concern to preserve social harmony.

[120] Hence, for example, Myburgh says, although on the basis of dated authority, that theft is not considered a crime among Xhosa-speakers, or assault among the Pedi and Sotho. *See* Myburgh, *Law and Justice, supra* note 119, at 296.

[121] *See* A. Tunc, *Introduction,* INTERNATIONAL ENCYCLOPEDIA OF COMPARATIVE LAW 49 § 1.6 (A. Tunc ed., Vol. XI Mohr 1981).

[122] *See* van Niekerk, *supra* note 55, at 40. The violation of certain norms, such as the bar on incest, is deemed to have a malign effect on the entire community, thereby requiring a punishment. *See* Labuschagne, *supra* note 118, at 85. *See, e.g.,* J.O. Ibik, *The Customary Law of Wrongs and Injuries in Malawi, in* IDEAS AND PROCEDURES IN AFRICAN CUSTOMARY LAW, *supra* note 53, at 305; *See* Isaac Schapera, *The Tswana, in* ETHNOGRAPHIC SURVEY OF AFRICA 54–55 (C.D. Forde ed., Part III 1953); R.D. COERTZE, DIE FAMILIE-, ERF- EN OPVOLGINGSREG VAN DIE BAFOKENG VAN RUSTENBURG 136 (Sabra 1971).

[123] *See* van Niekerk, *supra* note 55, at 40, and authorities cited therein.

[124] *See* H. ASHTON, THE BASUTO 266 (Oxford Univ. Press 1952) (requiring payment of double value for theft); Mönnig, *supra* note 58, at 327 (same); *id.* at 324–325 (requiring double value for damage to property); *Cele v Ndokweni* 1950 N.A.C. 162 (NE) (same).

[125] *See* Labuschagne, *supra* note 118, at 89; G.J. van Niekerk, *The Administration of Indigenous Criminal Law in Southern Africa – a Comparative Law Reform Study,* 24 DE JURE 277, 283 (1991).

[126] *See* Tunc, *supra* note 121, at 50, § 1.6. As Gluckman says of Barotse society, wrongs arise out of harmful acts by outsiders or out of a kinsman's failure to fulfil a status obligation. Gluckman, *supra* note 47, at 204 (citing P.P. HOWELL, A MANUAL OF NUER LAW: BEING AN ACCOUNT OF CUSTOMARY LAW, ITS EVOLUTION AND DEVELOPMENT IN THE COURTS ESTABLISHED BY THE SUDAN GOVERNMENT 22 (Oxford Univ. Press 1954)). *Cf.* Ibik, *supra* note 122, at 307–308.

In a famous case study from central Zimbabwe, Holleman showed how this goal was vital to settling a long-standing dispute between a father and his son.[127] Although the families in this community were generally loath to air their differences in public, a disgruntled father perpetrated a series of public outrages to force a hearing of his complaints against his son. Some of these offenses constituted what western law would regard as serious criminal acts. The court, however, chose to ignore the criminal element in favor of a compromise of personal interests in order to secure a lasting settlement between father and son.

Even under the common law, of course, it is difficult to distinguish crime and delict on the basis of the substance of the wrong or the social function of the ensuing correction, because the same act may give rise to both a criminal and a civil suit. Indeed, these actions may be brought in the alternative. Nonetheless, the courts must assess liability by very different criteria and employ radically different procedures.[128] According to the common law, for instance, the initiative for instituting a civil action lies with the aggrieved party, whereas, in criminal matters, a state functionary attached to the court as prosecutor must institute the action, and will thereafter be responsible for leading evidence and finding witnesses.

Some systems of customary law have evidently established a procedure of this sort, for traditional rulers may intiate actions of their own accord.[129] Nevertheless, a noticeable difference in the overall approach of customary and western courts is a much looser idea of relevance in customary courts. The facts in dispute do not have to be pared down to fit predetermined normative categories in order to fix the cause of action.[130] As a result, the parties are not required to define the scope of a claim before bringing a matter to the court, and, during a hearing, they may present whatever information they think is appropriate.[131] The degree of latitude depends on the aim of the trial: In the case of delict, customary law would expect the parties to attempt a compromise in order to restore their relationship,[132] whereas, in the case of crime, a wider community interest would suggest that private settlements are less likely, and a public hearing more necessary.[133] Much depends on the closeness of the parties' relationship.

---

[127] *See* Holleman, *supra* note 90, at 47. For similar accounts, see J.F. Holleman, African Interlude 86–94 (Nasionale Boekhandel 1958); M.F.C. Bourdillon, The Shona Peoples; an Ethnography of the Contemporary Shona with Special Reference to their Religion 147–167 (Mambo Press 1976); Mönnig, *supra* note 58, at 310–328.

[128] *See* Tunc, *supra* note 121, at 50, § 1.6.

[129] *See* Labuschagne, *supra* note 118, at 86–87; Coertze, *supra* note 122, at 136, 175; D.H. Reader, Zulu Tribe in Transition – the Makhanya of Southern Natal 299 (Manchester Univ. Press 1966). *See also* E.J. Krige, The Social System of the Zulus 228 (Longmans Green 1936). For civil cases, see id. at 230.

[130] *Cf.* D Taylor, "The Truth the Whole Truth Nothing but the Truth": Truth, Community and Narrative in African Procedural Law, 40 CILSA 215, 229 (2007).

[131] *See* Dlamini, *supra* note 47, at 3; Van der Merwe, *supra* note 116, at 147.

[132] *See* S.M. Poulter, Family Law and Litigation in Basotho Society 37 (Clarendon 1976).

[133] *See, e.g.,* Mönnig, *supra* note 58, at 304.

If traditional courts do not distinguish crimes and delicts in the same way as the common law, it becomes that much more difficult to insist on the procedural guarantees required under the Constitution. What is more, in distinguishing crime from other wrongs, the courts face the almost insoluble problem of deciding which law to use in order to classify. Customary law might take one view of an offense and the common law another.[134] Rape is a classic problem.[135] Customary law tends to regard it as a civil matter of adultery or illicit fornication,[136] whereas the common law, of course, treats it as crime. Which law must be used to classify?

16.5. CONCLUSION: PLURALISM CONSIDERED

When comparing the two systems of justice in South Africa, the President of the Congress of Traditional Leaders (CONTRALESA), Inkosi Patekile Holomisa, said that:

> Courts of traditional leaders are spread all over the countryside, particularly in the former homelands. The great majority of what would be considered petty crimes in the cities – common assault and theft of property of low value – are dispensed with as a matter of routine to the general satisfaction of the litigants. The town courts, especially the lower courts, are clogged with such cases to the detriment of speedy justice. Delays are due to several factors, such as litigants' inability to hire lawyers and heavy workloads for lawyers and presiding officers.
>
> It is the responsibility of the state to provide protection and justice to its citizens. That value is what informs the administration of justice in the original African judicial system. Why should citizens pay for what is inherently due to them? Modern justice is expensive; the more money you have the more chance of a favourable outcome.[137]

Given the parlous state of the formal justice system, and South Africa's situation of both de facto and de jure pluralism, we have little choice but to accept customary criminal law. Indeed, recognition of traditional rulers and their judicial powers compels that conclusion. It is difficult (if not impossible) to separate delict from crime, courts from the laws they administer, or traditional authorities from their judicial powers. In other words, customary-law justice comes as a package deal.

---

[134] For example, as a prelude to a customary marriage, the bride may be "abducted" by her suitor and carried off to his homestead. Viewed from a common-law perspective, this action may constitute a crime of kidnapping, whereas, under customary law, it is at most a delict if the marriage does not ensue. *See R v Swartbooi & Others* 1916 E.D.L. 170.

[135] *See* Bennett, *supra* note 14, at 107–108.

[136] *See, e.g.,* Koyana & Bekker, *supra* note 31, at 35–36 (citing the example of a rape case being settled by a process of reconciliation). *See also* K. Moult, Justice Served? Exploring Informal Justice Mechanisms to Address Violence Against Women (Univ. Cape Town 2004) (investigation into informal justice mechanisms in Khayelitsha, Thohoyandou and Mount Frere).

[137] *Why Should We Pay for Justice?*, Business Day (S. Afr.), May 31, 2005.

The state can comfort itself with the knowledge that acceptance of pluralism dovetails with its obligations, under § 34 of the Constitution, to provide access to justice for all,[138] and §§ 30 and 31 to allow freedom to practice a culture of choice.

As for concerns about due process and the proper role of the state, we have seen from the preceding discussion that, although it might appear as if the customary system usurps the state's monopoly on the use of force and offends the right to fair trial, closer inquiry reveals that the problem is not as serious as it might first seem. In fact, a closer comparison of the two systems might reveal the reverse: The common-law system of criminal justice offends customary ideas of due process, which themselves may come closer to realising fundamental rights than the common law.

For instance, § 35(3)(d) of the Constitution requires a trial to begin and end "without unreasonable delay." Proceedings in the magistrates' courts and the High Court, however, are notoriously slow, whereas those in traditional courts are likely to be speedier, if only because the predominantly oral nature of proceedings requires prompt action before memories fade. Paradoxically, the procedural safeguards available under the common law may conduce to the very delays and costs that the system seeks to avoid. In *Bangindawo & others v Head of the Nyanda Regional Authority & another*,[139] for example, the court held that the elaborate precautions associated with common law provided "fertile ground for the raising of technical points," whereas the less formal procedures of customary law had the advantage of leaving no room "for such technicalities and of having the real substance of disputes dealt with and laid to rest."[140]

Furthermore, courts working in a common-law tradition have a more superficial approach to disputes than their customary-law counterparts. To save time and costs, the former will seek to arrive at decisions as quickly as possible, and, to achieve this aim, make frequent use of the rule of relevance.[141] Such an approach, however, offends the customary conception of *audi alteram partem*, which will require a court to devote as much time as is needed to reach a settlement satisfactory to both the parties and the wider community in disputes concerning neighbors and kin.[142]

On the face of it, then, a pluralist approach to criminal justice not only provides an expedient solution to the state's difficulties in providing access to justice, but can also give more comprehensive effect to fundamental rights. Having accepted such a conclusion, however, we need to attend to the following problems.

---

[138] Section 34 provides that "[e]veryone has the right to have any dispute that can be resolved by the application of law decided in a fair public hearing before a court or, where appropriate, another independent and impartial tribunal or forum." S. AFR. CONST. 1996 § 34.

[139] 1998 (3) SA 262 (Tk), 1998 (3) BCLR 314.

[140] 1998 (3) SA at 279–80, 1998 (3) BCLR at 333. The applicants also argued that presiding officers were "untrained in law," but the Court dismissed this contention, holding that traditional courts were perfectly well equipped to conduct hearings.

[141] *See* Dlamini, *supra* note 47, at 3; Van der Merwe, *supra* note 116, at 147.

[142] What is more, a judge who ignored community opinion would not be considered to have reached a fair decision. *See, e.g.,* M. GLUCKMAN, POLITICS, LAW AND RITUAL IN TRIBAL SOCIETY 188 (Blackwell 1971).

First, there is a purely technical problem of deciding which system of criminal law to apply. Are all the people within a traditional court's area of jurisdiction subject to the customary law prevailing in that area, regardless of the system under which they personally might live? Should the solution be found in the principle of personality or even allegiance to a traditional leader?[143] The immediate answer, of course, is to prefer a principle of territoriality, because crime suggests an offense against the realm, not a particular person, therefore all people within the realm must obey the same system of law.[144]

This solution, however, does not answer the second, related question. If we allow traditional courts to apply both customary and common law, why should the same powers not be extended to the magistrates' courts and the High Court, giving prosecutors the option of charging accused persons with customary- or common-law crimes? (Until now, customary law in these courts has played a minor role in the form of the "cultural defence.")[145] If prosecutors are to be given this power, on what grounds should they exercise their discretion to choose customary or common law? Should weight be given to the accused's cultural orientation or the victim's? And how should that orientation be decided?

Thirdly, if we are prepared to apply customary criminal law, how are we to deal with the objection of a potentially discriminatory system of justice, one for people in rural areas and another for urbanites? (This was the initial concern expressed about the Traditional Courts Bill.) The problem was raised in *Mhlekwa & Feni v Head of the Western Tembuland Regional Authority & another*,[146] where the applicants' contention – that the different procedures in magistrates' and traditional courts constituted a violation of the right to equality before the law – was upheld on the basis that magistrates give a better guarantee of fair trial.[147]

---

[143] Bonds of allegiance are established through the processes of birth, marriage, immigration, and, in the past, conquest or capture in war. *See* A.C. MYBURGH, DIE INHEEMSE STAAT IN SUIDER-AFRIKA 11–15 (Univ. S. Afr. 1986); M.W. PRINSLOO, DIE INHEEMSE ADMINISTRATIEFREG VAN 'N NOORD-SOTHOSTAM 66–69 (Univ. S. Afr. 1981); A.C. MYBURGH & M.W. PRINSLOO, INDIGENOUS PUBLIC LAW IN KWANDEBELE 2–4 (Van Schaik 1985).

[144] As far as the South African courts were concerned, the civil jurisdiction of the traditional courts was based solely on residence within a ruler's area of jurisdiction, not political allegiance. *See Monete v Setshuba* 1948 N.A.C. (C&O) 22.

[145] The "cultural defense" may be based on the right to culture in sections 30 and 31 of the Constitution. A defense of this nature could affect the unlawfulness of the crime, the accused's capacity, *mens rea* or the question of sentencing. *See* P.A. Carstens, *The Cultural Defence in Criminal Law: South African Perspectives*, 37 DE JURE 312, 312 (2004) (with regard to witchcraft, *muti* killings and necklacing).

[146] 2001 (1) SA 574 (Tk), 2000 (9) BCLR 979.

[147] A right to a fair trial is required in section 35(3) of the Constitution. *See* 2001 (1) SA at 620–621, 2000 (9) BCLR at 1022. The respondents' arguments that the different standards of justice were justified by restoration of powers to traditional leaders, cultural expectations, and the benefits of lower costs and greater informality were all dismissed as giving no justification for violating section 9(1) of the Constitution. *Id.* at 621–624; 2000 at 1023–1026.

An immediate solution to this problem may be sought in a system of transferring cases, but, in this regard, the current bill is far from satisfactory. In criminal matters arising in magistrates' courts, prosecutors are given the sole discretion to decide whether cases may be transferred to small claims courts or traditional courts.[148]

The better, although more difficult, solution would be to attend to deficiencies in the overall justice system. Insofar as traditional courts are concerned, for example, attention needs to be paid to their tendency to discriminate against women[149] and outsiders (especially those of foreign ethnic groups).[150] There is also evidence that they succumb to coercive means to obtain their ends, thereby sacrificing ideals of restorative justice in favor of retribution.[151]

The Traditional Courts Bill attempts to address these problems by obliging all courts and tribunals to attack "systemic unfair discrimination and inequalities, particularly in respect of gender, age, race, as a result of past unfair discrimination, brought about by colonialism, apartheid and patriarchy." Moreover, when interpreting the Bill of Rights, it obliges the courts to promote the values of an "open and democratic society, based on human dignity, equality and freedom," and, when interpreting legislation or developing the common or customary law, to "promote the spirit, purport and objects of the Bill of Rights."[152]

Whether these laudable goals will be achieved, however, depends largely on training and supervision. Sadly, the bill fails to commit the state to definite support. Clause 17 provides that: "The Minister may, within the resources available at the magistrate's court in which jurisdiction the traditional court sits, assign one or more officers to assist a traditional court in performing its functions under this Act." Otherwise, the remedy is a system of appeals and reviews, which is scarcely any improvement on the Black Administration Act.[153]

Finally, we have very little hard evidence on which to base policy decisions about the functioning of traditional courts. Indeed, a cursory reading of the footnotes in this chapter will have disclosed the paucity and age of the materials. Fieldwork is needed.

[148] *See* Traditional Courts Bill, B15–2008 § 19(2)(b).
[149] *See* Moult, *supra* note 136.
[150] *See* Baker, *supra* note 11, at 176.
[151] For example, once arrested, a suspect has to prove innocence. *See* B.F. Ndaki, *What Is to be Said for Makgotla?, in* Southern Africa in Need of Law Reform, *supra* note 109, at 177–178.
[152] Traditional Courts Bill, B15–2008 § 3(2).
[153] Clause 13 allows for appeals to magistrates' courts, and Clause 14 provides a system of review by a magistrate if a traditional court acted *ultra vires*, showed gross procedural irregularity or bias. *Cf.* Project 90 Customary Law Report, *supra* note 33, at 29–31. Here, a Commissioner for Customary Courts, with largely administrative functions, was responsible for supervising customary courts.

17

Gacaca in Rwanda

Customary Law in Case of Genocide

Roelof H. Haveman

17.1. INTRODUCTION: A DAY IN COURT

A day in August, 2009, Aimable, a friend since my arrival in Rwanda, has asked me to join him to the *gacaca* where the killers of his family will stand trial. He was not in the country when the genocide started on April 6, 1994. Just a few hours before the airplane of the president was shot down – the catalyst event that started the genocide – he left the country. At the time, he was studying law in Kigali. During the Easter holidays, he and a girlfriend paid his family a visit. His friend had insisted on leaving the country immediately, totally in panic and without any clear reason. His family was angry about him leaving so soon, because they had not seen him for a long time. Three days later, his entire family was dead.

The place we are visiting is Gatare, one of those small villages on Lake Kivu's shore. We travel five and a half hours from Kigali to Cyangugu in the southwest of the country, bordering the Democratic Republic of the Congo. We spend the night in the guesthouse of catholic nuns. The congregation is divided, as some of the nuns had been actively involved in the genocide. The following morning we continue taking a dirt road to the north, along the lakeshore. Halfway, a soldier joins us to ensure Aimable's safety and security. Aimable does not know what to expect. Since 1994, he has been back to the village only three times, always with military protection.

Four men have been accused of killing and looting the property of Aimable's family. When we arrive, many of the villagers have already assembled. At least 200 men and women, young and old, are standing and sitting in the burning sun, with the green surrounding hills in the background. The four accused men are also present, ready to stand trial. As they are not in prison awaiting trial, they wear civilian clothes instead of the usual pink prison dress. One of them is an old man, who nervously looks at Aimable and then turns away. Another one is a heavily sweating younger man with a handkerchief on his head, hiding his eyes behind sunglasses that will never leave his face. The other two, more average-looking men, both middle-aged, are talking with some men in the audience.

On the veranda are sitting an old aunt of Aimable, her son – a young man who, together with his sister, survived the genocide – Aimable, and me. The young man, as the story goes, was not killed because he is a hermaphrodite whose life was spared because of his inability to produce children. His living hell would be on earth. The sister lives in Kigali and refuses to join the *gacaca*. Apart from them, there are a military guard, a government representative, and two Hutu women who were married to Tutsi killed during the genocide. The *Inyangamugayo*, the lay judges, four men and three women, each with a sash in the colors of the Rwandan flag, take their seats behind a table in the middle of the veranda.

After the victims of the genocide are remembered with a minute of silence, the president of the *gacaca* tribunal takes the floor. He leads the court session in a very strict manner. Three of the four accused men are sent in different directions, to prevent them from talking to each other when the trial proceeds with the hearing of the fourth accused. He is accused of having killed Aimable's mother and of having looted his family's property. The second man, the one with the handkerchief and sunglasses, is accused of having raped and killed several family members of Aimable and also of having looted their property. The third man is accused of murder and looting. They all deny the charges and their participation in the genocide. It soon becomes clear that the fourth accused man, the old and nervous man, stands trial without good reason; his wife and children have looted Tutsi's property, but there is no evidence whatsoever that he participated in the looting.

During the hearings, few people stand up to testify. A young man who worked in a restaurant near the houses of Aimable's family and saw what happened testifies against the accused. Another young man testifies for the accused, as does the wife of one of the accused men. The two Hutu women, married to Tutsi men, whose entire families, including husbands and children, were killed, testify in a very emotional way against three of the defendants.

Suddenly Aimable asks me for my telephone and starts dialing a number. He calls the hermaphrodite's sister, who lives in Kigali and fears to come back to her birth village to testify against her family's killers. She gives her evidence through the telephone, twice, with the loudspeaker on so that everybody can hear her very strong words against the accused. The audience is quiet as mice, not to miss any word.

Every time after an accused and witnesses have been heard, Aimable gets the floor. He denounces the *"ceceka"* mentality, the mentality of keeping silent against all odds, which, he says, turns the *gacaca* into a theater play. The vast majority of the audience listens attentively, nods affirmatively, laughs about the little jokes he makes during his speech. Aimable tries to bring a somewhat reconciliatory message; impressive for someone who lost his entire family and faces those accused of having killed them. All in all, it seems as if the population is not hostile. On the contrary, if an accused or witness tells a blatant lie, everybody laughs about the stupidity of it, mocking the liar. The survivors – *rescapées* – are listened to, with some compassion by all with the exception of a small group, maybe six men and one woman, who, as Aimable puts it, seem to have formed a coalition to exculpate the accused men and take the floor at every possible occasion with this goal in mind.

Almost no one in the audience accuses the men directly. However, from the response of the audience one may infer that, in fact, everybody knows what has happened and who was responsible. You know that I know that you know; we all know it, but for whatever reason – and there are many possible reasons – we do not talk about it. Therefore, Aimable does not think it is useless and does not consider it a bad theater play, although not a big hit either. No one directly admits who killed his family, but at least one has to re-think now what happened. It is not kept a secret and the discussion is out in the open. At least it is part of the village's history.

After his final speech, Aimable shakes hands with the *Inyangamugayo* and leaves the court's venue. He has said what he wanted to say. Together with the other survivors and a few friends, he leaves. The entire population remains staring at us, in silence, motionless, until we are out of sight.

On the way back we visit the church where Aimable's mother was killed, together with 7,000 others. He shows me the hill where he grew up, the hill where his grandparents and his brothers and sisters lived. They were all killed. He shows me where their houses stood. All were destroyed. The government has built a small village for the few survivors in the region on the spot of his parents' house. He refuses to go anywhere near.

17.2. THE TRADITIONAL GACACA

Gacaca refers to a kind of soft grass/herb – *umucaca* – on which traditionally a community – that is, the men – came together to discuss conflicts within or between families or inhabitants on a certain hill, and sometimes conflicts with "strangers."[1] The symbolism behind the name may be considered twofold. First, "*[l]e tapis d'umucaca sur lequel siège le conseil de Gacaca cache des pièges, les racines rampantes de cette plante sont traîtresses, elles font tomber les distraits qui s'y aventurent. Le symbolisme étant ici que la Gacaca doit être capable de déjouer les pièges, les 'intrigues sociales,'*"[2] meaning that the tapestry of the plant *umucaca* hides its treacherous roots, which

---

[1]   See F. Reyntjens, *Le* gacaca *ou la justice du gazon au Rwanda,* 40 POLITIQUE AFRICAINE 31, 31–41 (1990); FELIX NTAGANDA, LA JUSTICE PARTICIPATIVE (GACACA) ET LA JUSTICE INTERNATIONALE; OPPOSITION OU COMPLÉMENTARITÉ? 48 (mémoire DEA Université de Lyon 2003).

[2]   UNHCHR, *Gacaca, le droit coutumier au Rwanda, Rapport final de la première phase d'enquête sur le terrain* 9 (Kigali, June 31, 1996), cited in Ntaganda, *supra* note 1, at 48.

act as snares to easily make the absent-minded stumble; hence, the tapestry thwarts the snares, the social machinations. Secondly, "*[l]'umucaca est une plante toujours verte. Ni la chaleur de la saison sèche, ni l'humidité de la saison des pluies ne ternissent le vert d'umucaca. Cette couleur survit au changement des saisons,*"[3] or: the *umucaca* never loses its green color; it survives the heat of the dry season as well as the humidity of the rainy season. *Gacaca*, as a physical place to sit down but also as a symbol, has become the common name for the traditional justice system in Rwanda to solve conflicts in a community.

As far as it is possible to get a clear picture of customary law in ancient times,[4] it seems as if in the pre-colonial era – that is, until the end of the nineteenth century – customary law was structured along family lines: the nuclear family ("*Urugo*") as the basic unit with the male head of the household, and then the clan ("*Umuryango*")[5] with the oldest and wisest men of the clan acting as "judges."[6] These judges were called *Inyangamugayo*, which can be broadly translated as "person of integrity, fair, honest, wise, faithful, trustworthy."[7] On top of the pyramid was the royal court with the *Mwami*, the king, as the judge dealing with the most severe cases.[8]

During the colonial era, this traditional structure mainly remained untouched under the Germans and, after 1917, initially also under the Belgians. This changed in 1943 when the *Ordonnance législative no. 34 du 5 octobre 1943 sur les juridictions indigènes du Rwanda-Urundi*[9] – the edict on the indigenous jurisdictions – was issued, transforming the customary legal system into a formal structure. Next to some non-customary courts, this edict introduced as customary tribunals the "*tribunaux de chefferie,*"[10] "*tribunaux de territoire,*" and the "*tribunal du Mwami,*" all with career judges appointed by the colonial authorities or the *Mwami*. This heralded the marginalization of the role of the family and clan and therefore the disintegration of the traditional legal system.[11] Significant for this breakdown of the traditional system

---

[3] *Id.*

[4] Only a few reliable written sources about the *gacaca* can be found as the tradition was oral rather than written.

[5] The clan consisted of all descendants of the same ancestor until the fourth generation, including all entering and leaving the clan through marriages. *See* UNHCHR, *supra* note 2, at 9, *cited in* Ntaganda, *supra* note 1, at 26.

[6] *See* Ntaganda, *supra* note 1, at 25–31.

[7] Rwandans whom I asked for the meaning of the word *Inyangamugayo* explained that although there are many good connotations for this word, "integrity" is the core characteristic of someone who is called *Inyangamugayo*.

[8] *See* Ntaganda, *supra* note 1, at 25–31.

[9] Ordonnance of December 11, 1943, invoking *l'ordonnance législative du 5 octobre 1943 sur les juridictions indigènes du Rwanda-Urundi*.

[10] The *chefferie* was the colonial name for the territory under the authority of the chief of the clan.

[11] *See* Ntaganda, *supra* note 1, at 33–34 (mainly referring to MINEUR, JURIDICTIONS INDIGÈNES DU RWANDA-URUNDI (Astrida, Rwanda 1944)).

is that the edict provided in its article 5 that the tribunals of the chiefs and territory may be assisted by indigenous advisors to advise them on the customs.[12] The same marginalization of the traditional judge also happened with the *Mwami*, the king, in his own court.[13] The *ordonnance* ruled that, in addition to the *Mwami* as president of the court, two or more assessors had to be appointed; in case of absence of the *Mwami*, the deputy president could preside over the court.[14] Last but not least, the colonial "Resident" could replace the *Mwami* as president of the court, with the *Mwami* then being an assessor.[15] In fact, this meant that the *Mwami* in the eyes of his people had been reduced to an organ of administration next to or even below the colonial authorities, instead of the sole and divine authority. With the abolition of the kingdom in 1959 and the independence shortly after, this court of the *Mwami* – previously the summit of the traditional pyramid – disappeared altogether.[16]

It seems that the new government after independence did little to stimulate the *gacaca* as the traditional justice system. Nevertheless, it is clear that the *gacaca* as such stayed alive at least until the early 1990s. Elderly men stress that the focus of the *gacaca* was on reconciliation: "Acknowledgement of the committed fault and discussion about it were important elements in achieving reconciliation."[17] The *gacaca* were "based upon the assumption of collective responsibility" of the family as a whole, which had to bear the punishment together.[18] One old man remembered that the *gacaca* also dealt with murder, before referring it to a higher court; others claim that the *gacaca* only dealt with minor offenses and civil conflicts – about land and family affairs, for instance.[19]

The situation in the early 1990s, before the genocide took place, is not very clear. One scholar, Filip Reyntjens, reports in 1990 that in a sector in the countryside[20] where he attended a *gacaca*, on average there was one *gacaca* per week dealing

---

[12] See *Mineur*, JURIDICTIONS INDIGÈNES DU RWANDA-URUNDI, *supra* note 11, cited by Ntaganda, *supra* note 1, at 35 ("[L]es tribunaux de chefferie et de territoire peuvent se faire assister de conseillers indigènes traditionnels pour l'application des coutumes; ces conseillers auront une voix consultative seulement.").

[13] The marginalisation of the *Mwami* begun in the early 1920s, when it was ruled that a delegate of the Belgian resident had to assist the *Mwami* in his role as judge. In 1931, *Mwami* Musinga was dethroned and subsequently the proclamation of the new king Mutare III Rudahigwa was enacted without any traditional ceremony. ARTHUR MOLENAAR, GACACA, GRASS ROOTS JUSTICE AFTER GENOCIDE: THE KEY TO RECONCILIATION IN RWANDA? 17 (African Studies Centre Research Report 77, Leiden 2005).

[14] See Ntaganda, *supra* note 1, at 35 (primarily referring to MINEUR, JURIDICTIONS INDIGÈNES DU RWANDA-URUNDI, *supra* note 11).

[15] See *id.*

[16] See *id.* at 41.

[17] Molenaar, *supra* note 13, at 14.

[18] *Id.*

[19] See *id.* at 15–17.

[20] Two of my friends who spent their late teenage years living in Kigali before 1994 do not recall any *gacaca* in the city.

with small conflicts, including theft, destruction of property, and physical violence.[21] The *gacaca* mostly addressed conflicts between family members and neighbors, but also those involving relative strangers.[22] It arranged matters parallel to or maybe preceding state courts, with the *gacaca* functioning as an unofficial filter for the state system, and with the state courts as a kind of an unofficial court of appeal for the *gacaca*. In some cases, the *gacaca* dealt with matters that were not regulated in the official system, such as inheritance matters, in a traditional way.[23] Other differences noted between the *gacaca* and the lowest state tribunal, the *tribunal de canton*, include a greater social distance between the parties in the state tribunal compared to the *gacaca* (57% to 41% relative strangers), and a higher percentage of litigants being other than farmers (25% to 7%).[24] The number of cases dealt with by the *gacaca* was about fifteen times as high as the number of cases dealt with by the lowest state court level.[25]

It is interesting to note that, popular and customary as the *gacaca* may seem, already in 1990 Reyntjens warned that the *gacaca* cannot be called purely popular and even less traditional, rather semi-official and neo-traditional.[26] The ties between the *gacaca* and the state legal system are quite strong, for instance through the role the city counselor plays as the president of the tribunal, and because the *gacaca* anticipate that their decisions may be challenged in the *tribunal de canton* by one of the parties.

In sum, we can say that it is not entirely clear how often and regarding which conflicts *gacaca* were still used shortly before its "reinvention" to try genocide suspects. Whatever the exact situation was mid 1990s, it is clear that the *gacaca* were no longer as alive as in ancient times, and more semi-official and neo-traditional than genuinely customary.

17.3. THE TRANSFORMATION OF THE GACACA

Directly after the genocide was stopped in July 1994, many persons were detained and accused of complicity in the genocide. By the end of October 1996, a total of 86,200 prisoners were incarcerated in 19 Rwandan detention centers (among them 3,000 women and 2,000 adolescents),[27] many of them without a sound legal

[21] *See* Reyntjens, *supra* note 1, at 33–34.
[22] *See id.*
[23] *See id.* at 37–38.
[24] *See id.*
[25] *See id.* at 38–39.
[26] *See id.* at 39–40.
[27] *See* REPORT OF THE U.N. HUMAN RIGHTS FIELD OPERATION IN RWANDA (HRFOR), *noted in* U.N. Office for the Coordination of Humanitarian Affairs, Integrated Regional Information Network (IRIN) Emergency Update No. 56 on the Great Lakes (Dec. 13, 1996).

basis.[28] This number grew steadily to reach about 130,000 persons by the end of 1997.[29] At the same time, the judiciary had been diminished. The judicial system, already not quite well developed before 1994, was left in shambles after the genocide as a substantial part of the judiciary had been killed or had fled the country during and after the genocide.[30] Of 758 judges, only 244 were left after the genocide, and 12 out 70 prosecutors remained. Almost all of them were non-lawyers. There were only a handful of advocates/lawyers to defend the accused. Nevertheless, one tried to re-establish the judicial system. At the same time, the trials of genocide suspects had to start. The challenge was to build a new justice system, punish the guilty, and reconcile the population at the same time. The first law on genocide was published as early as 1996.[31] This law created so-called specialized chambers within the *tribunaux de base* (first instance or primary courts) and military courts with exclusive jurisdiction to try genocide cases. This law also introduced the categorization of crimes[32] and the guilty plea,[33] two aspects that have remained cornerstones of the genocide trials to date.

In the late 1990s it was estimated that trying all 125,000 detained suspects of the genocide in regular penal courts would take more than 200 years. Between December 1996 – when the first trials started – and July 1999, a total of 1,801 suspects had been tried.[34] Moreover, the faith in the classical justice system in Rwanda in those days was low.[35] As a result, continuing only with trials before regular courts was not an option. Amnesty was not considered an option either.[36] Considering

---

[28] The law relating to provisional modifications to the Criminal Procedure Code "legalized" this situation. This law was published on September 15, 1996, entered into force retroactively as of April 6, 1994, and in January 1998 was extended until December 1999. *See* Stef Vandeginste, Justice, Reconciliation and Reparation after Genocide and Crimes against Humanity: the Proposed Establishment of Popular Gacaca Tribunals in Rwanda 10, All-African Conference on African Principles of Conflict Resolution and Reconciliation, Addis Ababa (Nov. 8–12, 1999).

[29] The number dropped again to 125,000 by the end of 1998. *See* U.N. Econ. & Soc. Council, Comm'n on Human Rights, *Report on the Situation of Human Rights in Rwanda Submitted by the Special Representative, Mr. Michel Moussali, Pursuant to Resolution 1998/69,* ¶ 28, U.N. Doc. E/CN.4/1999/33 (Feb. 8, 1999).

[30] *See* Ministry of Justice of Rwanda: Gacaca Process: Achievements, Problems and Future prospects, *available at* http://www.inkiko-gacaca.gov.rw/PPT/Realisation%20and%20future%20persective.ppt.

[31] Organic Law N° 08/96 of 30/08/1996 on the Organization of Prosecutions for Offences Constituting the Crime of Genocide or Crimes against Humanity Committed Since Oct. 1, 1990.

[32] *See id.* § 4.2.

[33] *See id.* § 5.3.

[34] *See* Vandeginste, *supra* note 28, at 11–12 (giving a telling overview of the situation in 1999). For French-translated decisions of the courts and tribunals, *see* Avocats sans Frontières, Recueil de Jurisprudence Contentieux du Genocide (2002–2004).

[35] *See, e.g.,* Office of the President, *Report on the Reflection Meetings Held in the Office of the President of the Republic from May 1998 to March 1999 (Detailed document)* 67–74 (August 1999).

[36] The culture of impunity, which had been prevalent since 1959, was an important reason for denouncing amnesty. Impunity was considered a contributing factor to the re-occurrence of massacres in Rwanda because it had left killers in previous massacres untouched. Secondly, the "fight against

the sluggish speed of the International Criminal Tribunal for Rwanda, trying an expected 70 accused in 15 years, it would take the international tribunal 15,000 to 20,000 years to try all the suspects. The ICTR was also problematic in that it sat in Tanzania, far away from Rwanda, and conducted in a language most Rwandans do not (sufficiently) understand.

The *gacaca* as a tool to approach the genocide is mentioned as from shortly after the genocide. Apparently, immediately after the genocide, "old fashioned" *gacaca* emerged to deal with property crimes committed during the genocide;[37] killings were not discussed. A UNHCHR report of 1996, based on a field study the previous year, raised the possibility of *gacaca* dealing with minor offenses and collecting facts about the atrocities committed and then referring these cases to the classical tribunals. The report strongly advised against the *gacaca* itself dealing with the atrocities.[38] In November 1995, the *gacaca* was mentioned during a *National and International Dialogue Conference* in Kigali on "Genocide, Impunity and Accountability."[39] One of the specific objectives of this conference was to:

[e]xamine alternatives to the classical legal system for sanctioning participation in the genocide, with the objectives of establishing the truth, bringing people to acknowledge their wrongs and repent, thus facilitating national reconciliation. These alternatives include for example:

– exploring the use of Rwandan customary law;
– initiation of plea bargaining to obtain guilty pleas;
– seeking alternative sanctions (e.g. establishing work camps to rebuild infrastructure mechanisms for the rehabilitation of participants especially the children).[40]

The conference rejected any consideration of a blanket amnesty in order to fight the culture of impunity: "[t]here shall be no impunity for these crimes. Those who are guilty have a rendez-vous with justice."[41] In its recommendations, the conference

---

impunity" was the buzz-word in the international debate during those years, implying that each and every person involved in genocide, crimes against humanity, and war crimes have to be prosecuted and tried, as enemies of humankind, *hostes humani generis*.

[37] *See* Bert Ingelaere, *The Gacaca Courts in Rwanda*, *in* INTERNATIONAL INSTITUTE FOR DEMOCRACY AND ELECTORAL ASSISTANCE (IDEA), TRADITIONAL JUSTICE AND RECONCILIATION AFTER VIOLENT CONFLICT: LEARNING FROM AFRICAN EXPERIENCES 25, 35–36 (2008).

[38] *See* UNHCHR, *supra* note 2, as mentioned by e.g. *Report on the Situation of Human Rights in Rwanda Submitted by the Special Representative, Mr. Michel Moussali*, *supra* note 29, at 51 (repeating this opinion).

[39] *See* Office of the President, *Recommendations of the Conference Held in Kigali from November 1st to 5th, 1995 on: 'Genocide, Impunity and Accountability: Dialogue for a National and International Response'* (1995). One hundred and sixty-five persons participated in this meeting, from within and outside Rwanda.

[40] *Id.* at 9.

[41] *Id.* at 20.

focused mainly on an independent specialized court or, as introduced a year later, specialized chambers within the classical penal system. The categorization of crimes, guilty pleas, and the use of laymen in the courts were all raised during this conference.[42] For the less serious crimes, alternative forms of accountability were proposed without going into much detail.[43] "In particular, the Conference urges that in cases not involving crime against the person, customary Rwandan procedures such as the AGACACA be used, or adapted, to the extent possible."[44]

However, it seems that only as of 1998–1999 had the *gacaca* really gained ground in the form we now know it. After reflection meetings were held in 1998–1999 in the office of the president – attended by politicians from various parties, members of parliament, ministers and secretary generals, prosecutors, judges, police, military, scholars, and some individual citizens[45] – it was found necessary to look for a solution outside the classical criminal justice system, a solution in which the people should actively participate as, after all, "usually justice is done in the name of the people and for the people," and it is the people "who know the truth about the events which took place."[46]

> Regarding the offences of genocide and massacres, they were committed in public, by many people, in the people's eyes. So, it would be better if those offences were tried in public, the people participating in prosecuting and punishing those who committed them. Those who committed the crime together being tried and punished together. In this new justice, in which the people actively participate, leaders must not leave it to the people alone. Leaders know how people were killed and properties spoiled, and they should participate in helping to search for crimes and their perpetrators, punishing the perpetrators, thus being an example which will be followed by other people.[47]

This new justice in which the people actively participate should help rebuild the country, for instance, by introducing community service for convicts, eradicating the culture of impunity, fostering reconciliation, and the re-establishment of unity among Rwandans. "Rwandans can base that new justice on the Gacaca Rwandese heritage. Gacaca which was existing in Rwanda would serve as a basis when working

---

[42] *See id.* at 16–21.

[43] *See id.* at 21.

[44] *Id.* at 23.

[45] *See Report on the Reflection Meetings held in the Office of the President, supra* note 35. (The English in the Report is of rather low quality, and the citations with obvious mistakes have been corrected.) The meetings were held on various Saturdays between May 1998 and March 1999 in the president's office. The list of attendees mentions 164 names. Four topics were discussed: democracy, justice, economy, and security.

[46] *Id.* at 51.

[47] *Id.* at 51–52.

out the new Gacaca, which is adapted to the period in which Rwandans are living
and which enables them the objectives of real justice."[48]

Arguments raised against the *gacaca* are:

- Trying cases of genocide and massacres by *gacaca* would minimize the seriousness, "making them a simple offence."
- People who are not educated do not have the capacity to try genocide cases
  because they do not know how to implement the law or to carry out trials in an
  appropriate way.
- Nothing would prevent the people from being partial, for instance, because of
  family and friendship ties.
- Rwandans "are used not to tell the truth."[49]
- In some parts of the country, all those who were persecuted died, leaving none
  to testify.
- Trials by *gacaca* would be the origin of other disputes.
- As a result, those accused would kill all those who could accuse them.
- Trials by *gacaca* would not be in conformity with international laws.
- *Gacaca* should only participate in the investigations, leaving other proceedings
  to the classical penal system.[50]

Arguments raised for the *gacaca* include:

- Rwanda needs *gacaca* as a new way of making the population actively participate in justice.
- *Gacaca* give the power to the people, establish the unity of Rwandans, eradicate the culture of impunity, and punish those who should be punished.
- People can be educated on the law and how to carry out trials.
- The public character of the trials limits partiality, with people contradicting
  partial statements and giving concrete evidence.
- Instead of *gacaca* minimizing the seriousness of the crimes, it puts "the crime
  of genocide and massacres at the level in which it was committed": in public
  and with people actively participating, as the crimes had been committed in
  public with the active participation of "too many people."
- Considering the unusual character of the crime of genocide and its basis in
  "bad policy of the former leaders, which was based on ethnism [sic]," "different

[48] *Id.* at 52.
[49] The popular belief is that all Rwandans lie, which is even taught to children during *éducation civic* classes in secondary school. I do not have the impression that Rwandans lie more than other human beings, and the statement is of course particularly troublesome when Rwandans say it themselves.
[50] See *Report on the Reflection Meetings held in the Office of the President, supra* note 35, at 53–54.

means and unusual strategies" are needed to "help Rwandans to get out of the deadlock into which they were plunged by those tragic events."

- The aim is not only to repair any particular offense, but also to "eradicate the roots of killings in Rwanda, to rebuild Rwanda."

- "The people are not considering Government justice as theirs." The *gacaca* will "help Rwandans to believe and even actively participate in justice."[51]

It is interesting to note that most of these pros and cons raised during the reflection meetings have dominated the debate about the *gacaca* ever since and still do, and most of them have turned out to be valid, both for and against the *gacaca*. The choice for *gacaca* was not an easy one, but maybe had to be taken. As one scholar remarked when asked for his opinion on the *gacaca*:

> How to decide on a policy towards the gacaca proposed? From the analysis until now, it is clear that the proposal is simultaneously extremely promising and very dangerous; long thought-out and full of uncertainty; locally owned and weakly socially implanted; containing the seeds of reconciliation and potentially leading to increased conflict; preparing a decrease in the (current) prison population while possibly leading to increases in new detainees. There is no way to be sure of anything: it is a giant bet for the Rwandan authorities and population, as it would be for any donor supporting it (with that difference that for donors it is not a matter of life and death, whereas for the Rwandans it is).[52]

The reflection meeting, after having concluded that Rwanda should utilize a justice mechanism in which the people participate and based on the *gacaca* heritage, decided to install a special commission to study how to of implement the idea. The commission's report contains all principle elements that constituted the new *gacaca*,[53] a *gacaca* based on the past experience but adapted to the current situation.

17.4. THE GACACA: LEGAL FRAMEWORK

17.4.1. *Constituting Considerations*

The organization, competence, and functioning of *gacaca* courts have been written down in the law.[54] Since the introduction of the *gacaca* as a more or less official state

---

[51] *See id.* at 54–56.
[52] Peter Uvin, The Introduction of a Modernized Gacaca for Judging Suspects of Participation in the Genocide and the Massacres of 1994 in Rwanda 12, Discussion Paper prepared for the Belgian Secretary of State for Development Cooperation (without date, most probably 2000).
[53] *See id.* at 57–67.
[54] *See* Organic Law N° 16/2004 of 19/6/2004 Establishing the Organisation, Competence and Functioning of Gacaca Courts Charged With Prosecuting and Trying the Perpetrators of the Crime of Genocide and Other Crimes Against Humanity, Committed Between Oct. 1, 1990 and Dec. 31, 1994; Organic

tribunal system, six laws have passed parliament since 2001, each further refining the whole system. This shows the flexible nature and the rapid developing character of the *gacaca*, with decision makers trying to cope with problems that turned up during the process. The preamble of the law establishing the *gacaca* tribunals and determining their organization, functioning, and competence is clear on what moved the government to create *gacaca*:

> Considering the necessity to eradicate for ever the culture of impunity in order to achieve justice and reconciliation in Rwanda, and thus to adopt provisions enabling rapid prosecutions and trials of perpetrators and accomplices of genocide, not only with the aim of providing punishment, but also reconstructing the Rwandan Society that had been destroyed by bad leaders who incited the population into exterminating part of the Society,[55]

and "[c]onsidering the necessity for the Rwandan Society to find by itself, solutions to the genocide problems and its consequences,"[56] it is decided to adopt this law on *gacaca*, providing for "penalties allowing convicted persons to amend themselves and to favour their reintegration into the Rwandan Society without jeopardizing the people's normal life."[57]

The importance of finding a home-grown solution should not be underestimated. This comes out of resentment that the international community left Rwanda when the genocide started, leaving it to solve its problems itself – during the genocide as well as afterward – and out of pride that it could find a response that was not dictated by the international community.

More than 12,000 *gacaca* were established throughout the country, with about 250,000 persons elected as "judges," the so-called *Inyangamugayo* or persons of integrity in the villages. The number of *Inyangamugayo* later dropped to about 170,000, seemingly because some of those initially elected turned out to have been involved in the genocide, and the number of judges per bench was limited. One difference between the old and new *gacaca* became immediately clear: Whereas

---

Law N° 28/2006 of 27/06/2006 Modifying and Complementing Organic Law N° 16/2004 of 19/6/2004; Organic Law N° 10/2007 of 01/03/2007 Modifying and Complementing Organic Law N° 16/2004 of 19/6/2004; Organic Law N° 13/2008 of 19/05/2008 Modifying and Complementing Organic Law N° 16/2004 of 19/6/2004. These laws together are the revised version of the Organic Law N° 40/2000 of 26/01/2001 Setting Up "Gacaca Jurisdictions" and Organising Prosecutions for Offenses Constituting the Crime of Genocide or Crimes Against Humanity, Committed Between Oct. 1, 1990 and Dec. 31, 1994, and the Organic Law N° 33/2001 of 22/6/2001 Modifying and Completing Organic Law N° 40/2000 of 26/01/2001; two of these laws in their turn were an amendment to the Organic Law N° 08/96 of 30/08/1996 on the Organization of Prosecutions [in regular courts] for Offenses Constituting the Crime of Genocide or Crimes Against Humanity Committed since Oct. 1, 1990.

[55] Organic Law N° 16/2004 of 19/6/2004, preamble.

[56] This consideration did not appear in the 2000 version of the law. It is an often heard sentence: With the *gacaca*, Rwanda shows the world that it can handle its problems itself.

[57] Organic Law N° 16/2004 of 19/6/2004, preamble.

the old *gacaca* consisted exclusively of men, the new *gacaca* consisted of both men and women.[58]

The first "modern" *gacaca* to try genocide cases started with a pilot project in June 2002, with an information phase in 751 *gacaca* courts in 118 sectors,[59] and the trial phase starting March 2005. Nation-wide, the *gacaca* officially started in January 2005, with an information phase to gather information on victims, suspects, looted property, and so on, after which suspects were categorized; the proper trials started in mid-2006.[60]

While started with the idea that about 125,000 detained suspects had to be tried, extrapolation of the number of suspects "discovered" during the pilot phase of the *gacaca* led to an estimate that 750,000 suspects[61] had to be tried all over the country. This turned out to be a rather low estimation. At the end of the *gacaca* trials in mid-2010, the number turned out to be a little less than 1.2 million persons, due to new accusations during the *gacaca*.[62]

17.4.2. *The Crimes*

The crimes covered by the *gacaca* law are crimes against humanity and acts of genocide committed between October 1, 1990, the day the Rwandan Patriotic Army (RPA) – the armed wing of the Rwandan Patriotic Front (RPF) – invaded Rwanda and the war started, and December 31, 1994.[63] As Rwanda had ratified the relevant international conventions but not yet provided for sanctions, the basis of prosecution is the domestic penal code.

The crimes have been grouped in three categories.[64] The *first category* includes those who planned, organized, and supervised the crimes or incited others to

[58] This reflects an important change in society in which women have gained importance. This change was partly due to the fact that women formed the majority of the population after the genocide, as many men were killed or had fled the country, and partly due to an express policy of the government. Rwanda has the highest percentage of women in parliament of any country in the world, and the constitution determines that in all decisive organs in the state at least one-third of its members should be women. It speaks for itself that this change in female leadership is not generally accepted on the village level.

[59] Initially 12, soon broadened to 118 sectors.

[60] The information phase took more time than expected only in Kigali and was still on its way during 2007. *See* National Service of Gacaca Courts, Report on Data Collection, *available at* http://www.inkiko-gacaca.gov.rw/pdf/ikusanya%20english.pdf.

[61] In the pilot phase, about 60,000 persons were categorized, of whom about 7,000 were in cat. 1; 35,000 in cat. 2; and 16,000 in cat. 3. For numbers of the pilot phase, see Table Indicating the Achievements, *available at* http://www.inkiko-gacaca.gov.rw/pdf/Achievements.pdf.

[62] *See* Summary of Person Pro[s]ecuted for Having Committed Genocide, *available at* http://www.inkiko-gacaca.gov.rw/pdf/abaregwa%20english.pdf.

[63] *See* Organic Law N° 16/2004 of 19/6/2004.

[64] *See* Organic Law N° 13/2008 of 19/05/2008, art. 9. Initially there were four categories. *See* Organic Law N° 40/2000 of 26/01/2001, art. 51. These four categories have been refined and reduced to three by, broadly speaking, combining the initial second and third categories.

commit crimes, those who committed crimes as high-ranked officials within religious or state institutions or in militia, and those who allegedly committed rape and sexual torture. This category comprises an estimated 10,000 suspects of whom 7,000 are suspected of sexual torture and rape.[65] The *second category* entails those who distinguished themselves by the zealousness or excessive wickedness with which they took part in the genocide, as well as torturers, violators of corpses, those who "just" killed someone else, those who acted with the intention to kill but did not succeed, and those who engaged in other criminal acts against persons without the intention to kill. This category harbors about 450,000 persons. The *third category* is formed by those who committed acts against property. This category includes approximately 450,000 suspects.[66]

All these crimes include the persons who committed the acts as well as accomplices, that is, persons who have "by any means, provided assistance to commit offences."[67] Superiors are criminally responsible for the acts of their subordinates "if he or she knew or could have known that his or her subordinate was getting ready to commit this act or had done it, and that the superior has not taken necessary and reasonable measures to punish the authors or prevent that the mentioned act be not committed when he or she had means."[68]

It is interesting to note that the crimes as such are not crimes against humanity or acts of genocide under international law, although labeled so in the domestic law. After all, international law requires that an act has to be committed with the intent to destroy, in whole or in part, a national, ethnical, racial, or religious group to be considered genocide.[69] To establish a crime against humanity, it should be established that the acts were committed as part of a widespread or systematic attack directed against any civilian population, with knowledge of the attack.[70] The *gacaca* courts,

---

[65] Until Organic Law N° 10/2007 of 01/03/2007, the first category also included those who distinguished themselves by the zealousness or excessive wickedness with which they took part in the genocide, and violators of corpses. As at the end of the information phase of the *gacaca*, this category turned out to be too big – about 70,000–80,000 suspects – who were to be tried by the regular courts within a reasonable time (as first category cases are), the first category has been diminished, and these two groups have been shifted to the second category.

[66] These numbers are a rather rough estimation. The exact numbers are not yet known. A suspect that is accused of murder and looting counts in two categories. A number of persons until to date unknown have been tried by different *gacaca*, with the result that some suspects were counted more than once.

[67] Organic Law N° 16/2004 of 19/6/2004, art. 53.

[68] *Id.*

[69] This definition of genocide was laid down in the genocide convention and copied by all international instruments afterwards, including the ICC Statute. *See* Convention on the Prevention and Punishment of the Crime of Genocide, Dec. 9, 1948, 78 U.N.T.S. 277; Rome Statute of the International Criminal Court, July 17, 1998, 2187 U.N.T.S. 90.

[70] *See supra* note 69, art. 7 for the definition of crime against humanity as laid down in the statute of the ICC.

however, do not have to establish for each suspect that (s)he committed his or her act as part of a widespread attack or with the intent to destroy an ethnical group.[71] The overarching assumption in the law is that these acts were committed as part of a widespread or systematic attack or with the intent to destroy, in whole or in part, an ethnical group, and therefore constitute acts of genocide and crimes against humanity. Due to, for instance, the hate campaign on the radio, village meetings, and songs the years before and during the genocide, everybody knew that the aim of the killings was the extermination of the Tutsi. These acts are, so to speak, symbolically made into acts of genocide and crimes against humanity, without having to prove this. From a legal position, the crimes to be prosecuted and tried before the *gacaca* are in fact "ordinary" crimes, with similar penalties.

17.4.3. *The Sanctions*

The law provides for general sanctions for each category, which range from prison – in custody and suspended[72] – to community service[73] and/or the payment of damages. An important determining factor in the sanctions imposed is whether the suspect/ offender has confessed, pleaded guilty, repented, and apologized. In such cases, the punishment is substantially diminished in order to encourage confessions. For minors who were between fourteen and eighteen when they committed the crimes, maximum prison sentences are mitigated as noted later in the chapter.[74] Children who were younger than fourteen years when they committed a crime[75] cannot be prosecuted, but they can be placed in a solidarity camp.[76]

First-category offenders incur life imprisonment [young offenders: ten to twenty years]. When they have confessed and repented, they face a prison sentence between twenty and thirty years [six and a half to nine years for young offenders]. Community

---

[71] There is probably one exception, i.e., those who committed their crimes as high-ranked officials, as the law there speaks about "those offences," apparently referring to "the crime of genocide or crimes against humanity" in the heading of the provision.

[72] Article 14 of Organic Law N° 10/2007 of 01/03/2007 introduced the suspended sentence. The reason for the suspended sentence is that the number of persons convicted to prison is expected to be too high to harbor all of them in the prisons.

[73] *See* Organic Law N° 10/2007 of 01/03/2007, art. 14.

[74] *See* Organic Law N° 13/2008 of 19/05/2008, art. 20.

[75] *See* Organic Law N° 16/2004 of 19/6/2004, art. 79. The English text of the law reads: younger than 14 "at the time of the charges against them," which is a different criterion than "at the time of the events" as mentioned in art. 78. The French text reads: "au moment des faits leur reprochés." Reading the law other than "at the time they committed the crime" would create a gap.

[76] *Ingando* (in Kinyarwanda) are residential camps for groups of about 300 persons (e.g., students), which have a duration of three weeks to two months. The participants discuss in particular five themes: (1) analysis of Rwanda's problems, (2) history of Rwanda, (3) political and socioeconomic issues in Rwanda and Africa, (4) rights, obligations and duties, and (5) leadership. Released prisoners also undergo *Ingando*.

service is not possible.[77] Initially, the death penalty was possible. As of 1998, a total of twenty-two people had been executed in public execution ceremonies. Since then, more than 500 first-category offenders have been convicted to death, but no one has been executed. The death penalty was finally abolished in Rwanda in 2007.[78]

Second-category punishments are more differentiated, according to the specific act within this category and whether the offender confessed and repented.[79] The zealous murderers, torturers, those who committed dehumanizing acts on dead bodies, and those who refuse to confess face a prison sentence ranging from thirty years to life imprisonment [young offenders: ten to fifteen years].[80] If they confess, the prison sentence ranges from twenty to twenty-nine years [six to seven and a half years for young offenders], half of which is commuted into community service, whereas part of the remaining time in prison is commuted into a suspended sentence.[81] For those who "just" killed someone or had the intention to kill but did not succeed, the sentence is a prison term from fifteen to nineteen years [four and a half to five and a half years for young offenders]; community service is not possible. If they have confessed, the prison sentence ranges between eight and fourteen years [two and a half to five years for young offenders], half of which is commuted into community services, and part of the remaining time in prison is commuted into a suspended sentence.[82] Lastly, those who committed a crime against persons without any intention of killing them face a prison sentence of five to seven years [two and a half to three and a half years for young offenders], half of which is commuted into community service, and one-sixth of the remaining prison sentence is suspended.[83] For those who confessed, the sentence ranges from one to four years [six months to two and a half

---

[77] Within the group of confessors, a distinction has been made according to the moment the confession has been made: before the name [of the confessor] was included on the list of perpetrators drawn up by the cell *gacaca*: 20 to 24 years, and after that moment, when the suspect already appears on that list: 25 to 30 years. This distinction already existed for second-category cases, but has been introduced with regards to first-category offenders by article 13 of Organic Law N° 10/2007 of 01/03/2007.

[78] Organic Law N° 31/2007 of 25/07/2007. Recently parliament decided to abolish the solitary confinement that replaced the death penalty.

[79] *See* Organic Law N° 10/2007 of 01/03/2007, art. 14.

[80] Under the previous law, Organic Law N° 16/2004 of 19/6/2004, this was life imprisonment or death, so the maximum penalty has been lowered.

[81] In the group of confessors, a distinction has been made according to the moment the confession has been made: before the confessor's name was included on the list of perpetrators drawn up by the cell *gacaca*: 20 to 24 years and one-third of the remaining prison sentence suspended, and after that moment, when the suspect already appears on that list: 25 to 29 years and one-sixth of the remaining prison sentence suspended.

[82] In the group of confessors, a distinction has been made according to the moment the confession has been made: before the confessor's name was included on the list of perpetrators drawn up by the cell *gacaca*: 8 to 11 years and one-third of the remaining prison sentence suspended, and after that moment, when the suspect already appears on that list: 12 to 14 years and one-sixth of the remaining prison sentence suspended.

[83] In this case, half of the prison sentence is not suspended when it regards young offenders.

years for young offenders], half of which is commuted into community service and part of the remaining time in prison is commuted into a suspended sentence.[84] The community service part becomes void when the offender refuses to work or commits another crime, and (s)he shall have to serve the full prison sentence.[85]

As to the *third category*, the law provides that when the offender and the victim have agreed upon an "amicable settlement," the offender cannot be prosecuted.[86] In case of prosecution, the offender will be sentenced to civil reparation of the damages (s)he has caused,[87] that is, reparation of the property looted whenever possible, or repayment of the ransacked property, or carrying out the work worth the property to be repaired.[88]

Apart from prison and community service, offenders who were eighteen years and older when they committed the crimes "are liable to"[89] the withdrawal of civil rights, either perpetually or for the duration of the sentence, that is: the right to be elected; to become a leader; to serve in the armed forces; to serve in the National Police and other security organs; or to be a teacher, a medical staff, a magistrate, a public prosecutor, or a judicial council member.[90] The rights to be withdrawn and the duration depend on the category of the crime and whether the offender confessed.

The execution of punishments is an interesting example of the rapidly evolving law. In 2007, the death penalty was abolished and the suspended sentence introduced. These changes were made because the number of persons convicted to prison was expected to be too high to house all of them in the prisons. In late 2007, new discussions began regarding how to further alleviate the burden of the prisons, for instance through altering the sequence of the execution of sanctions – first community service, then the suspended prison part, and finally the prison part – and early release of convicted prisoners. In 2009, it was decided that convicts who served their community service in a group instead of alone, therefore spending more days per week on community service, would benefit from a substantial reduction of the period to be spent in community service.[91]

---

[84] In the group of confessors, a distinction has been made according to the moment the confession has been made: before the confessor's name was included on the list of perpetrators drawn up by the cell *gacaca*: 1 to 2 years and one-third of the remaining prison sentence suspended, and after that moment, when the suspect already appears on that list: 3 to 4 years and one-sixth of the remaining prison sentence suspended.

[85] *See* Organic Law N° 16/2004 of 19/6/2004, art. 74, partly amended by Organic Law N° 13/2008 of 19/05/2008, art. 18.

[86] *See* Organic Law N° 16/2004 of 19/6/2004, art. 52.

[87] *See id.* art. 75.

[88] *See id.* art. 95.

[89] I understand that "are liable to" (in the French text: "encourent") means: Rights may be, but are not necessarily, withdrawn.

[90] *See* Organic Law N° 10/2007 of 01/03/2007, art. 15. In the previous Organic Law N° 10/2007 of 01/03/2007, art. 76, the right to vote was also withdrawn.

[91] *See* the subsequent laws on the *gacaca* mentioned *supra*, note 54.

17.4.4. *The Procedure*

A small part of the first category of accused persons are tried before regular penal courts; the vast majority of the suspects of genocide and crimes against humanity – most of the first-category and all second- and third-category cases – are tried by the *gacaca* courts. There are three different levels of *gacaca*: the *gacaca* courts of the cell, the *gacaca* courts of the sector, and the *gacaca* courts of appeal.[92] Each *gacaca* court is made up of a General Assembly, a Bench, and a Coordination Committee.[93] Apparently there were also unofficial *gacaca* established in prisons by prisoners themselves according to the cells where suspects came from; the information gathered there may be used in the official *gacaca*.

Each bench consists of seven judges or *Inyangamugayo* and two substitutes.[94] They are the lay judges who try the cases before the *gacaca* courts. The members of the bench elect out of their midst the coordination committee, which serves as sort of a daily management team. The general assembly on the lowest level, that of the cell, consists of all the cell's residents of 18 years and older – at least 200 persons.[95] The general assembly for the sector is composed of all *Inyangamugayo* of the cell *gacaca* in that sector, together with the sector judges and the judges of the appeals *gacaca*.[96]

Three phases can be distinguished in the activities of the *gacaca*. The first phase, executed by the cell *gacaca*, is the making of a list of persons who reside in the cell, who resided in the cell before the genocide (and locations they kept moving to and routes they took), who were killed in the cell of residence or outside, who were victimized[97] and whose property was damaged, and the alleged authors of the offenses. This can be done on the basis of confessions, guilty pleas, files forwarded by the public prosecutor, evidences and testimonies, and other information. The second phase for the cell *gacaca* is to categorize the suspects in one of the three categories of crimes.[98]

---

[92] Organic Law N° 16/2004 of 19/6/2004, arts. 3–4, as amended by Organic Law N° 28/2006 of 27/6/2006, arts. 1–2.

[93] Organic Law N° 16/2004 of 19/6/2004, art. 5.

[94] *Id.* arts. 8, 13, as amended by Organic Law N° 10/2007 of 01/03/2007, arts. 1–2, again partly amended by Organic Law N° 13/2008 of 19/05/2008, art. 4. Before the first amendment, there were nine judges and five deputies. Initially the bench consisted of nineteen people. *See* Organic Law N° 40/2000 of 26/01/2001, art. 13.

[95] Organic Law N° 13/2008 of 19/05/2008, art. 3. If the number of 200 persons for the general assembly is not met, this *gacaca* court of the cell has to be merged with another neighboring *gacaca* court.

[96] Organic Law N° 16/2004 of 19/6/2004, art. 7.

[97] A victim is defined as "anybody killed, hunted to be killed but survived, suffered acts of torture against his or her sexual parts, suffered rape, injured or victim of any other form of harassment, plundered, and whose house and property were destroyed because of his or her ethnic background or opinion against the genocide ideology." *Id.* art. 34.

[98] *Id.* arts. 33–34.

On the basis of this categorization, suspects are subsequently tried by the cell *gacaca* (third category), sector *gacaca* (second category), or *gacaca* and regular state criminal courts (first category).[99] In order to fulfill these tasks, they have various competencies, such as to summon any person to appear in a trial, to order and carry out a search, to take temporary protective measures against the property of an accused, and to issue summons to the alleged authors of crimes and order detention or release on parole.[100]

Gacaca meet once a week if a quorum is – 5 of the 7 members of the bench and 100 members of the general assembly – is present, and are public except when decided differently.[101] Decisions are made in consensus and, if this turns out to be impossible, with an "absolute majority" of its members.[102] Decisions and deliberations of judges are made in secret, but a judgment must state its grounds,[103] and proceedings are public, except for rape and sexual torture cases. Acts of sexual torture and rape – first-category acts – cannot be confessed in public.[104] Victims of these acts (or in case of death or incapacity an interested party) choose one or more members of the seat to whom to submit her or his complaint, either in words or in writing, or, in case (s)he does not trust the members of the seat, to the public prosecution. In cases of rape and sexual torture, the trials take place behind closed doors; the judgment, however, is done in public.[105]

The steps to be taken during the proceedings before the *gacaca* courts have been laid down in the law, separately for the cell *gacaca* and the sector and appeals *gacaca*. In broad lines, they are as follows. The cell *gacaca*, which only deal with property crimes, start with a determination of the damaged property; they then link this to the owners and those accused of having damaged the property who can present their defense. This is followed by a response by the owner of the property, upon which the list of property, victims, and defendants is adopted. Subsequently, the bench explains to the defendants the modalities for granting the compensation by asking each defendant to decide on his or her means and the period of payment in case of conviction.[106]

---

[99] *See id.* (enumerating activities).

[100] *See id.* art. 39.

[101] *See id.* art. 17 *et seq.*, art. 23 as amended by Organic Law N° 28/2006 of 27/6/2006, art. 5. Article 38 of the 2004 law has been amended by Organic Law N° 13/2008 of 19/05/2008, art. 6.

[102] Organic Law N° 16/2004 of 19/6/2004, art. 24.

[103] *See id.* arts. 21, 25.

[104] Organic Law N° 13/2008 of 19/05/2008, art. 6.

[105] *See id.* For more detail about the trials of sexual violence cases, see Usta Kaitesi & Roelof Haveman, *Prosecution of Rape and Sexual Torture Before Gacaca, in* VICTIMOLOGICAL APPROACHES TO INTERNATIONAL CRIMES (Rianne Letschert, Roelof Haveman, Anne-Marie de Brouwer, & Antony Pemberton eds., Intersentia, forthcoming Oct. 2010).

[106] Organic Law N° 16/2004 of 19/6/2004, art. 68.

The sector and appeals *gacaca* start, in case of a confession, with the identification of the defendants and the plaintiff, and all charges against the defendant are read out loud, as well as the minutes of the defendant's confession. Each defendant may comment on the accusation. Then any interested party may testify for or against the defendant. Such a witness must take an oath "to tell the truth by raising his or her right arm, saying: 'I take God as my witness to tell the truth.'"[107]

The plaintiff describes all the offenses suffered and how they were committed, upon which the defendant responds. Then the bench of the *gacaca* establishes a list of the victims and the offenses each of them suffered, upon which the defendant can respond. The minutes of the hearing are read out loud, and when all agree, the parties to the trial – all who took the floor – and the bench put their signatures or fingerprints on the statement of the hearing. Finally, the hearing is closed or postponed if deemed necessary to obtain further information.[108] When there was no preceding confession, the defendant gets the opportunity to confess during the hearing.[109]

It is mandated that "[t]he hearing shall be carried out in calmness. Any person who takes the floor, must be characterized by politeness in speech and behavior before the persons of integrity, parties, witnesses and the audience at large."[110] For any parties that do not conform to this requirement, "the President of the session can give a warning to the troublemakers in the Court, eject or put him or her in detention for a period not exceeding forty eight (48) hours, according to the gravity of the offence. When the committed offence is a criminal offence, the Seat forwards the case to the security organs, for prosecution basing on the ordinary laws."[111]

The judgment contains, apart from information on the proceedings and identity of parties, the damaged property that requires reparation and the defendants responsible for this (cell *gacaca*) or the charges against the defendant (sector and appeals *gacaca*), the facts presented by the parties, the motives of the judgment, and the modalities and period for reparation (cell *gacaca*) or the offense of which the defendant is found guilty and the penalties pronounced (sector and appeals *gacaca*). The judgment is given at the same day of the final hearing or at a subsequent public hearing, the date and time of which all present in the hearing are informed.[112]

Similar to the ordinary penal system, there are three legal remedies against *gacaca* decisions and sentences: "opposition," "appeal," and "review of judgment."[113] All three remedies lead to full trials, and are not restricted to errors of law or procedural errors. Opposition is the remedy against a judgment *in absentia*, and is

---

[107] *Id.* art. 64.

[108] *See id.*

[109] *See id.* art. 65. *See also* art. 66 (trial *in absentia*).

[110] *See id.* art. 71.

[111] *Id.*

[112] *See id.* arts. 67, 69–70, 83.

[113] *Id.* arts. 85–93.

brought before the court that passed judgment in first instance. An opposition is only permissible if the party who was absent pleads a "serious and legitimate reason" for his absence during the trial.[114] Opposition can be made within fifteen calendar days from the day of notification of the judgment passed *in absentia*. Cell, sector, and appeals *gacaca* deal with opposition against their own judgments *in absentia*.[115]

Appeal – that is, a request to a higher court of law to reconsider a decision rendered by a lower court – can be lodged against all decisions of cell *gacaca* – except judgments relating to offenses against property – and sector *gacaca* at the sector *gacaca* and appeals *gacaca* respectively. Hence, the sector *gacaca* serve as the appeals court for sentences by the cell *gacaca* on perjury and unlawful pressure and threats on witnesses and judges, and for other decisions in general. The *gacaca* courts of appeal serve as the appeals court for sentences pronounced in the first instance by the sector *gacaca* in second-category cases. An appeal has to be lodged by the defendant, plaintiff, or any other person acting in the interest of justice within fifteen calendar days after the decision or sentence to be appealed against has been pronounced.[116]

Review is possible when new evidence turns up contrary to an initial judgment by a *gacaca* court or when a person has been given a sentence that is contrary to the legal provisions of the charges against him or her. A review can be lodged by the defendant, the plaintiff, or any other person acting in the interest of justice.[117]

17.5. SOME IMPORTANT CHARACTERISTICS

Three aspects in particular of the *gacaca* deserve special attention as these distinguish the *gacaca* from ordinary "classical" penal trials. These aspects are the use of lay judges, the participation of the population in the trials, and the place of reconciliation in the whole process.

17.5.1. *Lay Justice*

Gacaca is a form of lay justice. Lay justice is not uncommon in Rwanda historically. Before 1994 and up until the 2004 justice sector reforms, only about 5 percent of the

[114] *Id.*, art. 86.
[115] *See id.* It seems reasonable to assume that the regular criminal procedural rules apply here, i.e., that this notification must be personal, or otherwise within fifteen days from the date on which the sentenced person personally received the notice, and hence when (s)he becomes aware of the judgment that (s)he plans to oppose.
[116] *See id.* arts. 41–43, 23 (as amended by Organic Law N° 28/2006 of 27/6/2006, arts. 7–9), 89–92 (art. 90 as amended by Organic Law N° 28/2006 of 27/6/2006, art. 19).
[117] Organic Law N° 13/2008 of 19/05/2008, art. 24.

judges were lawyers.[118] The special genocide chambers that had been established in the 1990s also mainly consisted of lay judges. In October 2001, more than 250,000 *Inyangamugayo* were elected by the population to fill the benches of about 11,000 *gacaca* courts, later brought back to about 170,000 persons.[119] The *Inyangamugayo* are ordinary people from the villages. One report, for instance, revealed that 92 percent of the *Inyangamugayo* are farmers of whom 81 percent earn less than 5,000 RWF (approximately € 7) per month.

Together these *Inyangamugayo* form the lay benches of the 11,000 *gacaca* all over the country. Each bench – whether at cell level, sector level, or the appeals *gacaca* – consists of seven *Inyangamugayo* and two substitutes. The lay judges have to swear an oath before exercising their duties, including that they work for the consolidation of national unity, without any discrimination whatsoever.[120] An *Inyangamugayo* cannot judge in a case in which (s)he is involved in any way – for example, when the case concerns relatives, good friends, or sworn enemies.[121]

According to the law, *Inyangamugayo* are persons who have not participated in the genocide, are "free of the spirit of sectarianism" and from genocide ideology,[122] are of high morals and conduct, truthful, honest, and characterized by a "spirit of speech sharing." Government officials, politicians, soldiers, policemen, and magistrates cannot be elected as *Inyangamugayo*.[123]

Inyangamugayo can be replaced when they are absent from the sessions of the *gacaca* for three consecutive times without good reason, have been convicted to imprisonment for at least six months, have prompted "sectarianism" or genocide ideology, have done "any act incompatible with the quality of a person of integrity," or have revealed details of *in camera* proceedings.[124] Also the bench as a whole can be dissolved when it takes "sentimental decisions," lacks "consensus spirit," is

---

[118] In comparison, in 2006, 95 percent of the judges are lawyers and not surprisingly all very young. In comparison, before the genocide there was only one faculty of law which produced about twenty-five lawyers every two years. Moreover, judges were rather marginalized as the main power within the judiciary was with the prosecutors and police.

[119] *See, e.g.*, Presidential Order N° 12/01 of 26/6/2001, Establishing Modalities for Organizing Elections of Members of 'Gacaca Jurisdictions' Organs.

[120] Organic Law N° 16/2004 of 19/6/2004, art. 9.

[121] *Id.* art. 10.

[122] "Ideology of genocide consists in behaviour, a way of speaking, written documents and any other actions meant to wipe out human beings on the basis of their ethnic group, origin, nationality, region, colour of skin, physical traits, sex, language, religion or political opinions." Organic Law N° 10/2007 of 01/03/2007, art. 3.

[123] Organic Law N° 16/2004 of 19/6/2004, arts. 14–15, as modified and complemented by Organic Law N° 10/2007 of 01/03/2007, arts. 3–4.

[124] Organic Law N° 13/2008 of 19/05/2008, art. 5.

incompetent, or behaves incompatibly with *gacaca* courts activities.[125] Involvement in genocide has been an important reason for replacement of *Inyangamugayo*. An alleged 40 percent of the *Inyangamugayo* appointed turned out to have been involved in genocidal acts in 1994 themselves.[126]

17.5.2. *Participatory Justice*

The *gacaca* is a form of participatory justice. The participatory aspect of *gacaca* is demonstrated by the number of persons involved in the *gacaca* as *Inyangamugayo*, as accused persons, and as witnesses for and against the accused.

Officially, every citizen is obliged by law to take part in the *gacaca*.[127] This obligation is less strange than it seems at first glance when read in conjunction with the duty to testify. In the preamble to the law establishing the *gacaca*, it is made clear that every Rwandan citizen is obliged to testify regarding what he or she has seen or knows. The first substantive consideration reads that the crimes were "publicly committed in the eyes of the population, which thus must recount the facts, disclose the truth and participate in prosecuting and trying the alleged perpetrators."[128] The second one is of the same character, providing "that testifying on what happened is the obligation of every Rwandan patriotic citizen and that nobody is allowed to refrain from such an obligation whatever reasons it may be."[129]

The message is clear: Every citizen is obliged to participate in the *gacaca*, as all have been witnesses to the crimes. This is not different in many of the classical penal systems: In general, witnesses are obliged to testify. In Rwanda, persons who omit or refuse to testify on what they have seen or know, as well as persons who make a slanderous denunciation, face a prison sentence of three to six months.[130] A similar

---

[125] *See id.* Instructions N° 06/2005 of 20/7/2005 of the Executive Secretary of the National Service of Gacaca Courts on Dismissal of the Judge Inyangamugayo from the Gacaca Court Bench, Dissolution of a Gacaca Court Bench and Replacement of the Judges Inyangamugayo.

[126] *See, e.g.,* 28,000 *Leaders Implicated in Genocide,* THE NEW TIMES (Rwanda), Dec. 21–22, 2005. Since the information gathering started in March 2005, the number of "leaders" who have been suspected of involvement in the genocide has increased from 688 to 28,477 as of December. *Id.* If I understand this correctly, more than 90 percent of them are *Inyangamugayo.*

[127] *See* Organic Law N° 16/2004 of 19/6/2004, art. 29. The previous Organic Law N° 40/2000 of 26/01/2001 did not contain such a provision.

[128] Organic Law N° 16/2004 of 19/6/2004, preamble.

[129] *Id.* The preamble of the 2001 law reads: "Considering that the duty to testify is a moral obligation, nobody having the right to get out of it for whatever reason it may be."

[130] *See* Organic Law N° 16/2004 of 19/6/2004, art. 29, doubled in case of a repeated offense. The previous Organic Law N° 40/2000 of 26/01/2001 did contain a similar provision in article 32, with a prison sentence of 1 to 3 years maximum.

fate face those who exercise pressures[131] or attempt to do so or threaten[132] the witness or the members of the bench: three months to one year imprisonment.[133]

Participation of the population where the crimes took place is an important feature, adding to the reconciliatory function of the *gacaca*. In regular domestic and international criminal courts, the victim, who, apart from the offender, is the person most directly involved in the conflict, is denied full access to the proceedings. The victim's role is taken over by a representative of the state or, even worse, the international community. The proceedings take place not within the community where the crimes took place, which therefore also is a "party" in the conflict, but far away. In the ICTR case against Kayishema,[134] one of the witnesses, a woman from Kibuye, a place in the western province of Rwanda, reflects this notion when stating: "I kept imagining, 'How I wish this trial was taking place in Kibuye!' How I wish I had testified in front of the people of Kibuye whom [Kayisehema] had wronged, and not an audience made up of only foreigners. I felt like walking up to his chair, grabbing him, and bringing him with me to Rwanda."[135] The traditional criminal justice systems steal the conflict from those directly involved.[136] Participatory justice on the level where the crimes have been committed leaves the conflict where it belongs. Whether the *gacaca* indeed fulfills this function remains to be determined.[137]

An obligation to participate of course does not guarantee that the population in practice actively participates. The ideal situation would be that the population spontaneously and actively participates because they see the advantages of such involvement. Reality is different. A recent opinion survey on social cohesion in Rwanda by the National Unity and Reconciliation Commission (NURC)[138] shows

---

[131] "Anything aiming at coercing the Seat into doping against its will, translated into actions, words or behaviour threatening the Seat, and clearly meaning that if the latter fails to comply with, some of its members or the entire Seat may face dangerous consequences." Organic Law N° 16/2004 of 19/6/2004.

[132] "Words or actions clearly meant to threaten the witnesses or the Seat members for a Gacaca court, aiming at winning acceptance for his or her wish." *Id*

[133] *Id*. arts. 30–32.

[134] *See* Prosecutor v. Kayishema & Ruzindana, Case No. ICTR 95-1-A (appeal). Clément Kayishema was the *préfet* of Kibuye, a town in the west of Rwanda at Lake Kivu, who was sentenced to life for genocide and crimes against humanity.

[135] Helena Cobban, Amnesty After Atrocity? Healing Nations After Genocide and War Crimes 3 (Paradigm, 2007).

[136] *See, e.g.*, Nils Christie, *Conflicts as Property*, 17 Brit. J. Criminology 1 (1977). It may be interesting to study to what extent *gacaca* in this respect differ from regular traditional courts. But in fact this is very difficult to study, as little research is known on the effectiveness of criminal justice systems in general or of alternatives such as a truth and reconciliation commission. At the end of the day it seems to boil down to beliefs.

[137] For rather pessimistic views, see Bert Ingelaere, *The Gacaca Courts in Rwanda, supra* note 37; Bert Ingelaere, *Does the Truth Pass Across the Fire Without Burning? Locating the Short Circuit in Rwanda's Gacaca Courts*, 47 J. Mod. Afr. Stud. 507 (2009).

[138] National Unity and Reconciliation Commission (NURC), Social Cohesion in Rwanda, an Opinion Survey, Results 2005–2007 (Kigali 2008).

that between 2005 – the year that the *gacaca* were implemented nation-wide – and 2007, about one-third of the participants of the *gacaca* were actively involved[139] as witnesses[140] or *Inyangamugayo*.[141] In 2007, 62 percent of the participants reported themselves as mere "spectators."[142]

An assessment of whether this participation rate is high or low needs a more detailed study,[143] and, moreover, seems to depend on one's expectations. In any case, one may question whether it is only active participation that counts or the mere fact of being there and registering and digesting what is happening. Maybe the term "engagement," as used by Phil Clark,[144] is more suitable. It differs from the term "participation," which seems to signify an active attitude. The term "engagement" entails both an active and passive attitude. One can, for instance, be shamed by what one hears during the *gacaca* proceedings, without any active participation.

17.5.3. *Reconciliation: Confession, Guilty Plea, Repentance, Apology*

From the start, confession, guilty plea, repentance, and apology has played an important role in the discussions about trials of genocide suspects. It was introduced in 1996 in the first law on genocide trials for special chambers of the classical courts, and remained a core element in the *gacaca* proceedings. To this end, a special procedure has been introduced in the law, to which every person who has committed one of the three category crimes has recourse. To be accepted as a confession, guilty plea, repentance, and apology, the law determines that the defendant must:

1. give a detailed description of the confessed crime, how (s)he carried it out, where and when, witnesses to the fact, the persons victimized, where (s)he threw their dead bodies, and the damage caused;

---

[139] *Id.* at 24. (2005: 36%, 2006: 31%, 2007: 37%).

[140] *Id.* (2005: 25%, 2006: 21%, 2007: 29%).

[141] *Id.* (2005: 10%, 2006: 10%, 2007: 9%).

[142] *Id.* (2005: 63%, 2006: 68%, 2007: 62%). Only 1% throughout the years reported not being involved at all. Ingelaere concludes that "[i]n general a decrease in the active participation is evident." Ingelaere, *supra* note 137, at 510. However, Ingelaere bases his findings on the same numbers as the NURC survey for 2005 and 2006, but includes the year 2002, when the pilot phase of the *gacaca* had started and the total number of "spectators/no participation at all" was 54%, and excludes 2007, when the situation had improved significantly compared to 2006.

[143] Ingelaere for instance distinguishes between witnesses for and against the defence. *See* Ingelaere, *supra* note 137. Moreover, one should make a correction for those participants in the *gacaca* who during the genocide were elsewhere hence did not witness anything, which may explain in part the percentage of spectators/no participation at all.

[144] Phil Clark, *The Rules (and Politics) of Engagement: The Gacaca Courts and Post-Genocide Justice, Healing and Reconciliation in Rwanda, in* AFTER GENOCIDE: TRANSITIONAL JUSTICE, POST-CONFLICT RECONSTRUCTION AND RECONCILIATION IN RWANDA AND BEYOND (Phil Clark & Zachary D. Kaufman eds., Hurst 2008).

2. reveal the co-authors, accomplices, and any other information useful to the exercise of the public action;

3. apologize for the offenses that (s)he committed.[145]

The confession, guilty plea, repentance, and apology have to be done in front of the bench of the *gacaca*, the judicial police officer, or the public prosecution officer in charge of investigating the case. It shall be done orally during the *gacaca* session or in the form of a written statement (bearing his or her signature or fingerprint) before the court examines the substance of the case. An apology, however, "shall be made publicly to the victims in case they are still alive and to the Rwandan Society."[146]

As discussed earlier, offenders who confess, plead guilty, repent, and apologize enjoy a substantial reduction of their sentence. First-category offenders, however, only benefit from it when they confess before the moment the cell *gacaca* makes up the list of offenders at the end of the information phase. Offenders who confess only during the appeals proceedings also receive no benefit.[147]

How the confession procedure has worked out in practice is a topic of debate. Initially, before the *gacaca* took off, there was a high willingness to participate.[148] The number of confessions seemed to depend on many factors, ranging from individual considerations of wanting to clear one's conscience to organizational matters. In the early days of the trials, before the special chambers in classical courts, quite a few confessions were reported, so many that apparently the justice system had problems processing them all promptly. There could have been more, however:

> Had there been greater certainty that a guilty plea and confession would lead to prompt treatment of the case and eventually release, there might well have been many more confessions. Moreover, things were not helped by the inability of the Rwandan authorities to separate those who had confessed from those who had not. In order to encourage confession, it was surely necessary to separate those participating from the general prison population, so as to reassure them of safety and protection from reprisals. Once again, had this better been organised, the confession programme might have delivered more than it did.[149]

Another issue is the quality of the confessions: Do people tell the truth and how much of the truth do they tell? Many argue that, at best, confessions reflect only part of the

[145] Organic Law N° 16/2004 of 19/6/2004, art. 54.

[146] *Id.* arts. 59–63.

[147] *Id.* arts. 55–58 (art. 58 as amended by Organic Law N° 13/2008 of 19/05/2008, art. 12).

[148] *See* S. Gabisirege & S. Babalola, *Perceptions about the Gacaca Law in Rwanda: Evidence from a Multi-Method Study* 14, Special Publication No. 19, John Hopkins University School of Public Health, Center for Communication Programs (2001).

[149] William Schabas, *Post-Genocide Justice in Rwanda: a Spectrum of Options*, in AFTER GENOCIDE: TRANSITIONAL JUSTICE, POST-CONFLICT RECONSTRUCTION AND RECONCILIATION IN RWANDA AND BEYOND 207, 218, *supra* note 144.

crimes the confessor committed in practice, and not the most severe part. The opinion survey of the NURC shows that "[a] significant majority of survivors believe that there is a pact of silence that prevents many defendants from confessing (82%)."[150] Perhaps it is not surprising that only (but still) 34 percent of prisoners do believe this is true, and 62 percent of the general population.[151] With regard to witness testimonies, the NURC opinion survey shows that a vast majority of the population thinks that "*gacaca* allows for those who are unjustly accused to redeem themselves,"[152] but the survey also indicates "a low level of trust in testimonies made before the *gacaca* with a majority of the population across all groups believes that false accusations and false defense testimonies are quite common during the *gacaca* proceedings."[153]

Maybe the most difficult question to answer is whether the *gacaca*, through confessions and truth telling, contributes to reconciliation. The NURC opinion survey tries to give an answer. It indicates, for instance, that 99 percent of the population at large agrees that *gacaca* is an "essential step towards unity and reconciliation among Rwandans"; 92 percent of the survivors and 79 percent of the prisoners agree.[154] Asked whether the "*gacaca* will facilitate sustainable peace within Rwandan society," 97 percent of the population at large, 81 percent of the survivors, and 73 percent of the prisoners agree.[155] Ninety-one percent of the general population agree with the statement that "after the *gacaca* the families of the condemned and those of the victims will reconcile with each other"; among prisoners, this is 79 percent, whereas 71 percent of survivors support this statement. These findings make the researchers conclude that "[t]here is general optimism that reconciliation between families of victims and perpetrators will occur after the end of *gacaca*."[156]

However optimistic these more general findings may be, when looking in detail at specific issues, "a much more mixed picture emerges."[157] How to interpret this?[158] It

[150] NURC, *supra* note 138, at 67. Seventy-six percent of the survivors believe that defendants who refuse to confess maintain some sense of duty in what they did, against 26 percent of the prisoners and 49 percent of the general population. On both questions and among all groups, these opinions have not changed significantly since 2005 and seem firmly entrenched. *Id.*
[151] *Id.*
[152] *Id.* at 64. In 2007 the general population 97% (from 96% in 2005), survivors 94% (from 87% in 2005) and prisoners 78% (from 86% in 2005). *Id.*
[153] *Id.* at 66. Not surprisingly prisoners are most skeptical about witnesses for the prosecutor and survivors are most skeptical about witnesses for the defense. *Id.*
[154] *Id.* at 68.
[155] *Id.*
[156] *Id.* at 70. Ingelaere suggests that this may be because the question was "after" instead of "because of" *gacaca.* Ingelaere, *supra* note 137, at 511.
[157] NURC, *supra* note 138, at 76.
[158] An explanation for this friction may be that "[t]hese general statements are propagated during awareness raising campaigns with authorities. The population has very well understood and internalised these discourses. But when asked to reveal opinions on the actual practice, experience or expected outcomes, respondents portray less optimism." Ingelaere, *supra* note 137, at 511.

shows that asking questions and counting percentages on the one hand and interpreting the results on the other are two different exercises.[159] Terms such as "optimism,"
"shocking," and "low" all have to do with weighing results. When, for instance, the
NURC report speaks of "only 71% of survivors" who agree that families of survivors and of perpetrators will reconcile, this suggests that the researchers expected a
significantly higher percentage of survivors agreeing, whereas one could also state
that this percentage is quite high instead. When Ingelaere concludes that "[t]he
observation that 53% of the population replies affirmatively to the proposition that
'it is naïve to trust others' (…) after more than a year of Gacaca activities in 2006 is
revealing, almost shocking," he reveals having had quite optimistic expectations.[160]
The NURC opinion survey report is therefore right to put that it "is important for
analysts and policymakers to properly 'read' these sentiments [and] triangulate them
with other information or data that this survey cannot provide [For example (…)
motivations, fears and hopes of those minorities who reject the gacaca process and
doubt that it has any contribution to reconciliation (…)]."[161] Reality seems more
complex than one would wish, which makes a thorough evaluation of *gacaca* and
separate aspects extremely difficult.[162]

17.6. GACACA AS CUSTOMARY LAW

It is clear that the old *gacaca* were a form of customary law. But do the new *gacaca*,
established to try genocide cases, still deserve the label "customary," as its old name-
sake? Some scholars state that the new *gacaca* are indeed a continuation of the old

---

[159] Pitfalls are both in the facts as in the interpretation thereof. For an assessment of criticism on *gacaca*,
see Roelof Haveman, *Doing Justice to Gacaca*, in SUPRANATIONAL CRIMINOLOGY: TOWARDS A
CRIMINOLOGY OF INTERNATIONAL CRIMES 359 (Alette Smeulers & Roelof Haveman eds., Intersentia
2008); Roelof Haveman & Alphonse Muleefu, *The Fairness of Gacaca*, in DAWN ROTHE ET AL.,
STATE CRIME (forthcoming 2010).

[160] Ingelaere, *supra* note 137, at 511.

[161] NURC, *supra* note 138, at 79.

[162] Regarding the truth, for instance: What is the effect of the notion of "you know that I know that
you know," in particular in a society where "the" truth is often kept hidden (one of the core presumptions of Ingelaere, *supra* note 137). If it is true that the truth is hidden and adapted to what
the respondent thinks the authority wants to hear, what does this imply for responses to opinion
studies such as the NURC and Ingelaere surveys? To what extent is "the" truth revealed to the
researcher, or is it also the case here that respondents tell the version of the "truth" that they expect
the researcher wants to hear? Also, for instance, the difference between "the" truth and a "parties'
truth" – which has been highlighted as one of the differences between the adversarial and inquisitorial penal process models – might shed some brighter light on the role of the truth in *gacaca*.
A clear definition of the concept of reconciliation as used in the study is no less important. How
do the effects of the *gacaca* relate to other activities meant to promote reconciliation? Last but not
least, one should distinguish between short-, mid-, and long-term effects and on a micro, meso, and
macro level.

gacaca, although with more state influence and trying crimes of a nature unknown to the old *gacaca*.[163] Others are of the opinion that the new *gacaca* have nothing to do with the illustrious old ones, except for sharing its name.[164]

Let us first conclude that the answer to this question has very little to do with the legal question about the efficacy of the system. In many publications discussing the *gacaca* from a legal perspective, the question about the historical roots of the new *gacaca* is raised within the context of the perceived efficacy of the *gacaca* to try genocide cases. However, the new *gacaca* could be very effective without being a continuation of the old ones; or very ineffective without being a true continuation of the old ones; or very effective being a continuation of the old ones; or very ineffective being a true continuation of the old ones. Continuity has very little to do with the core question from a legal point of view, which is whether the new *gacaca* has turned out to be an efficient and effective way of dealing with a genocidal past, offering justice, reconciliation, retribution, or whatever goal has been set. In this regard, the only question that might be interesting to answer is whether an unaltered *gacaca* would have been better equipped to deal with the genocide than the modernized version. Which can be seriously doubted, at least when the goal is to try not only minor offenses but also crimes that constitute genocide.

The question of whether *gacaca* is or is not a continuation of the past seems more important within a (legal) anthropological framework, discussing how traditional conflict resolution mechanisms develop over time, and whether or not they stand firm under the influence of events that make society shake to its foundations, such as a genocide. First, we have to conclude that the *gacaca* survived the genocide; reports of the early years following the genocide show that in rural areas, *gacaca* re-emerged, in particular regarding property crimes committed during the genocide.

Another question is whether the *gacaca* survived its genocide version. It is too early to answer this question with certainty, the genocide *gacaca* not yet being closed down at the time of writing. However, one might consider the *abunzi* – conflict mediators at cell level – as a continuation of the *gacaca*, albeit with a new name – the name *gacaca* may be too much linked to the genocide. The *abunzi* were created by law in 2006[165] and have as their principal task to mediate in small civil disputes and minor criminal cases, mainly land disputes, disputes in the field of family, marriage and succession, domestic abuse, and petty theft. There are more than 30,000 *abunzi* committee

[163] *See, e.g.*, U.A. Karekezi, A. Nsimiyimana, & B. Mutamba, *Localizing Justice: Gacaca Courts in Post-Genocide Rwanda*, in My Neighbour, My Enemy: Justice and Community in the Aftermath of Mass Atrocity 69, 74 (E. Stover & H.M. Weinstein eds., Cambridge Univ. Press 2004).

[164] *See, e.g.*, Ingelaere, *supra* note 137, at 516. ("[T]he relation between the 'old' and the 'new' gacaca is not one of identity, or even of gradual continuity. There is a difference in kind.... The 'new' gacaca courts are in the truest sense an 'invented tradition.'").

[165] Organic Law N° 31/2006 of 14/08/2006 on the Organisation, Jurisdiction, Competence and Functioning of the Mediation Committee.

members in more than 2,000 cells nationwide;[166] they are elected by the population for two years, they are not paid, nor do they have to be paid for their services.[167]

Also with regard to the *abunzi*, one has to conclude that the involvement of the state is rather strong, for instance by regulating *abunzi* functioning in a written law and organizing official elections. Furthermore, efforts of international nongovernmental organizations (NGOs) and the government trying to let the *abunzi* anticipate decisions being taken in the classical courts[168] contribute to a breakdown of the customary character of the *abunzi* in a very similar way as the breakdown of the *gacaca* was achieved during and after the colonial period. It would be an interesting topic to study to what extent the *abunzi* indeed can be considered a continuation of the old *gacaca*, and, if considered too state-orchestrated by the population, whether the old *gacaca* will pop up again, *sub rosa*, as an informal conflict regulatory mechanism.

However, this still does not answer the question whether the genocide *gacaca* still can be considered customary law. The extent to which the new *gacaca* have drifted away from the traditional *gacaca* provide a strong indication. Then the question is: To what extent have they drifted apart? And does this mean that all ties with customary law have been cut off? Have *gacaca* become part of the classical (penal) system? Let me try to give the beginning of an answer, realizing very well that my knowledge about customary law in general is insufficient to give a conclusive answer. I will do this by mentioning some arguments why *gacaca* is no longer customary law, subsequently trying to show that these arguments are less absolute than often stated. Some considerations can be mentioned that show that the modern *gacaca* are not entirely disconnected from their ancient precursors and are more embedded in the everyday life of the population at large than the classical penal system is.

One of the most striking differences between the old and new *gacaca* is that in the latter, criminal rules of procedure and evidence have been written down in the law. By introducing rules of procedure and evidence in the law, the *gacaca* have seemingly become less customary and more legal and state-orchestrated than its traditional precursor. Although *gacaca* are much more than only a penal system, by codifying the procedural rules they seemingly have become, first and foremost, a state-run system to try those who were involved in the genocide. However, this difference is less striking than it may seem at first sight. As previously noted, the

---

[166] Each *abunzi* committee comprises of twelve members and three substitutes, and at least 30 percent of the members must be women in order to conform to the Constitutional mandate for gender representation in all decisive bodies in Rwanda.

[167] *See* Organic Law N° 31/2006 of 14/08/2006.

[168] For instance, in an effort to diminish the influx into the classical system and to keep citizens who do not agree with the decision of the *abunzi* from "appealing" to the classical legal system, the *abunzi* have been anticipating the decisions of the official state system. Thus, the *abunzi* have sort of taken over and formalized the filter function of *gacaca*, and consequently have been incorporated into the classical judicial system. *See supra* Section 17.2.

traditional *gacaca* as they existed before the genocide were already much less "alive" than in ancient times and had become semi-official and neo-traditional during the colonial and post-colonial era. This, in combination with the post-genocide society, with communities scattered and less homogenous and cohesive than before the genocide, with few people left with sufficient knowledge of the customary rules of the *gacaca*, partly explains why rules had to be written down.[169] These rules were less obvious and "unconsciously known" – less generally accepted among the population as *the* law – than before.[170] This shows more a continuum in the development of the *gacaca* than it being a fundamental breach with the old system.

Secondly, procedural rules being written down suggests an inflexible system instead of the flexible nature of customary oral procedures with each case at hand being adapted to its specific circumstances. To a certain extent this is true. The written law limits the power of the *gacaca* in genocide-related cases. The law determines the procedure to follow. However, this is only for a rather short period of time, that is, the years that the genocide-related cases are tried, in order to guarantee uniformity. Without these rules, the *gacaca* undoubtedly would have been criticized by international commentators much more fiercely than they already have been. Moreover, the written rules do not mean that there is no flexibility. On the contrary, consider the multitude of amendments to the *gacaca* law in a very short time span. Moreover, every time the *gacaca* face an unexpected problem, the *gacaca* lawyers of the *Service National des Juridictions Gacaca* (SNJG), assisting the *Inyangamugayo*, take the problem to "the garage" (in the words of the *gacaca* lawyers) to be fixed on the spot:

> [F]or any case that would prove difficult [the lawyers working at the SNJG] would have to return to the "garage", the name given to their meeting room in order to study and seek for means to resolve the problem within the limits of the law. They expressed commitment to finding legal solutions to any arising case, and expressed that they would deal with each case as it came up instead of seeking for a generalized solution.[171]

---

[169] Since 1990, the war and the genocide, which lasted from April to July 1994, left one million people dead and five million people displaced, both inside the country and in neighboring countries, for a total population in 1994 of about seven million.

[170] *Compare* A.W.B. Simpson, *The Common Law and Legal Theory*, in OXFORD ESSAYS IN JURISPRUDENCE, 2D SERIES (A.W.B. Simpson ed., Oxford Univ. Press 1973), *reprinted in* FOLK LAW: ESSAYS IN THE THEORY AND PRACTICE OF LEX NON SCRIPTA: VOL. I 119, 137 (A. Dundes Renteln & A. Dundes eds., Univ. Wisconsin Press 1995), (stating that a need for procedural authority grows when self-regulating authority more or less breaks down: "the only function served by rulings telling lawyers how to identify correct propositions of law is to assure acceptance of a corpus of ideas as constituting the law"). Turning this statement around, one may conclude that the formulation of procedural rules can be seen as a breakdown of the (authority of) customary law.

[171] Kaitesi & Haveman, *supra* note 105, § 5.2.

In terms of customary law, *gacaca* is "living law," law that is used in practice and developing on a daily basis, contrary to static codified rules. Although, it must be admitted, this law is adapted to reality by a state-run organization, the SNJG.

Closely related, thirdly, is the argument that the new *gacaca* try crimes that were not in the jurisdiction of the old *gacaca*. The law defines and hence limits the crimes that can be tried. The old *gacaca*, a least as they existed shortly before 1994, did not deal with severe crimes, such as murder. Genocide will certainly never have been part of its jurisdiction. However, we may well assume that in pre-colonial times more severe crimes were dealt with by *gacaca*, either directly or in preparing for the court of the *Mwami*, the king. Moreover, we can be sure that the acts constituting these crimes always have been, still are, and always will be against the customary law. This pertains to behavior that always belonged to the jurisdiction of the *gacaca*, such as looting and destroying cattle and houses (category-three crimes), but also to the crimes that were not in the jurisdiction of at least the most recent traditional *gacaca*: abusing, torturing, and killing people (category-two and category-one crimes). The need to codify these crimes therefore has less to do with a need to define the rejected behavior[172] than with the fact that "modern" legal rules – the principle of legality – demand that the punishable behavior is well defined in the law.[173] From this point of view, it may be considered a wise decision to have codified this part of the "law" to give it official legitimacy, as did the codification of the procedural rules.

Fourthly, another seemingly striking difference between the old and the new *gacaca* is that the goals are different: reconciliation and reparation for the traditional *gacaca*, retribution for the new *gacaca*. At first sight, this is undoubtedly true, at least when comparing the new *gacaca* with the *gacaca* that existed shortly before 1994. However, this difference becomes much less striking when one realizes that almost half of the cases tried by the new *gacaca* regard property crimes with a procedure that is aimed more at reparation and reconciliation than punishment, with the parties trying to come to an amicable settlement and the *Inyangamugayo* in many cases functioning as arbiters rather than as judges. Moreover, the penalties are more and

---

[172] This is not true for all crimes, however, for instance in cases of sexual violence when the coercion exercised was more of a psychological nature rather than physical. *See* Kaitesi & Haveman, *supra* note 105. It is interesting to note that, apart from the demarcation of jurisdiction between customary and state courts, many publications about customary law in particular deal with the question of how to ascertain whether a certain act, such as polygamy, breaking a promise to marry a girl, sex before 'marriage,' or killing an alleged witch, is considered against customary law, and whether it is to be tried by a customary tribunal or as a customary "crime" by a state court. Regarding Indonesia, see, *e.g.*, Roelof Haveman, The Legality of Adat Criminal Law in Modern Indonesia (Jakarta, Tatanusa 2002). *See also* Folk Law: Essays in the Theory and Practice of Lex Non Scripta: Vol. I, *supra* note 170, at 283–394 (with seven chapters under the heading "The Ascertainment of Folk Law," as well as various other contributions in the two volumes).

[173] *See, e.g.*, J. Fierens, *Gacaca Courts: Between Fantasy and Reality*, 3 J. Int'l Crim. Just. 896, 906–08 (2005) (arguing that the *gacaca* law is retroactive because genocide and crimes against humanity were not covered by the law at the time the acts were committed).

more limited in practice, in particular through the way they are executed, leading to sentences that – in nature and severity – are very soft compared to sentences for similar crimes in an "ordinary" situation. The introduction of community service can be seen as a sanction that bridges the old and new *gacaca*, community service being more restorative than punitive. In general, one may ask oneself whether punishments are only retributive. In particular in customary law, the distinction between "crimes" and "civil conflicts" is fluid, as are sanctions, varying somewhere between the extremes of retribution and reconciliation. Moreover, it may very well be that on a local level the goals of *gacaca* are perceived to be different from the official state goals, even differing from *gacaca* to *gacaca*, which adds to the "popular" and flexible character of the *gacaca*.[174]

Last but not least, when compared to the classical justice system and even more when compared to the international forum – the ICTR in Arusha – the new *gacaca* are much closer – physically and mentally – to traditional customary legal trials than to classical state justice. The *Inyangamugayo* are not state-appointed judges but ordinary people[175] elected by the community of which they themselves are members and in which the crimes have been committed. They do not wear black robes nor do they speak a legal language that is not understood by the vast majority of the population. Much more than classical courts, the *gacaca* are based on participation of the whole community, considering the "conflict" at hand not only an issue between the offender and the victim but as a matter for the whole community. This remains true, even when the participation of the population is more passive than active but at least can be engaged. Also physically the *gacaca* are closer to the population than the state courts.[176] This proximity seems exactly the reason for "ordinary Rwandans [to] prefer the Gacaca courts over the national courts and the ICTR for dealing with the genocide crimes." "[F]or the ordinary peasant the classical tribunals are both physically and psychologically remote institutions" which make them "prefer the justice of proximity, despite its problems."[177]

---

[174] *See, e.g.*, Clark, *supra* note 144, at 313.

[175] As mentioned earlier, elite members of the community – government officials, politicians, soldiers, policemen, and magistrates – cannot be elected, which adds to the "popular" character.

[176] Compare this to the ever-growing popularity of the law clinics all over the country, first at the national university, and the state-established *Maisons d'Access à la Justice*. Both of these institutions are attracting many ordinary people trying to find justice, which was almost inaccessible to them before.

[177] Ingelaere, *supra* note 37, at 51. A study from 2001, before the *gacaca* started, shows a similar outcome: 41 percent of the 1,676 respondents viewed the involvement of the community as an advantage of *gacaca* over the classical justice system, and 28 percent mentioned the faster pace of the *gacaca*. *See* Gabisirege & Babalola, *supra* note 148, at 13 (noting that "Rwandans attach a lot of importance to the Gacaca Law and are overwhelmingly in favour of the jurisdictions"). The opinion survey of the NURC shows that in 2007, 98 percent of the general population, 96 percent of the *rescapées*, and 83 percent of the prisoners agreed with the statement that "Gacaca allows us to adjudicate crimes against humanity and crimes related to the genocide more quickly and fairly than other existing judicial institutions." NURC, *supra* note 138, at 58.

`Gacaca, previously existing in Rwanda as customary law, definitely served as a basis when working out the new *gacaca*, "adapted to the period in which Rwandans are living" – that is, adapted to the specific circumstances of a post-genocide society. Let me keep on the safe side by concluding that the new *gacaca* are bouncing between the customary and classical state justice, having drifted too far away from the ancient *gacaca* to be called customary *strictu sensu*, but bearing too many customary law characteristics to be considered part of the classical (penal) system.

PART SIX

Customary Law, Human Rights, and Gender Equality

18

Customary Law, Gender Equality, and the Family

The Promise and Limits of a Choice Paradigm

Tracy E. Higgins and Jeanmarie Fenrich

18.1. INTRODUCTION

The legal regulation of the family under customary law is characterized by complexity within particular traditional legal systems and by diversity across the wider range of such systems within Africa. Customary law may determine the rights and obligations of spouses, the terms of marriage formation and dissolution, the implications of marriage for family membership, parental rights and obligations regarding children, custody of children upon marital dissolution, land acquisition, ownership and inheritance, and often governance structures within the community.[1] Virtually all of these legal norms have implications for gender equality.

This chapter explores the tension between the operation of traditional legal systems (whether formally recognized or not) and the increasingly widespread commitment among African states to gender equality, a commitment embodied in international treaties and many domestic constitutions.[2] Specifically, we consider whether a pluralist legal structure – one in which multiple family law paradigms are recognized – provides a means of reconciling the persistence of patriarchal customary norms with a state's commitment to gender equality. Assuming that at least one among multiple regulatory schemes complies with the substantive demands of gender equality norms, is the mere availability of an egalitarian option sufficient to satisfy international standards? What other conditions must be satisfied, if any, to ensure meaningful choice?

We begin with a brief sketch of international human rights law governing gender equality. We next describe in greater detail what we call the choice model of

---

[1] See Jeanmarie French & Tracy Higgins, *Promise Unfulfilled: Law, Culture, and Women's Inheritance Rights in Ghana*, 25 FORDHAM INT'L L. J. 259, 268 (2001) (citing Victor Essien, *Sources of Law in Ghana*, J. BLACK STUDIES 246, 248 (1994)).

[2] See infra Section 18.2. See, e.g., UGANDA CONST. 1995 art. 21; GHANA CONST. art. 17; TANZ. CONST. art. 13(5); S. AFR. CONST. 1996 § 9(3).

reconciling customary law with gender equality standards. As a means of explaining the model and exploring its limits, we next examine case studies from Ghana, Tanzania, and South Africa, each of which represents a somewhat different implementation. Finally, we offer some conclusions about the strengths and limitations of the model and some suggestions as to how it might best be implemented.

18.2. INTERNATIONAL LAW REGARDING GENDER EQUALITY

International and regional human rights treaties, including the Universal Declaration of Human Rights,[3] the United Nations Charter,[4] the International Covenant on Civil and Political Rights,[5] the International Covenant on Economic, Social, and Cultural Rights,[6] the African Charter on Human and Peoples' Rights ("African Charter"),[7] the Convention on the Elimination of All Forms of Discrimination Against Women (CEDAW),[8] and the Protocol to the African Charter on Human and Peoples' Rights on the Rights of Women in Africa ("African Protocol"),[9] all contain guarantees of equal rights without regard to sex.[10] In signing them, States undertake an obligation to eliminate discrimination against women in all areas, including the domestic, economic, political, and cultural fields.[11]

With respect to areas of customary law that conflict with gender equality norms, international law is clear that gender equality must take priority. Rather than simply focus on state action or formal legal gender equality, CEDAW requires that States "take all appropriate measures, including legislation, to modify or abolish existing laws, regulations, customs and practices which constitute discrimination against women."[12] In other words, States must affirmatively regulate customs and

---

[3] Universal Declaration of Human Rights at 71, G.A. Res. 217A III, U.N. Doc. A/180 (Dec. 12, 1948) [hereinafter UDHR].

[4] U.N. Charter, *signed* June 26, 1945, *entered into force* Oct. 24, 1945.

[5] International Covenant on Civil and Political Rights, *adopted* Dec. 19, 1966, *entered into force* March 23, 1976, U.N. Doc. A/6316, 999 U.N.T.S. 171 [hereinafter ICCPR].

[6] International Covenant on Economic, Social and Cultural Rights, *adopted* Dec. 19, 1966, *entered into force* Jan. 3, 1976, U.N. Doc. A/6316, 999 U.N.T.S. 3 [hereinafter ICESCR].

[7] African Charter on Human and Peoples' Rights, *adopted* June 27, 1981, *entered into force* Oct. 21, 1986, OAU Doc. CAB/LEG/67/3 Rev.5 (1982) [hereinafter African Charter].

[8] Convention on the Elimination of all Forms of Discrimination Against Women, *adopted* Dec. 18, 1979, *entered into force* Sept. 3, 1981, U.N. Doc. A/34/46, 1249 U.N.T.S. 13 [hereinafter CEDAW].

[9] Protocol to the African Charter on Human and Peoples' Rights on the Rights of Women in Africa, *adopted* July 11, 2003, *entered into force* Nov. 25, 2005, OAU Doc. CAB/LEG/66.6 (2003) [hereinafter African Protocol].

[10] UDHR, *supra* note 3, art 7; U.N. Charter, art. 55; ICCPR, *supra* note 5, arts. 2(1), 26; ICESCR, *supra* note 6, art. 3; CEDAW, *supra* note 8, arts. 2, 3, 5, 15, 16; African Charter, *supra* note 7, arts. 2, 3.

[11] *See* African Charter, *supra* note 7, art. 1, 18(3); CEDAW, *supra* note 8, arts. 2, 3, 15, 16; African Protocol, *supra* note 9, art. 9.

[12] CEDAW, *supra* note 8, art 2(f).

social practices in a way that promotes gender equality. The African Protocol similarly requires States to "enact and effectively implement appropriate legislative or regulatory measures, including those prohibiting ... all forms of discrimination particularly those harmful practices, which endanger the health and general well-being of women."[13] States must also devote the resources necessary for enforcement and must undertake education efforts and any additional steps necessary to ensure equal rights for women.[14] Under article 2(2) of the African Protocol, States commit to modify social and cultural patterns through public education and information strategies "with a view to achieving the elimination of harmful cultural and traditional practices and all other practices which are based on the idea of the inferiority or superiority of either of the sexes, or on stereotyped roles for women and men."[15]

These legal obligations apply specifically to women's rights in marriage and the ownership of property. CEDAW requires State parties to "take all appropriate measures to eliminate discrimination against women in all matters relating to marriage and family relations"[16] and to ensure that women have on an equal basis with men, "the same right freely to choose a spouse and to enter into marriage only with their free and full consent"[17] and "the same rights and responsibilities during marriage and at its dissolution."[18] The African Protocol similarly provides that States "shall ensure that women and men enjoy equal rights and are regarded as equal partners in marriage" and that States shall enact legislation to ensure that "no marriage shall take place without the free and full consent of both parties."[19] The Protocol also guarantees women the same rights as men with respect to seeking a separation, divorce, or annulment of the marriage.[20]

With respect to polygamy, the African Protocol provides that legislation should guarantee that "monogamy is encouraged as the preferred form of marriage" but

---

[13] African Protocol, *supra* note 9, art. 2(1)(b).
[14] *See, e.g.*, CEDAW, *supra* note 8, arts. 2(c), (e), (f); African Charter, *supra* note 7, arts. 1, 25.
[15] African Protocol, *supra* note 9, art. 2(2).
[16] CEDAW, *supra* note 8, art. 16(1).
[17] *Id.* art. 16(1)(b).
[18] *Id.* art. 16(1)(c). Interpreting this obligation, the Committee on the Elimination of all Forms of Discrimination Against Women adopted General Recommendation Number 21, which stated:

many countries in their legal systems provide for the rights and responsibilities of married partners by relying on the application of common law principles, religious or customary law, rather than by complying with the principles contained in the convention. These variations in law and practice relating to marriage have wide-ranging consequences for women, invariably restricting their rights to equal status and responsibility within marriage. Such limitations often result in the husband being accorded the status of head of household and primary decision maker and therefore contravene the provisions of the Convention.

General Recommendation No. 21 (13th Session, 1994), Equality in Marriage and Family Relations, ¶ 17 [hereinafter General Recommendation No. 21].
[19] African Protocol, *supra* note 9, art. 6(a).
[20] *Id.* art. 7(b).

that the rights of women in all types of marriage, including in polygamous marriages, are protected.[21] Although CEDAW does not expressly prohibit polygamy, in its
General Recommendation Number 21: Equality in Marriage and Family Relations,
the Committee on the Elimination of all Forms of Discrimination Against Women
("CEDAW Committee") found that "[p]olygamous marriage contravenes a woman's right to equality with men, and can have such serious emotional and financial
consequences for her and her dependents that such marriages ought to be discouraged and prohibited."[22] The CEDAW Committee further concluded that permitting
such marriages under customary law violates the provisions of the treaty.[23]

With respect to property rights, CEDAW requires State parties to ensure women
have equal rights to conclude contracts and administer property and guarantees "the
same rights for both spouses in respect of the ownership, acquisition, management,
administration, enjoyment and disposition of property."[24] The African Protocol also
guarantees married women "the right to acquire her own property and to administer
and manage it freely."[25] Upon dissolution of a marriage, women are also guaranteed
an equitable share of the joint property acquired during the marriage.[26]

In short, international human rights treaties recognize the centrality of the family to women's equality and oblige states to regulate the family accordingly. This is
true whether one views family as a product of private ordering or of the legal norms
created and enforced by the State. On either view, the State has an affirmative obligation to promote gender equality within the institution. At the same time, international human rights law also recognizes the importance of both religion and culture
to individual autonomy and obliges the State to protect the right to practices one's
religion and to observe culture rites and traditions.[27] Moreover, as an aspect of family
rights, international human rights law also protects family privacy.[28] The recognition
of these religious, cultural, and privacy rights implies a boundary to state regulation
of the family that may limit the degree to which the State may regulate the institution directly in the name of gender equality. The choice model we describe later in
this chapter represents one response to the apparent tension that exists at the level
of international human rights law between protecting individual autonomy and privacy on the one hand and promoting gender equality on the other. It may also be a
model particularly well-suited to pluralist legal regimes in Africa and elsewhere.

---

[21]   *Id.* art. 6(c).
[22]   General Recommendation No. 21, *supra* note 18, ¶ 14.
[23]   *See id.*
[24]   CEDAW, *supra* note 8, art. 16(1)(h).
[25]   African Protocol, *supra* note 9, art. 6(j).
[26]   *See id.* art. 7(d).
[27]   *See* ICCPR, *supra* note 5, art. 26.
[28]   *See* Barbara Stark, *When Globalization Hits Home: International Family Law Comes of Age*, 39 VAND.
       J. TRANSNAT'L L. 1551, 1572 (2006) (citing LOUIS HENKIN, THE AGE OF RIGHTS 150–151 [1990]).

18.3. LEGAL PLURALISM AND GENDER EQUALITY

Largely as a result of colonialism, legal pluralism characterizes the regulation of the family in much of sub-Saharan Africa.[29] By legal pluralism we refer simply to the existence of multiple alternative sets of regulatory norms for a particular domain, in this case the family.[30] At the most general level, the family law pluralism of most states in the region consists of various systems of customary or religious law as well as common or civil law.[31] The two types of systems, customary law on the one hand and civil or common law on the other, are premised on quite different conceptions of the relationships among the individual, the family, the clan, and the wider community. These different conceptions, in turn, have different implications for gender equality.

Informed by western notions of the family, the marital relationship, and individual autonomy, these civil and common law systems attempt to strike a balance between family privacy and state regulation. Of course, these systems were at one time characterized by substantial gender *inequality*, with legal norms calculated to reinforce male power and privilege within the family.[32] Over the past several decades, however, these colonial norms have been subject to statutory reforms equalizing the formal status of men and women in marriage, divorce, custody, and inheritance.[33] These reforms generally leave significant room for individuals to structure their own families in a variety of ways by allowing individuals to define contractually what the family relationship might look like as it pertains to obligations between spouses, the economic consequences of the marital relationship (through the use of prenuptial agreements), and inheritance (making a will rather than relying on the rules of intestate succession).[34] In this sense, we might say that the civil and common law systems themselves instantiate the choice model, even apart from a regime of legal

---

[29] *See generally* Jacques Frémont, *Legal Pluralism, Customary Law and Human Rights in Francophone African Countries*, 40 VICT. U. WELLINGTON L. REV. 149 (2009).

[30] *See* Sally Engle Merry, *Legal Pluralism*, 22 LAW & SOC'Y REV. 869, 879 (1988). *See also* Johanna E. Bond, *Constitutional Exclusion and Gender in Commonwealth Africa*, 31 FORDHAM INT'L L. J. 289, 291 (2008).

[31] *See* Bond, *supra* note 30, at 302.

[32] *See id.* at 297.

[33] *See, e.g.*, Domestic Violence Act (2007) (Sierra Leone); The Devolution of Estates Act (2007) (Sierra Leone); The Registration of Customary Marriage and Divorce Act (2007) (Sierra Leone); Equal Rights of Customary Marriage Law of 2003 (Liber.); Recognition of Customary Marriages Act of 1998 (S. Afr.); Intestate Succession Act, P.N.D.C. Law 111 (1985) (Ghana).

[34] *See* S. Afr. Law Commission Project 15, The Matrimonial Property Law with Special Reference to the Matrimonial Affairs Act, 1953, the Status of the Married Woman, and the Law of Succession in so far as it affects the Spouses (1982) (describing changes to rectify gender inequality in laws of marriages but exempting customary marriage). *See also* Tracy E. Higgins & Rachel P. Fink, *Gender and Nation-Building: Family Law as Legal Architecture*, 60 ME. L. REV. 375, 402 (2008).

pluralism. Nevertheless, despite the scope of individual choice permitted under these systems, the default norms governing family relationships in the absence of contractual arrangements generally conform to standards of gender equality and neutrality, providing for equal rights for spouses.[35] Moreover, most systems provide for judicial intervention when the particular private ordering would lead to manifest injustice or compromise the interest of children.[36]

With respect to the acquisition, ownership, and transfer of property, the common and civil laws also generally operate in a facially gender-neutral fashion. Here again gender hierarchy, particularly with regard to inheritance and property acquisition within marriage, previously characterized these legal regimes.[37] Indeed, in many states, married women were disallowed from owning property in their own names and/or from passing property to their children through inheritance.[38] Today, however, even intra-family transfer of ownership (whether between spouses, upon divorce, or across generations) generally functions without regard to the gender of the parties.[39]

Of course, among gender-neutral rules, some promote equality more effectively than others. For example, a presumption of community of property or joint owner-ship of marital assets is critical to the protection of women's economic status upon divorce. From a gender equality standpoint, such a system is far superior to a system of separate property, another facially gender-neutral alternative. Moreover, the effi-cacy of such gender neutral laws in promoting gender equality within the family depends in large part on the interplay between social conditions and applicable legal norms and presumptions. This is no less true of the common law than of customary law. Nonetheless, most modern common and civil laws governing the family are at least facially gender-neutral, distinguishing them from customary law to which we now turn.

Customary law is premised on a conception of the family very different from that implicit in civil and common law systems. Anglo-European family law systems are generally premised on the fiction that the family is somehow private or pre-political, not implicated in state power, and, to some degree, sheltered from it.[40] In customary

---

[35] *See* Bond, *supra* note 30, at 305, 320 (discussing that "exclusionary clauses have a disproportionately negative effect on women").

[36] *See id.* at 330–41 (discussing three modes of judicial intervention – limited intervention; formalist intervention; and activist intervention).

[37] *See, e.g.,* French & Higgins, *supra* note 1; Tamar Ezer, *Inheritance Rights in Tanzania: The Impoverishment of Widows and Daughters,* 7 GEO. J. GENDER & L. 599 (2006).

[38] *See* French & Higgins, *supra* note 1; Ezer, *supra* note 37.

[39] *See generally* Akua Kuenyehia, *Marriage, and Intestate Succession in the Context of Legal Pluralism in Africa,* 40 U.C. DAVIS L. REV 385 (2006).

[40] *See generally* Martha M. Ertman, *Marriage as a Trade: Bridging the Private/Private Distinction,* 36 HARV. C.R.-C.L. L. REV. 79 (2001) (exploring the connection between family law and private business law). *See also* Jana B. Singer, *The Privatization of Family Law,* 1992 WIS. L. REV. 1443 (1992); Tracy Higgins, *Reviving the Public/Private Distinction in Feminist Theorizing,* 75 CHI.-KENT L. REV. 847, 850–51 (2000); ROBIN WEST, PROGRESSIVE CONSTITUTIONALISM: RECONSTRUCTING

legal systems, the premise is entirely different: It is that the family itself gives rise to legal and political power, that these are a product of kinship ties, not a distinct and separate sphere.[41] Thus, the creation of nuclear families is not seen primarily as the privately determined union of two individuals, but rather the public linking of two families or clans.[42] Cattle and land are at stake as well as the lineage. In this sense, family formation is a political and legal act that has potentially broad implications. Customary law therefore assigns the control over the particulars of marriage not solely to the individuals who form the marital couple, but rather the extended family and community.[43] Within this customary family structure, both generational and gender hierarchy prevail, with parents and other elders within the family exercising considerable control over younger members and men exercising control over women.[44]

THE FOURTEENTH AMENDMENT 164–65 (1994) ("[A]t least a good deal of the time, in the name of guaranteeing constitutional protection of individual freedom, [the Constitution] also aggressively protects the very hierarchies of wealth, status, race, sexual preference, and gender that facilitate those practices of subordination."); Catharine A. MacKinnon, *Reflections on Sex Equality Under Law*, 100 YALE L.J. 1281, 1311 (1991) ("[T]he law's privacy is a sphere of sanctified isolation, impunity, and unaccountability").

[41] *See* T.W. Bennett, *Customary Law in South Africa* 294–296 (2004) (describing differences in African and Western conceptions of the family, Bennett writes: "The common law and customary law hold widely differing views as to when legal personality begins and ends. The common law is prepared to attribute rights to a child, even unborn, whereas customary law would consider survival at birth a minimum condition. On the question of death, the positions are reversed. According to the common law, physical death marks the termination of personality, whereas in customary law death is not an instant event that is measured physically.").

[42] *See, e.g.*, Women in Law and Development in Africa (WiLDAF), *Advocacy for Better Implementation of Women's Rights In Ghana*, (July 2002), *available at* http://www.wildaf-ao.org/eng/IMG/pdf/Advocacy_womens_rights_Ghana.pdf at 4/20 (noting that "under our [Ghana's] customary laws, marriage is a union between two families as opposed to a union between two individuals under monogamous marriages."); Marissa Herbst and Willemien du Plessis, *Customary Law v Common Law Marriages: A Hybrid Approach in South Africa*, 12.1 Electronic J. of Comp. L. 6 (2008), *available at* http://www.ejcl.org/121/art121–28.pdf ("The customary law initially was not concerned with consensus between the two marrying parties. The marriage was regarded as a union between two families rather than two individuals.").

[43] *See* Bennett, *supra* note 41, at 217 ("Customary marriage is not completed by the performance of a single act nor does it need the approval of a public authority. Instead, it can best be described as a (potentially lengthy) process that affects only the spouses and their families ... [for the Tswana], this process begins with a series of meetings between two families at which they negotiate terms.... Go-betweens and family elders are always available to testify to the celebration of a marriage, and the status of the union will be a matter of general repute, since members of the community have witnessed the negotiations, the wedding ceremony and the delivery of lobolo." (citations omitted)). *See also* Population Council/UNFPA, *Leave No Woman Behind Ethiopia* 10 (2007) *available at* http://www.popcouncil.org/pdfs/Ethiopia_LeaveNoWomanBehind.pdf (stating that in a survey conducted among over 3,000 girls and women aged 10 to 45 in the rural Amhara region in Ethiopia, "The vast majority of marriages were arranged and were not consented to by the bride. Overall, 94 percent of marriages were arranged by parents.").

[44] *See* Bennett, *supra* note 41, at 248–249 ("The term "patriarchy" signifies the authority and the range of special rights and privileges enjoyed by senior males. By implication, all women, as well as junior

As we have already suggested, these two systems, the common or civil law and the customary law, have different implications for gender equality. Again, although initially patriarchal, civil and common law norms have, for the most part, been altered through statutory reform so as to conform facially to norms of gender equality. Although a gendered division of labor may persist in a family premised on a gender-neutral legal model, the legal rules themselves do not dictate or reinforce gender hierarchy and, properly structured, can help undermine it. In contrast, customary law norms governing the family structure, rights to property, access to divorce, obligations to children, inheritance, and family and clan membership expressly create and sustain gender hierarchy. As such, these customary norms stand in tension with the guarantees of gender equality that exist under international law and are increasingly common in constitutions throughout Africa.[45]

Some states have avoided the conflict between customary law and equality guarantees by expressly exempting family law, whether customary or religious, from such guarantees under domestic constitution and by entering treaty reservations.[46] Yet, these exemptions and reservations effectively strip guarantees of gender equality of much of their relevance to women's lives by insulating the most important social institution – the family – from their reach. This is particularly true in rural communities where virtually all economic production takes place through the exploitation of family-owned land and labor.[47] In such a context, exempting family law (including family land rights, inheritance, as well as marriage and divorce) from the reach of gender equality commitments undermines women's economic as well as personal equality.[48]

Another means of resolving the tension between a state's commitment to gender equality and the entrenchment of customary law is to alter customary law by means of statute in a way that eliminates its patriarchal characteristics. Although often advocated by international treaty bodies and nongovernmental organizations,[49] such an

---

men, are subordinate. Patriarchal societies are remarkably common, and, in pre-colonial times, they were present in all parts of southern Africa.").

[45] *See, e.g.,* UGANDA CONST. 1995 art. 21; GHANA CONST. art. 17; CONST. TANZ. art. 13(5); S. AFR. CONST. 1996 § 9(3).

[46] *See, e.g.,* ZIMB. CONST. art. 23, § 3 (a)-(b) (providing that "(3) Nothing contained in any law shall be held to be in contravention of subsection (1)(a) [prohibiting discrimination] to the extent that the law in question relates to any of the following matters – (a) matters of personal law; (b) the application of African customary law in any case involving Africans or an African and one or more persons who are not Africans where such persons have consented to the application of African customary law in that case."); SIERRA LEONE CONST. 1991, art. 27 (4)(d) (providing that the protection from discrimination shall not apply "(d) with respect to adoption, marriage, divorce, burial, devolution of property on death or other interests of personal law").

[47] *See* Tiffany M. McKinney Gardner, *The Commodification of Women's Work: Theorizing the Advancement of African Women,* 13 BUFF. HUM. RTS. L. REV. 33, 35 (2007).

[48] *See, e.g., infra* Section 18.4. B.

[49] *See* Kuenyehia, *supra* note 39, at 395–404.

approach can be difficult to pursue politically and, even if successful on a formal level, may have only limited practical effect. More often than not, unpopular and radical statutory reform measures are simply ignored in favor of traditional practices, particularly where access to both information and courts is limited.[50] This approach also raises concerns with respect to individual autonomy and the pursuit of cultural and religious practices.

A third means of reconciling customary family law with a commitment to gender equality is to take advantage of the legal pluralism that survives as a legacy of colonialism in much of the region. If statutory marriage and customary marriage both exist as recognized legal family structures, individuals can, in theory, choose the framework under which they will create their family. For example, individuals can choose civil marriage, which might entail a presumption of community of property or foreclose polygamy.[51] Women might choose to include their names on title to land acquired during marriage rather than relying on the customary norm of land ownership.[52] So long as nonhierarchical choices are available, perhaps one can presume that individuals enter patriarchal customary relationships voluntarily. If individuals choose to embrace customary law within the privacy of the family, one might therefore conclude that the patriarchal character of that law does not create a problem for public norms of equality. Indeed, given the importance of individual self-determination and the protection of religious belief in international law and liberal constitutions, perhaps such a paradigm of choice can be regarded as rights-promoting in other respects as well.

Of course, for such a choice to be meaningful, at a minimum, the individual must be aware of the existence of alternative schemes. She must understand the implications of her choice and have meaningful access to a forum in which her rights under the alternative legal frameworks may be enforced. Yet, because of the nature and scope of customary law, these basic requirements may not be sufficient to ensure that such choices are freely made. Where custom operates most comprehensively, it defines status and relationships within the broader family, community, and governing hierarchies, including mechanisms for the allocation of land, for the determination of inheritance rights, and for dispute resolution more broadly.[53] In

---

[50] *See, e.g.*, French & Higgins, *supra* note 1, at 304–316, 326–337 (discussing resistance and lack of enforcement of statute altering the customary law systems of intestate succession).

[51] *See supra* note 33.

[52] *See* Lisa R. Pruitt, *Migration, Development, and the Promise of CEDAW for Rural Women*, 30 MICH. J. INT'L L. 707, 747 (2009) (stating "Customary laws dictate that land rights vest in the husband, and the wife's rights terminate if the marriage fails."). *See also* CYNTHIA GRANT BOWMAN & AKUA KUENYEHIA, WOMEN AND LAW IN SUB-SAHARAN AFRICA (2003) (discussing extensively women's perspectives on law in Sub-Saharan Africa, particularly with respect to family law, access to land, inheritance laws, and reproduction).

[53] *See* Bennett, *supra* note 41, at 164–166.

such circumstances, ensuring that individuals make an informed and free choice about family structure may require more substantial intervention.

The balance of this chapter describes and analyzes legal reforms intended to reconcile customary law and gender equality using a paradigm of choice. The examples are drawn from the areas of marriage (Ghana and South Africa) and land rights within families (Tanzania). The case studies are neither comprehensive nor representative, but rather are intended to illustrate common challenges and possible paths toward resolving – or at least lessening – the tension between customary law and international and domestic guarantees of women's rights.

18.4. REFORM EFFORTS IMPLEMENTING A CHOICE MODEL

18.4.1. *Multiple Forms of Marriage in Ghana*

In Ghana, three types of marriage exist: customary law marriage, statutory marriage entered into pursuant to the Marriage Ordinance,[54] and Islamic law marriage entered into pursuant to the Marriage of Mohammedans Ordinance.[55] Each one of these three forms of marriage provides different rights and carries different obligations,[56] though the Marriage of Mohammedans Ordinance applies only to marriages under Islamic law, leaving non-Muslims a choice between customary and ordinance marriage.

Although the formalities for a valid customary law marriage vary somewhat from one ethnic group to another in Ghana, all require the consent of the two families.[57] Other requirements can include the consent of the prospective husband and wife; the giving of presents and drinks by the man's family to the woman's family and acceptance of those presents and drinks by the woman's family; and, in some parts of Ghana, a dowry or bride wealth.[58] All customary marriages in Ghana are potentially polygynous.[59] In contrast, marriages entered into pursuant to the Marriage Ordinance are legally monogamous.[60] Moreover, a valid Ordinance marriage requires: agreement by the parties to the marriage (and not the consent of the families); celebration of the marriage before two or more witnesses as

54 Marriage Ordinance, Cap. 127 (1884) (Ghana).
55 Marriage of Mohammedans Ordinance, Cap. 129 (1907) (Ghana).
56 *See* French & Higgins, *supra* note 1, at 282.
57 *See* Akua Kuenyehia & Esther Ofei-Aboagye, *Family Law in Ghana and Its Implications for Women* in WOMEN AND LAW IN WEST AFRICA: SITUATIONAL ANALYSIS OF SOME KEY ISSUES AFFECTING WOMEN 26 (1998).
58 *See id.*
59 *See id.* at 25.
60 *See id.*; French & Higgins, *supra* note 1, at 282.

evidenced by a Marriage Certificate; a certificate issued after certain formalities; and consummation of the marriage.[61]

Primarily as a result of the requirement of monogamy, ordinance marriages provide women so married with a higher social status.[62] "Wives of such marriages are referred to as 'Mrs.' and they enjoy a certain measure of respect within the Ghanaian society. This kind of respect is not accorded to customary wives."[63] Apart from status, the benefits to women of ordinance marriage are somewhat less clear. Because all property acquired during marriage is presumed the separate property of the spouses, an ordinance marriage does not convey significant economic rights for women that differ from customary law marriages.[64] At the same time, the requirement that the husband obtain a divorce prior to a second marriage may afford the wife in an ordinance marriage a certain amount of bargaining power during that process.

Based on this simplified characterization, we might say that Ghana offers a quite basic model of choice: for non-Muslims, a choice between two marital regimes, one characterized by formal gender equality, the other by different and unequal rights for husbands and wives. Given this menu of legal options, can we regard Ghana as having satisfied its obligations with respect to gender equality in marriage, notwithstanding the fact that it continues to recognize manifestly unequal forms of customary marriage? In other words, does the fact that women have the legal option of an ordinance marriage mean that we should regard their entry into customary marriage as an exercise of individual autonomy?

To answer this question, we must look more closely at the situation in Ghana. Given the advantages for women of ordinance marriage over customary marriage, one might expect women to negotiate for ordinance marriage when they are marrying men who are not already married under customary law. Indeed, in Ghana, there appears to be little or no social cost to women who marry under the ordinance rather than under customary law.[65] This may be due to the relative insignificance of bride wealth in Ghanaian culture, leaving the family with no economic incentive to favor customary marriage over ordinance marriage for their daughters.[66] Thus, a woman fully informed of her options might be expected to choose customary law only if she wanted to marry a man who was already married to another woman under customary law. Conversely, men are likely to resist ordinance marriage even if they have no present intention of taking a second wife because customary marriage preserves

---

[61] Kuenyehia & Ofei-Aboagye, *supra* note 57, at 28.
[62] *See* Interview with Women Lawyers, in Accra, Ghana (June 4, 2001) ("Traditionally, you are respected if you are a Mrs.").
[63] Kuenyehia & Ofei-Aboagye, *supra* note 57, at 29.
[64] *See* French & Higgins, *supra* note 1, at 282.
[65] *See id.* at 282–284.
[66] *See id.* at 274.

that option. Indeed, our research suggests that the fact that customary marriages are
potentially polygynous shifts power in favor of the husband even if he never marries
an additional wife.[67] The mere threat that he can do so helps constrain his wife's
exercise of power.

Given these incentives, the very small percentage of marriages that take place
under the Marriage Ordinance provides a rough measure of women's lack of bargaining power in the marriage choice.[68] As one scholar explains, "The decision to
marry according to one system of law is rarely the exclusive choice of the woman.
She may, in fact, have little bargaining power to negotiate the relevant system of
law."[69] For women, then, the "choice" between ordinance marriage and customary
marriage may be no choice at all.[70] We do not mean to suggest that women would
never freely choose to enter customary marriage. Rather, we note that the mere existence of the legal choice does not guarantee that freedom. Put differently, the legal
availability of a more egalitarian form of marriage does nothing to alter the underlying inequality in bargaining power that exists as a result of men's greater economic,
social, and political power.

The example of Ghana suggests that the existence of legal pluralism in the laws
of marriage is not sufficient to ensure that the choice among formal options is made
freely and equally by the parties involved. In order for the choice to be meaningful,
the legal regime must somehow respond to and compensate for the underlying power
imbalance. As illustrated by the following example of land reform in Tanzania, one
way to do so is to employ presumptions favoring the more egalitarian legal norm.

18.4.2. *Women and Land Ownership in Tanzania*

Tanzania remains an agricultural economy with approximately 80 percent of the
population relying on access to land to support their livelihoods.[71] Thus, land is a

---

[67] *See id.* at 273–278 (discussing the asymmetrical power distribution between husbands and wives under
a customary marriage).

[68] *See* Kuenyehia & Ofei-Aboagye, *supra* note 57, at 25; *See* French & Higgins, *supra* note 1, at 284.

[69] Kuenyehia & Ofei-Aboagye, *supra* note 57, at 25.

[70] A similar pattern exists in Ghana with respect to the relative status of customary wives and "girlfriends"
or "concubines." Women in the latter category lack the legal standing and rights of customary wives and
therefore are unable to claim property upon the death of the man, even though they may have lived with
him for many years, had children with him, and existed as an economic unit. At the same time, because
of the informal and progressive nature of customary marriage rites, the line between a customary wife
and a girlfriend is sometimes indistinct. As a result, the existence or "completion" of a customary marriage is often disputed at the time of a man's death. Although registration of customary marriages facilitates the proof of such a marriage, men and their families often resist registration precisely to unsettle the
status of the wife and undermine her property claims. Here again, her "choice" whether to register the
marriage or not is an illusory one. *See* French & Higgins, *supra* note 1, at 308–311.

[71] *See* Tanzania Gender Networking Programme, Gender Profile of Tanzania: Enhancing
Gender Equality 62 (2007) [hereinafter Gender Profile of Tanzania]. *See also* J.M. Lusugga

vital asset for development, survival, and wealth accumulation.[72] Yet, under customary law, women are not able to own land in Tanzania.[73] Women gain access to land through male family members, such as their father, brother, or husband.[74] In such circumstances, women typically have usufruct rights only, meaning they can use the land for a certain period but do not own the land.[75] As acknowledged by the country's 1995 National Land Policy, "[u]nder customary land law, women generally have inferior land rights relative to men, and their access to land is indirect and insecure."[76]

In Tanzania, land is generally divided into three categories: village land, where customary tenure generally applies; reserved land, including land reserved by the government, such as national parks and areas set aside for future development; and general land, including all urban areas and other land that is neither village nor reserved land.[77]

In 1999, two new statutes, the Land Act and the Village Land Act, were passed to reform the land tenure system in Tanzania and to provide for greater gender equity with respect to both general land and village land.[78] Among other things,

Kironde, *Improving Land Sector Governance in Africa: The Case of Tanzania* (paper prepared for Workshop on Land Governance in support of the MDGs: Responding to New Challenges, Washington DC, March 9–10, 2009), at 6.

[72] *See* GENDER PROFILE OF TANZANIA, *supra* note 71, at 62; Kironde, *supra* note 71, at 1. *See also* Renee Giovarelli, *Customary Law, Household Distribution of Wealth, and Women's Rights to Land and Property*, 4 SEATTLE J. SOC. JUST. 801, 804 (2006) ("Property rights in land – whether customary or formal in nature – provide both economic access to key markets and social access to non-market institutions, such as household and community-level governance structures.").

[73] *See* GENDER PROFILE OF TANZANIA, *supra* note 71, at 62.

[74] *See* WOMEN ADVANCEMENT TRUST, MY LAND: WOMEN'S PERSPECTIVES ON SECURE TENURE IN TANZANIA 8 (2001) [hereinafter WOMEN ADVANCEMENT TRUST].

[75] *See id.*; Lorenzo Cotula, Food & Agric. Org of the U.N., *Gender and Law: Women's Rights in Agriculture*, FAO Legislative Study 36 (2002).

[76] Ministry of Lands, Housing and Urban Development, *National Land Policy*, Dar es Salaam, 1995, ¶ 4.2.5

[77] *See* Kironde, *supra* note 71, at 9–10. *See also* UN-Habitat, *Rights and Reality: Are Women's Equal Rights to Land, Housing and Property Implemented in East Africa?* 110 (2002) (explaining that "All land in Tanzania is declared to be public land vested in the President as trustee for and on behalf of all citizens of Tanzania. Public land is then divided into three categories: (a) general land ...; (b) village land; (c) reserved land.... The Commissioner for Lands can, in the name of the President, grant a right of occupancy for a term of maximum 99 years" although "customary rights of occupancy generally have no term limit."). *See also* Ingunn Ikdahl, *Go Home and Clear the Conflict: Human Rights Perspectives on Gender & Land in Tanzania*, in WOMEN'S LAND RIGHTS & PRIVATIZATION IN EASTERN AFRICA 49 (2008) (stating that "Today, the Village Land Act lays out the legal framework for procedures for most of Tanzania's rural land to be governed through a community-based land tenure management system."). For a more comprehensive overview of the complicated land tenure structure, history and policies of Tanzania, see Kironde, *supra* note 71; UN-Habitat, *supra*, chapter 4.

[78] In general, the Land Act covers general land and the Village Land Act addresses village land, although the Land Act also provides general principles and definitions that apply to both. *See* Kironde, *supra* note 71, at 8; UN-Habitat, *supra* note 77, at 109.

both laws state that the "right of every woman to acquire, hold, use, and deal with, land shall to the same extent and subject to the same restriction be treated as a right of any man."[79] The Land Act also addresses co-occupancy and the relationship between spouses and provides that where one spouse obtains land for the use and co-occupation of both spouses:

> there shall be a presumption that, unless a provision in the certificate of occupancy or certificate of customary occupancy clearly states that one spouse is taking the right of occupancy in his or her name only ... the spouses will hold the land as occupiers in common, and unless the presumption is rebutted ... the Registrar shall register the spouses as joint occupiers accordingly.[80]

The Land Act also provides that if land is registered in the name of one spouse alone but the other spouse contributes their labor to the "productivity, upkeep and improvement of the land," that spouse shall acquire an interest in that land by virtue of his or her labor.[81] The Village Land Act maintains that disputes related to customary rights of occupancy shall be decided based on the customary law of the community,[82] but, significantly, it provides that a rule of customary law shall be "void and inoperative ... to the extent to which it denies women ... lawful access to ownership, occupation or use of any such land."[83] These Acts have not altered the customary law of intestate succession, however, which continues to discriminate against women.[84] The Land Act and the Village Land Act came into effect on May 1, 2001.[85]

Additionally, the Constitution of Tanzania, as amended in 2000, also now expressly prohibits discrimination on the basis of sex.[86] The Constitution also provides that every person is entitled to own property.[87]

Based on the two Land Acts and the Constitution, women can now acquire and own land, and can register the land and obtain title, to the same extent as men.[88] The combination of laws goes beyond the simple choice model described above in

[79] The Land Act No. 5 of 1999, § 3(2) (Tanz.); The Village Land Act No. 4 of 1999, §3(2) (Tanz.).
[80] The Land Act No. 5 of 1999, § 161(1) (Tanz.). This is inconsistent with an earlier statute, the Marriage Act of 1971, which provides that property acquired in the name of one spouse alone is presumed to belong to that spouse exclusively. *See* Marriage Act of 1971, § 60 (Tanz.). This has led to calls for amending the Marriage Act to avoid confusion. *See, e.g.,* TANZANIA WOMEN LAWYERS ASSOCIATION, REVIEW OF GENDER DISCRIMINATIVE LAWS IN TANZANIA 16 (2009) [hereinafter TAWLA report].
[81] The Land Act No. 5 of 1999, § 161(2) (Tanz.).
[82] The Village Land Act No. 4 of 1999, § 20(1) (Tanz.).
[83] *Id.* § 20(2) (Tanz.).
[84] *See* Ezer, *supra* note 37, at 633.
[85] UN-Habitat, *supra* note 77, 121.
[86] TANZ. CONST. art. 13(1), (5).
[87] *See id.* art. 24(1).
[88] *See* GENDER PROFILE OF TANZANIA, *supra* note 71, at 62.

connection with marriage schemes in Ghana in several ways. First, the statutory scheme sets up a clear presumption in favor of joint occupancy at the registration stage.[89] This means that the spouses must opt out of, rather than into, joint occupancy. If the issue is left unaddressed or unresolved, the default will be joint occupancy.[90] Moreover, the new rules create an opportunity after the fact for a spouse who is not registered to establish that she contributed to the acquisition or maintenance of the property and thereby acquired an occupancy interest.[91] This provision is important because it reduces the significance of the form of the original title, something about which the woman might have been uninformed or powerless to alter. Later, in the context of marital dissolution, for example, she might be much better positioned to demonstrate the extent of her economic contribution. Finally, the Village Land Act overrides customary law insofar as it denies women the ability to own and occupy village land, though it does not specify the alternative rule that should govern.

How has this "choice plus presumptions" model affected women's access to land in Tanzania? A decade after the enactment of the reform statutes, women continue to be under-represented in land ownership and title registration.[92] According to one scholar, as of 2009, eight years after the Land Acts came into effect, "[l]ess than 15% of registered land is in the name of women or is jointly owned."[93] In practice, most women continue to abide by the customary law pursuant to which they have no secure right to occupy land in their own name and for the long term.

The Land Acts together have failed to adequately protect the interests of women for several reasons. First, both men and women may lack knowledge of the statutory law. Women whose interests are compromised by this lack of knowledge may be unable to access legal services, especially in rural areas.[94] NGOs working on land tenure issues indicate that women are often unaware of their rights under the Land Acts and therefore do not seek to enforce their rights to own property.[95]

[89] *See* The Land Act No. 5 of 1999, § 161(1) (Tanz.).
[90] *See id.*
[91] *See id.*
[92] *See* Kironde, *supra* note 71, at 13; Committee on the Elimination of Discrimination against Women, *Concluding Observations of the Committee on the Elimination of Discrimination against Women: United Republic of Tanzania*, ¶ 140, U.N. Doc. A/63/38 (July 16, 2008) [hereinafter CEDAW Tanzania report]; WOMEN ADVANCEMENT TRUST, *supra* note 74, at 8 (noting "while woman's rights may be protected on paper, the inequalities and prejudices a woman faces in her daily existence may in effect nullify her ability to take advantage of her rights.").
[93] Kironde, *supra* note 71, at 13.
[94] *See* GENDER PROFILE OF TANZANIA, *supra* note 71, at 63 ("The conflict between the customary and statutory law and other violations of the laws could have been resolved if the victims had better access to information about their rights and legal services.").
[95] *See* interview with NGO in Dar es Salaam (Jan. 28, 2010); interview with NGO in Morogoro (Jan. 29, 2010); WOMEN ADVANCEMENT TRUST, *supra* note 74, at 20. *See also* CEDAW Tanzania report,

According to one scholar, "[T]here is considerable ignorance of both the law and procedures related to land ownership and development and dispute resolution in both rural and urban areas."[96] One study found that 82.5 percent of those surveyed had no knowledge of the Land Act.[97] Even where women are aware of their legal rights, legal services are "too few, too far away and too expensive," especially for women in rural areas.[98] The Tanzanian government does not provide legal aid, and the NGOs that do provide such services are mainly located in urban areas.[99] Courts are also typically located only in urban areas, and the costs associated with traveling to such places and paying for lawyer's fees may be prohibitively expensive for women.[100]

These problems are common to any attempt to effect social change through legal reform, and addressing them is a necessary precondition to an effective implementation of our choice model, even at the most basic level. For choice to be at all meaningful as a safeguard of individual autonomy and access to gender equality, individuals must understand their legal rights and have the resources to enforce them when necessary. Yet, common as they are, these problems could be addressed, at least in theory, by the allocation of greater resources. Perhaps more troubling, from the standpoint of implementing the choice model, is the entrenchment of the customary law and traditional practices that the statutory law is attempting to change.[101] Women often face significant social pressure from their families and communities to maintain the status quo and to refrain from enforcing their statutory rights, even when they are aware of and understand those rights. As noted by one woman in Tanzania, the "laws do not discriminate," but "culture overshadows women, suppresses you."[102] According to NGOs working on these issues, "pursuant to customs and traditions they are not supposed to own land and women accede

supra note 92, at ¶ 140 (The Committee "is also concerned about women's limited knowledge of their property rights and their lack of capacity to claim them."). These interviews and the interviews that follow were conducted in Tanzania in January 2010 by Katherine Hughes, a Fellow at the Leitner Center, and in May 2010 by a delegation of Fordham Law School faculty and students. A complete report documenting the findings of this fieldwork is forthcoming. *See* Katherine Hughes & Elisabeth Wickeri, *A Home in the City: Women's Struggle to Secure Adequate Housing in Urban Tanzania*, 34 FORDHAM INT'L L.J. (forthcoming Mar. 2011).

[96] Kironde, *supra* note 71, at 15.
[97] *Id.*
[98] WOMEN ADVANCEMENT TRUST, *supra* note 74, at 21.
[99] *See* GENDER PROFILE OF TANZANIA, *supra* note 71, at 63.
[100] WOMEN ADVANCEMENT TRUST, *supra* note 74, at 21.
[101] *See, e.g.*, WOMEN ADVANCEMENT TRUST, *supra* note 74, at 11 ("Tradition and custom was by far the topic most cited by the women interviewed as a barrier to women's land rights."). *See also* TAWLA report, *supra* note 80, at 6 (noting that gender neutral statutes do not protect women because of implementation problems, including "the cultural backdrop and general negative attitudes").
[102] Interview with NGO, in Dar es Salaam, Tanzania (Jan. 26, 2010).

to this."[103] As a result of cultural norms, titles and residential licenses are typically kept in a husband's name alone,[104] leading to difficulty for women upon divorce, the death of a spouse, and when applying for loans.[105] One woman in Dar es Salaam explained that having her husband's name alone on the registration papers allowed him to "take the house and everything in it" upon their separation.[106] Men believe that they "worked hard every day to pay for [the housing or land]," so it belongs to them.[107] Attorneys in Tanzania noted that, due to the "patriarchal system," families continue to put only the husband's name on land registration papers, even where women earn the money to buy property.[108]

When women in Tanzania own property or a house, they often do so in secret.[109] Women will build a house in the name of a male relative because they do not want to be seen as owning property.[110] They fear that men will refrain from contributing to the marriage otherwise:[111] "Men do not want to stay in a wife's house."[112] According to women interviewed in Dar es Salaam, even educated women will allow title to be put in their husband's name "due to love" because it will otherwise bring shame upon the husband.[113] One woman noted that if a man included his wife on a title, "the relatives and friends will laugh at him and say he is not strong."[114] This pressure exists for women in urban areas as well as rural areas.[115]

Perhaps not surprisingly, this cultural resistance carries over to the government implementation of the reform measures. One author who conducted field research in Dar es Salaam reports that some officials involved in the registration process did not support joint titling because "the husband was already the owner."[116] This same author reports that bureaucrats in the ministry of land turned women away who came to include their name on a residential license because "they saw it as a household matter which was up to the couple to decide."[117] In an interview in Tanzania,

[103] Interview with NGO, in Morogoro, Tanzania (Jan. 29, 2010).
[104] *See* interview with Members of the Federation of the Urban Poor, Kurasini, Dar es Salaam, Tanzania (May 17, 2010).
[105] *See* interview with Mariam M., Dar es Salaam, Tanzania (May 19, 2010); interview with Tausi H., Dar es Salaam, Tanzania (May 19, 2010).
[106] Interview with NGO Client, in Dar es Salaam, Tanzania (May 2010).
[107] Interview with Felista Komba, Street Level Chairperson & Chair of Centre of Community Initiatives, Kurasini, Dar es Salaam, Tanzania (May 17, 2010).
[108] *See* interview with representatives of TAWLA, Dar es Salaam, Tanzania (May 18, 2010).
[109] *See* interview with NGO, in Dar es Salaam, Tanzania (Jan. 26, 2010).
[110] *See id.*; Interview with NGO, in Morogoro, Tanzania (Jan. 29, 2010).
[111] *See* interview with NGO in Dar es Salaam, Tanzania (Jan. 26, 2010).
[112] *Id.*
[113] Interview with NGO in Dar es Salaam, Tanzania (Jan. 28, 2010).
[114] Interview with Liz K., in Dar es Salaam, Tanzania (May 2010).
[115] *See* WOMEN ADVANCEMENT TRUST, *supra* note 74, at 12.
[116] Ikdahl, *supra* note 77, at 53.
[117] *Id.*

government officials acknowledged "We don't force both male and female names on the title. It is their decision."[118]

The Tanzanian experience with land reform suggests that even tilting the scales in favor of the egalitarian legal norms through the use of presumptions may not be sufficient to ensure a full and free choice. Rather, in order to compensate for unequal bargaining power, reinforced by entrenched social norms about appropriate behavior, the state must attend more carefully to the conditions under which individuals choose. Our third case study, from South Africa, entails a choice-based legal regime that combines presumptions with both procedural safeguards and substantive limits on the scope of inequality under customary law.

18.4.3. *Constrained Choice among Marriage Rules in South Africa*

The 1996 South African Constitution expressly prohibits gender discrimination.[119] It also protects the right to culture[120] and requires courts to apply customary law where applicable "to the extent that [the customary law] is consistent with the Bill [of Rights]."[121] The Promotion of Equality and Prevention of Unfair Discrimination Act also prohibits discrimination on the basis of gender and "any practice, including traditional, customary or religious practice, which impairs the dignity of women and undermines equality between women and men."[122] As we documented in an earlier report, notwithstanding these protections, women in South Africa often face legal, social, and sexual subordination in their marital relationship.[123]

The Recognition of Customary Marriages Act of 1998 ("RCMA")[124] was meant to change the earlier discriminatory policies of the colonial and apartheid regimes, which did not fully recognize customary marriages or which subjected such marriages to the repugnancy test.[125] The RCMA expressly recognizes customary law

---

[118] Interview with Bertha Mlouda, Principal Town Planner, Office of Settlements Regularisation, Ministry of Lands, Housing and Human Settlements Development, Dar es Salaam, Tanzania (May 25, 2010).

[119] *See supra* Section 18.2.

[120] *See* S. AFR. CONST. §§ 30, 31.

[121] *Id.* § 39(3). *See also* Bhe v. Magistrate, Khayelitsha, 2005 (1) BCLR 1 (CC) ¶ 41 (S. Afr.) ("[T]he Constitution put[s] it beyond doubt that our basic law specifically requires that customary law should be accommodated, not merely tolerated, as part of South African law, provided the particular rules ... are not in conflict with the Constitution.").

[122] Promotion of Equality and Prevention of Unfair Discrimination Act of 2000 § 8 (S. Afr.).

[123] Tracy E. Higgins, Jeanmarie Fenrich & Ziona Tanzer, *Gender Equality and Customary Marriage: Bargaining in the Shadow of Post-Apartheid Legal Pluralism*, 30 FORDHAM INT'L L. J. 1653, 1654 (2007).

[124] Recognition of Customary Marriages Act of 1998 (S. Afr.) [hereinafter "RCMA"].

[125] *See Gender Equality and Customary Marriage, supra* note 123, at 1653–1654; CENTRE ON HOUSING RIGHTS AND EVICTIONS, BRINGING EQUALITY HOME: PROTECTING AND PROMOTING THE INHERITANCE RIGHTS OF WOMEN 118 (2004); Bennet, *supra* note 41, at 38 (The repugnancy clause

marriages, including polygamous customary marriages, as valid marriages subject to civil law.[126] Such recognition is important to improve the situation of women in customary marriages because it provides these women with additional legal protections and allows them to utilize state mechanisms to enforce their legal rights. Yet such recognition also gives legal sanction to the institution of customary marriages, a highly gendered and patriarchal institution. This would seemingly conflict with South Africa's obligations to promote gender equality and prohibit customary practices that undermine equality between women and men.

The RCMA attempts to counter this in several ways. First, the act seeks to ensure that women enter and remain in these marriages by choice. Under the RCMA, for a customary marriage to be valid, both prospective spouses must "consent to be married to each other under customary law."[127] This means women must agree to the customary marriage or it will not be valid under the RCMA. With respect to exit, the RCMA formally equalizes women's access to divorce by providing that a court may grant a divorce on the basis of "the irretrievable breakdown of the marriage."[128] The RCMA thus provides women with the ability to choose to exit a marriage on the same basis as men and to do so in a civil court, where their rights regarding spousal support and child custody may be better protected than in a traditional court.

Second, the RCMA puts in place presumptions that favor egalitarian rules in the absence of an explicit agreement between the spouses. For example, the Act provides that absent agreement to the contrary, all property acquired by the couple during marriage shall be held in community.[129] As in Tanzania, the couple must affirmatively opt out of this joint ownership regime.

Third, the Act provides for judicial oversight and intervention at points where women are especially vulnerable.[130] In addition to procedural safeguards in divorce already noted, the Act provides for judicial oversight of the husband's decision to take additional wives. This is critical given that the RCMA preserves polygamy and does not condition it on the pre-existing spouse's approval. In order to marry an additional wife, the husband must seek judicial permission and the court must effect a division of property intended to protect the property interest of the existing wife.

---

subjects the relevant customary law to the requirement that the law not be "repugnant to the general principles of humanity observed throughout the civilized world.").

[126] The RCMA recognizes both marriages entered prior to enactment of the RCMA that were valid under customary law and those marriages entered into after enactment of the RCMA that comply with the Act's requirements. *See* RCMA §§ 2(1)-2(4).

[127] *Id.* § 3(1)(a)(ii).

[128] *Id.* § 8(1), (2). The RCMA defines irretrievable breakdown as meaning "that the marriage relationship between the parties ... has reached such a state of disintegration that there is no reasonable prospect of the restoration of a normal marriage relationship between them." *Id.* § 8(2).

[129] *See id.* § 10(2).

[130] *See id.* §§ 3(4), 4(5), 4(6), 4(7), 7(7)(b), 8(4).

In theory, this oversight can provide protection for women who otherwise have no control over the decision.

Finally, the Act also attempts to mitigate this tension between custom and equality by providing women in customary marriages with more substantive rights while they are in the marriage.[131] For example, the RCMA states: "A wife in a customary marriage has, on the basis of equality with her husband and subject to the matrimonial property system governing the marriage, full status and capacity, including the capacity to acquire assets and to dispose of them, to enter into contracts and to litigate, in addition to any rights and powers that she might have at customary law."[132] The RCMA thus goes further than Ghana's simple choice model or Tanzania's choice-plus-presumptions scheme by providing additional procedural safeguards with respect to entry and exit, and greater formal equality with respect to rights within marriage, even under customary law.

Does the RCMA go far enough to ensure that women's choice to enter customary marriage is substantially free and informed? We think it does not for several reasons. First, despite the requirement of consent, a woman's ability to choose whether or not to enter the marriage is not without important constraints. The RCMA also provides that for a valid customary marriage, "the marriage must be negotiated and entered into or celebrated in accordance with customary law."[133] Under customary law, this requires negotiation and approval by the families of the prospective spouses.[134] Thus, in practice, women are not typically making independent decisions regarding whether or not to enter into a customary marriage.[135] Rather, our interviews revealed that families continue to exert a great deal of control regarding the marriage decision, notwithstanding the RCMA.[136] In some cases, marriage negotiations take place between the families without the knowledge or involvement of either prospective spouse.[137] In other instances, the prospective husband will negotiate with the woman's family without her involvement.[138] More commonly now, a couple will agree to marry and then negotiations will take place between the families.[139] Even in these instances, however, the families exercise control over whether or not the marriage will take place through negotiation over the *lobolo*. *Lobolo* is "the property in cash

---

[131] *See, e.g., Id.*

[132] *Id.*

[133] *Id.* § 3(1)(b).

[134] *See* Higgins et al., *supra* note 123, at 1671; Bennett, *supra* note 41, at 195.

[135] *See* interview with the Queen of the GaMatlala Community, in Limpopo Province, S. Afr. (May 2006) ("[A]s a child, the woman takes direction from her parents").

[136] *See* interview with women in the GaMatlala Community, in Limpopo Province, S. Afr. (May 2006).

[137] *See* Higgins et al., *supra* note 123, at 1672.

[138] *See id.*

[139] *See* interview with Edward Ximba, Executive Director of the Shembe Church, Durban, KwaZulu-Natal Province, S. Afr. (May 2006).

or in kind ... which a prospective husband or the head of his family undertakes to give to the head of the prospective wife's family in consideration of a customary marriage."[140] Although *lobolo* is not required by the RCMA for a valid customary marriage, on the ground, it remains essential to customary marriage in South Africa.[141] Thus, when a woman and man agree to marry, her family can effectively block the marriage by demanding a *lobolo* payment that the man's family cannot afford to make. The prospective husband's family similarly can block the marriage by refusing to pay whatever *lobolo* is requested by the woman's family.[142]

With respect to exit from the marriage, we also believe that the RCMA does too little to equalize the position of the spouses. Under customary law, divorce is strongly discouraged and permitted only under very limited circumstances.[143] Rather, when a marriage breaks down, reconciliation is emphasized.[144] Although, in theory, this customary norm of reconciliation applies to both men and women in a marriage, customary law also permits polygamy.[145] As a result, men do not need to divorce to be able to enter into additional marital or informal relations.[146] Women have no such freedom under customary law. This means, of course, that men and women are in very different bargaining positions with respect to divorce under customary law. By preserving polygamy without conditioning it on the consent of existing spouses, the Act preserves the inequality with respect to divorce even while adopting the formally gender-neutral grounds of "irretrievable breakdown."

In addition, although by recognizing customary marriage the Act gives women access to judicial process in its dissolution, it also undermines this procedural safeguard by recognizing the role of traditional leaders in marital disputes. Specifically, it provides that "[n]othing in this section ... limit[s] the role, recognized in customary law, of any person, including any traditional leader, in the mediation, in accordance with customary law, of any dispute ... prior to the dissolution of a customary marriage by a court."[147] Given the emphasis traditional leaders place on reconciliation over divorce pursuant to customary law, this provision helps further reinforce the social norms trapping women in unhappy or even abusive marriages.

---

[140] RCMA § 1(iv).
[141] *See* Bennett, *supra* note 41, at 220–224.
[142] *See* Higgins et al., *supra* note 123, at 1673.
[143] *See id.*, at 1681. For example, divorce may be permitted if a woman fails to care for her husband by cooking and cleaning for him or if a man fails to provide food for his wife. *See* interview with Professor Maituffi, Member of South African Law Commission, in Pretoria, S. Afr. (May 2006).
[144] *See* interview with Paramount Chief, in Keerom Village, Barberton, Limpopo Province, S. Afr. (May 2006); interview with Ndebele King, in Limpopo Province, S. Afr. (May 2006).
[145] *See* Higgins et al., *supra* note 123, at 1684.
[146] *See id.*
[147] RCMA § 8(5).

Finally, the RCMA avoids altogether the issue of *lobolo*. Although the Act does not specify payment of *lobolo* as an element of a valid customary marriage, it does not attempt to regulate or discourage the practice, despite its gender-discriminatory impact. Yet, the payment of *lobolo* constrains not only a woman's ability to enter a marriage, but can affect her ability to leave it as well.[148] An unhappy or abused wife may be discouraged from leaving the marriage because her family may have to repay the *lobolo*: "It will be difficult to leave that marriage, difficult to go home because they will tell you to go back, because they paid."[149]

In sum, the RCMA takes several important steps toward promoting a fair and equal process with respect to entry into and exit from customary marriage and the choice between customary marriage and its more formally egalitarian counterpart under South African law. In our view, however, it still falls short of providing protections that are sufficiently robust to satisfy constitutional and treaty-based commitments to gender equality.

18.5. CONCLUSION

In the context of pluralist legal systems in states characterized simultaneously by commitments to customary norms and to human rights, a legal paradigm of choice has strong appeal. In theory, offering individuals the ability to structure their intimate lives according to their own priorities respects both individual autonomy and equality, so long as the individuals within the family unit are consenting and have opportunity for exit. In order to satisfy the demands of gender equality, such a model must include the option to structure the family in a fully egalitarian way. Individuals must also have adequate information about and access to this option.

These conditions are necessary but not sufficient to ensure gender equality in the decision-making process. A choice model as we envision it must also include specific measures to counteract patriarchal cultural norms and women's unequal bargaining power. These may include presumptions in favor of egalitarian rules, for example a presumption of joint ownership of property acquired within marriage and equitable division upon divorce. Limitations on the scope of choice may also be necessary to counteract systematic disadvantage. These may include, for example, a uniform standard for adjudicating and granting divorce or restrictions on polygyny. Finally, the model must include opportunities for intervention or review after the fact in order to avoid manifest injustice, for example, allowing a court to adjust the allocation of property upon divorce or the death of a spouse in order to protect the interests of all parties.

---

[148] *See* Higgins et al., *supra* note 123, at 1674.
[149] Interview with Nontsikelelo Tshongweni, in Khayelitsha Township, Western Cape Province, S. Afr. (June 2006).

Ideally, even the fully qualified choice model just described might not be preferable to a single egalitarian standard from the standpoint of gender equality. Nevertheless, given the entrenchment of legal pluralism in the domain of family law and the conflicting commitments it represents, the careful implementation of such a model may represent the best available step toward greater gender equality in the family.

19

African Customary Law and Women's Human Rights in Uganda

Dr. Ben Kiromba Twinomugisha

19.1. INTRODUCTION

One of the major achievements in the development of human rights has been the recognition that women's rights are human rights and that issues of gender equality should form an integral part of international relations. It is now recognized that women's human rights are inalienable and an indivisible part of universal human rights, which includes the right to full and equal participation with men in the political, civil, economic, social, and cultural life at all levels. The Convention on the Elimination of all Forms of Discrimination against Women (the Women's Convention) covers women's human rights in all aspects of their lives.[1] At the regional level, the Protocol to the African Charter on Human and Peoples' Rights on the Rights of Women in Africa pays special attention to women's human rights in Africa.[2] These international and regional instruments, to which Uganda is a party, provide a framework for the elimination of gender-based discrimination generally and the protection of women's right to equality in particular.

In Uganda, there has been some progress in the advancement of women's status through law and policy strategies. Women are now visible at decision-making levels, although some analysts have attributed this to the bureaucratic or paternalistic concession of the ruling National Resistance Movement ("NRM") government benefiting mainly the elite.[3] In 1995, a new constitution was promulgated with a number of progressive provisions regarding women's issues and concerns. Unlike the 1962 and 1967 constitutions, "sex" was for the first time included as a ground for impermissible

---

[1] Convention on the Elimination of all Forms of Discrimination against at 193, *adopted* Dec. 18, 1979, *entered into force* Sept. 3, U.N. Doc. A/34/46 1249 U.N.T.S. 13 [hereinafter CEDAW].

[2] Protocol to the African Charter on Human and Peoples' Rights on the Rights of Women in Africa, *adopted* July11, 2003, entered into force Nov. 25, 2005, OAU Doc. CAB/LEG/66.6 (2003) [hereinafter African Protocol].

[3] *See* J. Asiimwe, *Making Women's Land Rights a Reality in Uganda: Advocacy for Co-ownership by Spouses*, 4 YALE HUM. RTS. & DEV. L.J. 171 (2001).

discrimination.[4] In addition to other articles in the Bill of Rights, which apply to both women and men, a whole article was specifically devoted to women's human rights.[5] The 1995 Constitution accords women "full and equal dignity of the person with men"[6] and obliges the state to "provide the facilities and opportunities necessary to enhance the welfare of women to enable them to reali[z]e their full potential and advancement."[7] Women also have a "right to affirmative action for the purpose of redressing the imbalances created by history, tradition or custom."[8]

African customary law has been recognized as a source of law in Uganda in civil matters. The Judicature Act empowers the High Court to apply customary law "which is not repugnant to natural justice, equity and good conscience and not incompatible either directly or by necessary implication with any written law."[9] Though the Constitution does not contain an explicit reference to customary law, it enshrines the right to culture whereby, "[e]very person has a right as applicable to belong to, enjoy, practise, profess, maintain and promote any culture, cultural institution, language, tradition ... in community with others."[10] The Constitution also recognizes the institution of traditional or cultural leaders in any area of Uganda in accordance with the culture, customs, and traditions of the people to whom it applies.[11] However, the Constitution declares that it is the supreme law and prohibits application of any custom that is inconsistent with any of the provisions of the Constitution.[12] The Constitution recognizes only those customary values and practices that are consistent with fundamental rights and freedoms, human dignity, and democracy.[13] In fact the Constitution specifically prohibits "cultures, customs or traditions which are against the dignity, welfare or interest of women or which undermines their status."[14] Uganda does not have detailed rules regarding the application of customary law, however, or for resolving any conflicts that may arise between customary law and statutory law, including women's human rights. Yet, it has the responsibility to ensure freedom from discrimination and a woman's right to equality as discussed in this chapter.

Against this background, this chapter explores the relationship between customary law and women's human rights in Uganda. It argues that customary law is a

[4] *See* UGANDA CONST. 1995 art. 21.
[5] *See id.* art. 33.
[6] *Id.* art. 33(1).
[7] *Id.* art. 33(2).
[8] *Id.* art. 33(5).
[9] The Judicature Act, (1996) Cap. 13 Laws of Uganda, § 15.
[10] UGANDA CONST. 1995 art. 37.
[11] *See id.* art. 246(1).
[12] *See id.* art. 2.
[13] *See id.* Objective XXIV.
[14] *Id.* art. 33(6).

living system of law that is adaptable to changing conditions over time. This chapter rejects the uncritical approach that treats all aspects of customary law as discriminatory and thus a violation of women's human rights. Consequently, it argues that African customary law and women's human rights are not irreconcilable; rather, there are certain positive aspects of customary law that may be empowering for women in Uganda. This chapter is divided into six parts. The first part is this introduction. The second part reflects on the development of customary law and the parameters for its application in Uganda. The third part examines the responsibility of the state to eliminate discrimination against women and ensure their right to equality. The fourth part discusses the interface between customary law and women's human rights in Uganda. The fifth part considers some of the strategies that may be employed to ensure that customary law is consistent with the protection of women's human rights. The final part contains concluding remarks.

19.2. UNDERSTANDING CUSTOMARY LAW

19.2.1. *What Is Customary Law?*

There is no single definition of customary law agreed on by lawyers, jurists, and anthropologists.[15] Customary laws are derived from the morals, values, and traditions of indigenous ethnic groups. These norms and values have passed on from one generation to the next. Customary law includes customs and traditions of the people, which play a crucial role in shaping their culture. Culture encompasses a system of beliefs, languages, and laws that give individuals their unique character. Culture is an expression of a people's identity and way of life. Customary laws help people understand their background, who they are and – in a wider sense – their culture. Accordingly, customary law in Uganda has been defined as "a rule or set of rules, established, accepted and binding on the members of a given society in their social relations. Customary law may exist and operate on its own or side by side or complementary to another different nature of law. The latter is now the general situation in Uganda creating a mixed grill of law."[16]

One advantage of customary law is that it is flexible and changes with time and circumstances. Customary law represents law that originates with the people in the most direct sense. The customary law system gives a sense of ownership to the people who subscribe to it. Customary law is largely unwritten and its validity is a

---

[15] *See* C.M.N. White, *African Customary Law: The Problem of Concept and Definition*, 9 J. Afr. L. 86 (1965).

[16] J.M.N. Kakooza, *The Application of Customary Law in Uganda*, 1 Uganda Living L.J. 23, 24 (2003).

question of social practice to be tested by social observation.[17] Customary law itself and the culture in which it is based is not static; it is influenced by the evolution of the social, economic, and political conditions in which it operates. As a regime of personal status and identity, it applies to most people in Uganda irrespective of whether they are in rural or urban locations, depending on the degree of westernization adopted by the relevant person.[18] It is important to note that customary law is not uniform.[19] Uganda has diverse ethnic and social groupings, with a wide range of customary laws and practices to which they ascribe.

19.2.2. *The Development of Customary Law in Uganda: A Bird's Eye View*

During colonial rule (1894–1962), customary law was isolated from the law imported from Britain and relegated to a secondary position. The British colonialists applied a dual system of law: English law applied to people of English descent and to Africans who "opted out" of customary (native) law, whereas customary laws were allowed to continue to apply to native populations. Though the British did not abolish customary law, they limited its application. Customary law was permitted to develop side by side with English law but was only applicable if it was not repugnant to justice and morality, or inconsistent with any order in council or ordinance.[20] Recognition of customary law had very little to do with the well-being of the local people; it was useful as an instrument of colonial rule.

The colonialists viewed African customary values and practices as undermining the status of women. Customary practices such as polygamy and bride price, where money or property is paid by the groom's family to the bride's family at the time of the marriage, were seen as equating women to "chattels." In *R v. Amkeyo*,[21] the court considered whether a woman married under customary law was a wife for purposes of giving evidence against her husband. The court held that, in Africa, there was no marriage as in "Christendom"; it was a misnomer to call customary law marriage a "marriage" given that taking a woman by a native was like buying a chattel. The

---

[17] On early writings about the nature and legal status of customary law, see W. TWINING, THE PLACE OF CUSTOMARY LAW IN THE NATIONAL LEGAL SYSTEMS OF EAST AFRICA (Univ. Chicago Press 1963); C. Ogwurike, *The Source and Authority of African Customary Law*, 3 U. GHANA L.J. 11 (1966); A. Nekam, *Aspects of African Customary Law*, 62 NW. U. L. REV. 45 (1967).

[18] *See* C.A. Odinkalu, Pluralism and the Fulfilment of Justice Needs in Africa 4, Open Society Institute, Africa Governance Monitoring and Advocacy Project (2005).

[19] *See* C. Nyamu-Musembi, *Local Norms, Institutions and Women's Property Rights in Rural Kenya*, 9 E. AFR. J. PEACE & HUM. RTS. 255 (2003).

[20] Orders in council were laws made by the colonial government through the Privy Council without going through the full parliamentary process. Ordinances were made by the colonial governor or other local authority. *See generally* H.F. MORRIS & J.S. READ, UGANDA: THE DEVELOPMENT OF ITS LAWS AND CONSTITUTION (1966).

[21] (1917) 7 E.A.L.R. 14.

court condemned bride price as wife purchase and concluded that, because the woman did not participate in the marriage arrangements, there was no consent in the legal sense. It has been pointed out that the colonialists were not genuinely interested in women's human rights, however, but were convinced that polygamy would be harmful to their own interests, for example, by promoting idleness among male natives, which would affect the colonialists' source of labor.[22]

Other commentators link the marginalization of women to the colonial policy of land ownership. It is argued that colonialism engendered inequalities in customary ownership of land by systematically tilting the balance in favor of men and transferring the pre-colonial land rights from women exclusively to men.[23] To achieve their objectives of capital accumulation, the colonial administration introduced and promoted cash crop production for export. This undermined the food sufficiency that had existed previously and that had ensured women and their families' good nutrition and health.[24] In most pre-colonial societies, including Uganda, women contributed heavily to subsistence production, and customary laws allowed them greater independence in relation to food production and processing.[25] Although there were significant limitations placed on a woman's ownership rights, custom permitted a woman considerable independent control of the products of her own labor.[26]

Uganda obtained independence on October 9, 1962. As discussed earlier, the post-independence legal system recognizes customary law in civil matters to the extent it is not incompatible with written law or "repugnant to natural justice, equity or good conscience." Customary law has remained resilient in spite of the existence of statutory law.

19.3. WOMEN'S HUMAN RIGHT TO EQUALITY

Freedom from discrimination generally and a woman's right to equality in particular is provided for in the 1995 Constitution and a number of human rights instruments to which Uganda is a party. According to the Women's Convention, states parties "condemn discrimination against women in all its forms [and] agree to pursue by all appropriate means and without delay a policy of eliminating discrimination against women."[27] States parties are enjoined to "adopt appropriate legislative and other

---

[22] *See* M. Mamdani, Citizen and Subject: Contemporary Africa and the Legacy of Colonialism (Princeton Univ. Press 1996).

[23] *See* M. Chanock, *Paradigms, Policies and Property: A Review of the Customary Law of Land Tenure, in* Law in Colonial Africa (K. Mann & R. Roberts, eds., James Currey 1991).

[24] *See* W. Kaberuka, The Political Economy of Uganda 1890–1979: A Case Study of Colonialism and Underdevelopment (Vantage Press 1990).

[25] *See* M. Turshen, The Political Economy of Disease in Tanzania (Rutgers Univ. Press 1984).

[26] *See* M. Edel, The Chiga of Western Uganda (Oxford Univ. Press 1957).

[27] CEDAW, *supra* note 1, art. 2.

measures, including sanctions where appropriate, prohibiting all discrimination against women"[28] and to "establish legal protection of the rights of women on an equal basis with men."[29] The Convention obliges states parties "to ensure the full development and advancement of women, for the purpose of guaranteeing them the exercise and enjoyment of human rights and fundamental freedoms on a basis of equality with men."[30] States parties are obliged to "take all appropriate measures ... to modify or abolish existing laws, regulations, customs and practices which constitute discrimination against women."[31] The states parties agreed to "modify the social and cultural patterns of conduct of men and women,"[32] in order to achieve "the elimination of prejudices and customary and all other practices which are based on the idea of the inferiority or the superiority of either of the sexes or on stereotyped roles for men and women."[33]

The International Covenant on Civil and Political Rights (ICCPR) also guarantees all persons equality before the law and freedom from discrimination on any ground, including sex.[34] At the regional level, the African Charter on Human and Peoples' Rights (ACHPR) obliges states parties to "ensure the elimination of every discrimination against women and also ensure the protection of the rights of the woman ... as stipulated in international declarations and conventions."[35] States parties are obliged to ensure that cultural values and practices that are permitted by domestic law respect women's right to equality and are free from discrimination.

The Women's Protocol to the ACHPR (hereinafter "the Protocol") also obliges states parties to "combat all forms of discrimination against women through appropriate legislative, institutional and other measures."[36] Like the Women's Convention, the Protocol enjoins states parties "to modify the social and cultural patterns of conduct ... with a view to achieving the elimination of harmful cultural and traditional practices."[37] As a party to all these human rights instruments, Uganda has the responsibility to take appropriate measures to comply with the obligations therein. The state must take steps to eliminate both de jure and de facto discrimination accentuated by negative customary law and practices.

---

[28] *Id.* art. 2(b).

[29] *Id.* art. 2(c).

[30] *Id.* art. 3.

[31] *Id.* art. 2(f).

[32] *Id.* art. 5(a).

[33] *Id.*

[34] *See* International Covenant on Civil and Political Rights, *adopted* Dec. 19, 1966, *entered into force* March 23, 1976, U.N. Doc. A/6316, 999 U.N.T.S. 171 [hereinafter ICCPR].

[35] African Charter on Human and People's Rights art. 18(3), *adopted* June 27, 1981, *entered into force* Oct. 21, 1986, OAU Doc. CAB/LEG/67/3 Rev. 5, (1982) [hereinafter African Charter].

[36] CEDAW, *supra* note 2, art. 2(1).

[37] *Id.* art. 2(2).

The 1995 Constitution guarantees all persons equality before and under the law "in all spheres of political, economic, social and cultural life" and prohibits discrimination on grounds of sex.[38] Pursuant to the Constitution, the Parliament of Uganda enacted the Equal Opportunities Commission Act 2007, which establishes the Equal Opportunities Commission ("EOC") to monitor, evaluate, and ensure that policies, laws, plans, programs, activities, practices, traditions, cultures, usages, and customs "are compliant with equal opportunities and affirmative action in favour of groups marginalized on the basis of sex ... gender ... or any other reason created by history, tradition or custom."[39] The mandate of the EOC includes the examination of "any law, proposed law, policy, culture, tradition, usage, custom or plan which is likely to have effect of nullifying or impairing equal opportunities to persons in employment or enjoyment of human rights."[40] The EOC is also mandated to prepare and establish guidelines for "the avoidance of acts, practices, usage, customs, tradition or cultures that undermine equal opportunities."[41] However, the powers of the EOC are restricted because it cannot investigate any matter involving behavior that is considered to be immoral and socially harmful or unacceptable by the majority of the cultural and social communities in Uganda.[42]

19.4. CUSTOMARY LAW AND WOMEN'S HUMAN RIGHTS

Customary law is primarily a matter of personal law. It deals with personal matters that concern the family and the clan such as land, marriage, divorce, and succession. Thus, customary law in Uganda continues to play a significant role in women's lives, especially in domestic relations. The position of the majority of women continues to be defined by customary rules deeply embedded in historical, economic, and social experiences. Consequently, the inclusion of customary law as part of the human rights debate is becoming increasingly important. Various commentators have questioned the impact of customary practices on women's human rights. Some scholars view African culture and, by implication, customary law as antagonistic and diametrically opposed to human rights.[43]

It cannot be denied that many customary norms and practices are discriminatory and thus violate women's human right to equality. However, it is wrong to treat all customary norms and practices as negative. Narrow interpretations of African

---

[38] UGANDA CONST. 1995 art. 21(1)-(2).

[39] The Equal Opportunities Commission Act, (2007) Laws of Uganda, § 14(1)(f). Unfortunately, the EOC has not been constituted.

[40] *Id.* § 14(2)(b).

[41] *Id.* § 14(2)(f).

[42] *See id.* § 15(6)(d).

[43] *See, e.g.,* E. Mayambala, *Changing the Terms of the Debate: Polygamy and the Rights of Women in Kenya and Uganda,* 3 E. AFR. J. PEACE & HUM. RTS. 200 (1996).

customary law that present it as rigid, inflexible, and oppressive ignore its potential to improve the quality of life of disadvantaged and marginalized groups, such as rural women. Such interpretations fail to appreciate that customary law is capable of transformation in response to changing circumstances. Over time, the negative aspects are discarded. For example, the Bakiga of South Western Uganda condemn pre-marital sex. According to custom, if a girl became pregnant, her brother would throw her over Kisiizi Falls.[44] This practice was later abandoned when a pregnant girl dragged her brother over the falls with her and both perished. Today, when a girl becomes pregnant she is sent out of the home and delivers the baby at the paternal aunt's (*shwenkazi*) place. After delivery, the girl returns home and may even continue with her education. Thus, as other examples that follow illustrate, a more critical understanding of customary law is needed with efforts to preserve positive aspects of customary law that enhance women's human rights and to discard practices that are discriminatory.[45]

19.4.1. *Women's Land Rights under Customary Tenure*

In most areas of Uganda, customary laws and practices have always largely defined access to physical resources such as land. According to the World Bank, "[c]ustomary systems of land tenure have evolved over long periods of time in response to location-specific conditions. In many cases they constitute a way of managing land relations that is more flexible and more adapted to location-specific conditions than would be possible under a more centralized approach."[46]

Under customary tenure in pre-colonial times, both men and women in a family had full user rights to land as long as they did not sell it. After death, land passed on to the customary heir to manage the land in trust for both the present and future generations of family members. The basic rule under customary tenure was that land sales were not allowed except where there was a compelling reason to do so. The customary system also had provisions for protecting the rights of women and children. Although these rights were unwritten, they were part of the social obligations of living within the clan, and clan elders enforced them. Women were free to utilize the land for production of food for their children and families. Under customary law, a woman's land rights were respected, even after the death of her husband. Even if her husband married other wives, a woman would be guaranteed sufficient land to farm and provide for herself and her children. Although women

---

[44] *See* Edel, *supra* note 26.
[45] On this view, see also S. Tamale, *The Right to Culture and the Culture of Rights: A Critical Perspective on Women's Sexual Rights in Africa*, 16 FEMINIST LEGAL STUD. 47 (2008).
[46] *Land Policies for Growth and Poverty Reduction*, World Bank Policy Research Report (2003).

did not have inheritance rights as such, they enjoyed security of tenure rooted in their structural roles as lineage women.[47]

In most areas of Uganda where land is held under customary tenure, women can still access the available land for production of food and other crops. This is a positive aspect of customary law that should be preserved. A major criticism of customary land tenure is that women lack ownership and control of the land. The bases of customary ownership have been eroded since the time of colonialism, making women's access to land even more precarious as the protections traditionally ensured by the clan system have been peeled away.[48] In Apac District in Northern Uganda, for example, management of land has shifted from the elders, who held the land in trust, to the small family unit where the head is usually assumed to be a man, who becomes the sole individual owner and can sell the land.[49] Where land registration systems have been put in place, the situation may even be worse, because titling of land gives men absolute ownership to the exclusion of women.[50] The men may sell or mortgage the land thereby depriving women of their access rights.

It should be noted that traditional patrilineal descent remains dominant, especially in the rural areas of Uganda, and is characterized by male control of decision making about who will inherit the estate. In many ethnic groups in Uganda, pursuant to customary law, inheritance of land is largely through the male issue.[51] In such a situation, women do not inherit family property. Women are regarded as being unable to own land in their own right and instead serve as mere trustees for their male kin.[52] This practice is discriminatory and violates women's right to equality; it must be discarded. Following pressure from the women's movement in Uganda, Parliament included provisions in the Land Act aimed at protecting the rights of women, children, and persons with disabilities regarding customary land. The Act provides as follows:

> Any decision taken in respect of land held under customary tenure, whether in respect of land held individually or communally, shall be in accordance with the

[47] *See* Perpetua Wambui Karanja, *Women's Land Ownership Rights in Kenya*, 1991 THIRD WORLD LEGAL STUD. 109.

[48] *See* A.M. Tripp, *Women's Movements, Customary Law, and Land Rights in Africa: The Case of Uganda*, 7 AFR. STUD. Q. 1 (2004).

[49] *See* Judy Adoko, Land Rights: Where We Are and Where We Need to Go: A Review of the Situation of Land Rights in Apac District in Uganda and of Opportunities for Land Rights Protection Work, Report by Land and Equity Movement in Uganda (2005).

[50] *See id.*

[51] Even statutory law is discriminatory in the area of inheritance. For example, the Succession Act provides that in determining a legal heir, a paternal ancestor shall be preferred to a maternal ancestor and where there is equality, a male heir shall be preferred to female. The Succession Act, Cap. 162 Laws of Uganda, § 2(n).

[52] *See* Asiimwe, *supra* note 3. *See also* L. Khadiagala, *Negotiating Law and Custom: Judicial Doctrine and Women's Property Rights in Uganda*, 46 J. AFR. L. 1 (2002).

customs, traditions and practices of the community concerned, except that a decision which denies women or children or persons with a disability access to ownership, occupation or use of any land or imposes conditions which violate articles 33
[women's rights], 34 [children rights] and 35 [rights of persons with disabilities] of
the Constitution on any ownership, occupation or use of any land shall be void.[53]

The women's movement had pressed for a provision that required spouses to co-
own land. Unfortunately, this provision, which would have significantly enhanced
women's security of land tenure, was not included in the Act. However, the Land
Act contains a "consent clause" that prohibits the sale, transfer, mortgage, or other
dealings "in the case of land on which the person ordinarily resides with his or her
spouse and from which they derive their sustenance, except with the prior written
consent of the spouse."[54]

Although these provisions are progressive from the point of view of women's right
to equality, their implementation may prove difficult. This is because no serious
attempt was made to understand the systems of inheritance and the customary practices relating to land ownership before the Act was enacted. As has been noted elsewhere, statutory changes, though helpful, generally have no practical effect on the
great majority of the population, who are governed by customary law in family and
personal matters.[55] Laws that seek to protect women's property rights must be written and implemented in a way that recognizes and respects the positive cultural
practices of the people. The starting point of any effort at law reform should be to
involve both men and women at the grassroots level in the discussion of the merits
and demerits of customary practices and any proposed legislation so that they can
own it.

19.4.2. *Female Genital Mutilation (FGM)*

According to the World Health Organization (WHO), FGM comprises all procedures that involve partial or total removal of the external female genitalia, or other
injury to the female genital organs for non-medical reasons.[56] In Uganda, FGM
is practiced among the Sabiny and Pokot communities of Eastern Uganda. The

---

[53] The Land Act, Cap. 227 Laws of Uganda, § 27.
[54] *Id.* § 39(1)(a)-(c)(1).
[55] *See* A.M. Richardson, *Women's Inheritance Rights in Africa: The Need to Integrate Cultural Understanding and Legal Reform*, 11 HUM. RTS. BRIEF 19 (2004).
[56] For the definition of the various types of FGM, see World Health Organization, Female Genital Mutilation, http://who.int/mediacentre/factsheets/fs241/en/ (last visited Sept. 20, 2008). Type I is the excision of the prepuce with or without excision of part or the entire clitoris. Type II is the excision of the clitoris together with partial or total excision of the labia minora. Type III is excision of part or all the external genitalia and stitching or narrowing of the vaginal opening (infibulation). Type IV is unclassified and includes stretching (elongation) of the clitoris and/or labia.

practice involves incising the clitoris and/or labia minora; it is a rite of passage into adulthood and is associated with "women's sexual purity." FGM is usually carried out on young girls and is internationally recognized as violation of the human rights of girls and women.[57] WHO is of the view that the customary practice

> reflects deep-rooted inequality between the sexes, and constitutes the extreme form of discrimination against women. It is usually carried out on minors and is a violation of the rights of children. The practice also violates a person's rights to health, security and personal integrity, the right to be free from torture, cruel, inhuman and degrading treatment, and the right to life when the procedure results in death.[58]

Apart from the constitutional provisions that prohibit cultural practices that violate women's human rights, there is no legislation in Uganda against FGM.[59] There is no doubt that most types of FGM violate women's human rights. The consequences of the practice on women's health and human dignity are well documented. However, in some instances, the attitude of WHO and other anti-FGM campaigners to the practice of FGM reflects a lack of understanding of the nature and value of African cultural practices. For example, WHO lumps the practice of elongating the labia minora, which is practiced among the Baganda and other Bantu communities in Uganda, within Type IV of FGM.[60] A study on sexual pleasure among the Baganda, however, found that this customary practice has enhanced sexual pleasure among Baganda women and expanded their perceptions of themselves as sexual beings. The study found that the practice enhances the erotic experience of both the male and female because "when the elongated labia are touched and manipulated in the correct manner during foreplay or mutual masturbation, they may be the source of immense pleasure to the couple."[61] Most of the women interviewed in the study did not consider the practice harmful, contrary to the attitude of WHO.[62] Thus, it has been argued that the customary practice of labia elongation does not violate women's rights except where a woman is coerced into the practice.[63] Arguably, a practice that enhances both women's and men's sexuality should be preserved.

---

[57] *See id.* On the implications of FGM for women's human rights, see also REBECCA J COOK ET AL., REPRODUCTIVE HEALTH AND HUMAN RIGHTS: INTEGRATING MEDICINE, ETHICS AND LAW (Oxford Univ. Press 2003).

[58] World Health Organization, *supra* note 56.

[59] *See, e.g.,* UGANDA CONST. 1995 art. 32(2); The Children Act, Cap. 59 Laws of Uganda, § 7 (making it unlawful to subject a child to social or cultural practices that are harmful to a child's health). However, Parliament recently passed the Prohibition of Female Genital Mutilation Bill, No. 16 of 2009, that criminalizes FGM, but is yet to be assented to by the President of the Republic of Uganda for it to become law.

[60] *See* World Health Organization, *supra* note 56.

[61] Tamale, *supra* note 45, at 49.

[62] *See id.*

[63] *See* K.K. Mwenda, *Labia Elongation Under African Customary Law: A Violation of Women's Rights?,* 10 INT'L J. HUM. RTS. 341 (2006).

The practice of FGM is far more complex culturally and socially than may be imagined. The practice is so deeply embedded in the girl's place in her community that to forgo the act would deprive her of the one moment the entire village celebrates her existence as a woman. The girl feels that if she does not undergo the practice she will forever be treated as a child and nobody may marry her. Some women and girls may view this practice as enhancing their status in society. Countless interventions to eradicate FGM in Uganda have been attempted but failed; instead the practitioners have "gone underground," with youthful males forcing reluctant girls to undergo the practice. Having a law prohibiting FGM is not enough. It is important to try to understand the origins of the practice and the principles on which it is based. The underlying positive aspects of the practice of FGM, especially the celebration of the rite of passage, must be preserved. This may require symbolic rituals to replace the mutilation procedure. A grassroots basic education program that incorporates human rights principles and highlights the health consequences of the practice may be undertaken to facilitate this change.

19.4.3. *Customary Marriages*

Most societies in Africa recognize customary marriages. African customary marriages may vary from one ethnic group to another and also within the group but are largely based on similar social principles. In most, there is a requirement for marriage gifts, which have, in a derogatory manner, been called "bride price" or "bridal wealth."[64] Notwithstanding the *R. v. Amkeyo* case discussed earlier, it is wrong to tag a "price" to customary marriages because they do not have any connotations of purchase. Under customary law, a bride is not a commodity to be sold and bought on the market. These terms were deliberately coined to undermine African cultural identity. The marriage gifts signify the bond uniting the families of the husband and wife and are an incentive for the husband and wife to perform their marital obligations. The marriage gifts are also a way of appreciating the efforts of the girl's parents in bringing her up in a dignified manner. In any case, marriage gifts in contemplation of marriage are common in many western marriages as well. A girl may, for example, receive a diamond ring worth thousands of pounds from a prospective suitor.

Under customary law, a man is entitled to marry more than one wife, provided that he fulfills the rites and customs of the ethnic group from which he has chosen the bride.[65] Some commentators have argued that because customary marriages are polygamous or "potentially polygamous," they undermine women's right to

---

[64] A petition has been filed in the Constitutional Court challenging the constitutionality of "bride price." *Mifumi (U) Ltd and Others v. Attorney General and Another*, Constitutional Petition No. 12 of 2007.

[65] *See* The Customary Marriage (Registration) Act, Cap. 248 Laws of Uganda, § 4(2).

equality.[66] With respect to the practice of polygamy, which has continued unabated in spite of the harms associated with it, it has been observed that:

> In the first place, the recognition of polygamy treats women as second-rate citizens entitled to fewer rights than men. No consideration whatsoever is given to the effect the subsequent marriage or marriages has [sic] on the wife, not only in terms of tangible deprivation of material and sexual satisfaction, but also in relation to intangible values like self esteem. By recognizing and endorsing this practice, society fails to recognize that the wife has been wronged. The failure to recognize a wrong to the wife usually results in society failing to provide a remedy for women to opt out of polygamous marriages.[67]

Another scholar has argued that polygamy is a harmful cultural practice because it promotes rivalry between co-wives, which may lead to violence or even homicide.[68] She concludes that many manifestations of polygamy render women's rights, especially the right to equality, meaningless.[69]

In the months of June and July 2008, I interviewed sixty women in polygamous marriages in six randomly sampled parishes in Kashambya and Rwamucucu subcounties in Kabale District, South Western Uganda, with widely varying responses. The majority of women (80%) said that they willingly entered the relationship knowing that their husbands were married. However, 20 percent of the women said they were forced into the relationship because they simply wanted somebody to cater for their daily needs. Forty women (66.6%) stated that they enjoy the relationship because the younger wives assist them, especially in preparing meals and "providing sexual satisfaction to their husbands." One woman whose husband has two more wives in the same homestead stated: "It is better for my husband to officially marry another wife than continue having mistresses behind my back." On further probing, the woman told me that when she is sick, she is relieved when the husband sleeps in a co-wife's house. Other women had mixed reactions to the institution of polygamy, however. One woman said that though she entered the relationship voluntarily, she is not comfortable because the husband favors her co-wife by regularly buying her clothes, meat, salt, and other necessities. Other women were critical of polygamy because it has the potential of spreading HIV/AIDS in the family.

It can be concluded from these findings that the customary practice of polygamy is complex. Banning the practice may be counterproductive. It may be necessary to involve women and men in the discussion of polygamy so that they can freely debate the advantages and disadvantages of the practice.

---

[66] *See* Mayambala, *supra* note 43, at 201.

[67] *Id.* at 214.

[68] *See* Lillian Tibatemwa-Ekirikubinza, *Multiple Partnering, Gender Relations and Violence by Women in Uganda,* 4 E. Afr. J. Peace & Hum. Rts. 15 (1997).

[69] *See id.*

19.5. RECONCILING CUSTOMARY LAW AND WOMEN'S HUMAN RIGHTS

Opinion is still divided as to whether human rights should have universal application.[70] Some commentators argue that cultural values and practices should be exempt from the application of human rights norms. In my view, the universalism versus cultural relativist debate was theoretically settled by the 1995 Constitution, which is largely premised on the universal application of human rights. The Vienna Declaration also underlines this point: "While the significance of national and regional particularities and various historical, cultural and religious backgrounds must be borne in mind, it is the duty of States, regardless of their political, economic and cultural systems, to promote and protect all human rights and fundamental freedoms."[71]

The state has the responsibility to bring its domestic practice, including customary laws, in conformity with the Constitution and both international and domestic human rights law. It is obliged to remove any inconsistency between human rights law and customary practices. In so doing, the state should guard against the view that culture and human rights are irreconcilable. As previously noted, one cannot ignore the stark reality that cultural values and practices still govern the lives of the majority of the population. There is a need to recognize that culture is constantly evolving and can only be meaningfully tackled on a case-by-case basis. As the Uganda Constitutional Commission observed,

> Culture is dynamic and develops as people develop. It interacts with other cultures and in the process cultures change.... [Cultural practices] are subject to change, modification and even abolition according to the contemporary demands of common good, human rights, morality, development and nation-building. Every society, therefore has a duty to identify those cultural practices which when judged with contemporary values should be kept, and those which should be eliminated, or modified or substituted. This is the only way equality can be asserted and any discrimination by culture eliminated.[72]

Thus, although Uganda's constitutional framework upholds the universal application of human rights, universalism does not mean an uncritical application of the western concept of human rights in African communities without regard for their

---

[70] On cultural relativism, see, e.g., A. An-Na'im, *Problems of Universal Cultural Legitimacy for Human Rights, in* HUMAN RIGHTS IN AFRICA: CROSS-CULTURAL PERSPECTIVES (A. An-Na'im & F. Deng, eds., 1990); K. Mickelson, *How Universal is the Universal Declaration?*, 47 UNIV. NEW BRUNSWICK L.J. 19 (1998).

[71] World Conference on Human Rights, June 14–25, 1993, *Vienna Declaration and Programme of Action,* ¶ 5, U.N. Doc. A/CONF.157/23 (July 12, 1993).

[72] REPUBLIC OF UGANDA, THE REPORT OF THE UGANDA CONSTITUTIONAL COMMISSION: ANALYSIS AND RECOMMENDATIONS 170 (1993).

customary values and practices. Human rights can be used as a yardstick to identify those positive and negative aspects of customary law and practices. Where some practices negatively impact on women's human rights, they should be modified or discarded. The question is: How should this be done?

19.5.1. *Legislative Strategies*

The legislature can play a critical role in the promotion and protection of human rights in Uganda. However, it is important to be cautious when advocating for the development of customary law through law reform. As has been observed with respect to the South African experience,

> While legislative development of customary law appears attractive, both in order to update and ensure compatibility with the Constitution, such an undertaking runs the risk of arresting further development. It also risks imposing homogenous rules on communities that do not at present apply homogenous rules. While legislation has the advantage of legal certainty and consistency, it risks the loss of diversity and difference and the alienation of communities that value their particular practices. Careful consideration will, therefore, have to be given the question of whether this is appropriate and desirable, and if so, how this is to be done.[73]

Though restatements may not have binding legal authority,[74] they are a starting point for any meaningful law reform. In my view, a systematic recording and restatement of African customary law provides a fairly accurate account of the customary law of each ethnic group at the time of recording, which can be used by the legislature as a starting point of reform and by the judiciary as an authoritative guide.[75] The restatement of customary laws provides a basis for increasing the pool of knowledge about these laws, and thereby providing a more informed view of the customary practices involved. The restatement highlights the common principles under customary laws that affect the majority of the population, especially women and children.

It is important to note that a restatement may serve as an awareness-raising exercise among the clan elders and local council (LC) members[76] who preside over

---

[73] Evadné Grant, *Human Rights, Cultural Diversity and Customary Law in South Africa*, 50 J. AFR. L. 2, 19 (2006).

[74] *See id. See also* W. Twining, *The Restatement of African Customary Law: A Comment*, 1 J. MOD. AFR. STUD. 221 (1963).

[75] On reform and development of customary law, *see generally* M. Pieterse, *Killing it Softly: Customary Law in the New Constitutional Order*, 33 DE JURE 35 (2000); W. Lehnert, *The Role of the Courts in the Conflict Between African Customary Law and Human Rights*, 21 SAJHR 241 (2005).

[76] A local council is a form of local government within the districts of Uganda. There are five levels of LCs, the lowest being at the village level (LC I) and the highest at the district level (LC V). These LCs handle administrative issues and cases especially those of a customary nature. It should be noted that although women are members of LCs, their voices may not be heard because they are overshadowed

customary law cases to appreciate the implications of customary principles on human rights. Those spearheading the restatement of customary law and eventually legal reform must be conscious of the fact that most customary practices serve the interests of the dominant classes in society.[77] It is thus necessary to involve women and other marginalized groups in the clarification and documentation of customary laws and practices to ensure that their voices are heard. Women must be involved in the articulation of both positive and negative aspects of customary law.

19.5.2. *Judicial Strategies*

Customary law and practices that are discriminatory and violate the right to equality can be challenged in the courts of law. The 1995 Constitution provides that "[j]udicial power is derived from the people"[78] and shall be exercised "in the name of the people and in conformity with law and with the values, norms and aspirations of the people."[79] As organs of the state, the courts are obliged to respect, uphold, and promote the rights and freedoms enshrined in the Constitution.[80] The judiciary is therefore duty-bound to nullify discriminatory practices that undermine women's human rights and uphold those practices that conform to the Bill of Rights. In so doing, the courts are conforming to an important aspiration for women: to live a meaningful and dignified life.

Indeed, there are instances where the courts have annulled discriminatory legal provisions. For example, in *Uganda Association of Women's Lawyers and Others v Attorney General*,[81] the petitioners challenged the constitutionality of sections 4, 5, 21, 22, 23, and 26 of the Divorce Act.[82] Section 4 spells out the grounds for divorce. Whereas the section permits a husband to petition for divorce on the ground of adultery, a wife has to combine a claim of adultery with other grounds such as

---

by their male peers. *See generally* USAID, Telling Our Story: Uganda – Giving Women a Voice in Local Government, http://www.usaid.gov/stories/uganda/fp_uganda_women.html (last visited Jan. 19, 2010).

[77] *See* C.I. Nyamu, *How Should Human Rights and Development Respond to Cultural Legitimization of Gender Hierarchy in Developing Countries?*, 41 HARV. INT'L L.J. 381, 405 (2000).

[78] UGANDA CONST. 1995 art. 126(1).

[79] *Id.*

[80] *See id.* art. 20(2).

[81] Constitutional Petition No. 3 of 2003 (Unreported).

[82] The Divorce Act, Cap. 49 Laws of Uganda. Section 4 spells out the grounds for divorce. Whereas the section permits a husband to petition for divorce on only one ground (adultery), the wife has to combine it with other grounds such as desertion, bigamy, bestiality, sodomy, or cruelty. Under section 5, the husband shall make the alleged adulterer a co-respondent. Sections 21, 22, and 23 concern damages for adultery and alimony. Section 26 provides that where dissolution of marriage is pronounced on account of the wife's adultery, and the wife is entitled to any property, the court may order that all or part of the property be settled for the benefit of the husband.

desertion, bigamy, bestiality, sodomy, or cruelty. Under section 5, the husband shall make the alleged adulterer a co-respondent. Sections 21, 22, and 23 concern damages for adultery and alimony. Section 26 provides that where dissolution of marriage is pronounced on account of the wife's adultery, and the wife is entitled to any property, the court may order that all or part of the property be settled for the benefit of the husband. The Constitutional Court unanimously held that the provisions were inconsistent with the equality and non-discrimination provisions of the Constitution, and were in effect null and void. The court noted that the divorce law was archaic in content and a colonial relic in substance "where the traditional patriarchal family elevated the husband as the head of the family and relegated the woman to a subservient role, of being a mere appendage of a husband without a separate legal existence."[83] In *Law and Advocacy for Women v Attorney General*,[84] the Constitutional Court also annulled various sections of the Succession Act for discriminating against women in respect of inheritance.

The courts have also upheld customary practices that are consistent with the Bill of Rights. In *Bruno Kiwuwa v. Ivan Serunkuma & Juliet Namazzi*,[85] the plaintiff instituted a suit to prevent celebration of a Christian marriage of the first and second defendants. The plaintiff argued that the defendants, like the plaintiff, were Baganda by tribe and belonged to the same *Ndiga* (sheep) clan and were therefore prevented by an established custom to marry. The plaintiff further argued that article 37 of the Constitution and sections 14 and 15 of the Judicature Act mandate the court to enforce the custom in question, which is enjoyed by the Baganda as a tribe. The defendants contended that the said custom did not apply to them because they intended to contract marriage under the Marriage Act and not a customary marriage to which such a custom would apply. The issue before the court was whether the defendants could lawfully contract a marriage under the Marriage Act. The court found that the custom in question related to the institution of marriage among the Baganda and protects the family, which is the very basic unit of any human society. The court held that the custom was not incompatible with any written law, especially the Marriage Act, and was not repugnant to natural justice, equity, and good conscience.

The court noted that a marriage under the Marriage Act could be barred on the ground of an established custom. The court observed that it is duty-bound to promote the application and observance of customary laws that enhance the dignity and well-being of Ugandans.[86] The court found that observance of the custom in question

---

[83] Constitutional Petition No. 2 of 2003, Judgment of Mar. 10, 2004.
[84] Constitutional Petitions Nos. 13 of 2005 and 5 of 2006.
[85] High Court Civil Suit No. 52 of 2006.
[86] *See Uganda Const.* 1995 Objective XXIV(a).

does not violate the right to marry and found a family[87] and declared that the defendants' intended marriage was illegal, null, and void by reason of the said custom.[88]

Preventing a marriage on grounds that the couple belongs to the same clan is intended to prevent inbreeding. For the Baganda, marriage is permitted only within the *mamba* (lung fish) clan, which has two "branches." In my view, this precedent should not be applied in all circumstances. Some clans are so huge that the argument of preventing inbreeding may not hold. The court held that the custom in question amounted to a just cause. This would be understandable if the couple intended to marry either under the Customary Marriage (Registration) Act or the Marriage of Africans Act, where customary law governs marriages. The custom in question does not fall within the prohibited degrees of relationship under the Marriage Act. Thus, the court should have applied the Marriage Act and permitted the marriage.

In other jurisdictions, courts have also applied customary law, subject to the Constitution and relevant legislation. For example, in the South African case of *Bhe and others v. The Magistrate, Khayelitsha and others,*[89] an application was made on behalf of two daughters of Ms. Bhe and her deceased partner. It was contended that the customary rule of male primogeniture unfairly discriminated against the two children in that they could not inherit the deceased estate of their late father. The Constitutional Court held that the rule of primogeniture discriminates unfairly against women and illegitimate children and declared it unconstitutional and invalid. The Court observed that a court engaged in the adjudication of customary law must be mindful of its obligations to promote the spirit of the Bill of Rights. In a partially dissenting opinion, Justice Ngcobo noted that the Court has an obligation under the Constitution to develop customary law so as to bring it in line with the Bill of Rights, in particular the right to equality. Accordingly, the dissent argued that the principle of primogeniture should not be struck down but instead should be developed so as to be brought in line with the right to equality by permitting women to succeed to the deceased's estate as well. In respect of inheritance under customary law, the court in the Tanzanian case of *Ndewawiosia d/o Ndeamtza v. Imanuel s/o Malasi*[90] also observed as follows:

> This custom which bars daughters from inheriting clan land and sometimes their own fathers' estate has left a loophole for undeserving clansmen to flourish within

[87] *See id.* art. 31.
[88] In a comment on the *Kiwuwa* case, Kakungulu-Mayambala agrees with the court on a ground that observing the custom protects the family. He argues that the right to marry and found a family is not absolute; it can be limited on grounds of public interest as per Article 43 of the Constitution. *See* R. Kakungulu-Mayambala, *Bruno Kiwuwa v. Ivan Serunkuma & Juliet Namazzi: An Appraisal of the Right to Marry and Found a Family in Uganda*, 13 E. Afr. J. Peace & Hum. Rts. 334 (2007).
[89] 2005 (1) SA 580 (CC), 2005 (1) BCLR 1 (S. Afr.).
[90] (1968) H.C.D. 149 (Tanz.).

the tribe.... These men are not entitled to take property towards acquisition of which they have contributed absolutely nothing.... In Tanzania ... and elsewhere the idea of equality between men and women has gained much strength.... The time has come when the rights of daughters in inheritance should be recognized.[91]

Women's rights activists and other public-spirited individuals may challenge negative customary practices in court on a case-by-case basis on the ground that such practices are discriminatory and violate the right to equality. The Ugandan Constitution allows any person who claims that his or her right has been violated to seek redress through court, including compensation.[92] The Constitution also provides for the concept of public interest litigation (PIL), whereby "[a]ny person or organisation may bring an action against the violation of another person's or group's human rights."[93] PIL recognizes the vulnerability of disadvantaged persons or groups such as the indigent who may not be in position to file actions in their own names. Thus, a person is not required to have a personal interest or injury before lodging an application or petition alleging a violation of women's human rights. Individuals or civil society organizations working for the public good can bring to the attention of the court the actual or potential impact of negative customary practices on women's human rights. Litigation assists in placing issues on the agenda before the judiciary and the court of public opinion. Thus, the judiciary has a fundamental role to play: either to strike down negative customary practices or to develop them to be consistent with the Bill of Rights.

19.5.3. *Learning from Grassroots Women*

Grassroots women's groups, especially in the rural areas, should be involved in any efforts to reform or develop customary law. In Kigezi, as elsewhere in Uganda, grassroots women engage in daily acts of resistance against discriminatory customary practices and rules.[94] For example, in a bid to defeat the customary practice that promotes inheritance of property only by men, women often have more children in order to produce sons who would improve their access to land. Field research found that most of the rural women (90%) in Kashambya and Rwamucucu sub-counties in Kabale District desire many children for various reasons including provision of

---

[91] *Id.*

[92] *See Uganda Const.* 1995 art. 50(1).

[93] *Id.* art. 50(2). On public interest litigation in Uganda, see B.K. Twinomugisha, *Exploring Judicial Strategies to Protect the Right of Access to Emergency Obstetric Care in Uganda,* 7 Afr. Hum. Rts. L.J. 283 (2007).

[94] *See* Tripp, *supra* note 48, at 15.

domestic and farm labor, inheritance of property, and security in the home.[95] One woman stressed that because Bakiga custom does not allow inheritance of property by girls, having a son ensures that her "share" of the property is passed over to him. Unfortunately, this can partly explain why some rural women are reluctant to use modern family-planning methods, as the following conversation with a woman in a polygamous relationship revealed.

INTERVIEWER: Have you ever heard of any modern method of family planning?
WOMAN: Yes.
INTERVIEWER: Which methods?
WOMAN: Pills, injection, tubal litigation (sic).
INTERVIEWER: Have you ever used any of the methods?
WOMAN: How can I go for family planning when I have only two children? Besides, they are all girls. What if I become sterile? Do you want "my land" to be taken by my co-wife when I join my ancestors [die]?[96]

Some rural women's reluctance to use modern family-planning practices may point to an understanding of their situation. A woman may have to seriously consider the impact of not having an additional child in light of her economic situation, her status in her community, and her security in the family as dictated by custom. Domestic violence is a real problem in Africa.[97] For example, Focus Group Discussions (FGDs) revealed that the majority of women fear that they may be subjected to domestic violence if their husbands discover that they are using contraceptives. Consequently, some women use contraceptives discreetly. One woman told me that she hides the contraceptive pills and swallows them only when her husband is not at home or when she is alone in the garden.[98] Some women who use the injection (Depo Provera) stated that they fake malaria and visit the nearby health center, where they receive this injection from health professionals.[99]

It should be noted that the majority of customary practices in Uganda do not exalt ownership of land by women. Owning land bestows power on the owner, and the majority of men loathe women who have power. FGDs revealed that men view women who own land in reasonable amounts as deviant and improper.[100] Such women are in Rukiga language called *kyeyombekyeire*, a woman who is

---

[95] *See* interviews at Kitanga and Kyehinde in Kashambya (July 18, 2008); interviews at Kitojo and Ibumba in Rwamucucu (July 20, 2008).

[96] Interview at Kamusiza in Kashambya (July 25, 2008).

[97] On domestic violence in Africa, see generally D. GREEN, GENDER VIOLENCE IN AFRICA: AFRICAN WOMEN'S RESPONSES (St. Martin's Press 1999).

[98] *See* Female FGD at Nyakarambi in Rwamucucu (June 12, 2008).

[99] *See id.*

[100] *See* Male FGD at Rwara in Kashambya (June 18, 2008).

usually single, independent, and disobedient of male authority. However, women of Kashambya and Rwamucucu sub-counties explained how they secretly purchase land using names of their trusted relatives and friends.[101] The women can sell or pledge the land to meet their pressing needs such as health care and education of their children.[102] These examples show that in their small but significant way, rural women are tackling negative customary practices that perpetuate their inequality and subordination. These women are not merely passive victims desperately waiting for outsiders to liberate them from patriarchy and oppressive customary practices. They instead resist and struggle on their own using different strategies. Rural women's resistance and struggles have the potential to change negative customary laws and practices. There is thus a need to learn from rural women and build on their struggles so as to meaningfully tackle such practices.

19.6. CONCLUSION

Uganda's Constitution and international human rights law recognize both women's human rights and the right to culture, and, by implication, customary law. However, the law only recognizes positive customary rules and practices that enhance women's dignity and well-being. Uganda has the responsibility to ensure that its domestic practice – including customary laws – conform with the Bill of Rights. The state must transform and modify customary laws and practices that are discriminatory and violate women's human right to equality. However, it is wrong to treat all customary norms and practices as negative. There is a need to identify and preserve those customary values and practices that enhance the quality of life of women. It does more harm than good to abolish customary laws and practices without taking into account their actual meaning and significance to the people who subscribe to them. Thus, stakeholders such as rural women must be involved in any efforts to reform or develop customary law.

---

[101] *See* Female FGDs at Noozi in Rwamucucu (June 19, 2008); female FGDs at Ruyumbu in Kashambya (June 20, 2008).

[102] *See id.*

Women's Rights, Customary Law, and the Promise of the Protocol on the Rights of Women in Africa

Johanna E. Bond

20.1. INTRODUCTION

The existence of plural legal systems in Commonwealth Africa presents both challenges and opportunities for women's rights activists in the region.[1] Because statutory, customary, and religious laws operate as parallel systems of law in many countries, women enjoy different rights within each system of law. Customary law is dynamic, often unwritten law that governs in some countries in certain areas of law, such as family law matters. In a few cases, customary law has evolved to reflect human rights norms of gender equality.[2] In other cases, courts have invalidated customary laws that discriminated against women.[3] In many other cases, customary law continues

---

[1] A longer version of this chapter appears in 83 S. CAL. LAW REV. 425 (2010) (*reprinted in relevant part with permission*).

[2] *See, e.g.,* Tinyiko Shilubana v. Sidwell Nwamitwa (CCT 03/07) [2008] ZACC 9, 39 (4 June 2008) *available at* http://www.saflii.org/za/cases/ZACC/2008/9.html (Van der Westhuizen, J.) (finding that the Royal Family had the authority to develop its law in an effort to "affirm constitutional values in [the] traditional leadership [of] its community"). In *Shilubana v. Nwamitwa*, the Constitutional Court of South Africa considered whether to uphold the traditional authorities of the Royal family of the Valoyi's decision to grant a daughter the right to succeed her father's chieftaincy title. *See id.* at 2. The Chief died without a male heir and was initially succeeded by his brother instead of his eldest child, daughter Ms Shilubana. At the time of her father's death, Ms. Shilubana could not inherit the title under Customary law. *See id.* at 3. The elders modified the rule almost thirty years later to allow the daughter's chieftaincy, arguing it was necessary "to bring [the community's] customs and traditions in line with the new constitutional order." *Id.* at 17. Proponents of the decision argued that such change was common in customary law, as it is a changing, flexible system "develop[ed] over time to meet the changing needs of the community." *Id.* at 17. The Court ultimately decided, after conducting a balancing test between the nature of the law and the process by which the change occurred, that the traditional authorities had the power to develop their customary law under the Constitution. *See id.* at 37. The case serves as a prime example of both the dynamic nature of customary law and the ability of customary law to incorporate gender equality norms.

[3] *See, e.g.,* Bhe v. Magistrate, Khayelitsha, 2004 (18) BHRC 52 (CC) (S. Afr.) 593, *available at* http://www.mangaung.co.za/docs/Shibi%20Case.pdf (Langa, DCJ) (The Court found that the principle of primogeniture violated the right of women to human dignity as guaranteed by the Constitution.).

to impinge on women's rights to equality within family law.[4] This chapter will assess the extent to which international and regional human rights treaties may prove useful in the ongoing effort to reform customary law so that it conforms to internationally recognized gender equality norms.

The Convention on the Elimination of All Forms of Discrimination Against Women ("CEDAW")[5] and the African Charter on Human and Peoples' Rights ("African Charter"),[6] the two primary human rights treaties in the fight for gender equality in Africa, neglect issues of culture and gender equality, respectively.[7] In contrast to these substantive gaps in CEDAW and the African Charter, the Protocol to the African Charter on the Rights of Women in Africa ("the Protocol")[8] is a promising new tool for promoting gender equality on the continent.[9] The Protocol provides both strong substantive rights and important procedural rights to ensure that women have a voice in the ongoing examination and reformulation of cultural practices and customary law.[10] For example, Article 17 of the Protocol obligates States Parties to "enhance the participation of women in the formulation of cultural policies at all levels."[11]

Because it provides for women's agency in the formulation of cultural policies, the Protocol reflects theoretical advances in both the conception of women's self-identity and the potential of dialogical processes to promote rights.[12] I argue that the Protocol offers African feminists, among others, largely unexplored procedural, dialogical rights that have the potential to engage women in the public discourse that shapes African customary law.[13] Unfortunately, the transformative power of dialogue, or rights talk, is constrained by the power disparities among discursive participants, particularly traditional leaders and rural women.[14] For this reason, the value

---

[4] See generally, Johanna E. Bond, Constitutional Exclusion and Gender in Commonwealth Africa, 31 FORDHAM INT'L L.J. 289 (2008).

[5] Convention on the Elimination of Discrimination Against Women, adopted Dec. 18, 1979, entered into force Sept. 3, 1981, U.N. Doc. A/34/46, 1249 U.N.T.S. 13 [hereinafter CEDAW].

[6] African Charter on Human and Peoples' Rights, adopted June 27, 1981, entered into force Oct. 21, 1986, OAU Doc. CAB/LEG/67/3 Rev.5 (1982) [hereinafter African Charter].

[7] See discussion infra Part I.A-B and accompanying notes.

[8] See Protocol to the African Charter on Human and Peoples' Rights on the Rights of Women in Africa, adopted July 11, 2003, entered into force Nov. 25, 2005, OAU Doc. CAB/LEG/66.6 (2003) [hereinafter African Protocol].

[9] See ROSEMARY SEMAFUMU MUKASA, THE AFRICAN WOMEN'S PROTOCOL: HARNESSING A POTENTIAL FORCE FOR POSITIVE CHANGE 5 (Jacana Media (Pty) Ltd 2008) ("[T]he African Women's Protocol is a potential force for changing the lives of African women for the better.").

[10] See discussion infra.

[11] See African Protocol, supra note 8, art. 17.

[12] See discussion infra.

[13] See discussion infra.

[14] See discussion infra.

of deliberation is limited in the context of African customary law.[15] Despite this limitation, however, localized deliberation still has a role to play in identifying the most effective and viable methods of *implementing* women's human rights. The Protocol, therefore, has the potential to engage traditional leaders in dialogue about localized implementation of human rights norms, which will lead to greater internalization of those norms at the local level.[16]

Section 20.2 in this chapter identifies some of the shortcomings of CEDAW and the African Charter in negotiating potential conflicts between multiculturalism, as embodied in plural legal systems, and equality. Section 20.3 explores the Protocol's corresponding potential to effectively mediate such conflicts through its substantive provisions and highlights the procedural rights in the Protocol, which allow women to systematically engage with cultural meaning and facilitate enculturation of human rights norms among traditional leaders. I argue, however, that local deliberation about customary law offers both promise and pitfalls in the struggle for women's equality rights in the region. Many proponents of local deliberation do not adequately account for the very real power disparities that pervade localized discussions of customary law and have the potential to corrupt the outcome of deliberation.[17]

To maximize the potential of localized deliberation, non-governmental organizations (NGOs) and the state must facilitate the dialogue and structure it in a way that encourages the active participation of a diverse group of women, including those in rural areas. Women must have a voice in the implementation of equality standards and cultural practices and norms. Effective, facilitated dialogue, together with careful litigation, will allow women to shape the customary law and cultural practices that dramatically affect their daily lives. The Protocol provides a vehicle for improving women's rights through both litigation and deliberative processes designed to encourage women's engagement with and reformulation of the normative content of customary law.

Because the countries of Commonwealth Africa share a similar history, this chapter focuses on those countries.[18] As post-colonial states, many of the African

---

[15] *See* discussion *infra*.
[16] *See* Sally Engle Merry, *New Legal Realism and the Ethnography of Transnational Law*, 31 LAW & SOC. INQUIRY 975, 990 (2006) ("The concept of vernacularization was developed to explain the nineteenth-century process by which national languages in Europe separated, moving away from the medieval transnational use of Latin and creating a new and more differentiated sense of nationhood in Europe [Anderson 1983]. Human rights language is similarly being extracted from the universal and adapted to national and local communities.").
[17] *See generally* Seyla Benhabib, *The Law of Peoples, Distributive Justice and Migrations*, 72 FORDHAM L. REV. 1761 (2004).
[18] Commonwealth Africa includes the following countries: Botswana, Cameroon, The Gambia, Ghana, Kenya, Lesotho, Malawi, Mauritius, Mozambique, Namibia, Nigeria, Seychelles, Sierra Leone, South Africa, Tanzania, Uganda, Zambia, and Zimbabwe (departed in 2003). A full list of Commonwealth member states is available at http://www.thecommonwealth.org/Internal/191086/142227/members/.

Commonwealth countries continue to negotiate the boundaries between state and community-based law.[19] During the colonial period, British colonial authorities established a plural legal system in which the "received" or British law operated alongside indigenous customary law and religious law in certain areas like family law.[20] Thus, for the indigenous population, African customary law or religious law governed issues such as marriage, divorce, custody, burial, and inheritance.[21] To date, many African states have retained this structure of parallel legal systems.[22]

Some countries have attempted to integrate or unify these parallel systems of family law during the post-independence period.[23] Ghana, for example, established a unified law of inheritance in 1985, although implementation of the unified law has been spotty, particularly in rural areas.[24] Similarly, Tanzania passed a law integrating its marriage law under the 1971 Law of Marriage Act.[25] Despite these and other examples

[19] *See* Boaventura de Sousa Santos, *The Heterogeneous State and Legal Pluralism in Mozambique*, 40 LAW & SOC'Y REV. 39, 45–46 (2006) ("Whereas in colonial society it was easy to identify the legal orders and their spheres of action ... in present-day African societies the plurality of legal orders is much more extensive and the interactions between them much denser.... The boundaries between the different legal orders become more porous and each one loses its "pure," "autonomous" identity and can only be defined in relation to the legal constellation of which it is a part.").

[20] *See id.* at 870 ("In Africa, the British and the French superimposed their law onto indigenous law, incorporating customary law as long as it was not 'repugnant to natural justice, equity, and good conscience'....").

[21] *See* Bart Rwezaura, *Tanzania: Building a New Family Law Out of a Plural Legal System*, 33 U. LOUISVILLE J. FAM. L. 523, 523 (1994–1995) ("As would be expected, the majority of people for whom indigenous law was applicable were African, while Europeans and people of other cultures preferred Western law. Africans who adopted the Islamic faith also acquired an additional system of law (besides African customary law) that courts could apply to them in some contexts").

[22] *See* Johanna E. Bond, *Constitutional Exclusion and Gender in Commonwealth Africa*, 31 FORDHAM INT'L L.J. 289, 290 (2008) ("The history of colonialism in the region has created a plural legal system in which multiple systems of law – statutory, customary, and religious – operate simultaneously.").

[23] *See* Mark J. Calaguas et al., *Legal Pluralism and Women's Rights: A Study in Postcolonial Tanzania*, 16 COLUM. J. GENDER & L. 471, 491 (2007) (citing Bart Rwezaura, *Tanzania: Building a New Family Law Out of a Plural Legal System*, 33 U. LOUISVILLE J. FAM. L. 523, 523–524 [1995]) ("The movement for the unification of laws during the early postcolonial period in East Africa was most pronounced in the area of family law, which had been particularly beleaguered by the choice of law problems created by the plural legal system inherited from the British.").

[24] *See* Jeanmarie Fenrich & Tracy E. Higgins, *Promise Unfulfilled: Law, Culture and Women's Inheritance Rights in Ghana*, 25 FORDHAM INT'L L.J. 259, 268 (2001) ("Until 1985, customary law governed intestate succession for the vast majority of estates, providing rules of succession that largely excluded spouses. This regime was radically altered in 1985 by a statute intended to protect more fully the interests of spouses, particularly widows.").

[25] *See* Rwezaura, *supra* note 21, at 526 ("In the pursuit of these twin objects [i.e., integration and reform] the LMA introduced a number of statutory provisions that are applicable to all married couples, irrespective of the form of marriage they may have contracted. These provisions include, for example, the requirement for mutual consent to marriage, provisions regarding capacity for marriage [including minimum age], the abolition of extrajudicial divorce and the empowerment of courts to make orders regarding reallocation of property on divorce and the upbringing of children. But, the LMA also gave recognition to existing procedures for contracting religious and customary marriages and did not seek to abolish polygamy.").

of integration, many Commonwealth African countries have retained fairly rigid divisions between parallel legal systems.[26] In a number of countries, those divisions are, in fact, constitutionally sanctioned.[27] A handful of Commonwealth African countries' constitutions preserve the separation between statutory and customary or religious law by specifically excluding the latter from constitutional non-discrimination protection.[28] These constitutions, thus, perpetuate the separation between public law and private, familial law, an area in which the state will not intercede to prevent gender discrimination.[29] These states have embraced a strong form of multiculturalism, ceding the authority to govern family law to local communities and removing the backstop of constitutional non-discrimination rights. Some states embrace a weak form of multiculturalism in which deference to community law is tempered by far-reaching equality rights or specific statutory overrides, such as Ghana's integrated inheritance law.[30] Wherever states fall on this continuum, women within indigenous African communities continue to engage with cultural norms, sometimes pushing them incrementally closer to national and international standards of gender equality.[31]

---

[26] See, e.g., Anne Hellum, Human Rights and Gender Relations in Postcolonial Africa: Options and Limits for the Subjects of Legal Pluralism, 25 LAW & SOC. INQUIRY 635, 637 (2000) ("Botswana has, with certain modifications, kept a dualistic system of laws with a corresponding set of customary and general law courts.").

[27] See Bond, supra note 22, at 290.

[28] See, e.g., ZIMBABWE CONST. art. 23 (amended Sept. 14, 2005), available at http://www.parlzim.gov.zw/cms/UsefulResourses/ZimbabweConstitution.pdf.

   (1) Subject to the provisions of this section –
      (a) no law shall make any provision that is discriminatory either of itself or in its effect; and
      (b) no person shall be treated in a discriminatory manner by any person acting by virtue of any written law or in the performance of the functions of any public office or any public authority.
   (3) Nothing contained in any law shall be held to be in contravention of subsection (1)(a) to the extent that the law in question relates to any of the following matters –
      (a) matters of personal law;
         [Paragraph as amended by section 3 of Act 5 of 2005 – Amendment No. 17]
      (b) the application of African customary law in any case involving Africans or an African and one or more persons who are not Africans where such persons have consented to the application of African customary law in that case.

   Id.

[29] See Bond, supra note 22, at 318.

[30] See Fenrich & Higgins, supra note 24, at 287 ("According to the Memorandum accompanying Law 111, the law was intended 'to provide a uniform intestate succession law that will be applicable throughout the country irrespective of the class of the intestate and the type of marriage contracted by him or her.'" (quoting Memorandum, Intestate Succession Law, P.N.D.C. L. 111 (1985) (Ghana))).

[31] See, e.g., Bhe v. Magistrate, Khayelitsha, 2004 (18) BHRC 52 (CC) (S. Afr.) 633, available at http://www.mangaung.co.za/docs/Shibi%20Case.pdf (declaring Section 23 of the Black Administration Act 38 of 1927 to be inconsistent with the Constitution and invalid). In the Bhe case, Ms. Bhe brought suit in the interest of the deceased's female descendants, her two minor daughters. See id. at 594. Under the Black Administration Act, "the children did not qualify to be heirs in the intestate estate of their deceased father." Id. at 597. The Court found that the principle of primogeniture violated the right of women to human dignity as guaranteed by the Constitution. See id. at 622.

20.2. GAPS IN COVERAGE: CEDAW AND THE AFRICAN CHARTER

Early efforts to promote global women's rights focused on the repressive nature of culture and custom in the global south.[32] For many years, human rights activists in the global north cast women in developing countries exclusively as victims of a foreign, exotic culture.[33] Although women in the global north struggled to resist discrimination in their homes, workplaces, schools, and other venues, this discrimination was not widely viewed as a manifestation of discriminatory culture.[34] According to this view, gender discrimination in the global north was not embedded in the very fabric of social relations as it was in the global south, including Africa. Modern, western liberalism came to be viewed as "cultureless," and women in the global south became defined exclusively as victims of, rather than agents of or participants in, culture and local custom.[35]

Culture, defined broadly, is "an historically transmitted pattern of meanings in symbols, a system of inherited conceptions expressed in symbolic form by means of which men [and women] communicate, perpetuate and develop their knowledge and attitudes toward life."[36] Although conceptually distinct from culture, customary law is a legal expression of cultural norms and values.[37] Like culture, customary law

---

[32] *See* Radhika Coomaraswamy, *Identity Within: Cultural Relativism, Minority Rights and the Empowerment of Women*, 34 Geo. Wash. Int'l L. Rev. 483, 484 (2002) ("Many women acquiesce because they see their group identity as the most important aspect of their lives.").

[33] *See* Tracy E. Higgins, *Anti-essentialism, Relativism and Human Rights*, 19 Harv. Women's L.J. 89, 91 (1996) ("Addressing this tension, this Article endeavors to sort out the degree to which feminism, by virtue of its own commitments, must take cultural defenses seriously, particularly when articulated by women themselves."). *See also* Ratna Kapur, *The Tragedy of Victimization Rhetoric: Resurrecting the "Native" Subject in International/Post-Colonial Feminist Politics*, 15 Harv. Hum. Rts. J. 1, 6 (2002) (noting that "[w]omen in the Third World are portrayed as victims of their culture, which reinforces stereotyped and racist representations of that culture and privileges the culture of the West.").

[34] *See* Leti Volpp, *Feminism Versus Multiculturalism*, 101 Colum. L. Rev. 1181, 1186–87 (2001) ("Part of the reason many believe the cultures of the Third World or immigrant communities are so much more sexist than Western ones is that incidents of sexual violence in the West are frequently thought to reflect the behavior of a few deviants – rather than as part of our culture. In contrast, incidents of violence in the Third World or immigrant communities are thought to characterize the cultures of entire nations.").

[35] Karen Engle states "Third world feminist critiques have also challenged the extent to which structural bias feminism denies women's agency in its representation of women as victims." Karen Engle, *International Human Rights and Feminisms: When Discourses Keep Meeting*, in International Law: Modern Feminist Approaches 47, 62 (Doris Buss & Ambreena Manji eds., 2005). *See also* Madhavi Sunder, *Piercing the Veil*, 112 Yale Law Journal 1399, 1415–1417 (2003) (describing an historicist view in which religion and culture constitute "law's past.").

[36] Abdullahi Ahmed An-Na'im, *Toward a Cross-Cultural Approach to Defining International Standards of Human Rights: The Meaning of Cruel, Inhuman, or Degrading Treatment or Punishment*, in Human Rights in Cross-Cultural Perspectives: A Quest for Consensus 19, 23 (Abdullahi Ahmed An-Na'im ed. 1992) (*quoting* Clifford Geertz, Interpretation of Culture 89 (1973)).

[37] "Sometimes termed customary law, indigenous law is the system of norms which governs the lives of millions of African people, particularly (but not exclusively) in the rural areas." Thandabantu Nhlapo,

is dynamic and changes based on social, economic, and legal developments.[38] It is internally contested, and powerful elites often determine the dominant cultural interpretation and provide what is seen as a definitive interpretation of customary law.[39]

Although CEDAW and the African Charter have been successfully invoked to challenge discriminatory customary laws on the continent, both treaties have gaps in the coverage of the human rights that they protect. CEDAW was drafted in the 1970s, in an era during which many women's rights activists in the global north focused primarily on formal inequality based on gender.[40] As a result, it privileges gender as an analytical focal point.[41] The African Charter is also the product of a particular historical moment, and its drafting was informed by anti-colonial struggles on the continent.[42] Thus, the Charter's text privileges culture over gender equality.[43] The Protocol, in contrast to both CEDAW and the African Charter, represents a

---

Indigenous Law and Gender in South Africa: Taking Human Rights and Cultural Diversity Seriously, 1994–95 THIRD WORLD LEG. STUD. 49, 53 (1994–1995).

[38] *See* Alice Armstrong et al., *Uncovering Reality: Excavating Women's Rights in African Family Law,* 7 INT'L J. L. & FAM. 314, 327 (1993) (describing living law, Rwezaura explains that it is the "flexible and highly negotiable ... custom representing the law governing the actual social life of the people in their day to day lives often changing in response to changing conditions [Rwezaura, 1992]."). *See also* Nhlapo, *supra* note 37, at 53. Nhlapo notes: "Nowadays it is accepted that indigenous law has undergone profound changes through various kind of interaction with European culture and with both the colonial and apartheid states. The process has led to the growth of "official" customary law which consists of rigid rules, embedded in judicial decisions and statutes, which have lost the characteristics of dynamism and adaptability which distinguished African custom." *Id.*

[39] *See* An-Na'im, *supra* note 36, at 28 ("A third and more significant feature of cultural dynamism is the ambivalence of cultural norms and their susceptibility to different interpretations. In the normal course of events, powerful individuals and groups tend to monopolize the interpretation of cultural norms and manipulate them to their own advantage.").

[40] See CEDAW, *supra* note 5, at 193. *See* Judith Resnik, *Foreign as Domestic Affairs: Rethinking Horizontal Federalism and Foreign Affairs Preemption in Light of Internationalism,* 57 EMORY L.J. 31, 52 (2007).

[41] *See* Bond, *supra* note 22, at 73 ("With the exception of some voices from the global South, the international women's human rights community's focus on 'women' to the exclusion of other identity categories, such as ethnicity, race, class, religion, and sexual orientation, has resulted in a limited understanding of women's human rights.").

[42] *See* Adrien Katherine Wing & Tyler Murray Smith, *The New African Union and Women's Rights,* 13 TRANSNAT'L L. & CONTEMP. PROBS. 33, 53–54 (2003) ("Conceived in 1963, on the heels of Africa's break from the colonial yoke, the OAU was established to unite the nations of the continent against the foreign intervention and racial subrogation that defined the period."). "It appears that the Charter was conflicted from the beginning given its attempt to reconcile deep-seated African values (which arguably subjugate women's gender roles) and the emerging global values of non-discrimination. In many ways, the Charter embraced the OAU principle of protecting state sovereignty." *Id.* at 58.

[43] *See* Deborah A. Wean, *Real Protection for Women? The African Charter on Human and Peoples' Rights,* 2 EMORY J. INT'L DISP. RESOL. 425, 456 (1987) ("African women may realistically expect to face a similar problem in light of the fact that proponents of the Charter seemed to be more concerned with the inequities of race than the inequities of sex in African society.").

more current view that explicitly values both the positive aspects of culture and equality rights for women.[44]

During CEDAW's drafting phase, many human rights activists did not view women as active members or beneficiaries of cultural communities.[45] In the 1990s, a critical mass of women's rights activists in the global south and a segment of the women's rights community in the global north – particularly activists from communities of color – popularized a more complicated picture of discrimination, one that more accurately represented their experiences of discrimination along multiple axes of discrimination such as gender and race or ethnicity.[46] This led to a better understanding of the intersectional, mutually reinforcing forms of discrimination against women.[47] Consistent with this more nuanced understanding of women's experiences of discrimination, the mainstream human rights movement also began to value the multiple aspects of women's identity, including women's membership in religious and cultural communities.[48]

The drafting of CEDAW, however, pre-dated this more accurate and complex understanding of women's identity.[49] A simpler, narrower notion of discrimination as against women *qua* women, without attention to the multiple sites of oppression in women's lives, is embodied in the convention's text.[50] Only a handful of

[44] *See* Mukasa, *supra* note 9. The author notes that:

  While the CEDAW's effectiveness was undermined in some quarters because it was considered to be a western woman's instrument, the African Women's Protocol is a homegrown instrument developed by African women for African women. On the other hand, where the African Charter on Human and Peoples' Rights (ACHPR) went overboard is in its wholesale embrace of African traditions, values and customs without acknowledging that some of these customs discriminate against and harm women; the African Women's Protocol outlaws traditions such as FGM, widow inheritance and child marriages.
    Id. at 7.

[45] *See* Celina Romany, *Black Women and Gender Equality in a New South Africa: Human Rights Law and the Intersection of Race and Gender*, 21 Brooklyn J. Int'l L. 857, 857–858, 860 (1996) ("Feminist theory and the knowledge derived from a common experience of subordination has exposed the male-centered values upon which the international human rights framework is built.... However, feminist methodology, particularly when applied to the cross-cultural magnitude of the world, must guard against its essentialist impulses.... A feminist critique that merely focuses on gender or grants as an afterthought the existence of other forms of subordination, retains the abstract contours of the liberal self it aims to attack while politically alienating key allies in securing global social justice.").

[46] *See, e.g.,* Kimberle Crenshaw, *Demarginalizing the Intersection of Race and Sex: A Black Feminist Critique of Antidiscrimination Doctrine, Feminist Theory and Antiracist Politics*, 30 U. Chi. Legal F. 139, 139–167 (1989); Trina Gillo, *Anti-Essentialism and Intersectionality: Tools to Dismantle the Master's House*, 10 Berkeley Women's L.J. 16 (1995); Angela Harris, *Race and Essentialism in Feminist Legal Theory*, 42 Stan. L. Rev. 581, 585 (1990).

[47] Bond, *supra* note 22, at 75. *See also* Penelope E. Andrews, *Globalization, Human Rights, and Critical Race Feminism: Voices from the Margins*, 3 J. Gender, Race & Just. 373 (2000).

[48] *See* Sunder, *supra* note 35, at 1404 ("[D]espite law's formal refusal to acknowledge claims of internal dissent, women are nonetheless claiming their rights to challenge religious and cultural authorities and to imagine religious community on more egalitarian and democratic terms.").

[49] *See supra* note 40 and accompanying text.

[50] *See* Berta Esperanza Hernandez-Truyol, *Human Rights Through a Gendered Lens: Emergence, Evolution, Revolution, in* Women and International Human Rights Law, Vol. I, 4 (Kelly D.

CEDAW's articles even address culture, and those that do primarily treat culture as uniformly regressive and bad for women.[51] Because CEDAW largely fails to consider the power and meaning of cultural and community membership in women's lives, it has the potential to create a backlash in any given conflict between gender equality rights and cultural rights.[52] In its dismissal of culture as a potentially positive aspect of women's lives, the treaty also fails to provide states and communities with the tools to effectively mediate or resolve such conflicts.[53]

The African Charter also fails to offer a meaningful mechanism for women's rights activists in Africa to reconcile the conflicts that sometimes arise between women's equality rights and the right to culture in indigenous African communities.[54] Because the Charter fails to comprehensively protect women's rights, it offers African women's rights activists very little ammunition in the struggle for gender equality.[55] Although the Charter itself is of limited use, the Protocol offers new hope to activists in the region. With more expansive rights protections for African women, the Protocol will not only provide a new source for normative rights claims, but will also lead to a broader interpretation of the more limited rights within CEDAW and the African Charter. There are three primary reasons why the Protocol offers significant promise for promoting women's rights in Africa while simultaneously respecting and promoting cultural rights and, particularly, women's rights to define and re-define the normative content of custom and customary law. I discuss each in greater detail in subsequent sections of the chapter.

First, the Protocol offers credibility within the region.[56] African women played a large role in drafting and promoting the Protocol; as such, it provides a convincing

Askin and Doreen M. Koenig, eds. 1999) (noting that "the Women's Convention has been criticized by many feminists as being outdated....").

[51] *See* discussion *infra* Part I.A and accompanying notes.

[52] *See* Mukasa, *supra* note 9, at 42 ("Furthermore, Article 17 empowers African women by giving them the right to live in a positive cultural context and to embrace participation in the determination of cultural policies. This provision provides African women with a tool to address one of the biggest challenges for efforts to implement the CEDAW ... the co-existence of multiple legal systems with customary and religious law governing personal life and prevailing over positive law and even constitutional guarantees.").

[53] There are, however, several advantages to using CEDAW to promote women's rights. The CEDAW Committee, for example, is a well-established United Nations institution with a proven track record. Some of the more recent regional instruments, like the Protocol to the Rights of Women in Africa, must rely on new or chronically underfunded institutions for enforcement.

[54] *See* Mukasa, *supra* note 9, at 35 ("Another area of inadequacy stems from the charter's warm and wholesale embrace of African tradition and customs, without taking into account the fact that some of these very traditions discriminate against women").

[55] *But see* Ephrahim v. Pastory & Anor, High Ct. Civ. App. 70/89 (22 Feb. 1990) (Tanz.) in which the Tanzanian High Court relied on both CEDAW and the African Charter in upholding women's rights.

[56] *See* Mukasa, *supra* note 9, at 14 ("Significantly, the Women's Protocol is also the outcome of a political negotiation process between African heads of state, giving it an added degree of legitimacy and credibility in comparison to other international agreements – it is an instrument that has been developed by Africans for Africans.").

response to charges of western imperialism.[57] As Rosemary Semafumu Mukasa remarks: "The Protocol is a homegrown instrument developed by Africans for African women. It legitimates the fight against gender oppression as an African struggle. No longer can detractors claim that women's rights are transplants from the western world with no roots in African values and norms."[58]

Second, the Protocol has strong substantive provisions for the protection of women's rights in the region. Professor Alpha Oumar Konare, Chairperson of the African Union Commission, observes, "The Protocol is arguably one of the most progressive and visionary rights instruments for gender equality not just in Africa but internationally."[59] The Protocol's substantive rights provisions explicitly value *both* cultural rights and rights to gender equality.[60]

Third, the Protocol provides an intriguing, but infrequently discussed, procedural right that, if properly operationalized, could lay the foundation for an engaging grassroots discourse that promotes women's voices in the ongoing process of cultural definition and the articulation of customary norms.[61] By "procedural" right, I am referring not to a formal due process right but rather to a right to be part of a more informal process of defining and articulating cultural norms. The Protocol's procedural provisions open the door for systematic engagement with traditional leaders concerning implementation of women's human rights at the local, community level.[62]

---

[57] *See* Fareda Banda, *Global Standards: Local Values*, 17 INT'L J. L. POL.& FAM. 1, 17 (2003) ("These sub-regional initiatives have been followed up at the regional level with the drafting of the Draft Protocol to the African Charter on the Rights of Women in Africa. A joint initiative of the African Commission and Women in Law and Development in Africa (WILDAF), the Draft Protocol was drafted by a working group chaired by the Special Rapporteur on the Rights of African Women."). Banda, however, also notes that NGOs were excluded from the drafting process at various points. Although not a perfectly inclusive process, the drafting of the Protocol afforded African women more of an opportunity to shape treaty language than that enjoyed by women in the drafting and adoption of the African Charter *Id.*

[58] Mukasa, *supra* note 9, at 5.

[59] Alpha Oumar Konare, *Preface, in* BREATHING LIFE INTO THE AFRICAN UNION PROTOCOL ON WOMEN'S RIGHTS IN AFRICA ix (2006).

[60] For example, Article 17 of the African Protocol recognizes the positive aspects of culture but states, "1. Women shall have the right to live in a positive cultural context and to participate at all levels in the determination of cultural policies. 2. States Parties shall take all appropriate measures to enhance the participation of women in the formulation of cultural policies at all levels."). African Protocol, *supra* note 8, art. 17. "One of the Protocol's greatest strengths is that it is an African instrument that outlaws negative traditional practices and enshrines the right of women to live in a positive cultural context." Mukasa, *supra* note 9, at 5.

[61] Article 17 states, "Women shall have the right to live in a positive cultural context and to participate at all levels in the determination of cultural policies." African Protocol, *supra* note 8, art. 17.

[62] *See* discussion *infra* Section 20.2.

Before turning to the shortcomings of CEDAW and the African Charter and
the advantages of the Protocol, however, a few caveats are necessary. Human
rights commentators from the global north often discuss culture as if it existed
only in foreign legal systems, where it operates as a dominating force in the lives
of "other" women.[63] Culture implies "other"; in this popular hegemonic narrative, the West becomes constructed as modern and free of the regressive and
oppressive burdens of culture.[64] Women in places like Africa become simplistically characterized as exotic victims of a uniformly regressive culture.[65] There is
a clear colonialist and ethnocentric bias in this construction. The second caveat
reflects the recognition that talking about culture as conflicting with equality implies that equality and culture cannot be coexistent.[66] This is not true.
Equality exists within cultures, but real conflicts do arise. Because academics
have struggled to reconcile these sometimes competing rights, commentators
occasionally leave the impression that they cannot and, in fact, do not coexist.[67]
The final caveat I will offer stems from the difficulty of talking about culture
in Africa from an outsider's perspective.[68] This is inherently problematic but
should not foreclose the possibility of sustained cross-cultural discourse. It is
critical, however, to talk about these issues in way that is both respectful of

[63] *See* Volpp, *supra* note 34, at 1198 ("The relative status of women across communities is still used to
assess the progress of culture. And the discourse of feminism versus multiculturalism assumes that
women in minority communities require liberation into the "progressive" social customs of the West.
The idea that "other" women are subjected to extreme patriarchy is developed in relation to the vision
of Western women as secular, liberated, and in total control of their lives.").

[64] *See id.* at 1198–1199 ("But the assumption that Western women enjoy complete liberation is not
grounded in material reality. Rather, Western women's liberation is a product of discursive self-rep-
resentation, which contrasts Western women's enlightenment with the suffering of the 'Third World
woman.'").

[65] Ratna Kapur observes, "[The focus on the victim subject] encourages some feminists in the international arena to propose strategies which are reminiscent of imperial interventions in the lives of the
native subject and which represent the 'Eastern' woman as a victim of a 'backward' and 'uncivilized'
culture." Kapur, *supra* note 33, at 6.

[66] *See* Volpp, *supra* note 34, at 1193 ("Recognizing that feminism exists within communities of color
breaks down the equation between multiculturalism and antifeminism inherent in the notion of "feminism versus multiculturalism." [This equation breaks down as well when we realize that gender-
subordinating values are also valued in the dominant culture of the West.]").

[67] Some scholars critique the application of a rights discourse to culture, emphasizing that individual autonomy rights inherently undermine a cultural focus on community identity and collective
decision-making. *See* Coomaraswamy, *supra* note 32 ("Many scholars from the third world argue that
human rights discourse is not universal but a product of the European Enlightenment and its particular cultural development.... ").

[68] *See generally* Makau Mutua, *Savages, Victims, and Saviors: The Metaphor of Human Rights*, 42 HARV.
INT'L L.J. 201 (2001).

and deferential to those women whose daily lives are most directly affected by customary law.[69]

20.2.1. CEDAW: *The Problems of Scope and Reservations*

CEDAW has often proven to be a successful tool for improving women's rights around the world, used effectively in legislative reform efforts, test case litigation, and grassroots organizing across the globe.[70] It includes both civil and political rights and economic, social, and cultural rights.[71] Although it was drafted in the late 1970s, the document includes forward-looking language that would later help dismantle the public/private distinction in international human rights law.[72] CEDAW's inclusion of affirmative action provisions, or "temporary special measures" in the language of the treaty, has opened the door for interpretations of equality that go beyond mere formal equality.[73]

Although its successes are noteworthy, CEDAW is not without flaws. As a document drafted in the late 1970s, it largely reflects a "second-generation" feminist understanding of gender as the primary – if not sole – site of oppression.[74] It fails to acknowledge that women may face multiple forms of discrimination, such as that based on, among other things, race, ethnicity, culture, religion, or sexual orientation.[75] Similarly, it does not reflect the multidimensional and intersectional role of

[69] The vast majority of women in Africa view customary law as the controlling authority in their lives. In Ghana, for example, one study revealed that 80 percent of women were married according to customary law. *See* Fenrich & Higgins, *supra* note 24, at 284.

[70] *See* Bringing Equality Home: Implementing the Convention on the Elimination of All forms of Discrimination Against Women 10 (Ilana Landsberg-Lewis ed., United Nations Development Fund for Women 1998) ("Some of the most significant constitutional gains have been won in countries where there has been a broader national move for constitutional renewal, a recent ratification of CEDAW, and an interest from women's NGOS in using CEDAW as an advocacy tool. CEDAW principles have been integrated into new constitutions and added to more established constitutions through amendments.").

[71] *See* Harold Hongju Koh, *Why America Should Ratify the Women's Rights Treaty (CEDAW)*, 34 Case W. Res. J. Int'l L. 263, 266 (2002) ("The Convention affirms the rights of all women to exercise on an equal basis their 'human rights and fundamental freedoms in the political, economic, social, cultural, civil or any other field.'") (*quoting* CEDAW, art. 1).

[72] *See* Vicki C. Jackson, *Transnational Discourse, Relational Authority, and the U.S. Court: Gender Equality*, 37 Loy. L.A. L. Rev. 271, 275–276 (2003) "([CEDAW's] substantive provisions target not only intentional acts of discrimination but acts which effect substantive inequalities; they reach both private and state conduct; and they obligate states not merely to refrain from discrimination but actively to seek to redress and remedy private discrimination against women.").".

[73] *See* Rebecca J. Cook, *Accommodating Women's Differences Under the Anti-Discrimination Convention*, 56 Emory L.J. 1039, 1044–1046 (2007) ("The General Recommendation on Temporary Special Measures proposes evolution beyond the male comparator or reference point as the standard for determining equality.").

[74] *See supra* note 46.

[75] *See id.*

African women as both members of their cultural communities and as advocates for gender equality within those communities.[76]

CEDAW, in fact, rarely mentions culture. The only positive reference to culture appears in Article 13, which provides that women should enjoy an equal right to "participate in recreational activities, sports and all aspects of culture."[77] Other references to culture appear in Article 5, which prohibits gender stereotyping.[78] Article 2 contains another passing reference to culture and states' obligations to change culture to conform to equality norms.[79] With the exception of Article 13, CEDAW treats culture as a uniformly negative influence on women's lives. It largely fails to recognize the possibility of a positive culture that benefits women – as well as men – by providing a sense of community and identity that stems from association with others who share foundational values.[80] Sally Engle Merry comments, "When [CEDAW] committee members or the convention invoke culture in CEDAW proceedings, it is more often as an obstacle to change than as a resource or a mode of transformation."[81] By treating culture as a static obstacle rather than a fluid source for transformation, as the CEDAW experts sometimes do, Merry argues that the Committee members miss a valuable opportunity to reformulate culture in a way that promotes women's equality rights.[82] CEDAW's limited view of culture, as expressed in the text of the treaty and by some CEDAW Committee experts, contributes to backlash against the treaty and interferes with implementation and internalization of gender equality norms in the African region.[83] Indeed, "a more

---

[76] *See id.*

[77] CEDAW, *supra* note 5, art. 13.

[78] CEDAW, art. 5(a) states that States parties agree "[t]o modify the social and cultural patterns of conduct of men and women, with a view to achieving the elimination of prejudices and customary and all other practices which are based on the idea of the inferiority or the superiority of either of the sexes or on stereotyped roles for men and women." *Id.* art. 5(a).

[79] CEDAW, art. 2(f) requires States parties "[t]o take all appropriate measures, including legislation, to modify or abolish existing laws, regulations, customs and practices which constitute discrimination against women." *Id.* art. 2(f).

[80] *See* Ayelet Shachar, *Religion, State, and the Problem of Gender: New Modes of Citizenship and Governance in Diverse Societies*, 50 McGILL L.J. 49, 49 (2005) ("Both examples highlight the fact that minority group members may wish to benefit from affiliation with more than one legal and cultural system.").

[81] SALLY ENGLE MERRY, HUMAN RIGHTS AND GENDER VIOLENCE 91 (The University of Chicago Press 2006). Merry notes also "The [CEDAW] experts tend to see culture as a barrier to women's human rights." *Id.* at 90.

[82] *See id.* at 91 ("When culture is discussed as a resource, or when there is recognition that the goal of the CEDAW process is cultural reformulation, a far more fluid and contested idea is implied.").

[83] *See* Ravi Mahalingam, *Women's Rights and the "War on Terror": Why the United States Should View CEDAW as an Important Step in the Conflict with Militant Islamic Fundamentalists*, 34 CAL. W. INT'L L.J. 171, 195 (2004) ("These countries have taken a cultural relativist approach in defending their reservations, arguing that CEDAW represents the active imposition of western secular values or "cultural imperialism" upon non-western countries.").

nuanced critique of particular practices or gender stereotypes is less likely to evoke nationalist defenses and justifications and more likely to build on local movements of resistance and contestation."[84]

The CEDAW Committee has attempted to address the conflict that some-times arises between culture and equality through its general recommendations.[85] Although there is no general recommendation devoted exclusively to the messy issues that arise in the context of equality and culture, the issue does surface within the context of several recommendations. General Recommendation 21, for exam-ple, addresses equality in marriage and states "Whatever form [the family] takes, and whatever the legal system, religion, custom, or tradition within the country, the treatment of women in the family both at law and in private must accord with the principles of equality and justice for all people...."[86] Similarly, the general recom-mendations that address violence against women and female genital mutilation also argue, correctly albeit simplistically, that states should not allow custom or culture to justify these harmful practices.[87] Despite the Committee's willingness to address conflicts between custom and equality in its general recommendations, the treaty itself is less effective than some regional and sub-regional initiatives that directly address the potential conflict between culture and equality rights in the text of the treaty itself and consider the importance of local context.[88]

In addition to these textual shortcomings of CEDAW, States Parties' reservations to CEDAW's substantive provisions often shield family law and customary or reli-gious law from scrutiny by international monitoring bodies, such as the CEDAW Committee.[89] A large number of States Parties have entered significant reservations to the treaty, including some reservations to core treaty provisions.[90] A few states, for

---

[84] Merry, *supra* note 81, at 100.
[85] General Recommendations "are documents explaining how a particular treaty should be interpreted and applied." Women, Law & Dev. Int'l and Human Rights Watch Women's Right Project, Women's Human Rights Step By Step 170 (1997).
[86] CEDAW, General Rec. 21, para. 13.
[87] CEDAW Committee, General Rec. 14, 1990 (noting that "continuing cultural, traditional and eco-nomic pressures ... help to perpetuate harmful practices"); CEDAW General Rec. 19, 1992 ("States parties in their reports should identify the nature and extent of attitudes, customs and practices that perpetuate violence against women...").
[88] Merry, *supra* note 81, at 104 ("The [CEDAW] Committee's lack of attention to local situations impedes productive collaboration with grassroots activists....").
[89] *See* Yakare-Oule Jansen, *The Right to Freely Have Sex? Beyond Biology: Reproductive Rights and Sex Determination*, 40 AKRON L. REV. 311, 323–324 (2007) ("According to General Recommendation 21 on Equality in Marriage and Family Relations, no reservations can be made to this article [16], as that would be inconsistent with the principles of CEDAW. Yet, as practice has shown, this article is a favor-ite amongst State Parties when it comes to reservations and declarations of interpretation.").
[90] *See* Anne F. Bayefsky, *General Approaches to Domestic Application of International Law, in* HUMAN RIGHTS OF WOMEN 352 (Rebecca Cook ed., 1994) ("First, although over 120 states have ratified the Convention, many have done so conditionally. Approximately 40 states have made a total of roughly

example, have made reservations to Article 2 of the Convention, which contains a broad obligation to change laws and practices to conform to the equality standard embodied in the treaty.[91] Many more states have made reservations to Article 16, which obligates states to eliminate discrimination within marriage and family life.[92] These reservations contravene the "object and purpose" of the treaty and should be discouraged through aggressive objections by other States parties.[93] Otherwise, reservations such as these will continue to hamper implementation of the treaty.

Despite the proliferation of reservations to the treaty, CEDAW has made a positive contribution to women's rights in the region.[94] Because there have been few women's rights cases involving challenges to customary law in the region, it is difficult to generalize about CEDAW's effectiveness in reforming customary law. In some cases, the treaty has clearly proved to be an important resource for women's rights activists campaigning for law reform in the region. In others, the treaty has been unpersuasive in domestic courts. The Protocol, however, provides an important new source of women's human rights law in the region and supplements CEDAW in crucial ways, as I discuss later in the chapter.

105 reservations and declarations to the convention. Many of the substantive reservations are wide-ranging and profoundly affect the integrity of the convention.").

[91] *See* Vedna Jivan & Christine Forster, *What Would Ghandi Say? Reconciling Universalism, Cultural Relativism and Feminism through Women's Use of CEDAW*, 9 S.Y.B.I.L. 103, 108 (2005) ("As of November 2002, fifty-five State parties had entered reservations to CEDAW.... Reservations to CEDAW, however, are most often made on the grounds that national law, tradition, religion or culture are incongruent with some of its articles or principles. Thus, most of the reservations lodged relate to Articles 2, 5 or 16. Article 2 identifies the range of measures that State parties should take to eliminate gender discrimination.").

[92] *See* Marie Egan Provins, *Constructing an Islamic Institute of Civil Justice that Encourages Women's Rights*, 27 Loy. L.A. Int'l & Comp. L. Rev. 515, 522–23 (2005) ("Article 16 directs states to eliminate discrimination against women in matters of marriage and family relations.... The committee declares reservations to Article 16 ... incompatible with CEDAW and thus impermissible. Significantly, twelve parties have made reservations to CEDAW Article 2 and/or Article 16, explicitly asserting that these provisions are incompatible with Sharia.").

[93] *See* Jessica Neuwirth, *Inequality Before the Law: Holding States Accountable for Sex Discrimination Under the Convention on the Elimination of All Forms of Discrimination Against Women and Through the Beijing Platform for Action*, 18 Harv. Hum. Rts. J. 19, 25 (2005) ("The CEDAW Committee has said that article 2 is central to the object and purpose of the Convention and that reservations to article 16 are incompatible with the Convention and therefore impermissible.") (*citing* U.N. Div. for the Advancement of Women, *Reservations to CEDAW, available at* http://www.un.org/women-watch/daw/cedaw/reservations.htm (last visited Feb. 10, 2005)); Arthur M. Weisburd, *The Effect of Treaties and Other Formal International Acts on the Customary Law of Human Rights*, 25 Ga. J. Int'l & Comp. L. 99, 127 (1996) ("State objections to reservations under that instrument [CEDAW] are especially important, since they are the principal means of raising questions regarding the permissibility of reservations; the Committee lacks authority to compel states to abandon even impermissible reservations.").

[94] *See* Claude E. Welch, Jr., *Human Rights and African Women: A Comparison of Protection under Two Major Treaties*, 15 Hum. Rts. Q. 549, 573 (1993) ("Progress in greater women's rights in Africa, though slow, can be seen in the application of the Women's Convention and the African Charter.").

20.2.2. *Substantive Shortcomings of the African Charter on Human and Peoples' Rights*

Whereas CEDAW – both in its text and in the Committee's general recommendations – has failed to explicitly value culture in women's lives, the African Charter
has failed to adequately protect women's rights.[95] The right to culture is enshrined
in a number of international and regional human rights treaties.[96] Article 27 of the
Universal Declaration of Human Rights recognizes that "everyone has the right freely
to participate in the cultural life of the community."[97] Article 15.1 of the International
Covenant on Economic, Social and Cultural Rights ("ICESCR") provides that individuals have the right to take part in cultural life.[98] The International Covenant on
Civil and Political Rights ("ICCPR") provides specific protection for members of
ethnic, linguistic, or cultural minorities to enjoy their own culture.[99]

Drafted after these international documents, the African Charter built on the
existing protection of cultural rights and expanded that protection.[100] The Charter
emphasizes cultural rights and attempts to balance fundamental, universal rights on
the one hand, and to provide an African "fingerprint" on traditional articulations of
fundamental rights on the other hand.[101] As such, the Charter embodies a conscious
effort to filter traditional human rights through an African lens.[102] Like the ICESCR,

---

[95] *See* Mukasa, *supra* note 9 at 7.

[96] *See* Laurence Juma, *Reconciling African Customary Law and Human Rights in Kenya: Making a Case
for Institutional Reformation and Revitalization of Customary Adjudication Process*, 14 ST. THOMAS L.
REV. 459, 491–492 (2002) ("The International Covenant on Civil and Political Rights (ICCPR) offers
protection to cultural rights and provides that people have a right 'in community with the other members of their group, to enjoy their own culture to profess and practice their own religion or to use their
own language.' Several other treaties and regional instruments recognize the rights to culture.").

[97] Universal Declaration of Human Rights art. 27, G.A. Res. 217A III, U.N. Doc. A/180 (Dec. 2, 1948).

[98] *See* International Covenant on Economic, Social and Cultural Rights art. 15(1), *adopted* Dec. 19,
1966, *entered into force* Jan. 3, 1976, U.N. Doc. A/6316, 999 U.N.T.S. 3:

  1. The States Parties to the present Covenant recognize the right of everyone:
     (a) To take part in cultural life; ...

[99] *See* International Covenant on Civil and Political Rights art. 27, adopted Dec. 19, 1966, *entered into
force* March 23, 1976, U.N. Doc. A/6316, 999 U.N.T.S. 171 (members of minority groups "shall not
be denied the right, in community with other members of their group, to enjoy their own culture, to
profess and practice their own religion, or to use their own language.").

[100] *See* Angela M. Lloyd, *The Southern Sudan: A Compelling Case for Secession*, 32 COLUM. J. TRANSNAT'L
L. 419, 428–429 (1994) ("By addressing both rights and affirmative duties, the African Charter expands
the scope of human rights in ways unaddressed by other international human rights regimes.").

[101] Makau Mutua argues, "The transplantation of the narrow formulation of Western liberalism cannot
adequately respond to the historical reality and the political and social needs of Africa." Makau Mutua,
The Banjul Charter: The Case for an African Cultural Fingerprint, in CULTURAL TRANSFORMATION
AND HUMAN RIGHTS 70 (An-Na'im, ed. 2002).

[102] "It is also crucially important not to forget the fact that traditional conceptions of human rights in the
African context subsume the interests of the individual concern and must be expanded to encom-
pass the family and community." J. Oloka-Onyango, *Human Rights and Sustainable Development in
Contemporary Africa: A New Dawn, or Retreating Horizons?*, 6 BUFF. HUM. RTS. L. REV. 39, 42 (2000).

the Charter explicitly values cultural rights.[103] As such, the Charter stands in stark contrast to CEDAW.

Although the African Charter offers robust protection of cultural rights, it lacks effective women's rights guarantees.[104] As Sibongile Ndashe observed, "The absence of cases pertaining to women's human rights before the African Commission have, for a long time, been a cause of concern and it had been speculated that the unclear and potentially ambiguous provisions of the charter relating to women's rights were a deterrent."[105] The Commission has yet to examine a single petition alleging a violation of women's rights.[106] The Charter, however, has been invoked in conjunction with CEDAW in domestic women's rights litigation, such as the Botswana case, *Unity Dow v. Attorney General.*[107] Although women's rights activists have relied on the Charter in a handful of cases, the treaty's lack of specificity on women's rights and its emphasis on African cultural values and traditions suggest that its usefulness is limited to enforce women's rights.

Aside from a general non-discrimination provision in Article 2 and an equal protection provision in Article 3, the Charter's primary vehicle for the promotion of women's rights is Article 18.[108] Article 18 begins by describing the family as the "natural unit and basis of society" and "the custodian of morals and traditional values recognized by the community."[109] In more expansive language, Article

---

[103] *See id.* at 58 ("The distinctive character of the African Charter has been extolled by numerous authors, particularly with respect to the recognition of economic, social, and cultural rights.").

[104] *See* Mukasa, *supra* note 9, at 41 ("[T]he ACHPR went overboard in its wholesale embrace of African tradition, values and customs without acknowledging that some of these customs and traditions discriminate against women....").

[105] Sigongile Ndashe, *Strategic Litigation: A Tool for Domesticating the Protocol?, in* BREATHING LIFE INTO THE AFRICAN UNION PROTOCOL ON WOMEN'S RIGHTS IN AFRICA, *supra* note 59, at 61.

[106] Ibrahima Kane, *Harmonising the Protocol with National Legal Systems, in* BREATHING LIFE INTO THE AFRICAN UNION PROTOCOL ON WOMEN'S RIGHTS IN AFRICA, *supra* note 59, at 57 (*stating* "[I]t is not mere coincidence that that human rights' Commission has not examined a single petition about the violation of women's rights in 16 years.").

[107] In the *Dow* case, the Botswana High Court considered Botswana's constitutional and human rights obligations and concluded that a Botswana woman married to a foreign national could pass on Botswana citizenship to her children. *See* Lisa Stratton, *The Right to Have Rights: Gender Discrimination in Nationality Laws,* 77 MINN. L. REV. 195 (1992).

[108] *See* Rachel Rebouché, *Labor, Land and Women's Rights in Africa: Challenges for the New Protocol on the Rights of Women,* 19 HARV. HUM. RTS. J. 235, 236–37 (2006).

[109] African Charter on Human and Peoples' Rights, *adopted* June 27, 1981, *entered into force* Oct. 21, 1986, OAU Doc CAB/LEG/67/3 Rev. 5 [hereinafter African Charter]. Article 18 states in relevant part:

   The family shall be the natural unit and basis of society. It shall be protected by the State which shall take care of its physical health and morals.

   The State shall have the duty to assist the family which is the custodian of morals and traditional values recognized by the community.

   The State shall ensure the elimination of every discrimination against women and also ensure the protection of rights of the woman and the child as stipulated in international declarations and conventions. *Id.* art. 18.

18(3) then states, "The State shall ensure the elimination of every discrimination against women and also ensure the protection of the rights of women and the child as stipulated in international declarations and conventions."[110] By framing the family as the guardian of traditional values and morals and by articulating a non-discrimination right in this limited context, the drafters suggest a limited role for non-discrimination. Article 18 also lacks specificity and has been widely criticized as unhelpful for women in the region.[111] "[T]he Charter places emphasis on traditional African values and traditions without addressing concerns that many customary practices, such as female genital mutilation, forced marriage and wife inheritance, can be harmful or life threatening to women."[112] An introductory note to the Draft Protocol explicitly acknowledges that the drafting of the Protocol was, in part, a response to the perceived inadequacy of the Charter's limited protection of women's rights.[113]

Because the text of the treaty provides more extensive protection to cultural rights than to gender equality rights, the African Charter fails to adequately protect women's rights when there is a potential clash between cultural rights and equality rights.[114] By strongly privileging rights to culture over equality rights, the Charter forces women's rights advocates to look elsewhere for support.[115] In contrast to the Protocol, the Charter does not explicitly, or even implicitly, value women's voices in the localized determination of cultural policies.

[110] *Id.* The Charter also authorizes the African Commission on Human and Peoples' Rights to "draw inspiration from international law on human and peoples' rights," including, presumably, CEDAW. *Id.* art. 60.

[111] "By ignoring critical issues such as custom and marriage, it has been argued that the Charter inadequately protects women's human rights." Manisuli Ssenyonjo, *Culture and the Human Rights of Women in Africa: Between Light and Shadow*, 51 J. AFRICAN L. 39, 44 (2007). *See also* FAREDA BANDA, WOMEN, LAW AND HUMAN RIGHTS IN AFRICA 67 (2005) ("Despite the existence of the African Charter and the extensive ratification of CEDAW by African states, it had over time been clear that the issue of gender was not being seriously considered at the institutional level, with little being done by the African Commission, which is responsible for monitoring the Charter, to make states parties accountable for gender-based discrimination occurring within their boundaries.").

[112] Ssenyonjo, *supra* note 111, at 44.

[113] Banda, *supra* note 111, at 67 (2005) ("To date, no African instrument relating to human rights proclaimed or stated in a precise way what are the fundamental rights of women in Africa. There is a vacuum in the African Charter....") (*citing* Drafting Process of the Draft Protocol on the Rights of Women in Africa (Item 8(e)) DOC/OS/(XXVII)/159b at 1)).

[114] *See* Itoro Eze-Anaba, *Domestic Violence and Legal Reforms in Nigeria: Prospects and Challenges*, 14 CARDOZO J.L. & GENDER 21, 31 (2007) ("It did not take into consideration critical issues such as custom and marriage.... More importantly, the Charter promoted African traditional values and traditions without due consideration to the harmful effects of some traditional values on women.").

[115] *See* Mukasa, *supra* note 9, at 35 ("The charter extols 'the virtues of historical tradition and the values of African civilization,' without addressing its vices, which include FGM, child marriages and widow inheritance.").

As discussed earlier, CEDAW, too, fails to provide adequate means for resolving heated contests between equality rights and rights to enjoy one's culture.[116] It largely ignores the issue of culture except where it is seen as uniformly regressive in women's lives.[117] This limited view of culture leads to a narrow perception of women's self-identity and can create a backlash against women's rights.[118] The Protocol, by contrast, explicitly values the positive aspects of culture and offers expansive and detailed protection against violations of women's human rights, including those that stem from customary law, tradition, and cultural practice.[119] As such, it strikes an appropriate balance between valuing women's membership in cultural communities and preventing those cultural communities from harming or discriminating against female members. The Protocol, moreover, promotes the notion that women, as social agents, must play a significant role in determining cultural policies. In the context of customary law, it values women's voices in formulating and reformulating cultural norms where other international and regional treaties do not.

20.3. THE POTENTIAL OF THE PROTOCOL: SUBSTANCE AND PROCESS

20.3.1. *Regional Credibility of the Protocol*

CEDAW lacks the regional credibility of the Protocol.[120] The Protocol reflects the voices of African women who played a role in drafting it.[121] As such, it is likely to be a more palatable source of human rights obligations than international treaties that are seen as imports of the West.[122] As Abdullahi Ahmed An-Na'im remarks, "Most African and Asian countries did not participate in the formulation of the Universal

---

[116] *See* discussion *supra* Section 20.1.1 and accompanying notes.

[117] *See id.*

[118] In her discussion of Swaziland, Sari Wastell provides a compelling example. Wastell describes the vehemence with which many Swazis resisted the country's proposed constitution. "This ambivalence was the result of different and cross-cutting political and cultural factors, but the most important was the fact that human rights discourse, as understood by ordinary Swazis, seemed to express a value system that was opposed to Swazi culture." Mark Goodale, *Introduction: Locating Rights, envisioning law between the global and the local, in* THE PRACTICE OF HUMAN RIGHTS: TRACKING LAW BETWEEN THE GLOBAL AND THE LOCAL 34 (2007).

[119] There is, of course, the difficult issue concerning *who* decides whether a particular cultural tradition is positive or negative. Ideally, local women within the communities that practice the tradition in question will evaluate the costs or benefits of the practice.

[120] *See* Mukasa, *supra* note 9, at 41 ("While CEDAW's effectiveness was undermined in some quarters because it was considered a Western women's instrument, the African Women's Protocol is a home-grown instrument developed by Africans for African women.").

[121] *See id.* at 29 ("In the case of the African Women's Protocol, the NGOs played a pivotal role in its initiation, elaboration, and subsequent adoption.").

[122] *See* Mukasa, *supra* note 9, at 41.

Declaration of Human Rights because, as victims of colonization, they were not members of the United Nations."[123] An-Na'im accepts the universal applicability of human rights law, but he emphasizes the centrality of local context in the internalization of human rights norms.[124] He recognizes that universal norms may become particularized to the extent that they require localized modes of implementation. He states, "[I]t is reasonable to assume that the prospects for practical implementation of a given regime of human rights as a normative system are related to the degree of its legitimacy in the context of the culture(s) where it is supposed to be interpreted and implemented in practice."[125]

The Protocol enjoys regional credibility largely because of the role African women's rights activists played in drafting the document.[126] In 1996, the African Commission voted to appoint a Special Rapporteur on the Rights of Women in Africa.[127] The Commission later charged the Special Rapporteur and two Commissioners with the task of convening a working group to draft a Protocol on women's rights.[128] "As the drafting process went along, input came from NGOs throughout the continent, government legal experts and the Women's Unit of the Organization of African Unity."[129] Although women's rights activists criticized this early stage of drafting as insular and inaccessible,[130] broader coalitions of NGOs had an impact on later drafts. Drafters

[123] Abdullahi Ahmed An-Na'im, *Human Rights in the Muslim World, in* THE PHILOSOPHY OF HUMAN RIGHTS 315, 317 (Patrick Hayden ed., Paragon House 2001).

[124] *See id.* at 317–318 ("Concern for the lack of universal participation in formulating international human rights instruments does not lead me to invalidate those existing instruments.... I adopt a constructive approach to the problem of the cultural legitimacy of human rights norms.... The proposed new interpretation will have to be undertaken in a sensitive, legitimate manner, and time will be required for its acceptance and implementation by the population at large."). *See also* Elizabeth M. Bruch, *Whose Law Is It Anyway? The Cultural Legitimacy of International Human Rights in the United States*, 73 TENN. L. REV. 669, 680–87 (2006) (offering an excellent description of An-Na'im's approach).

[125] Abdullahi Ahmed An-Na'im, *State Responsibility to Change Religious and Customary Laws, in* HUMAN RIGHTS OF WOMEN 171 (Rebecca J. Cook ed. 1994).

[126] *See* Fareda Banda, *Blazing a Trail: The African Protocol on Women's Rights Comes Into Force*, 50 J. AFRICAN L. 72, 73 (2006) ("As the drafting process went along, input came from NGOs throughout the continent...."); Mukasa, *supra* note 9, at 5 ("The Protocol is a homegrown instrument developed by Africans for African women. It legitimizes the fight against gender oppression as an African struggle.").

[127] *See* Banda, *supra* note 126, at 73 ("[T]he African Commission agreed to the setting up of a working group to look into the matter of women's legal disenfranchisement. To lead the working group, it appointed the Special Rapporteur on the Rights of African Women....").

[128] *See* Banda, *supra* note 111, at 68 ("The African Commission mandated the Special Rapporteur and two other Commissioners to convene a working group to draft an additional protocol on women's rights.").

[129] Banda, *supra* note 126, at 73.

[130] *See* Fareda Banda, *The Protocol on the Rights of Women in Africa, in* THE AFRICAN CHARTER ON HUMAN AND PEOPLES' RIGHTS 445 (Malcom Evans and Rachel Murray ed., Cambridge University Press 2008) ("The Special Rapporteur convened a small working group to assist her in the elaboration

incorporated broad concepts of women's rights, drawing on rights provisions in the Southern African Development Community's ["SADC"] Addendum on Violence Against Women and the African Charter on the Rights and Welfare of the Child.[131]

The drafting process was not without difficulties. Several states, including Algeria, Egypt, Libya, and Sudan, attempted to limit the reach of the Protocol's equality provisions.[132] Rights related to sexual orientation were excluded from the final draft.[133] Tunisia and Sudan objected to the provision requiring that the minimum age for marriage be eighteen years of age.[134] The issue of polygamy was particularly contentious, with NGOs proposing an outright ban and states defending the practice as an important right under both customary and Islamic law.[135] The final version included a requirement that States Parties encourage monogamy as the preferred form of marriage.[136] Like all negotiated international instruments, some of the Protocol's provisions reflect a compromise between conservative government representatives and consulting NGOs.[137]

Regardless of these compromise provisions, however, the Protocol embodies a progressive vision of women's rights on the continent, one in which African women played a significant role in creating.[138] As a regional document, the Protocol mediates between global or international approaches to rights and more localized approaches. The regional and national NGOs that played a role in the drafting process "navigate[d] the divide between the local and the global, translating global approaches into local terms and seeking to give local groups voice in global settings."[139]

---

of the instrument. The initial lack of extensive consultation was to become a source of tension and unhappiness as the drafting process evolved.").

[131] *See* Banda, *supra* note 126, at 446–447.

[132] *See id.* at 447 ("Most challenging was the resistance offered by Algeria, Egypt, Libya and Sudan to the use of the word 'same' as indicating equality....").

[133] *See* Banda, *supra* note 111, at 78.

[134] *See id.*

[135] *See id.* at 76.

[136] *See* African Protocol, *supra* note 8 ("[M]onogamy is encouraged as the preferred form of marriage and that the rights of women in marriage and family, including in polygamous marital relationships are promoted and protected....").

[137] *See, e.g.*, Banda, *supra* note 126, at 449 ("Looking at the final version of the Protocol, it would appear than an unsatisfactory compromise was reached, recognizing the equal rights of men and women to pass on nationality to their children 'except where this is contrary to a provision in national legislation or is contrary to national security interests.'").

[138] The drafting process involved largely women from the urban elite. Knowledge of the Protocol is still limited in rural areas. Thus, although the Protocol incorporates many of the concerns of African feminists, it should not be understood as a fully representative and inclusive document. *See also* Banda, *supra* note 126, at 72 ("The entry into force of the Protocol ... marked the culmination of years of lobbying for a document which would promote and protect the human rights of the continent's women by African women's rights advocates.").

[139] Merry, *supra* note 81, at 104.

As such, the Protocol offers an effective rebuttal to those who view human rights, particularly the rights of women, as a hegemonic import from the west.[140]

20.3.2. Substantive Provisions of the Protocol

The Protocol entered into force on November 25, 2005.[141] As of January 2010, twenty-seven countries had ratified the Protocol.[142] National, regional, and international campaigns continue to increase the number of ratifications and to promote enforcement of the Protocol within national legal systems.[143] These campaigns are especially important for women's rights activists, because the Protocol's provisions build on and, in some cases, expand the rights contained in CEDAW.[144] In the case of violence against women, the value of the Protocol lies in the specificity with which it prohibits gender-based violence, extending protection well beyond CEDAW.[145]

---

[140] See, e.g., Makau Mutua, Terrorism and Human Rights: Power, Culture, and Subordination, 8 BUFF. HUM. RTS. L. REV. 1, 4–5 (2002) ("The international law of human rights ... seeks the universalization of European cultural, philosophical, and political norms and social structures.... In this script of human rights, democracy and western liberalism are internationalized to redeem savage non-Western cultures from themselves, and to alleviate the suffering of victims, who are generally non-western and non-European.").

[141] Mukasa, supra note 9, at 4 (2008). The Heads of State and Government of the African Union adopted the Protocol on July 11, 2003, but it did not enter into force until fifteen countries had ratified it, which happened when Benin ratified on Nov. 25, 2005.

[142] See African Protocol, supra note 8. The countries that have ratified the Protocol include: Angola, Benin, Burkina Faso, Cape Verde, The Comoros, Democratice Republic of Congo, Djibouti, The Gambia, Ghana, Guinea-Bissau, Lesotho, Liberia, Libya, Malawi, Mali, Mauritania, Mozambique, Namibia, Nigeria, Rwanda, Senegal, Seychelles, South Africa, Tanzania, Togo, Zambia, and Zimbabwe.

[143] See, for example, the work of Equality Now, available at http://www.equalitynow.org/. Equality Now "has for the past two years been coordinating the campaign for popularization, ratification and domestication of the African Protocol on Women's Rights. It is registered as an NGO in Kenya." BREATHING LIFE INTO THE AFRICAN UNION PROTOCOL ON WOMEN'S RIGHTS IN AFRICA, supra note 59, at 98. Another organization, Association des Juristes Maliennes (AJM), has been "involved in the drafting and lobbying for the ratification of the Protocol and continues to undertake activities aimed at popularizing the Protocol among their members and other legal practitioners." Id. at 95–96.

[144] See Fareda Banda, Remarks by Fareda Banda: Sex, Gender, and International Law, 100 AM. SOC'Y INT'L L. PROC. 243, 244 (2006) ("The African Protocol on Women's Rights takes CEDAW as its jumping-off point.... Building as it does on CEDAW, it is worth noting that the Protocol contains rights not found within CEDAW....").

[145] Although CEDAW brings violence against women within the purview of the Convention through General Recommendation 19, the Protocol specifically addresses harmful traditional practices, which can be a source of violence against women, particularly in rural areas of Africa. Article 5(b) requires states to take action to ensure "prohibition, through legislative measures backed by sanctions, of all forms of female genital mutilation, scarification, medicalisation and para-medicalisation of female genital mutilation and all other practices in order to eradicate them...." African Protocol, supra note

The Protocol is a response to many of the substantive gaps of CEDAW and the African Charter, seeking to correct CEDAW's neglect of culture and the African Charter's prioritization of culture and neglect of gender equality.[146] Although not without shortcomings, the Protocol is a significant step forward in terms of meaningfully grappling with the potential conflict between culture and equality.

The Protocol contains a number of innovative provisions that move the culture/equality conversation forward in important ways. First, the Protocol explicitly values culture and custom at the same time that it promotes gender equality, which reflects an understanding of the self as multidimensional, contested, and intersectional.[147] In particular, the Protocol explicitly values the positive aspects of culture, referring to culture and tradition that are not harmful to women. Article 17, for example, recognizes women's right to "live in a positive cultural context and to participate at all levels in the determination of cultural policies."[148] By viewing women both as members of cultural communities and as gender-equality-seeking individuals, the Protocol reflects the lived reality of women's lives. As such, it avoids some of the backlash that CEDAW generates by focusing on gender equality to the exclusion of other axes of women's oppression such as race, ethnicity, class, sexual orientation, and disability.[149]

Many of the Protocol's articles, including *inter alia* those related to violence, elimination of harmful practices, and marriage, offer strong protection for women's equality rights. When there is a perceived conflict between customary law or practice and gender equality, the Protocol overwhelmingly resolves the conflict in favor of equality.[150] For example, the Protocol will not allow the right to culture

8, art. 5(b). *See also* Banda, *supra* note 144, at 244 ("Building as it does on CEDAW, it is worth noting that the Protocol contains rights not found within CEDAW, including those referring to violence against women. (CEDAW has made up for this by way of two general recommendations on violence.) The definition of violence is widely drawn and includes economic harm. Interestingly, pornography and sexist advertising are proscribed. Female genital cutting (mutilation) is explicitly outlawed even when performed in a medical establishment – thus putting paid to the idea that it is only a problem if done in an unhealthy environment.").

[146] *See* discussion *supra* Section 20.1.1–20.1.2 and accompanying notes.

[147] *See* African Protocol, *supra* note 8, art. 1, ("Discrimination against women" means any distinction, exclusion or restriction or any differential treatment based on sex and whose objectives or effects compromise or destroy the recognition, enjoyment or the exercise by women, regardless of their marital status, of human rights and fundamental freedoms in all spheres of life....").

[148] *Id.*

[149] *See generally*, Johanna E. Bond, *International Intersectionality: A Theoretical and Pragmatic Exploration of Woman's International Human Rights and Violations*, 52 EMORY L.J. 71 (2003).

[150] *See* Banda, *supra* note 111, at 81 ("On the issue of culture, the document is firm in its injunction that culture is to be rooted in principles of equality and democracy, and that women are to be consulted about the content of the cultural norms that are to operate within their societies.") (*citing* the Preamble to the Protocol and Article 17).

to trump gender equality rights and specifically disallows traditional practices if they are harmful to women.[151] But it does so within a framework that explicitly values the positive aspects of custom and culture, likely reducing the backlash that often results from external threats to community values and norms.[152] In addition to recognizing the positive value of culture, the Protocol also provides procedural protections that offer women a voice in the determination of cultural policies and practices.[153]

20.3.3. *Benefits of the Protocol's Procedural Rights*

Article 17 of the Protocol, which states that women have the right "to participate at all levels in the determination of cultural policies," offers the strongest protection for women's right to engage with and influence cultural policies.[154] Article 17 also requires that States Parties "take all appropriate measures to enhance the participation of women in the formulation of cultural policies at all levels."[155] It is worth noting, however, that drafters could have used stronger obligatory language, such as a requirement that states "ensure" rather than "enhance" the participation of women in the formulation of cultural policies. Although the drafters failed to utilize the most compelling language in this instance, the Protocol's specific mention of "communication" in several places is another discursive method of challenging gender-based stereotypes.[156] These procedural provisions, which are often overlooked in discussions of women's rights, offer an underutilized vehicle to promote women's engagement with the laws and policies that often determine the outcome of family law disputes.

The emphasis on women's participation in the determination of cultural policies is an attempt to create decisional space for women to interpret and engage

---

[151] *See* African Protocol, *supra* note 8, art.
[152] *See* An-Na'im, *supra* note 36, at 5 ("Those of one cultural tradition who wish to induce a change in attitudes within another culture must be open to a corresponding inducement in relation to their own attitudes and must also be respectful of the integrity of the other culture. They must never appear to be imposing external values in support of the human rights standards they seek to legitimize within the framework of the other culture.").
[153] *See* African Protocol, *supra* note 5, art. 17:

  1. Women shall have the right to live in a positive cultural context and to participate at all levels in the determination of cultural policies.
  2. States Parties shall take all appropriate measures to enhance the participation of women in the formulation of cultural policies at all levels.
  Id.

[154] *Id.* art. 17(1).
[155] *Id.* art. 17(2).
[156] *See, e.g., id.* art. 2(2), 4(2)(e).

with cultural meaning.[157] These provisions reflect an understanding of the importance of women's agency in articulating the normative content of customary law and seek to enhance women's participation in the discourse around culture and custom. Because the Protocol does an excellent job of framing women's equality norms in the context of custom and culture, the real discursive value of Article 17 is its potential to engage traditional leaders in the exploration of localized methods for implementation of equality rights.

NGOs have a crucial role to play in operationalizing the Article 17 right of women to participate in the formulation of cultural policies. As Sally Merry observes, "Movement activists, NGO leaders, and government officials create programs and institutions that are a blend of transnational, national, and local elements as they negotiate the spaces between transnational ideas and local concerns."[158] Merry proposes a strategy for NGOs attempting to "translate" ideas between global and local spaces. This translation strategy is useful for NGOs seeking to facilitate discourse between, for example, traditional leaders and grassroots women in Africa. Among other things, NGOs should use culturally relevant "images, symbols, and stories" to frame the discourse. "Frames are ... ways of packaging and presenting ideas that generate shared beliefs, motivate collective action, and define appropriate strategies for action."[159] Framing strategies will help NGOs to structure the dialogue, introduce ideas that challenge patriarchal traditions, and, when appropriate, search for frames that are culturally resonant.[160]

Merry is not alone in her emphasis on the importance of participation. Recent strains of feminist legal and political theory also underscore the importance of the procedural, participatory protections.[161] I argue that, although important, these participatory, dialogical rights may lead to outcomes that are a product of power

---

[157] *See* Banda, *supra* note 111, at 252–54 ("The preamble of the Protocol makes it clear that 'positive African values' have to be based on 'the principles of equality, peace, freedom, dignity, justice, solidarity and democracy.'").

[158] Merry, *supra* note 81, at 134.

[159] *Id.* at 136.

[160] Choosing culturally resonant frames is not always appropriate. *Id.* ("This is precisely the problem human rights activists confront: If they frame human rights to be compatible with existing ways of thinking, they will not induce change.").

[161] *See* SEYLA BENHABIB, THE CLAIMS OF CULTURE 11 (Princeton University Press 2002) ("[O]nly those norms and normative institutional arrangements can be deemed valid only if all who would be affected by their consequences can be participants in a practical discourse through which the norms are adopted."); IRIS MARION YOUNG, INCLUSION IN DEMOCRACY 121–122 (Oxford University Press 2000) ("For these reasons many recent calls for greater political inclusion in democratic processes argue for measures that encourage more representation of under-represented groups, especially when those groups are minorities or subject to structural inequalities."). *See generally* Angela M. Banks, *Expanding Participation in Constitution Making: Challenges and Opportunities,* 49 WILLIAM & MARY L. REV. 1043 (2008).

dynamics rather than true deliberation.[162] As a result, I see the value of discourse not in substantively defining equality norms but in exploring localized modes of implementation and acculturating traditional leaders to international human rights norms such as those embodied in the Protocol.[163] It is the discursive search for localized modes of norm implementation, rather than norm definition, which holds the greatest promise for promoting women's equality rights in the region. For example, in a paper presented at the *Customary Law Revisited: The Role of Customary Law in the 21st Century* conference in Botswana in October 2008, Amelia Vukeyia, an attorney with the AIDS Law Project in South Africa, provides a compelling example of discursive collaboration between the state, civil society, and traditional leaders. The government of South Africa has, in collaboration with NGOs, systematically engaged traditional leaders in dialogue concerning efforts to combat the spread of HIV/AIDS in the country. In its effort to implement the National Strategic Plan on HIV, the government articulated a commitment to "facilitate & sustain dialogue with cultural, religious and traditional leaders."[164] According to Vukeyia, the dialogue has been productive and has led to a deeper understanding of the issues on all sides.[165]

20.4. CONCLUSION

Although imperfect in its substantive coverage, the Protocol fills critical lacunae left by CEDAW and the African Charter. Whereas CEDAW oversimplifies issues of culture and custom, the African Charter fails to adequately protect women's rights under the treaty. Provisions in the Protocol strike an appropriate balance between culture and equality when conflicts arise, recognizing the positive aspects of culture while invalidating customs that are harmful to women.

[162] Monique Deveaux, *A Deliberative Approach to Conflicts of Culture*, 31 POLITICAL THEORY 780, 785 (2003) ("James Bohman notes that although idealized versions of deliberative democracy require 'the inclusion of everyone affected by a decision,' failure to account for the effect of social in-equalities on civic participation and political inclusion can render the norm of inclusion ineffectual." (*citing* JAMES BOHMAN, PUBLIC DELIBERATION: PLURALISM, COMPLEXITY AND DEMOCRACY 16, 18 (MIT Press 2000))).

[163] *See* Merry, *supra* note 81, at 219 ("Human rights ideas and feminist ideas are appropriated by national elites and middle-level social activists and translated into local terms. Those who are most vulnerable, often the subjects of human rights, come to see the relevance of this framework only through the mediation of middle-level and elite activists who reframe their everyday problems into human rights terms.").

[164] *See* Amelia Vukeya, Customs and HIV/AIDS in South Africa: Engaging the Traditional Leadership as a Prevention Strategy, Presentation at the Leitner Center for International Law and Justice Program: Customary Law Revisited: The Role of Customary Law in the 21st Century (Oct. 23, 2008).

[165] *See id.*

Largely unnoticed procedural provisions in the Protocol hold great promise for facilitating women's critical engagement with the customs and practices that shape their lives. These provisions, if effectively operationalized, will give women a much needed voice at the table in discussions regarding the normative content of customary law. Insight from political philosophy, particularly discourse ethics and its critics, demonstrates the need for state and civil society involvement in the architecture of the discourse. Such involvement is necessary to minimize dramatic power disparities between traditional leaders and grassroots, rural women. Through careful and sustained engagement with traditional leaders, such as that envisioned by the Protocol, grassroots women may find a liberating, collective voice in the ongoing examination of customary law.

From Contemporary African Customary Laws to Indigenous African Law

Identifying Ancient African Human Rights and Good Governance Sensitive Principles as a Tool to Promote Culturally Meaningful Socio-Legal Reforms

Dr. Fatou K. Camara

"The German experience should be regarded as a lesson. Initially, after the codification of German law in 1900, academic lectures were still based on a study of private law with reference to Roman law, the Pandectists and Germanic law as the basis for comparison. Since 1918, education in law focused only on national law while the legal-historical and comparative possibilities that were available to adapt the law were largely ignored. Students were unable to critically analyse the law or to resist the German socialist-nationalism system. They had no value system against which their own legal system could be tested."[1]

21.1. INTRODUCTION

Identifying indigenous African laws and practices is of the greatest importance, as Africans truly need to take stock of their past laws if they want to implement much-needed culturally based socio-legal reforms. Customary laws are thought to reflect the founding ancestors' values. It is this very belief that gives them most of their strength in the mind of their followers. In Senegal, a popular proverb states the following: "If you don't know where you are heading, go back to where you came from." (*Soo xamul foo jëm dellul fi nga jogé*, Wolof).[2] Hence, socio-legal reforms gain tremendous leverage if they can be understood as a restoration of the customary laws of old rather than a radical departure from the past. Similarly, problematic "traditions" might be discredited by historical research that reveals their lack of such

---

[1] Willemien du Plessis, *Afrika en Rome: Regsgeskiedenis By Die Kruispad*, DE JURE 289–305 (1992).

[2] Professor Paul Ngom, former head of the History of Law department of Cheikh Anta Diop University's Law Faculty, once said, in answer to that proverb, "When a big wind has erased all footsteps, how do you find the way back?" Big winds (slave trade, colonization, civil wars) have indeed swept away much of Africa's memory of its past, hence the need for researchers with a proper methodology.

pedigree. It is therefore useful to sift through the confusing mix of today's African customary laws, in order to establish which laws are indigenous, what their original or early meanings might have been, and how, why, and when they have changed over time.

Despite the fact that its authority comes from its supposedly ancient roots, customary law is a dynamic body of law that is constantly evolving and adapting itself to changes in the economy and the socio-political environment. The trans-Atlantic and trans-Saharan slave trades, the civil wars and famines they caused, the colonial conquest, and, more recently, the post-colonial dictatorships all affected the internal dynamics of African societies, and consequently the customary law. Most of the changes brought about by these external forces were not changes for the better.[3] Accordingly, this chapter argues that whenever the ancient law is more human-rights-friendly than the current customary law, it would be useful to draw attention to that and use that "discovery" to promote respect for human rights in a particular community. This chapter offers a method for sifting through the mix of today's African customary laws in order to uncover rules of the past that can be used to dismiss harmful current practices – either based on or blamed on customary law. Such a process can also help legitimize positive changes within the society by showing how such changes are rooted in ancient practices. Framed in this manner, legal reform can be understood as cleaning up the house as opposed to destroying it.

Improving customary norms through historical inquiry may seem more time-consuming and difficult than merely eliminating antiquated rules, but this process can be properly understood as central to the much awaited "African Renaissance." Although many political leaders invoke the African Renaissance as a way of deflecting external criticism and creating political insulation, this use distorts the true meaning of the word "renaissance."[4] Renaissance is used by historians to describe the "rebirth" of classical ideas in Europe in the thirteenth to sixteenth centuries. The revival of these long-forgotten concepts was due to the rediscovery of ancient Greek and Roman literature. In fact, the "Renaissance men" (to cite but a few,

---

[3] The following rule clearly did not survive the endemic violence that ripped the continent apart with the slave trades (trans-Saharan and trans-Atlantic): "Many African societies had social codes of conduct during war with regards to children and women. For instance, among the Wapare and Wachagga (Tanzania), killing women and children during war was forbidden. The soldiers were allowed to either leave the women and children untouched or take them as their wives and adopted children. The latter was the practice in many instances." C. K. OMARI & D.A.S. MBILINYI, AFRICAN VALUES AND CHILD RIGHTS: SOME CASES FROM TANZANIA 23 (1996).

[4] French President Nicolas Sarkozy used the term "African renaissance" in his speech in South Africa, Feb. 28, 2008. NEPAD (the *New Partnership for Africa's Development*), a project developed by the Presidents of Algeria, Senegal, and South Africa, also calls itself "the African renaissance project." THE NEW PARTNERSHIP FOR AFRICA'S DEVELOPMENT (2001), http://www.un.org/africa/osaa/reports/nepadEngversion.pdf.

Petrarch, Da Vinci, Erasmus, Cervantes, Shakespeare, Montaigne, Martin Luther, Galileo, Copernicus, Kepler, and Newton) had the humility and the sagacity to take the time to study and research the texts of masters of philosophy, science, technology, and the arts, even though those masters, such as Plato, Aristotle, Euclid, Ptolemy, and Cicero, were "pagans" who had lived more than a thousand years earlier. Therefore, it stands to reason that if Africans wish to correctly use the concept of the Renaissance, they must understand that it means learning from the great African philosophers, lawmakers, and artistic and technological geniuses of the past. African customary law, properly situated in its historical context, is bound to reflect and retain some of the principles of past times characterized by peace, prosperity, and great artistic, intellectual, and technological development.[5]

In the spirit of this African Renaissance, the first section of this chapter will introduce a research methodology aimed at enabling scholars, tribunals, and states to go beyond the apparent differences within African customary laws to identify common indigenous core principles. The second section will focus on different ways in which research results can be used to promote culturally meaningful socio-legal reforms.

This chapter focuses primarily on Ancient Egypt because it is the most well-documented ancient African state. Comparing ancient Egyptian laws and practices to various African customary laws reveals many similarities.[6] The comparison is

[5] Although the concept of a golden age is a tricky one, one cannot dismiss the fact that some periods in time have been more prosperous than others in any given community in terms of intellectual development and artistic or technical achievements. The Pyramids texts, the Pyramids, and the Charter of Kurukan Fugan (the orally transmitted constitution of the empire of Mali – 1235–1645 – available at: http://www.oecd.org/dataoecd/56/56/38874847.pdf) are such landmarks.

[6] Cheikh Anta Diop offers a valid explanation of the importance of focusing on Ancient Egypt when he writes the following:
"The history of Black Africa will remain suspended in air and cannot be written correctly until African historians dare to connect it with the history of Egypt. In particular, the study of languages, institutions, and so forth, cannot be traced properly; in a word, it will be impossible to build African humanities, a body of African human sciences, so long as that relationship does not appear legitimate.... Imagine, if you can, the uncomfortable position of a Western historian who was to write the history of Europe without referring to Greco-Latin Antiquity and try to pass that off as a scientific approach." CHEIKH ANTA DIOP, THE AFRICAN ORIGIN OF CIVILIZATION, MYTH OR REALITY XIV (1974). According to Diodorus Siculus, Egyptians came from Ethiopia and retained the customs and manners of Ethiopians. DIODORUS SICULUS, THE LIBRARY OF HISTORY BOOKS 2.35–4.58 (C. H. Oldfather trans., 2000), *available at* http://www.homestead.com/wysinger/strabo.html (stating that "Now the Ethiopians, as historians relate, were the first of all men and the proofs of this statement, they say are manifest. For they did not come into their land as immigrants from abroad but were natives of it and so justly bear the name "autochthones" ... furthermore, that those who dwell beneath the noonday sun were, in all likelihood, the first to be generated by the earth, is clear to all, since, in as much as it was the warmth of the sun which, at the generation of the universe, dried up the earth when it was still wet and impregnated it with life, it is reasonable to suppose that the region which was nearest to the sun was the first to bring forth living creatures ... The Aithiopians say that the Egyptians are settlers from among themselves and that Osiris was the leader of the settlement. The customs of the Egyptians, they say, are for the most part Aithiopian, the settlers having preserved their old traditions.");

limited mostly to West African states and communities with the aim of explaining and illustrating the research methodology that could be applied to other indigenous African communities. Given a rule or a practice that is common to ancient Egypt and other indigenous African communities, its purpose in ancient Egypt may suggest an explanation for the practice that is independent of Islamic, Christian, or post-colonial jurisprudences. Documenting the existence of an earlier indigenous model can help situate and, indeed, challenge the authenticity of the changes that later occurred.

21.2. THE RESEARCH METHODOLOGY

The research is divided into two stages. The first stage consists of collecting reliable data (21.2.1.), and the second stage concentrates on processing collected material (21.2.2).

21.2.1. *Returning to African Antiquity and Pre-Colonial Time: Going Beyond the Fracture Points: Islam, the Slave-Trades, and Colonization*

Advocates of customary laws sometimes characterize them as having been formulated by the great ancestors and handed down, virtually unchanged, from one generation to the next. In reality, customary laws have evolved over time as African societies have changed. These changes reflect shifting sources and structures of power.

After the Muslim conquest of the Middle East and North Africa during the seventh and eighth centuries, Islam spread into West Africa along the trans-Saharan trade routes. It was introduced into the royal courts by Berber merchants and Muslim scholars who gradually ingratiated themselves to their hosts. Throughout the Middle Ages, Islam remained the religion of rulers and traders – an Islam of chiefs and lords in the midst of a peasantry still committed to their ancestral religion.[7] Christianity, which was introduced into sub-Saharan Africa in the fifteenth century by European missionaries, did not prosper in West Africa until the time of the colonial conquest in 1890. Until then, indigenous law remained the operative law throughout West Africa. Even in areas with high Muslim density, as in

HERODOTUS, HISTORY, Book II, (George Rawlinson trans. 440 BCE), *available at* http://classics.mit. edu/Herodotus/history.2.ii.html (indirectly answers the question of Ancient Egyptians skin color (and whether or not they were indigenous Africans or immigrants) when he argues the point of the origin of the Dodona oracle in Greece: "The Dodonaeans called the women doves because they were foreigners, and seemed to make noise like birds. (...) Lastly, by calling the dove black the Dodonaeans indicated that the woman was an Egyptian."). For more details on the ethnic origins of ancient Egyptians, see also Diop, *supra* note 6; Mubabinge Bilolo, *Aristotle and the Melanity of Ancient Egyptians*, ANKH, JOURNAL OF EGYPTOLOGY AND AFRICAN CIVILIZATIONS, n°6/7, 139–160, (1997–1998).

[7]   J.C. Froelich, *Les Musulmans d'Afrique Noire*, 18–19 (1962).

Niani, the capital of the empire of Mali, shari'a law was not applied. In its hey-
day, in the thirteenth century, the Mali Empire covered most of West Africa. It
included Guinea and Mali (the heart of the empire), Senegal, the Gambia, a part
of Mauritania, Côte d'Ivoire, Burkina Faso, Guinea Bissau, and Sierra Leone. It
extended eastward from the Atlantic coast to the Niger River bend; from Timbuktu
it extended southward to the Hausa inland, in what is now North Nigeria. The
emperors of Mali were all Muslims, but religious freedom was the rule throughout the empire. During his visit to that great West African empire in the fourteenth century, the famous Moroccan traveler Ibn Battuta wrote about the fact
that although the Mansa (emperor) and the people of the towns he stayed in were
Muslims, shari'a law was totally disregarded.[8]

Islam, however, did play a role in some imperial courts. In the empire of Ghana
(3rd–11th century) the rulers were not Muslim, but members of the aristocracy were.
This divisive factor led to the contestation of the legitimacy of the matrilineal system
of transfer of political power.[9] In Mali, as well, the patrilineal Islamic law clashed with
the matrilineal indigenous law for the succession to the throne.[10] Islam also served
to legitimize military coups, as was the case in the West African Songhai Empire
(14th–16th century). The Songhai kingdom began its rise as a great power during the
reign of Sonni Ali Ber (1464–1492), an enlightened ruler who did not allow Muslim
leaders to dictate the policy of the empire. They later had their revenge by helping
the usurper Askia Muhamad (1493–1528) put a new dynasty on the throne of the
Songhai Empire, the Askia dynasty. The Askia rulers remained highly subservient to
the power of Muslim religious leaders.[11] The rulers who, like the Askia or the kings
of Kano (Nigeria), needed Muslim religious leaders to stay in power did not hesitate
to impose patriarchal rules that did not exist under the indigenous law.[12]

Between the seventeenth and late nineteenth centuries, African states were undermined as a direct consequence of the intensification of the trans-Atlantic slave trade,
causing Africa to sink deeper into political chaos. At the same time, warlords looking

[8] *See* IBN BATTUTA, VOYAGES, III. INDE, EXTREME-ORIENT, ESPAGNE ET SOUDAN 423 (1997).
[9] *See* SÉKÉNÉ MODY CISSOKO, HISTOIRE DE L'AFRIQUE OCCIDENTALE 26 (1966).
[10] *See* Cissoko, *supra* note 9, at 68.
[11] *See id.* at 99–101.
[12] The following account of the new laws established by the king of Kano (Nigeria) after his conversion to Islam is quite telling: "According to the Chronicle of Kano (composed in 1890 on the basis of
ancient sources and published by Palmer), in the second half of the fourteenth century, forty Wangara
from Mali brought Islam to Kano and converted the sovereign (sarki), who built a mosque and made
it mandatory to observe the five prayers, then drove the head of the pagans away telling him to go
lead the blind. Towards 1400, the sarki brought in helmets and chainmail armour. At the end of the
fifteenth century, according to the Chronicle of Kano, sarki Muhammad Rimfa launched twelve
basic reforms, among which were the confinement of women (*Kulle*), the appointment of *eunuchs* in
state positions, the public celebration of the two major Muslim holidays, etc." VINCENT MONTEIL,
L'ISLAM NOIR 78 (1964).

to create theocratic Islamic empires through the sword emerged.[13] It is important to note that the Islamicization of the masses did not come by way of these jihads; that feat was achieved by the colonial upheaval. "Islam was the first beneficiary of colonialism; it progressed more in fifty years of European administration than it did in ten centuries of history."[14] Indeed, it was not until the late nineteenth century that Islam really began to penetrate the masses. People who were uprooted, isolated, and lost found that adhering to the Muslim community offered a sense of cohesion as well as mutual aid. Customary laws were thus gradually influenced by Islamic jurisprudence as interpreted by local Muslim leaders.

One should also note that the slave trade and colonization badly damaged intergenerational transmission of customary norms and the knowledge of their historical and social context. This disruption facilitated the cooptation of customary law by colonial powers.[15] For example, the "native's court of justice" that was implemented by the colonial authorities served only to further empower the colonial authorities. They controlled the appointment and dismissal of the court members as well as the judgments rendered. In order to be accepted, customary laws had to pass the repugnancy test – that is, the custom applied was not "barbarous" – and the compatibility test, that is, the custom applied is not incompatible with colonial statutes. The colonial rulers, however, did not care if their appointees correctly applied the appropriate

[13] For example, in 1725, the Muslim scholar Karamoko Alfa Diallo set up a theocratic Muslim state in Fouta Djallon (Guinea). In 1776, the ruling dynasty in Fouta-Toro (Senegal River Valley) was overthrown by an army of Toucouleur Muslims led by Souleymane Baal in a movement called the tooroodo revolution. The revolution installed the almamiyat (Almamy is the title of the king of Fouta who had to be a Muslim scholar and a great marabout) and Islam was declared the state religion. In 1802, Usman Dan Fodio founded the Fulani Empire of Sokoto (Northern Nigeria) and based it on the precepts of Islam. Following his example, in 1810, the Fulani Cheikhou Amadou extended his authority throughout the Macina, from Djenné to Timbuktu. The Toucouleur El Hadj Omar Tall spent formative years in Mecca and Medina (1827 to 1833), and upon his return home attacked Muslims who were too tolerant or ignorant, also taking aim at the Quadri brotherhood. In 1849, he proclaimed holy war against the so-called pagan kingdoms, but did not spare the kingdoms led by "fake Muslims" either. In 1861–1862, he conquered the Bambara kingdom of Segou and destroyed the Muslim kingdom of Macina. He died in 1864. In Guinea, Samory Toure (1830–1900) carved himself a Muslim empire of which he was the Almamy. At its height, his empire stretched from Guinea to Burkina Faso through the north of Côte d'Ivoire.

[14] Froelich, *supra* note 7, at 75 (original text: "Le premier bénéficiaire de la colonisation fut l'Islam qui progressa plus en cinquante ans d'administration européenne qu'en dix siècles d'histoire.").

[15] Famous African writer and promoter of the African oral tradition, Amadou Hampaté Bâ explains in the following text how colonial powers extirpated African tradition from the Africans' minds: "Formerly, that knowledge (the African knowledge) was regularly handed down from generation to generation, through initiation rites and various forms of traditional education. The impact of colonisation, an external, extra-African cause, put a stop to this regular transmission. Coming in with its superior technology, its own methods and its own values, colonisation did all it could in order to substitute the African way of life to its own. As nothing is ever planted on fallow land, colonial powers were forced to "uproot" the African tradition in order to plant their own traditions." AMADOU HAMPATÉ BA, ASPECTS DE LA CIVILISATION AFRICAINE, 26 (1972).

custom.[16] Consequently, rules issued from the statutory customary law courts do not necessarily reflect legal norms that existed before the colonial period.[17]

Relentlessly attacked on all fronts – judicial, political, economical, religious, and educational – the indigenous "African way of life" has literally been torn apart. How can the remaining bits and pieces of our ancient rules be identified and reinterpreted in a way that is useful for African societies today?

As one of the earliest documented African civilizations, ancient Egypt can be used as a type of blueprint against which subsequent developments within customary law can be measured and evaluated.

Law historians have many tools with which to reconstruct ancient and precolonial African laws. Those tools are mainly archaeological excavations, written sources, and oral tradition. To start, Africans have written about themselves since the invention of script. Papyruses, brick walls, stones, and other artifacts covered with Egyptian hieroglyphics are now widely translated. Roman and Greek scholars such as Herodotus, Aristotle, Diodorus Siculus, Strabo, or Plinus the Old have also left written testimony about the parts of Africa where they have visited and/or conducted research. Forty Arab authors, dating from the seventh to the sixteenth century, are considered sources of African history.[18] European explorers, mainly from Portugal, France, Holland, England, and Spain, have also written voluminous accounts of the Africans they encountered, dating from the late fifteenth century.[19] Comparing these various sources to African oral tradition, myths, legends, tales, and pictorial art enables the conscientious researcher to identify ways in which Islam, Christian missionaries, slave traders, or colonial authorities have influenced early norms. Such a study may reveal that certain accepted customary norms actually lack the ancient pedigree ascribed to them and instead reflect practices imported in the service of a particular regime. Conversely, it may reveal that other norms, characterized as Western or un-African, in fact have roots in African tradition.

21.2.2. *The Identification Process: Tracing Common Features Back to the Earliest African Civilisations*

Cross-cultural study has called attention to four features common to many indigenous African communities: the matriarchal system, the feminization of spirituality,

---

[16] In Senegal, it has been noted that many native's court's appointees of the Muslim faith would judge all cases according to Muslim law, without the litigants consent and even when they forcefully asked for the application of their own customary laws. *See* SERGE GUINCHARD, DROIT PATRIMONIAL DE LA FAMILLE AU SÉNÉGAL, 43 (1980).

[17] *See* Paul Kuruk, *African Customary Law and the Protection of Folklore*, COPYRIGHT BULLETIN, vol. XXXVI, n°2, 23 (2002), *available at* http://unesdoc.unesco.org/images/0012/001277/127784e.pdf.

[18] *See* LOUISE MARIE DIOP-MAES, AFRIQUE NOIRE, DÉMOGRAPHIE, SOL ET HISTOIRE 85–93 (1996).

[19] *See also* Diop-Maes, *supra* note 18.

the place of women in the decision-making process, and circumcision as a coming-of-age ritual. Each of these features is relevant to the critique of current customary laws and practices as inconsistent with human rights norms, specifically the norm of gender equality. After examining their historical origins, I turn to these modern debates in the next section in order to illustrate how ancient principles can be applied to current laws in a way that lessens or eliminates the conflict with human rights.

21.2.2.1. The Matriarchal System

The gender issue is at the heart of ancient African culture. Indeed, matriarchy is the socio-political system that was Africa's trademark for as long as the various parts of the continent remained free of external attacks.[20] A woman was the seat of power, the provider of riches, the guardian of life, the embodiment of justice, generosity, and fairness, the healer, and The Mother God.[21]

By matriarchy, I do not mean the tyranny of the female sex over the male.[22] Rather, a matriarchal society is a society where the maternal values of caring, courage, compassion, nurturance, and fertility (prosperity) are predominant. Ancient African societies premised on women's values and contributions also provided them with greater freedom. In his paper, *Rural Women in the Socio-political Transformations*,[23] Mutiso outlines the weight put on a woman's spiritual knowledge, whereas patriarchy embodies the supremacy of pure strength. Women were the priestesses whose

---

[20] *See* Cheikh Anta Diop, *Africa's Cultural Unity in* Towards the Africa Renaissance, Essays in African Culture & Development: 1946–1960 129–136 (1996). *See also* Cheikh Anta Diop, L'unité Culturelle De L'Afrique Noire – Domaine Du Patriarcat Et Du Matriarcat Dans L'Antiquité Classique (1982).

[21] *See* Runoko Rashidi, *African Goddesses: Mothers of Civilization, in* Black Women in Antiquity 72–88 (2002) (arguing that, in the earliest times, in Africa, religious concepts were developed in which the female deity played a major role. He describes her the following way, "[S]he had an all encompassing influence and was universally acknowledged as the greatest and ultimate seat of power. She was both the giver and sustainer of life"); Rosalind Jeffries, *The Image of Woman in African Cave Art, in* Black Women in Antiquity, *supra*, 98–122 (studying "The Primal Mother in Cave Painting," "The Primal Mother in Sculpture," "Akan, Benin, Mother Creator").

[22] *See* Christian Jacq, Les Egyptiennes, 11 (1996) (stating that matriarchy constitutes dictatorship of women over men. In order to refute the fact that the ancient Egyptian socio-legal system was indeed a matriarchy, Jacq starts quite interestingly by listing all the elements of a matriarchy, and then dismissing those that contradict his own (false) definition of matriarchy. He states that Egyptian women's autonomy is such that when visiting Egypt, Geographer Diodorus of Sicily, alleges that the Egyptian wife has full authority over her husband. He further states that the mother of Pharaoh occupies a central place in the process of power and that naming one's mother is more important than naming one's father. All these signs of a matriarchal system are dismissed because they do not lead to the existence of an abusive female power system. There is no proof of a tyranny exercised by the female sex over the other.).

[23] Gidbon Mutiso, *Rural Women in the Socio-Political Transformations, in* The Civilization of the Woman in African Tradition (1975).

role was to protect the community from all evil and to seek good luck and prosperity. They were the main intermediaries with the spirits of the land.[24] Consequently, in indigenous African culture, women were respected in body and mind, without being required to cover their bodies or stay out of public view. On the contrary, African women could go out in public freely, without male chaperones, barely covered, and completely self-confident. There is a Senegalese saying, from the Coniagui community, which emphasizes the freedom African women enjoy: "The moon is a woman because she is brave enough to go out at night."[25] Jacq reports that Pharaoh Ramses III asserted he had made it so that the Egyptian woman is free to go wherever she wants to go, without anybody bothering her on her way.[26] Jacq comments that this Pharaoh's edict was not an innovation, but a reminder of a societal fact that was established from the start of the Egyptian civilization. He further states that it was at the very beginning of the pharaoh's monarchy that women enjoyed a total freedom of movement, without being secluded in a dark room of the house, under the implacable authority of a father or of an almighty husband.[27]

Visiting the West African empire of Mali in the fourteenth century, Ibn Battuta was as surprised as Diodorus Siculus had been 500 years ago while visiting Egypt. Ibn Battuta testifies that in Mali, women enjoyed more consideration than men. Women, including married women, could go about freely without either a veil or a chaperone and interact with men; children named themselves after their maternal uncle (actually they named themselves after their mother, but coming from a patriarchal society Battuta was trained to ignore women); and inherited from their maternal uncle, not from their father.[28] In the southern region of Burkina Faso, the Lobi children took their mother's name and inherited from their maternal uncle who was responsible for their education. The same situation appears among the Toundjours and the Danembous, in the north of Chad, in the Kanem region, among the Miéné, Mérié, and Bandjabi of Gabon, the Serers and Lebou of Senegal, the Agni and Baoulé of the Ivory Coast, and the Kabré of northern Togo.[29]

As a rule, in many indigenous African communities, marriage does not deprive a woman of her legal capacity. Consequently, she keeps the right to work and to manage her property herself. Her husband is neither her guardian and keeper nor her lord and master. He is a "brother" and a friend.[30] The fact that spouses are

[24] *See id.* at 528.
[25] Monique Gessain, *Une Société Matrilinéaire Dans un Monde Patrilinéaire, in* Côtés FEMMES, APPROCHES ETHNOLOGIQUES 117 (1986) (the original text, prior to translation, is: "Les Coniagui disent de la lune; "c'est une femme puisqu'elle est assez courageuse pour sortir la nuit.").
[26] *See Jacq, supra* note 22, at 11.
[27] *See id.*
[28] *See* Battuta, *supra* note 8, at 403–426.
[29] SOCIAL COMMISSION, THE CIVILIZATION OF THE WOMAN 582 (1975).
[30] *See* FATOU KINÉ CAMARA & SALIOU SAMBA MALAADO KANJI, L'UNION MATRIMONIALE DANS LA TRADITION DES PEOPLES NOIRS 129–36 (2000).

encouraged to demonstrate the same deep care, affection, and merciless teasing that mark a siblings' relationship is documented as far back as ancient Egypt.[31] The fact that spouses frequently referred to each other as "my brother" or "my sister" misled some Egyptologists into thinking that those were incestuous unions.[32] In Senegal, A. B. Diop reports that the mother of the bride will tell her son-in-law the following: "This woman is not your wife, she is your sister."[33]

Thus, women are sisters and wives; they are also priestesses and key economic players. Moreover, indigenous African women have at times enjoyed more freedom and greater equality that they do today.

21.2.2.2. The Participation of Women in the Political and Decision-Making Processes

Matriarchy means that women are necessarily the ones who fashioned the laws that ruled their communities. According to Diodorus of Sicily, Queen Isis was praised for having given mankind its first laws and for having taught them to practice justice and banish violence from their midst.[34] As a matter of fact, women organized a socio-political system based on the ideals of fairness, kindness, and harmony. Those ideals were to be achieved with the participation of everyone in the decisions that have a direct impact on their life and on the destiny of their community. Not being excluded by their womenfolk from the conduct of public affairs, men, as a social category, did not reject that system. Cheikh Anta Diop argues that the acceptance of the matriarchal system by men is based on the fact that matriarchy is a harmonious dualism, which promotes the well-being of both sexes in a sedentary society. He insists on the fact that it is not a system based on the "absolute and cynical triumph of woman over man."[35] Actually it was a system based on what the ancient Egyptians called Maat.[36]

In ancient Egyptian theology, the creation is not static or complete – it is in perpetual motion, perpetual renewal, and therefore in constant danger of falling into chaos or freezing into nothingness. Maintaining order and harmony on earth and

---

[31] *See* CHRISTIANE DESROCHES-NOBLECOURT, LA FEMME AU TEMPS DES PHARAONS 210 (1986).

[32] This is not to say that such unions did not exist, but only between the pharaoh and his half-sister because of the matrilineal system that made it mandatory for the pharaoh to either have royal blood through his mother or marry a princess whose mother was a royal queen, even if they had the same father. *See* Théophile Obenga, *Sexualité, Amour et Mariage en Egypte et en Grèce dans l'Antiquité*, ANKH, JOURNAL OF EGYPTOLOGY AND AFRICAN CIVILIZATIONS, n°14/15, 9–33 (2005–2006).

[33] ABDOULAYE BARA DIOP, LA FAMILLE WOLOF 140 (1985) (the saying prior to translation is "*Ndaw si du sa jabar, sa jigéen la*").

[34] *See* Diodorus, *supra* note 6, at, Book 1, Section 1, VIII.

[35] Diop, L'UNITÉ CULTURELLE DE L'AFRIQUE NOIRE, *supra* note 20, at 114.

[36] *See* Fatou Kiné Camara & Abdoullah Cissé, *Arbitrage et Médiation Dans Les Cultures Juridiques Africaines: Entre La Propension à Dénouer et la Mission de Trancher*, REVUE DE L'ARBITRAGE n°2, 285–316 (2009).

sky is directly dependent on the respect accorded to Maat, the principle of justice, an idea including both truth and fairness. In ancient Egypt, Maat is a goddess, that is, a divine principle – a woman, crowned with an ostrich feather, a symbol of the principle of equality of all before the law. Queens are the natural living women who embody the sacred principle of Maat. Among Pharaoh's official titles are the following; "son of Ra" and "brother of Maat." Maat is also called "daughter of Re."[37] As the embodiment of Maat on earth, the queen is the supreme authority to whom even the Pharaoh must listen because he is not above the law and even less above Maat. The queen's role is to watch over Pharaoh as well as to ensure his consistent adherence to the rule of Maat so that truth and fairness reign supreme. Accordingly, Queen Tiyi, the wife of Amenhotep III (1386–1349 BCE), is explicitly mentioned in a number of official acts,[38] thus making clear her official status as co-ruler. Tellingly, a text of the tomb of Khérouef reads: "She is similar to Maat (The Universal Rule) following Ra (The Divine Light)."[39] This was not an exception. In ancient Egypt, the male and female sovereigns had equal responsibility in the governance of the kingdom.[40] Desroches-Noblecourt notes that official art conveyed the same meaning of a ruling couple – a man and a woman with equal power. She states that one only has to see the magnificent schist sculpture, in full size, of Pharaoh Menkaure and his wife, Kamérèmèbti II, side by side, of the exact same size, directing their gaze toward the infinite, for confirmation of the strict equality of the two characters.[41] Obenga also notes that the indigenous queens of Egypt bore political titles that indicate they exercised sovereignty over the whole kingdom of Egypt.[42]

According to the Political Commission's report at the 1972 Abidjan colloquium entitled "The Civilization of the Woman in African Tradition,"[43] the example of the Akan woman (Ivory Coast) illustrates the African tradition of women's participation in decision making. According to Akan law, the Akan woman is the depository of most temporal and spiritual powers. As owner of the *chair* (meaning the throne), she plays an important role in succession politics, because it is the king's mother or sister's responsibility to nominate his successor, along with the help of

---

[37] A. M. Ali Hakem, *La Civilisation de Napata et de Méroé*, Histoire Générale de l'Afrique 233 (1987).

[38] *See* Jacq, *supra* note 22, at 99.

[39] *See id.*

[40] *See* Desroches-Noblecourt, *supra* note 31, at 43–77.

[41] *See id.* at 58.

[42] *See* Obenga, *supra* note 32, at 20–21.

[43] In July 1972 a Colloquium on "the Civilization of the Woman in African Tradition" was organized by the Society of African Culture under the patronage of the government of the Republic of Ivory Coast. There were sixty delegates and papers. They were from France, the United States, and thirteen African countries: Cameroon, Chad, Congo, Dahomey (currently Benin), Gabon, Ivory Coast, Kenya, Nigeria, Senegal, Togo, Upper-Volta (currently Burkina Faso), Uganda, and Zaïre (currently the Democratic Republic of Congo).

the government council.[44] The values of African indigenous laws have been carried down throughout the years. An example of this is the Egyptian Goddess Isis and the meaning of her name. According to Charles S. Finch, "The second important deity in the Osirian drama is Isis, whose Egyptian name 'AST' means 'throne, seat, or abode.'"[45] The women controlled the throne, were the owners of "The Chair," and thus the embodiment of power. Another example is in Southern Cameroon, specifically the Bamileke's community, where the *Mefo*, the mother of the ruler, receives the respect paid to the chief and is responsible for important duties. She presides over the other women and takes part in the decisions of the government council. In the Wolof and Seereer kingdoms of Senegal, the *lingeer* (i.e., the female sovereign, a female relative of the king on his maternal side) had significant political powers.[46] The *lingeer* are princesses of royal blood with a total legitimacy to rule. Their legitimacy can even be higher than that of the male ruler because the royal blood is transmitted through women as it is a matrilineal system of succession.

In the Wolof and Seereer kingdom of the Senegambia, the effectiveness of the *lingeer's* political power was noted with surprise and spite by the French colonial governors who, in the nineteenth century, encountered the resistance of the kingdom of Waalo in their conquest of what later became the colony of Senegal. Governor Soret wrote the following: "Fara Penda, blind old man, *brak* (king) of Waalo, is king of name only, it is Princess Ndyômbôt, married to the king of Trarzas, who now rules...."[47] Governor Thomas, who replaced Governor Soret, makes the same bitter conclusion – the *brak* has changed but the power is still in the hands of the *lingeer*: "[It] is to the princess Ndyômbôt, the *de facto* ruler, that the colonial authority is obliged to turn to when it has claims or when it seeks compensation for some losses."[48]

The power of these women is not a mere power of influence; it is a constitutionally recognized right to participate openly in public affairs. The Charter of Kurukan Fuga, the orally transmitted constitution of the empire of Mali, states in article 16:

---

[44] *See* SOCIÉTÉ AFRICAINE DE CULTURE, THE CIVILIZATION OF THE WOMAN IN AFRICAN TRADITION 597 (1975).

[45] Danita Redd, *Black Madonnas of Europe: Diffusion of the African Isis, in* BLACK WOMEN IN ANTIQUITY 162 (2002).

[46] *See* GASPARD THÉODORE MOLLIEN, L'AFRIQUE OCCIDENTALE EN 1818 69 (1967); HENRY GRAVRAND, LA CIVILISATION SEREER – COSAAN, 267 (1983); BOUBACAR BARRY, LE ROYAUME DU WAALO 263, 275 (1985); JEAN BOULÈGUE, LE GRAND JOLOF – XIIIE–XVIE SIÈCLE 61–62 (1987); BASSIROU DIENG, L'ÉPOPÉE DU KAJOOR 15 (1993).

[47] Barry, *supra* note 46, at 263 ("Fara Penda, vieillard aveugle, brak du Waalo, n'en est le roi que de nom ; c'est la princesse Ndyômbôt, mariée au roi des Trarzas qui dirige maintenant..." Mémoire du gouverneur Soret, April 14, 1839").

[48] *Id.* at 275 (quoting "[C'] est à la princesse Ndyômbôt qui gouverne de fait que l'autorité coloniale est obligée de s'adresser lorsqu'elle a des réclamations à faire ou à demander la réparation de quelques préjudices." Mémoire laissé par Thomas lorsqu'il a cessé les fonctions de gouverneur par intérim au Sénégal, Memoirs left by Governor Saint-Louis Thomas, Dec. 11, 1845).

"Women, in addition to their daily occupations, must be associated with all our governments."[49] Simi Afonja provides confirmation of the effectiveness of this constitutional law in Nigeria by stating that in cities and villages, women were represented in the council of leaders in the executive and the judiciary.[50] She also states that in each Ibo village, women had their own council.[51] In the kingdom of Dahomey (Benin), there was a women's assembly and a men's assembly. Both assemblies sat separately but had the same prerogatives. In a historical instance, women ordered mobilization and war against the invading French army after the men had decided it was best to surrender. After the women's assembly convened, the men's assembly accepted the women's decision.[52]

Again, such is the case in Kiganda (Uganda), where the royal women played an important part in running the kingdom, which is stressed by Liz Dimock, who nevertheless is mindful of the existence of a patriarchal hierarchy. She calls "anomalous" the high status of the women of all politically important families, starting with the queen mother and queen sisters, who not only had their own estates but also held their own courts.[53]

Queens and other women of noble blood are not the only women who have a say in the decision-making processes of their community. Ordinary women are also involved in public affairs. In the Ivory Coast, women acted as Supreme Court judges, in the sense that they were in charge of stating what the law ultimately was. Besides, not one official act, from granting asylum rights to collecting taxes, was legally perfect without their consent. Any transaction would be void if they did not approve of it.[54]

---

[49] The Charter of Kurukan Fuga art. 16, available at http://www.wildaf-ao.org/eng/IMG/pdf/THE_ CHARTER_OF_KURUKAN_FUGA__Anglais_1.pdf.

[50] *See* Simi Afonja, *Les Femmes Nigérianes et Les Affaires Publiques Dans la Société Traditionnelle*, *in* THE CIVILIZATION OF THE WOMAN IN AFRICAN TRADITION 371 (1975).

[51] *See id.* at 373.

[52] *See* CHEIKH ANTA DIOP, L'AFRIQUE NOIRE PRÉCOLONIALE 33 (1987).

[53] *See* Liz Dimock, *Women's Leadership Roles in the Early Protestant Church in Uganda: Continuity with the Old Order*, *in* THE AUSTRALIAN REVIEW OF AFRICAN STUDIES XXV(2), 10 (2003) (stating that "In this patriarchal hierarchy, anomalous high-status women included the female relatives of the *Kabaka* (king), the royal women, along with those of clan heads and chiefs, the politically important families. The royal women included the *Namasole* (Queen Mother), the *Lubuga* (Queen Sister), the royal wives, and princesses, descended from past or present *Kabakas* many of whom had their own estates, and in the case of the *Namasole* and the *Lubuga*, held their own court.").

[54] *See* Madeleine Hiba & Joséphine Dikéblé, *The Woman in the Traditional Political Life of Societies in the Center, East and Southeast of the Ivory Coast States*, *in* THE CIVILIZATION OF THE WOMAN IN AFRICAN TRADITION 383 (1975) (quoting "Toute transaction qui a trait à l'occupation d'un lopin de terre par une personne étrangère doit faire l'objet d'un conseil de famille. Le dernier mot revient à la femme. Sans son consentement cette concession est nulle et sans effet. L'autorisation du droit d'asile, la perception des impôts fonciers, sont faites par le chef mais avec l'accord des femmes. La femme a droit de regard sur la chose de la communauté. C'est elle qui autorise les attributions. Son refus entraîne la nullité de toute transaction.").

In sum, a case can be made that, in indigenous African jurisprudence, women and men are equals (brothers and sisters). African social organization frequently embraced the principle of man and woman working harmoniously together for the well-being of their community. This structure did not imply the pitting of man's skills against a woman's know-how. Rather, gender parity was about blending the experiences and accepting differences. The African woman played an important role in the political life of her community. Her actions were associated with those of the man, according to the ruling principle of harmony, with the idea that all beings have equal rights and should therefore live in peace and solidarity. Gender parity demanded that at the highest level, men be surrounded by women (spouse, mother, sisters, etc.) who would guide and counsel them.

21.2.2.3. The Femininisation of Spirituality

"In the beginning was Mother."[55]

Sculptures portraying a black woman, completely naked or bare-breasted, with a suckling infant on her knees, are a familiar part of African art. In Ancient Egyptian art, that image of Isis and her infant son, Horus, is famous.[56]

Indigenous African theology relies on the mother figure to convey the idea of Creation and of the origins of all God's creatures. God is the One who gave birth to the earth, moon, and sky. In Ancient Egyptian theology, *Nuut* is the Universal Mother who swallows the sun each night and gives birth to it each morning. *Nuut* is the "Primordial Mother" because she gave birth to the first human couples, which acquired godlike status as the first ancestors – Isis, Osiris, Nephtys, and Seth. *Roog* is the name the Seereer, a Senegalese ethnic group,[57] gave to God. The Seereer say, "*Nqoox Paal, Yaay um Roog*" ("The black bull's mother [is] God"); for the Seereer, God/*Roog* is a mother.

Sacred myths also play an important part in conveying the values of those who created such myths. Accordingly, African myths convey respect for women and their role in society. In contrast to the patriarchal tales of Genesis, many indigenous African myths place women as the giver of life and the savior of mankind.[58]

---

[55] Mutiso, *supra* note 23, at 527.
[56] The place of women in African traditional religion and in Ancient Africa's religious art is particularly well documented in these papers: "Egypt's Isis: The Original Black Madonna" by Eloise McKinney-Johnson; "African Goddesses: Mothers of Civilization" by Runoko Rashidi, "The Image of Woman in African Cave Art" by Rosalind Jeffries, "Black Madonnas of Europe : Diffusion of the African Isis" by Danita Reed. *See generally,* IVAN VAN SERTIMA, BLACK WOMEN IN ANTIQUITY (2002).
[57] *See* CHEIKH ANTA DIOP, NATIONS NÈGRES ET CULTURE: DE L'ANTIQUITÉ NÈGRE EGYPTIENNE AUX PROBLÈMES CULTURELS DE L'AFRIQUE NOIRE D'AUJOURD'HU 392–401 (1999) (establishing facts that confirm that the Seereers originated from ancient Egypt). *See also* ABOUBACRY MOUSSA LAM, DE L'ORIGINE EGYPTIENNE DES PEULS (1993) (tracing the Egyptian origin of the Peul).
[58] *See* SOCIÉTÉ AFRICAINE DE CULTURE, *supra* note 44, at 597.

Sacred African stories do not bring the woman out of any man's body part[59] or even a male god's body part.[60] In the African Creation stories, the Primordial Mother created man and woman. They are the First Twins, like Osiris and Isis; hence, the special status of twins and their mothers in many African communities. The ancient Egyptian genesis even goes as far as to state that men were created for women, in order to give love to women. In a papyrus dating from the time of the Ramesside dynasty (thirteenth–twelfth century BCE), God proclaims: "I am the one who has made the primeval waters in order for the Celestial Cow to come into existence. I am the one who has made the Bull for the Cow in order for the joy of love to come into the world."[61] Indigenous African theology also lacks the patriarchal structure of the Muslim and Judeo-Christian religions, which influenced greatly many African communities. For example, priestesses and female guardian spirits are common in the indigenous faith, whether called voodoo, animism, or paganism. They usually perform the most important rituals and prayers for prosperity, fertility, and protection from disasters: "The woman presides over fetish convents, initiation rites, and agricultural rites for fertility. She orders the moon, the sun and the rain."[62]

21.2.2.4. Circumcision as a Coming-of-Age Ritual

Although traditional African societies are not segregated societies, at some point girls and boys undergo separate initiation rites. After a child has reached the age of seven, he or she is enrolled in an age group where he or she will be taught further about societal norms and values. The group is defined solely by age and not other characteristics, such as class, caste, or ethnic origin. The age group forms a brotherhood or a sisterhood, creating a web of solidarity that helps comfort and assist each member throughout their life. Undergoing the initiation rites together, with circumcision being part of the initiation rituals, and having their blood mix on the circumciser's knife makes the initiates of a same group blood-brothers and blood-sisters.

It is important to make the distinction between female circumcision and excision. Male circumcision consists of removing the prepuce, otherwise known as the hood of the penis. In the case of a female circumcision, it is also only the hood of the prepuce that is cut off, whereas excision consists of cutting off a part or the whole of the clitoris. In that sense, excision can be somewhat compared to a castration.[63]

---

[59] According to the Biblical story of the creation of Eve, who was brought into being for and named by Adam.

[60] According to Greek mythology, Athena was not created by any woman, but leapt from the head of Zeus, already an adult, dressed in full armor.

[61] SARWAT ANIS AL ASSIOUTY, ORIGINES EGYPTIENNES DU CHRISTIANISME ET DE L'ISLAM, RÉSULTATS D'UN SIÈCLE ET DEMI D'ARCHÉOLOGIE 239–240 (1989).

[62] SOCIÉTÉ AFRICAINE DE CULTURE, *supra* note 44, at 597.

[63] Camara & Kanji, *supra* note 30, at 261–276.

In the indigenous African communities where circumcision is practiced as a vital part of the initiation rituals, the procedure marks the passage from adolescence to adulthood. Therefore, it is not performed at infancy, but at an age between fourteen and twenty-one years old, when young men and women feel they are ready to be tested and to become trustworthy members of the adult community. Circumcision is a practice that Greek historians[64] attribute solely to Africans – specifically Ethiopians and Egyptians – African immigrants, and a few others who borrowed the practice from an African culture.[65]

For certain African communities, circumcision is a vital part of an initiation ritual, though not an aspect of religious practice. In contrast, although the origins of excision are obscure, in Islamic literature, the practice is said to have come from Abraham's wife, Sara, who excised Hagar out of jealousy. That story suggests a Semitic origin of excision.[66]

In sum, in many African societies throughout history, women held key positions in the religious, economic, political, and social arena. Situating customary norms within this more complete historical context reveals many of their patriarchal features to be inconsistent with other, more egalitarian – and perhaps older – standards. Thus, one could argue that the reempowerment of African women is not only dictated by modern human rights conventions; it is also at the root of the much-awaited African Renaissance.

---

[64] *See* Herodotus, *supra* note 6, at 104; *see also* STRABO, GEOGRAPHY XVIII.i.12–13, available at http://www.fordham.edu/halsall/ancient/romanegyptl.html.

[65] *See* Herodotus, *supra* note 6, 104, available at http://www.homestead.com/wysinger/strabo.html:
"For the people of Colchis are evidently Egyptian, and this I perceived for myself before I heard it from others. So when I had come to consider the matter I asked them both, and the Colchians had remembrance of the Egyptians more than the Egyptians of the Colchians; but the Egyptians said they believed that the Colchians were a portion of the army of Sesostris. That this was so I conjectured myself not only because they are dark-skinned and have curly hair (this of itself amounts to nothing, for there are other races which are so), but also still more because the Colchians, Egyptians, and Ethiopians alone of all the races of men have practised circumcision from the first. The Phenicians and the Syrians who dwell in Palestine confess themselves that they have learnt it from the Egyptians, and the Syrians about the river Thermodon and the river Parthenios, and the Macronians, who are their neighbours, say that they have learnt it lately from the Colchians. These are the only races of men who practise circumcision, and these evidently practise it in the same manner as the Egyptians. Of the Egyptians themselves however and the Ethiopians, I am not able to say which learnt from the other, for undoubtedly it is a most ancient custom; but that the other nations learnt it by intercourse with the Egyptians, this among others is to me a strong proof, namely that those of the Phenicians who have intercourse with Hellas cease to follow the example of the Egyptians in this matter, and do not circumcise their children."
Id. See also Strabo, *supra* note 64 (confirming the African origin of circumcision by stating, "They (the Egyptians) circumcise the males, as also the females, as is the custom also among the Jews, who are of Egyptian origin, as I said when I was treating of them.").

[66] *See* Sami A. Aldeeb Abu-Sahlieh, *Muslims' Genitalia in the Hands of the Clergy: Religious Arguments about Male and Female Circumcision*, *in* MALE AND FEMALE CIRCUMCISION: MEDICAL, LEGAL, AND ETHICAL CONSIDERATIONS IN PEDIATRIC PRACTICE 151 (1999).

21.3. THE RESEARCH OBJECTIVE: AN AFRICAN RENAISSANCE

An African Renaissance cannot be achieved with Africans turning their backs on the past. The way forward is to adapt ancient law to a modern context (see Section 21.3.1) through the use of positive teachings of the great ancestors and interpreting them in view of modern human rights standards. In addition, African governments would add to the legitimacy of positive legal reforms[67] by identifying their indigenous base wherever possible (see Section 21.3.2.).

The next section applies the traditional principles explicated earlier to three contexts in which customary norms seem to conflict with human rights.

21.3.1. *Adapting Ancient Law to Modern Context*

21.3.1.1. Regulating Male and Female Circumcision

The foregoing analysis suggests that circumcision (male and female), and not excision (nor castration), is the truly indigenous African practice. It is also worth noting that the fact that circumcision was performed in matriarchal societies, such as in ancient Egypt, where men and women were given equal rights and opportunities, suggests that it might be implemented in a way for both sexes that does not undermine equality. A proposal to replace excision with circumcision has the added advantage of making communities feel that their culture is given due respect. That approach was successfully applied by a Seattle hospital in 1996. The mother of a Somali baby girl wanted her excised. The mother made it clear that if the procedure was not performed in the hospital, she would find a native midwife to do the job or fly back to Somalia just to have it done. The doctors understood the importance of this tradition for the Somali woman through drawing a parallel to Judaism and its belief that a male infant must be circumcised in order to be a member of the faith. Consequently, hospital authorities proposed circumcision instead of excision, and the mother was only too happy to accept. The process used by the Seattle hospital illustrates how an attitude of respect for a culture, combined with thorough research of that culture, can go a long way toward appeasing everyone.[68]

There is still, however, one important element of the indigenous African circumcision one must not overlook. The procedure was not generally performed on

---

[67] A positive legal reform is a reform that enhances human rights, democracy, and good governance.

[68] *See* Carol M. Ostrom, *Doctors at Seattle Hospital Consider Circumcising Muslim Girls,* Seattle Times, Sept. 29, 1996, *reprinted in* WOMEN LIVING UNDER MUSLIM LAW DOSSIER 17, 135–38 (1997) (noting that the circumcision did not take place, though, because of public outcry).

infants; rather, it was performed on adolescents or young adults[69] as a coming-of-age ritual. Louis Diéne Faye states the following rule: "Initiation is never given to a non-circumcised. It is an obligatory passage for access to the circle of adults."[70] He further explains that circumcision was undergone between the age of seventeen and twenty or so[71] because, not only was it the ideal age for socialization and the development of the individual gifts manifested since birth, it was also the age of marriage and pro-creation.[72] As a matter of fact, circumcision was the obligatory ritual that gave access to the initiation school called *Ndut* in Seereer.[73] *Ndut* is a school that will give initi-ates the qualities the community expects of mature men. Among such qualities are courage, self-control, discretion, technical skills, and religious consciousness.[74] *Ndut* means "hut,"[75] but the word is also synonymous to "bird nest." The analogy draws attention to the fact that the teenager who enters the *Ndut* is like the little bird in a nest, in a position of complete dependence. On leaving the nest, he will fly on his own.[76]

This use of the practice is not necessarily inconsistent with international human rights norms, which require, at a minimum, that such procedures be performed only with the informed consent of the individual. Dione gives testimony to the adherence to the rule of informed consent in the Seereer community, where teen-agers who decided to become circumcised had to wait a period of four years, dur-ing which they would need to show that they are ready and willing to undergo the ordeal.[77] African communities that still practice circumcision should be encour-aged to delay the procedure until the age of legal majority, unless circumcision of the child is advised for a valid medical reason. Compliance with this norm could be encouraged by a revivalist campaign in which the main arguments will

---

[69] *See* http://exploring-africa.blogspot.com/2008_11_15_archive.html (showing Ancient Egyptian paint-ings of a circumcision and explanations. Visual renditions of ancient Egyptian traditions of circumci-sions largely show us those done to male candidates who are clearly young adults.).

[70] Louis Diéne Faye, *Education et Mariage, Le Monde Seereer* 37 (2006).

[71] Lat Dior Ngoné Latyr Diop, a celebrated damel (elected king of Kajoor – a pre-colonial Senegalese kingdom) for the heroic resistance he opposed to the French colonial invasion of his kingdom, went through the circumcision ritual at the age of nineteen (he is believed to be born in the year 1842, and his circumcision took place in 1861). A year later, in 1862, he was elected king. Thiam and Ndiaye, 1976, p. 110; IBA DER THIAM & NADIOUR NDIAYE, HISTOIRE DU SÉNÉGAL ET DE L'AFRIQUE 110 (1976). *See also* MARIE CASANOVA, LAT DIOR, LE DERNIER SOUVERAIN DU CAYOR 11–23 (1976).

[72] *See* Faye, *supra* note 70, at 38. *See also* Salif Dione, L'appel du Ndut ou l'initiation des Garçons Seereer 15 (2004).

[73] Seereer is the language of a Senegalese ethnic group that is said to originate from Ancient Egypt.

[74] *See* Faye, *supra* note 70, at 38.

[75] The secluded hut where the circumcised are going to be taught to become men worthy of the trust of their companions and of their community.

[76] *See* Faye, *supra* note 70, at 38.

[77] *See* Dione, *supra* note 72, at 20–25.

be based on culture, history, and the wisdom of the great ancestors in addition to international standards.

As far as excision is concerned, experience has shown that banning it without an adequate campaign does not cause the practice to end, but pushes it underground. In Senegal, where female circumcision and excision are criminal offenses,[78] and where remarkable NGOs relentlessly campaign in favor of their abolition, studies have shown that the courts have treated very few cases of excision, and that the practice is on-going.[79] Conversely, a more moderate approach that differentiates between female circumcision and excision, allowing the former to be performed by doctors while strictly forbidding the latter, could go a long way to eradicating the more extreme practice.

21.3.1.2. Promoting Respect for All Faiths, Including Animism

Feminists have long criticized religious fundamentalism as a threat to gender equality.[80] However, in view of the important roles that women play in traditional African religions, advocates of women's rights are well-served by promoting respect of all belief systems and an equal treatment from the state toward all faiths, rather than a skepticism of religion. For example, a project in Senegal of creating a Temple for Initiated Women is a step toward the full recognition of the traditional religion and the prominent place women held in it as saintly figures, holy spirits, healers, and priestesses. Initiated women are the women who hold the holy secrets transmitted during initiation rites and training.[81] Healing, rainmaking, divination, sacred

---

[78] Article 299 bis (law n°99–05) (Jan. 29, 1999) (Sen.).

[79] *See generally* Abdoulaye Kâ, Les Decisions de Justice Rendues en Matière d'excision au Sénégal (2008); Abraham Ndioukane, Les decisions de justice rendues en matière d'excision au Sénégal (2008).

[80] *See, e.g.*, SONIA CORRÊA & REBECCA REICHMANN, POPULATION AND REPRODUCTIVE RIGHTS, FEMINIST PERSPECTIVES FROM THE SOUTH, 3 (1994) (quoting writings from DAWN (Development Alternatives with Women for a New Era), which sound like an unheeded alarm: "Fundamentalism is not an isolated Southern phenomenon but a global issue. Apart from its specific religious, cultural and political bases, certain features are common to fundamentalism across all world regions. It is always constructed around a notion of purity and impurity in which 'the other' is perceived as intrinsically evil and must be eliminated or 'cleansed'. Fundamentalist discourse naturalizes the family, sexuality and gender relations and excludes women from the public sphere. Everywhere, fundamentalism uses women's bodies as a battlefield in its struggle to appropriate state power. Fundamentalism is not a religious movement, but a political phenomenon with impacts at national and international levels.").

[81] The young people of the village of Baback Sereres, in the Thies region in Senegal, held a meeting on October 15, 2007, to discuss the project. In a letter summarizing the views expressed in that meeting, they wrote the following in support of the project: "Culture, which can be defined as the ways of doing things, the way of life, the beliefs, in short the ways in which a group sees the world, occupies a major place in the life of people. However the phenomena of Westernization, combined with the attempts at Islamisation, have caused the negation of the existence of Black-African cultures. Without

singing and dancing, initiatory tales, the hidden meanings of mythical stories, and the coded language of the initiates constitute a wealth of knowledge that will be lost and forgotten unless a temple is built to shelter it and the women who hold it.

The Temple for Initiated Women's project is an undertaking by the women of the village of Baback Sereres, assisted by the researcher Issa Laye Thiaw, a native of the village. The Temple project aims at developing the culture and the spiritual values of the Seereer community. The Seereer have a long-standing tradition of resisting conversion to Islam and the Christian faith, which has enabled them to retain many elements of the indigenous African culture, for example the matrilineal inheritance system. For the project's initiators, learning the moral values and spiritual knowledge that have been bequeathed by the ancestors will help promote the emancipation of Senegalese women. By its sheer existence, the Temple for Initiated Women will subtly convey a feminist message. Furthermore, women playing the roles of officially acknowledged spiritual leaders would enhance the community's respect for them.

The existence of the Convention on the Protection and Promotion of the Diversity of Cultural Expressions ("CCD"), adopted on October 20, 2005 by the UNESCO General Conference, and entered into force in March 2007, gives an added value to the project. Indeed, the CCD represents a new and important platform for promoting culture in the wider context of sustainable development.[82] The CCD rightly defines culture as one of the mainsprings of development – the cultural aspects of development being as important as its economic aspects. Accordingly, the preamble emphasizes the need to incorporate culture as a strategic element in national and international development policies and encourages national authorities to assume responsibility on the matter of protecting their people's cultural heritage.[83] The preamble specifically puts to light the importance of traditional knowledge as a source of intangible and material wealth, and in particular the knowledge systems of indigenous peoples, and its positive contribution to sustainable development, as well as the need for its adequate protection and promotion. Furthermore, the preamble underlines the importance of culture for social cohesion, including its potential for

---

culture it is impossible to reach development." *See* Fatou K. Camara, *The Temple for Women Initiates: An Alternative Religious and Cultural Institution,* app. 1, available at www.brandeis.edu/hbi/pubs/FKCamaraPaper%20FVCorrigee.doc.

[82] It is important to note that the Convention clearly points out that no one can invoke the provisions of this Convention in order to infringe on human rights and fundamental freedoms as enshrined in the Universal Declaration of Human Rights or guaranteed by international law, or to limit the scope thereof. *See* Convention on the Protection and Promotion of the Diversity of Cultural Expressions art. 2, entered into force March 18, 2007, 2440 U.N.T.S. ___, UNESCO reg. number I-43977 [hereinafter CCD].

[83] The states who are parties to this convention are under the obligation to endeavor to create in their territory an environment that encourages individuals and social groups: to create, produce, disseminate, distribute, and have access to their own cultural expressions, paying due attention to the special circumstances and needs of women as well as various social groups, including persons belonging to minorities and indigenous peoples. *See* CCD, *supra* note 82, art. 7.

the enhancement of the status and role of women in society. These principles, for which the CCD stands, need to be acted on to give them substantial meaning. The Temple for Initiated Women's project gives the CCD such a meaning.

21.3.2. *Justifying Modern Law with Ancient Concepts*

21.3.2.1. Gender Parity in Representative Assemblies

Ancient practices in which women were more fully included in governmental decision making can be called on to promote legal reforms when implementing a gender-equal democracy. Upholding the principle that all human beings are created equal does not mean that differences should be overlooked. Indeed, a gender-blind system may systematically under-represent women because of societal inequality that undermines women candidates. Recognizing this, the Protocol to the African Charter on Human and People's Rights on the Rights of Women in Africa, in article 9, poses the right for women to participate in the political and decision-making process, as well as their right to be represented equally with men at all levels in all electoral instances. Article 9 specifically calls for states parties to ensure increased and effective representation and participation of women at all levels of the decision-making processes.

In Senegal, a women's rights association (COSEF, Conseil Sénégalais des Femmes "Council of Senegalese Women")[84] organized a seminar entitled "A Day for the Study of a Politically and Culturally Adapted Law on Gender Parity In All Our Assemblies." A panel of jurists, traditionalists, sociologists, historians, and human rights activists was asked to study three models for gender parity implementation. One model proposed was the "dual seat" system, where each candidate would pair with another candidate of the opposite sex to campaign with; thereby, electing one would mean electing the other to the same seat. Another model presented was that of a dual chamber system in all Houses of Representatives at the local and national levels. One chamber would be an all-male chamber and the other would be all female. Both chambers would not necessarily have the same number of representatives,[85] but they would have the same powers and prerogatives. The third model was called "the zebra list," where all candidate lists are arranged by alternating gender from top to bottom. The "zebra list of candidates" was the model feminist activists favored because they said it was the simplest to carry out and could be voted on without any prior modification to the Constitution. It also puts to rest a concern many women

---

[84] *See* Conseil Sénégalais des Femmes, http://www.ongafrique.com/cosef.html.
[85] Many political leaders, of both genders, claim that they cannot put more women on the lists of candidates because women are reluctant to enter into politics, especially in certain areas where women follow strict patriarchal Islam-based customary laws.

in politics had expressed, namely the fact that their male counterparts would claim that there was a substantial number of women candidates on the list, without specifying that those women were almost all on the bottom of the list at places where it was unlikely they would get elected. Consequently, the "zebra list" makes sure that there is not only the same number of male and female candidates on the list, but also that both have the same chances of getting elected due to the alternating form of the list.[86]

After COSEF led an exhaustive campaign for gender parity in the 2007 legislative election, the National Assembly passed a statute for gender parity on the national lists of candidates.[87] The Constitutional Council, however, rejected that statute on the grounds that it was discriminatory and thus unconstitutional.[88] A constitutional amendment was passed by Parliament in November 2007 allowing Parliament to pass laws using affirmative action in order to promote equal access for men and women to official mandates and posts. In Senegal, the campaign for gender parity in electoral assemblies has been successful, in terms of public and political awareness of the issue, because COSEF feminist activists made sure to claim the issue as an African cultural heritage issue. On December 8, 2006, that message was reflected in the President of the Republic's address to the National Assembly. In his message, the President urged the House of Representatives and political party leaders to increase the number of women on the lists of candidacies for the upcoming legislative election. He chose, among other arguments, the very historical facts COSEF had put forward such as the matriarchal heritage and the female leaders of famous Senegalese pre-colonial kingdoms, such as Yacine Boubou, Ndieumbët Mbodj, and her sister Ndaté Yalla,[89] as well as a famous priestess who led a non-violent resistance to the exactions of the French army in the southern part of Senegal during World War II.[90]

[86] The conclusions of the colloquium were not printed; therefore, I can only give testimony of the discussions that took place as organiser and participant. *See Avant Projet de Loi Modifiant le Code électoral pour instituer la Parité à la Candidature aux Elections Législatives, Régionales, Municipales et Rurales, available at* http://www.fes-sn.org/IMG/pdf/Parite__texte_definitif___1_.pdf (2007) (providing the model of law that was written according to the specifications); *see also* Friedrich Ebert Stiftung Senegal, http://www.fes-sn.org/-Documents-.html

[87] *See* Statutory Law n°23/2007 (Mar. 27, 2007) (introducing parity on the list of candidates for proportional representation vote) (Sen.).

[88] *See* Decision n°1/c/2007 (Apr. 27, 2007) (Sen.).

[89] Ndieumbët Mbodj(1840–1846) and her younger sister Ndate Yàlla (1846–1855) have been the ruling *lingeer* of the kingdom of Waalo. Ndate Yalla was deposed as a result of the French colonial conquest. Yacine Boubou is another famous *lingeer* of the late seventeenth century. The *lingeer* is the eldest female kin, on the maternal line, of the elected male ruler. She can be his mother, his sister, his aunt, or his cousin. She will reign alongside him with equal, if not more, political power.

[90] Aline Sitoye Diatta (1920–1943) is a priestess from Casamance (the southern region of Senegal) who preached passive resistance against the French. She was deported and confined in a prison by the French authorities in 1943, and died in prison, allegedly from harsh treatment.

COSEF's campaign for a statutory law that makes it mandatory for all representative assemblies to have an equal number of male and female members is a good illustration of the way African historical figures and past laws can be called on to justify modern laws of good governance, open democracy, and respect for human rights. COSEF based its claim for gender parity not only in the women's rights international convention, but also in the indigenous African law that promoted female leadership. The cultural aspect of the claim became extremely popular, so much so that the President of the Republic endorsed it with the same justifications COSEF had put forward.

21.4. CONCLUSION

No one can be ignorant of the challenges of implementing the changes listed in this chapter. Yet, understanding these changes as consistent with important aspects of African tradition can help overcome the challenges. This is true for two reasons. First, insofar as the current, often-patriarchal norms of customary law command respect because of their supposed ancient pedigree, the historical reading presented here can offer a more gender-equal alternative by which to challenge customary law on its own terms. Second, identifying gender equality as authentically African gives credibility to those who seek to enforce the obligation of African states to meet their human rights obligations. Opponents of change may brand these advocates as outsiders to African culture. However, the evidence presented here reveals them to be perhaps its most authentic champions.

Index

520 *Index*

CEDAW. *See* Convention on the Elimination of All Forms of Discrimination Against Women
CEDAW Committee (Committee on the Elimination of all Forms of Discrimination Against Women), 426
cell *gacaca*, Rwanda, 404–405, 407
Central and Local Courts Proclamation, Lesotho, 148
certainty, legal, 54–56, 373–376
Certification judgment, South Africa, 36, 43
changeability of customary law, 15–17, 35–37
Chanock, M., 89, 97, 250
Chapter XXII, 1992 Constitution of Ghana, 280
Charter of Kurukan Fuga, Mali Empire, 505–506
The Cheyenne Way: Conflict and Case Law in Primitive Jurisprudence, 86–87
Chie, Raymond, 192, 193, 195–196
Chief Pilane v. Chief Linchwe case, South Africa, 350–351
chiefs. *See also* chieftaincy in Botswana; chieftaincy in Ghana; chieftaincy in Lesotho; traditional leaders
    exalted role of in land management and allocation functions, 319–321
    in Liberia, 183–184, 185–191
    in Sierra Leone, 172, 180–181
    in traditional courts, South Africa, 231–232, 233, 237–238, 239
Chiefs' Ordinance of 1904, Ghana, 273–274
Chieftaincy Act 1961, Ghana, 278
Chieftaincy Act 1971, Ghana, 279
Chieftaincy Act 2008, Ghana, 207, 222, 280–281
chieftaincy in Botswana, 247–265
    customary law regarding, 250–251
    future of, 258–264
    historical antecedents, 252–254
    legislation regarding, 255–258
    legitimacy of, 255–258
    nature of, 251–252
    overview, 4, 247–250
    post-1966 pressures and survival of, 254–255
chieftaincy in Ghana, 266–292
    anthropological overview of main ethnic groups, 267–270
    during colonial administration, 273–277
    conflicts within, 283–286
    in court system, 206
    current problems and challenges, 286–291
    as customary arbitrators, 207
    Houses of Chiefs, 222–223
    land management in Kumasi, 91–93, 100–101

legal regulation of chieftaincy, 270–282
    overview, 4–5, 266–267
    post-colonial era, 277–282
    pre-colonial era, 271–272
chieftaincy in Lesotho
    appointment of chiefs, 145
    authority of in Basutoland, 134–136
    Basutoland National Council, 138–139
    in colonial times, 137–138
    competition among chiefs, 133
    overview, 146–147
    structure of Code of Lerotholi, 139–141
    as symbol of traditionalism, 150–151
Chieftainship Act 1968, Lesotho, 145
Chieftainship Amendment Act of 1970, Botswana, 256–257
Chieftainship Amendment Act of 1987, Botswana, 257
child custody, 114–115, 122
children, in inheritance law in Namibia, 157–160. *See also* inheritance; succession
Chitambala v. R case, Rhodesia, 227–228
choice model, 423–445
    constrained choice among marriage rules in South Africa, 440–444
    international law regarding gender equality, 424–426
    legal pluralism and gender equality, 427–432
    multiple forms of marriage in Ghana, 432–434
    overview, 423–424, 431–432
    reform efforts implementing, 432–444
    women and land ownership in Tanzania, 434–440
choice of law, 66
Chronicle of Kano, 498
circumcision
    as coming of age ritual in indigenous Africa, 508–509
    regulating male and female, 510–512
Ciskei Region, South Africa, 242–243
citizens, obligation of to participate in Rwandan *gacaca*, 409–411
citizenship, and customary land tenure, 300–301, 309–310
civil law
    confinement of Kenyan customary law to, 109–113
    gender equality under, 427–432
    in Ghana, 217–220
    recognition of customary laws, 22
    role of customary laws within, 20
    in South African traditional courts, 229, 239–241

role of dialogue in combating HIV/AIDS, 492
tradition in constitutional law, 40
ubuntu in transitional justice process, 77
utility of chiefs as vote banks, 263–264
South African Law Reform Commission, 228
South African National Civic Organisation
(SANCO), 242
South African traditional courts, 227–246
criticisms of, 231–233
distinction between civil and criminal cases,
239–241
future of, 241–246
issue of legal representation, 234–236
main advantages of, 230–231
overview, 4, 227
as real courts of law, 227–230
reconciliation versus retribution, 241
recording and codification, 236–238
sovereignty, state, 370
spiritual purification and cleansing rituals, 78
spirituality, femininisation of, 507–508
spouse, use of term in South African succession
legislation, 348, 349
standard, test of repugnancy as, 113–114
Standard Six Certificate, South Africa, 237
standardization, in self-stating customary laws, 168
state control over customary courts, in post-
colonial era, 67
state law
acceptance of CEDAW, 480–481
versus customary land tenure, 299–305
versus customary law, 11–12
international law regarding gender equality,
424–426
invalidation of customary laws, in Kenya, 112
legal pluralism and gender equality, 427–432
policies of state agents, 27–30
recognition of by customary law, 25–26
revival of African jurisprudence as supplement
to, 77–78
role of customary laws within, 18–25
survival of some customary law norms as, 75
state monopoly on use of force, 370–373
statutory marriage, Ghana, 432–434
statutory reform of customary laws, and gender
equality, 430–431
stock theft cases, Botswana, 261
stool, in chieftaincy in Ghana, 268
Stool Revenue (Akyem Abuakwa) Act 1958,
Ghana, 278
Sub-Saharan Africa. *See* customary land tenure

*Sub-Saharan Africa: From Crisis to Sustainable
Growth* (1989), World Bank, 324
substantive provisions of Protocol to the African
Charter on the Rights of Women in
Africa, 476, 488–490
succession. *See also* customary law of succession,
South African; male primogeniture
principle of succession
attempt to phase out customary laws regarding,
Kenya, 126–127
chieftaincy in Lesotho, 147, 150–151
traditional leadership in Ghana, 283–286
Succession Act, Uganda, 454, 462
Succession Bill, Kenya, 126–127
Sunon Asogli Power (Ghana) Limited, 291
superiors, responsibility of in Rwandan
gacaca, 400
supplement to official law, customary law as,
77–78
supranational laws, 21
Supreme (High) Court (Civil Procedure) 1954,
Ghana, 209
Supreme Court, Ghana, 209
Supreme Court of Appeal, South Africa, 41–42
Supreme Court Ordinance of 1876, Ghana,
204–205, 208–209, 278
suspended sentences, Rwanda, 401
Swaziland, 485
swearing, thunderbolt, 173
*Swynnerton Report: A plan to intensify the
development of African agriculture in
Kenya*, 323

Tanganyika, repugnancy clause in, 115–116
Tanzania
codification of customary laws, 94
inheritance law, 463–464
Law of Marriage Act, 470
living customary law, 39
women and land ownership, 434–440
Tawana Moremi II, Batawana paramount
chief, 263
Taylor, Justice of the Supreme Court of
Ghana, 214
Temne customary law, Sierra Leone, 181–182
Temple for Initiated Women, Senegal, 512–513
tengdanas, Ghana, 270
tenure, land. *See* land tenure
territoriality principle, in application of criminal
law, 385
testation, freedom of, 349–350

CPSIA information can be obtained at www.ICGtesting.com
Printed in the USA
LVOW120013300413

331451LV00002B/2/P